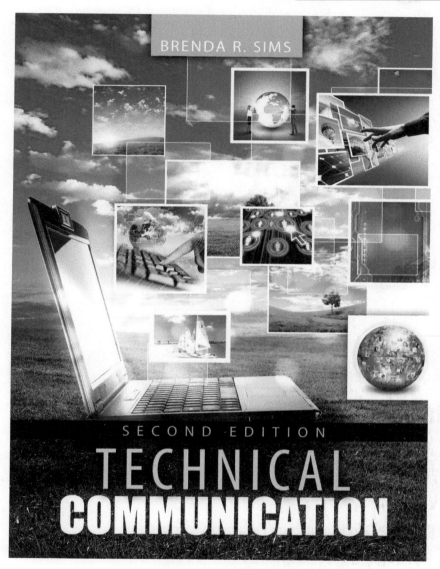

BRENDA R. SIMS

SECOND EDITION

# TECHNICAL
# COMMUNICATION

**Kendall Hunt**
publishing company

Cover image © Shutterstock, Inc.

**Kendall Hunt**
publishing company

www.kendallhunt.com
Send all inquiries to:
4050 Westmark Drive
Dubuque, IA 52004-1840

Printed in the United States of America
10 9 8 7 6 5 4 3 2

# Dedication

To my parents for teaching me the value of hard work

# contents

## CHAPTER 6

### Organizing Information for Your Readers .................................................. 135

## CHAPTER 7

### Writing Easy-to-Read Documents.................................................................. 185

# CHAPTER 8

## Using Reader-Focused Language

# CHAPTER 9

# CHAPTER 10

## CHAPTER 11

### Creating Effective Visual Information for Your Readers ..................... 297

## PART 3  Using the Writer's Tools to Correspond with Your Reader

## CHAPTER 12

### Writing Reader-Focused Letters, Memos, and Emails ..................... 351

# CHAPTER 13

# PART 4  Using the Writer's Tools to Create Effective Documents and Presentations

# CHAPTER 14

## CHAPTER 15

## Writing Reader-Focused Formal Reports ....................................... **461**

## CHAPTER 16

## Writing Persuasive Proposals ............................................................. **529**

# CHAPTER 17

## Writing Writer-Focused Definitions and Descriptions......................561

# CHAPTER 18

## Writing User-Focused Instructions and Manuals..........................589

# CHAPTER 19

## Creating User-Focused Websites ...................................623

# chapter *one*

## Technical Communication and Your Career

iStockphoto 2008.

*A*s you begin reading this book, you may wonder, *Why do I need a technical communication course? I came to college to learn about my major, not writing.* Indeed, many of you reading this book probably came to college to study engineering, computer science, biology, chemistry, business, or other technical and professional fields. You probably didn't come to college solely to learn to write. However, in any field, you will demonstrate your competence, in part, through your writing.

Let's consider a mechanical engineer, Ernie Chavez, who works as a piping specialist for an energy company. Ernie spends an average of 40 percent of his time writing. He begins most of his piping analysis projects with a written proposal to a plant manager. If the manager approves the project, Ernie will report his progress and possible changes in written progress reports to the plant manager. Ernie usually closes a project with a final report of his work, his conclusions, and the cost of the completed project. Like you, Ernie went to college not to learn to write but to learn his profession; yet writing, he now realizes, is vital to succeeding as a professional engineer.

Let's also consider Jennifer Nowakowski, a computer programmer in the research and development division of a company specializing in software applications for the hotel and restaurant industries. Jennifer and her team have developed a prototype of a software application for inventorying restaurant food and supplies. Before they can test the prototype, they must write a proposal for company executives, introducing the prototype and asking for the funds they need to test it. If they write persuasively, the proposal may convince the executives to fund the test.

In this chapter, you will learn that writing is important to your career and how your workplace will affect your writing. You will also learn the characteristics of effective technical communication.

## HOW WILL WRITING IMPACT YOUR CAREER?

> When you effectively communicate ideas in writing, you have a greater opportunity to ensure that your coworkers and managers understand the value of your work.

Like Ernie and Jennifer, you will have to communicate your ideas effectively to perform your job and succeed in your career. You can't assume that your managers and your coworkers will value and approve your work simply because you did it. Instead, you must effectively communicate your work, ideas, and progress to those with the authority to implement your ideas or to those who supervise you (Barabas 1990). You may also need to persuade others that your work has value. When you effectively communicate ideas in writing, you will have a greater opportunity to ensure that your coworkers and managers understand the value of your work. Your managers may even evaluate you indirectly or directly on how well you communicate in writing.

In many workplaces, "it is not the performance of an employee that counts, but rather managers' perceptions of that performance" (Couture and Rymer 1993, 7). Managers often develop this perception through an employee's written and oral communication skills; supervisory evaluations of communication skills correlate well with employees' overall competence within the organization (Scudder and Guinan, in Couture and Rymer) and "effective writing" is a typical measure of a professional's performance (ibid.). Your managers will develop a perception of your skills, your knowledge, and your value to the organization, in part, through your writing.

If you are like the typical college graduate, technical communication—specifically, writing—will fill about 20–60 percent of your time as a professional. For professionals in technical fields, writing will fill at least 40 percent of your time at work (University of Maryland 2001).

As a professional, you not only will spend much of your time writing, but you also will need to write effectively to succeed in your career. A survey of 120 U.S. companies revealed that writing is an essential skill for hiring and promotion; 70 percent of the respondents reported that two thirds or more of their employees had writing responsibilities (College Board 2004). Although communicating well does not automatically lead to success in the workplace, it is an important factor. You may find that you can enhance your reputation with your managers, your peers, and your organization through your written and oral communication. In a labor force filled with mediocre writers, a professional who communicates effectively stands out and succeeds (Hansen and Hansen, 2001).

Whether you are proposing a new idea to your manager or recording a project's history for the permanent files, clear communication gives you visibility and credibility with your managers, your peers, and ultimately, your organization. Poor communication gives you visibility, too—but without credibility. If you communicate poorly, others may have difficulty understanding your ideas; and your ideas and your work may ultimately fail to receive the recognition they deserve.

 ## HOW DOES THE WORKPLACE AFFECT WHAT AND HOW YOU WRITE?

Several workplace factors will affect you and your writing tasks. These factors include
- your organization's and your manager's expectations
- your readers' needs and expectations
- collaborative work
- time and budget limitations
- ethical considerations

### What Do My Organization and Manager Expect?

When you become a professional, your organization and your manager will have certain expectations about your documents. They may state or write these expectations explicitly, or they may imply their expectations. Your organization or manager expect the format, organization, or style of a document to meet certain criteria or established guidelines, or your manager will have certain preferences about format and style. For example, many organizations have a standard format or established template for progress reports or for

TAKING IT INTO THE *workplace*

## Visiting with a Professional in Your Field

You can best learn how communication will impact your career by talking with professionals. To learn more about communication in your field, locate a professional working in your major field. For example, if your major is computer science, find a computer programmer or systems analyst. If your field is construction management or building construction, find a project manager for a construction project. You could contact these professionals in person, by telephone, or by email.

## Assignment

Once you have located a professional, set up an interview to discuss how communication, specifically writing, impacts his or her career. If you cannot interview the professional in person, suggest a telephone or email interview. At the interview, ask the professional the following questions:

- What types of writing do you do at work?
- What steps do you take when creating a document?
- How do time and budget affect your writing?
- What percentage of your week do you spend on communication tasks?
- Do you collaborate with others when you write? If yes, describe the collaboration.
- How has communication impacted your career?

You may also develop some questions of your own. You may want to ask the professional to give you some document samples that he or she has written. After the interview:

iStockphoto 2008.

1.  Write a memo to your classmates about what you learned.
2.  Email your memo to your instructor and to your classmates.

meeting minutes. Some organizations have a standard cover page and a formatted layout for letters and memos. Many organizations also have a style sheet that dictates style and design elements (font, color, and graphics guidelines) that the organization expects you to follow when creating documents for internal and external readers. Find out whether your organization or manager has specific expectations about style and design and meet those expectations to the best of your ability.

This book suggests formats as well as style and design guidelines for many workplace documents. If your organization or manager does not have explicit written guidelines, use the sample documents and style guidelines presented in this book. These documents and guidelines will help you become familiar with conventions that you may encounter in the workplace. Once you are in the workplace, supplement these sample documents and guidelines by gathering examples of effective documents written by your coworkers to use as models. Your organization and your manager will appreciate that you are creating documents that align with other company documents and that you are working to be part of the organization's corporate culture.

## What Do My Readers Need and Expect?

As a student, you generally know your reader—your instructor—and what he or she expects. However, in the workplace, you may or may not know your readers. They may be your managers or your coworkers. They may be company executives whom you've never met. They may be clients, users, or even potential customers. You may never meet your readers.

The readers for many of your documents may be more than one person or group, and each individual or group may have different expectations of your documents. Your readers may include people who live and work in countries and cultures other than your own and whose expectations of you and your documents differ from readers in your own country. As a professional, you must account for these differences to create effective documents.

This book will help you learn how to determine what your readers expect and how to meet those expectations. It also will help you consider what international readers will expect from your documents and how to write for them.

## How Will a Collaborative Environment Affect My Communication?

When communicating in the workplace, you frequently will work with others to produce a document: 87 percent of college graduates surveyed by Lisa Ede and Andrea Lunsford, authors of *Singular Texts/Plural Authors: Perspectives on Collaborative Writing* (1990), said they sometimes collaborated with others to produce documents. Technical professionals and technical communicators collaborate on most documents except correspondence, progress reports, and meeting minutes. They collaborate by:

- planning a document with others, either within or outside of their organization
- coauthoring or writing as part of a team
- reviewing and revising documents

## Planning Documents with Others

Before a large document project, many organizations create a team to determine the purpose, readers, schedule, and format. The team may comprise only writers; however, in most cases, the team consists of members from different areas of the organization. An organization might select team members according to the function they will perform in the document production; the team might have a subject-matter expert, a writer, a graphics expert, and an editor.

When team members plan documents together, they can identify and answer important questions about global issues early in the document cycle—before writing begins—issues such as budget limitations, deadlines, document design, and readers' expectations and needs. In early planning sessions, team members can establish a schedule for producing the document and agree about areas of responsibility. Once the team has planned the document, set the schedule, and assigned areas of responsibility, one or more persons may actually produce the document. In some collaborative situations, the team plans the document, but only one person actually does the writing (Raign and Sims 1993).

## Coauthoring or Writing as Part of a Team

In some organizations and writing situations, several people write a document. These people collaborate in one of three ways:

- Each person is responsible for writing a particular section of the document while one team member does the final edit (Raign and Sims 1993).
- Each person is responsible for writing a particular section, and the team edits the document collectively. Team members send the draft of their sections to the entire team for comments and edits.
- Team members write the document together.

Most teams find the first and second methods of collaboration more efficient. Regardless of the method, successful teams decide on the document's style, design, and schedule early in the writing process.

### Reviewing and Revising Documents Collaboratively

Even if you don't work as part of a team, you probably will collaborate with others when reviewing and revising most documents. You may even collaborate with others by reviewing their documents—documents that you didn't help plan or write. The review can be a formal process by which the writers and other interested parties meet to review the document and suggest revisions. These people may meet more than once before formally approving the document. Even if you are not writing as part of a team, you may take part in a formal review of your documents. William Sims, a licensed professional engineer, reports that newly hired and unlicensed engineers write under the signature of a licensed engineer; so a senior or licensed engineer must review and approve many documents (Sims 2008). Collaboration of this type does not involve teamwork; instead, collaboration takes place at the reviewing or revising stage.

The review process may be informal. When it is, coauthors and interested parties receive a copy of a document to review. Often, these reviewers make comments and suggestions through email or in a shared file accessible to all reviewers. The authors then use this file to make revisions. This book will help you develop techniques for successfully collaborating with others to create effective documents.

## What Do My Time and Budget Allow?

The workplace will probably limit the amount of time you can spend on creating documents. Your manager and your organization will expect you to write quickly and efficiently. You will be expected to finish documents on time and within budget. Every professional must contend with time and budget limitations; but like successful professionals in your field, you can learn to write effective documents despite these constraints.

Your budget and schedule may force you to spend extra hours at work or to submit a document before you are ready. For example, your manager may ask you to write the documentation for a new software application that your company is marketing. He or she may require you to have the document ready for user testing within a month, even though you normally would need two months. You may have to adapt an idea or a document to meet budget requirements. This book suggests ways to streamline your writing process, to prioritize layout and design decisions, and to use online resources to help you submit documents on time and within budget.

## What Ethical Issues Should I Consider?

As a professional, you may face ethical considerations about the language, graphics, or information that you or your coworkers use in workplace documents. For example, how will you report the test results of a new airbag design when the testing shows serious design flaws and redesigning the airbag would delay the production of a new car model? The language you use could affect how your readers perceive the design problem and, ultimately, how they decide to act. The language you choose could force the company to spend thousands or millions of dollars to correct the design flaws. Your decision could also cause the company to lose sales to a competitor or to install the flawed airbag in automobiles—possibly endangering lives.

As a professional, you may face similar ethical issues. This book will help you analyze the ethical implications of the language, graphics, and information you select for your writing and to understand how language affects readers' perceptions or endangers lives. It will also give you four moral standards to apply when facing ethical challenges in the workplace.

## WHAT MAKES TECHNICAL COMMUNICATION EXCELLENT?

You read and use technical documents every day; although few of these documents are excellent. As a professional, you want your technical documents to be excellent. Technical communication is excellent when it successfully conveys your intended message and meets the needs and expectations of your readers. You best convey your message and meet the needs of your readers when your technical communication
- includes honest, ethical information
- addresses specific readers
- uses clear, concise language
- uses a professional, accessible design
- includes complete, accurate information
- follows the conventions of grammar, punctuation, spelling, and usage

Figure 1.1 presents an example of excellence in technical communication.

### Includes Honest, Ethical Information

Technical communication is excellent when it successfully conveys your intended message and meets the needs and expectations of your readers.

Excellent technical communication is honest, ethical, and complete. Honesty is at the heart of ethical information. When you communicate ethically, you have "done the right thing." You have communicated out of the "intrinsic rightness of the behavior," not only to keep your job or to receive personal or monetary gain (Dombrowski 2000, 42). You have communicated ethically if you have given readers honest, complete information and if you have not misled them.

## FIGURE 1.1

**Brochure Demonstrates Excellence in Technical Communication**

Figure 1.1 is an excerpt from a brochure titled "Zero Harm." This brochure provides readers with an overview of the company's commitment to safety. The brochure demonstrates excellence in technical communication through the information, attention to specific readers, language, and design.

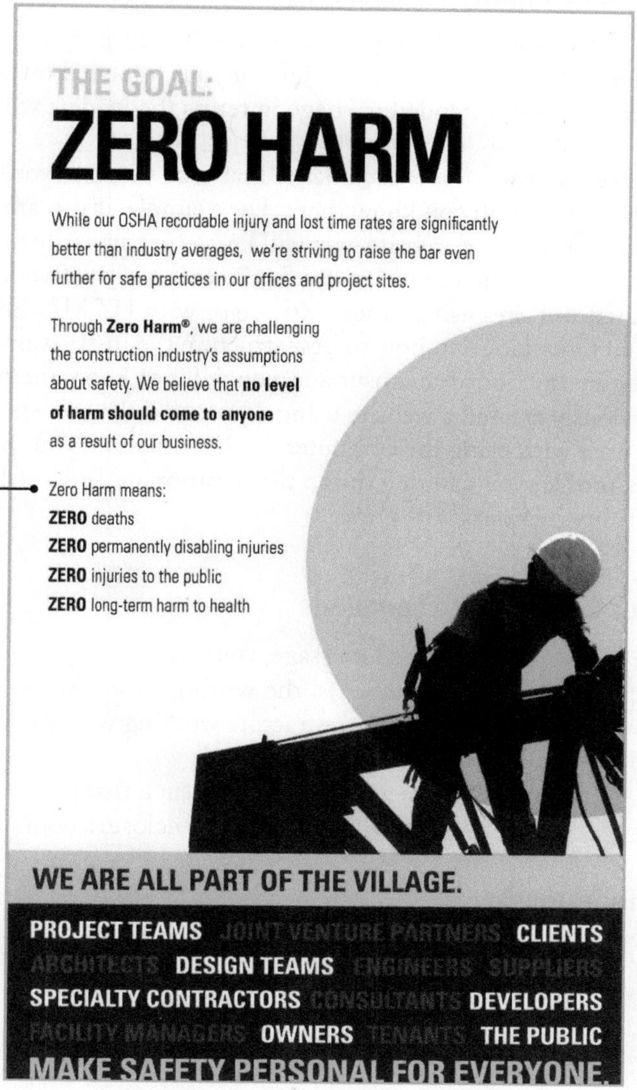

THE GOAL:

# ZERO HARM

While our OSHA recordable injury and lost time rates are significantly better than industry averages, we're striving to raise the bar even further for safe practices in our offices and project sites.

Through **Zero Harm®**, we are challenging the construction industry's assumptions about safety. We believe that **no level of harm should come to anyone** as a result of our business.

Zero Harm means:
**ZERO** deaths
**ZERO** permanently disabling injuries
**ZERO** injuries to the public
**ZERO** long-term harm to health

**WE ARE ALL PART OF THE VILLAGE.**

PROJECT TEAMS   JOINT VENTURE PARTNERS   CLIENTS
ARCHITECTS   DESIGN TEAMS   ENGINEERS   SUPPLIERS
SPECIALTY CONTRACTORS   CONSULTANTS   DEVELOPERS
FACILITY MANAGERS   OWNERS   TENANTS   THE PUBLIC
MAKE SAFETY PERSONAL FOR EVERYONE.

**Source:** Courtesy of Balfour Beatty Construction

Technical communication is dishonest when you misinform readers or intentionally omit important information—perhaps information that could kill or injure someone. If you are dishonest, you and your organization may face legal charges.

## Addresses Specific Readers

Your technical documents can accomplish their purpose only when they
- meet the needs and expectations of your intended readers
- convey your intended message in terms the readers will understand

Before you can create documents that will succeed, you must identify your readers. This task is easy when you know them. For example, if you are writing instructions to help your coworkers create a website, you will know (or can easily find out) what they know about the task. You can find out if they are familiar with the software they will be using or if they have created websites using other software or with HTML. You can then determine how much detail to include and how to best structure the instructions. However, if you are writing the same instructions for consumers, you will not know them. You may not know if they have previously created a website using different software; you may not even know how familiar they are with using the computer. In this situation, you should create a reader profile. With this profile, you can determine the appropriate level of language and detail to include in your instructions.

## Uses Clear, Concise Language

To convey your intended message, your technical documents must be clear. For readers to use your technical documents, the writing must also be concise. Let's look at an example from some instructions to contractors working with electrical transformers:

> The transformers are configured such that operating personnel are exposed to live 12.47kv when any of the enclosure doors are opened.

This instruction is not clear or concise, possibly endangering the users. The instruction would be clearer if written like this:

> Danger: **To avoid being exposed to live 12.47kv, close all enclosure doors.**

When technical communication isn't clear and concise

- **It can be dangerous.** The original instruction to the contractors does not tell them to keep the doors closed. If one of the operating personnel opened the doors, he or she could be severely burned or, worse, killed.
- **It can be unethical.** When technical communication is unethical, readers can get hurt; and you and your organization may face serious legal charges.
- **It can be expensive.** When technical communication isn't clear and concise, either the writer or the reader wastes time, and in the workplace, time is money. For example, Melissa Brown, a documentation manager for a marketing company, reports that by including a tips supplement in software documentation, her company was able to reduce the number of calls to technical support (Blain and Lincoln 1990). Her company saved substantial money simply by including this tips section (Redish 1995).

## Uses a Professional, Accessible Design

You can use design to create more effective documents and to achieve your intended purpose. An effective design

- **Helps readers locate information and understand how you have organized the document.** Most readers of technical documents do not read the entire document; instead, they look for specific information within it. When a document is effectively designed, readers can efficiently locate information and navigate through a document.
- **Creates a positive, professional impression of your document and your organization.** When a technical document has an attractive, professional design, readers are more likely to read it, and you are more likely to achieve the intended purpose: a professional design that conveys information and creates a positive impression of you, your information, and your organization. A sloppy, unprofessional design, likewise, creates a negative impression of you and your organization, and it makes your information suspect.
- **Gives your documents an attractive, inviting appearance.** When faced with a page or screen filled with only words, your readers may not read it. Readers are more likely to read and use your document when it incorporates design features that create an attractive, inviting appearance.

## Includes Complete, Accurate Information

Even when the design is effective and the language is clear and concise, a technical document can only succeed if the information is complete and accurate. A successful technical document gives readers all the information they need to understand the problem, to perform the required task, to understand an unfamiliar topic, or to make a decision. You will best know what information to include and not to include when you identify and create a reader profile. Successful technical communicators don't *assume* what the readers know; they *find out* what the readers know. Then, the writer can include complete information to help the readers accomplish their goals.

Effective technical documents also give readers accurate information. If your technical document gives readers inaccurate information, you confuse or annoy them. Documents with inaccurate information can be expensive for the organization or dangerous to the reader. For example, a U.S. construction company executive didn't proofread a contract before it was signed. In the contract, the company agreed to complete a project for $200,000 instead of $2,000,000. The contract writer simply left out a zero. Although the company was able to amend the contract, it unnecessarily spent thousands of dollars in legal fees and lost much goodwill with its client.

## Follows the Conventions of Grammar, Punctuation, Spelling, and Usage

Effective technical communication follows the conventions of grammar, punctuation, spelling, and usage. When your technical documents and your correspondence don't follow these conventions, readers may misread your communications. When you don't follow these conventions, you send negative, unprofessional signals to your readers. For example, if you send an email filled with spelling and punctuation errors to a potential client, he or she may assume that you and your organization do sloppy work and may question the accuracy of your technical information. These errors may also cause readers to focus on your writing rather than on the information you are trying to convey. These same errors may cost you a promotion as your managers may evaluate your ability to communicate. In a survey of 402 companies, executives identified writing as the most valued skill in an employee (Hansen and Hansen 2001). Although following the conventions of correctness isn't all that makes up good writing, many managers will evaluate your writing solely on its correctness.

 **WHAT'S AHEAD IN THIS BOOK?**

*Technical Communication* will help you to write effectively as a professional. Part I explains your role as a writer in the workplace and introduces some issues that you may face as a technical professional. The chapters in Part I focus on
- understanding how to analyze and write for readers
- understanding how to collaborate effectively
- facing ethical challenges

Part II discusses the "tools" that a writer needs to create effective technical documents. You may have learned how to use some of these tools in other writing courses; others, however, will be new to you. In Part II, you will learn about tools for

- researching information using primary and secondary sources
- organizing information for your readers
- writing easy-to-read documents
- using reader-focused language
- building persuasive arguments
- designing reader-focused documents
- creating effective visual information

Once you understand the writer's role and you have the tools to write effectively, you can begin to correspond with your readers and to create effective documents and presentations. In Part III, you will learn specific guidelines for writing effective letters, memos, and emails. You will also learn how to write effective job correspondence.

In Part IV, you will learn about the types of work-related documents you are likely to write; you will also learn how to prepare and deliver memorable presentations. You will learn about writing

- informal reports
- formal reports
- proposals
- definitions and descriptions
- instructions and manuals
- websites

Throughout the book, you will see tip boxes that summarize critical information to help you apply principles presented in the chapters and Taking It into the Workplace boxes that present up-to-date research in technical communication from the vantage point of the workplace professional. Each box includes an assignment where you will learn about communicating and writing in the workplace.

Along with these features, the book includes examples of student and professional writing. It also includes exercises and case studies to give you practice and will improve your writing skills, including some teamwork exercises.

# CASE STUDY ANALYSIS

## Embarrassing Typo Costs County $40,000[1]

### Background

In 2006, county officials in Ottawa County, Michigan were preparing for the November 7 elections. Citizens would be voting on a proposed state constitutional amendment to ban affirmative action programs that give preferential treatment to individuals or groups based on race, gender, and other characteristics. The county printed 180,000 ballots, at a cost of approximately $0.30 each. The county mailed about 10,000 of these ballots to absentee voters. On October 3, Ottawa County Clerk Daniel Krueger noticed a typo—a very embarrassing typo. The "*l*" was missing in the word public.

"My first thought was, 'Oh, crap,'" Krueger said, as reported in the *Holland Sentinel*. "We had about five or six people proofread it. It's just one of those words. Even after we told people it was there, they still read over it. It happens occasionally."

Because the error occurred on a statewide proposed amendment, Krueger decided to reprint the ballots. The cost to the county general fund was $40,000. Krueger said, "It needed to be reprinted" as the proposal was statewide and controversial. In other cases of misprints, the county had decided to use the ballots with errors, but those typos typically consisted of misspelled names, omissions, or incorrect numbers.

The Michigan Secretary of State Bureau of Elections representative Kelly Chesney told the *Holland Sentinel*, "The county made the right decision. It happens every election. There are 1,500 local election officers running our elections. They check and double check, but mistakes happen. Unfortunately, sometimes there is human error involved."

### Assignment

Pretend you are Ottawa County Clerk Daniel Krueger. Write a letter to the county commissioners explaining what went wrong in the ballot printing process and how you plan to ensure it doesn't happen again. Hand in your letter to your instructor. (For information on writing letters, see Chapter 12.)

[1] Compiled from hollandsentinel.com/stories/101006/local_20061010013.shtml.

1. Locate a Web page that demonstrates some or all of the characteristics of excellent technical communication. In a memo to your instructor, discuss the following
   - Who will read or use the Web page?
   - How is the page an example of technical communication?
   - Does the page demonstrate any or all of the characteristics of excellent technical communication?

   Include the URL of the Web page in your memo.

2. **Collaborative Exercise:** Form a team with two or three class members. Locate a manual for a consumer product. You might select a manual for a microwave, a bicycle, or a cell phone. In a memo to your instructor, answer these questions.
   - Who will use the manual?
   - Does the manual demonstrate the characteristics of excellent technical communication? If so, which characteristics does it demonstrate? If not, why?
   - How would you improve the manual to make it excellent?

   Include a copy of the manual with your memo.

# Part 1

# Understanding Your Role as a Writer

# chapter *two*

## Writing for Your Readers

A U.S. company that manufactures deodorant created a marketing campaign for its product in Japan. The campaign featured a smiling octopus dabbing deodorant under its eight arms. A typical U.S. consumer might think an octopus was cute putting deodorant under each arm; however, the Japanese didn't see the octopus as having eight arms. They saw the octopus as having eight legs—not a place consumers would typically apply deodorant. To the Japanese consumer, this marketing campaign looked odd.

Another U.S. company introduced a baby food product in Africa. The baby food jar included a picture of a baby—appropriate in many Western countries. In Africa, however, consumers expect the label on a food product to have a picture of exactly what is in the jar: *WYSIWYG* (What You See Is What You Get). To them, the product looked like food made from babies—an appalling thought. To clearly market their product to African consumers, the food company should have pictured the food on the jar (Barthon 2007).

How can you avoid similar problems in your technical communication? You must find out what your readers know about the subject of your documents and predict how they will respond to you as the writer, your organization, the visual information, and the document. This information about your readers will influence all aspects of a document—its purpose, organization, design, tone, graphics, and content. This chapter presents guidelines to help you determine the purpose of your documents and to develop a reader profile.

## DETERMINE YOUR PURPOSE FOR WRITING

Before you begin writing, think about why you are writing and what you want the document to accomplish. For example, Randy, a mechanical engineer, is writing a feasibility report about repairing a turbine that vibrates excessively. The vibrations are damaging surrounding equipment and reducing productivity. The purpose of Randy's report is to present three options for repairing the turbine and to persuade the plant manager and the executives in the home office to choose the third option, a $1 million plan to perform a high-speed balance of the turbine rotor. The first option is to operate the turbine in its current condition and minimize the vibration damage by increasing the overhaul frequency of the surrounding equipment. This option will increase maintenance costs and will not permanently solve the problem. The second option is to limit the turbine load to reduce the damage from the vibrations. This option will cause the company to lose revenue.

Randy will send his report to the executives in the home office and to the plant manager (his supervisor). Randy has worked in the home office but has recently been promoted and transferred to the plant where the turbine is located. He wants to favorably impress the executives and the plant manager. He also wants to establish a good working relationship with his readers and demonstrate that he is capable of solving problems in a timely, reasonable manner. Figure 2.1 shows the questions (and answers) that Randy might ask as he prepares to write his report.

You will face similar writing situations where you will have to ask questions to determine the document's purpose. For some documents, the purpose will be clear from the beginning; but for other documents, the purpose will be apparent only after you have asked questions about your readers and about the document's purpose. Sometimes, the purpose you identified at the beginning of the writing process will change as you gather information about readers' needs. In this situation, you may discover the document has a long-term goal such as maintaining the reader's goodwill or establishing a positive working relationship.

FIGURE 2.1

**Questions Randy Might Ask to Determine the Purpose of His Report**

| Questions Randy Might Ask | Possible Answers |
|---|---|
| What is the purpose of the document? | • To present three options for repairing the turbine<br>• To persuade readers to fund the third option (performing a high-speed balance of the turbine rotor at a cost of $1 million) |
| Does the document have a long-term goal? If so, what is that goal? | • Yes: to convince the executives in the home office and the plant manager that I can solve problems and that I am capable of doing my new job<br>• To establish a good working relationship with the plant manager and with the home office |

To determine your purpose for writing, ask yourself these questions
- What do I want this document to accomplish?
- Why am I writing this document?
- What do I want readers to know or to do after reading this document?

## IDENTIFY YOUR READERS

As you determine your purpose for writing, identify your readers—one of your most important tasks. Your document will accomplish your purpose only when it meets the reader's needs and expectations. The time you spend identifying and understanding your readers and their purpose for reading varies from one writing situation to another. For example, if you know your readers or if you have previously worked with them, you will not need much time to identify your readers and their purpose for reading. However, if you have never met or worked with your readers, plan to spend some time finding out about them and their purpose for reading your document. This section poses three questions to help you identify your readers.

Know Your Readers
- Are they internal or external?
- What do they know about the subject?
- Will multiple groups of readers read or use your document?

- Are your readers internal or external?
- What do your readers know about the subject?
- Will multiple groups of readers read or use your document?

## Are Your Readers Internal or External?

*Internal readers* work for your organization. *External readers* work outside your organization. Your readers' internal or external location affects the information, formality, and language you will use.

### Writing for Internal Readers

The organizational hierarchy will give you clues about the readers' technical knowledge and educational background; this hierarchy may tell you what the readers need to know about the subject matter.

Let's consider the organizational hierarchy at Randy's plant (see Figure 2.2). Below the plant manager, the organization has four areas: environmental staff, production superintendent, support superintendent, and administrative staff. The technical expertise of the people in the production and support groups varies based on their roles, experience, and education. Individuals at the same horizontal level in production have the same level of expertise and similar educational backgrounds. However, the plant operators in this group have a different level of expertise and education. They are technicians who have high-school diplomas and extensive on-the-job experience. They don't have the educational background of the engineers and production supervisors, who have engineering degrees.

Your readers' vertical level in the organizational hierarchy will tell you whether the readers have more authority in the organization than you. If you know where they are in the hierarchy, you can better determine the appropriate tone for a document. If you and your readers are at the same level, you probably will use an informal tone; but if your readers are several levels above you, you would use a more formal tone. Because these readers may know little about the specific project you are writing about, you will need to provide background information.

### Writing for External Readers

External readers may be customers, clients, or other professionals. In large organizations, external readers may also work for your organization, but not in your specific department or division. When writing for most external readers, use a formal tone and format. For

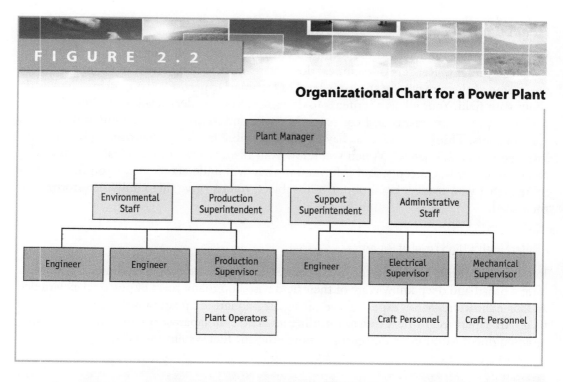

F I G U R E   2 . 2

**Organizational Chart for a Power Plant**

example, organizations generally expect informal memos when corresponding internally, but when corresponding with external readers, they use a formal tone and format. For example, if writing an email to an external reader, you should include an electronic letterhead or company logo (if available), but you might not include the letterhead or logo in an email to an internal reader. If you are corresponding with an external reader with whom you have worked for an extended time, you may use a less formal, friendlier tone.

When using email to correspond with external readers, remember to use a professional tone. If your working relationship with these readers is new or if email will serve as a matter of record, use a formal tone. Some organizations will expect you to use a formal tone in every email to external readers. In paper documents, organizations generally use different formats for internal and external readers. For example, if you are writing a proposal for someone within the company, you might use a memo format with the pages stapled together. However, if you are sending a proposal to a customer outside your organization, you might use a color layout, a table of contents, tabs between the sections, and an attractive, well-designed cover.

## What Do Your Readers Know about the Subject?

Will your readers understand the technical terms you use? Will they understand the concepts you present? Readers of technical documents have varying levels of technical expertise. Some of them may have the same level of technical expertise as you; others know little about your field. Your job as a writer is to determine your readers' levels of technical expertise and then to use terms and concepts they will understand or define unfamiliar terms and concepts. Think of readers as having three possible levels of expertise: high, mid, and low (see Figure 2.3 below). When you know your readers' level of technical expertise, you can choose words, concepts, and information they will understand. Once you have determined what your readers know about your subject, you can give them only the information they need.

### Readers with a High Level of Expertise

Readers with high-level technical knowledge are usually experts or technicians. *Experts* have a broad and deep knowledge of their field based on many years of practical experience and/or education. Most experts have an undergraduate or postgraduate degree in their field. An expert might be a surgeon reading an article on laparoscopy in a medical journal or an engineer working on designing a more efficient fuel system for a car.

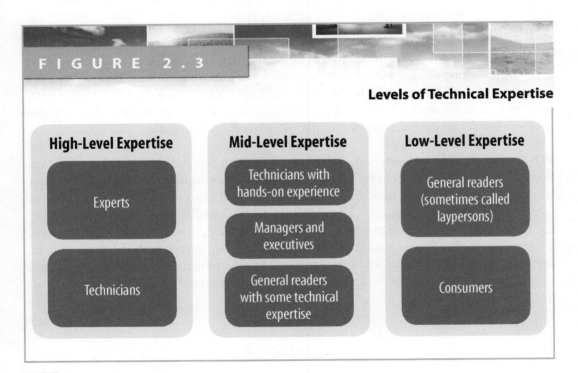

**FIGURE 2.3**

**Levels of Technical Expertise**

| High-Level Expertise | Mid-Level Expertise | Low-Level Expertise |
|---|---|---|
| Experts | Technicians with hands-on experience | General readers (sometimes called laypersons) |
| Technicians | Managers and executives | Consumers |
| | General readers with some technical expertise | |

Experts
- understand technical terms and information in their fields
- understand abbreviations and technical vocabulary commonly used by experts in their field
- expect few, if any, explanations of technical terms or information
- expect a direct presentation of the information
- want to know and understand the theory and research behind conclusions and recommendations

Figure 2.4 presents a document for expert readers. The document uses technical terms and abbreviations familiar to medical experts. It directly presents the information and includes information on the research.

*Technicians* have practical technical knowledge gained from hands-on experience and training. These readers may apply or implement the expert's ideas. For example, technicians perform procedures in labs or they maintain mechanisms and systems or they construct what an expert has designed. For example, a technician might build the fuel system designed by the engineer or work in a lab to identify disease-causing organisms.

Technicians
- understand technical vocabulary and concepts of the field
- expect practical, procedural information, not theories
- may need explanations of some technical vocabulary and concepts

Figure 2.5 illustrates a document that technicians might read and use. It explains how to identify microfilaria; the technicians reading this document understand the technical vocabulary.

## Readers with Mid-Level Expertise

Readers with mid-level expertise might be technicians with hands-on experience, managers, or general readers with some technical expertise. The technicians may have less formal education and training than the technicians with a high level of expertise; however, they have extensive hands-on experience. These technicians
- understand some terms and concepts in the field because of their practical experience
- are interested in practical, how-to information, not theories
- need explanations of some technical terms and concepts

Figure 2.6 would be appropriate for these technicians. It explains how to prepare blood smears in a laboratory. Technicians reading these procedures have practical experience in taking blood samples and analyzing those samples. These procedures include step-by-step instructions for carrying out the procedure, but they do not explain the theory behind the procedures.

FIGURE 2.4

## Excerpt from a Document for Experts

The writer uses technical terms and does not define or explain them.

Zoonotic filarial infestations occur worldwide, and in most reported cases the involved species are members of the genus *Dirofilaria*. However, zoonotic *Onchocerca* infections are rare and to date only 13 cases (originating from Europe, Russia, the United States, Canada, and Japan) have been described. In all of these cases only 1 immature worm was found, and the causative species was identified as *O. gutturosa, O. cervicalis, O. reticulata,* or *O. dewittei japonica* on the basis of morphologic and in some cases serologic parameters (*1–4*). *O. cervicalis* and *O. reticulata* are found in the ligaments of the neck and extremities of horses, *O. gutturosa* is typically found in the nuchal ligaments of cattle, and *O. dewittei japonica* is found in the distal parts of the limbs and adipose tissue of footpads of wild boars.

The writer presents information directly.

We identified the causative agent of a zoonotic *Onchocerca* infection with multiple nodules in a patient with systemic lupus erythematosus (SLE) who had been receiving hemodialysis. The parasite was identified in paraffin-embedded tissue samples by PCR and DNA sequence analysis.

The writer uses abbreviations.

### The Study

The patient was a 59-year-old woman with SLE who had developed multiple nodules on the neck and face over several years. Because of major renal insufficiency, she also had been receiving hemodialysis 3 times per week (3.5 hours) for >10 years. The first clinical differential diagnoses were cutaneous SLE, nephrogenous

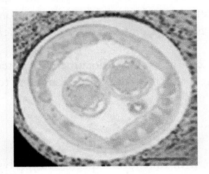

dermatopathy, calciphylaxis, and calcinosis. The clinical picture was obscured by secondary inflammations and ulcerations caused by self-inflicted trauma. Multiple sampling attempts by cutaneous core biopsies resulted in histologic diagnosis of unspecific, secondary inflammatory changes. Deep surgical excision of 1 subcutaneous nodule on the scalp indicated subcutaneous helminthosis. The patient was treated with ivermectin and subjected to 2 plastic surgeries for facial reconstruction, after which she recovered.

**Source:** Koehsler, Martina; Soleiman, Afschin; Aspock, Horst, Auer, Herbert, and Walochnik, Julia. *"Onchocerca jakutensis* Filariasis in Humans." *Emerging Infectious Diseases Journal,* CDC, volume 13.11 (November 2007).

FIGURE 2.5

## Document for Technicians with High-Level Expertise

### Bench Aids for the diagnosis of filarial infections — Introduction

World Health Organization 1997

**Introduction**

Several species of filarial worms infect humans in the tropical and subtropical regions of the world. The adult worms inhabit various tissues and organs of the body and are inaccessible for identification. Consequently, diagnosis of filarial infections depends primarily on the identification of the larval stage of the parasite (microfilaria). Most species of microfilaria circulate in peripheral blood; however, some are found in the skin.

**The microfilaria**

At the light-microscopic level and with the aid of a variety of stains, a microfilaria appears as a primitive organism, serpentine in shape and filled with the nuclei of many cells. In many, but not all, species, the body may be enveloped in a membrane called a sheath (**sh**). Where a sheath is present it may extend a short or long distance beyond either extremity of the microfilaria. In some species, depending on the stain used, the sheath displays a characteristic staining quality which aids in species identification. The nuclei of the cells that fill the body are usually darkly stained and may be crowded together or dispersed. The anterior extremity is typically devoid of nuclei and is called the cephalic or head space (**hs**); it may be short or long. Along the body of the microfilaria there are additional spaces and cells that serve as anatomical landmarks. These include the nerve ring (**nr**), excretory pore (**ep**), excretory cell (**ec**), and anal port (**ap**). In some species, an amorphous mass called the innerbody (**ib**) and four small cells called the rectal cells (**R-1, R-2, R-3, R-4**) can be seen, usually with the aid of special stains. These structures and their positions are sometimes useful for species identification. The shape of the tail and the presence or absence and distribution of nuclei within it are also important in species identification.

**Periodicity**

Some species of microfilariae circulate in peripheral blood at all hours of the day and night, while others are present only during certain periods. The fluctuation in numbers of microfilariae present in peripheral blood during a 24-hour period is referred to as periodicity. Species that are found in the blood during night-time hours but are absent at other times are designated **nocturnally periodic** (e.g. **Wuchereria bancrofti, Brugia malayi**); those that are present only during certain daytime hours are designated **diurnally periodic** (e.g. **Loa loa**). Microfilariae that are normally present in the blood at all hours but whose density increases significantly during either the night or the day are referred to as **subperiodic**. Microfilariae that circulate in the blood throughout a 24-hour period without significant changes in their numbers are referred to as **nonperiodic** or **aperiodic** (e.g. **Mansonella** spp.).

The periodicity of a given species or geographical variant is especially useful in determining the best time of day to collect blood samples for examination. To determine microfilarial periodicity in an individual, it is necessary to examine measured quantities of peripheral blood collected at consecutive intervals of 2 or 4 hours over a period of 24–30 hours.

The writers include practical information to help technicians identify microfilaria.

The writers use technical terminology, yet define some terms and concepts technicians will not understand.

**Source:** Downloaded from the World Wide Web, November 2008: www.cdc.gov/eid/content/13/11/1749.htm. *CDC Bench Aids.*

**FIGURE 2.6**

**Procedures for Technicians with Mid-Level Expertise**

### Specimen Processing

**Preparing Blood Smears**

If you are using venous blood, blood smears should be prepared as soon as possible after collection (delay can result in changes in parasite morphology and staining characteristics).

**Thick smears**

Thick smears consist of a thick layer of dehemoglobinized (lysed) red blood cells (RBCs). The blood elements (including parasites, if any) are more concentrated than in an equal area of a thin smear. Thus, thick smears allow a more efficient detection of parasites (increased sensitivity). However, they do not permit an optimal review of parasite morphology. For example, they are often not adequate for species identification of malaria parasites: if the thick smear is positive for malaria parasites, the thin smear should be used for species identification.

The writers include procedural information.

Prepare at least 2 smears per patient!

1. Place a small drop of blood in the center of the pre-cleaned, labeled slide.
2. Using the corner of another slide or an applicator stick, spread the drop in a circular pattern until it is the size of a dime (1.5 cm$^2$).
3. A thick smear of proper density is one which, if placed (wet) over newsprint, allows you to barely read the words.
4. Lay the slides flat and allow the smears to dry thoroughly (protect from dust and insects!). Insufficiently dried smears (and/or smears that are too thick) can detach from the slides during staining. The risk is increased in smears made with anticoagulated blood. At room temperature, drying can take several hours; 30 minutes is the minimum; in the latter case, handle the smear very delicately during staining. You can accelerate the drying by using a fan or hair dryer (use cool setting). Protect thick smears from hot environments to prevent heat-fixing the smear.
5. Do not fix thick smears with methanol or heat. If there will be a delay in staining smears, dip the thick smear briefly in water to hemolyse the RBCs.

**Source:** Downloaded from the World Wide Web, November 2008: www.dpd.cdc.gov/DPDx/HTML/Diagnostic Procedures.htm. *DPDx Blood Diagnostic Procedures.*

*Managers and executives* (upper-level managers) run the organization or a division or department of that organization; their jobs are to ensure that the organization runs efficiently and achieves its goals. Managers and executives want to know the bottom line: how the information will affect the organization now and in the future. They need information to make decisions; they do not have time to wade through theory and research in the same way experts do. Instead, managers need to know how the information relates to the organization so they can make an informed decision. Some managers, especially mid-level managers, take the information to upper-level management or executives. If you know that a manager will present your information and document to executives, include an executive summary at the beginning of the document and use headings and lists to highlight information that will help the manager present the information.

Managers may or may not have a background related to your field. They may have earned a degree in your field, but their knowledge may not be up-to-date. Before writing for managers and executives, find out if they will understand the technical vocabulary.

Managers and executives generally
- read to gather information for decision making
- expect conclusions, recommendations, and implications to appear near the beginning of the document or in an executive summary (see Chapter 15 for information on executive summaries)
- scan documents for the information they need for decision making
- need definitions and explanations for most technical terms and information
- prefer simple graphics that clearly summarize the information

Figure 2.7 instructs managers on how to plan for emergencies. This excerpt from FEMA's *Emergency Management Guide for Business and Industry* (2008) gives managers information to use when establishing an emergency planning team.

*General readers* with mid-level expertise may be interested, but not formally educated in your field. They may have degrees in related areas. These readers have read widely in your field and understand basic terms and concepts. Think of them as *sophisticated* general readers format like Experts, etc.

## Readers with Low-Level Expertise

*General readers* have little, if any, technical knowledge. The general reader, sometimes called a *layperson*, reads technical information outside his or her area of expertise. All of us become general readers at some time; for example, if engineers read a brochure about blood clots, they are general readers because they are not medical experts or technicians. Likewise, if a medical expert reads a document about testing the structural integrity of pipes, he or she is a general reader in that situation. General readers are also *consumers* who may read and use product instructions. For example, the instructions for changing the default settings in a software program would be aimed at general readers, not at experts or technicians. General readers
- do not understand basic technical vocabulary or concepts
- need basic technical vocabulary and concepts defined
- expect examples and analogies
- expect a simple, direct presentation
- learn from simple graphics

FIGURE 2.7

**Document for Managers**

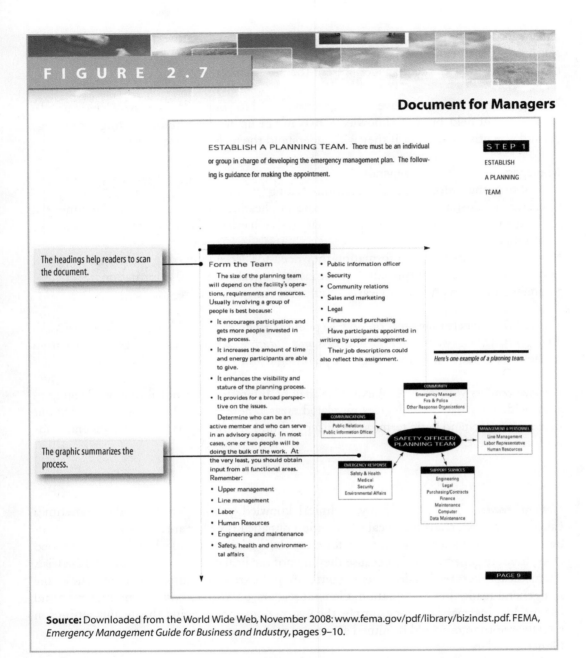

ESTABLISH A PLANNING TEAM. There must be an individual or group in charge of developing the emergency management plan. The following is guidance for making the appointment.

STEP 1
ESTABLISH
A PLANNING
TEAM

The headings help readers to scan the document.

**Form the Team**

The size of the planning team will depend on the facility's operations, requirements and resources. Usually involving a group of people is best because:

- It encourages participation and gets more people invested in the process.
- It increases the amount of time and energy participants are able to give.
- It enhances the visibility and stature of the planning process.
- It provides for a broad perspective on the issues.

Determine who can be an active member and who can serve in an advisory capacity. In most cases, one or two people will be doing the bulk of the work. At the very least, you should obtain input from all functional areas. Remember:

The graphic summarizes the process.

- Upper management
- Line management
- Labor
- Human Resources
- Engineering and maintenance
- Safety, health and environmental affairs

- Public information officer
- Security
- Community relations
- Sales and marketing
- Legal
- Finance and purchasing

Have participants appointed in writing by upper management.

Their job descriptions could also reflect this assignment.

*Here's one example of a planning team.*

PAGE 9

**Source:** Downloaded from the World Wide Web, November 2008: www.fema.gov/pdf/library/bizindst.pdf. FEMA, *Emergency Management Guide for Business and Industry*, pages 9–10.

When you write for general readers, you must determine what they already know and understand. You want to gather as much information as possible about them because the more you know about their background, education, reading ability, and attitudes, the better you can anticipate what they will understand and what type of vocabulary you should use.

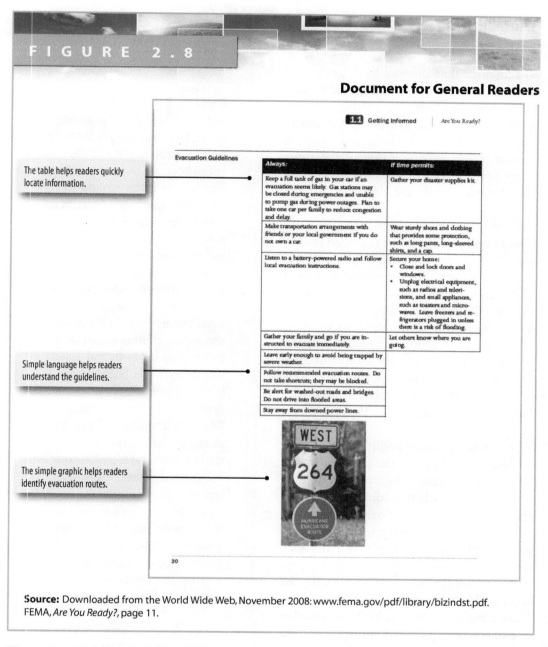

# FIGURE 2.8

**Document for General Readers**

Figure 2.8 above is an excerpt from a document prepared by Homeland Security and FEMA that tells families how to plan for disasters. This document uses simple, nontechnical language. Compare the language in this document with the language in Figure 2.7 for managers.

## Will Multiple Groups of Readers Read or Use the Document?

Often, more than one person or group will read your documents. The *initial reader,* such as an administrative assistant or even a department head, may skim the document to determine who in the organization should receive it. Judging from the summary, cover letter, title, or introduction, the initial reader sends the document to the primary reader.

The *primary reader* is the intended reader: for example, the technician who will use the instructions, the executive who will make the decision, and so on. The primary reader will use the document to complete a task, to gather information, or to make a decision. Some primary readers use the document to make a decision, but may read only certain sections and then send the document to a secondary reader, who has only a minor interest in the document.

The *secondary reader* might be a technical adviser whose opinion the decision maker seeks. Such a reader assumes the role of primary reader when reading the sections that draw on his or her area of expertise. For example, the primary reader of a proposal might be a manager, and the secondary reader might be a technical expert who assumes the role of primary reader for the Problems section of a document. The Dow Chemical website, in the interactive document analysis found online, illustrates a document for multiple readers. Follow these tips in the sidebar at right when writing for multiple groups of readers.

**TIPS FOR WRITING FOR MULTIPLE GROUPS OF READERS**

- **Divide the document into distinct sections so readers can go directly to the sections that apply to them.** For example, you might have a Getting Started section for general readers and an Advanced Techniques section for technicians.
- **Use devices that help readers locate information in the document.** These devices include indexes, tables of contents, executive summaries, headings, and tabs (Holland, Charrow, and Wright 1988).
- **Put definitions of technical vocabulary, explanations of technical concepts, and other technical details in footnotes, appendices, or other special sections that readers can easily find** (Holland, Charrow, and Wright 1988). Clearly label these sections with headings, icons, or color so readers can locate them.
- **Direct the language and presentation of a single document to readers with the lowest level of technical expertise.** This technique works especially well for instruction and policy manuals.
- **If you have the time and the budget, write separate documents for each group of readers.** This option benefits readers by allowing you to organize and direct the document to one group of readers. However, few organizations have the budget or time for this option.
- **Put the document online so you can compartmentalize it for readers with various levels of knowledge.** Include good navigation tools so readers can easily locate the sections they need.

# DETERMINE YOUR READERS' PURPOSE, NEEDS, AND PREFERENCES

Just as you have a purpose for writing your document, your readers have a purpose for reading it. They approach your document with questions and expectations about the information and perhaps the style of the document. They have specific needs that you must consider when writing and designing your document.

You may wonder how you can determine your readers' expectations and needs. If possible, talk to them. This method, however, is not always possible because of the number of readers, their geographic location, or your relationship to them. You may not know your readers or they may not be expecting the document, so gathering information directly from them may not be feasible or appropriate. If you are writing for a large group, find out about your readers by talking with a representative sample. Or, contact people who know your readers or have previously written for or worked with them.

Let's consider Randy and his feasibility study for repairing the turbine. Randy knows the secondary readers at the home office, but he doesn't know the primary reader, the plant manager, well. How can he determine the manager's needs and preferences? He can ask both the plant manager and coworkers who have worked with the plant manager. He can also look at reports previously prepared for the manager. The following sections provide guidelines to help you meet your readers' purposes, needs, and preferences.

## Think about Your Readers' Purposes for Reading

You have a purpose for writing, and your readers have a purpose for reading. Readers have one or more of these purposes for reading a technical document
- to gather information
- to answer a specific question
- to make a decision
- to perform a task or specific action

To determine your readers' purposes, consider some of the questions they might ask.

Let's consider Randy's readers. His primary reader is the plant manager; his secondary reader is the vice president of production in the home office. Figure 2.9 below lists the questions Randy thinks these readers will ask. Randy thinks the plant manager (the primary reader) is concerned with certain aspects of the recommendation: the cost of the recommended option in terms of time and personnel, whether the recommended option will solve the problem, and why Randy thinks option 3 is the most feasible. The vice president (the secondary reader) is most concerned with the financial impact of the solution on the plant and the company budgets, the impact of the turbine shutdown on other plants, and the effect of the chosen option on the company's overall production of electricity.

**FIGURE 2.9**

### Questions That Randy's Readers Might Ask

**Primary Reader: The Plant Manager**
- What are the three options?
- What is the cost of each option?
- How much time and personnel will each option take?
- What are the criteria for evaluating each option?
- What are the advantages and disadvantages of each option?
- How much downtime, if any, will each option cause the plant?
- What is the most cost-effective option over the long term?
- How and why is option 3 better than the other options?
- Is option 3 technically sound? Will it repair the turbine and solve the vibration problem?
- Can the plant personnel perform the high-speed balance or will we have to hire an outside company?

**Secondary Reader: Vice President of Production**
- What impact will option 3 have on the production of electricity in the northern district?
- Will the other plants have to generate additional electricity while the turbine is being repaired? If so, for how long?
- How much does option 3 cost?
- Is the cost within the plant's budget? If not, how much can the plant contribute?
- Is option 3 cost effective?
- Has the plant considered all possible options?
- Is option 3 a long-term solution?

## Consider Your Readers' Physical Surroundings and Time Constraints

Think about how and where readers will use the document and what time constraints they face. Readers' physical surroundings can influence your choices such as the cover, binding, headings, page size, paragraph divisions, and type size. For example, some readers work in noisy, distracting areas; others work in environments where documents are likely to get dirty and pages get bent and torn. By considering readers' surroundings, you can design and organize the document to meet their needs. For example, if you know your readers will use your instructions in a warehouse, you put the instructions in a sturdy binding or notebook and laminate the pages so readers can clean the pages. If you know your readers will use your reference manual at a small computer workstation, use a relatively small page size that fits next to the computer and put the manual in a three-ring binder that lies flat or put the manual online.

Along with considering where readers will use the document, think about the time readers have to read your document. For example, your readers may receive many documents each week and have little time to read them. To help readers locate information quickly, organize and design your document to be easily accessible. If your readers are executives who receive many proposals, include tabs for the major sections so they can quickly flip to the sections they need. You should also include an executive summary that briefly makes the case for your proposal. If you are presenting your information on the company intranet or website, include concise summaries of long passages so readers can decide whether to read in more detail (Fugate 2001). Use several design devices to help busy readers find information in your document
* headings and subheadings
* tabs that separate the major sections
* table of contents and index for longer, formal documents
* page designs with ample white space
* graphics that summarize information
* summaries at the beginning of documents and major sections
* overviews at the beginning of documents and major sections

## Consider Your Readers' Preferences

Your readers may have preferences about style, format, design, and media (paper, email, or other electronic formats). For example, some people like to receive documents by way via email, and others prefer a hardcopy. Organizations also have preferences. Some want the organization's logo to appear in particular colors on every cover page. Some expect all documents to be printed in a specific typeface. How do you find out about these preferences?
* Talk to your readers when possible.
* Talk with others who have written for or worked with your readers.
* Look at documents that your readers or their organizations have written.

As you talk with readers and their coworkers and examine their documents, look for their preferences in style, format, design, and media. You may discover other preferences, but these four areas give you a starting place. Once you have identified preferences, decide whether and how you can accommodate them. If you are writing to more than one person or group, these preferences may be incompatible. They may contradict your organization's policies for technical documents or they may be inconsistent in style.

## Consider Your Readers' Culture

Consider your readers' culture to ensure that you don't unknowingly offend or mislead them. Ask these questions:

- Are the readers from a non-U.S. culture? If so, what cultural characteristics will affect your document?
- How fluent are the readers in written English?
- What choices do you need to make about document organization? Deductive or inductive? Degree of specificity? Type of information to include about you and your organization? Appropriate tone, formality, and graphics?[1]

For more information on considering readers' cultures, see the table on understanding the differences between U.S. and non-U.S. written communication on the next page.

Learn about your readers:
- Ask for help from people who have worked with them or know them.
- Talk with the readers themselves.
- Examine other documents prepared for your readers and ask about the documents' effectiveness.

# ANALYZE YOUR READERS' ATTITUDES AND EXPECTATIONS

When you understand your readers' attitudes and expectations, you make better decisions about the appropriate information, tone, design, and organization. You can determine the attitudes and expectations of readers whom you or your coworkers know. When you or your coworkers don't know your readers, you cannot easily analyze their attitudes. Imagine yourself in their place to determine how interested they might be in the subject or how they might react to your document or to your organization. Do some research. The following sections suggest techniques for analyzing your readers' attitudes about your document's subject and about you and your organization.

[1] Tebeaux and Driskill (1999). Used by permission of Baywood Publishing Company, Inc.

| Characteristic | How U.S. Readers and Writers Approach This Characteristic | When Writing for U.S. Readers | How Non-U.S. Readers and Writers Approach This Characteristic | When Writing for Non-U.S. Readers |
|---|---|---|---|---|
| Importance of individual or groups | • Organizations expect written communication to be accurate and to document activities and decisions.<br>• Employees see themselves as individuals who are not defined by their jobs or their organizations. | • Use I rather than We.<br>• Address letters to a primary reader.<br>• Sign your letters. | • Employees prefer face-to-face communication.<br>• Employees see themselves as members of an organization, not as individuals. | • Use We rather than I.<br>• Sign your letters with your company name, not your name. |
| Value of business life and personal relationships | • Business life and goals have a higher priority than personal life and goals.<br>• Work and personal life are separate.<br>• Documents are precise and have an objective, direct tone. | • Focus on the technical information with little, if any, reference to your personal life or goals.<br>• If you mention personal information related to you or your reader, place it after the technical information. | • Personal relationships are more important than business relationships.<br>• Work and personal life are intertwined.<br>• Readers and writers emphasize the responsibility shared by the group.<br>• Documents have a subjective, indirect tone. | • Work to build a personal relationship with the readers and their organization.<br>• Expect to conduct business during social activities. |
| Effect of job rank or status | • The distance between managers and subordinates is less formal.<br>• Managers and subordinates usually develop close working relationships. | • Address your managers by their first names.<br>• Generally, use less formal communications such as email and memos to correspond with your manager. | • The relationship between manager and subordinate is formal. Job status is important.<br>• Managers and subordinates have a formal working relationship. | • Do not be too informal. If you have never met your reader, use his or her title, such as Ms., Mr., or Dr.<br>• Generally, use more formal documents, such as letters to communicate. Avoid email. |
| Expectations related to context | • Readers expect documents to contain comprehensive, information—all the reader needs to understand the document and make a decision.<br>• These readers are from a low-context culture. | • Spell out all the details.<br>• Include only business-related information. | • Readers value documents where the details are implicit. The implicit information is conveyed via other forms of communication developed through a personal relationship.<br>• These readers are from a high-context culture. | • Omit obvious information to avoid insulting the reader. For example, in a high-context culture, a cup of hot coffee would not include the warning "Beware of hot contents" because everyone knows a cup of coffee is hot. |
| Expections about uncertainty | • Readers value and expect clear guidelines, goals, and information. They are uncomfortable with uncertainty.<br>• Readers expect specific timelines and deadlines. | • Begin with the most important ideas.<br>• State your points clearly, directly, and objectively.<br>• Set firm deadlines.<br>• Highlight important information in bulleted lists.<br>• Confirm details and verbal decisions in writing. | • Readers are comfortable with uncertainty.<br>• Readers do not expect firm deadlines and timelines. Instead, deadlines and timelines are relative and flexible.<br>• Readers rely less on written guidelines and goals and more on a mission statement or code of conduct. | • Place the main point at the end of the document.<br>• De-emphasize the main points.<br>• Suggest a deadline or a timeline, rather than stating a required, firm deadline or timeline. |

[2] Adapted from Elizabeth Tebeaux and Linda Driskill "Culture and the Shape of Rhetoric" Protocols of International Document Design," *Exploring the Rhetoric of International Professional Communication: An Agenda for Teachers and Researchers*. Ed. Carl R. Loritt with Dixie Goswami. New York: Baywood. 1999. Used by permission of Baywood Publishing Company, Inc.

## Analyze Your Readers' Attitudes about the Subject

Your readers' attitudes about your subject may be negative, positive, neutral, skeptical, or enthusiastic. If their attitude is positive or enthusiastic, your task is easier. For example, you won't have to entice the readers into your document or figure out how to convince them to read or use it. If their attitude is negative, skeptical, or neutral, you must motivate readers to read your document or persuade them to accept your recommendations. For example, if you know readers will resist your recommendations, you would present the benefits or reasons for the recommendations before actually presenting them. When readers have positive attitudes about your subject, you want to reinforce those attitudes. When attitudes are negative, however, you want to change them.

To anticipate readers' attitudes toward a document, think about how they will feel about the topic. For example, a software user who is troubleshooting while installing software is motivated to read a troubleshooting guide. In contrast, a company executive may be skeptical or unenthusiastic about reading an unsolicited letter from an unknown inventor requesting funding for a new way to measure ozone. Imagine yourself in the readers' situation so you can analyze attitudes toward your document. You can also
- ask for help from people who have worked with your readers or who know them
- talk with your readers about what information to include
- read background documents and information related to the topic to find out what your readers thought of those documents and information

Consider Randy's feasibility report for repairing the turbine. In analyzing his readers' attitudes, he begins with the plant manager who is unhappy about spending more money on the turbine because less than a year ago the plant spent $750,000 to repair it. Those repairs caused the plant to be offline for more than six weeks. The manager is nervous about spending more money and losing more production time. Randy works directly with the manager but is new to the plant and still must prove his abilities to gain the manager's confidence. He decides to meet with the manager to get feedback about the three options. Randy also decides to talk with some former coworkers in the home office; they worked with the manager for several years. Randy's task with the vice president of production is easier. He reported directly to her for six years, so he emails his recommended solution to her to get her feedback. He believes that she is likely to agree with him but will expect him to analyze all three options and justify their costs.

## Analyze Your Readers' Attitudes toward You and Your Organization

Your readers' attitudes toward you and your organization influence their reactions to your document. These attitudes reflect the readers' previous experiences with you or your organization. If readers have had a good experience working with you or your organization, they will probably look favorably on your document even before reading it. If readers have had a negative experience with you or your organization, you face a challenge: You will have to use part of your document to regain their confidence. If you don't know your readers, find out if your coworkers have worked with them. If your coworkers have had positive experiences with your readers, you probably can assume the readers will have a favorable attitude toward you and your organization. If the experience was negative, you need to design and organize the document to regain their confidence.

Even if your readers don't know you, they have a preconceived attitude about your organization. Think about your attitude toward the Internal Revenue Service (IRS). Would you be enthusiastic about receiving a letter from them? Most of us would not look forward to that. Correspondence from the IRS often is unwelcome information about filing tax forms or paying back taxes and penalties. Even though most of us don't know anyone at the IRS, we have a preconceived attitude about the organization and what it does. Likewise, your readers may have a preconceived attitude about your organization.

Let's look at what Randy discovered about the plant manager's attitude toward him and the plant. Because the manager is an internal reader, Randy knows the manager is interested in the future of the plant and its reputation with the home office—both issues that relate directly to the manager's credibility and job performance. Randy knows the manager respects his abilities but will not accept his recommendation based solely on these abilities. Randy has been working at the plant for only two months, so the manager will expect solid evidence to support Randy's recommendations.

## CREATE A READER PROFILE

Think about your readers throughout the writing process. Identify them and anticipate as best you can how they will respond to your document. After drafting the document, if possible ask one or more of the primary readers to read your draft and give you their reaction. If their response is not positive, ask them for advice on how to change your document to meet your goals.

To help you anticipate your readers' reactions, create a reader profile sheet like the one on this book's website (below).

DOWNLOAD A READER PROFILE SHEET ONLINE AT

WWW.GRTEP.COM

# CASE STUDY ANALYSIS

## Microsoft's Clippy

### Background

In Microsoft Office 1997, Microsoft introduced Clippy. If you used an earlier version of Microsoft Word, you may have seen Clippy, an animated paperclip with large, winking eyes. Clippy was the software user's link to the online help system. Clippy was operated by a type of software called a wizard. *Wizards* help readers complete tasks by asking questions. Originally, Clippy offered online help to the user without being asked. Clippy would appear on the screen and ask, "What would you like to do?" Many Office users found Clippy annoying. One user complained that "it pops up without warning—even when you don't want it or don't need it" (quoted in Shroyer 2000). Another user complained that Clippy "wouldn't be so obnoxious if you could control it. As is, it moves all over the place and gets in the way" (quoted in Shroyer 2000). Because so many users reacted negatively to Clippy, *PC World* published articles telling users how to turn off Clippy (Li-Ron 1998). In October 1998, Microsoft gave customers the code to remove Clippy from the system (Shroyer 2000).

What went wrong? Why did users reject Clippy? They rejected Clippy, in part, because the software designers assumed that users couldn't work without supervision. In reality, the users found Clippy's help intrusive. The users knew what they were doing; if they didn't, they asked for help (Shroyer 2000). The software designers assumed that all users knew less than they did and would welcome help from Clippy. These designers' misguided assumptions frustrated many users.

The software designers at Microsoft learned from their users; in Office 2000 and later versions, Clippy was more user friendly. Clippy sat in one corner of the screen, and the user could turn off Clippy by simply clicking. Clippy became the "office assistant," and users could change Clippy to the character they wanted.

### Assignment

- How could the designers at Microsoft have better anticipated how users would react to Clippy?
- Select a software program and do the following:
  - Find an example of an automatic function—one the user does not or cannot easily change or turn off.
  - Is that function user friendly? If not, how could the designers have made the function more user friendly?
  - Be prepared to share your findings with your instructor and your class.

TAKING IT INTO THE *workplace*

## Readers and the Web
### The Changing Demographic of Internet Users

Americans are overwhelmingly turning to the Internet to gather information, to connect with family and friends, and to conduct business. According to a study by Pew Research, the fastest growing group of Internet users in the U.S. are those aged 50 and older. Those users nearly doubled from 22 percent in April 2009 to 42 percent in May 2010 (Madden 2010). Once thought of as "relatively slow to adopt new technologies" and to view computers as "tools" (Fugate 2001, 40), these older Americans now embrace the Internet. Unlike their younger counterparts, older readers prefer email for maintaining contact with friends, family, and colleagues; yet they do "rely on social network platforms to help manage their daily communication" (Madden). A 2012 Pew Research study reports that once adults age 65 and older" are given the tools and training needt to start using the internet, they become fervent users of the technology".[3] Companies, government agencies, and nonprofit groups want to capture the attention of this growing group of Internet users.

## Assignment

Assume that you work for your city. You want to learn more about how the over 50 age group in your city uses the Internet. You want to know what they like and don't like in a website and how they prefer to receive information about city services—what information do they like to gather online and what information do they prefer to receive through email or traditional mail. To gather that information, you decide to survey a small group of citizens over age 50.

1. Develop a questionnaire for citizens over age 50 in your city. In the survey, ask questions about how they prefer to receive information from the city, what types of information they expect to be on the city website, etc. (To learn about writing questionnaires, see Chapter 5.)
2. Ask at least five citizens over 50 to complete the questionnaire.
3. Summarize your findings in an email to the city manager.

[3] Source: Zichuhr, Kathryn and Mary Madden. "Older adults and internet use: for the first time, half of adults ages 65 and older are online." Pew Research Center's Internet & American Life Project, 6 June 2012

# EXERCISES

1. Write two paragraphs about one of these topics or about a topic that you select.
   • a car accident you were involved in
   • a grade you received
   • a class you took
   • the relationship between body fat and aerobic exercise
   • the relationship between ozone and vehicle emissions
   • cheese production
   • safety precautions for women walking alone at night

   Write each paragraph for a different reader. The readers should have different purposes for reading and different levels of knowledge about the topic. Refer to the online Reader Profile Worksheet (URL at bottom of page 43) as you analyze your readers and determine their needs and expectations.

2. The following passage appears in a brochure on property tax appraisals written for homeowners. These homeowners have different educational backgrounds and levels of expertise about property tax appraisals. Most of these homeowners are general readers and will read these paragraphs to understand property appraisals, which determines their home's fair market value or what an appraiser believes is the home's value were it to be put up for sale.

   **What Is Market Value?**
   Section 1.04 of the Texas Property Tax Code defines *market value* as follows:

   Market value means the price at which a property would transfer for cash or its equivalent under prevailing market conditions if
   a. exposed for sale in the open market with a reasonable time for the seller to find a purchaser
   b. both the seller and the purchaser know of all uses and purposes to which the property is adapted and for which it is capable of being used and of the enforceable restrictions on its use

c. both the seller and the purchaser seek to maximize their gains and neither is in a position to take advantage of the exigencies of the other

Write a memo to your instructor explaining why this paragraph about market value doesn't adequately respond to readers' needs and levels of expertise. Comment on the specific language that readers might not understand.

3. Find an article for expert readers on a topic related to your major field of study. Make sure you understand the article and then complete this assignment:
   a. Write a memo to your instructor describing the probable educational background of the article's primary readers, their level of technical expertise, and their purpose for reading the article.
   b. Select a 200- to 300-word passage that you find particularly interesting and rewrite it for readers with a low level of technical expertise.
   c. Attach a copy of the article to your memo and rewritten passage. Turn both into your instructor.

4. **Collaborative exercise:** Working with a team, locate two ads for the same type of product. For example, you might locate ads for coffee from Starbucks and Folgers, or ads for a hybrid vehicle and a traditional vehicle. When you have found the ads, complete the following steps:
   a. Profile the intended readers of each ad. Use the online Reader Profile Worksheet online as your guide.
   b. Be prepared to discuss how effectively the ads address the attitudes and expectations of the intended readers.

DOWNLOAD THE READER PROFILE WORKSHEET ONLINE AT

WWW.GRTEP.COM

## Informing Students about Financial Aid

### Background

Although this assignment is a team project, your instructor may modify it to be an individual assignment. Your team has received the following assignment from the scholarship and financial aid office at your college or university:

> Our school is losing many good students because they cannot afford the cost of tuition, books, and living expenses. Many of these students are unaware of the scholarships and other forms of financial aid that are available. Students don't know they can apply for scholarships based only on merit, scholarships based on merit and financial need, and scholarships and grants based solely on financial need. Scholarships and other forms of financial aid help students stay in school. Students, however, may be unaware of these scholarships, think they don't qualify, or think that applying for financial aid is too much trouble.

### Assignment

Your assignment is to create a document aimed at students at your college or university informing them that scholarships and financial aid are available to qualifying students. Determine the most appropriate media for presenting this information to students: website, student newspaper, flier, email, or letter. Whatever media you select, your document should motivate students with financial difficulties to come to the scholarship and financial aid office for information.

Follow these steps to complete the assignment:
1. Complete the online Reader Profile Worksheet at the URL below.
2. Visit your college or university's website or financial aid office to gather information about scholarships and financial aid at your university.
3. Determine the most appropriate format for your readers.
4. Turn the document in to your instructor. Include the completed Reader Profile Worksheet.

 DOWNLOAD THE READER PROFILE WORKSHEET ONLINE AT

WWW.GRTEP.COM

# chapter *three*

## Collaborating in the Workplace

iStockphoto 2008.

As a professional in the workplace, you will work as part of a team. The team might collaborate to design a new product, to propose a project, to solve a problem, or to write a procedure. The type and level of the collaboration will depend on the project, its purpose, and the team's work style. Professionals collaborate because teams usually create better and more efficient solutions, products, designs, and written documents than individuals working alone. However, for many professionals, collaboration is frustrating and time-consuming because they don't know how to collaborate effectively and efficiently. As a student, you may have experienced this frustration when working with a team.

This chapter presents guidelines to help you to collaborate effectively and efficiently and to understand collaborative writing in the workplace.

You can write collaboratively in many ways in the workplace: as part of a team where members equally share writing responsibilities or as part of a team where one member is the primary writer. You may not be part of a team, however, to work collaboratively. You can also collaborate by writing for others. Let's begin by discussing that type of collaboration.

## Collaborating When Writing for Others

When you collaborate by writing for others, you write all or most of a document while other professionals supply the information you need to write, design, and perhaps, publish. A good example of this type of collaboration is Paul's work on a proposal for a new telecommunications system for the Northwest Medical Center. Paul collaborates with technical specialists and salespeople to gather the information for the proposal and to plan the document. He will talk with the medical center's administrators and work with graphic designers on the layout and graphics. After Paul has gathered the information and discussed his plans with his associates, he will draft, revise, and publish the document himself. The technical specialists and the salespeople will not write any of the proposal. Once Paul has completed it, the salespeople will present it to the Northwest Medical Center. Paul's name won't appear on the document.

> Workplace teams may use their expertise, the stages of the writing process, or the sections of the document to set up team members' responsibilities.

You can also write collaboratively by preparing a document for someone else's signature. You collaborate with that person to determine what he or she wants in the document. As you write, you and that person collaborate to be sure the document meets his or her expectations. In these situations, you have the ultimate responsibility for gathering and analyzing the information needed for the document. You might collaborate with other professionals to obtain information, but you are responsible for using your expertise to write a document that will carry someone else's signature. A good example of this type of collaboration occurs in Rhonda's job. She is a new engineer for an architectural engineering company, and she is responsible for preparing construction specifications. She recently wrote specifications for protecting the underground pipes of a water-pumping station the company is designing. She researched the protection required for the pipes, wrote the specifications, and the project manager signed off on the specification document.

## Collaborating as a Team Member

When you collaborate as a team member, you work with one or more people to produce a document. Workplace teams may use any of the following criteria to set up team members' responsibilities:

- team members' expertise
- stages of the writing process
- sections of the document

### Collaborating Based on Team Members' Expertise

Some teams divide the work based on team members' expertise or job functions. For example, if you work in marketing, you would be responsible for information related to marketing. Consider the team in Figure 3.1. The biologist is the subject-matter expert and responsible for gathering the information needed to draft the document, while the other team members are responsible for their job functions—marketing, legal, and writing. For this team, the biologist gathers the information, the legal specialist answers the legal questions, and the marketing specialist provides the marketing information. The technical communication specialist writes, revises, and produces the document. In this setup, the team divides the work based on each person's expertise or job function.

When collaborating based on expertise, team members may not share the writing responsibility equally. For example, Neil collaborated with coworkers in engineering and management to prepare a proposal. They analyzed the writing situation together, brainstormed what to include in the proposal, and outlined the proposal. Then Neil wrote all sections of the proposal, except the plan of action and the budget. The team members did not share the writing responsibility equally, but each contributed. In some team writing projects, you may have more or less responsibility because of your job function or technical expertise.

### Collaborating Based on Stages of the Writing Process

Instead of dividing the work based on members' job functions, teams may collaborate based on the stages of the writing process. As Figure 3.2 shows, team members work together to plan the document: Together they analyze the writing situation and organize the information. After the team has planned the document, some members draft the document. Others prepare the graphics. Once those team members responsible for drafting the document and preparing the graphics have completed their work, some (or perhaps all) of the team members revise the document. Finally, the entire team proofreads the document. Teams often collaborate in this fashion to work more efficiently. When teams draft as a group, the work is inefficient and time consuming. By dividing the work based on the stages of the writing process, teams work more efficiently.

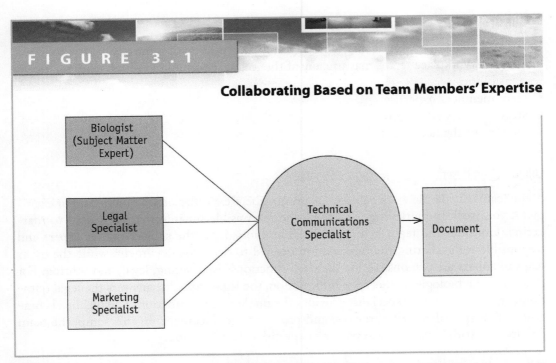

## FIGURE 3.1

**Collaborating Based on Team Members' Expertise**

- Biologist (Subject Matter Expert)
- Legal Specialist
- Marketing Specialist

→ Technical Communications Specialist → Document

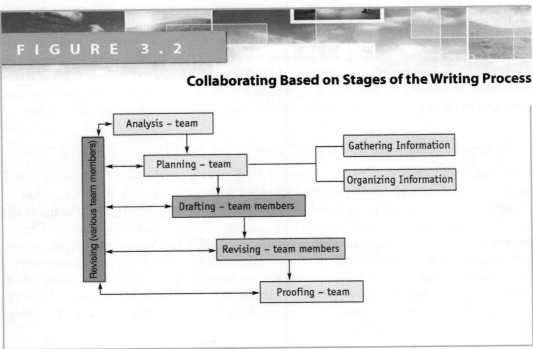

## FIGURE 3.2

**Collaborating Based on Stages of the Writing Process**

- Analysis – team
- Planning – team
  - Gathering Information
  - Organizing Information
- Drafting – team members
- Revising – team members
- Proofing – team

Revising (various team members)

## Collaborating Based on Sections of the Document

Teams may collaborate based on sections of the document, where each team member is responsible for preparing one or more sections. For example, if a team of four is writing a four-chapter manual, each person might write one chapter. This method of collaboration is common with large projects, such as proposals or manuals. However, this method leads to uneven style, inconsistencies, or unnecessary repetition. To avoid these problems, teams should use style sheets when planning the document and edit the document for consistency.

 ## MANAGING THE PROJECT AND CONDUCTING EFFECTIVE TEAM MEETINGS

At the beginning of a team project, your team needs to decide how to manage the project and conduct the meetings. First, hold a planning meeting to determine how your team will operate. At this meeting, team members define the task, take care of basic housekeeping, and set the team's schedule. These duties appear in the Tips for the First Team Meeting. By taking care of these tasks at the first meeting, you foster effective and efficient collaboration.

### Conducting Effective Face-to-Face Meetings

When possible, your team should meet face-to-face. As Michael Schrage, author of *No More Teams! Mastering the Dynamics of Creative Collaboration* (1995), explains, his favorite collaboration tool is the face-to-face meeting. For example, a Silicon Valley engineering firm decided it would only hold face-to-face meetings when problems arose; otherwise, employees would handle all business over the Internet. After "60 days, they went back to holding weekly meetings" because they were only getting together to argue (Quain quoting Schrage 1997). The more we use technology to collaborate, the more important face-to-face meetings become.

In the workplace, many people consider meetings their biggest waste of time (Quain quoting Schrage 1997). You may have been on a team where meetings were, indeed, a waste of time, perhaps because some team members arrived late, others were unprepared, or a few talked on their cell phones or searched the Internet during meetings. However, meetings are valuable tools for effective collaboration when teams establish and stick to some simple guidelines. Review the Tips for Conducting Effective Face-to-Face Meetings.

- **Define the writing project.** What is your team assigned to do? What document, or deliverable, will your team complete? All team members should understand and agree on the task, the readers, the purpose, and the document's scope. Allow ample time to define the task as this step lays the foundation for the project.
- **Set a schedule.** Set a time table for completing each member's tasks. The time table should include deadlines for turning in drafts.
- **Trade phone numbers and email addresses.** All team members need to know how to contact the others. This contact information is especially important if members work in different geographic locations—for example, if members work in different buildings, cities, states, or even countries.
- **Select a team leader, sometimes called a project manager.** The team leader serves as a liaison between the team and the clients and/or management. (In school, the team leader represents the team when contacting the instructor.) The team leader keeps the team on task, sets up and conducts team meetings, coordinates the team's work, and coordinates communication with management and clients.
- **Decide on each team member's task or role** (if the tasks or roles aren't already assigned). Even though the team is responsible for the final document, each member will have a primary responsibility for a task that best fits his or her technical expertise or abilities. Each member should understand each team member's responsibilities and how each member's task relates to the work of the team.
- **Decide how the team will communicate and meet.** Will you communicate by phone, email, text message, or website? Will you meet in person or meet using media such as videoconferencing, online meeting software, or a combination? Team members need to know how each member's work is progressing so the team and the team leader can track progress. Team meetings and communications help the team identify and resolve problems more efficiently and effectively.
- **Decide what software the team will use to create the document and the graphics.** Make sure all team members can easily access the software they need.
- **Decide how you will share files.** Your team needs a place where members can store files for members to "check out." You might use a shared folder on the organization's intranet, or other online file-sharing locations. For example, your team might use Google Docs to manage and share documents.
- **Create a style sheet.** Style sheets save time for everyone because all team members use the same format when writing their individual sections. Style sheets simplify revisions and proofreading. As your team creates its style sheet, review the design and style questions listed in Figure 3.3. Consider using the styles function of your wordprocessing software.

- **Decide how to evaluate each member's contribution.** In most workplaces, team members do not evaluate each other's contributions. Instead, the team is evaluated on the result of their work: the deliverable. In some work environments and in some classrooms, you may be asked to evaluate each team member's contribution. In those cases, your team should decide on the evaluation criteria. Sometimes, you will be given a form to use; your team will not create the form or establish the criteria. Consider keeping a log of your work and your contributions. This log will help you document your work. Figure 3.4 shows a sample log.

**TIPS** FOR CONDUCTING EFFECTIVE FACE-TO-FACE MEETINGS

- **Arrive on time.** When you are on time, you show respect for the other team members. When members arrive late, the leader must take time to summarize what the team has accomplished during the late member's absence.
- **Tell your team leader if you will miss the meeting.** If you know you will miss a meeting, let your team leader know as soon as possible.
- **Be prepared.** If you have a task to complete before the meeting, complete it. You show disrespect for your teammates when you are unprepared and you may delay the schedule.
- **Stick to the agenda.** The leader of the meeting should
  - Establish an agenda before the meeting.
  - Send the agenda to team members before the meeting.
  - Keep the team focused on that agenda during the meeting. If the team needs to discuss an issue not on the agenda, set up another meeting or wait until you have completed all the agenda items. Then, if you have time, discuss the new item.
- **Take minutes.** One team member should take minutes during the meeting and send copies of them to each team member after the meeting. *Minutes* are a record of decisions made at the meeting. Minutes give you a written record of what the team decided. They are especially valuable on long projects and for those who miss the meeting. (See Chapter 14 for information on writing minutes.)
- **Make sure every member understands his or her task at the end of the meeting.** At the end of the meeting, the leader should:
  - Summarize the decisions made during the meeting.
  - Make sure each member knows his or her assigned task.

FIGURE 3.3

**Questions to Consider When Creating a Style Sheet**

**Design Questions**
- What page layout and page size will be most effective for the readers and the document's purpose?
- What typeface and size will we use for the text and the headings?
- Where will the headings appear on the page? Will they be indented? If so, how far will they be indented?
- What page margins will we use?
- What bullet style will we use? Will we indent the list? If so, how far?
- What file format will each team member use to submit drafts? Will we use a word processing or desktop-publishing program?
- Will we use color? If so, where? What will our budget allow?

**Style Questions**
- What, if any, abbreviations or technical terminology will we use?
- Will we use words or numerals for chapter numbers, section numbers, and other enumerations? Will we use Arabic or Roman numerals?
- What terminology will we use when referring to the readers, to the organization, or to the team? Will we use second-person pronouns when referring to the readers?
- What conventions will we use when writing? (For example, if your team is writing software documentation, how will you refer to specific function keys or to the arrow keys on the keyboard? Will you use icons?)
- How will we refer to figures and tables?

## Setting a Schedule

After the team has defined its task and assigned roles, it establishes a schedule for completing the project. A schedule will clarify
- each member's responsibility
- how each member's work relates to the work of the whole team
- when each member should complete his or her work

# Project Log

Your Name: _Meredith Mitchell_

Project Title: _Social Media Practices of Small Businesses in Colorado_

**Log of Your Independent Work**

| Activity | Date | Number of Hours |
|---|---|---|
| Conducted research for Results section | March 10 | 3 |
| Wrote Results section | March 12 | 2.5 |
| Reviewed draft of document | March 15 | 1.5 |

**Log of Your Work with the Team**

| Activity | Date | Number of Hours |
|---|---|---|
| Met with Debra to discuss the research for the Results section | March 11 | 1.5 |
| Met with team to discuss the Results section | March 11 | 1 |
| Met with team to go over the draft of the document | March 16 | 2 |

**Comments about your contributions:**

If possible, the schedule should allow for the unexpected, such as losing a team member due to a transfer to another project, illness, or personal emergency. At any stage of the process, the team may face unexpected problems. For example, the information that team members gather may be insufficient, or a draft may fail to meet the team's or management's expectations. Unexpected problems will frustrate even the most organized team; however, a schedule with built-in flexibility will alleviate some of the frustration.

##  COLLABORATING EFFECTIVELY

A project schedule should list specific, reasonable dates for completing individual tasks and allow time for meetings or other communication to discuss individual work—especially drafts. The schedule also should encourage team members to communicate frequently. Usually a team establishes a project due date and works backward to set intermediate deadlines. For example, if the project is due on April 12, April 8 may be the deadline for a completed draft, April 1 for a revised draft, and March 20 for a first draft.

As you collaborate on a writing project, the relationships that develop among team members will affect the project. Collaboration is more likely to go smoothly if team members respect and understand each other. For example, if one team member likes to communicate by email, team members might agree to use it when they want to provide information to each other. By agreeing to use email, they show respect for and understanding of one of the team members. If you have never worked with some or all of the team members, you and they might spend some time getting to know each other and each team member's expertise. As team members work together, they should frequently share relevant project information. Such contact will help all members feel they are important, valued members of the team. This section presents guidelines to help team members to collaborate successfully:

- Encourage team members to share their ideas.
- Listen intently and respectfully to all team members.
- Share information willingly.
- Consider cultural differences.
- Disagree respectfully and politely.
- Critique team members' work respectfully.

## Encourage Team Members to Share Their Ideas

You and the other team members bring unique creativity and expertise to the project. Together, you and the others represent a wealth of knowledge and ideas. To best use this knowledge, all members must share their knowledge and ideas. Even when ideas clash, team members can learn from one another. From this conflict, teams create more innovative solutions, ideas, and documents. All team members should feel comfortable expressing their ideas—even when those ideas differ from the prevailing views expressed by the majority.

Some team members may be shy or quiet and may feel uncomfortable expressing their ideas during team meetings. If you see that some members aren't participating in discussions, ask them to participate and help the team include them in the discussions. You might say, "Rob, what do you think of that approach?" or "What are your ideas about the project, Sue?" You might direct the discussion toward the shy or quiet members by saying "Let's hear what John has to say on the topic" or "We've heard some good ideas from Linda and Patrick. Let's hear what Juan has to say."

## Listen Intently and Respectfully to All Team Members

Have you ever tried to express your ideas about something in which you were truly interested while some listeners talked to others as you were speaking? Have you ever spoken to a group that didn't give you their undivided attention? Have you ever talked to listeners who appeared to hear what you were saying, but when you asked for comments, you discovered they hadn't really heard you? Their comments revealed that their minds had been elsewhere. Such situations are always frustrating. In a collaborative setting, they discourage participants from sharing their ideas. Each person needs to know the team will listen to and consider his or her ideas. Members should not expect the team to accept any or every idea that is presented, but they should expect everyone to listen and participate.

To encourage all team members to share their ideas, listen intently and respectfully to everyone. Use both nonverbal and verbal signals to let speakers know you are paying attention. The tips on the following page will help you to be an active listener.

## TAKING IT INTO THE *workplace*

### Cell Phones at Work: Convenience or Nuisance?

"Despite their overwhelming presence in today's society, cell phones perpetually straddle the line between modern convenience and disruptive nuisance. The phone calls, text messages, pictures and other data relayed to family members, friends, doctors, or even co-workers while on the job are the source of many interrupted business meetings or disgruntled employees" (McCorvey 2010, 1). You probably have been annoyed by someone who doesn't use good cell phone etiquette. This lack of etiquette is particularly problematic when cell phone users excessively or inappropriate use their cell phones at work. J. J. McCorvey suggests these guidelines for cell phone etiquette at work.

- **"The 'vibrate' function is your best friend.** When working in a professional atmosphere, the vibrate function should be a default. No one likes a loud ringer—especially when left unanswered" (McCorvey 2010, 2).
- **"No phone use during meetings."** Save the phone calls and texts for after the meetings. Many people believe that texting is acceptable in meetings; however, "texting can be as annoying as talking" (Flynn 2001).
- **"Letting calls go to voicemail isn't a sin."** According to a Pew Research survey of 1,500 adults, 24 percent of them said they felt obligated to take a call—even if it interrupted an important meeting (McCorvey 2010, 2). When you answer calls, especially personal calls, during a meeting, you are saying that the call is more important than the meeting and the people attending the meeting.
- **"Maintain low tones."** Keep your voice low if you must answer a phone call at work, or find a quiet area to talk. Your loud phone conversation annoys others who are trying to get work done (McCorvey2010, 2).
- **Use language and content appropriate for work.** Professional communication is not the same as communication at home. Your coworkers may be offended if you use expletive-filled language or discuss inappropriate topics on your cell phone (McCorvey 2010).

## Assignment

Many organizations are putting cell phone policies into place for their employees. These policies address cell phone etiquette, company-owned cell phones, and the security of the organization's information if accessed on a cell phone (Flynn 2001; McCorvey 2010). Your assignment is to
- Find at least two articles that discuss cell phone policies at work
- Summarize these articles in a memo to your instructor. Be sure to appropriately cite the articles.

## Share Information Willingly

Encourage others to share their ideas if you are willing to do the same. If you discover information that may help another member or affect what a member is doing, share that information willingly and in a timely manner. When you share such information, your team members are more likely to reciprocate, leading to good working relationships.

## Consider Cultural Differences

In the classroom and in the workplace, you may collaborate with people from other cultures. A person's culture will affect how he or she collaborates. The key is to remain open to collaboration with people from other cultures and to learn about those cultures without jumping to hasty or incorrect conclusions. Learn about your team members' cultures before your first meeting.

Team members from other cultures may
- Have difficulty speaking up or asserting themselves. Their culture may value silence more than speech.
- Be unwilling to disagree, to question others, or to be questioned. Some people of other cultures do not respond with a definite "no."
- Hesitate to ask the team to clarify information or to admit that they don't understand.

> Team members from other cultures may
> - have difficulty speaking up,
> - be unwilling to disagree, or
> - hesitate to ask for clarification.

## Disagree Respectfully and Politely

Robert I. Sutton, Stanford professor and author on innovation and business practices, writes, "Treating people with respect rather than contempt makes good business sense" (Sutton 2007, 92). One of the benefits of collaboration is the diversity of ideas and the conflicts that naturally occur. Conflicts are a healthy part of working with others. Conflict can help a team discover the best way to handle a project or the best way to organize a report. To encourage healthy conflict and disagreeing respectfully, review the tips below.

## TIPS FOR BEING AN ACTIVE LISTENER

- **Maintain eye contact with the speaker.** You let speakers know that you are actively listening when you maintain eye contact with them. Speakers who receive little eye contact feel their listeners are being inattention.
- **Avoid body language that may distract the speaker or other team members.** To signal that you are actively listening, look at the speaker and avoid distracting gestures.
- **Let the speaker finish his or her statements before you ask questions.** You encourage all team members to participate by allowing speakers to finish their statements before you ask questions or make comments. If you continually interrupt, speakers may become distracted or assume you aren't listening; or they may think you believe what you have to say is more important than what they have to say. Such interruptions discourage team members from sharing their ideas, especially those who are shy or timid.
- **Use phrases that indicate you agree with the speaker.** If you agree with the speaker, use expressions such as "I agree," "Good idea," or "I like that" to let the speaker know. These phrases also encourage those who are shy or uncomfortable sharing their ideas.
- **Ask questions when you want something clarified or when you want more information.** By asking questions, you get more information to determine whether you agree or disagree with the speaker. Your questions also encourage other team members to share their ideas and ask questions.
- **Ask questions relevant to the speaker's topic.** Effective team members ask questions to understand what a speaker has said and to connect ideas.
- **Occasionally paraphrase or summarize what the speaker has said.** By paraphrasing, you make sure you understand what the speaker has said and give the speaker the opportunity to correct any misunderstanding. If you disagree, paraphrase what the speaker has said. You may discover that you actually agree.

- **Focus on the issue, not on the individual.** When disagreeing with or criticizing the work of a team member, avoid personal remarks and insults. Remember that others members have feelings. You show respect for those feelings by respectfully and politely criticizing the ideas, not the person. Consider the difference in these approaches.
  - **Focus on the individual:** *If you paid attention to details, you would notice that I sent the email at 3:32 p.m. today.*
  - **Focus on the issue:** *I sent the email today at 3:32p.m.*
- **Don't take positions you cannot support.** Be careful not to overstate or exaggerate your ideas or your position:
  - **Overstated:** *This process will solve all our problems.*
  - **Not overstated:** *With this process, we can begin to solve some of our problems.*
- **Look for points with which you can agree when disagreements arise.** You may only disagree with part of a team member's idea or comment. If so, look for and focus on points with which you can agree. In this way, you can avoid conflict or at least minimize it.
- **Be open to criticism of your ideas.** Just as you will criticize and disagree with your team members, they, too, will criticize and disagree with your ideas. Be prepared to listen and be open to this criticism. Think of your writing and your ideas as belonging to the team, not to you. By distancing yourself emotionally from your work, you won't automatically take it personally when team members criticize your writing or ideas. This objectivity frees you to discuss the most effective way to write the team's document or present the best ideas for the team's project, rather than trying to protect and defend your document and your ideas. When the team begins to evaluate your ideas, participate in the discussion and be willing to look at your draft or your ideas objectively—even offer suggestions for improving your own work. However, be prepared to persuade team members to use your ideas if you feel they are overlooking important points.
- **Support the team decision.** Once you have had your say and the team has made a decision, support that decision fully. If you feel the decision is unethical, talk with a mentor.

## Critique Team Members' Work Respectfully

When you critique your team members' work, think about how you like having your work critiqued. You will gain your team members' respect when you critique their work respectfully. Comment on their work without offending or attacking them. When you offend a

**TIPS FOR RESPECTFULLY CRITIQUING THE WORK OF YOUR TEAM MEMBERS**

- **Make positive comments.** When possible, begin with a positive comment. When you critique the work of a team member, comment on the strengths of his or her work. For example, you could say you are suggesting ways to improve a basically good draft. Focus on the positive qualities of a draft or an idea, and tell the team member about those qualities when you suggest changes.
- **Focus on the big picture before commenting on the local issues.** For example, critique the content, the organization, or the layout before critiquing the specifics of style or grammar.
- **Recommend specific ways to improve the work.** When critiquing team members' work, give them specific information they can use to revise their work. Briefly state why you recommend the change.
- **Comment on the work, not on the team member/writer.** Avoid subjective comments about the writer or the writer's work. Instead, give objective comments. For example, criticize a specific part of an idea instead of making a broad, subjective comment that you can't support. Consider the difference in tone of these comments below:
  - **Subjective and offensive:** *I don't like the writing in your draft. It's not well done and too formal.*
  - **Objective and polite:** *The draft might be stronger and friendlier if we included more second-person pronouns.*
  In the subjective, offensive comment, the team member uses subjective, unnecessarily negative language. In the objective, polite comment, the team member uses diplomatic language and offers a specific suggestion for improving the document.
- **Be honest, yet polite.** Your goal as an individual and as a team member is to produce an effective deliverable that meets the expectations of your readers and managers. Even when you know a recommendation or critique may upset a team member, you should be honest. However, always present your comments politely.

team member, you may impede progress. Your goal is to create an effective document that meets the expectations of your team and management, not to evaluate the writer. As you critique the work of members, follow the tips listed on the previous page.

## USING ELECTRONIC TOOLS TO COLLABORATE MORE EFFICIENTLY

Electronic tools help teams communicate efficiently. With these tools, team members can work at different times and locations and still collaborate. They can work on a project when a face-to-face meeting isn't convenient or possible. For instance, you might be working on your draft at 7:30 a.m. in New York while your team members are still sleeping in California. You email your draft to your team members by 8 a.m., Eastern time, so they can work on it when they arrive at the office at 8 a.m., Pacific time. Electronic tools also allow team members to track and store revisions and changes to documents as a project progresses.

Teams have several types of tools available to facilitate collaboration. These tools
- **Help members comment on and track document changes.** You are probably familiar with this function in Microsoft Word. Using this function, teams track document drafts and ensure that all members work on the most current draft.
- **Enable members to meet online instead of in person.** Teams meet virtually using Web and video conferencing software. You may have used Skype on your laptop. If your team meets online, be sure to use the software's recording function so you have a record of all aspects of the meeting. This software can be as simple as two members meeting via webcam or as sophisticated as an entire team meeting via videoconferencing software that lets members show slides and use a virtual (digital) whiteboard. These whiteboards allow team members to share data in real time. With the whiteboard, members in different locations can "mark" on the same document or screen as if they were in the same room; or a team member in one location can show a PowerPoint presentation to members at another site.
- **Help members share files efficiently and securely.** Teams can also upload files to secure sites or to community sites where members access and manage files from anywhere, using, for example, Google Docs or SharePoint. Teams password protect their files so only members can access them. Some organizations, however, require that the documents be housed on a company intranet to ensure the information is secure.

Your team should find out what tools are available for collaboration and for sharing and storing files and determine the most effective tools for your team and your project.

# CASE STUDY ANALYSIS

## Collaborating on a Public Relations Dilemma

### Background[1]

Big Lake Steam Electric Station, a power plant near a small Texas town, uses steam to generate electricity. The plant's main steam pipe carries steam to a turbine, which drives a generator that produces electricity. The Big Lake manager observed that sections of this main steam piping system were sagging. The main steam system uses constant support hangers (a spring-type hanger) to carry the weight of its pipes and reduce the effect of the piping system on the plant equipment. Since the late 1960s when the plant was built, engineers have learned that these spring-type hangers alone cannot support the weight of the pipes over time. To compensate, engineers recommend using a combination of spring-type hangers and rigid supports (hangers without springs; see Figure 3.5). Without rigid supports, the sagging worsens, and the weight of the pipes transfers to the plant equipment. This equipment is not designed to carry the weight and will be permanently damaged if the sagging continues. Knowing the damage that continued sagging will cause, the Big Lake manager asked the corporate engineers to study the problem and recommend solutions. The corporate engineers's survey of the Big Lake plant revealed that the main steam piping system was sagging over 6.5 inches. Their survey also indicated that the sagging would worsen and eventually damage the plant equipment.

## Corporate's Solution for Repairing the Plant

In early July, the corporate office engineers suggested two solutions: the first solution would only stabilize the pipes, while the second would stabilize the pipes and correct the sagging.

[1] This case study is based on an actual situation that occurred at a power plant owned by a utility company in Dallas, Texas. This case, written by Brenda R. Sims, is adapted from Richard Louth and Ann Martin Scott, eds., *Collaborative Technical Writing: Theory and Practice* (St. Paul, Minn.: ATTW, 1989). Courtesy of the Association of Teachers of Technical Writing.

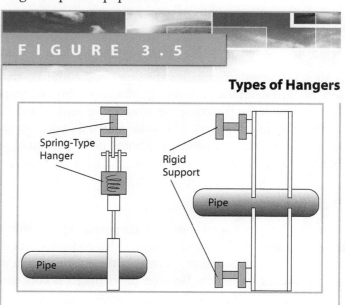

**FIGURE 3.5**

**Types of Hangers**

Spring-Type Hanger

Rigid Support

Pipe

Pipe

- **Solution 1:** Replace two of the spring-type hangers with rigid supports in the area where the main steam system was sagging. Cost: $132,100.
- **Solution 2:** Shorten the piping system by cutting out and removing a short section of the piping, then adding rigid supports, thus pulling up the lowest portion and eliminating the sag. Cost: $403,600.

## Solution 1: Replacing Two Spring-Type Hangers

This solution would stabilize the pipes, but would not eliminate the existing sagging. To implement this solution, engineers would run a computer stress analysis on the pipes to verify that the existing sagging does not result in stresses that exceed allowable limits. This analysis would require about 40 hours, but the plant would not have to shut down during the analysis. If the engineers verify that the stress levels are acceptable, subcontractors could replace the spring-type hangers during the regularly scheduled fall maintenance shutdown. With this solution, plant personnel would lose no work time.

Although this solution would be relatively inexpensive and could occur without ordering an unscheduled shutdown, corporate did not recommend this solution because
- It would not correct the existing sag, resulting in a permanent low point in the piping system. Low points can trap water and cause water hammer.
- The plant would have to install a manual drain at the low point. Periodically, plant personnel would have to manually drain the low point.
- Corporate fears that during busy periods, plant personnel would forget to drain the low points, creating additional problems.

## Solution 2: Shortening the Main Piping System and Adding Rigid Supports

This solution would stabilize the pipes and eliminate the sagging and the possibility of a low point. Therefore, even though the cost is higher, corporate recommends this solution. In the long term, the company would save money and time by shortening the pipes and adding the rigid supports. This solution would take two weeks beyond the regularly scheduled fall maintenance shutdown. Some plant personnel would have to take vacation time or time off without pay.

## Discussions about the Solutions

The Big Lake manager met with corporate representatives on July 23 to discuss the feasibility of the solutions and to express his concerns over the cost in downtime and money. The manager believes that shortening the piping system would cost the plant and the electric consumer too much. Because the manager is concerned about the time involved with both solutions, corporate sent him a memo after the meeting outlining the work needed to shorten and reweld the section of the piping system and to replace the spring-type hangers with rigid supports.

## An Emergency Plant Shutdown and the Chosen Solution

On August 30, before the plant manager had decided how to repair the sagging pipes, the Big Lake plant experienced a boiler tube leak unrelated to the sagging pipes. Plant personnel had to shut down the plant to repair the leak. While waiting for the plant to cool to begin repairing the leak, one of the spring-type hangers broke, causing the steam piping system to sag an additional two feet. The damaged hanger was temporarily repaired so the plant could resume operation and the plant manager could have more time to decide how to handle the sagging pipes.

Ten days after the unscheduled shutdown, the Big Lake manager rejected the second solution (shortening the piping system and adding rigid supports), primarily because of its high cost. He selected the first solution (replacing the spring-type hangers with rigid supports) because the repairs could be done during the regularly scheduled fall maintenance shutdown and because the plant would avoid additional downtime and the expense of the second solution.

### Citizen Concern about the Plant Shutdowns and the Sagging Pipes

The August 30 plant shutdown concerned the community's citizens because the plant employs a large portion of the town's population. When the plant manager first discovered the pipe sagging problem, the citizens feared that the sagging pipes could close the plant permanently and that if the sagging causes the pipes to rupture, the released steam could injure plant personnel.

Because these fears were unwarranted, the Big Lake manager placed an announcement on the local radio and television stations to explain that the Big Lake plant would remain open and that the plant personnel were safe. The citizens feared that the plant could close permanently, leaving the plant personnel without jobs. The citizens also feared that if the plant did remain open, the personnel would be in danger from the sagging pipes and would be laid off without pay when the pipes were eventually repaired. Now the Big Lake manager had to convince citizens that the plant needs only minor repairs that could be handled during a scheduled shutdown and that plant personnel were safe.

## Assignment

Your team will write a letter from the plant manager to the town's citizens. This letter will appear in the local newspaper. The purpose of the letter is to
- convince the citizens that the plant will remain open
- convince the citizens that the sagging pipes would not cause them to rupture and would not endanger plant personnel
- explain the type of repairs the plant manager has planned for the plant

You will collaborate with your team to
- decide what to include in the letter
- discuss the ethical dilemma, if any, the plant manager faces
- draft a letter on behalf of the plant manager
- comment on the individual letters that each team member will write

## Deciding What to Include in the Letter and Considering the Ethics of the Situation

Your team should discuss the Big Lake situation and complete the steps below.
1. List the characteristics of the readers of the letter, the citizens of the small Texas town near Big Lake. The team should answer the following questions to determine the readers' characteristics:
   - Why are the citizens interested in the Big Lake situation?
   - What is their current attitude toward the plant?
   - How would closing the plant affect the town's citizens?
   - What will the citizens want to know about how the sagging pipes will be repaired?
   - What rumors have many of the citizens heard about the sagging pipes and how these pipes affect the plant and its personnel? Are these rumors accurate?
2. Decide what information your team will include in the letter.
3. Using the Chapter 2 online worksheet, Ethical Communication, determine if the information you plan to include is ethical. If not, decide how your team will revise that information. Each team member should write an individual version of the letter and email a copy of it to your team members and the instructor.

## Critiquing the Drafts

Your team will respond to each other's letters using the comment and track changes functions of your word processing software.
1. Read each team member's letter.
2. Using the comment and track changes function, critique each team member's draft.
3. Email the marked draft to the writer.
4. Be prepared to discuss your comments with your teammates.

## Writing the Final Draft

Your team will give one final draft of the letter to your instructor. To prepare this final draft, your team should follow the guidelines for effective collaboration presented in this chapter. Your team has several options for preparing the draft.

- Write the draft using sections from the individual letters written by the team members.
- Revise sections of the individual letters to create the final draft.
- Write the final draft using only ideas from the individual letters.

Once your team has completed the final draft, give your instructor a copy.

# EXERCISES

DOWNLOAD A WORKSHEET FOR EFFECTIVE COLLABORATION AT

WWW.GRTEP.COM

1. Interview a professional in your major field of study to gather information about the kinds of collaboration you can expect as a professional. This professional can help you gather information on the kinds of collaboration that you might encounter in the workplace. For example, if you are majoring in mechanical engineering, interview an engineer about collaborative projects in his or her job. Before the interview
   - Call the professional for an appointment.
   - Gather some background information on the professional's job.
   - Create a list of questions about collaborative work, for example.
     - How often do you collaborate with coworkers?
     - On what types of projects do you collaborate?
     - What are some advantages and disadvantages you've encountered when collaborating?
     - What do you think is the most important consideration when working as a team?
   
   After the interview, write a memo to your instructor summarizing the information you gathered about collaboration.

2. You have probably worked on a team in other courses, in a volunteer organization, or on a job. Think of some of your best and worst experiences when collaborating. Be prepared to discuss these experiences in class. Based on these experiences, prepare a list of guidelines for an effective team experience. Assume these guidelines will be used by people in your class, in your volunteer organization, or at your job. As you prepare your list, remember to include what to do and what not to do.

3. You will work on a team during this course, or you may work on a team in a volunteer organization. Prepare an evaluation form that your team or the organization might use to evaluate the contributions of each team member. Once you have completed the form,
   - Save it as a PDF.
   - Write an email to your instructor.
   - Attach the PDF to the email.

4. Select a culture different from your own. Find websites with information about the culture and customs of that country. Look for customs that might affect how people from that country would collaborate. Be prepared to share your findings with your classmates.

5. **Collaborative exercise.** The city council wants to encourage more people to visit your city. The council has hired your team to write a brochure promoting the city. The council wants the brochure to include information about the city's history, attractions, entertainment, shopping, restaurants, and hotels. At the first team meeting, your team should
   • Select a team leader.
   • Trade phone numbers and email addresses.
   • Decide on each team member's task.
   • Set a schedule for doing research and for future meetings.
   • Create a style sheet.
   • Determine how the team will share files.

   After team members have gathered the information needed to draft the brochure, the team should
   • Organize the information into an outline.
   • Determine who will write each section of the outline (the team leader may assign sections, or team members may select the sections each wants to write).
   • Set a schedule for completing the drafts of the sections and for revisions.

   After your team has completed the brochure,
   • Write a memo to your instructor describing how collaboration affected your work and your team's brochure.
   • Use specific information from your project log to support and illustrate the information that you included in the memo (see Figure 3.4).
   • Attach a copy of the brochure to your memo.

 DOWNLOAD A PROJECT LOG ONLINE AT

WWW.GRTEP.COM

# REAL WORLD EXPERIENCE

## Creating a Cell Phone Etiquette Policy for Your Team

As you learned in Taking It into the Workplace, cell phone use negatively impacts meetings and coworkers. Working with a team that you are currently collaborating with either on a class project, a volunteer project, or a work project, write a cell phone policy.

- The policy should address the following cell phone activities: making and receiving phone calls, reading and sending text messages, accessing the Internet, and playing games. Your team may gather information about how organizations are dealing with these activities. Cite all sources that you use as you create your policy.
- All team members should agree with the policy. As you create the policy, remember to listen and disagree respectfully.
- The policy should be easy to read.

Once your team has agreed to a policy, draft the policy and turn it into your instructor.

## chapter *four*

# Facing Ethical and Legal Challenges

iStockphoto 2008.

In the workplace, you may face decisions where you will have to consider your values—what you believe is right and wrong. At the heart of these decisions is doing the right thing. However, doing the right thing may not always be clear cut. For example, you may feel pressured to compete at any cost, to sacrifice safety to get a product out on time, or to sidestep environmental regulations to cut costs. You might be tempted to distort statistical data to make the results of a study appear more favorable, or you might be intimidated into manipulating the language of an annual report to make your company look more profitable.

When faced with these situations, your resolve to do the right thing may be difficult to maintain. Most likely, your organization will expect you to follow standard business ethics and to know and to do the right thing, but ethical dilemmas will still arise.

*Ethics* is the study of values, often called principles of conduct, that apply to a person or group. Ethics, according to Aristotle, is the study of what is involved in doing good. When we say that someone has acted ethically, we usually mean that the person has done the right thing. When you behave ethically, you act out of the "intrinsic rightness of the behavior"; you don't do something just to keep your job or to receive personal or monetary gain (Dombrowski 2000, 42).

When you face ethical decisions that are not clear cut, the following frameworks can help you weigh the consequences of your actions:[1]
- the morality of an action
- the consequences of an action
- the rights of the people involved
- the care for relationships

Along with these frameworks, you must also consider the laws related to your action. The law cannot always tell you how to act ethically; certainly, the law cannot give you ethical constraints that come only from the fine-tuning of your own judgment and conscience (Shimberg 1980). The law can give you clearly defined legal restraints. Paul Dombrowski, author of *Ethics in Technical Communication*, explains that "ethics cannot be reduced to politics or the law because it must guide us when the law or political rules are silent" (2000, 45). The law often sets up only minimal legal restraints for behavior, whereas ethics implies "high standards of honest and honorable dealing and of methods used" in professions and businesses (Golen, Powers, and Titkemeyer 1985, 76).

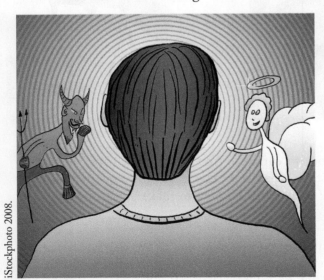

When you look at the morality of an action, you consider whether the action itself is morally right or wrong.

iStockphoto 2008.

## Morality of an Action

If you look at the *morality of an action*, you consider whether it violates your moral duty. Instead of looking at the consequences of the

[1] I base these moral standards on the scholarship of Paul Dombrowski; Mark Wicclair and David Farkas; Steven Golen, Celeste Powers, and M. Agnes Titkemeyere; and Tom Beauchamp and Norman Bowie.

action, you consider the action itself to decide whether it is morally wrong. Some actions are wrong "just for what they are and not because of their bad consequences" (Wicclair and Farkas 1984, 16). For example, we consider lying and stealing to be morally wrong even when no one is harmed or the lying and stealing produce positive consequences.

## Consequences of an Action

If you look solely at the *consequences of an action,* you use what ethical theorists call the *standard of utility.* According to this standard, you select the course of action that produces the greatest good for the greatest number of people or the least amount of harm for the fewest number of people (Wicclair and Farkas 1984). Regardless of whether an action is morally right or wrong, the standard of utility "prohibits actions that produce more bad than good" (Wicclair and Farkas 1984, 18).

> The standard of utility helps you select the course of action that produces the greatest good for the greatest number of people or the least amount of harm for the fewest number of people. (Wicclair and Farkas 1984).

Let's consider how the government of Great Britain in 2001 dealt with an outbreak of foot-and-mouth disease, a highly contagious viral disease that infects cattle, sheep, and other animals. Because foot-and-mouth disease is difficult to control, it can devastate herds of livestock, damaging agricultural industries and severely limiting the production of meat and dairy products. To stop the disease outbreak, the British government called for the slaughter of thousands of livestock in contaminated areas. By slaughtering even healthy livestock in the affected areas, government officials hoped to save thousands of other livestock and family farms. The government was using the standard of utility: It chose the least amount of harm for the fewest livestock and farmers. The government didn't focus solely on whether the action was right or wrong; it considered how it could produce the greatest good for the greatest number of people.

## Rights of the People Involved

If you look at the impact of an action on others, you consider whether you are violating the *rights of the people involved* (Wicclair and Farkas 1984). This standard means that people have the right to be treated fairly and to expect similar cases to be treated alike.

Employees in any company have a right to a reasonably safe workplace and to be informed of potential dangers in that workplace. Consumers expect to be informed of risks they may encounter as a result of a product. For example, when you visit an amusement park, you may see a sign that reads: People with back or heart problems should not ride this roller coaster. Pregnant women should not ride this roller coaster. By posting this sign, the park is considering the welfare of visitors who may ride the roller coaster. These visitors have a right to know the inherent dangers of the roller coaster. The park cannot know the health of its visitors, but it can fully disclose the dangers so that visitors can make informed decisions. Similarly, when you buy a product, you have the right to know that the information accompanying that product is complete and accurate.

## Care for Relationships

If you look at the *care for relationships*, you consider how the action affects relationships with others, especially those closest to us—our families, our coworkers, and our communities. For example, after the hijacked planes crashed into the World Trade Centers in New York in September 2001, some motion picture companies stopped the release of movies that portrayed hijacking and terrorism. Movie executives based their decisions not on whether the movies were good or bad, but instead on their care for those who had lost loved ones in the tragedy.

## APPLYING THE FRAMEWORKS

When facing an ethical decision, you may find that the frameworks discussed above conflict. This dilemma can make an ethical decision difficult to assess and even more difficult to make.

For example, let's consider Susan, a quality control engineer for an automobile manufacturer. She is responsible for testing a newly designed side impact airbag, which company executives are eager to put into next year's models. Susan's tests of the new design have not been completely successful. Test results showed that all the airbags inflated on impact, but 10 airbags out of every 100 tested inflated to 60 percent capacity. The partially inflated airbags would protect passengers from most of a collision's impact, but those passengers might receive more injuries than passengers whose airbags inflated fully. If the passengers with partially inflated airbags were children, the injuries could be especially serious.

Susan asks for more time to further test the airbags; however, company executives reply that they must get the airbags in the new models. Susan feels pressured to certify that the airbags are safe. Her ethical decision is not clear cut.
- If she looks at the situation using the *moral standard*, her choice is simple. She cannot report that the airbags are safe and ready to be installed.

- If she looks at the situation through the ***standard of utility*** (the greatest good for the greatest number), her choice is more complex. If she says the airbags are safe, more lives will be saved with the airbags than without them. However, if an installed airbag only partially inflates, someone—especially a child—could be injured or even killed.
- If she considers ***the rights of those involved,*** the consumers and her company have the right to know the results of the tests, regardless of the impact on sales.

What should Susan do? What would you do? Because moral standards often conflict, this chapter will help you ask the right questions so you can assess a situation and make a difficult ethical decision like the one facing Susan.

##  UNDERSTANDING YOUR LEGAL RESPONSIBILITIES

As a professional, you are responsible for knowing and following four bodies of law:
- copyright law
- trademark law
- liability law
- contract law

### Copyright Laws

In school, you have a responsibility to research and write papers ethically, without plagiarizing. ***Plagiarism*** is the intentional or unintentional use of another person's words, photographs, music, or graphics without acknowledging that you have used that work. If you plagiarize, you could receive a failing grade or be expelled from school.

Plagiarism is an ethical issue, not a legal issue. Unlike plagiarism, copyright is a legal matter. ***Copyright laws*** give the "owner" of intellectual property—such as words, graphics, music, or photographs—the sole right to "copy" the work that he or she has created and to profit from or prohibit the sale or distribution of that work. For example, if your roommate writes a report, he or she has the right to copy that report; but if you want to use that report, you must get permission from your roommate.

The copyright laws protect authors even if they haven't registered that work with the U.S. Copyright Office. Copyright exists from the moment an author creates the work. Some companies encourage employees to reuse company-created information. The reused information is sometimes called ***boilerplate***. Companies call the practice of reuse ***repurposing*** or ***single sourcing*** of information. They allow it because the repurposing saves time and eliminates errors.

For example, if you work for AT&T, you can legally copy information from the AT&T website and use that information in AT&T marketing documents. However, if you work for AT&T and find information or a graphic on the Verizon website, you cannot copy that information or graphic to the AT&T website without Verizon's written permission. Without written permission, you would be violating Verizon's copyright.

You may wonder why you have to get permission from Verizon instead of from the person who created the information or graphic. Anything that an employee creates while on the job belongs to the company, not to the employee. This concept is called "work made for hire." Because the creator of the information or graphic worked for Verizon, the information or graphic copyright belongs to Verizon, not to the individual.

Copyright law does not give the owner all rights. In some limited instances, copyrighted material may be used without permission. The law provides for the "fair use" of small parts of copyrighted material without the owner's written permission. For example, if you include a statement from a website in your report and you cite the source, you are following the *fair use* guidelines. These guidelines also allow you to use copyrighted material without written permission for purposes such as education or news reporting. The guidelines in Figure 4.1 will help you determine fair use.

## TIPS FOR FOLLOWING COPYRIGHT LAWS

- **Follow fair use guidelines.** Do not rely on excessive amounts of material borrowed from other sources unless that information is repurposed from your company. Fair use guidelines do not apply to graphics, so you must always seek written permission to use a graphic.
- **When in doubt about fair use, obtain written permission.** The fair use guidelines can be confusing because the law does not provide a specific number of words, lines, or notes that you may legally use without permission. If you are unsure whether you are following fair use guidelines, ask for permission to use the material. If you cannot gain permission, do not use the copyrighted material.
- **Cite the source of material that does not belong to you or your organization.** The U.S. Copyright Office notes that simply acknowledging the source of the copyrighted material does not substitute for obtaining permission. By citing your sources, you also fulfill your ethical responsibility to be honest.
- **Ask for guidance from legal counsel.** If you need help understanding copyright laws, ask your organization's legal counsel for help. Don't guess or assume that you are following the law correctly.

Be wary of using other people's written information and making only cosmetic changes to it. You could be guilty of violating copyright laws, and you certainly would be guilty of violating the author's rights and your moral duty to be honest. If you need more information on copyright laws, go to the website for the U.S. Copyright Office, www.copyright.gov.

## Trademark Laws

Trademark laws protect the owner(s) of a brand name or logo used for a product. Companies use trademarks and registered trademarks to protect the identity of their products:

- *Trademarks* protect words, names, symbols, or devices that distinguish a company's goods and services from those manufactured or sold by others. Trademarks also indicate the source of the goods or services (Office 2012). If the product is trademarked, the company includes the ™ symbol after the product name. This symbol indicates a company has applied for a registered trademark with the U.S. Patent and Trademark Office or is simply claiming the rights to the trademark.
- *Registered Trademarks* indicate a company's application for a trademark has been approved by and thus registered with the U.S. Patent and Trademark Office. The company can use the ® after the product name. For example, Frito-Lay has a registered trademark for Doritos® brand tortilla chips.

# FIGURE 4.1

## What Is Fair Use?

The U.S. Copyright website explains that the law sets out four factors to consider when determining fair use:

- **The purpose and character of the use, including whether such use is of a commercial nature or is for nonprofit educational purposes.** For example, fair use guidelines are applied more liberally to schools and more conservatively to for-profit organizations.
- **The nature of the copyrighted work.** If the work is essential to the public, fair use guidelines are applied more liberally than if the work is non-essential to the public.
- **The amount and substantiality of the portion used in relation to the copyrighted work as a whole.** For example, 2 pages of a 100-page document are a small portion, while 2 pages of a 4-page document are a large portion. The law does not specify a specific amount or percentage that you may use without written permission.
- **The effect of the use on the potential market for or value of the copyrighted work.** If the use of the copyrighted material would hurt the owner's potential for profit, then you have probably violated fair use guidelines.

Source: Downloaded from the World Wide Web, January 15, 2011: www.copyright.gov/fls/fl102.html. U.S. Copyright Office, "Fair Use," p. FL-102.

You are responsible for protecting your company's or your client's trademark and for using the trademark and registered trademark symbols accurately.

## Liability Laws

Liability laws protect the public from inaccurate information from authors, editors, or publishers. These groups are responsible for injury that occurs from defective information, even if they give out the information unknowingly. If a company violates a liability law, it could face a liability lawsuit for "personal injury, death, property damage, or financial loss caused by a defective product" (Helyar 1992).

## Contract Laws

A contract formalizes an agreement between two parties by making it a legal promise. You will want to consider these areas of contract law: [2]

- **Express Warranties.** An *express warranty* is an oral or written statement (such as an advertisement) for a product. For example, if a washing machine manufacturer claims that a washer/dryer combination doesn't require an exterior vent, that claim is an expressed warranty. If a salesperson says the combination washer/dryer works great, he or she is not making an express warranty; such a statement would be considered a personal opinion.

- **Implied Warranties.** An *implied warranty* is an implied promise that a product is fit for the particular purpose of the buyer. This warranty is not written or spoken, but is implied. For example, by its nature, a cell phone is fit for making phone calls, and a car is fit to carry passengers. You might see an implied warranty in the graphics included in product advertisements or manufacturing information.

**TIPS FOR PROTECTING A TRADEMARK**

- **Use the trademark or registered trademark symbol.** Each time you include the name of a trademarked product, use the appropriate symbol. If you are unsure whether a product is trademarked, go to the website for the U.S. Office of Patent and Trademarks, www.uspto.gov.

- **Use a footnote the first time you use a trademark.** At least once in a document, preferably near the beginning, follow the trademark or registered trademark symbol with an asterisk or footnote number. At the bottom of the page in a footnote, state that the product is a trademark or registered trademark. For example, a footnote might read: [1] Kleenex is a registered trademark of Kimberly-Clark Corporation.

- **Use the trademark as an adjective, not as a noun.** For example, you would write: Doritos® tortilla chips, not simply Doritos®. Likewise, you would write: Dr. Pepper™ soft drink, not Dr. Pepper™.

- **Don't do anything to hurt the spirit of the trademark or to alter the trademark.** Do not change the trademark in any way. For example, if the trademark uses a particular color or font, do not change that color or font.

# TIPS FOR FOLLOWING LIABILITY LAWS

You can protect your organization and yourself from possible liability suits by following these tips adapted from Pamela S. Helyar, author of *Product Liability: Meeting Legal Standards for Adequate Instructions* (1992).

- **Use language and graphics that the users will understand.** For example, if you are writing a manual that children will use, include simple, clear graphics that children can easily follow. If you are writing a manual for nonnative speakers of English, use simple language free of *idioms* (expressions whose meanings are different from the standard or literal meanings of the words they contain: e.g., going cold turkey).

- **Tell the user how the product works and what it can and cannot do.** Make sure that your users understand what the product does. You can be liable if you do not also explain what the product cannot do.

- **Warn the users of risks when using the product.** State the specific dangers in using the product. Use direct, clear language. Don't assume that readers will know the danger. You are responsible for directly stating that danger.

- **Make sure that users can easily see the warnings.** For example, if you are warning users of the risk of cutting their fingers or toes with a lawn mower, put the warning both in the instruction manual and, more important, on the mower.

- **Tell users what the product can do and what it can't or shouldn't do.** Tell users what the product is designed to do and what it isn't designed to do. Put this information not only in the instruction manual that will accompany the product, but also in materials that a potential buyer will see. For example, a manual for a gas barbecue grill states: "For outdoor use only. Never operate grill in enclosed areas, as an explosion or a carbon monoxide buildup might occur, which could result in injury or death" (Coleman 1999). While most users would know that they should operate a barbecue grill only outside, the manufacturer could be liable if it didn't warn users of the risk of using the grill indoors.

- **Inform users of all aspects of owning the product, from maintaining to disposing of the product.** When purchasing some products or services, the user may have ongoing responsibilities; you must inform the user of these responsibilities. For example, most car manuals provide owners with a maintenance schedule. Along with the schedule, the manual usually includes a statement such as, If your vehicle is damaged because you failed to follow the recommended Maintenance Schedule and/or to use or maintain fluids, fuel, lubricants, or refrigerants recommended in this Owner's manual, your warranty may be invalid and may not cover the damage.

- **Test the product and the accompanying product information.** Perform usability testing to make sure the product is safe and that the instructions and product information are accurate. For information on usability testing, see Chaper 18.

## MAKING ETHICAL DECISIONS

Now that we have defined ethics and considered the moral and legal standards, let's examine two guidelines to help you work through ethical dilemmas:

- **Use a decision-making model** to help you work through ethical dilemmas.
- **Ask the right questions** to help you decide whether an action is ethical.

### Use a Decision-Making Model

Before making a decision, gather all related information about the situation and the people involved. Many companies suggest that their employees follow a model to help them work through an ethical dilemma. By following a model, you can make more informed ethical decisions. In Figure 4.2 Raytheon gives its employees a quick test to use when facing an ethical problem. If your workplace does not have a stated model for making ethical decisions, follow the tips in the sidebar to the right.

### Ask the Right Questions

When you face an ethical decision, determine the appropriate action by asking the right questions. Your company executives may have a series of questions they expect you to consider when making decisions. For example, Kraft Foods gives employees four simple questions to ask themselves when confronted with an ethical workplace dilemma (see Figure 4.3). Proctor & Gamble has a *Worldwide Business Conduct Manual.* In this manual, the company states the

## TIPS FOR MAKING ETHICAL DECISIONS

- **Gather all related information.** Make sure you have all the facts and that your facts are accurate. You don't want to risk losing your job or your reputation by basing a decision on inaccurate or incomplete information.

- **Think first; then act.** Once you are satisfied you have all the facts and they are accurate, think about all the possible choices and use the questions in the section, Ask the Right Questions. Once you are satisfied you have made the ethical choice, take action or communicate your decision.

- **Find out all you can about the people affected by your decision and those who will read your communication.** You can then determine the best way to approach these people if you want to argue for change or you need to suggest a course of action that they may not want to consider.

- **Talk to people whom you trust.** They may help you consider alternative, yet ethical choices. If you feel you cannot trust anyone in your organization, talk to someone whom you trust outside the organization. Don't face the situation alone.

- **Aim to establish a reputation as a hardworking, loyal coworker with integrity.** Then, when you do take a stand on an ethical issue, your coworkers and managers will take your stand seriously.

core of its business ethic is "doing the right thing." To help employees do the right thing, Proctor and Gamble instructs employees to ask the questions in Figure 4.4.

If your company does not have a manual or guidelines for making ethical decisions, ask the following questions to help you recognize your fundamental ethical responsibilities:

- Is it legal?
- Is it consistent with company policy and my professional code of conduct?
- Am I doing the right thing?
- Am I acting in the best interests of all involved?
- How will it appear to others? Am I willing to take responsibility publicly and privately?
- Will it violate anyone's rights?

When making an ethical decision, ask yourself these questions:
- Is it legal?
- Is it consistent with company policy and my professional code of conduct?
- Am I doing the right thing?
- Am I acting in the best interests of all involved?
- How will it appear to others?
- Am I willing to take responsibility publicly and privately?
- Will it violate anyone's rights?

## Is It Legal?

You must follow all laws that apply to you, your product, and your organization. You must follow all laws that relate to ideas and products. For example, if you use a graphic from a website, you should assume the information is copyrighted. If it is, you are legally obligated to obtain permission to use that graphic. If you use copyrighted ideas or graphics without permission, you are, in essence, stealing from the owners.

## Is It Consistent with Company Policy and My Professional Code of Conduct?

Your company or organization expects you to follow its policies and guidelines. You are responsible for knowing those policies. If you do not know if an action is consistent with company policy, ask a manager or a mentor. Likewise, your profession may have a code of conduct. If so, you should also abide by that code. To learn more about professional codes of conduct, read the section in this chapter titled Taking It into the Workplace.

## Am I Doing the Right Thing?

You have a duty to be honest and truthful with your employer and the public and to report problems and information that could either negatively or positively influence your company, its employees, and its products or services.

## FIGURE 4.2

### Raytheon Quick Test for Ethical Decisions

## When facing an ethical problem, ask yourself these questions:

- Is the action legal?
- Is it right?
- Who will be affected?
- Does it fit Raytheon's values?
- How will I feel afterwards?
- How would it look in the newspaper?
- Will it reflect poorly on the company?

When in doubt, ask—and keep asking until you get an answer.

Source: Downloaded from the World Wide Web, October 25, 2007: www.raytheon.com/stewardship/ethics/ethics_answers/test/index.html. Raytheon Company, Raytheon Business Ethics and Compliance Information, Ethics Quick Test and Decision-Making Model.

## FIGURE 4.3

### Kraft Foods Guide to Ethical Dilemmas

## Integrity: Doing What Is Right

### Ask Before Acting

- Is it legal?
- Does it follow company policy?
- Is it right?
- How would it look to those outside the company? For example, how would it look to our customers, the people in the communities where we work, and the general public?

### Remember These Rules

- Know the legal and company standards that apply to your job.
- Follow these standards—always.
- Ask if you are ever unsure what's the right thing to do.
- Keep asking until you get the answer.

Kraft Foods is the world's largest manufacturer and marketer of consumer packaged goods.

Source: Provided courtesy of Kraft Foods and downloaded from the World Wide Web, Jan. 1, 2008: http://www.kraft.com/assets/pdf/KraftFoods_CodeofConduct.pdf.

FIGURE 4.4

**Proctor and Gamble's Business Code of Conduct**

The core of the Company's business ethic is "doing the right thing." In addition to complying with any applicable legal requirements and the requirements described elsewhere in this Manual, you should ask the following questions in making decisions:

- Is my action the "right thing to do?"
- Would I feel comfortable if my action were reported broadly in the news, or were reported to a person whose principles I respect?
- Will my action protect the Company's reputation as an ethical company?
- Am I being truthful and honest?

If the answer to any of these questions about the action you are considering is not an unqualified "Yes," then simply do not take the action.

Source: Downloaded from the World Wide Web, Jan. 1, 2008: www.pg.com/company/our_commitment/corp_gov/WBCMREDUCED_Single_Page.pdf. Proctor & Gamble Worldwide Business Conduct Manual, p. 10.

You will be dishonest and untruthful if you manipulate the language to hide facts, to make data say what you or your managers want, or to leave out unfavorable information. For example, you would be acting unethically if you only reported the positive results of patient tests with an experimental drug while hiding or otherwise not reporting negative results.

When facing an ethical dilemma, ask yourself whether the proposed action is the right thing to do. If it is right, is it right only for this particular situation or for all similar situations? If the action is right now, is it right for everyone else in the same situation (Golen, Powers, and Titkemeyer 1985)? For many situations, this answer will be clear. For example, if you manufacture a baby stroller and you know that it can collapse and injure or kill a child, you can clearly see that your company cannot sell the stroller.

# TAKING IT INTO THE *workplace*

## Understanding Ethics in Your Profession

Many professional organizations have developed a code of conduct or a code of ethics for their members. These codes give members standards for ethical behavior in their profession. While these codes are hard to enforce, they do guide the organization's members in ethical professional behavior. Many businesses have also adopted codes of conduct or ethics. These codes give members guidelines for ethical behavior and inform the public about how its members will conduct business.

## Assignment

Assume that you are a recent college grad and have started a new job. You plan to join a professional organization in your field. Your assignment is as follows:

1. Find a professional organization in your field.
2. Find out if the organization has a code of ethics. (If not, find another organization related to your field.) Most professional organizations post their code of ethics on their website.
3. Bring a copy of the code of ethics to class.
4. Be prepared to answer these questions about the code:
   - Does the code provide a model for making ethical decisions?
   - How effectively does the code protect the interests of the public? Of the professional organization? What specific words or phrases demonstrate this effectiveness?
   - How can the professional organization enforce the code?
   - Does the code help the members make ethical decisions? If so, how? If not, what would you include in the code?

iStockphoto.com 2008

Other situations are more complex. For example, suppose you see a coworker use her company credit card to charge personal items. The company has a policy that states employees may use the card only for company business and employees may not charge personal items on the card. This coworker conscientiously pays the balance on the credit card each month, so the company doesn't incur any interest charges. Should you tell her supervisor? If you were her supervisor, would you want to know? After all, she pays the balance each month; the company isn't being hurt. Is it right for her to use the credit card for personal charges?

Ask yourself this question: If it is right in this situation, is it right for everyone else in the same situation? If you can answer "yes," then your action is probably ethical. If you answer "no," then the action is probably unethical. If you are still uncertain, consider your options, ask more questions, or even talk to someone you trust and respect. This person may be able to help you look at the situation objectively.

## Am I Acting in the Best Interests of All Involved?

Ideally, in any given situation, the best interests of all involved will coincide, making it easy to identify the right action. However, you may face a situation where these interests conflict. If so, you may have an ethical dilemma. When you face ethical problems, think about all the consequences and how these consequences will affect those involved now and in the future.

Consider how the Red Cross handled donations to the victims of the September 11, 2001 terrorist acts. In radio and television ads across the United States, the Red Cross asked for donations to help the victims. The Red Cross received millions of dollars—more money than it had ever received for disaster relief. Executives with the Red Cross decided that because they had received record amounts of money, they would put some of the money aside for future disasters. They reasoned that the money would still go to disaster victims, just not to victims of the 9/11 tragedies. When donors discovered that their money wasn't going to the victims, they felt that the Red Cross had misled them and was mishandling the money.

Did the Red Cross act in the best interests of the victims or the organization? By earmarking some of the 9/11 donations, the Red Cross intended to protect the interests of future victims. However, did it act in the best interests of the donors and the 9/11 victims? By not disclosing to the public what it was doing and by not using the money as the donors expected, the Red Cross lost the trust of many current and potential donors and, in turn, possibly hurt the interests of future victims.

### How Will It Appear to Others? Am I Willing to Take Responsibility Publicly and Privately?

When you face an ethical decision, ask yourself this question: How will this decision or action appear to others? Even what you may consider to be an innocent action can result in the appearance of wrongdoing. If you don't want others to know what you have decided or done, you should reconsider your decision and perhaps seek advice. With any decision you make, you should be willing to take responsibility both publicly and privately. Consider these additional questions when analyzing a possible action or communication:

- Will it reflect poorly on me or my organization?
- How would it look in the local newspaper?
- How will I feel afterward?

### Will It Violate Anyone's Rights?

When faced with ethical dilemmas at work, consider whether the action violates the rights of your organization, other employees, the public, or others involved with the situation or communication. These people have a right to be treated fairly and to receive "what is due or owed" and what they deserve or "can legitimately claim." (Wicclair and Farkas 1984, 16). Your organization, your coworkers, and the public also have the right to expect similar situations to be treated similarly, so consider whether you would act or communicate in the same way in similar situations. As you consider others' rights, look at any expressed or implied warranties that your decision may affect.

 ## FOLLOW THE PRINCIPLES FOR ETHICAL COMMUNICATION

As an employee, you are expected to follow company policies and to avoid actions that conflict with those policies. You are also expected to act with integrity. When you act with integrity, you put honesty above any financial objective, marketing target, or effort to compete (Kraft Foods 2009). To communicate with integrity, follow the principles for ethical communication listed in the Ethics Note on the following page.

### Follow All Relevant Laws

Follow all laws related to intellectual property and to your product or service. Read these guidelines to ensure you know the laws and you are following the laws related to intellectual property:

- **Obtain permission for copyrighted information or graphics.** Do not plagiarize. If you can't get written permission, don't use it.

- **Protect yourself and your organization by honoring all trademarks.** Use trademark and registered trademark symbols. Do not alter the trademark. Follow the Tips for Protecting a Trademark earlier in this chapter.
- **Follow all guidelines related to liability laws.** Follow the Tips for Following Liability Laws earlier in this chapter.
- **Honor the expressed and implied warranties related to your products, goods, and services.**

## Follow Company Policies and/or Your Professional Code of Conduct

Determine if your employer has a code of conduct; ask your manager, ask a human resources representative, or search your company's website and intranet. If your company does not have a stated code of conduct, read company policies to determine if your action will violate a company policy. You can also turn to your professional code of conduct for guidance. If you cannot find a stated company or professional policy or code of conduct, ask your manager or another trusted company official for help.

## Be Honest

You have an ethical responsibility to be honest. You may feel pressure to lie about your company's or another company's products, information, or services. If you lie, you are not doing the right thing. You may have to resist a manager's pressure to lie about an action, a product, a service, or a test result. Even if you have to go over the manager's head, you have a responsibility to tell the truth.

## Do Not Mislead Your Readers

A misleading statement or graphic leads readers to make false conclusions or to think that conditions exist when they don't. These misleading statements or graphics are the same as lying: You, in essence, are giving readers untruthful information.

You can mislead readers in several ways:

- **Creating false impressions.** You can create false impressions with language and graphics. For example, an owner's manual for a glass cooktop states, "Clean only with OvenBrite." This statement leads owners to assume that only the OvenBrite brand will work. This statement creates a false impression; it is not true. You may be tempted to use terms such as "highly energy efficient," "best on the market," "innovative," or "state-of-the-art" to make a product or service sound better than it is. Rather than using these terms, include specific information. For example, instead of saying an appliance is "highly energy efficient," give the appliance's Energy Star rating. You can also create false impressions with graphics. For example, look at the graphic comparing cereals in Figure 4.5. The graphic begins at 8, rather than 0. The chart implies that Best Brand has one-third less sugar than Brands A and B because the readers don't see the entire chart. Actually, Best Brand has only about 5 percent less sugar than the competing brands.
- **Exaggerating.** If you write, "This new oven offers features to meet all your cooking needs," you are exaggerating because no oven will meet users' every cooking need. Indeed, the oven may have some advanced features not common to all ovens, but it can't meet every need. This statement creates false impressions, especially for novice cooks.
- **Using euphemisms.** You use a euphemism when you substitute a mild or less negative word for a harsh or blunt word. For example, a company might use the phrase "involuntarily separated" instead of "fired" or "laid off." Euphemisms can mislead readers.
- **Deemphasizing important information or emphasizing misleading information.** You mislead readers when you deemphasize information, especially negative information, or emphasize misleading or incorrect information through page layout, type size, or color. For example, an advertisement for a drug that controls heart rate emphasizes that the drug is safe. The word "safe" appears in a bright-red band and in excessively large, 36-point type. Yet, at the bottom of the page, in excessively small, 6-point black type, the ad warns that a defibrillator and emergency equipment should be available for the user. Clearly, the drug is not completely safe; however, the reader may never see the warning because the ad deemphasizes the important, life-saving information.

## Use Clear, Precise Language

You have a responsibility to write as clearly and precisely as possible and to make your information easy to find. Clear, precise language helps your readers understand your message.

You can mislead or deceive readers if your language is unclear. For example, you are write an instruction manual for a cordless vacuum cleaner and you tell readers that the vacuum is "great for unexpected spills and messes and convenient for small, routine cleanup jobs around the house." This information is not clear unless you explain what you mean by "spills and messes." Many readers may consider spills of milk or juice a job for the vacuum

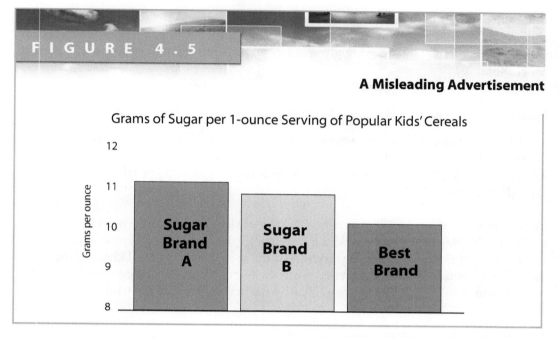

**FIGURE 4.5**

**A Misleading Advertisement**

Grams of Sugar per 1-ounce Serving of Popular Kids' Cereals

when, in fact, the vacuum is designed to clean up only dry materials. Instead, the instruction manual should say, "Use your vacuum to pick up dry materials. Do not use the vacuum to clean up spills of liquids and other wet materials. If you use the vacuum to pick up wet materials, you could be electrocuted."

## Include All the Information That Readers Need or Have a Right to Know

You have an ethical responsibility to give your readers all the information they need or have a right to know. If you intentionally or unintentionally omit information, you are not acting ethically. For example, you may be tempted to tamper with research data to make it look precise by smoothing out or omitting irregularities so the data appear statistically significant. You have a responsibility to give readers the untampered data with its irregularities, regardless of its statistical significance.

Professionals may be pressured to omit information that readers have a right to know. For example, in a memo about the O-rings that led to the 1986 Challenger space shuttle disaster, the writers' memo included the following sentence: "The conclusion is that secondary sealing capability in the SRM field joint cannot be guaranteed." This sentence misleads readers because it doesn't give them enough information to correctly assess the risks. A more accurate sentence might have said: "The conclusion is that the secondary seal is not effective at temperatures below 50 degrees Fahrenheit, so the joint is highly vulnerable to catastrophic failure at such temperatures" (Winsor 1990, 15). The first sentence is technically accurate, but it doesn't give readers enough information to arrive at a correct conclusion.

## Take Ownership of Your Writing

When appropriate, include references to you, the writer. Your writing is more effective when you include personal pronouns or references such as I, we, or the organization's name. Identifying the speaker or actor is a "necessary ingredient for ethical communication" (Rubens 1981, 335).

When you omit references to a person, you may mislead the readers. For example, if you write, "Each spreadsheet was checked for accuracy," the readers don't know who checked the accuracy of the spreadsheet. If you checked the spreadsheet, write, "I checked the accuracy of each spreadsheet." In the revised sentence, you appropriately take ownership of your work. If you didn't check the accuracy, identify the person who did the work.

## Acknowledge the Work of Others

You may use the work of others in a report or presentation. For example, you may work with a team on a project or you may refer to someone else's research. Your readers want to know who did the work, so you should acknowledge their work. If you don't acknowledge the work of others, your readers may assume that you performed all the work. When you take credit for work you did not do or do not acknowledge work done by others, you are acting unethically.

- If you use or refer to someone else's work in your research or writing, tell readers who did the work. If you don't properly acknowledge others' work, you are plagiarizing.
- If you are reporting on work done collaboratively, acknowledge everyone who worked on the project. Consider how you would feel if one of your coworkers didn't acknowledge your work to your manager or didn't cite your part in a project.

## Avoid Discriminatory Language

You have an ethical responsibility to use language that does not discriminate against people because of their gender, age, physical appearance, physical or mental ability, religion, sexual orientation, or ethnicity. Discriminatory language reflects negatively on you and your organization. For more information on avoiding discriminatory language, see Chapter 8.

# CASE STUDY ANALYSIS

## The Human Radiation Experiments[3]

### Background

From the 1940s to the 1970s, patients, some terminally ill, were injected with pluto-nium—mostly without their knowledge or consent—at Oak Ridge Hospital, the University of Rochester, the University of Chicago, and the University of California. In the years following the atomic bombings of the Japanese cities Hiroshima and Nagasaki, the U.S. military and nuclear weapons industry wanted data on the biological effects of plutonium and radioisotopes. To determine these effects, Manhattan Project scientists injected 18 unsuspecting patients with plutonium. All these patients had already been diagnosed with terminal diseases and weren't expected to live more than 10 years. Some of the patients, according to investigators at the Atomic Energy Commission, had not granted informed consent. The patients who had granted consent did so under false pretenses because the word plutonium was classified during World War II. Those patients who survived did not even know that they had been injected with plutonium until 1974.

These experiments continued during the Cold War, when the U.S. military wanted to know how much radiation a soldier could endure before becoming disabled even though research-ers were aware of the hazards of working with plutonium early as January 5, 1944. From 1960 to 1971, scientists at the University of Cincinnati performed experiments on 88 can-cer patients ranging in age from 9 to 84. These patients were repeatedly exposed to massive doses of radiation, yet medical researchers from the 1930s through the 1950s had deter-mined that whole-body radiation was ineffective in treating most cancers. These patients had tumors that would resist radiation—a fact that the doctors already knew (Braffman-Miller 1995). Most of these patients were uneducated, had low IQs, and were poor. The researchers in charge of these experiments wrote in 1969 that "directional radiation will be attempted since this type of exposure is of military interest" (quoted in Braffman-Miller 1995, 6). The doctors did not use this procedure to treat tumors. Instead, they used it to study how radiation exposure might affect soldiers. These researchers also denied patients treatment for the nausea and vomiting that resulted from the radiation. These researchers instructed the hospital staff to ignore these symptoms: "DO NOT ASK THE PATIENT WHETHER HE HAS THESE SYMPTOMS" (see Figure 4.6). Instead, the staff were to record the symptoms' time, duration, and severity without treating the patient. Publicly, the researchers at the University of Cincinnati claimed the purpose of their research was to study ways to treat cancer. However, in a report to the Department of Defense, they

[3] Braffman-Miller (1995); U.S. Department of Energy

wrote that the purpose of their study was to understand better the influence of radiation on "combat effectiveness of troops and to develop additional methods of diagnosis, prognosis, prophylaxis and treatment of [radiation] injuries" (quoted in Braffman-Miller 1995, 5).

In 1966, Dr. George Shields and Dr. Thomas E. Gaffney at the University of Cincinnati formally questioned the purpose of the experiments. These doctors pointed out that the researchers deceived patients and were hiding the real purpose of their experiments. Their memos appear in Figures 4.7 and 4.8. Ultimately, the experiments were continued with some revisions.

## Assignment

1. Read the memo written by Dr. George Shields (Figure 4.7). Be prepared to answer these questions in class:
   - What was the purpose of this memo?
   - What was Dr. Shields's ethical dilemma?
   - Dr. Shields recommended disapproving the study; however, he stated that if the study was continued, the researchers should change the language used to inform patients of the risk. What language did he propose? Would this language have ensured that all involved were treated ethically? Explain your answer.

2. Read Dr. Thomas Gaffney's memo (Figure 4.8). Be prepared to answer these questions in class:
   - What was the purpose of this memo?
   - What was Dr. Gaffney's ethical dilemma?

3. Consider the ethical dilemma faced by the scientists who continued the experiments. Be prepared to answer these questions in class:
   - What was their ethical dilemma?
   - Were these scientists acting in the best interests of the patients or of the staff caring for these patients? Explain your answer.
   - Were these scientists and those who funded the research acting for the greater good—that of protecting soldiers who might be exposed to radiation? Were they acting ethically because they might have saved the lives of thousands of soldiers by sacrificing a few terminally ill cancer patients?
   - Did the patients need to know the purpose of the experiments? Explain your answer.
   - Should the scientists have disclosed the adverse effects of whole-body radiation to the patients? To the public? Explain your answers.

FIGURE 4.6

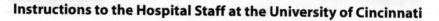

## Instructions to the Hospital Staff at the University of Cincinnati

INSTRUCTIONS FOR RECORDING OF SYMPTOMS
FOLLOWING IRRADIATION

DEPARTMENT OF RADIOLOGY
GENERAL HOSPITAL

Date: _____

PATIENT_____ NO. _____ WARD _____

TIME OF THERAPY _____

This patient has just received total body radiation for therapeutic purposes. It is possible that the symptoms listed below may develop within the next several days. Please note carefully the time at which these symptoms develop and note their duration and severity.

DO NOT ASK THE PATIENT WHETHER HE HAS THESE SYMPTOMS

|  | Time of Onset | | Duration | Severity |
|---|---|---|---|---|
|  | Date | Hr. | | |
| Anorexia | | | | |
| Nausea | | | | |
| Vomiting | | | | |
| Abdominal Pain | | | | |
| Diarrhea | | | | |
| Weakness | | | | |
| Prostration | | | | |
| Mental Confusion | | | | |

E.L. Saenger, M.D., line 207
H. Perry, M.D., line 200

FIGURE 4.7

## Memo from Dr. George Shields

TO:      Dr. Edward A. Gall

FROM:    Dr. George Shields

DATE:      March 13, 1967

SUBJECT: Protection of Humans with Stored Autologous Marrow

I regret that I must withdraw myself from the subcommittee studying this proposal, for reasons of close professional and personal contact with the investigators and with some of the laboratory phases of this project. The following comments are sent to you in confidence, at your request.

This protocol is difficult to evaluate. The purpose of the study is obscure, as is the relationship of the experimental groups to the purposes. The significance of the study in relation to the health of the patients under study may be considerable if the investigators succeed in prolonging the lives of these patients with malignant disease, but the risk of treatment may be very high if the authors' hypothesis (that bone marrow transfusions will ameliorate bone marrow depression due to radiation) is incorrect. The radiation proposed has been documented in the authors' own series to cause a 25% mortality.

I recommend that this study be disapproved, because of the high risk of this level of radiation. Admittedly it is very difficult, in fact impossible, to balance potential hazard against potential benefit in experiments of this sort. The stakes are high. Our current mandate is that we evaluate the risks on some arbitrary scale. I believe a 25% mortality is too high (25% of 36 patients is 9 deaths), but this is of course merely an opinion.

If it is the consensus of the investigators and the review committee that a 25% mortality risk is not prohibitive, then the experiment could be reconsidered from the standpoint of informed consent - provided the patient is appraised of this risk in a quantative fashion. I believe that the conditions of informed consent will have been observed if the authors change "all patients are informed that a risk exists, but that all precautions to prevent untoward results will be taken" to the equivalent of "all patients are informed that a 1 in 4 chance of death within a few weeks due to treatment exists, etc."

Finally, although it is not our concern directly, a comment as to experimental design is indicated in this particular protocol. The authors' stated purposes are vague in the first page of the application, but on the last page three purposes are listed since it would require an untreated group and no reference has been made by the authors to such an untreated group of patients.

The second purpose can be fulfilled by this protocol only with the retrospective group (Group 1). The evaluation of bone marrow transfusion in the treatment of bone marrow depression would require a concomitant control group of patients treated only with radiation. It is apparent that the authors feel the radiation risk is too high to re-expose another group to this level of radiation without some effort at radio-protection, and therefore the authors have chosen to use the retrospective group as a control. There is considerable question whether this retrospective group will be entirely similar and therefore whether it will serve the second purpose.

The third purpose, "to determine whether autologous bone marrow therapy may play a role in treatment of bone marrow depression following acute radiation exposure in warfare or occupationally induced accidents," is not the subject of this experiment because normal individuals are not being tested. It is problematic whether the information gained in this study will apply to normal individuals following acute radiation exposure. Therefore it is my definite opinion that the third purpose of this experiment would not justify the risk entailed.

For these several reasons I feel that the experimental design is inadequate, and because of the high risk inherent in this level of radiation, I think experimental design should be a proper subject for our consideration in this instance.

**FIGURE 4.8**

**Memo from Dr. Thomas E. Gaffney**

To:  Dr. Edward Gall, Chairman
      Clinical Research Committee
From:  Dr. Thomas E. Gaffney,
Date:  4/17/67

I cannot recommend approval of the proposed study entitled "The Therapeutic Effect of Total Body Irradiation Followed by Infusion of Stored Autologous Marrow in Humans" for several reasons.

The stated goal of the study is to test the hypothesis that total body irradiation at a dose of 200 rad followed by infusion of stored autologous marrow is effective, palliative therapy for metastatic malignancy in human beings. I don't understand the rationale for this study. The applicants have apparently already administered 150-200 rad to some 18 patients with a variety of malignancies and to their satisfaction have not found a beneficial effect. In fact, as I understand it, they found considerable morbidity associated with this high dose radiation. Why is it now logical to expand this study?

Even if the study is expanded, its current design will not yield meaningful data. For instance, the applicants indicate their intention to evaluate the influence of 200 rad total body radiation on survival in patients with a variety of neoplasms. This "variety," or heterogeneity, will be present in a sample size of only 16 individuals. It will be difficult if not impossible to observe a beneficial effect in such a small sample containing a variety of diseases all of which share only CANCER in common.

This gross deficiency in design will almost certainly prevent making meaningful observations. When this deficiency in experimental method is placed next to their previously observed poor result and high morbidity with this type of treatment in a "variety of neoplasms," I think it is clear that the study as proposed should not be done.

I have the uneasy suspicion, shared up by the revised statement of objective, that this revised protocol is a subterfuge to allow the investigators to achieve the purpose described in their original application; mainly, to test the ability of autologous marrow to "take" in patients who have received high doses of total body radiation. This latter question may be an important one to answer but I can't justify 200 rad total body radiation simply for this purpose, "even in terminal case material".

I think there is sufficient question as to the propriety of these studies to warrant consideration by the entire Research Committee. I recommend therefore that this protocol and the previous one be circulated to all members of the Committee and that a meeting of the entire Committee be held to review this protocol prior to submitting a recommendation to the Dean.

Sincerely,

Thomas E. Gaffney, M.D.

# EXERCISES

DOWNLOAD A WORKSHEET FOR ETHICAL AND LEGAL CHALLENGES AT

WWW.GRTEP.COM

1. **Collaborative exercise:** You and your team will decide on the language to use in a report on the test results of a new battery-powered smoke detector. The situation is as follows:

   > Testing revealed that the battery-powered smoke detectors did not always sound when the battery was low. Specifically, 75 percent of the smoke detectors emitted a sound to indicate a low battery, and 20 percent of the detectors emitted a sound so weak that a homeowner could not hear it beyond 20 feet. Your supervisor, Donna Dimaggio, and her manager want to start production of the smoke detectors within two weeks. They are waiting for your test results. Because earlier reports from other employees did not indicate problems with the smoke detectors, your supervisor assumes your test results will be insignificant. She and her manager will be displeased if their division can't begin manufacturing these smoke detectors; this division has not shown a profit in the last three quarters. If the division doesn't begin showing a profit, the company may downsize or eliminate
   > the division.

   Your team should complete the following tasks:
   - Determine what language choices you have for reporting the test results.
   - Use the principles for ethical communication to analyze these language choices. Write a memo to your instructor listing each choice and explaining the consequences of each choice. (For information on writing memos, see Chapter 12.)
   - Write a memo to the supervisor reporting the test results and recommending a course of action.

2. **Collaborative exercise:** Working with a team, research a current issue that involves ethics. For example, you might research an issue related to bioethics, sustainability, or social media.
   a. In a memo to your classmates.
      - Describe the issue.
      - Explain the ethical dilemma.

- Analyze the possible actions and consequences of those actions.
- Suggest the ethical course of action and the consequences.

b. In a memo to your instructor, present your analysis and suggest the ethical action you would take. Your instructor may ask you to present your analysis in class.

3. Find a website, advertisement, or product information that you believe misleads the reader.
- Print the page and bring it to class.
- Write a memo to your instructor explaining why the information misleads the reader.
- Attach a copy of the page to your memo.

4. After the 9/11 attacks on the World Trade Center, the Red Cross solicited donations for the victims of these attacks. It received approximately $250 million—more money than it had ever received for disaster relief. Executives with the Red Cross decided that because they had received record donations, they would set some of the money aside for future disasters. They reasoned that the money would still go to disaster victims, just not to victims of the 9/11 attacks. However, when donors discovered that their money wasn't going to the victims, they felt the Red Cross had misled them and was mishandling the money. By proposing to earmark some of the donations, the Red Cross executives intended to protect the interests of future victims. According to the Red Cross website, the Red Cross abandoned the proposal to earmark the monies because it "proved very unpopular."[4] Be prepared to discuss these questions in class:
- Would earmarking some of the monies for other disaster victims be ethical? Explain your answer.
- Which principles of ethical communication support your answer?

5. **Collaborative exercise:** Form a team with two or three of your classmates. Find a company's code of conduct and analyze how effectively (or ineffectively) the code states the company's ethical goals. Many companies post their codes on their websites.
- Does the code describe appropriate behavior expected of employees? Does the code describe inappropriate behavior?
- Does the code provide instruction and/or guidance to help employees decide if behavior is appropriate or inappropriate?
- Does the code specifically state the penalties for not following the code? If so, analyze the penalties. Are they fair? Do they protect all involved?
- How does the code address employees who report misconduct?

[4] Source: Myths and Legends about the American Red Cross, http://www.redcross.org

As a team, write a memo to your instructor summarizing what you have learned. Include a copy of the code with your memo.

6.  During the summer, you begin work as an intern for Centurian, Inc., a software company. You got the job on the recommendation of your best friend's dad. You really appreciate the opportunity to work for this company and hope that they will ask you to return during the winter break. As part of your responsibilities, you help maintain the company's website. As you begin your work on the site, you find that it contains several copyrighted graphics and images. The image on the homepage is a copyrighted image that the company has apparently not asked for or received permission to use. You also find that the company has used passages from another company's product literature without citing sources.
    • Is it unethical for you to ignore your findings? Why or why not?
    • If you report the findings, what are the possible consequences?
    • Be prepared to discuss your ideas with the class.

7.  Read the information in Figure 4.9. This information accompanies a drug used to treat arthritis. Consider whether the information is presented ethically. Be prepared to discuss your answers in class.
    • Does this information leave the readers with a clear impression of the side effects of the drug?
    • Does it directly answer the question about whether the drug damages heart valves?
    • Has the manufacturer ethically presented the information? Explain your answer.

FIGURE 4.9

<u>Medication Guide</u>
<u>for</u>
<u>Non-Steroidal Anti-Inflammatory Drugs (NSAIDs)</u>
(See the end of this Medication Guide for a list of prescription NSAID medicines.)

**What is the most important information I should know about medicines called Non-Steroidal Anti-Inflammatory Drugs (NSAIDs)?**

**NSAID medicines may increase the chance of a heart attack or stroke that can lead to death.**
This chance increases:
- with longer use of NSAID medicines
  - in people who have heart disease

**NSAID medicines should never be used right before or after a heart surgery called a "coronary artery bypass graft (CABG)."**

**NSAID medicines can cause ulcers and bleeding in the stomach and intestines at any time during treatment. Ulcers and bleeding:**
- can happen without warning symptoms
- may cause death

**The chance of a person getting an ulcer or bleeding increases with:**
- taking medicines called "corticosteroids" and "anticoagulants"
- longer use
- smoking
- drinking alcohol
- older age
- having poor health

**NSAID medicines should only be used:**
- exactly as prescribed
- at the lowest dose possible for your treatment
- for the shortest time needed

**What are Non-Steroidal Anti-Inflammatory Drugs (NSAIDs)?**
NSAID medicines are used to treat pain and redness, swelling, and heat (inflammation) from medical conditions such as:
- different types of arthritis
- menstrual cramps and other types of short-term pain

**Who should not take a Non-Steroidal Anti-Inflammatory Drug (NSAID)?**
**Do not take an NSAID medicine:**
- if you had an asthma attack, hives, or other allergic reaction with aspirin or any other NSAID medicine
- for pain right before or after heart bypass surgery

**Tell your healthcare provider:**
- about all of your medical conditions.
- about all of the medicines you take. NSAIDs and some other medicines can interact with each other and cause serious side effects. **Keep a list of your medicines to show to your healthcare provider and pharmacist.**
- if you are pregnant. **NSAID medicines should not be used by pregnant women late in their pregnancy.**

29

FIGURE 4.9

**Document for Exercise 7** *continued*

- if you are breastfeeding. **Talk to your doctor.**

**What are the possible side effects of Non-Steroidal Anti-Inflammatory Drugs (NSAIDs)?**

| Serious side effects include: | Other side effects include: |
|---|---|
| • heart attack<br>• stroke<br>• high blood pressure<br>• heart failure from body swelling (fluid retention)<br>• kidney problems including kidney failure<br>• bleeding and ulcers in the stomach and intestine<br>• low red blood cells (anemia)<br>• life-threatening skin reactions<br>• life-threatening allergic reactions<br>• liver problems including liver failure<br>• asthma attacks in people who have asthma | • stomach pain<br>• constipation<br>• diarrhea<br>• gas<br>• heartburn<br>• nausea<br>• vomiting<br>• dizziness |

**Get emergency help right away if you have any of the following symptoms:**

- shortness of breath or trouble breathing
- chest pain
- weakness in one part or side of your body
- slurred speech
- swelling of the face or throat

**Stop your NSAID medicine and call your healthcare provider right away if you have any of the following symptoms:**

- nausea
- more tired or weaker than usual
- itching
- your skin or eyes look yellow
- stomach pain
- flu-like symptoms
- vomit blood
- there is blood in your bowel movement or it is black and sticky like tar
- skin rash or blisters with fever
- unusual weight gain
- swelling of the arms and legs, hands and feet

These are not all the side effects with NSAID medicines. Talk to your healthcare provider or pharmacist for more information about NSAID medicines.

**Other information about Non-Steroidal Anti-Inflammatory Drugs (NSAIDs)**

- Aspirin is an NSAID medicine but it does not increase the chance of a heart attack. Aspirin can cause bleeding in the brain, stomach, and intestines. Aspirin can also cause ulcers in the stomach and intestines.

- Some of these NSAID medicines are sold in lower doses without a prescription (over – the –counter). Talk to your healthcare provider before using over –the –counter NSAIDs for more than 10 days.

**NSAID medicines that need a prescription**

| Generic Name | Tradename |
|---|---|
| Celecoxib | Celebrex |
| Diclofenac | Cataflam, Voltaren, Arthrotec (combined with misoprostol) |
| Diflunisal | Dolobid |

30

Source: Downloaded from the World Wide Web, November 2008: www.fda.gov/cder/foi/label/2008/020998s026lbl.pdf.

# Part 2

# Knowing the Tools of the Writer

# chapter *five*

## Researching Information

*B*ill Garcia, a food company engineer, must determine why water pipes in one of the manufacturing plants are vibrating and recommend a solution. Before making an appointment to visit the plant, Bill thinks about the information he will need to make a solid recommendation and to write an effective report. He knows he will need to do more than inspect the system; but with the amount of information available to him, he feels overwhelmed. He's not quite sure where to begin or what sources will best suit his purpose. He needs a plan for selecting appropriate research techniques and sources.

Bill's dilemma is not unusual. You, too, may face a similar dilemma as a student and as a professional. As a student, you might need to answer an abstract question, such as "What causes the hiccups?" or "How do greenhouse gases affect the health of people living in heavily populated urban areas?" As a professional, you will likely answer applied questions, such as Bill's question of "How can we solve the problem of vibrating pipes at our plant?" This chapter presents guidelines to help you effectively research information.

Bill thinks about his document's purpose. He decides that he is writing primarily to recommend a viable solution to the problem of the vibrating pipes. His solution must be not only cost effective and feasible, but also well supported with research and testing. Bill has a long-term goal as well—to establish his reputation as a problem solver and to develop positive relationships with his supervisor and the plant manager.

As a professional, you may also conduct research to complete documents or projects. For some documents, you will need only a single fact or figure; for others, you may need to do research using several information-gathering techniques. How do you decide which techniques to use? You could ask questions like those in Figure 5.1 as you plan your research.

After considering the readers' needs, the purpose, and the subject, develop a detailed plan for your research. Some writers like to draw an informal flow chart listing the steps in the process. Others prefer to list the questions they must answer first and then the steps needed to answer those questions. Let's go back to Bill's situation. After determining the type of information he needs, he decides to interview the plant manager and operations personnel, observe the vibrating pipes, examine company files and archives for instances of similar problems, investigate technical literature on similar problems and their solutions, and test the pipes. Before calling the plant manager, Bill writes these steps in an informal flow chart (see Figure 5.2). Having planned his research to suit his purpose, Bill is ready to select the techniques he will use to gather information.

Like Bill, you will need a plan. Figure 5.3 shows the steps you could follow when planning your research. As you work through the planning process, you may decide you have to return to one or more of the steps. The planning process is not linear. You may have to revisit a step because, for example, you don't have enough information or a source isn't credible.

## Select the Right Research Method for Your Topic and Your Readers

As you plan your research, decide on the most appropriate methods for gathering information. You might begin by asking these questions:
- **What types of tools can you use?** You use tools to locate information in secondary sources—sometimes called *research media*. For example, will you use online catalogs or databases, or reference works such as encyclopedias, indexes, or abstract services?

FIGURE 5.1

## Questions to Consider When Planning Your Research

| | |
|---|---|
| **Consider your readers' needs** | • Who are the primary readers? Are there secondary readers? If so, who?<br>• Do the needs of the primary and secondary readers differ? If so, how?<br>• What do your readers expect from your research? What questions might they ask while reading your document?<br>• What do your readers know about the subject? Are they experts, technicians, managers, or general readers?<br>• What are your readers' attitudes toward the subject of your document?<br>• How will your readers use your research findings? |
| **Consider the purpose** | • What is the purpose of your research and your document?<br>• What do you want to accomplish or find out? |
| **Consider your subject** | • What, if anything, do you know about the subject?<br>• What information, if any, are you missing? What do you still need to find out?<br>• Where can you get the information you need?<br>• How much time do you need to gather the missing information or to conduct the research? Will the project allow you this much time? Do you need to adjust the project scope? Do you need to ask for more time? |

FIGURE 5.2

## Bill's Research Plan

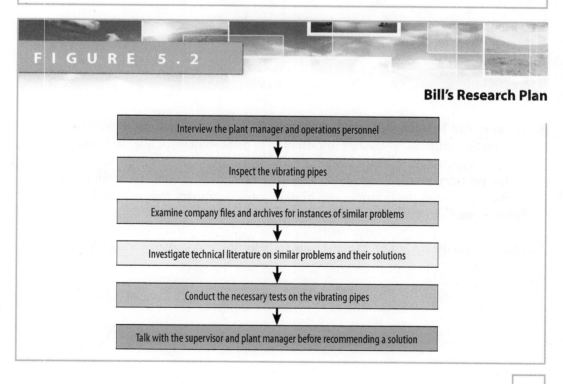

FIGURE 5.3

**Planning Your Research**

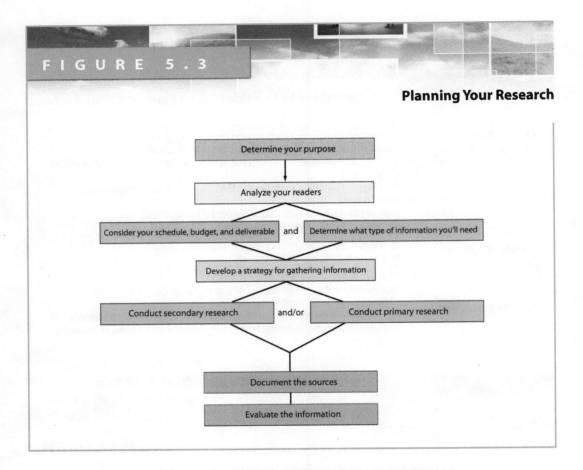

- **What research media will you use?** Where can you find the information? For example, will you find reliable, up-to-date information in print sources, online databases, websites, discussion groups, or perhaps blogs?
- **What primary research methods can you use?** Should you use primary research methods to gather the information? Should you use primary research methods to verify information from secondary sources?

Use the ideas in the tip box on the next page for selecting and implementing a research plan.

## TIPS FOR SELECTING AND IMPLEMENTING YOUR RESEARCH PLAN

- **Determine the appropriate methods for gathering reliable, up-to-date information.** For example, if you want to find out if people are stopping at an intersection, you would observe the intersection at different times of day. However, if you want to know how many accidents have occurred at that intersection, you would search websites or government documents. The information you need determines how you will gather the information.
- **Take detailed notes.** Don't rely on your memory or on haphazard notes. Write down or record all needed information in a detailed, systematic manner. As you take these notes, include sufficient bibliographic information so that your readers can locate the same information.
- **Record your data accurately and thoroughly.** Regardless of the value of the information (or data) you find, if you don't record it accurately and thoroughly, the information is useless. Write it on paper or enter it into an electronic file. If you are conducting an interview or making an observation, record the interview or video the observation; make sure to get permission before recording an interview or observation. If you are searching websites, cut and paste the website URLs and save them with your notes. Bookmark the websites so you can easily return to them.
- **Record your information in a timely manner.** Don't rely on your memory; instead, record information in a timely manner. For example, if you conduct an interview, record the information during the interview—either in written notes or in a recording. If you find information on a website, cut and paste or bookmark the URL immediately; don't wait until you are ready to use that information. You may find that you cannot find the site or you may waste valuable time relocating it.
- **Verify information by using more than one method.** Good researchers rely on more than one or two methods to verify information. Consider driving directions on the Internet; these directions are often incorrect. If you want to provide directions for your coworker to a restaurant that you have never visited, you might get the directions online, look at a map, call the restaurant to verify the directions, or try the directions yourself.
- **Be persistent and patient.** You have probably become frustrated trying to find information on the Internet or in the library. Even experienced researchers have trouble locating information—especially *reliable* information. Be persistent and patient as the information may not be easy to find.

# SELECT APPROPRIATE PRIMARY RESEARCH TOOLS

*Primary research* (sometimes called original or firsthand research) is gathering information for the first time—not relying on research previously conducted by others. If you interview an expert or conduct an experiment, you are using primary research tools. In this section, you will learn some of the more common primary research tools such as
- interviews
- inquiry letters and emails
- surveys and questionnaires
- observations and experiments

## Interviews

You can gather valuable firsthand information from informal and formal interviews. *Interviews* give you the opportunity to gather information from an expert, to hear firsthand observations of a situation, and to discover the experiences of the interviewee. For example, Bill plans to interview the plant manager and the operations personnel who have observed the vibrating pipes. From these interviews, he hopes to determine the characteristics of the problem, such as how frequently the pipes vibrate or whether the vibration is associated with any particular plant operation.

### Informally Interview Coworkers and Colleagues

*Informal interviews* are a valuable tool for information gathering. They may be informal conversations in the office, by telephone, or by email. For many writing situations, informal interviews are the primary means of gathering information. For example, Bill will informally interview the plant manager and other engineers to determine what they know about vibrating pipes and how to stop the vibration. Review the tips on the following page for conducting successful informal interviews.

### Formally Interview People Whom You Don't Work With or Know Well

*Formal interviews* are the best choice for gathering accurate and thorough information from people whom you don't work with or know well. Bill will probably set up formal interviews with the plant manager and the operations manager because he doesn't work regularly with them. They will want to gather statistics and data about the vibrating pipes before talking to Bill, and a formally scheduled interview will give them the lead time they need. Read the Tips for Effective Formal Interviews later in this chapter as you prepare for

## TIPS FOR CONDUCTING INFORMAL INTERVIEWS

- **As you plan your research, write down questions that you intend to ask.**
- **Make a list of all the people who could answer your questions.** From this list, select people whom you work with or know well to interview informally. (Set up formal interviews with people whom you don't work with or know well.)
- **Interview people when they are least busy.** When people are less busy, they share information more fully and freely and answer your questions more accurately.
- **Be willing to return the favor.** If you are open to answering your coworkers' questions, they in turn will be more willing to answer yours.
- **If you use email to interview, ask your interviewees if they would like to have the questions inserted directly into the email message or attached in a file.** You can also do both. The interviewees can then decide which format they prefer.

and conduct formal interviews. Too frequently, beginners go to an interview with only a notepad and pencil, expecting to ad lib the questions. Although this strategy (or lack of it) occasionally works for experienced interviewers, most researchers who arrive at an interview without a written list of questions will leave without enough information.

## Inquiry Letters and Emails

Instead of an interview, you can send an inquiry letter or email. Many people prefer the ease of an email inquiry; they can simply click on the Reply button to respond. Be aware, however, that because many respondents receive junk email, they may ignore your inquiry if they do not know you or recognize your email address. If the interviewee is busy or dislikes writing, you risk receiving incomplete answers to which you will have to follow up. On the other hand, many organizations and experts will respond to inquiry emails and send you detailed answers to your questions. If your topic is sensitive or confidential, send a more formal inquiry letter.

Although inquiry letters and emails are convenient, they are not as useful as face-to-face interviews for several reasons:
- In most cases, you cannot ask follow-up questions or ask the respondent to clarify.
- The respondent may misunderstand your question.
- Because the respondent has not agreed to answer your inquiry, he or she may not respond.

## Surveys and Questionnaires

*Questionnaires*, sometimes called surveys, are a research tool for gathering information from a large group of people. Use a questionnaire to gather information about a group's preferences, attitudes, or beliefs. For example, if you plan to change the company's health plan, you might send a questionnaire to employees to determine their opinions about the current company health plan. You can also use questionnaires to develop a profile of a group. For example, you could gather demographics about consumers as you ask them what product brand they prefer or what news source they prefer. Questionnaires, however, have these disadvantages:

- The response rate for questionnaires is poor, usually only 15 to 20 percent.
- You can't guarantee that the respondents are a representative sample, so you must draw careful conclusions from the information you gather from a questionnaire. The respondents who choose to respond may have a bias about the subject (Plumb and Spyridakis 1992).
- You won't know if respondents misinterpret a question because questionnaires don't allow you to follow up and clarify, as you can in an interview (Plumb and Spyridakis 1992).

If you use a questionnaire, remember that you are asking the respondents to do you a favor with little, if any, benefit to them, so make sure the questionnaire is as efficient and simple as possible.

# TIPS FOR EFFECTIVE FORMAL INTERVIEWS

| | |
|---|---|
| **Determine the purpose of the interview** | **Before the interview**<br>• **Identify the purpose of the interview.**<br>• **Identify the specific information you want to gather.**<br>Think about Bill's interview with Richard Hampton, operations manager at the plant. Bill might identify the purpose of this interview as follows:<br>*The purpose of my interview with Richard Hampton is to identify the frequency of the vibration, its effect on the plant's operation, and which operations seem to trigger the vibration. I also want to know what he believes is causing the vibration.* |
| **Contact the interviewee to set up the interview** | **When you call or email**<br>• **State the purpose of your interview,** so the interviewee can tell you whether he or she can give you the needed information. If you need the information by a specific date, tell the interviewee.<br>• **Be flexible about the time.** If possible, let the interviewee determine the time and date for the interview.<br>• **Hold the interview at the interviewee's office or at a location most convenient for the interviewee.** Make the interview location convenient for the interviewee even if it is inconvenient for you.<br>• **Ask permission to record the interview** if you plan to use audio- or video-recording equipment.<br>• **Offer to submit questions ahead of time.** |
| **Prepare for the interview** | **Before the interview**<br>• **Find out as much about your subject and the interviewee as possible.**<br>• **Plan your questions.**<br>• **Gather background information.** Look at secondary sources. You look unprepared if you ask questions that the professional literature answers.<br>• **Plan specific, open-ended questions.** Avoid questions that can be answered with yes/no.<br>   • **Yes/no question:** *Can greenhouse emissions affect children's health?*<br>   • **Open-ended question:** *How do greenhouse emissions affect children's health?*<br>• **Avoid leading, biased questions.**<br>   • **Leading/biased:** *Don't you agree that greenhouse emissions are one of the greatest dangers to children's health in large cities?*<br>   • **Impartial:** *How do you see greenhouse emissions as affecting children's health in large cities?*<br>• **Write each question on a separate notecard.** You can also put the questions on a file on your laptop or other electronic device. Be sure to use wide margins so you can see the questions and summarize the answers. |
| **Prepare yourself** | **Before the interview**<br>• Give yourself plenty of time to arrive early for the interview.<br>• Arrive on time (or a little early).<br>• Check your video- and audio-recording equipment if you plan to use it. |

| Conduct the interview | **At the beginning of the interview** |
|---|---|
| | • Thank the interviewee for agreeing to do the interview. |
| | • State the purpose of the interview. |
| | • Tell the interviewee how you plan to use the information. |
| | • Respect cultural differences. Make sure you use the appropriate level of formality, politeness, and other behaviors in the given culture. (See Chapter 2.) |
| | **During the interview** |
| | • Let the interviewee do most of the talking. |
| | • Maintain eye contact. Your interviewee will give you more information if you seem sincerely interested. |
| | • Use your prepared questions. |
| | • Ask follow-up questions, such as |
| |     • *Can you give me an example?* |
| |     • *What additional actions would you suggest?* |
| | • If you don't understand an answer, ask the interviewee clarifying questions, such as |
| |     • *Can you give an example?* |
| |     • *Can you simplify?* |
| |     • *Would you go over that again, please?* |
| | • Verbally summarize the interviewee's answers to make sure you understood. |
| | • If the interviewee gets off the subject, be prepared to respectfully move the interview back to the intended focus. You might say, *Thank you for that interesting information. I know our time is short, so let's move on to the next question.* |
| | • Take notes only as necessary. Write only the important information. Don't write so much that you can't maintain some eye contact with the interviewee or that the interviewee has to wait while you complete your notes. |
| | **At the end of the interview** |
| | • Ask the interviewee for final comments. |
| |     • *Would you like to add any other information?* |
| |     • *Can you suggest other sources or people whom I should interview?* |
| | • Ask permission to quote the interviewee (if you have not already done so). |
| | • Ask for the interviewee's correct title and position. |
| | • Ask if you may contact the interviewee again if you have questions or need to verify information. |
| | • Offer to send the interviewee a copy of your notes, so he or she can review the information for accuracy. |
| | • Thank the interviewee for his or her time. |
| | • Leave promptly. |
| Follow up | **After the interview** |
| | • Write down the information that you want to remember from the interview. |
| | • Write the interviewee a thank-you note within two or three days. |

## Determining the Purpose, Sample Group, and Method

Before you begin preparing the questions for your questionnaire, ask yourself these questions:

- **What is the purpose of this questionnaire?** What do I want to learn?
- **What kinds of questions will I ask?**
- **What is the target group I want to question?**
- **How will I select the target population (the intended respondents)?** Will I select them at random? See Figure 5.4 for questions you might ask your target group.
- **How many questionnaires will I send?** The more questionnaires you send, the more responses you will receive.
- **How will I administer the questionnaire—by mail, by email, by phone, online, or in person?** Mailed questionnaires take less time, but they are expensive, and fewer people will respond. You will generally receive more and quicker responses when you administer the questionnaire by email, by phone, online, or in person. However, some respondents are uncomfortable, even annoyed, by phone questionnaires. By phone or in person, respondents may respond with less candor than with mail or email questionnaires. If you personally deliver a questionnaire, the response rate may be higher, but the geographic area you can survey is greatly reduced.

## FIGURE 5.4

### Selecting the Target Group

To identify the target group you will survey, answer these questions.
- Do group members need a certain level of education? If so, what level?
- Should group members be a certain age? If so, what age?
- Must group members live in a specific geographic area? If so, where?
- Is the target group best represented by males, females, or both genders?
- Should group members have a certain level of subject knowledge? If so, what knowledge level?
- Must group members be savvy users of a certain type of tool or software? If so, what tool or software?
- Must group members share a particular language? If so, what language?
- Must group members have a certain income level? If so, what level?

FIGURE 5.5

## Types of Questions Used in Questionnaires

| Type of Question | Type of Answer | Example |
|---|---|---|
| **Multiple choice** | Respondents select from one or more alternatives | What is your classification?<br>_____ Freshman _____ Junior<br>_____ Sophomore _____ Senior _____ Graduate |
| **Yes or no** | Respondents select "yes" or "no" | Would you use the express rail service to commute to your office?<br>_____ Yes _____ No |
| **Likert scale** | Respondents rank their answers on a scale. Select an even number of choices. Plumb and Spyridakis (1992) recommend including no fewer than 3 and no more than 11 choices. | The online reporting system has made my job easier. Circle your response.<br><br>Strongly disagree    Disagree    Agree    Strongly agree |
| **Semantic differential scale** | Respondents rate their answers on a continuum of opposing concepts. Limit the choices to no fewer than 3 and no more than 11. Use this type of question to measure attitudes and feelings. | Your technical communication class is<br><br>Easy _____ Hard<br><br>Interesting _____ Boring<br><br>Current _____ Out of date |
| **Ranking** | Respondents rank (prioritize) their answers. | Rank the importance of the following factors when you purchase a new car. Put a 1 next to the most important factor, a 2 next to the second most important factor, and so on.<br>_____ Fuel economy _____ Safety ratings<br>_____ Price _____ Consumer satisfaction ratings<br>_____ Size _____ Dealership<br>_____ Color _____ Upgrades available |
| **Formal rating scale** | Respondents rate an item or quality on a specific scale, usually 1 to 5 or 1 to 10. | How do you rate your satisfaction with your new vehicle? Please circle only one rating, with 1 being not satisfied and 5 being satisfied.<br><br>   1        2        3        4        5<br>Not satisfied                    Satisfied |
| **Checklists** | Respondents check one answer. With an expanded checklist, respondents may check more than one response. (See the example to the right.) Plumb and Spyridakis (1992) point out that "to ensure that all respondents interpret the questions similarly, the question instructs respondents to 'Check all that apply.' The 'Other' response option is provided in case the researcher has not considered all possible activities" (1992, 633). | Which of the following activities describes tasks you complete daily using a computer? (Check all that apply.)<br>_____ Check and send email<br>_____ Surf the Internet<br>_____ Communicate with friends<br>_____ Pay bills<br>_____ Watch videos<br>_____ Get directions<br>_____ Get news and weather<br>_____ Check my stocks<br>_____ Use word processing software<br>_____ Prepare spreadsheets<br>_____ Other (please explain) _____ |
| **Short answer/ essay** | Respondents answer open-ended questions using phrases or sentences. | How well do you think telecommuting will work in your department? What do you believe are the advantages and disadvantages of telecommuting? |

- **Write unambiguous questions.** If respondents can interpret a question in more than one way, your results will be meaningless.
- **Use simple, plain language.** Plumb and Spyridakis recommend avoiding "technical terms, acronyms, and abstract or ambiguous words" (1992, 631).
- **Avoid questions that influence your respondents' answers or that indicate your opinion.** For example, the following questions unnecessarily influence, or lead readers:
  - **Impartial**: *Is curbside recycling an environmentally sound idea?*
  - **Leading/Biased**: *Is curbside recycling a waste of the city's valuable tax dollars?*
- **Before you finalize the questionnaire, test your questions on a small group of respondents to make sure the questions are clear and unambiguous.** Rewrite any problem questions. If you have time, test the questionnaire a second time. Once you send out the questionnaire, you can't revise it.
- **Ask only necessary questions.** Respect your respondents' time. Respondents often ignore questionnaires that are long or that seem to waste their time.
- **Attach a cover letter or cover email.** Clearly and concisely explain the purpose of your questionnaire.
- **Explain the significance of the questionnaire.** Persuade your respondents that their responses will benefit them, their workplace, or their community.
- **Tell the respondents when you will pick up the questionnaire or when they should return it.** Include this information in the cover letter or email. Include a self-addressed, postage-paid envelope for returning the questionnaire if you're using the mail, or use an electronic format. Your respondents will be more likely to complete the survey and return it to you in a timely manner if they can simply drop it in the nearest mailbox or respond to an email.
- **In the cover letter or email, thank respondents for their time.**

## Preparing Effective Questions

Both closed- and open-ended questions are appropriate. *Closed-ended questions* elicit answers that you can count or quantify. With closed-ended questions, you limit respondents' answers to only the responses that you provide. With open-ended questions, respondents answer with their own words. A questionnaire that uses closed-ended questions might include

- multiple-choice questions
- yes/no questions
- ranking questions that ask respondents to arrange items in order of preference
- ranking questions that ask respondents to rate items on a scale

Because closed-ended or quantitative questions yield totals and percentages, you can use software to read and tabulate the answers. Such questions are particularly valuable when you have a large number of respondents. Figure 5.5 illustrates the kind of closed-ended questions you might include in a questionaire.

*Open-ended questions* yield answers that you can't easily quantify, but they may give you valuable information that you can't gain through closed-ended questions. Open-ended questions tend to elicit more accurate information because they don't limit the respondents to the writer's suggested answers (Anderson 1985). For example, for the question, "Why didn't you use the Fleet Assistance Program when you bought your 2012 car?" respondents can list their reason, which might not be one the question writer had considered.

Figures 5.6A and 5.6B show a sample cover letter and accompanying questionnaire. The questionnaire includes both closed- and open-ended questions. As you write your questionnaire, consult the Tips for Preparing an Effective Questionaire on the previous page.

**TIPS** FOR CONDUCTING AN EFFECTIVE EXPERIMENT

- **Establish a hypothesis.** A *hypothesis* is an assumption. For example, to determine the efficacy of calcium supplements in preventing bone density loss (osteoporosis), you might test the following hypothesis: *Women will lose less bone density when taking 1500 milligrams per day of calcium than women who do not take a calcium supplement.*
- **Test the hypothesis.** You will need an experimental group and a control group. For example, to test your hypothesis, you would need an experimental group of women who take 1500 milligrams of calcium for one year and a control group that takes no calcium supplements for one year. You would conduct bone density tests on each woman in each group before and after the experiment.
- **Analyze the data.** Once you have all the data from the experiment, you must understand the data so you can determine whether your hypothesis is true.
- **Report the data.** After you analyze the data, you report what you have learned. (You will learn about report writing in Chapters 14 and 15.)

## Observations and Experiments

Once you have gathered adequate background information, you may decide to observe the problem or situation. In our example at the beginning of the chapter, for instance, Bill might personally observe the vibrating pipes and then conduct appropriate tests. These direct observations and tests will help Bill pinpoint the problem.. If you directly observe people and situations as part of your research, remember these guidelines:

**FIGURE 5.6A**

**Sample Cover Letter for a Questionnaire**

January 30, 2012

Department of English
University of North Dakota
Grand Forks, ND 58201

Name
Title
Company Name
Address

Dear _____ :

I am researching the types of writing done by entry-level employees and the types of software they use to write. You are receiving this questionnaire because you have hired graduates with a technical communication certificate from the University of North Dakota. Your responses will help us better understand how to prepare graduates for the workforce. I will use this information in a recommendation report for the faculty and lab staff in the technical communication program.

I am specifically interested in the following information
- whether entry-level employees are prepared for the types of writing done in the workplace
- the types of writing done by entry-level employees in the workplace
- the types of software they use for writing tasks
- whether our curriculum is preparing entry-level employees for their writing tasks
- whether our labs provide relevant software training

Please take a few minutes to complete this questionnaire. Your response will remain anonymous. If possible, return the survey by email to labsurvey@ndsu.edu. I appreciate you taking time to respond.

Sincerely,

Elizabeth Smidt
Technical Communication Student

FIGURE 5.6B

**Technical Communication Questionnaire**

1. Describe the work of your company (manufacturing, service, health care, high tech, etc.).
   _____

2. How many employees work for your company?
   ____ fewer than 10          ____ 100–200
   ____ 10–25                  ____ 200–300
   ____ 25–50                  ____ 300–400
   ____ 50–100                 ____ more than 400

3. What types of documents do entry-level employees write? Check all that apply.
   ____ email                             ____ feasibility reports
   ____ letters and memos                 ____ progress/status reports
   ____ PowerPoint™ presentations         ____ procedures
   ____ proposals                         ____ white papers
   ____ definitions                       ____ Web pages
   ____ product descriptions/definitions  ____ manuals
   ____ other (please explain) _____

4. What types of software do entry-level employees use to prepare documents? Check all that apply.
   ____ word processing
   ____ Web design and development
   ____ spreadsheet
   ____ desktop publishing
   ____ graphics
   ____ other (please explain) _____

5. How would you rate the preparedness of your entry-level employees for writing tasks (1 = Not prepared and 5 = Well prepared)?
   1          2          3          4          5

6. How would you characterize the writing skills of your entry-level employees?
   Poor            Good            Very good            Excellent

7. What percentage of writing tasks do entry-level employees perform in a collaborative setting?
   ____ none            ____ 50–70%
   ____ less than 20%   ____ more than 70%
   ____ 20–50%

8. Do you provide additional writing training for entry-level employees within their first year of employment?
   ____ Yes          ____ No

9. Please provide any comments that would help us better prepare our graduates.
   _____

- **Gather background information.** Before you observe, gather as much background information as possible. Without this information, you may not know what to look for and, therefore, waste your time.
- **Know what to look for.** Do your homework. Find out what you are looking for and where to find it.
- **Take notes as you observe.** As you observe, answer the questions Who? What? When? Where? Why? How? Record your observations immediately; don't rely on memory.

An *experiment* is a controlled observation where you test a hypothesis. If you decide to conduct an experiment, take your time to carefully design the experiment. You will only obtain valid results if you have designed an effective and reliable experiment. Follow the Tips on the previous page for Conducting an Effective Experiment. To learn about experimental design in your field, visit a website on research methods used in your field.

##  SELECT APPROPRIATE SECONDARY RESEARCH TOOLS

*Secondary research* is gathering information from previously documented research or studies. For example, if you want to research the climate of Mars, you would look at scientific reports that contain the analyzed data from the Mars *Pathfinder*. You can find valuable secondary information by searching the Internet or your college or university library. College and university libraries have resources (on site and online) to help you locate information: books, periodicals, trade publications, newspapers, databases, maps, films, computer databases, video and sound recordings, indexes, abstracts, and government documents. This list is only a sampling of the many resources available to you on the Internet and from your college or university libraries.

In the workplace, you may also find information in your organization's library. Some organizations call this library an *information resource center*. These centers collect information related to the organization's business. For some organizations, the information resource center has specialists who will do the research for you. For example, you might email a question such as "How many megawatts of power did Reliant generate between January and March of 2011?" The staff then researches the question and emails you the answer. Other organizations have staff that suggest where you can look for the information. If your organization does not have an information resource center, you can conduct research over the Internet or in company archives.

Secondary research involves gathering information from previously documented research or studies.

When you use a library or an information resource center, follow these guidelines.

- **Talk to reference librarians.** Reference librarians are your most valuable library resource. They can help you locate the appropriate resources and teach you how to use them. They are willing to suggest new ways to locate information or to tell you if your library doesn't have the information you seek. Reference librarians can save you time and frustration.
- **Take detailed notes.** Don't rely on your memory or on haphazard notes. Write down all needed information in a detailed, systematic way. As you take these notes, include accurate, complete bibliographic information—enough information for your readers to locate the same information.
- **If you are using Internet resources, record the URL and save a copy of the site's homepage.** Websites come and go, and your saved copy of the homepage may be the only proof that the information did exist.

The following sections discuss secondary resources and strategies for finding information in those resources.

## Understanding the Secondary Resources Available to You

You may better understand the wealth of secondary resources by categorizing them into the following groups: online catalogs, databases, search engines and subject directories, reference works, and abstract services. You can use these resources to find information in traditional sources: books, periodicals, reports, trade publications, and government documents. You can also use some of these resources to find information on the Internet. The following sections briefly describe each of the resources. When you understand the resources available, then we will discuss strategies for effectively and efficiently using these resources.

### Online Catalogs

Use an online catalog to search for library holdings. An *online catalog* is a database of any holding (item) housed at the library. You can search the holdings from your desktop; you don't have to go to the library building. With many online catalogs, you can find out if the item you need is available and where it is located.

### Online Databases

Use *online databases* to search in journals, trade magazines, conference proceedings, newspapers, government publications, etc. To access these databases, you go through commercial or government services that offer a variety of databases. Your college or university pays for access to database services. These databases gather information from a variety of fields. For example, if you are doing research in biology, you would use databases that gather information related only to biology. These databases help you narrow your search. You might be tempted to google the information; this approach can be frustrating because the information is not filtered. If you use the databases at your library, the information will be filtered by subject and will likely be more credible.

## Indexes

*Indexes* (**or** *indices)* are lists of books, newspapers, periodical articles, or other works on a particular subject. Indexes also list the documents available from the government.

**Periodical indexes** offer you an excellent source of some of the most current research information. (*Periodicals* are magazines and journals.) Although periodicals offer excellent information, you may have trouble identifying articles related to your topic. Periodical indexes simplify this task. These indexes list articles classified according to title, subject, discipline, and/or author. For example, the following indexes list articles in particular fields or by discipline.

- *Agricultural Index*
- *Business and Periodicals Index*
- *Applied Science and Technology Index*
- *Engineering Index*

You can also use a directory search engine to access periodicals. Many search engines contain a searchable directory of specialty search engines; you can search using the terms "journals" or "periodicals."

When you need periodicals, ask your reference librarian which indexes will best help you find the information you need. Once you have gathered a list of potential articles, you have to locate them. Check your library's online catalog to determine if your library carries the periodical you need. Be sure to check the volume number or years of the periodical; sometimes libraries don't carry all the volumes or may be missing some. If your library doesn't have the periodical or volume that you need, you may locate the article by using the following sources:

- **Interlibrary loan.** The interlibrary loan office will help you locate articles not owned by your library. This office will locate the article and request that another library loan or photocopy it.
- **Online document delivery services.** You access these services on the Internet. These services search a database of periodicals. If the service has the article you need, it faxes or emails the article to you, usually within an hour. These services may charge a fee; however, if you're in a hurry, the article may be worth the fee.

**Newspaper indexes** list many types of information, but newspapers don't cover most subjects in depth. Newspapers may summarize some topics, especially local issues and present statistics, trends, and demographic information. Many major newspapers are indexed by subject. You can access many newspapers on the Internet.

# TAKING IT INTO THE *workplace*

## Copyright Laws and Your Research

Passed by the U.S. Congress, the Copyright Act of 1976 and the Digital Millennium Copyright Act of 1998 protect the authors of published and unpublished works. The European Union passed a similar directive in 2001, the EU Copyright Directive. Under U.S. law, the author of a work is entitled to the profits if someone sells or distributes the work, except in cases of "fair use." For example, the information on a website may be copyrighted: the text, artwork, music, photographs, and audiovisual materials (including sounds). You can use copyright-protected works without the author's permission if you follow the fair use guidelines established by the Copyright Act of 1976. This law protects you if you use a small portion of an author's work to benefit the public. Fair use allows you to use works for education, research, criticism, news reporting, and scholarship purposes that are nonprofit in nature. To determine fair use, consider these factors:

- **The purpose of the use.** Is the use for commercial, nonprofit, or educational purposes? If you are using the work for commercial purposes, you may be violating the copyright law. You are responsible for knowing if the work is copyrighted.

- **The nature and purpose of the copyrighted work.** If the information is essential for the good of the public, you may be able to use the copyrighted work without the author's permission.

- **The amount and substantiality of the portion of the work used.** The law doesn't give us strict guidelines, so you must use your judgment to determine how much of a copyrighted work you can use without the

iStockphoto 2008.

author's permission. For example, if you use 400 words of a 1,000-word document, you are not following fair use guidelines. If you use 400 words of a 100,000-word document, you are following fair use guidelines. If you are using even a part of a copyrighted graphic, you must get permission. You can't use a portion of a copyrighted graphic.

- **The effect of the use on the potential market for or value of the copyrighted work.** If your use of the copyrighted document hurts the author's potential to profit from the work or hurts the potential value of the work, you have violated fair use guidelines.

As you write and create documents—online or in print—ask yourself these questions:

- Have you relied on information from copyrighted works? If so, do you have permission from the author(s) to use the work?
- Have you appropriately cited sources or acknowledged that you have used the work by permission of the author?
- Are you unfairly profiting from the copyrighted work of the author(s)?
- Have you asked for legal advice? If you don't know whether you can legally use a portion of work, ask for advice from legal counsel. If you ask for advice, you may prevent legal action against you or your employer.
- Are you doing the right thing? (For more information on ethics and doing the right thing, see Chapter 4.)

## Assignment

Visit these websites to learn more about U.S. copyright laws.

- U.S. Copyright Office: www.copyright.gov
- Copyright Clearance Center: www.copyright.com

After visiting these websites, write a memo to your instructor answering these questions:

- How do you know if a document is copyrighted?
- What is the Copyright Clearance Center? How can students and businesses use the center's website?
- How do you register a copyright?
- How long is a copyright protected?
- What works are protected by copyright?
- What is not protected by copyright?
- How does copyright affect you when conducting research?

- **Use more than one search engine.** Search engines are not identical; they index only a portion of the information available online. Use more than one search engine to make sure you get the most reliable, up-to-date information. If you don't find the information you need or if you get limited results, try a different search engine.
- **Use varied keywords or search phrases.** Vary the keywords. For example, if you are looking for information on greenhouse gases, you might use the terms greenhouse gases, greenhouse effect, greenhouse gas emissions, global warming, or climate change. By using all these terms, you will gather more information.
- **Use discipline-specific websites when possible.** Once you find a list of links, select the websites that are discipline specific. Let's consider the greenhouse gas example. If you search for greenhouse gas emissions, you will find links to information from the U.S. Environmental Protection Agency (EPA), Wikipedia, the U.S. Department of Energy (DOE), and *Science Daily*. The specialized websites would be the EPA, DOE, and *Science Daily*, not Wikipedia.
- **Download only what you need.** Many websites include graphics, video files, and sound. If you only need the text, download only that information. Graphics, video files, and sound take up valuable memory on your computer or flash drive.
- **Save or print what you need before the information changes or goes away.** Note the URL or copy and paste it and the date you accessed the information. Keep an electronic file of the URLs where you have accessed information. You will appreciate this file when you prepare your works cited or list of references.
- **Consider the ethics of using information from the Internet.** Information, videos, sounds, and graphics that you download from the Internet may be the intellectual property of an author or company. The information may be copyrighted. Make sure you credit the source and/or get permission to use the information, video, sound, or graphic.

**Government document indexes** list information available from the U.S. government. The U.S. government publishes documents on business, science, the environment, engineering, health, and many other topics. You can find documents published by federal agencies and departments such as the Department of Labor, the Department of Housing and Urban Development, the Environmental Protection Agency, and the Internal Revenue Service. You can find these documents through libraries that are registered repositories for U.S. government documents. Many university and some large public libraries are repositories. They usually have a separate reference librarian and staff for the government documents

FIGURE 5.7

## Government Printing Office Website

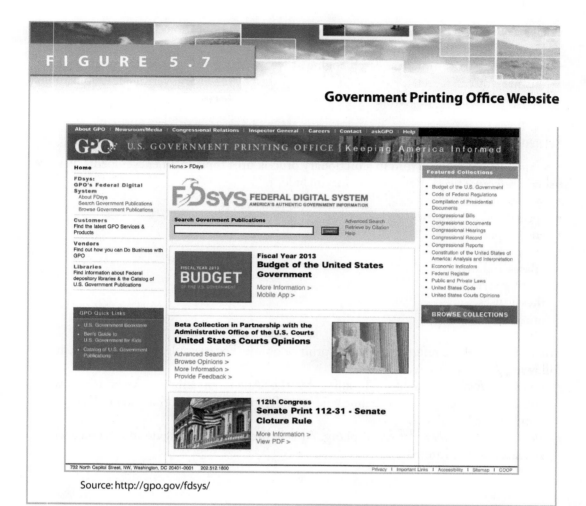

Source: http://gpo.gov/fdsys/

because they are cataloged separately. Some libraries also house publications published by state agencies. These publications provide information on topics such as food, nutrition, agriculture, animal science, natural resources, and state demographics, among others.

Government documents may be listed in a separate online catalog at your library. Unlike other documents in the library, government documents are classified according to the Superintendent of Documents system (not the Library of Congress system). Think of government documents as a library within the library. You can also find many government documents on the Internet. If your library is a government depository library, the librarians and staff of this section of the library will help you locate government documents and resources, and possibly state governments and agencies.

- Use www.gpoaccess.gov to search for government publications. As you can see in Figure 5.7, this site is searchable and easy to use.
- Use the U.S. government's search engine at www.USA.gov. Once on the main page for this site, you can search for all documents published by the U.S. government (publications .usa.gov/USAPubs.php).

## Reference Works

Any time you look up a word in a dictionary or look up a topic in an encyclopedia, you are using a *reference work*. Reference works include
- general dictionaries
- specialized dictionaries
- encyclopedias
- almanacs
- atlases and maps
- writing style manuals
- thesauruses
- other reference tools

You can access these reference works in print or online. For example, you might look at the following guides to reference works
- *Guide to Reference*, published online by the American Library Association, www .guidetoreference.org/. This online guide to reference sources in print and on the Internet is organized by subject.
- *Internet Public Library* at www.ipl.org. At this site, you can navigate to reference works available on the Internet.

## Abstract Services

*Abstract services* go one step beyond indexes. Along with bibliographic information, abstract services include an article summary. Abstracts can save you time. By reading the abstract before you locate the article, you can decide whether the article contains the kind of information you are seeking. Some abstract services cover a specific field, such as *Chemical Abstracts* and *Computer Abstracts*. Other abstract services are broader, such as *Dissertation Abstracts*. Your library's website has links to many services where you can read abstracts and decide whether to get the full-text version of an article.

FIGURE 5.8

## Questions for Evaluating Online Sources[1]

| Is the Online Source ... | Questions to Ask | Comments |
|---|---|---|
| **Written or prepared by reliable authors?** | • Who created the website or the information?<br>• What are the credentials of the author(s)?<br>• If you don't recognize the name of the author(s), company, or organization, did you find the site through another reliable source?<br>• Does the site contain biographical information on the author(s)?<br>• Can you find references to the author's, company's, or organization's credentials or work through other search engines or databases? | Anyone, whether qualified or not, can publish information online and all voices appear equal.<br>• Be wary of using information from an author, company, or organization you don't recognize, or from a source that you cannot verify as credible.<br>• If you cannot find who operates a website, find information from another source. |
| **Published by a reliable group?** | • Who is the website's publisher?<br>• What makes the publisher qualified to produce the site?<br>• Is the publisher affiliated with a reputable group or organization?<br>• Does the domain name give you information about the publisher and its purpose? For example, epa.gov tells you that the publisher is a government institution.<br>• Does the website include contact information for the publisher? | If the website is published from a personal account with an Internet service provider, the site may contain unreliable information. If the information looks interesting or valuable, verify that information through other sources. If you cannot verify it, don't use it. |
| **Up-to-date?** | • When was the website or document created or published?<br>• When was the site or document updated or revised? Has it been updated in the last three months?<br>• Are the links up-to-date? Do the links work?<br>• Is the site "under construction" or only partially complete? | If the website has not been updated in the last three months, the information may not be up-to-date or reliable. If the site or item is "under construction," you may want to use another site or source. If the links don't work, the site may not contain up-to-date information. |
| **Presented clearly and accurately?** | • Is the site well constructed? Does it have a professional appearance and design?<br>• Does the site follow basic rules of grammar, spelling, and punctuation?<br>• Do the authors cite sources? Do they support all claims with appropriate evidence?<br>• Does the information appear biased? | If a site looks unprofessional, its information may be unreliable. If the site doesn't follow the basic rules of grammar, spelling, and punctuation, the information may be unreliable or inaccurate. If the authors do not cite sources or support their claims, use other sources. A reliable site<br>• has a professional, well-constructed design<br>• follows the basic conventions of grammar, punctuation, and spelling<br>• supports all claims<br>• documents sources<br>• presents unbiased information or tells you when authors are stating opinions |

Some questions adapted from *Web Site Evaluation*, published by the University of North Texas Libraries.

## EVALUATE THE SOURCES AND THE INFORMATION

To find as much relevant information on your topic as possible, use a combination of sources. You will probably find ample information using this combination, but you must evaluate the quality of the sources and the information. Just because the information is published in print or online doesn't mean it is reliable. Some information may be out-of-date, incomplete, incorrect, misleading, or biased. The source of the information may not be reliable or credible. Use these questions to evaluate the information:

> Just because information is published in print or online doesn't mean it is reliable. Some information may be out-of-date, incomplete, incorrect, misleading, or biased. The source of the information may not be reliable or credible.

- **Is the information reliable and unbiased?** Does the author or source have a financial or political interest in the information? If the author or source has such an interest, the information may be biased and unreliable.
- **Is the source credible?** Does the author or source include their credentials? Are the credentials credible, relevant, and verifiable? Can you find a section such as "About Us"?
- **Is the information up-to-date?** You want to base your research and your conclusions on the most current information. You could sacrifice your professional reputation by basing your decisions or research on out-of-date information.
- **Is the information complete?** Does information seem to be missing? Have the researchers or authors covered all areas of the topic?
- **Is the information sufficiently detailed for your research?** Look for information that is sufficiently detailed for your research and your readers. Avoid overly simple or overly complex information for you, your readers, and your research.
- **Is the information accurate?** You can verify accuracy by using more than one source or conducting observations or experiments. You should also make sure that estimates used in your research are accurate.

You may find information from the Internet to be the most difficult to evaluate. Anyone can publish anything on the Internet—and the disreputable sources maybe just as prominent as the reputable ones. At first glance, disreputable sources may look equally reliable, so you must learn how to sort the reliable from the unreliable, the reputable from the disreputable sources. Few, if any, standards regulate publications that appear on the Internet. Many online publications have no overseeing editorial board. Currently, no market forces drive incompetent or unreliable publications off the Internet, so carefully evaluate the online sources you use in your research. As you evaluate these sources, consider the following guidelines and questions listed in Figure 5.8:

- **The Internet may not contain all the information available about your topic.** Even in this digital age, not all printed records have been transferred to digital storage; you may find important information about your topic in traditional print sources, such as journals, books, and trade publications. Although many journals are now available online, some excellent journals are still only available by subscription or in print. Until all print sources are transferred to digital records, be sure to include print sources as part of your search strategy.
- **No search engine indexes all available online information.** Therefore, use a combination of search engines and online tools.
- **Some online sources are out-of-date.** You cannot tell whether a site is current by simply looking at it. Check when the site was last updated.
- **Some search engines and subject directories typically index sites that have many links to them** (Lawrence and Giles 1999). Search results, then, will be populated with results from the more popular sites. A site's popularity may have nothing to do with the quality or reliability of its information.

## CASE STUDY ANALYSIS

### Prominent Doctor Admits to Creating Phoney Research[2]

### Background

When his department chair asked him to clear up some research data discrepancies, Dr. Andrew Friedman—a prominent surgeon and researcher at Brigham and Women's Hospital and Harvard Medical School—pulled patient files and frantically wrote in information to support his research findings. His deception was discovered days later when he confessed to colleagues and managers that he had manipulated data. Because his research had been published in some of the nation's top medical journals, he retracted his articles.

As a result of his deceptive research practices, Dr. Friedman was punished with a $10,000 fine, a one-year suspension of his medical license, and exclusion from federally funded research for three years. However, because he was from a family prominent in medicine and research and he had a highly regarded personal reputation that included groundbreaking work, awards, honors, and more than 100 published works, he was hired as a drug

[2] Source: Compiled from information found at www.msnbc.msn.com/id/8474936.

consultant with pharmaceutical companies for the next three years. During that time, he also volunteered with the American Red Cross and attended ethics and record-keeping lectures.

Later, he petitioned to have his license reinstated and was hired at Ortho-McNeil Pharmaceuticals as director of women's healthcare. In that position, he designed and reviewed clinical trials on hormonal birth control, including writing the information inserts for products. He also gave lectures and appeared as a media expert on hormonal birth control methods.

Dr. Friedman attributed his deceptive research to the professional pressure he was under to publish articles in addition to maintaining his surgical, patient, teaching, and lecture schedule.

## Assignment

1. Working with a team, write a procedure for Brigham and Women's Hospital that details a way to ensure research and articles prepared by the institution's doctors are not falsified or plagiarized.
   a. Use information found in this chapter to support your procedure.
   b. Have one student present your team's procedure to the class.
2. Assume you are the hiring director at Ortho-McNeil Pharmaceuticals. Draft a press release that explains why you have faith in in the company's decision to hire Dr. Friedman. Specifically address concerns that patients might have about drug research conducted by Dr. Friedman. Turn in your press release to your instructor.

# EXERCISES

DOWNLOAD A WORKSHEET FOR RESEARCHING INFORMATION ONLINE AT

WWW.GRTEP.COM

1. Use a search engine to find five websites about a current topic in your field. For example, if you are majoring in engineering, you might research using ethanol to fuel vehicles. If you're majoring in biology or chemistry, you might look at the impact of acid rain on the water quality of our rivers and lakes. Visit each website and follow these instructions.
   • Print the site's homepage.
   • Locate the contact information of the site's publisher.
   • Write a memo to your instructor evaluating the site's reliability. Use the questions in Figure 5.8, to guide your evaluation.

2. Using the topic you selected for Exercise 1, develop a research strategy for turning that topic into a report.
   • Make sure you have appropriately narrowed the topic.
   • Prepare a preliminary bibliography of the sources you might use for your report. Include at least five print sources, five websites, and five articles.
   • Determine what primary sources will be appropriate for your topic.
   • Write a memo to your instructor explaining your strategy. Be sure to list your planned secondary sources with complete bibliographic information.

3. Conduct a formal interview of someone who works with a nonprofit organization that does service (philanthropic) work on your campus or in your community. The purpose of the interview is to learn the following:
   • types of services the organization performs
   • purpose of the organization
   • qualifications and skills of the volunteers
   • current needs of the organization
   • examples of work done by the organization
   After the interview, write a memo to your classmates summarizing your interview. Send a copy of your memo and interview questions to your instructor.

4. Using search engines, answer the following questions related to your major. Print a copy of the homepage of any website. Put your answers in a memo to your instructor.
   - Name two professional organizations in your field.
   - What publications do each of the professional organizations publish? (For example, do they publish a journal or magazine?)
   - How often do the publications appear—monthly, quarterly, annually?
   - Do the organizations have discussion groups or electronic mailing lists? If so, how do you join? Print a copy of the instructions for joining the discussion groups or electronic mailing lists.
   - Do the organizations have a code of ethics? If so, print a copy of the code and attach it to the memo to your instructor.
   - Do the organizations have a student membership rate?

5. **Collaborative exercise:** Working with a team, find a topic for a report you will write for your classmates. You might consider any of the following topics:
   - Tackle a problem on your campus, such as parking, crowded classrooms, etc. What is the problem? Why is it a problem? Whom does the problem affect? How would you solve the problem?
   - Discuss a community problem. What is the problem? Why is it a problem? Whom does the problem affect? How would you solve it?
   - Identify an environmental issue. What is the problem? How does the problem affect the environment? What solutions have been proposed? Which solutions are feasible? What solution would you suggest?

   Once you have decided on a topic, your team should take the following steps:
   - Plan a research strategy. Email a summary of your plan to your instructor.
   - Select at least one primary research tool for gathering information. Decide who will conduct this research.
   - Select appropriate secondary research methods. Use a variety of methods and media and take detailed notes.
   - Evaluate the sources. Send an email to your instructor summarizing your evaluation.
   - Prepare a report for your classmates explaining the problem or issue that you researched and your proposed solution. (See Chapters 14 and 15 for information on reports.) Your instructor may want you to present your report orally. If so, review Chapter 20.

6. Many colleges and universities teach courses online. You may be taking one of them. Working either individually or with a team, prepare a questionnaire to evaluate the value of online courses. Follow these steps.
   1. Plan your questionnaire using these questions:
      - What is the purpose of the questionnaire?
      - Who is the target group?
      - How many questionnaires would you send?
      - What would be the best way to administer the questionnaire?
   2. Develop the questionnaire. Include a combination of closed- and open-ended questions.
   3. Administer the questionnaire to a representative sample of the target group.
   4. Analyze the results.
   5. Make an oral presentation for your class summarizing the purpose and results of your questionnaire.

# REAL WORLD EXPERIENCE

## Discovering Job Prospects in Your Field

### Background

Soon you will graduate from college and start looking for a job in your field. You want to learn more about what to expect when you begin job hunting. Answer the following questions:

- What are the job prospects in your field, internationally and nationally?
- What areas of specialization seem to have the best employment prospects?
- What types of skills and knowledge do employers expect from new college graduates?
- What annual salary should I expect to receive for an entry-level job?
- What websites can I use to look for a job and post my résumé?

### Assignment

1. Develop a research plan to answer the questions above about employment in your field.
2. Find secondary sources giving you employment and salary information. Include two citations from each of the following sources:
   - government or state publications
   - periodical publications such as trade magazines, journals, or newspapers
   - websites
3. Use a primary research tool to gather information and answer the questions listed in the Background section above. You may use any of the following tools:
   - Interview a professional in your field or a job recruiter in your institution's job placement center.
   - Survey faculty and employers in your field.
   - Send letter or email inquiries to two or more employers or professionals. Save a copy of the inquiry and the responses. If you don't receive responses, select another tool.
4. Write a memo to your classmates discussing the answers to the questions. Include a works cited page to document your sources. Give your memo and your works cited page to your instructor. (See Chapter 12 for information on writing a memo.)

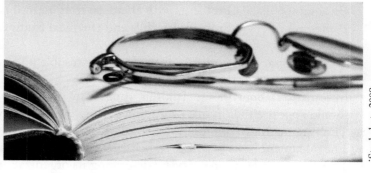

# chapter *six*

## Organizing Information for Your Readers

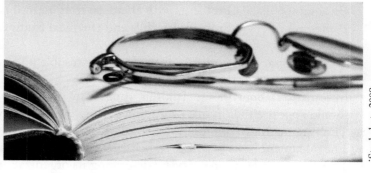

iStockphoto 2008.

$\mathcal{P}$aul Das sits at his desk looking at the pages of data he has collected for a manual on minimizing pollution from waste disposal sites. Paul works in a research laboratory where he and his coworkers develop technology for cities to use in treating and managing wastewater and solid and hazardous waste. They have a contract with the U.S. Environmental Protection Agency (EPA) to prepare this manual. After 18 months, they have completed their research on ways to minimize pollution. Paul is ready to begin writing the manual. He considers the ways he can organize the information and realizes that structuring it is more than preparing the outline. It is a process that goes beyond the data he has collected; it involves understanding the readers, the expectations of his workplace, and his purpose. In this chapter, you will learn guidelines for effectively organizing your documents.

Have you ever tried to read a document where the paragraphs were organized illogically? Did you have trouble locating the information you needed? Documents with an illogical organization make the reader's task difficult—whether that task is to follow a procedure, make a decision, or gather information (Felker, Pickering, Charrow, & Holland 1981). A logical organization helps readers remember, understand, and follow a document (Duin 1988a). For example, consider a section that one of Paul's coworkers prepared for the manual on minimizing pollution (see Figure 6.1). Let's look at the information in each paragraph of Figure 6.1:

| | |
|---|---|
| Paragraph 1 | Introduction to the use of chemicals to stabilize or destroy waste |
| Paragraph 2 | More information about using chemicals to stabilize or destroy waste |
| Paragraph 3 | The process of chemical fixation |
| Paragraph 4 | An alternative to applying chemicals to in situ landfills |
| Paragraph 5 | Firms that provide the chemicals to stabilize the waste |
| Paragraph 6 | Problems with chemical fixation in the landfills |
| Paragraph 7 | Problem landfills and chemical fixation |

As these paragraphs are organized, readers have trouble understanding how one paragraph relates to the next for the following reasons:

- Information about in situ landfills appears in paragraphs 4 and 6. This information should appear either in one paragraph or in two successive paragraphs.
- The paragraphs do not follow a logical order.
- The document lacks headings to help readers locate the major topics.
- The document lacks an overview describing its organization.

The information would be easier to follow in a general-to-specific organization as in Figure 6.2:

| | |
|---|---|
| Paragraph 1 | Introduction to the use of chemicals to stabilize or destroy waste |
| Paragraph 2 | The process of chemical fixation |
| Paragraph 3 | Problems with chemical fixation in the landfills |
| Paragraph 4 | An alternative to applying chemicals to in situ landfills |
| Paragraph 5 | Use of stabilized waste materials in in situ landfills |

**Illogically Organized Information**

## Chemical Fixation

[1] The application of chemicals to destroy or stabilize hazardous materials and potential pollutants has been a common practice for many years, particularly for industrial wastes. Generally, chemical treatment is quite waste-specific. Thus, an effective system in one case may be ineffective or totally inapplicable in another.

[2] Since the 1970s, several processes involving chemicals have been developed which may be effective on a broader range of wastes. Some of these newer processes are more effective on liquids and thin sludges while others function best with heavier sludges and solids. These processes rely on the reactions of such materials as Portland cement, lime, and common silicates to encapsulate, solidify, or cement waste material.

[3] Each of these processes involves the mixing of a chemical agent such as cement, lime, or silicates with the waste material. With liquid water, the agent absorbs the waste. With solids, the agent coats the surface of the solids to cement them together. With sludges, the agent absorbs and cements the waste. Some of these processes rely mainly on the ability of the chemical system to insulate each particle of pollutant from adjacent leaching fluids; others rely on the formation of a relatively impermeable mass to exclude leaching fluids from passing through the waste.

[4] An alternative to the application of chemical fixation agents to the in situ landfill is to use these agents for stabilizing waste materials. These waste materials can then serve as cover for a problem landfill. After proper processing, these waste materials can be spread, graded, and thereafter cemented into a stable, relatively impermeable cover.

[5] The earliest commercially prominent stabilization system was a process offered by Chemfix for applying to hazardous liquids and sludges. Now, stabilization processes are offered by other firms such as the Environmental Technology Corporation, IU Conversion Systems, Inc., and the Dravo Corporation. The latter two firms primarily offer systems for stabilizing sulfur dioxide scrubber sludge.

[6] We have included information on stabilizing waste materials with chemical agents because, in particular instances, the process is a viable means for controlling potential pollutants. However, this process is not feasible for in situ landfill problems because the success of the system depends on the intimate mixing of the chemical agents and the material to be stabilized; without this mixing, the municipal refuse cannot be coated and encapsulated, and the normal landfill processes of degradation and leaching cannot occur. To ensure the mixing of the chemicals with the refuse would require excavating the entire landfill, which provides little advantage over excavating and relocating the landfill to an environmentally sound site.

[7] An ideal situation would be a problem landfill located near a source of chemically stabilized waste material. The material would be readily available for applying to the landfill as a cap. The chemically stabilized material would then be applied at an approximate compacted thickness of 0.6 m, with appropriate drainage swales to remove surface water.

Source: Tolman, Andrews L., et al. *Guidance Manual for Minimizing Pollution for Waste Disposal Sites.* EPA-600/2-78-142. (Washington: GPO, Aug. 1978) 52.

## Logical, Reader-Focused Organization

**Chemical Fixation**

Overview

[1] The application of chemicals to destroy or stabilize hazardous materials and potential pollutants has been a common practice for many years, particularly for industrial wastes. Chemical treatment is generally waste specific. Thus, an effective system in one case may be ineffective or totally inapplicable in another. Since the 1970s several firms have developed chemical fixation processes that may be effective on a broader range of wastes[1]. In this section, we discuss how chemical agents destroy or stabilize waste and when chemical agents are ineffective.

Heading

### How Chemical Agents Destroy or Stabilize Waste

[2] To destroy or stabilize waste, each of these chemical fixation processes mixes a chemical agent, such as Portland cement, lime, or silicates, with the waste material. With liquids, the chemical agent absorbs the waste. With solids, the agent coats the surface of the solids to cement them together. With sludges, the agent absorbs and cements the waste. Some of these processes rely mainly on the ability of the chemical system to insulate each particle of pollutant from adjacent leaching liquids; others rely on the formation of a relatively impermeable mass to exclude leaching fluids from passing through the waste.

Heading

### When Chemical Agents Are Ineffective

Information on existing landfills is in successive paragraphs 3 & 4.

[3] Although chemical fixation is a viable means of controlling potential pollutants, this process is not feasible for existing landfill problems because the success of the process depends on the intimate mixing of the chemical agents and the material to be stabilized. Without this mixing, the municipal refuse cannot be coated and encapsulated, and the normal landfill processes of degradation and leaching cannot occur. To ensure chemical mixing with the refuse would require excavating the entire landfill, providing little advantage over excavating and relocating the landfill to an environmentally sound site.

Similar information is now grouped in paragraphs 4 & 5.

[4] An alternative to applying chemical fixation agents to an existing landfill is to use these agents to stabilize waste materials not currently in a landfill. These waste materials can then serve as cover for a problem landfill. After proper processing, these waste materials can be spread, graded, and thereafter cemented into a stable, relatively impermeable cover.

[5] When such waste material serves as cover, the problem landfill must be near a source of chemically stabilized waste material. The material would be readily available for applying to the landfill as a cap. The chemically stabilized material could then be applied at an approximate compacted thickness of 0.6 m, with appropriate drainage swales to remove surface water.

[1] Chemfix offered the earliest commercially prominent stabilization system for hazardous liquids and sludges. Now other firms such as Environmental Technology Corporation, IV Conversion Systems, Inc., and Dravo Corporation offer stabilization processes. IV Conversion and Dravo offer systems for stabilizing sulfur dioxide scrubber sludge.

Source: Adapted from Section 4, "Plume Management," in Andrews L. Tolman, Antonio P. Ballestero Jr., William W. Beck Jr., and Grover H. Emrich, *Guidance Manual for Minimizing Pollution from Waste Disposal Sites*, EPA-600/2-78-142 (Washington: GPO, Aug. 1978) 48-51. Reprinted by permission of Texas AgriLife Research.

In the second version, the writer grouped closely related information into five instead of seven paragraphs. For example, the information on existing landfills now appears in successive paragraphs. The document begins by introducing chemical fixation, moves to more specific information about how chemicals stabilize or destroy hazardous waste, and ends with specific information about when chemical fixation is ineffective. The document gives readers an overview at the beginning and includes informative headings that helps readers locate information.

 ## DECIDE HOW TO ORGANIZE YOUR DOCUMENT[1]

You may have several options for organizing information. By recognizing these options, you can select the one that will work best for your readers. Ask yourself this question to determine the most effective organization: Can I group similar information? When you combine similar (closely related) information, you help your readers locate the information they need and receive the intended message of your document. For example, the document writers in Figure 6.3 group three areas of related information: the definition of acid rain in one section, wet deposition in another, and dry deposition in the final section.

You need to understand how your readers and your workplace context may impact how you will organize your documents. Once you understand those factors, follow these guidelines to determine how to group similar information and effectively present it to your readers:
- Use the standard patterns of organization.
- Outline your information.
- Use overviews to tell readers what you are writing about.
- Make the organization visible with headings and lists.

### Consider Your Readers

Even though your information seems to suggest a particular organizational pattern, that pattern may not work for your readers. To analyze your readers' needs and expectations, ask yourself the following questions before you decide how to organize the document:
- **Can I put important information at the beginning of the document?** Most readers prefer to read the important information—or a summary of that information—at the beginning. For instance, proposal readers like to know at the beginning what you are proposing. They don't want to wait until the middle or the end to learn your proposed solution. Whenever possible, place the most important information or a summary of it at the beginning.

---

[1] Based on a suggested approach to arranging business documents created by Selzer (1989).

FIGURE 6.3

**Document That Groups Similar Information**

## What is acid rain?

"Acid rain" is a broad term referring to a mixture of wet and dry deposition (deposited material) from the atmosphere containing higher than normal amounts of nitric and sulfuric acids. The precursors, or chemical forerunners, of acid rain formation result from both natural sources, such as volcanoes and decaying vegetation, and man-made sources, primarily emissions of sulfur dioxide ($SO_2$) and nitrogen oxides (NOx) resulting from fossil fuel combustion. In the United States, roughly 2/3 of all $SO_2$ and 1/4 of all NOx come from electric power generation that relies on burning fossil fuels, like coal. Acid rain

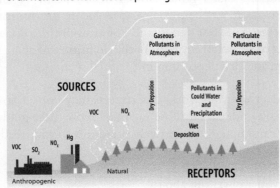

occurs when these gasses react in the atmosphere with water, oxygen, and other chemicals to form various acidic compounds. The result is a mild solution of sulfuric acid and nitric acid. When sulfur dioxide and nitrogen oxides are released from power plants and other sources, prevailing winds blow these compounds across state and national borders, sometimes over hundreds of miles.

## Wet deposition

Wet deposition refers to acidic rain, fog, and snow. If the acid chemicals in the air are blown into areas where the weather is wet, the acids can fall to the ground in the form of rain, snow, fog, or mist. As this acidic water flows over and through the ground, it affects a variety of plants and animals. The strength of the effects depends on several factors, including how acidic the water is; the chemistry and buffering capacity of the soils involved; and the types of fish, trees, and other living things that rely on the water.

## Dry deposition

In areas where the weather is dry, the acid chemicals may become incorporated into dust or smoke and fall to the ground through dry deposition, sticking to the ground, buildings, homes, cars, and trees. Dry deposited gases and particles can be washed from these surfaces by rainstorms, leading to increased runoff. This runoff water makes the resulting mixture more acidic. About half of the acidity in the atmosphere falls back to earth through dry deposition.

Source: Downloaded from the World Wide Web, November 2008: www.epa.gov-acidrain-what-index.html.

- **Can I order the information from the simplest to the most complex, the easiest to the most difficult, or the most familiar to the least familiar to clarify it for readers?** If you structure the information so that readers begin with what they already know or understand and move to what they don't know or understand, you will help them remember your information.
- **Will readers scan the document or read it selectively?** Readers rarely read technical and professional documents from beginning to end. Therefore, choose an organization that helps readers locate the information they need without reading the whole document. Make your organization visible to readers by using headings and lists.
- **Can I begin with the least controversial or surprising information and move to the most controversial or surprising?** For most readers, you will want to begin with the information that will least surprise or upset them, especially if you are trying to persuade them to take some action or adopt your viewpoint. When possible, establish common ground with your readers by beginning with information that is noncontroversial or unsurprising.

## Consider Your Workplace Context

The *workplace context* is the social and cultural conventions and expectations of a workplace. Your manager, your organization's policies, your field, or your coworkers may influence how you organize information in your documents. You may not be the sole decision maker in determining how you will organize your documents. Before you decide how to organize a document, consider the workplace conventions and expectations. These questions may help you:

- **How will my manager want me to organize the information?** Your manager may expect a particular organization. If you are in doubt about what he or she expects, discuss your plans with your manager or the person who asked you to write the document.
- **Does my organization have a predetermined organization for similar documents?** For some documents, your company or group will determine the organization before you begin writing, perhaps because you are responding to another document or because you have been given a preset format (Felker et al. 1981). In these situations, you may not have much control over the organization of sections or the overall document. However, within paragraphs, you can organize sentences logically (Felker et al. 1981). You can find out whether your workplace has a predetermined organization by looking at similar documents, searching the company's intranet, asking your manager, or reading the organization's style manual.

You can use any of these standard patterns for organizing information:

- spatial order
- chronological order
- general-to-specific order
- classification
- partition
- comparison and contrast
- problem and solution
- cause and effect
- order of importance

The first two patterns are sequential: The items you arrange follow each other in physical location (spatial order) or in time (chronological order). The other seven patterns require you to choose the main point and then group the subpoints in a specific way. You can use more than one pattern in a document. For instance, you can use partition to break a whole into parts and then use spatial order to describe the parts. You may encounter a writing situation where none of the standard patterns are appropriate. In such a situation, try grouping related information.

## Spatial Order

Use *spatial order* to describe an object, mechanism, or physical location. You use spatial order when you include words that indicate location, such as "east of the location," "to the right," or "below." When using spatial order, follow an organizational principle such as left to right, top to bottom, or inside to outside. For example, in Figure 6.4, the writers show how radon

**TIPS** FOR USING SPATIAL ORDER

- **Describe the object, mechanism, or location as if readers were looking at it.** Tell your reader how you are describing the object with words such as "beginning at your right."
- **Use words that help the reader follow the organization.** Give the reader a "roadmap" to follow. For example, use phrases such as "from the right," "north view," or "left to right."
- **Use graphics when possible to help readers follow your organization.** Graphics help readers follow the spatial organization of your document. For example, imagine trying to follow a description of a physical site without a picture or drawing. If you use graphics, be sure to introduce and explain them.

# FIGURE 6.4

**Information Organized Spatially**

## HOW DOES RADON GET INTO YOUR HOME?

*Any home may have a radon problem.*

Radon is a radioactive gas. It comes from the natural decay of uranium that is found in nearly all soils. It typically moves up through the ground to the air above and into your home through cracks and other holes in the foundation. Your home traps radon inside, where it can build up. Any home may have a radon problem. This means new and old homes, well-sealed and drafty homes, and homes with or without basements.

Radon from soil gas is the main cause of radon problems. Sometimes radon enters the home through well water (see page 8). In a small number of homes, the building materials can give off radon, too. However, building

*RADON GETS IN THROUGH:*

1. *Cracks in solid floors.*

2. *Construction joints.*

3. *Cracks in walls.*

4. *Gaps in suspended floors.*

5. *Gaps around service pipes.*

6. *Cavities inside walls.*

7. *The water supply.*

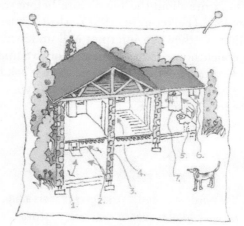

materials rarely cause radon problems by themselves.

Nearly 1 out of every 15 homes in the U.S. is estimated to have elevated radon levels. Elevated levels of radon gas have been found in homes in your state. Contact your state radon office (www.epa.gov/radon/whereyoulive.html) for general information about radon in your area. While radon problems may be more common in some areas, any home may have a problem. The only way to know about your home is to test.

Radon can also be a problem in schools and workplaces. Ask your state radon office (www.epa.gov/radon/whereyoulive.html) about radon problems in schools, daycare and childcare facilities, and workplaces in your area (also visit *www.epa.gov/radon*).

Source: Downloaded from the World Wide Web, November 2008: www.epa.gov/radon/pubs/citguide.html#howdoes

gets into a home. They begin at the left and move to the right of the house. The writers use numbers in the list to correspond to the numbers in the graphic. Spatial order works well for instructions, feasibility reports, definitions, and accident reports.

## Chronological Order

When you read information arranged in order of occurrence or sequence, you are reading information arranged *chronologically*. Chronological order occurs most frequently in instructions, process descriptions, and event descriptions. Use reverse chronological order when you write a résumé. Figure 6.5 demonstrates chronological order to describe three methods to create stem cells. This figure demonstrates two types of information that are often best organized chronologically: a procedure (how to do something) and a sequence of events (how something happens).

## General-to-Specific

When you use *general-to-specific* organization, you assume that readers need to understand the general topic before they can understand the specific information. For most information, you will want to "write about the 'big picture' before you describe the parts and pieces that make up the whole" (Felker et al. 1981). Most readers also need the conclusion or recommendations first, so they can interpret and understand the specific information in the context of the conclusions or recommendations (Samuels 1982). When you solve a problem or make a recommendation, you come to that solution, recommendation, or conclusion last; however, for your readers to understand your work, they need the solution, recommendation, or conclusion first.

### TIPS FOR USING CHRONOLOGICAL ORDER

- **Use words and phrases that give readers a "mental roadmap" of the chronological sequence.** Use signposts such as Step 1, Step 2, or Phase 1, Phase 2, etc. You could use an introduction to present the major parts of the sequence. Then use the parts as headings to guide your readers.
- **Use graphics when appropriate to illustrate the chronology.** If you use a graphic, introduce and explain it.
- **Explain the steps, events, or phases when appropriate for your readers and your purpose.** When organizing information chronologically, you are telling what happened in the order it happened. You do not have to explain why or how. For some information or readers, you need to analyze the steps or the events. For example, if you are telling a new cook how to make a cake, you need to explain some of the steps; for example, what you mean by "sifting the dry ingredients" or "creaming the butter and sugar." If you are explaining a workplace accident, the information may not be useful without your analysis of why the accident happened.

FIGURE 6.5

### Information Organized Chronologically

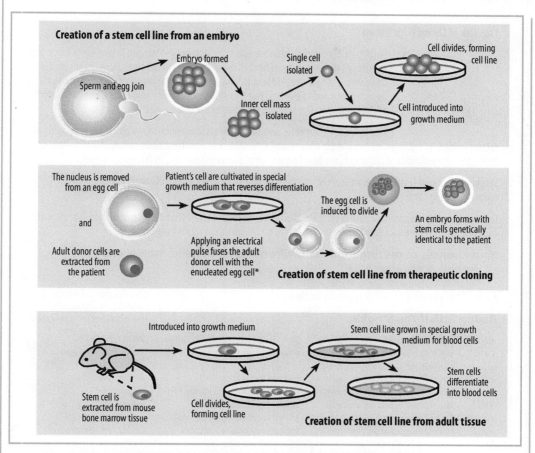

**Creation of a stem cell line from an embryo**

Sperm and egg join → Embryo formed → Inner cell mass isolated → Single cell isolated → Cell introduced into growth medium → Cell divides, forming cell line

The nucleus is removed from an egg cell

and

Adult donor cells are extracted from the patient

Patient's cell are cultivated in special growth medium that reverses differentiation

Applying an electrical pulse fuses the adult donor cell with the enucleated egg cell*

The egg cell is induced to divide

An embryo forms with stem cells genetically identical to the patient

**Creation of stem cell line from therapeutic cloning**

Stem cell is extracted from mouse bone marrow tissue → Introduced into growth medium → Cell divides, forming cell line → Stem cell line grown in special growth medium for blood cells → Stem cells differentiate into blood cells

**Creation of stem cell line from adult tissue**

*Alternatively, the nucleus from the adult donor cell could be directly injected into the egg cell.*

Source: learn.genetics.utah.edu/archive/stemcells/sccreate/.

Figure 6.6 is an excerpt from a document that uses a general-to-specific organization. The document begins with general information on the risk of living with radon and moves to specific (and technical) information about the increased risk if you smoke. You will see this specific information in the table.

FIGURE  6.6

## Information Organized from General to Specific

### The Risk of Living With Radon

Radon gas decays into radioactive particles that can get trapped in your lungs when you breathe. As they break down further, these particles release small bursts of energy. This can damage lung tissue and lead to lung cancer over the course of your lifetime. Not everyone exposed to elevated levels of radon will develop lung cancer. And the amount of time between exposure and the onset of the disease may be many years.

Like other environmental pollutants, there is some uncertainty about the magnitude of radon health risks. However, we know more about radon risks than risks from most other cancer-causing substances. This is because estimates of radon risks are based on studies of cancer in humans (underground miners).

Smoking combined with radon is an especially serious health risk. Stop smoking and lower your radon level to reduce your lung cancer risk.

Children have been reported to have greater risk than adults of certain types of cancer from radiation, but there are currently no conclusive data on whether children are at greater risk than adults from radon.

### Your chances of getting lung cancer from radon depend mostly on:

- How much radon is in your home
- The amount of time you spend in your home
- Whether you are a smoker or have ever smoked

> Scientists are more certain about radon risks than from most other cancer-causing substances.

### Radon Risk If You Smoke

| Radon Level | If 1,000 people who smoked were exposed to this level over a lifetime*... | The risk of cancer from radon exposure compares to**... | WHAT TO DO: Stop smoking and... |
|---|---|---|---|
| 20 pCi/L | About 260 people could get lung cancer | 250 times the risk of drowning | Fix your home |
| 10 pCi/L | About 150 people could get lung cancer | 200 times the risk of dying in a home fire | Fix your home |
| 8 pCi/L | About 120 people could get lung cancer | 30 times the risk of dying in a fall | Fix your home |
| 4 pCi/L | About 62 people could get lung cancer | 5 times the risk of dying in a car crash | Fix your home |
| 2 pCi/L | About 32 people could get lung cancer | 6 times the risk of dying from poison | Consider fixing between 2 and 4 pCi/L |
| 1.3 pCi/L | About 20 people could get lung cancer | (Average indoor radon level) | (Reducing radon levels below 2 pCi/L is difficult.) |
| 0.4 pCi/L | About 3 people could get lung cancer | (Average outdoor radon level) | |

Note: If you are a former smoker, your risk may be lower.

* Lifetime risk of lung cancer deaths from EPA Assessment of Risks from Radon in Homes (EPA 402-R-03-003).

** Comparison data calculated using the Centers for Disease Control and Prevention's 1999-2001 National Center for Injury Prevention and Control Reports.

Source: Downloaded from the World Wide Web, November 2008: http://www.epa.gov/radon/pubs/citguide .html#howdoes

## Classification

*Classification* is a means of grouping items into categories. In its simplest form, classification is grouping like items into a broad category or group. If you can find items that share common characteristics, you may be able to classify the information into meaningful categories (groups) and subcategories. To classify information, identify the broad group to which that information belongs. For example, Figure 6.7 classifies food we should eat to be healthy into six groups: grains (orange), vegetables (green), fruits (red), oils (yellow), milk (blue), and meat and beans (purple).

## Partition

*Partition* is the division of an item into its individual parts. For example, Figure 6.8 illustrates how you might partition the skin into its three layers: epidermis, dermis, and subcutaneous layer.

## Comparison and Contrast

You may need to compare or contrast two or more options. When you examine these options, you'll need standards, or criteria, for making comparisons. For example, if you were deciding which apartment to rent, you might compare apartments based on size, cost, amenities, and location. You might even rank these criteria in order of importance to help you select the best apartment for you, your budget, and your needs.

FIGURE 6.7

**Information Organized by Classification**

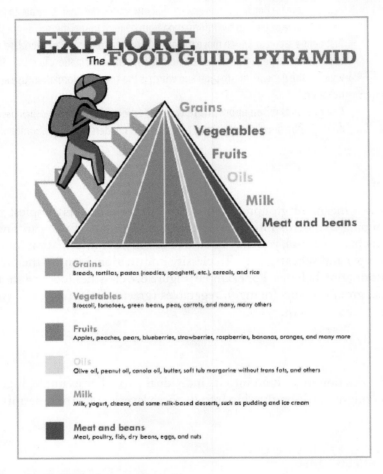

EXPLORE The FOOD GUIDE PYRAMID

Grains
Vegetables
Fruits
Oils
Milk
Meat and beans

Grains
Breads, tortillas, pastas (noodles, spaghetti, etc.), cereals, and rice

Vegetables
Broccoli, tomatoes, green beans, peas, carrots, and many, many others

Fruits
Apples, peaches, pears, blueberries, strawberries, raspberries, bananas, oranges, and many more

Oils
Olive oil, peanut oil, canola oil, butter, soft tub margarine without trans fats, and others

Milk
Milk, yogurt, cheese, and some milk-based desserts, such as pudding and ice cream

Meat and beans
Meat, poultry, fish, dry beans, eggs, and nuts

Source: U.S. Department of Agriculture.

**Information Organized by Partition**

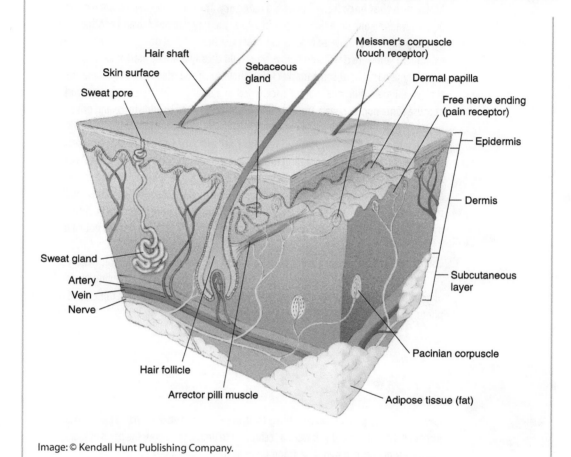

Hair shaft

Skin surface

Sweat pore

Sebaceous gland

Meissner's corpuscle (touch receptor)

Dermal papilla

Free nerve ending (pain receptor)

Epidermis

Dermis

Sweat gland

Artery

Vein

Nerve

Subcutaneous layer

Hair follicle

Arrector pilli muscle

Pacinian corpuscle

Adipose tissue (fat)

Image: © Kendall Hunt Publishing Company.

## TIPS FOR USING CLASSIFICATION

- **Make sure each item fits in only one category.** Categories should not overlap. The classification shown in Figure 6.7 works because the categories are mutually exclusive.
- **Make sure that each item fits into a category.** The categories should not overlap. If you have even one item that doesn't fit into a category, you need to add another category or you may have selected a basis for classification that doesn't fit the items. For example, if you were classifying homes, you could classify them by market value because every home has at least some market value. However, if you tried to classify homes by their exterior building materials of brick, wood, or aluminum siding, it would not work because some homes have a stucco exterior. You would need to add stucco and other building materials to your list of categories.
- **Classify the items in ways suited to your readers' and your purpose.** Choose a principle for classifying and dividing that fits the information and your purpose. When creating the food pyramid, the U.S. Department of Agriculture thought not only about all foods the readers could eat. It also focused on the foods that people should eat within the groups. So they changed the "fats" category to "oils" and made that section of the pyramid the smallest. In some graphics of the pyramid, the fat category does not have a label.
- **Use graphics to illustrate the categories and subcategories.** A graphic helps your readers understand how you have classified the information. Use the following types of graphics to illustrate your classifications: diagrams, pictographs, charts, tables, and photographs. Use color to show the categories, as in Figure 6.7.

## TIPS FOR USING PARTITION

- **Choose a principle for partitioning that meets your readers' needs and your purpose.** For example, if you want a technician to understand how the parts of a machine function, you might partition them by function.
- **Organize the parts in a way that your readers find helpful.** You help readers use and understand your document if you discuss each group of parts logically. For example, if you are discussing the parts of the cell, you could use spatial order, beginning with the parts on the right and moving clockwise to the parts on the left.
- **Use graphics to illustrate the parts.** A graphic helps your readers understand how you have partitioned the information.

## TIPS FOR USING COMPARISON AND CONTRAST

- **Choose criteria for comparing and contrasting.** For example, if you are going to compare cars, you might use the criteria of cost, fuel efficiency, and safety.
- **Evaluate each option using the criteria.** Draw your conclusions only after you have evaluated all options.
- **Organize your comparison or contrast in a way that helps your readers and meets your purpose.** In comparing cars, you could arrange the document so readers can easily gather information to decide which car to purchase. You might organize by criteria to group information about cost in one section and information about fuel efficiency in another. You could also organize by options and group information about one car in one section, information about a second car in another, and so on.
- **When appropriate, use graphics to illustrate your comparison or contrast.** Use graphics to summarize when you are comparing or contrasting.

## TIPS FOR USING PROBLEM AND SOLUTION

- **Identify the problem before you discuss the solution.** Before your readers can understand and appreciate your solution, they must first know the problem. Emphasize the problem's significance to your readers and the parts of the problem that your solution addresses.
- **Show how your solution will solve the problem.** Your readers will see the solution's value only if they understand how it relates to the problem. Give specific details revealing how the solutions will resolve the problem.
- **Group the stages of your solution into meaningful categories.** If your solution has several stages, help your readers by grouping the stages into mutually exclusive, nonoverlapping categories.
- **Give readers ample evidence that your solution will solve the problem.** If you are trying to persuade readers to adopt a solution that you recommend, give them the evidence and reasoning they need to accept it. Even if the solution is already in place, persuade readers that it is worthwhile and effective.
- **When appropriate, use graphics to illustrate or clarify the problem or the solution.** Graphics help you summarize or clarify the problem or the solution.

You may use the comparison and contrast pattern in many documents, but especially in feasibility reports. ***Feasibility reports*** compare two or more options. As you report the comparisons, you can organize by options or by the criteria used to compare the options. Figures 6.9 and 6.10 illustrate how you might organize a document comparing apartment complexes. Figure 6.9 is organized according to options. Notice that the information about Sunrise Apartments appears in one section, and the information about Sunset Apartments appears in another section. This organization has the advantage of presenting the whole picture for each option in one section and emphasizes the criteria in the other.

In Figure 6.10 the writer has organized according to the criteria used to compare the apartment complexes. The writer groups the information about the distance from campus, the monthly rent, and the amenities of both apartments in separate sections. This organization emphasizes the criteria and helps the reader easily compare options, based on individual criteria. The advantage of this organization is the point-by-point comparision.

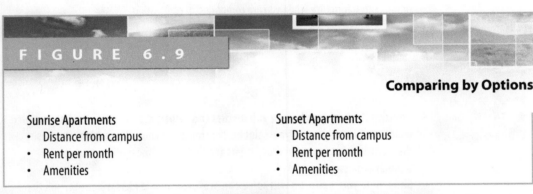

**FIGURE 6.9**

**Comparing by Options**

Sunrise Apartments
- Distance from campus
- Rent per month
- Amenities

Sunset Apartments
- Distance from campus
- Rent per month
- Amenities

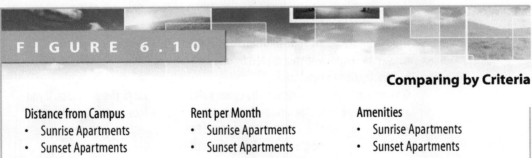

**FIGURE 6.10**

**Comparing by Criteria**

Distance from Campus
- Sunrise Apartments
- Sunset Apartments

Rent per Month
- Sunrise Apartments
- Sunset Apartments

Amenities
- Sunrise Apartments
- Sunset Apartments

FIGURE 6.11

## Document That Uses Comparison/Contrast

To eliminate contaminants in landfills, leachate can be collected and then rexycled through the landfill. Recycling accelerates the stabilizing of the landfill. The three most widely used recycling methods are

*The writers introduce the three options.*

- spray irrigation
- overland or at-grade irrigation
- subgrade irrigation

### Spray Irrigation

*The writers organize by the three options, using a heading to indicate each option. Under each heading, the writers first define the option and then use the criteria of odor and cost to organize the paragraph. In each paragraph, the writers discuss the criteria in the same order.*

Spray irrigation uses nozzles to spray effluent onto the landfill surface. Spray irrigation has one advantage over the other two methods: it effects some leachate treatment during the spraying by aerating and infiltrating the soil surface. However, it does not eliminate odor and is expensive. Spray irrigation has a total cost of $68,900 the first year and $28,000 each subsequent year.

### Overland Irrigation

Overland irrigation spreads effluent with trenches, spreading basins, or gaged pipe. During the irrigation, leachate is pumped into the ground. Overland irrigation does not eliminate odor but costs less than spray irrigation. Overland irrigation costs $7,100 the first year and $2,500 each subsequent year.

### Subgrade Irrigation

Subgrade irrigation uses a tile field or well. In the tile field construction, perforated pipe is buried in gravel-lined trenches to spread the leachate. The wells use an injection system. Unlike spray or overland irrigation, subgrade irrigation avoids local odor problems. It also is less expensive than the other two methods. Subgrade irrigation costs $12,350 the first year and $1,550 each subsquent year. Table 1 compares the cost of the three methods.

Table1. Cost of Leachate Recycling Methods*

*The table summarizes information on one of the criteria: cost.*

| Method | Capital Costs | Annual Operation and Maintenance Costs | Annual Power Costs | Total Cost First Year |
|---|---|---|---|---|
| Spray Irrigation | $30,900 | $3,500 | $24,500 | $68,900 |
| Overland Irrigation | $ 4,600 | $2,500 | 0 | $ 7,100 |
| Subgrade Irrigation | $10,800 | $1,550 | 0 | $12,350 |

*Source: Pound, C. E., R. W. Crites, and D. A. Griffes, *Cost of Wastewater Treatment by Land Application*. EPA-430/9-75-003.

Source: Adapted from Section 4,"Plume Management," in Andrews L. Tolman, Antonio P. Ballestero Jr., William W. Beck Jr., and Grover H. Emrich, *Guidance Manual for Minimizing Pollution from Waste Disposal Sites*, EPA-600/2-78-142 (Washington: GPO, Aug.1978) 48-51. Reprinted by permission of Texas AgriLife Research.

Figure 6.11 shows a document in which the writer organizes by options to compare three methods for recycling leachate in a landfill. The writer uses the criteria of cost and odor to compare and contrast these methods.

## Problem and Solution

You can use the *problem-and-solution* pattern to explain both actual and proposed solutions. This pattern is frequently used in proposals and progress reports.

The document on biological pollutants in Figure 6.12 illustrates the problem-and-solution pattern. The writer begins by identifying the problem of biological pollutants and their health effects, then concludes with solutions for reducing these pollutants in and around the home.

## Cause and Effect

You can use the *cause-and-effect* pattern to help readers understand the consequences or the causes of a particular action or series of actions. Depending on your purpose, you can move from the cause to the effect or from the effect to the cause. For example, you can talk about a leak (effect) in a building and then explain the cause (hail damage to the roof). You can also discuss the hail damage (cause) and predict the effect (a leak).

Figure 6.13 presents a document from the Centers for Disease Control with a cause-and-effect organization. The document explains the most common causes of poor oral health and discusses the impact of each condition on the patient's quality of life.

## Order of Importance

You can organize information according to its *importance*. Use either a descending or an ascending order. You begin with the most important and move to the least important (descending), or you begin with the least important and move to the most important (ascending). With descending organization, you get the reader's attention with the most important point. Use ascending order to persuade a reader who may be hostile or may disagree with you.

## TIPS FOR USING CAUSE AND EFFECT

- **Identify either the cause or the effect near the beginning of the document.** Near the beginning, tell your readers what you are trying to do in the document: to explain the causes of a specific effect or the effects of a specific cause. If your readers know how you have organized the information, they can better understand it.
- **Show how the cause directly relates to the effect or how the effect directly relates to the cause.** Ensure that your readers understand the links between the cause and the effect or between the effect and the cause. Don't expect readers to infer the connection; explain it.
- **Group the causes or effects into logical categories.** Grouping helps readers understand the relationships among causes and effects.
- **When appropriate, use graphics to illustrate or clarify the effect or the cause.** Graphics help you summarize or clarify the cause and the effect. Graphics are especially effective for showing how the cause and effect relate.

## TIPS FOR USING ORDER OF IMPORTANCE

- **Give readers a context for the information.** State the main point or topic at the beginning.
- **Tell readers how you are organizing the information.** Clearly tell readers that you are beginning with the most important information or that you are ending with the most important information.
- **Tell readers why one point is more or less important than another.** Don't assume your readers will see the information in the same order of importance as you.
- **Use graphics when appropriate.** Graphics help you clarify the information.

FIGURE 6.12

**Information Organized from Problem to Solution**

## What Are Biological Pollutants?

The writers identify the problem.

Biological pollutants are living organisms. They promote poor indoor air quality and may be a major cause of days lost from work or school, and of doctor and hospital visits. Some pollutants can even damage surfaces inside and outside your house. Biological pollutants can travel through the air and are often invisible.

## What Can You Do About Biological Pollutants?

**Control Water**

Fix leaks and seepage. If water is entering the house from the outside, your options range from simple landscaping to extensive excavation and waterproofing.

**Maintain and Clean All Appliances That Come In Contact With Water**

Have major appliances, such as furnaces, heat pumps and central air conditioners, inspected and cleaned regularly by a professional, especially before seasonal use.

The writers identify four solutions.

**Clean Surfaces**

Clean moist surfaces, such as showers and kitchen counters. Remove mold from walls, ceilings, floors, and paneling.

**Control Dust**

Always wash bedding in hot water (at least 130°F) to kill dust mites. Launder bedding at least every 7 to 10 days. Clean rooms and closets well; dust and vacuum often to remove surface dust.

Source: Adapted from U.S. Environmental Protection Agency, 2008. http://www.cpsc.gov/cpscpub/pubs/425.html.

FIGURE 6.13

## Information Organized from Cause to Effect

### Oral Health and Quality of Life

Diseases and disorders that damage the mouth and face can disturb well-being and self-esteem. The effect of oral health and disease on quality of life is a relatively new field of research that examines the functional, psychological, social, and economic consequences of oral disorders. Most of the research has focused on a few conditions: tooth loss, craniofacial birth defects, oral-facial pain, and oral cancer. The impact of oral health on an individual's quality of life reflects complex social norms and cultural values, beliefs, and traditions. There is a long tradition of determining character on the basis of facial and head shapes. Although cultures differ in detail, there appear to be overall consistencies in the judgment of facial beauty and deformity that are learned early in life. Faces judged ugly have been associated with defects in character, intelligence, and morals.

The writers identify the causes.

### The Impact of Craniofacial-Oral-Dental Conditions on Quality of Life

#### Missing teeth

People who have many missing teeth face a diminished quality of life. Not only do they have to limit food choices because of chewing problems, which may result in nutritionally poor diets, but many feel a degree of embarrassment and self-consciousness that limits social interaction and communication.

#### Craniofacial birth defects

Children with cleft lip or cleft palate experience not only problems with eating, breathing, and speaking, but also have difficulties adjusting socially, which affect their learning and behavior. The tendency to "judge a book by its cover" persists in the world today and accounts for many of the psychosocial problems of persons affected by craniofacial birth defects.

The writers identify the effects.

#### Oral-facial pain

The craniofacial region is rich in nerve endings sensitive to painful stimuli, so it is not surprising that oral-facial pain, especially chronic pain conditions where the cause is not understood and control is inadequate, severely affects quality of life. Conditions such as temporomandibular (jaw joint) disorders, trigeminal neuralgia, and postherpetic neuralgia (chronic pain following an attack of shingles affecting facial nerves) can disrupt vital functions such as chewing, swallowing, and sleep; interfere with normal activities at home or work; and lead to social withdrawal and depression.

#### Oral Cancer

Surgical treatment for oral cancer may result in permanent disfigurement as well as functional limitations affecting speaking and eating. Given the poor prognosis for oral cancer (the five-year survival rate is only 52 percent), it is not surprising that depression is common in these patients.

Source: Downloaded from the World Wide Web, November 2008: www.cdc.gov-oralhealth-ublicationsfactsheets-sgr2000_fs5.htm.jpg

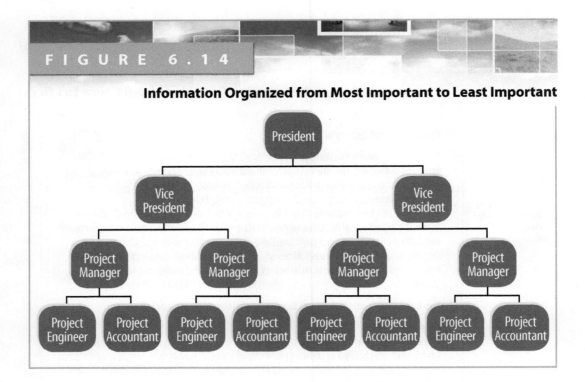

**FIGURE 6.14**

### Information Organized from Most Important to Least Important

The graphic shown in Figure 6.14 moves from the most important to the least important question for the readers. It shows a company's organizational hierarchy. When decisions are made in a company, decisions of minor importance related to day-to-day activities might be made at the project engineer or project manager level. However, decisions of major importance will be made at a higher level.

## PREPARE AN OUTLINE

Once you have analyzed your readers' and your workplace's expectations and have determined the standard pattern(s) you will use, outline your document. An outline helps you identify sections that are organized illogically or are incomplete.

An outline gives you a plan to follow as you write. Remember, though, that the outline is flexible. You may need to change your outline while you write as more information is uncovered, for example, or as sections are added or subtracted. You may also decide to write the sections out of sequence or to begin with the section you know the most about or for which you have gathered all the necessary information. You can use informal or formal outlines.

## A Document before the Writer Expands the Information

### Diagnosing Babesiosis[1]

Babesiosis, also known as Malignant Jaundice, is a tick-transmitted disease of dogs. Babesiosis is caused by a protozoan organism, Babesia canis, that enters and destroys the red blood cells. The principal carrier of babesiosis from infected to non-infected dogs is the brown dog tick. The disease can also spread through blood transfusions or, in rare cases, from an infected female dog to her pups before birth.

When a dog becomes infected with the Babesia organism, it may become critically sick and die in a few days; or it may become a carrier without showing any signs of the disease. The most specific signs for babesiosis are

- bloody urine
- jaundiced mucous membranes and skin

Other signs include poor appetite, listlessness, fever, weight loss, and pale mucous membranes from anemia; however, these signs also occur with other diseases.

A veterinarian can diagnose babesiosis by finding the microscopic organisms in the red blood cells. If a diagnosis is not possible with this method, the veterinarian must test the blood serum for Babesia antibodies. Even if a dog tests positive for babesiosis, the veterinarian cannot treat it because the most effective drugs for treating babesiosis are unavailable in the United States.

[1] Source: Adapted from W. Elmo Crenshaw and Bruce Lawhorn, *Tick-borne Diseases of the Dog*, L-22667, rpt. 10M-7-88 (College Station: Texas Agricultural Extension Service, n.d.).

## An Informal Outline

An *informal outline* may simply be a list of what you plan to include in a document. Informal outlines don't include sentences or parallel structure. Instead, they may be lists of initial thoughts and pieces of information that you write down but don't organize. These outlines may also be the topics you plan to discuss in the document in the order you plan to discuss them. Informal outlines may be sufficient for short reports, instructions, and correspondence.

> Informal outlines may be a list of initial thoughts and pieces of information that you write down but don't organize. These outlines are useful for short reports, instructions, and correspondence.

FIGURE 6.16

**Informal Outline**

**Ehrlichiosis**
- Ehrlichiosis is a frequently diagnosed tick-borne disease
- The symptoms of ehrlichiosis are depression, poor appetite, weight loss, fever, enlarged lymph nodes, pale mucous membranes, and bleeding tendencies
- Ehrlichiosis has either an acute form or a chronic form. Acute form may cause death within a few days of infestation or may last for 3 to 6 weeks. If dog survives acute, the disease may become chronic
- Diagnose ehrlichiosis through finding the rickettsial organism in blood cells or testing blood serum for ehrlichia antibodies

**Babesiosis**
- Babesiosis is caused by Babesia canis, which is transmitted by the brown dog tick
- Babesiosis is treated with drugs not currently available in the U.S.
- Babesiosis symptoms: poor appetite, listlessness, fever, weight loss, and pale mucous membranes from anemia, bloody urine, and jaundiced mucous membranes and skin
- Diagnose babesiosis by finding Babesia canis in blood cells or its antibodies in blood serum

**Borreliosis**
- Borreliosis, or lyme disease, was first diagnosed in 1975
- Borreliosis signs include intermittent lameness in one or more legs from swelling, pain in the joints of the legs and feet, and fever
- Borreliosis usually occurs in dogs less than 4 years old
- Treat borreliosis with antibiotics

**Prevention**
- Most effective prevention is treatment such as dipping, spraying, or using powders to kill ticks before they can cause the anemia or spread disease
- The lawn where the dog lives should also be sprayed to eliminate ticks
- The pet owner should carefully follow the label instructions for any dip, spray, or powder or have a professional treat the dog

Let's look at how a writer takes the first draft of a document on babesiosis (see Figure 6.15) and expands it into a final draft. The writer begins with an informal outline (see Figure 6.16). Use an informal outline to create a draft for a formal outline. This draft helps you learn incomplete or illogical.

## A Formal Outline

A *formal outline* differs from an informal outline in two ways:
- It has a more detailed organization of information.
- It uses numbers and letters.

Because a formal outline establishes a hierarchy among pieces of information, you can easily convert topics and subtopics into document headings or into a formal document's table of contents. As you prepare your outline, determine what format you will use for it; then use parallel structure for the topics and subtopics.

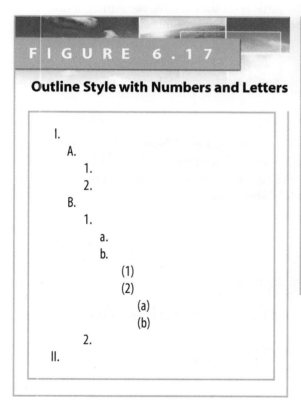

**FIGURE 6.17**

**Outline Style with Numbers and Letters**

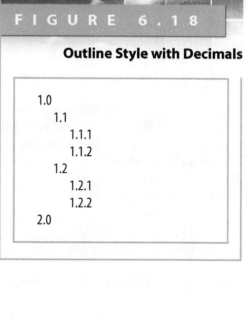

**FIGURE 6.18**

**Outline Style with Decimals**

## Selecting an Outline Format

If you are writing an outline that you will not show to others, use any format you can read, understand, and follow. If you will use your outline when collaborating or if your document requires a table of contents, select one of the formal outline formats: topic outline or sentence outline.

*Topic outlines* use phrases for the topics and subtopics. For example, a topic outline might use the phrase "signs of ehrlichiosis." *Sentence outlines* use sentences for the topics and subtopics: "A dog with ehrlichiosis may exhibit any one of seven signs."

Once you have selected a format, decide how you will number the outline—with a combination of numbers and letters (see Figure 6.17) or with decimals (see Figure 6.18).

## Using Parallel Structure

The statements of topics and subtopics in a formal outline should have a parallel structure. *Parallel structure* means that the items of the same level should have the same grammatical structure. The items in the following numbered list are *not* parallel:

A. Logging on to the network
   1. Find the login prompt
   2. Typing your login
   3. Passwords
   4. What you will see if you login correctly

Items 1, 2, 3, and 4 have different grammatical structures. Item 1 begins with a verb; item 2 begins with a different verb form; item 3 begins with with a noun; and item 4 begins with a pronoun. These differences obscure the writer's reason for listing the items in this sequence. The list is clearer when the items have a parallel structure:

A. Logging on to the network
   1. Find the login prompt
   2. Type your login
   3. Type your password
   4. Look for the message "Welcome to the network"

Now items 1, 2, 3, and 4 have the same grammatical structure; each item begins with a verb.

## Using an Outline to Analyze Your Organization and Your Information

You can use a draft of a formal outline to analyze the information you have gathered and the organization you plan to use. Let's consider the information for the document on tick-borne dog diseases (see Figure 6.16) and put it in a draft for a formal outline (see Figure 6.19). The draft reveals several problems:

- **The information is incomplete and inconsistent.** The sections on the three diseases contain different kinds and amounts of information. The sections on ehrlichiosis and babesiosis each have three subsections, but the subsections are different. The section on borreliosis has only two subsections. All three sections should have the same subsections for consistency and completeness.
- **Section II has only one subsection.** Each section of an outline should have at least two subsections.
- **The draft lacks parallel structure.** See the parallelism errors marked in blue on Figure 6.19.

Figure 6.20 shows a revised version of the outline with the improvements noted in blue:

- **The information is complete and consistent.** The sections on the three diseases contain consistent information on signs, diagnosis, and treatment. Ehrlichiosis is the only one of the three diseases that has a chronic stage; thus, the section on ehrlichiosis contains a subsection on the stages of the disease.
- **Section II has two subsections, instead of one.**
- **The structure is parallel.**

**Draft of a Formal Outline**

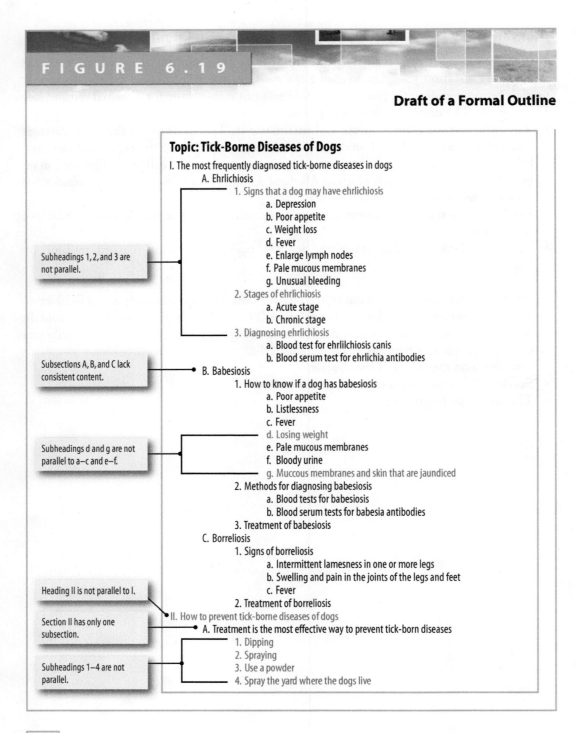

**Topic: Tick-Borne Diseases of Dogs**

I. The most frequently diagnosed tick-borne diseases in dogs

    A. Ehrlichiosis

        1. Signs that a dog may have ehrlichiosis

            a. Depression

            b. Poor appetite

            c. Weight loss

            d. Fever

            e. Enlarge lymph nodes

            f. Pale mucous membranes

            g. Unusual bleeding

        2. Stages of ehrlichiosis

            a. Acute stage

            b. Chronic stage

        3. Diagnosing ehrlichiosis

            a. Blood test for ehrlilchiosis canis

            b. Blood serum test for ehrlichia antibodies

    B. Babesiosis

        1. How to know if a dog has babesiosis

            a. Poor appetite

            b. Listlessness

            c. Fever

            d. Losing weight

            e. Pale mucous membranes

            f. Bloody urine

            g. Muccous membranes and skin that are jaundiced

        2. Methods for diagnosing babesiosis

            a. Blood tests for babesiosis

            b. Blood serum tests for babesia antibodies

        3. Treatment of babesiosis

    C. Borreliosis

        1. Signs of borreliosis

            a. Intermittent lamesness in one or more legs

            b. Swelling and pain in the joints of the legs and feet

            c. Fever

        2. Treatment of borreliosis

II. How to prevent tick-borne diseases of dogs

    A. Treatment is the most effective way to prevent tick-born diseases

        1. Dipping

        2. Spraying

        3. Use a powder

        4. Spray the yard where the dogs live

*Callout notes:*

Subheadings 1, 2, and 3 are not parallel.

Subsections A, B, and C lack consistent content.

Subheadings d and g are not parallel to a–c and e–f.

Heading II is not parallel to I.

Section II has only one subsection.

Subheadings 1–4 are not parallel.

FIGURE 6.20

**Revised Formal Outline**

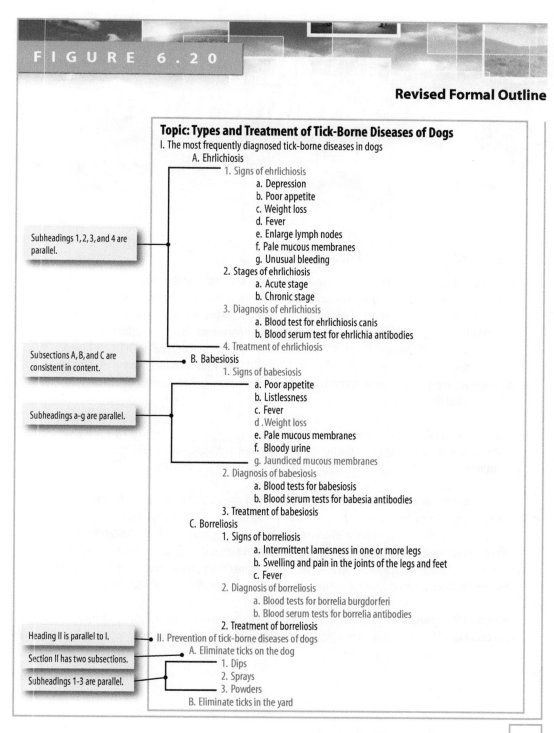

**Topic: Types and Treatment of Tick-Borne Diseases of Dogs**

I. The most frequently diagnosed tick-borne diseases in dogs
- A. Ehrlichiosis
  - 1. Signs of ehrlichiosis
    - a. Depression
    - b. Poor appetite
    - c. Weight loss
    - d. Fever
    - e. Enlarge lymph nodes
    - f. Pale mucous membranes
    - g. Unusual bleeding
  - 2. Stages of ehrlichiosis
    - a. Acute stage
    - b. Chronic stage
  - 3. Diagnosis of ehrlichiosis
    - a. Blood test for ehrlichiosis canis
    - b. Blood serum test for ehrlichia antibodies
  - 4. Treatment of ehrlichiosis
- B. Babesiosis
  - 1. Signs of babesiosis
    - a. Poor appetite
    - b. Listlessness
    - c. Fever
    - d. Weight loss
    - e. Pale mucous membranes
    - f. Bloody urine
    - g. Jaundiced mucous membranes
  - 2. Diagnosis of babesiosis
    - a. Blood tests for babesiosis
    - b. Blood serum tests for babesia antibodies
  - 3. Treatment of babesiosis
- C. Borreliosis
  - 1. Signs of borreliosis
    - a. Intermittent lamesness in one or more legs
    - b. Swelling and pain in the joints of the legs and feet
    - c. Fever
  - 2. Diagnosis of borreliosis
    - a. Blood tests for borrelia burgdorferi
    - b. Blood serum tests for borrelia antibodies
  - 2. Treatment of borreliosis

II. Prevention of tick-borne diseases of dogs
- A. Eliminate ticks on the dog
  - 1. Dips
  - 2. Sprays
  - 3. Powders
- B. Eliminate ticks in the yard

Callout boxes:
- Subheadings 1, 2, 3, and 4 are parallel.
- Subsections A, B, and C are consistent in content.
- Subheadings a-g are parallel.
- Heading II is parallel to I.
- Section II has two subsections.
- Subheadings 1-3 are parallel.

## Organization Does Make a Difference

Do you spend more time outlining and planning your documents than you do checking the grammar, sentence structure, and spelling of your documents? If you spend more time outlining and planning, you will probably create a more effective document. Researchers have found a positive correlation between outlining (and/or other writing plans) and the quality of the document (Perl 1979; Taylor and Beach 1984; Kellogg 1988; Spivey and King 1989). Effective writers prepare outlines and "spend more time on macrowriting issues such as organization" (Baker 1994, 457). Less effective writers "spend less time on outlining and more time on microwriting issues (sentence structure, grammar, spelling)" (Baker 1994, 457; Hayes and Flower 1987).

Readers process information on two levels:
- **microprocessing** (focusing on the meaning of individual words and sentences)
- **macroprocessing** (focusing on the relationship of paragraphs and sections)

Readers can more easily remember and process information when a document has an effective macrostructure (or organization) than when a document has an ineffective organization (Lorch and Lorch 1984). An effective organization allows readers to more easily relate word- and sentence-level information to the document as a whole. Without an effective organization, readers relate individual sentences and words—local information—only "to the immediately preceding ones"; the readers don't have a clear organization in which to integrate the local information (Baker 1994, 457; Kintsch 1989).

What does this research mean for your writing? If you want readers to understand your documents and better recall the information, use a logical, clear organization that gives readers a mental roadmap (Baker 1994).

## Assignment

Let's test Baker's theory that outlining does make a difference. For your next assignment, do the following:
- Prepare an informal or formal outline.
- Write a document based on the outline.
- Send an email to your instructor answering these questions:
  - Did you spend more time on writing the outline and planning or on editing the document?
  - Did you change the outline after you began writing?
  - Did the outline help you write a more reader-focused document? Explain your answer.

Remember to prepare the outline before you write the document.

##  USE OVERVIEWS TO TELL READERS WHAT YOU ARE WRITING ABOUT

Your readers want to know what they are reading. At the beginning of a document and at the beginning of each section, provide an overview to tell readers what is coming.

*Overviews* are introductory statements that describe what a document is about, what it may be used for, or how it is organized. Overviews preview the topic and organization of your document. They help readers in the following ways:
- If readers must read the document, overviews help them understand its contents.
- If readers aren't sure whether the document is what they need, overviews help them decide.
- If readers are trying to locate specific information, overviews help them locate the sections they need.

Place overviews immediately before the text they describe or summarize. That text might be a short document, a specific section of a document, or an individual chapter or section.

For shorter documents, such as memos, email, and letters, overviews may be unnecessary. Instead, a topic sentence at the beginning can function as an overview. Use overviews in three ways (Felker et al. 1981):

- Point out the type of information presented in the document.
- Identify the specific sections included in the document.
- Give instructions about how to use the document.

## Overviews Point Out the Types of Information in the Document

Consider the overview in Figure 6.21 from the *Earthquake Safety Guide for Homeowners* published by the Federal Emergency Management Agency (FEMA 2005). This overview tells readers about the two types of information in the guide: (1) common weaknesses that can result in damage to a home by earthquakes and (2) steps homeowners can take to correct those weaknesses. By reading the overview, readers can decide whether the document contains the information they need.

## Overviews Identify the Specific Sections of the Document

Write overviews that identify the sections of the document and describe the information they contain. These overviews particularly help readers by explaining the text's organization and by providing signposts to that organization (Felker et al. 1981). Figure 6.22 includes signposts in the overview to *Electric and Magnetic Fields*. Such overviews are especially useful in long documents, in documents divided into sections, and in documents written for more than one type of reader (Felker et al. 1981).

## Overviews Tell Readers How to Use the Document

In some overviews, you tell readers how to use the document. This type of overview combines signposts with instructions for using the document. Figure 6.23 shows an overview with instructions for a software manual. In the first paragraph, the writer lists the manual's major sections and tells readers how to use each section. This type of overview clearly tells readers "what the document is about, who should use the different parts of it, and when they should use it" (Felker et al. 1981, 14).

FIGURE 6.21

## An Overview Introduces the Types of Information in the Document

**Earthquakes**, especially major ones, are dangerous, inevitable, and a fact of life in some parts of the United States. Sooner or later another "big one" will occur. Earthquakes:
- Occur without warning
- Can be deadly and extremely destructive
- Can occur at any time

As a current or potential owner of a home, you should be very concerned about the potential danger to not only yourselves and your loved ones, but also to your property.

The major threats posed by earthquakes are bodily injuries and property damage, which can be considerable and even catastrophic. Most of the property damage caused by earthquakes ends up being handled and paid for by the homeowner.
- In a 2000 study titled HAZUS 99: Average Annual Earthquake Losses for the United States, FEMA estimated U.S. losses from earthquakes at $4.4 billion per year.
- Large earthquakes in or near major urban centers will disrupt the local economy and can disrupt the economy of an entire state.

However, proper earthquake preparation of your home can:
- Save lives
- Reduce injuries
- Reduce property damage

As a homeowner, you can **significantly reduce** damage to your home by fixing a number of known and common weaknesses.

This booklet is a good start to begin strengthening your home against earthquake damage. It describes:
- Common weaknesses that can result in your home being damaged by earthquakes, and
- Steps you can take to correct these weaknesses.

The overview tells readers what types of information they will find in the document.

Source: FEMA, *Earthquake Safety Guide for Homeowners*. FEMA 530, September 2005. Page 1.

## FIGURE 6.22

### An Overview Identifies the Specific Sections of the Document

The overview clearly describes the contents of each section.

Reports about possible health effects from exposure to electric and magnetic fields (EMF) continue to concern some employees and TXU customers. The following sections will help you to understand this issue:

- The first section "What is EMF?" defines and describes electric and magnetic fields.
- The second section "What About Scientific Studies?" describes existing and planned scientific studies of EMF.
- The third section "What Are We Doing?" describes what TXU and the industry are doing to address the EMF issue.

Source: *Electric and Magnetic Fields.* Used by permission of Energy Future Holdings, Dallas, TX.

## FIGURE 6.23

### An Overview Tells Readers How to Use the Document

The sections are identified by title.

**Which Sections Should I Use?**

This manual has three major sections: *Getting Started, Learning the Basics, and Using the Advanced Features.*

**Getting Started**
*Getting Started* will help you install and start the software. Complete this section before moving to the other sections of the manual.

**Learning the Basics**
If you are new to spreadsheets, try working through the lessons in *Learning the Basics* to learn spreadsheet fundamentals.

The overview clearly tells the readers how to use each section.

**Using the Advanced Features**
After you are familiar and comfortable with the fundamentals, you can move to *Using the Advanced Features.* This section is appropriate for more experienced users.

Headings are subtitles within a document. If you have prepared a formal outline, you can use the outline's entries as headings and subheadings. Headings help readers in several ways:

- They indicate the organization and scope of a document—a service that especially helps readers who want to determine whether a document contains information they need.
- They help readers locate specific information.
- They give readers clues to the information in specific sections.

Figures 6.24 and 6.25 show how adding headings helps reveal content. The document in Figure 6.24 has no design elements other than the title and paragraph breaks. It doesn't include headings or lists to help readers locate information, so they can't read selectively or easily locate specific information. Readers interested in specific information must read until they find that information. For example, if you want to know how to treat canine epilepsy, you must read six paragraphs before finding that information. In Figure 6.25 you locate that same information, by scanning the document until you see the heading Treatment of Canine Epilepsy.

Readers process a document from top to bottom unless the writer gives them clues about the organization (Duin 1988). Without these clues, readers may assume information near the beginning is more important than information near the end; they may read the information near the beginning especially closely, recalling it better than they recall information near the end. The document's format in Figure 6.25 gives readers clues through headings and lists. The headings visually categorize information so readers don't have to process the document from top to bottom. Instead, readers scan the document for the information they need. The document's format in Figure 6.24 gives readers no clues about content and forces them to process the entire document until they find the information they want.

## Make Your Headings Informative

Effective headings inform readers, giving them enough information to decide whether a section contains the information they need. Compare the headings in the left and right columns:

| | |
|---|---|
| Introduction | How to Use This Manual |
| Body | Description of the Rehabilitation Clinic |
| Part 2 | How to Set Up the Scanner |
| Donation Limitations | How Often Can You Give Blood? |

The headings in the left column give few, if any, clues about the information in the sections. "Body" doesn't give readers any clues to the information in that section. "Body" could refer to a human body, a body of people, or the body (main part) of the document. Because the headings in the left column give limited, if any, clues about the section's information, they can't help readers locate specific information. In contrast, the headings in the right column describe the information readers will find in each section.

## Use Grammatically Parallel Headings

Write parallel headings for the formal outline and use them in your document. All the main headings in a document have equal rank, so they all should have the same grammatical structure. All the subheads at the same level under a main heading also have equal rank and should have the same grammatical structure.

Figure 6.26 shows the levels you might have in a document and some sample headings that correspond with those levels (the headings are from the revised formal outline presented in Figure 6.20). Notice that both main headings have the same grammatical structure, a noun or noun phrase followed by a prepositional phrase. The three subheadings under the main heading 1, "The most frequently diagnosed tick-borne diseases in dogs," are parallel in grammatical structure with each other but not with the subheadings under the main heading 2, "Prevention of tick-borne diseases of dogs." Subheadings or sub-subheadings in any section of a document must be parallel, or grammatically equal, only with each other, not with all other subheadings or sub-subheadings. Subheadings under main heading 1 need not be parallel with subheadings under main heading 2, and so on. Even if you include the multiple-word sub-subheadings at the beginning of a document, you can still use single-word sub-subheadings at the end.

## USE LISTS TO EMPHASIZE IMPORTANT INFORMATION

Lists allow you to break up long sentences and to emphasize important information. Let's look at two examples from the document on canine epilepsy in Figures 6.24 and 6.25. The original document contains the following sentence:

> During a partial seizure, the dog may exhibit turning of the head to one side, muscular contractions of one or both legs on the same side of the body, or bending of the body to one side.

We cannot easily follow the sentence above because of the long series of symptoms. The sentence becomes easier to read when the series appears in a list:

FIGURE 6.24

**Document with No Headings or Design Elements**

## Canine Epilepsy

Epilepsy is a disorder characterized by recurrent seizures. Seizures, also known as fits or convulsions, occur when an area of nerve cells in the brain becomes overexcitable. This area is often called a seizure focus. The mechanism responsible for developing this focus is unknown.

A dog can inherit or acquire canine epilepsy. Inherited epilepsy affects about 1% of the canine population. Breeds which may inherit epilepsy include the beagle, Belgian shepherd, German shepherd, dachshund, and keeshond. Researchers also suspect a genetic factor in the following breeds: cocker spaniel, collie, golden retriever, Labrador retriever, Irish setter, miniature schnauzer, poodle, Saint Bernard, Siberian husky, and wire-haired fox terrier.

Acquired epilepsy may occur months to years after an injury or illness that causes brain damage. In many cases, the dog is completely normal except for occasional seizures. Causes of acquired epilepsy include trauma, infection, poisons, hypoxia (lack of oxygen), and low blood sugar concentrations.

A dog with inherited epilepsy has generalized seizures that affect its entire brain and body. The dog usually falls on its side and displays paddling motions with all four limbs. During or immediately after the seizures, the dog may also exhibit loss of consciousness (i.e., the dog will not respond when you call its name), excessive drooling, and urinating or passing of feces. The seizure of inherited epilepsy usually occurs between the ages of 1 and 3 years. Seizures that occur before 6 months or after 5 years of age probably result from acquired epilepsy.

A dog with acquired epilepsy has partial seizures. A partial seizure affects only one part of the body, and the dog may not lose consciousness. During a partial seizure, the dog may exhibit turning of the head to one side, muscular contractions of one or both legs on the same side of the body, or bending of the body to one side. These signs are localizing because they help to determine the location of the seizure focus in the brain. The localizing sign may occur only briefly, after which the seizure becomes generalized. If the seizure becomes generalized, you or your veterinarian may have difficulty distinguishing between acquired and inherited epilepsy. The first seizure may occur at any age.

You can treat epilepsy by giving anticonvulsant medication orally several times a day. This treatment is effective in 60 to 70% of epileptic dogs. Unfortunately, the medication will not completely eliminate the seizures. Instead, the medication reduces the frequency, severity, and duration of the seizures. Most veterinarians recommend that dogs receive the anticonvulsant medication when the seizures occur more often than once every 6 weeks or when severe clusters of seizures occur more often than once every 2 months. To successfully treat epilepsy, you must consistently give the medication as directed by the veterinarian and continue the medication without interruption. If you discontinue the medication, status epilepticus could occur, resulting in the dog's death. Status epilepticus is a series of seizures without periods of consciousness. If this condition occurs, contact a veterinarian immediately.

Source: Adapted from S. Dru Forrester and Bruce Lawhorn, *Canine Epilepsy* (College Station: Texas Agricultural Extension Service, n.d.).

## Document Broken Up with Headings and Design Elements

## Canine Epilepsy

Epilepsy is a disorder characterized by recurrent seizures. Seizures, also known as fits or convulsions, occur when an area of nerve cells in the brain becomes overexcitable. This area is often called a seizure focus. The mechanism responsible for developing this focus is unknown.

### Types of Canine Epilepsy

A dog can inherit or acquire canine epilepsy. Inherited epilepsy affects about 1% of the canine population. Breeds which may inherit epilepsy include the beagle, Belgian shepherd, German shepherd, dachshund, and keeshond. Researchers also suspect a genetic factor in the following breeds: cocker spaniel, collie, golden retriever, Labrador retriever, Irish setter, miniature schnauzer, poodle, Saint Bernard, Siberian husky, and wire-haired fox terrier. Acquired epilepsy may occur months to years after an injury or illness that causes brain damage. In many cases, the dog is completely normal except for occasional seizures. Causes of acquired epilepsy include trauma, infection, poisons, hypoxia (lack of oxygen), and low blood sugar concentrations.

### Characteristics of Inherited Epilepsy

A dog with inherited epilepsy has generalized seizures that affect its entire brain and body. The dog usually falls on its side and displays paddling motions with all four limbs. During or immediately after the seizures, the dog may also exhibit some or all of the following signs:
- loss of consciousness (i.e., the dog will not respond when you call its name)
- excessive drooling
- urinating or passing of feces.

The seizure usually lasts no longer than 1 or 2 minutes. The first seizure of inherited epilepsy usually occurs between the ages of 1 and 3 years. Seizures that occur before 6 months or after 5 years of age probably result from acquired epilepsy.

### Characteristics of Acquired Epilepsy

A dog with acquired epilepsy has partial seizures. A partial seizure affects only one part of the body, and the dog may not lose consciousness. During a partial seizure, the dog may exhibit one or more of the following localizing signs:
- turning of the head to one side
- muscular contractions of one or both legs on the same side of the body
- bending of the body to one side.

These signs are localizing because they help to determine the location of the seizure focus in the brain. The localizing sign may occur only briefly, after which the seizure becomes generalized. If the seizure becomes generalized, you or your veterinarian may have difficulty distinguishing between acquired and inherited epilepsy. The first seizure may occur at any age.

### Treatment of Canine Epilepsy

You can treat epilepsy by giving anticonvulsant medication orally several times a day. This treatment is effective in 60 to 70% of epileptic dogs. Unfortunately, the medication will not completely eliminate the seizures. Instead, the medication reduces the frequency, severity, and duration of the seizures. Most veterinarians recommend that dogs receive the anticonvulsant medication when the seizures occur more often than once every 6 weeks or when sever clusters of seizures occur more often than once every 2 months.

To successfully treat epilepsy, you must
- consistently give the medication as directed by the veterinarian
- continue the medication without interruption.

If you discontinue the medication, status epilepticus could occur, resulting in the dog's death. Status epilepticus is a series of seizures without periods of consciousness. If this condition occurs, contact a veterinarian immediately.

Source: Adapted from S. Dru Forrester and Bruce Lawhorn, *Canine Epilepsy* (College Station: Texas Agricultural Extension Service, n.d.).

FIGURE 6.26

Levels of Headings

**Title: Types and Treatments of Tick-Borne Diseases of Dogs**
    Main Heading 1:  Most frequently diagnosed tick-borne disease in dogs
        Subheading 1: Ehrlichiosis
            Sub-subheading 1:  Signs of ehrlichiosis
            Sub-subheading 2:  Stages of ehrlichiosis
            Sub-subheading 3:  Diagnosis of ehrlichiosis
            Sub-subheading 4:  Treatment of ehrlichiosis
        Subheading 2: Babesiosis
            Sub-subheading 1:  Signs of babesiosis
            Sub-subheading 2:  Diagnosis of babesiosis
            Sub-subheading 3:  Treatment of babesiosis
        Subheading 3: Borreliosis
            Sub-subheading 1:  Signs of borreliosis
            Sub-subheading 2:  Diagnosis of borreliosis
            Sub-subheading 3:  Treatment of borreliosis
    Main Heading 2: Prevention of tick-borne disease in dogs
        Subheading 1: Eliminate ticks on the dog
            Sub-subheading 1:  Dips
            Sub-subheading 2:  Sprays
            Sub-subheading 3:  Powders
        Subheading 2: Eliminate ticks in the yard

During a partial seizure, the dog may exhibit one or more of the following signs:
- turning the head to one side
- muscular contractions of one or both legs on the same side of the body
- bending the body to one side

With the list, we can easily follow the sentence because the page layout directs our eyes.

## TIPS FOR WRITING EFFECTIVE HEADINGS

- **Identify the section's primary topic.** The heading should clearly identify the information that follows. For example, in Figure 6.24, the heading Characteristics of Inherited Epilepsy clearly identifies the characteristics of only inherited epilepsy.
- **Use parallel headings.** Look again at Figure 6.24. Each heading has the same grammatical structure: a noun combined with a prepositional phrase. These headings, therefore, are parallel.
- **Use key words to tell readers the section's topic.** Often writers use key words such as Budget as headings. In many instances, these key words adequately inform readers of the following information. If you use single-word headings, make sure the headings clearly identify the information that follows.
- **Use questions to tell readers the section's topic and create a friendly tone for less-formal documents and non-expert readers** (Felker et al. 1981). Draw readers into your document and add a friendly tone by using question-style headings. For example, on a university website, you might find a heading such as How Do You Pay Your Bill Online? or How Do You Drop a Class? The pronoun you adds a personal, informal tone to the headings, yet the headings are still clear and informative.
- **Use "how-to" headings for instructions.** How-to headings help readers locate the tasks or procedures they need. For example, in a fax machine manual, you might see a heading such as How to Use a Shared Phone Line or How to Set Up the Fax Header.

## TIPS FOR WRITING EFFECTIVE LISTS

- **Use a number when the list has an implied sequence, a hierarchy, or a specified number of items.** For example, if you are writing instructions, use numbers to indicate the sequence of the steps. If you have a subordinate (sub)list, use lowercase letters or bullets to indicate that sublist:
  1. List item
     1. Sub item
     2. Sub item
  2. List item
     1. Sub item
     2. Sub item
- **Use a symbol, usually a bullet, when you do not have an implied sequence, a hierarchy, or a specified number of items.** For most business and technical documents, use a round or square bullet. If you have a sublist, use dashes or hollow bullets:

- List item
  - Subitem
  - Subitem
- List item
  - Subitem
  - Subitem

- **Align the list correctly.** Look at the lists in Figure 6.27. In the left column, the lines of text align below the bullet or number. However, in the right column, the lines of text align below the text, and the bullet or number stands out. The right column is easier to follow.
- **Break up long lists.** Most readers can only remember about seven items; so if your list has more than seven items, break the list into two or more smaller lists.
- **Make your lists parallel.** Look again at Figure 6.25. Notice the lists of characteristics of acquired epilepsy. Each item has the same grammatical structure: a noun combined with a prepositional phrase. These list items, therefore, are parallel.
- **Punctuate the lead-in correctly.** Although standards vary among organizations, the most commonly used lead-in is a complete clause followed by a colon, as in the following example:

  To log in to the network, complete these steps:

  If you cannot use a complete clause, do not use the colon—or any punctuation—after the lead-in:

  To successfully treat epilepsy, you must
  - Consistently give the medication as directed by the veterinarian.
  - Continue the medication without interruption.
- **Use correct punctuation and capitalization in your lists.** The rules for punctuating lists vary, so use the style what your organization prefers. If your organization has no preference, follow these guidelines:
  - *If the list items are phrases,* begin each list item with a lowercase letter and do not use a period or comma at the end of the item. You do not need the period or comma because the white space after the last list item signals the end of the list.
  - *If the list items are complete sentences,* begin each list item with a capital letter and end the list with a period.
  - *If the list items are phrases followed by complete sentences,* begin each list item with a capital letter and end the initial phrase with a period. Begin the complete sentence with a capital letter and end the sentence with a period. You can use italics and/or bold to emphasize the phrase, as in the example below.
  - *If the list includes two types of grammatical structures such as phrases and complete sentences,* begin each list item with a capital letter and end each item with a period, as in the example below.
    - *Increased fuel economy.* The new hybrid design will increase fuel economy by 15%.
    - *Increased cargo room.*
    - *Improved navigation systems.* The newly designed vehicle includes a built-in compass and a GPS navigation system.

FIGURE 6.27

**Aligning Lists Correctly**

| **Incorrectly Aligned** | **Correctly Aligned** |
|---|---|
| Text | Text |
| • subtext | • subtext |
| • subtext | • subtext |
| | |
| Text 2 | Text 2 |
| • subtext 2 | • subtext 2 |
| • subtext 2 | • subtext 2 |

# CASE STUDY ANALYSIS

## Online Sources and Presidential Campaigns

### Background

In 2004, presidential election campaigns were changed forever by making online sources immediately accessible to citizens across the nation. Webpages and blogs allowed campaign headquarters to post online news stories, posters, videos, letters, donation requests, and more, so workers at the grassroots level could access the information. The 2004 campaign effectively showed that using online sources could make a virtually unknown candidate a household name in a short time; the impact of the strategic shift has been likened to the Nixon/Kennedy televised debate.

With this new strategy, campaigns changed how they marketed the candidates. The information was managed and controlled after it was disseminated. Traditional campaign sources—television, radio, print, and mail—create an awareness and desire for a product through branding and consistent use of typography, design, color, and wording. However, once information is posted online, it is "owned" by the people who use it. Candidates cannot control how people at the grassroots level change or use the information. This online format results in an "over-the-back fence" feel to discussions carried on in coffee shops, town halls, and blog pages across the country.

### Assignment

1. Imagine you are creating information to be downloaded from a presidential candidate's website. What would you do to ensure that your candidate's political profile remains consistent and accurate after your information is posted and disseminated? Write a memo using a problem-and-solution pattern to answer this question.

2. Write a memo to your campaign manager explaining how information organized for the Internet is different from information organized for print.

# EXERCISES

1. Select an appropriate criterion you can use to compare or contrast two or more items or groups of items. Some suggested items appear below. Prepare a formal outline. Using your outline, write a brief document in which you compare or contrast the items.
   - apartment complexes near your campus
   - dorms on your campus
   - coffee shops near your campus
   - grocery stores in your community
   - state parks in your home state
   - Internet service providers

2. Partition a single object into its parts. Use one of the items listed below, or select one of your own: lawn mower, bicycle, refrigerator, tools, equipment, or instrument that us use in your major field of study, microwave, or cell phone.

   Specify the particular brand or model of the object. For example, you will not partition a generic printer; instead, you might partition an HP Officejet Pro L7680 printer. Partition the object into at least two levels of parts—main parts and subparts. For instance, you might partition the printer into the control panel and the paper tray. Once you have partitioned the object, create a diagram (or locate a diagram from the manufacturer's online literature) showing the partitions, as in Figure 6.8.

3. Using the partitions and the diagram you used for Exercise 2, write a description of the parts of the item. Use spatial order to describe the parts.

4.  Determine the most effective classification principle for a topic and specific readers. Select one of the following topic-and-reader combinations or create a combination of your own:
    - types of financial aid available to students at your college or university
      *Readers:* students or parents
    - restaurants
      *Readers:* visitors to your community
    - types of jobs available in your major field after graduation
      *Readers:* graduating college seniors

    Prepare a formal outline (as in Figure 6.20), a diagram, or a description of your classification. Remember that the classification categories must not overlap.

5.  Prepare a document that explains the cause of some situation or event. Address your document to a specific reader, such as a friend, family member, or classmate. Search the Internet for information on your topic. Document information that you use from the Internet. Select one of the following topics, or choose one of your own:
    - comets
    - global warming
    - hurricanes
    - eclipses of the sun or moon
    - tsunamis

6.  Prepare a document that explains the effects of a situation or event for a specific reader, such as a friend, family member, or classmate. Select one of the following topics or choose one of your own:
    - writing skills and your job
    - recycling
    - the U.S. government's budget deficit
    - mercury levels in water and food

7.  Select a problem in your community, on your campus, or at your workplace, and determine an appropriate solution. Prepare a formal outline of the problem and your proposed solution. Your outline should have at least two levels. Using the outline, write a letter detailing the problem and solution to the appropriate community leader, to your local or campus newspaper, or to the appropriate person on campus or at your workplace. (For information on writing letters, see Chapter 12.)

8. A friend asks you to describe a process or procedure. Using chronological order, write a description of the process or procedure for your friend. You can use one of the processes or procedures below or select one of your own:
   - how to create a slideshow using Microsoft PowerPoint®
   - how to create a wiki
   - how to use a tool or equipment in a chemistry or biology lab
   - how to create and edit a graphic using graphics software (you must select a specific software)

9. **Collaborative exercise:** You and your team select a topic from the list below or choose one of your own: reasons pilots should or should not carry firearms, reasons your college should or should not offer more courses online, reasons your college should add more parking, or potential effects of global warming on your community.

   Write a memo to your instructor or to your classmates. Use the order-of-importance pattern to organize the memo. (For information on writing memos, see Chapter 12.)

10. Interview (in person or by email) someone in your field to find out how his or her workplace or manager influences the way he or she organizes documents. (For information on setting up and conducting interviews, see Chapter 5.) Ask the following questions; you may also add questions of your own.
    - Does your workplace or field have a predetermined organization for some of the documents you write? If so, what types of documents? How does the organization compare with the guidelines you learned in college?
    - Does your workplace use templates that give you a specific organization for a document? If so, which documents?
    - How frequently does your manager expect you to organize a document in a particular way? What do you do when you disagree with the organization that he or she expects?
    - If your workplace or manager does not have a required organization, how do you decide on an organzation for the document? What if you have never written such a document? Where do you find out about the organization? From a company archive? From a website? From a coworker?

    Write a memo to your instructor summarizing the information you gathered from the interview. (For information on writing memos, see Chapter 12.)

11. Find two documents on the Internet. One document should include overviews and headings; the other document should not include overviews and headings. Print a copy of the documents and complete the following:
    - Highlight the overview(s).
    - Highlight the headings.
    - Write a memo to your instructor explaining how the overviews and headings make the document easier to read. (For information on writing memos, see Chapter 12.)
    - Write headings for the document that lacks headings or overviews.

12. Using Tips for Writing Effective Lists, rewrite the following sentences into lists:
    a. Compost is organic material that can be used as a soil amendment or as a medium to grow plants. Mature compost is a stable material with a content called humus that is dark brown or black and has a soil-like, earthy smell. It is created by combining organic wastes (e.g., yard trimmings, food wastes, manures) in proper ratios into piles, rows, or vessels; adding bulking agents (e.g., wood chips) as necessary to accelerate the breakdown of organic materials; and allowing the finished material to fully stabilize and mature through a curing process.[2]
    b. Before installing your virtual private network (VPN), you will begin by importing your browser favorites. If you use Internet Explorer® at home, you have an "import" choice under the file menu that opens a wizard. If you use another browser, you can save these favorites one at a time by opening the document you sent from work, clicking each favorite in your home computer browser and adding it to your favorites list instead of importing the entire list.

[2] Adapted from www.epa.gov/epaoswer/non-hw/composting/basic.htm.

## Working with a Team to Illustrate the Standard Patterns of Organization

Working with your team, complete the following for each standard pattern of organization:
- Find at least two documents that illustrate each of the standard patterns of organization.
  - You could search the Internet or look at documents from businesses in your community or offices on your campus.
  - Make sure the documents follow the tips for that pattern.
  - Make a copy of each document.
- Be ready to make a class presentation, slide show, or other kind of talk that will define and illustrate the document organization. (See Chapter 20 on making presentations).
  - Define each pattern.
  - Explain how each document illustrates the pattern.
  - Include appropriate graphics.
  - Cite the document's source.

# chapter *seven*

## Writing Easy-to-Read Documents

iStockphoto 2008.

*Y*ou read every day—text messages, websites, social media, textbooks, magazines. Some of the writing is effective, but much is ineffective. Because you read so much ineffective writing, you may be used to wordy, indirect sentences that contain unnecessary words, ineffective verb phrases, and buried actions and actors. Many writers think this type of convoluted writing impresses readers. However, readers of technical documents prefer a clear, direct style that doesn't require them to search for information or to guess at meaning. Clear, concise writing not only helps you convey your intended meaning, but also makes you sound professional, makes a positive impression, and gains the respect of your managers, coworkers, and readers. In this chapter, you will learn guidelines to help you write easy-to-read sentences and paragraphs.

## FOCUS ON ACTORS AND ACTIONS[1]

In most of your writing, you will tell a story involving actors and actions. In even the most convoluted writing, you usually can find actors acting. Let's look at a passage in which the writer has buried the actors and actions:

> It is Sabrina's proposal for the adoption of updated software by the accounting department. This software provides assistance in the preparation of the annual budget.

Who are the real actors? In the first sentence, *Sabrina* and *the accounting department* are the actors although the sentence does not describe their actions. In the second sentence, the actor seems to be *software*, but because of the sentence structure, we can't be sure whether the software or the accounting department is preparing the budget.

What actions does the paragraph writer mention? In the first sentence, the actions appear in the nouns *proposal* and *adoption*. In the second sentence, the actions appear in nouns *assistance* and *preparation*. The writer buries the action in nouns, instead of using verbs.

Let's look at a revised version of the passage:

> Sabrina proposed that the accounting department adopt updated software. The accounting department personnel can use this software to prepare the annual budget.

In this revised passage, the actors (*Sabrina* and *accounting department personnel*) are the subjects, and the actions (*proposed*, *adopt*, *use*, and *prepare*) appear in verbs. The revised passage illustrates two powerful style principles: (1) Make actors the subjects of your sentences and (2) Put the action in verbs.

 ## MAKE THE ACTORS THE SUBJECTS OF YOUR SENTENCES

Most readers expect the actor to appear as the subject. (An **actor** is a noun—a person, a place, or a thing.) Think of the subject as a fixed location (see Figure 7.1), usually located before the verb.

In the following example, the writer buries the actor in the pronoun. By revising the sentence to make the actor the subject, the writer creates a more direct statement (the symbol ≠ means *is different from*; the symbol = means *is the same as*).

---

[1] I base this concept on Williams (2006).

## FIGURE 7.1

**Locating Actors and Action**

| Subject | | Verb |
|---------|---|------|

**Reader-focused sentence**

| Subject = Actor | | Verb = Action |
|-----------------|---|---------------|

**Nonreader-focused sentence**

| Subject ≠ Actor | | Verb ≠ Action |
|-----------------|---|---------------|

Actor ≠ subject   **Our expectation** is to implement the new social media policy on Monday, January 20.

Actor = subject   **We** expect to implement the new social media policy on Monday, January 20.

In some sentences, the actor doesn't appear in the sentence. The writer of the first sentence below knew what person or group selected a new organizational plan and adopted a new budget. The readers, however, do not know the identity because the writer doesn't include that information. The second sentence tells the readers that the executive committee selected the plan and adopted the budget.

Actor ≠ subject   In March, **a new organizational plan** was selected and a new budget was adopted.

Actor = subject   In March, **the executive committee** selected a new organizational plan and adopted a new budget.

## Use People as Subjects Whenever Possible

Make people the subjects of your sentences whenever possible. For some sentences, you may not be able to do that. For example, if you are describing a piece of equipment, you might make the equipment the actor or you might make your company the actor. When you use people as actors, you lessen the distance between you and the readers and eliminate ambiguity. Look at this passage:

**People ≠ subject**   The prescription drug card program will be eliminated, effective at year-end. Beginning January 1, prescriptions will be purchased from local pharmacies and will be paid at 100% after a $100 deductible. This means that all prescriptions purchased from local pharmacies must be paid in full and the receipts saved. A claim form and your receipts should then be mailed in for reimbursement.

Readers must infer who is purchasing, eliminating, paying, and so on. They could confuse the actions that they are to perform (purchasing, paying, saving, and mailing) with the actions that the pharmacy or insurance company will perform (eliminating, paying, and reimbursing). Look at the revision below in which people are the subjects:

**People = subject**   You will begin using a new prescription drug program on January 1. Instead of using your prescription drug card, you will purchase your prescriptions from your local pharmacy. The company will pay 100% of your prescriptions costs after you pay the $100 deductible. To take advantage of this new program, follow these four steps:

1. Pay for the prescriptions that you obtain from your local pharmacy.
2. Save the receipts.
3. Complete the attached claim form.
4. Mail the completed form and the receipts in the envelope provided, so we can reimburse you.

In the revised version, each sentence has people as actors. The passage now clearly explains what readers must do and what the company will do.

Let's look again at the unrevised prescription passage. The object of the action is the subject of these sentences because the writer uses passive-voice verbs instead of active-voice verbs. In the **passive voice**, the subject is acted upon. In the **active voice**, the subject performs the action.

When you use the passive voice, readers must search for the actors or assume who is doing the acting. When you use the active voice, the actor is the subject of the sentence, as your readers expect. Notice how the active voice changes the two passive-voice sentences:

| | |
|---|---|
| **Passive voice** | subject = object of the action<br>The **prescription drug card program** *will be eliminated* effective at year-end. |
| | subject = object of the action<br>Beginning January 1, **prescriptions** *will be purchased* from local pharmacies and *will be paid* at 100% after a $100 deductible. |
| **Active voice** | subject = actor<br>You *will begin* using a new prescription drug program on January 1. |
| | subject = actor<br>Instead of using your prescription drug card, you *will purchase* your prescriptions from your local pharmacy. |

In the active-voice sentences, the actor—*you*—is the subject. Active-voice sentences tell the readers who is performing the action and use fewer words than passive-voice sentences.

Passive-voice sentences have these characteristics:
- The actor and the subject are not the same. The actor may be missing or may appear in a prepositional phrase beginning with *by*.
- The verb consists of a form of the verb *to be* plus the past participle of the main verb. (The verb *to be* has eight forms: *is, am, are, was, were, be, being,* and *been*.)
- The object of the action appears as the subject.

Let's look at another passive-voice sentence. In this sentence, the subject (*proper procedures*) and the actor (*the front-desk staff*) aren't the same. The actor appears in a prepositional phrase. The verb (*be learned*) consists of the verb *be* plus the past participle *learned*.

| Passive voice | The **proper procedures** for closing the resturant *must be* |

<small>subject</small>

<small>prepositional phrase</small> <small>actor</small>

*learned* by the front-desk staff.

In the active-voice sentence below, the subject (*front-desk staff*) is also the actor. The verb does not have a form of *to be*. This and other active-voice sentences have these characteristics:
- The actor and the subject are the same.
- The verb does not consist of a form of *to be* plus the past participle of the main verb.
- The object appears after the verb.

<small>subject = actor</small> <small>object</small>

| Active voice | **The front-desk staff** *must learn* the proper procedures for presenting a guest's check. |

The active voice makes the actor the subject, so readers can read and understand sentences quickly and easily.

## When to Use the Passive Voice

You may have to choose between the active and the passive voice. Let's look at an example:

| Passive voice | During the last six months, more than 3,000 coats *were distributed* to children across the city. |

In this example, the more important information is not who distributed the coats, but who received them. The sentence writer used the passive voice because he or she wanted to focus on the children (the object) rather than on the people (the actors) who distributed the coats.

**TIPS FOR CHANGING A PASSIVE-VOICE SENTENCE INTO AN ACTIVE-VOICE SENTENCE**

- Identify the actor.
- Make the actor the subject of the sentence.
- Follow the actor with the action (the verb).
- Follow the action (the verb) with the object or the receiver of the action.

Before you decide to use the passive voice, answer these questions. If you answer *no* to the first question or *yes* to the second, the passive voice may be appropriate:
1. Do your readers need to know who is acting?
2. Do you want to focus attention on the object rather than on the actor? (We discuss this situation later in this chapter in the context of using the old/new pattern.)

Readers expect the action of a sentence to be expressed by a verb. Many writers, however, bury the action in nouns, as in this sentence:

Action in noun
　　　　　　　　　　　　　　　　　*verb*
　　　　　　　　The **police** *are conducting* an investigation of the robbery that occurred this morning.

You must look beyond the verb *are conducting* to find the action *investigation*. The sentence names this action in the noun *investigation* instead of using the verb *investigate*. The verb *are conducting* doesn't give you the information you need. To improve this sentence, eliminate the verb *are conducting* and express the primary action in the verb *investigate*:

Action in verb
　　　　　　　　　　　　　　　　　*verb*
　　　　　　　　The **police** *are investigating* the robbery that occurred this morning.

In this revised sentence, you don't have to search for the primary action. It appears in the verb where you expect to find it. The revised sentence is also shorter and more direct.

## Identifying Sentences Where the Verb Does Not Express the Action

Most sentences in which the verb does not express the action have one or both of these characteristics: (1) a noun expresses the primary action and/or (2) the verb is a form of *to be*.

If a noun expresses the primary action, you may be able to identify that noun from its suffix: *-tion, -ment, -ion, -ance, -ence,* or *-ery*. However, the noun may not end in a suffix because some verbs (for example, *hope, result,* and *change*) do not change form when used as nouns.

Let's look at some sentences in which nouns express the primary action. When revised, these sentences are clearer and more concise:

Action in noun
　　　　　　　　Her **discovery** of the missing bolts *happened* on Friday while she was cleaning the lab.

Action in verb
　　　　　　　　**She** *discovered* the missing bolts on Friday while she was cleaning the lab.

The second sentence is more direct and reader-focused because the action appears in the verb *discovered*. Now the sentence also has an actor in the subject.

Let's look at another example. In this example, the verb (*was*) is a form of *to be*, and the action of the sentence appears in the noun *discussion*. Notice that the noun ends in *–sion*. When the verb *discussed* expresses the action, the sentence is more effective and reader-focused. This revised sentence focuses on the actor, which now appears as the subject.

| | |
|---|---|
| Action in noun | There was a **discussion** of the recycling guidelines by the city council. |
| Action in verb | **The city council** *discussed* the recycling guidelines. |

## Keep the Actor and the Action Together

Once you have successfully expressed the action in a verb, keep that verb and the actor or subject together. If several words separate the subject from the verb, readers may have to reread the sentence. Consider this example:

| | |
|---|---|
| Actor and action separated | Our **branch managers,** because they have insufficient managerial experience or manage-ment training, *cannot motivate* unproductive employees. |

By the time you finally read the action (*cannot motivate*), you may have forgotten the actor (*branch managers*) because nine words separate the actor from the action. The sentence is easier to understand when the actor and the action are together:

| | |
|---|---|
| Actor and action together | Because they have insufficient managerial experience or management training, **branch managers** *cannot motivate* unproductive employees. |

## EMPHASIZE THE IMPORTANT INFORMATION IN YOUR SENTENCES

Readers can read documents more quickly if you emphasize the important information in your sentences. Emphasize the most important information by putting it at the end of the sentence or putting unfamiliar technical terms at the end of the sentence.

## Put the More Important Information at the End

The natural stress point of most sentences comes at the end. When reading a sentence aloud, you tend to raise the pitch of your voice near the end and stress the last few words (Williams 2006). When writing, take advantage of this natural stress point to emphasize important information. In the examples below, the more important information appears in bold and the less important in italics.

You have not sent us your **December progress report**, *according to our records*.

The profits in January **increased by 15 percent**, *for example*.

In both of these sentences, unimportant information appears at the end. By moving these phrases to the sentence beginning, you emphasize the more important information about the progress report and the 15 percent profit increase:

*According to our records*, you have not mailed us your **December progress report**.

*For example*, the January profits **increased by 15 percent**.

## Put Unfamiliar Technical Terms at the End

Readers will better understand unfamiliar technical terms if you put them at the end of sentences (Williams 2006). If you put them near the beginning, readers don't have a context for understanding unfamiliar terms. Consider these sentences:

| | |
|---|---|
| **Unfamiliar technical terms at the beginning** | **Fast-twitch fibers and slow-twitch fibers** are two basic types of muscle fibers. |
| **Unfamiliar technical terms at the end** | Muscles have two types of fibers: **fast twitch and slow twitch.** |

In the first sentence, the unfamiliar terms (*fast-twitch fibers and slow-twitch fibers*) appear at the beginning, and the familiar term *muscle* appears at the end. When we put the familiar term (*muscle*) at the beginning, the sentence gives readers a context for the unfamiliar terms *fast twitch* and *slow twitch*.

This section presents guidelines to show readers how the sentences in your paragraphs tie together:

- Put old information near the beginning of sentences.
- Use topics to tie sentences together.
- Use transitions.
- Repeat or restate key words or phrases.

> When you write or read your own paragraphs, you understand how the sentences fit together. However, your readers probably don't.

## Put Old Information Near the Sentence Beginning

*Old information* has previously appeared in a paragraph. *New information* has not yet appeared in the paragraph. In the following paragraph, the old information appears at the beginning of the second through fifth sentences. However, the third and seventh sentences begin with new information. The old information appears in bold.

> [1]When your muscles contract, the muscles' thick and thin filaments do the actual work. [2]**Thick filaments** are made of a protein called myosin. [3]At the molecular level, a **thick filament** is a shaft of myosin molecules arranged in a cylinder. [4]**Thin filaments** are made of another protein called actin. [5]**The thin filaments** look like two strands of pearls twisted around each other. [6]During **contraction**, the thick myosin filaments grab on to the thin actin filaments by forming crossbridges. [7]Making the sarcomere shorter, **the thick filaments** pull the thin filaments past them. [8]In a **muscle fiber**, the signal for contraction is synchronized over the entire fiber so that all of the myofibrils that make up the sarcomere shorten simultaneously.[2]

In the first two sentences, you can easily see how they relate and you can follow the pattern of the paragraph. However, this pattern breaks down in sentence 3 and again in sentence 7 because the writer introduces new information (*molecular level* and *Making the sarcomere shorter*) at the sentence beginning. Let's look at a visual representation of the information in the paragraph (see Figure 7.2). The new information appears in red. In sentence 3, notice that the word *molecular* does not appear in sentences 1 or 2. Likewise, in sentence 7, the word *sarcomere* does not appear in sentences 1 through 6. Therefore, these words are *new* information to the reader—information that has not yet been introduced.

---

[2] Reprinted courtesy of HowStuffWorks.com.

If we revise the paragraph to put the old information before the new information in sentences 3 and 7, the paragraph is easier to read.

[1]When your muscles contract, the muscles' thick and thin filaments do the actual work. [2]**Thick filaments** are made of a protein called myosin. [3]A **thick filament** is a shaft of myosin molecules arranged in a cylinder. [4]**Thin filaments** are made of another protein called actin. [5]**The thin filaments** look like two strands of pearls twisted around each other. [6]During contraction, the thick myosin filaments grab on to the thin actin filaments by forming crossbridges. [7]**The thick filaments** pull the thin filaments past them, making the sarcomere shorter. [8]In a **muscle fiber**, the signal for contraction is synchronized over the entire fiber so that all of the myofibrils that comprise the sarcomere shorten simultaneously.[3]

In the paragraph below, the old information appears in bold. The writer consistently presents new information near the sentence beginning, followed by old information near the end. Therefore, when you reach the end of a sentence, you don't know how the new information relates to the information in the previous sentence (that is, old information).

**Old information in the wrong place**

The Carter Blood Center will begin a recognition program for plasma donors. One suggestion based on feedback from **plasma donors** is to give plaques with annual updates of **plasma donation** totals. Attached is a photograph of a sample plaque that the **Center** will present to **donors**. The dated and numbered brass plates indicate the **donation** year and the number of units **donated**.

The writer can clarify the relationship between the old and the new information by moving the old information near the sentence beginning:

**Old information in the correct place**

The Carter Blood Center will begin a recognition program for plasma donors. For the **program, donors** suggested that the Center give plaques with annual updates of plasma donation totals. A photograph of a sample **plaque** is attached. The **plaque** includes dated and numbered brass plates that indicate the donation year and the number of units donated.

In the revised paragraph, the information flows logically from one sentence to another. You don't have to figure out how the sentences relate because the writer connects them by putting old information near the beginning of the sentences.

[3] Adapted and reprinted courtesy of HowStuffWorks.com.

FIGURE 7.2

**Understanding the Old/New Pattern (new information appears in red)**

| Sentence # | First part of the sentence | Second part of the sentence |
|---|---|---|
| 1 | When your muscles contract | the muscles' thick and thin filaments do the actual work. |
| 2 | Thick filaments | are made of a protein called myosin. |
| 3 | At the molecular level, | a thick filament is a shaft of myosin molecules arranged in a cylinder. |
| 4 | Thin filaments | are made of another protein called actin. |
| 5 | The thin filaments | look like two strands of pearls twisted around each other. |
| 6 | During contraction, | the thick myosin filaments grab on to the thin actin filaments by forming crossbridges. |
| 7 | Making the sarcomere shorter, | the thick filaments pull the thin filaments past them. |
| 8 | In a muscle fiber, | the signal for contraction is synchronized over the entire fiber so that all of the myofibrils that comprise the sarcomere shorten simultaneously. |

## Use Topics to Tie Sentences Together

You can relate sentences by topic. The first sentence in a paragraph introduces the topic. The second sentence comments on that topic, and the third, fourth, fifth, and subsequent sentences comment further on that topic. In a well-written paragraph, the writer signals the topic by mentioning it in the subject position of each sentence.

In the following paragraph, the sentence's subject appears in boldface, but the topic, *Personal Identification Number (PIN)*, shifts position from sentence to sentence:

Shifts in topic

Your **Personal Identification Number (PIN)** should arrive within three days after the card. The **bank** will allow cardholders to personalize their PINs once they activate their cards. The **company** selected a four-digit number for your PIN.

The topic of the paragraph's first sentence, *Personal Identification Number* (*PIN*), appears as the subject, and the remainder of the sentence provides information about the topic. The second sentence, however, does not comment on that topic. Instead, it introduces a new topic (*the bank*) as the subject. The third sentence introduces another new topic (*the company*). The paragraph would be more effective with consistent topics in the sentences's subjects:

Revised

Your **Personal Identification Number (PIN)** should arrive within three days after the card. Your **PIN** is a four-digit number that the bank has selected for you. Your PIN can be personalized after you activate your card.

In the revised version, the common topic appears as the subject of each sentence. Readers can easily relate the old information to the new in each sentence. The writer uses passive voice in the third sentence to place the common topic in the subject position. This writer appropriately uses the passive voice, *be personalized,* to tie together related information. Sometimes, you can only put a common topic into the subject position by using the passive voice.

## Use Transitions

*Transitions* are words, phrases, and even sentences that connect one idea or one sentence to another. Transitions indicate relationships of time, cause and effect, space, addition, comparison, and contrast. Figure 7.3 lists common transitions that writers use to connect ideas.

When using transitions to tie your sentences together, put the transition at or near the sentence beginning. When you put a transition after the verb or near the sentence end, you weaken the effect of the transition and frequently create an awkward sentence, as in this example:

Awkward

The flight test results concerned the project manager. The manager asked the research and development team to retest the new plane, **therefore**.

Because the transition (*therefore*) occurs at the end of the second sentence, you do not see the cause-and-effect relationship until you reach the end of the sentence. By putting the transition at the end, the sentence also fails to stress the important information. The transition is more effective at the beginning of the second sentence, as in the following example:

| Revised | The flight test results concerned the project manager. **Therefore,** the manager asked the research and development team to retest the new plane. |

Although transition words help readers to see relationships, use these words in conjunction with the other techniques presented in this chapter to tie your sentences together. Transition words alone aren't enough to tie all your sentences together. If you find that you use transition words in sentence after sentence, revise your paragraphs to eliminate some of the transition words.

## Repeat or Restate Key Words or Phrases

To help readers remember information and understand your point, tie sentences together by repeating or restating key words or phrases.

**FIGURE 7.3**

**Common Transitions**

| Time | before, while, during, after, next, later, first, second, then, subsequently, the next day, meanwhile, now |
|---|---|
| Cause and Effect | because, therefore, since, thus, consequently, due to, if … then, so |
| Place | below, above, inside, outside, behind, at the next level, internally, externally |
| Addition | furthermore, in addition, also, moreover, and |
| Comparison | likewise, as, like, similarly, not only … but also |
| Contrast | conversely, on the other hand, unlike, although, however, yet, nevertheless, but |

## Repeating Key Words and Phrases

Tie sentences together by repeating key words or phrases. However, avoid overusing this technique. The following sentences effectively repeat key words:

> The accident on the space station **depleted** the oxygen **supply**. Due to the **depleted supply**, the crew had to limit physical activities.

> The city council **recommended** that the city redraw the district lines. This **recommendation** upset many citizens.

In the first example, the second sentence repeats two words from the first, *depleted* and *supply*, to tie the sentences together.

In the second example, the verb *recommended* in the first sentence is echoed in the second by the noun *recommendation*. The repetition allows the writer to put old information at the beginning of the sentence.

## Restating with Pronouns

Use pronouns to refer to nouns that appear in a previous sentence. Pronouns not only tie your sentences together, but also avoid the monotony that results when the same noun appears several times in a sentence or paragraph.

> Muscles have two types of fibers: fast twitch and slow twitch. Fast-twitch fibers contract faster. **They** also have greater anaerobic capacity.

## Restating with Summary Words

Tie sentences together by using words that summarize ideas or information presented earlier. *Summary words* allow you to restate information, usually in a few words. In the example below, the subject of the second sentence (*this new equipment*) summarizes the equipment mentioned in the first sentence:

> The computer lab purchased 6 new laser printers and 12 new computers. **This new equipment** will allow the lab to better serve the technical communication students.

Summary words concisely restate the information from the previous sentence and put old information at the beginning of the new sentence.

## CASE STUDY ANALYSIS

### Bad Writing Costs State Governments Big Money[4]

### Background

Poor writing costs taxpayers big money. A report released by the National Commission on Writing says that poor writing skills cost state governments nearly $250 million annually in employee training programs to improve writing skills.

In a survey conducted by the Commission, human resource managers listed clear writing as one of the most important skills needed by state government employees. However, only 33 percent of managers at the state level reported that their administrative employees had adequate writing skills. Consequently, many employees at the state level must take writing classes, at a cost of as much as $400 per employee.

The consequences of poor writing skills cost taxpayers money because of
- slower response times
- time-consuming and costly rewrites and printing
- time lost in reading and rereading unclear documents
- additional hires required to answer citizens' questions about unclear documents

### Assignment

1. Find an example of a poorly written document distributed by your state or local government.
2. Highlight sentences and paragraphs that are unclear and that do not follow the guidelines presented in this chapter.
3. Revise the document. Make sure your revision follows the clear writing guidelines in this chapter.
4. Hand in both the original document and your revised document.

---

[4] Compiled from information downloaded from the World Wide Web: http://www.usatoday.com/news/washington/2005-07-04-employees-lack-skills_x.htm. "Report: State employees' lack of writing skills cost nearly $250M," Copyright 2005, The Associated Press.

**TAKING IT INTO THE** *workplace*

## How Are Your Proofreading Skills?

You probably feel relieved when you write the last word of a document. However, when you write that last word, you aren't finished—that is, you're not finished if you want to ensure that the document is coherent and error free. You still need to revise and proofread it. If you have time, ask your classmates, friends, or coworkers to help you revise and proofread your documents. Most writing professionals agree that revising and proofreading your own work "is not the best way to go" (Hansen 1997, 16). However, often you'll write under deadlines or won't be able to find someone to help you revise and proofread your document. When you revise (sometimes called edit) your own documents, James B. Hansen, author of *Editing Your Own Writing* (1997), suggests these tips:

- **Use a style sheet or style guide.** If you, your team, or your company does not have a style sheet or guide, create your own or use an established style guide, such as *The Chicago Manual of Style*.
- **Create a checklist.** Checklists help you locate your particular writing problems. For example, if you tend to misuse the comma, a checklist helps you isolate comma errors.
- **Wait a day or two before revising and proofreading.** If possible, don't revise or proofread your document immediately after you write it (Hansen 1997). By waiting, you can understand what the document actually says rather than what you intend it to say.
- **Revise and proofread longer documents on paper.** If possible, revise and proofread your documents, especially those over two pages, on paper instead of on screen. "Reading speed can drop as much as 30 percent on a computer screen" (Hansen 1997, 16; Krull and Hurford 1987; Gomes, 1994). You are more prone to overlook problems and errors on a screen.
- **Read the document more than once.**

## Assignment

Using a document that you are writing for your technical communication class or for another class you are taking, follow the tips above and revise and proofread that document before you turn it in to your instructor. You can also use the "Worksheet for Writing Easy-to-Read Documents" online at www.grtep.com

# EXERCISES

DOWNLOAD A WORKSHEET FOR WRITING EASY-TO-READ DOCUMENTS ONLINE AT
WWW.GRTEP.COM

1. Rewrite these sentences to make the actor the subject.
   a. Attempts were made by the engineering staff to complete the project.
   b. The new building will allow 20 new businesses to relocate downtown.
   c. There have been threats from other landowners nearby due to the trash and mud in the streets caused by unauthorized employees using this lot.
   d. There is no alternative except to recall the product.
   e. Working together will ultimately allow us to finish the new product by the deadline.
   f. It is extraordinarily important that we turn in our application by the deadline.

2. Change these sentences from the passive to the active voice. Follow the guidelines in Tips for Changing a Passive-Voice Sentence into an Active-Voice Sentence.
   a. The merit raises were approved by the board of directors.
   b. Dues must be paid within 90 days by all members.
   c. Please notify this office as soon as a shipment date is known.
   d. Parking on-site is allowed for hotel guests.
   e. Reduction in the size of the deficit has been accomplished.
   f. The ethics training was completed by the new employee.

3. Rewrite these sentences to put the action in the verb.
   a. We must provide support for the three candidates from our district who are running for president, vice president, and senator.
   b. Our expectation was to begin the interview at 10:00 a.m.
   c. The detectives are conducting an investigation of the burglary that occurred this morning.
   d. Failure to pay the fine within 15 days may result in a warrant being issued for your arrest.
   e. The team has taken into consideration the results of the usability tests.
   f. To ensure the safety of all visitors and employees, we will conduct a test of the new evacuation procedures on May 16.

4. Rewrite these sentences to put the more important information and technical terms near the end of the sentence.
   a. The outcome of the election changed because of some unfortunate comments about the city manager, according to the press release.
   b. Business owners in the downtown district are suing the developer for faulty foundations and poor street drainage, however.
   c. Water pipes in the older condominiums may freeze and burst when the temperature drops below 20° F.
   d. Myosin and actin are tiny filaments inside your muscles.
   e. Creatine phosphate is broken down by the muscles.
   f. Epithelial cells slide over the cornea and patch the injury if your cornea is scratched by dirt.

5. For each sentence below, (a) identify the problems in the sentence and (b) rewrite the sentence to eliminate the problems.
   a. Because of the clerk's inability to help us with the equipment, there was a delay in the repairs that we had to do the next day.
   b. Because the team did not have sufficient time to complete the project, it was not surprising that it was unable to prepare a satisfactory report.
   c. It is our intention to begin the project when the new equipment arrives.
   d. A reinvestigation of the employee's travel expenses by the accounting department is necessary before reimbursement from the company can be provided.
   e. The opening of an international branch will increase our budget for the new year, however.
   f. Our international sales offices, which are located in Germany, China, Canada, and Brazil, have increased sales by 15 percent.
   g. There has been a decrease in the number of infants killed because of the redesigned car seats.
   h. Updates to your account can be accessed on the Internet in five business days.
   i. The water quality reports will be ready next month after the staff has received the test results from the Department of Health, according to the press release.

6. Complete the following for each paragraph on the next 2 pages:
   • Underline the old information.
   • Make sure the paragraph has an effective topic sentence.
   • Rewrite the paragraph so the old information appears before the new information.
   • Make sure the paragraph follows the guidelines presented in this chapter for writing effective sentences and paragraphs.

a.  Almost everyone has had the unpleasant experience of a mosquito bite. Severe skin irritation can occur through an allergic reaction to the mosquito's saliva; this is what causes the red bump and itching. But a more serious consequence is the transmission of certain serious diseases, such as malaria, dengue fever, and several forms of encephalitis. Not only do mosquitoes carry diseases that afflict humans, but they also transmit several diseases and parasites to which dogs and horses are susceptible. These include dog heartworms and Eastern Equine Encephalitis. There are about 200 species of mosquitoes in the United States, all of which live in specific habitats, exhibit unique behaviors, and bite different types of animals. Despite these differences, all mosquitoes share some common traits, such as a four-stage life cycle. After the female mosquito obtains a blood meal (male mosquitoes do not bite), she lays her eggs directly on the surface of stagnant water, in a depression, or on the edge of a container where rainwater may collect and flood the eggs. When the eggs hatch, mosquito larvae, or "wigglers," emerge. Living in the water, the larvae feed and develop into the third stage of the life cycle, called pupae, or "tumblers." The pupae also live in the water, but no longer feed. Finally, the mosquitoes emerge from their pupa case and the water as fully developed adults, ready to bite.

b.  There are many rules regarding evidence presentation in both civil and criminal trials that the judge must apply in deciding which evidence may be admitted and the form and manner in which it may be admitted. These rules are complicated and not easily understood by the layperson. They have been developed through hundreds of years of experience so that we may have fair and orderly trials. When a question is asked that either attorney believes is in violation of these rules, he or she may object. Therefore, no juror must allow him- or herself to be prejudiced for or against one side or the other based on objections made by an attorney to the introduction of evidence. A judge's ruling does not mean that he or she is taking sides. The judge is merely deciding that the law does or does not allow the question or the form of the question to be answered. At times, the jury is excused from the courtroom or the judge speaks to the lawyers about questions of law, beyond the hearing of the jury while questions of law are being discussed. The law provides that certain matters of law be discussed out of the jury's presence. When a trial is interrupted for these reasons, do not feel that your time is being wasted or that information is being withheld from you. Oftentimes, these hearings expedite the case.[5]

---

[5] Adapted from jury instructions from Collin County Courts. http://www.texasjudge.com/juryduty/index.html.

c.    Insect repellents are available in various forms and concentrations. Aerosol and spray products are intended for skin applications as well as for treating clothing. Liquid, cream, lotion, spray, and stick products enable direct skin application. Products with a low concentration of the active ingredient may be appropriate for situations where exposure to insects is minimal. A higher concentration of the active ingredient may be useful in highly infested areas, or with insect species that are more difficult to repel. And where appropriate, consider nonchemical ways to deter biting insects—screens, netting, long sleeves, and slacks.[6]

d.    Acid rain looks, feels, and tastes like clean rain. The harm to people from acid rain is not direct. Walking in acid rain, or even swimming in an acid lake, is immediately no more dangerous than walking or swimming in clean water. However, the pollutants (sulfur dioxide [$SO_2$] and nitrogen oxides [$NO_X$]) that cause acid rain also damage human health. These gases interact in the atmosphere to form fine sulfate and nitrate particles that can be transported long distances by winds and inhaled deep into people's lungs. Fine particles can also penetrate indoors. Scientific studies have identified a relationship between elevated levels of fine particles and increased illness and premature death from heart and lung disorders, such as asthma and bronchitis. Based on health concerns, $SO_2$ and $NO_X$ have historically been regulated under the Clean Air Act, including the Acid Rain Program. By lowering $SO_2$ and $NO_X$ emissions from power generation, the Acid Rain Program will reduce the levels of fine sulfate and nitrate particles and so reduce the incidence and the severity of these health problems: asthma and bronchitis. Due to decreased mortality, hospital admissions, and emergency room visits, the public health benefits of the Acid Rain Program are estimated to be valued at $50 billion annually when fully implemented.[7]

[7] Adapted from the U.S. Environmental Protection Agency, Office of Pesticide Programs, Using Insect Repellants Safely. 25. Nov. 2001. http://www.epa.gov/pesticides/citizens/inspectrp.htm.

[8] Adapted from U.S. Environmental Protection Agency, Clean Air Market Programs, "Effect of Acid Rain: Human Health." Online. 25 Nov. 2001. Available: http://www.epa.gov/airmarkets/acidrain/effects/health.html

# *eight*

## Using Reader-Focused Language

©Blend Images, 2013. Used under license from Shutterstock, Inc.

As technical professionals and communicators, we have a responsibility to communicate not only objective, accurate information, but also to use language that our readers will understand and that communicates our intended meaning. When we don't use reader-focused language, our communication can have unintended consequences.

To ensure that your readers understand your intended meaning, follow the guidelines in this chapter for creating reader-focused language. Reader-focused language is

- specific and unambiguous
- concise
- simple
- positive when appropriate
- inoffensive
- sensitive to readers' culture and language

To understand your documents and respond appropriately, readers need specific and unambiguous language. Without such language, they may misunderstand or misinterpret what you write. When you use specific, unambiguous language, you convey your intended meaning precisely.

## Using Specific Language

Specific language is clear and precise; vague language is often unclear and is always imprecise. Specific language clarifies the meaning and eliminates questions that readers will ask when the language is vague.

| | |
|---|---|
| **Vague** | A microscope in the lab isn't working properly. |
| **Specific** | In the forensic lab, the capture window on VWR 8607070 monocular microscope shows only black and white images. |

After reading the vague sentence, a reader would wonder: Which microscope? Which lab? What is wrong with the microscope? The specific sentence answers all those questions. It identifies the lab where the microscope is located, the specific microscope, and the problem.

To make your language specific, include examples and details. Use *such as* or *for example* to introduce examples.

| | |
|---|---|
| **Vague** | For its mission, the relief organization needs food and supplies. |
| **Specific** | For its mission to the area damaged by hurricane Katrina, the relief organization needs food and supplies such as <br> • canned milk <br> • bottled water in one-gallon plastic containers <br> • canned meat such as tuna, chicken, or ham spread <br> • ready-to-use baby formula and disposable diapers <br> • gauze, bandages, and rubbing alcohol |

The vague sentence is imprecise because it does not tell the readers the specific food and supplies needed by the relief organization. However, from the specific sentence, the readers know exactly what the organization needs.

Consider another example.

| | |
|---|---|
| Vague | KH&S will replace the masonry frames with the correct metal frames. We must have these frames soon so we can complete the first floor of both buildings on schedule. |
| Specific | To complete the first floor of both buildings on schedule, KH&S must replace the masonry frames with the correct metal frames by 11/26/2012. |

The vague sentence includes the word *soon* instead of a date. *Soon* could mean by tomorrow, in a month, or in three months. When you don't specify a date, readers assign their own meaning to *soon*. In the specific example, the writer uses a date to ensure that readers understand what is meant by *soon*. Notice how the date appears at the end of the sentence to emphasize its importance.

## Using Unambiguous Language

Your readers need unambiguous language. Unambiguous language conveys only one meaning. Ambiguous language results from
- misplaced modifiers
- dangling modifiers
- stacked nouns
- faulty word choice
- inconsistent technical terminology

### Eliminate Misplaced Modifiers

*Modifiers* are words, phrases, or clauses that refer to other sentence elements. These elements are called *referents*. Misplaced modifiers appear to modify the wrong referent, causing ambiguity. To eliminate ambiguity, place the modifier as close as possible to the correct referent. Let's analyze the following examples:

| | |
|---|---|
| Ambiguous | Our manager suggested to the vice president that we register for the class in Orlando. |

Can you say for certain whether the class is being held in Orlando? The meaning is ambiguous because of the location of the prepositional phrase *in Orlando*. To prevent the ambiguity and possible misreading, place the prepositional phrase next to the word it modifies or rewrite to clarify the meaning.

| Unambiguous | Our manager suggested to the vice president in Orlando that we register for the class. |
| --- | --- |
| Unambiguous | While in Orlando, our manager suggested to the vice president that we register for the class. |
| Unambiguous | Our manager suggested to the vice president that we register in Orlando for the class. |
| Unambiguous | Our manager suggested to the vice president that we register for the Orlando class. |

By moving the location of Orlando, we change the meaning of the sentence.

Consider the examples below. In the first example, the misplaced modifier describes the *veterinarian* as *chubby and overweight* instead of the *dog*. In the second example the misplaced modifier implies the *lab technicians* are *growing in the sterile solution* instead of the *bacteria*.

| Ambiguous | **Chubby and overweight**, the veterinarian says my dog needs a new diet and more exercise. |
| --- | --- |
| Unambiguous | The veterinarian says my **chubby and overweight** dog needs a new diet and more exercise. |
| Ambiguous | **Growing in the sterile solution,** the lab technicians observed the bacteria. |
| Unambiguous | The lab technicians observed the bacteria **growing in the sterile solution.** |

## Eliminate Dangling Modifiers

A *dangling modifier* occurs when the modifier does not have the correct referent in the sentence, as in the following example:

| Dangling | **Trying to put out the fire**, the fire extinguisher broke. |
| --- | --- |

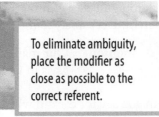

To eliminate ambiguity, place the modifier as close as possible to the correct referent.

In the sentence above, the writer incorrectly implies the fire extinguisher is putting out the fire. To eliminate the dangling modifier, rewrite the sentence to add the person in either the main clause or in the modifier:

| Correct | Trying to put out the fire, I broke the fire extinguisher. |
|---|---|
| Correct | As I was trying to put out the fire, the fire extinguisher broke. |

You can create dangling modifiers when switching from the indicative mood (a statement of fact) to the imperative mood (a command or request, usually with an understood *you* subject). To identify dangling modifiers in those situations, look for a passive-voice construction following a modifier, as in the following example:

| Dangling | **To access related websites**, the underlined link should be clicked on. |
|---|---|
| Correct | To access related websites, click on the underlined link. |

To correct the dangling modifier, the writer changes the passive voice (*be clicked*) to active voice with an understood referent—in this case, *you*.

## Eliminate Stacked Nouns

You create ambiguity when you use two or more nouns to modify another noun. When you use a "stack" of nouns as a modifier, you create hard-to-read and ambiguous passages. Look at this example:

| Stacked nouns | The consultant suggested the manager set aside time for a **fitness center member evaluation**. |
|---|---|

The sentence is ambiguous: Is the consultant suggesting that the manager evaluate the members or the fitness center? Or is the consultant suggesting that the members evaluate the fitness center? To eliminate the ambiguity, unstack the nouns:

| Correct | The consultant suggested that the manager set aside time to evaluate the members of the fitness center. |
|---|---|
| Correct | The consultant suggested that the manager set aside time for the members to evaluate the fitness center. |

Our language often uses one noun to modify another, as in *fitness center, space shuttle, software manual,* or *school superintendent*. However, whenever possible in your writing, avoid using a noun to modify another noun.

## Eliminate Faulty Word Choice

Let's look at another ambiguous sentence. In this one, the ambiguity occurs because of the word choice:

Ambiguous      We were **held up** at the bank.

Unambiguous   We were delayed at the bank.

The ambiguous sentence has two possible meanings: We were either delayed or we were robbed. To eliminate the ambiguity, select the verb *delay*, which has only one meaning in this context.

Take another example. In the example below, the ambiguity occurs because *tragedy* refers either to the type of play or to the quality of the children's performance.

Ambiguous      The seventh graders will present Shakespeare's *Hamlet* in the school auditorium on Friday at 8 p.m. Parents are invited to attend this **tragedy**.

Unambiguous   The seventh graders will present Shakespeare's *Hamlet* in the school auditorium on Friday at 8 p.m. They invite all parents to attend the performance.

In the unambiguous example, the writer uses *performance*, which can have only one meaning in the sentence. Carefully select the words in your documents to make sure readers will understand them in the way you intend.

## Use Technical Terminology Consistently and Appropriately

Readers of technical documents expect writers to consistently use the words that refer to technical concepts, instructions, and equipment. For instance, you could confuse readers of a computer manual if you use the words *screen* and *monitor* interchangeably. Pick one term or the other and use it consistently. When you write instructions or describe equipment, consistent language is especially important. For example, if you write a procedure that explains how to select a *typeface*, but the software itself uses the word *font*, you confuse readers who don't know that *typeface* and *font* are synonyms will be confused.

*Technical terminology*—or jargon—is the specialized vocabulary of a particular field, profession, or workplace. For instance, professionals in the restaurant business use the term *back server* for employees who clear guests' tables during and after meals. Horticulturalists use the scientific rather than the common name for a plant—for example, referring to a pecan tree as *Carya illinoinensis* or a daylily as *Hemerocallis.* Technical terminology offers a concise way to convey technical information. However, readers unfamiliar with the technical terms will find them confusing or will misinterpret them. You solve this problem for readers by defining technical terms in parentheses the first time you use them or by defining them in a glossary. But if your readers do not read your document from beginning to end, they will not see your parenthetical definition. If your readers can begin reading at a point in the document after the definition, then define new terms in a glossary or use nontechnical terms.

How will you know whether to use technical terminology in your documents? Ask yourself these questions:

## TIPS FOR USING TECHNICAL TERMINOLOGY

- **Use technical terminology only if your readers have detailed knowledge of the topic.** You can assume, for example, that an engineer knows what the abbreviation psi (pounds per square inch) means; however, someone without an engineering background may not understand it.
- **Use technical terminology for expert readers.** Expert readers expect technical terminology.
- **If your readers have casual or little knowledge of your topic or of your field, avoid technical terminology they won't understand.** If you cannot avoid using such terminology, define the word, concept, instruction, piece of equipment, etc., in familiar language.
- **Use technical terminology consistently.** Once you have selected the term you will use in the document, use that term consistently throughout the document.

- Will all my readers understand the technical terminology and abbreviations? Will they misunderstand or be confused by any of the technical terms and abbreviations? For example, ATM to most of us means *automated teller machine.* However, ATM also stands for *asynchronous transfer mode.* If you use ATM to mean asynchronous transfer mode and your readers are unfamiliar with the abbreviation, they will misunderstand your meaning.
- How can I help readers who don't understand the technical terminology and abbreviations? Will I define terminology and explain abbreviations in parentheses the first time I use them or will I refer readers to a glossary for technical terminology?
- Will my readers expect me to use technical terminology and abbreviations?

Readers want to read your documents without wading through unnecessary words. Therefore, use only the words needed to help your readers to understand the information. You write concisely when you eliminate redundancy and unnecessary words.

## Eliminating Redundancy

Your language is redundant when you use words or phrases that unnecessarily repeat the meaning of other words in the sentence. Redundancy occurs when you use doubled words or words that imply other words (redundant modifiers).

### Doubled Words

Redundancies can occur in pairs—two words with the same meaning combined by *and* — as in the following example:

| | |
|---|---|
| Redundant | Please give our recommendation **thought and consideration** because the proposed relocation can **help and benefit** the engineering division to better serve the southern region. |
| Concise | Please consider our recommendation because the proposed solution can help the engineering division better serve the southern region. |

Each pair of doubled words (*thought and consideration* and *help and benefit*) uses two words when one word will do. *Thought* and *consideration* have a similar meaning, as do *help* and *benefit*. To be concise, use only one of the words in each pair. Figure 8.1 lists common doubled words. When you see these doubled words in your writing, revise to use only one word and delete the word *and*.

### Words That Imply Other Words

Redundancy also results from words that imply other words in the sentence; these *redundant modifiers* repeat all or part of the meaning of other words in a sentence. (*Modifiers* are a word or a group of words that describe, limit, or qualify another word.) Examples of redundant modifiers include (the redundant words appear in bold type)

| | |
|---|---|
| Redundant | **end** result, **very** unique, **absolutely** free, **completely** eliminate |

## FIGURE 8.1

**Examples of Doubled Words**

| | | |
|---|---|---|
| advice and counsel | each and every | hope and trust |
| agreeable and satisfactory | fair and equitable | null and void |
| aid and assistance | fair and reasonable | opinion and belief |
| any and all | first and foremost | prompt and immediate |
| assist and help | full and complete | thought and consideration |
| basic and fundamental | help and benefit | true and accurate |
| due and payable | help and cooperation | |

For more examples, see Figure 8.2.

The sentences below illustrate the positive effect of eliminating words that imply other words:

Redundant    The proposed budget cuts will not affect the **final outcome** of our current projects or our **future plans** for improving the street drainage.

Concise    The proposed budget cuts will not affect the **outcome** of our current projects or our **plans** for improving the street drainage.

In the redundant sentence, the modifier *final* is unnecessary because it repeats the meaning of *outcome* (an outcome is always final), and the modifier *future* is unnecessary because it repeats the meaning of *plans* (all plans involve the future). Let's look at another example:

Redundant    The geology students analyzed a rock that was **pink in color, cylindrical in shape**, and **61 pounds in weight**.

Concise    The geology students analyzed a **pink, cylindrical** rock that weighed **61 pounds**.

The prepositional phrases in the redundant sentence repeat the meaning of *pink*, *cylindrical*, and *61 pounds*.

**Examples of Redundant Modifiers and Concise Alternatives**

| Instead of These Words . . . | Use These Concise Alternatives |
| --- | --- |
| absolutely essential | essential |
| absolutely free | free |
| anticipate in advance | anticipate |
| basic fundamentals | fundamentals |
| circle around | circle |
| consensus of opinion | consensus |
| continue on | continue |
| decrease down | decrease |
| end result | result |
| final outcome | outcome |
| free gift | gift |
| future plans | plans |
| green (red, black, etc.) in color | green (red, black, etc.) |
| human volunteer | volunteer |
| mail out | mail |
| past history | history |
| past memories | memories |
| past experience | experience |
| personal opinion | opinion |
| reduce down | reduce |
| repeat again | repeat |
| quite unique | unique |
| rarely ever | rarely |
| round (square, oval, etc.) in shape | round (square, oval, etc.) |
| return back to | return |
| seldom ever | seldom |
| small (large, medium, etc.) in size | small (large, medium, etc.) |
| true facts | facts |
| twenty (ten, two, etc.) in number | twenty (ten, two, etc.) |
| very latest | latest |
| very unique | unique |

## Eliminating Unnecessary Words

Wordy phrases make documents unnecessarily long. Even when readers understand a wordy phrase, they prefer concise writing. Readers want to read and understand technical and professional documents as quickly as possible, so eliminate any words not necessary to convey your meaning and purpose. Figure 8.3 lists examples of wordy phrases and suggests concise alternatives.

At first, you may not notice the wordy phrases that appear in your writing because you have used them or read them so many times. Make a special effort to spot these phrases and replace them with more concise, effective words.

You may also eliminate wordy phrases instead of replacing them. Figure 8.4 lists phrases that you usually can eliminate. Let's look at the effect of wordy phrases on sentence length and clarity. In each of the concise versions, the sentences are clearer and more concise.

| | |
|---|---|
| Wordy | **As a matter of fact, there is** an old warehouse that the emergency relief groups can use to house the hurricane victims **at this point in time**. |
| Concise | The emergency relief groups can use the old warehouse to house the hurricane victims. |
| Wordy | **It should be pointed out that** there are three candidates whom our organization **without further delay** will endorse, **despite the fact that we are not in a position** to contribute any money to their campaigns. |
| Concise | Our organization will endorse three candidates although we cannot contribute money to their campaigns. |
| Wordy | **It should be noted that** mercury levels in the river have increased this year. **In accordance with** your request, our department will **take into consideration** whether **it is essential** to conduct a study **with regard** to possible sources of this pollution. |
| Concise | Mercury levels in the river have increased this year. As you requested, our department will consider whether to study possible sources of this pollution. |

# FIGURE 8.3

**Revising Wordy Phrases**

| Instead of These Wordy Phrases . . . | Use These Concise Alternatives |
| --- | --- |
| a limited number | a few (or the specific number) |
| a majority | most (or the specific number) |
| a number | many (or the specific number) |
| at a later time (date) | later |
| at the conclusion of | after, following |
| at this point in time | now, currently |
| by means of | by |
| concerning the matter of | about |
| conduct an investigation | investigate |
| conduct a study | study |
| despite the fact that | although, even though |
| due to the fact that | because |
| have the ability to | can |
| have the capability to | can |
| has the capacity for | can |
| has the opportunity to | can |
| in accordance with your request | as you requested |
| in connection with | about, concerning |
| in order that | so that |
| in order to | to |
| in reference to | about |
| in regard to | about |
| in the event that | if |
| in the near future | soon (or give a specific time or date) |
| in this day and age | today, now |
| in view of the fact that | because |
| is able to | can |
| is in a position to | can |
| it is crucial that | must, should |
| it is important that | must, should |
| it is incumbent upon | must, should |

**Revising Wordy Phrases** *continued*

| Instead of These Wordy Phrases . . . | Use These Concise Alternatives |
|---|---|
| it is my (our) understanding that | I (we) understand that |
| it is necessary that | must, should |
| it is my (our) recommendation that | I (we) recommend that |
| it is possible that | may, might, can, could |
| make reference to | refer to (or referred) |
| not withstanding the fact that | although |
| on a weekly (daily, monthly, yearly) basis | weekly (daily, monthly, yearly) |
| prior to | about |
| relative to | to |
| subsequent to | after |
| take into consideration | consider |
| there is a chance that | may, might, can, could |
| there is a need for | must |
| until such time as | until |
| we are not in a position on to | we cannot |
| will you be kind enough to | please |
| with reference to | about |
| with regard to | about |
| with respect to | about |

## USE SIMPLE WORDS

You may want to impress your reader, but resist the temptation. Avoid words you rarely use when talking or writing. Many writers think they will impress readers by using *fancy*, less familiar words, such as those listed in Figure 8.5. In technical communication, however, you are more likely to impress readers not with fancy words, but with simple, clear, everyday words.

Your readers prefer familiar words, for example:

## FIGURE 8.4

**Commonly Used Phrases You Can Usually Delete**

| | |
|---|---|
| as a matter of fact | it is interesting to note that |
| I believe | it should be noted that |
| I hope | it should be pointed out that |
| in my opinion | thanking you in advance |
| in other words | the fact that |
| I should point out that | there are |
| I think | there is |
| it is essential | to the extent that |
| it is evident | |

| | |
|---|---|
| Less familiar words | **Pursuant to our conversation** on December 15 |
| Simple, familiar words | **As we discussed** on December 15 |
| Less familiar words | The accounting office will **endeavor** to **procure** our **compensation** checks. |
| Simple, familiar words | The accounting office will **try** to **find** our **paychecks**. |

With technical documents, readers usually need to gather information quickly and with the least amount of effort. Documents that contain fancy, less familiar words take longer to read than documents that employ simple, familiar words.

## USE POSITIVE LANGUAGE WHEN POSSIBLE

When possible, tell readers what something *is*, instead of what it *is not*. Similarly, readers would rather be told what to *do*, rather than what *not to do*. Readers grasp positive language more easily and accurately than negative language. The presence of several negative constructions in a sentence or paragraph slows the pace of reading because readers have to work harder to gather the information and meaning. Figure 8.6 lists some negative phrases and their positive counterparts. You'll discover more as you write.

FIGURE 8.5

**Revising Fancy Phrases**

| Instead of These Fancy Words . . . | Use These Simple Words |
|---|---|
| accumulate | gather |
| apparent | clear |
| ascertain | learn, find out |
| cognizant | aware |
| commence | begin, start |
| commitment | promise |
| deem | consider |
| endeavor | try |
| facilitate | help, ease |
| herewith | here |
| indebtedness | debt |
| initiate | begin |
| locality | place |
| optimum | best, most |
| proceed | go |
| procure | buy, get |
| subsequent to | after, next, later |
| sufficient | enough |
| terminate | end |
| utilize | use |
| whenever | when |

As the following examples show, positive language leads to clearer and often more concise sentences:

Negative     **Do not discontinue taking** the medicine until **none** of the medicine remains.

Positive     **Continue taking** the medicine until it is **all** gone.
or
**Take all** the medicine.

| | |
|---|---|
| **Negative** | Fourteen team members were **not** absent. |
| **Positive** | Fourteen team members **were present**. |
| | |
| **Negative** | Six of the 20 team members did **not attend** the meeting. |
| **Positive** | Fourteen of the 20 team members **attended.** |
| | |
| **Negative** | Even though the area was experiencing severe thunderstorms, the planes **were not late.** |
| **Positive** | Even though the area was experiencing severe thunderstorms, the planes **arrived on time**. |

### FIGURE 8.6

**Examples of Making Negative Language Positive**

| Instead of Saying What Something Is Not ... | Say What It is |
|---|---|
| did not succeed | failed |
| not many | few |
| not all | most |
| not on time | late, delayed |
| not late, not delayed | on time |
| not continue | discontinue |
| not discontinue | continue |
| not efficient | inefficient |
| not sad | happy |
| not accurate | inaccurate |
| not approve | disapprove |
| not disapprove | approve |
| not now | later |
| not familiar | unfamiliar |
| not absent | present |

## USE UNOFFENSIVE LANGUAGE

Communication is in large part perception. When you use offensive language, your readers also perceive your attitude as offensive—even if you do not intend it to be. When you avoid offensive language, you are considerate of your readers and you help break down stereotypes and misperceptions.

## TIPS FOR USING NONSEXIST LANGUAGE

- **Replace gender-specific nouns with nongender-specific nouns when referring to job functions or occupations.** Gender-specific nouns exclude one gender. For example, instead of *chairman* or *chairwoman*, use *chair* or *chairperson*. Instead of *waitress*, use *server*.
- **Use plural nouns to eliminate gender-specific pronouns.** The following examples illustrate how using plural nouns results in nonsexist language:

  | | |
  |---|---|
  | **Sexist** | **Each employee** should maintain **his** equipment and uniforms. |
  | **Nonsexist** | **Employees** should maintain **their** equipment and uniforms. |

  | | |
  |---|---|
  | **Sexist** | **Each teacher** must pass the qualifying test before **she** can receive a contract. |
  | **Nonsexist** | **Teachers** must pass the qualifying test before **they** receive a contract. |

- **To eliminate gender-specific pronouns, use *you* and *your* or the understood *you*.** Often you can avoid sexist language by using second-person pronouns (*you, your*) or the understood *you*. Use second-person pronouns to address your readers directly, as in the following examples:

  | | |
  |---|---|
  | **Sexist** | The user should read the troubleshooting section of the manual before **she** calls the help line. |
  | **Nonsexist** | **You** should read the troubleshooting section of the manual before **you** call the help line. |
  | | *or* |
  | | Read the troubleshooting section of the manual before **you** call the help line. |

- **Use *he or she* or *she or he* to avoid gender-specific pronouns.** Whenever possible, use plural nouns or second-person pronouns to avoid gender-specific pronouns. However, when you can't avoid gender-specific pronouns, use *he or she* or *she or he*. Even though these constructions are awkward, they are clear and inoffensive.

## Use Nonsexist Language

Sexist language inappropriately favors one gender over another. For example, if you refer to firefighters as *firemen*, then you are favoring male firefighters and leaving out female firefighters. This section describes ways to eliminate sexist language. When using nonsexist language, you may find personal pronouns can be especially troublesome. Many writers use *he/she* or *s/he* to eliminate nonsexist language, but these expressions are awkward, especially when they appear several times in a paragraph. The tips on the prior page will help you avoid he/she and s/he constructions and sexist language.

## Use Unoffensive Language When Referring to Persons with Disabilities

You may need to write for or about persons with disabilities—persons who have a physical, sensory, emotional, or mental impairment. When referring to persons with disabilities, focus on the person, not the disability. In her article "People First Language,"[1] Kathie Snow (2008) writes that "the words used to describe a person have a powerful impact on the person's self-image."

**TIPS FOR FOCUSING ON THE PERSON, NOT THE DISABILITY**

*These tips are adapted from Kathie Snow's article, "People First Language."*[1]

- **Use language that focuses on the person, not on the person's disability.** For example, write *people with disabilities* not *the handicapped, the crippled, or the disabled. Handicapped* and *crippled* calls to mind dated, negative images. Similarly, we should write *She has a brain injury* rather than *She is brain damaged*.
- **Refer to the person first, then the disability.** For example, write *the child with autism* instead of *the autistic child*.
- **Use positive, accurate language when referring to persons with disabilities.** For example, rather than writing *She is emotionally disturbed* write *She has a mental-health condition*.

[1] Adapted from Snow, www.disabilityisnatural .com. Used with permission.

 ## CONSIDER YOUR READERS' CULTURE AND LANGUAGE

Many companies do business internationally. When communicating with people in other countries, companies encounter two problems: cultural differences and language interference (Mirshafiei 1994). For example, miscommunication often occurs when people in the United States communicate with people whose cultures value "detailed, subjective analyses" and "philosophical argumentation" (1994, 281). In Middle Eastern cultures, writers

---

[1] Adapted from www.disabilityisnatural.com. Used with permission.

often use what people in the United States regard as overstatement and exaggeration; these writers are "highly rhetorical and use a highly complex and decorative language" (Mirshafiei 1994, 281) that people in the United States often find bewildering. Likewise, many Middle Eastern readers may not understand American writers' tendency for directness and individualism. Misunderstanding and miscommunication result when readers and writers don't understand the cultures that drive and dictate communication styles.

Japanese writers often use "telepathic communication," an indirect communication style that avoids direct confrontation. Telepathic communication allows writers to imply conflicting opinions and keep the communication smooth (Mirshafiei 1994, 281). When the Japanese communicate with people in cultures that expect and value direct, clear, language, miscommunications occur. For example, communication problems occur between people in the United States and people in Japan because the Japanese telepathic communication style conflicts with the direct style that American readers use and expect.

When you communicate with international readers, remember that their culture shapes their communication style, just as your culture shapes yours. An unfamiliar communication style is not inherently wrong or right; it is only different. Do your best to minimize this difference and eliminate potential miscommunications by adapting your communications to your readers' expectations and culture.

## Consider How Your Language Differs from Your Readers' Language

Along with cultural differences, consider language interference. Your international readers will not understand the idioms and technical or workplace language that you use with readers from your country or workplace. *Idioms* are expressions whose meanings differ from the literal or standard meanings of their words. Examples of American idioms include *put up with*, *turn over a new leaf*, and *know the ropes*. International readers can't translate idioms literally; they must memorize their meanings. For example, you might say to your roommate, "Let's run down to McDonald's and grab a burger." You don't literally mean that the two of you should dash to the restaurant and snatch a sandwich from the server. Instead, you mean Let's drive the car to McDonald's and buy something to eat.

When you write for international readers, consider the words and phrases you use so your readers will understand what you mean. Even international readers who speak English well do not understand all the expressions you use. For instance, in the United States, people say *line up* outside a theater box office, but people in England say *queue up*. In everyday speech, you use many words and phrases that international readers will not understand.

## TIPS FOR WRITING FOR INTERNATIONAL READERS

- **Avoid *idioms*—expressions whose meaning is different from the standard or literal meaning of their words.** Most U.S. readers, for example, would realize that *dig in their heels* means that people stubbornly refuse to change their positions. International readers, however, would be more likely to interpret the expression literally and think that people dig holes in the ground with their feet.

- **Only use workplace and technical language that international readers will be familiar or comfortable with.** Avoid terminology that is likely to be unfamiliar to your readers. For example, when writing for readers in Europe, use metric measurements such as kilometers rather than miles.

- **Avoid *localisms*—phrases familiar only to people living in a specific area.** For example, many people in the southern part of the United States use the phrase *fixin' to* as in *I am fixin' to eat lunch*. This phrase sounds odd to people who are not from the South and certainly would sound odd to international readers.

- **Avoid brand names.** Brand names are a type of localism. Many Americans mistakenly use the brand name *Kleenex* to refer to all facial tissues and the brand name *Coke* to refer to all soft drinks. Such brand names will baffle some international readers.

- **Avoid metaphors and allusions.** Metaphors and allusions may refer to or imply a concept or information that is familiar to American readers, but are unfamiliar to international readers. For example, you might write, "After the heated debate, John smoldered for weeks." Some international readers will not understand that *smoldered* is a metaphor for angry.

- **If you must use expressions and terminology that international readers will misinterpret or misunderstand, explain what the words mean.** Try to find and use the corresponding word or phrase in the readers' native language. You can also have your document translated into your readers' language, if there is one. If you select this option, be sure the translator knows the readers' language, country, and culture well enough to translate idioms and workplace and technical language correctly, not just literally.

- **Write simple, clear, complete sentences.** Divide long sentences into two or more shorter sentences. International readers or readers who aren't native speakers of your language will comprehend information more easily in short sentences than in long ones.

- **Use a version of Simplified Technical English.** If nonnative English speakers will read your technical documents, consider using a version of Simplified Technical English. To learn more about Simplified Technical English, see "Taking It into the Workplace," later in this chapter.

Avoid workplace language or technical terminology that would be baffling to international readers—especially to people who have never been to your country or your workplace. For example, the expression *boot up* (referring to turning on the computer and starting its operating system) will be unclear and even humorous to some international readers.

To minimize language interference, follow the tips on the previous page when writing for international readers.

## Writing Your Document for Translation and Localization

You may write a document or website that will be translated into another language. To make your document easy to translate, follow these techniques:

- Use short sentences.
- Use the simplest verb form.
- Use consistent terminology.
- Avoid abbreviations and acronyms.
- Use the active voice.
- Use simple language.
- Use words that have only one meaning.
- Do not use metaphors, localisms, or idioms (including brand names).

### TIPS FOR LOCALIZING DOCUMENTS

- **Avoid country-specific information.** For example, 800 phone numbers are country-specific to the United States.
- **Use the date and address formats appropriate for the locale.** For example, some countries use the 24-hour clock; so you would use multiple formats such as 2:00 p.m./14:00.
- **Know the format for numerical values in the locale.** For example, two million dollars could appear as $2,000,000.00 in American English, $2.000.000 in Spanish, and $2 000 000 in French.
- **Use international symbols.** For example for *stairs*, use ⌐ or for *information*, use ⓘ.
- **Use graphics that you know readers will understood in their language.**

Even when a document's words have been translated word for word, the document still may be ineffective. The document must be adapted to fit the economic, technical, and marketing realities of a particular country or region. For example, a U.S. company that produces heart treatment equipment "introduced its products with a cartoon of happily smiling hearts" (Klein 1997). Although these smiling hearts worked for U.S. readers, German readers were offended by the light treatment of heart disease. Readers in different locales have different rules, data, and cultural expectations.

## What Is Simplified Technical English?

Developed primarily for nonnative English speakers, Simplified Technical English gives writers a basic set of grammar rules, style points, and vocabulary words. The objective of Simplified Technical English is "clear, unambiguous writing" (Boeing 2012, 1). Simplified Technical English was developed by the Aerospace and Defense Industries Association of Europe (ASD). Other versions of simplified languages include Attempto Controlled English, Global English, and the U.S. government's Plain Language specification.

The ASD Simplified Technical English was first published in 1986 as *The AECMA Simplified English (E) Guide*. The guide offers these guidelines for Simplified Technical English:
- simplified grammar and style rules.
- a limited set of approved vocabulary with restricted meanings—each word has a limited number of clearly defined meanings and a limited number of parts of speech (Boeing, 2012).
- guidelines for adding new technical words to the approved vocabulary.

The ASD Simplified Technical English requires writers to use
- active voice
- articles (such as *a* and *the*) wherever possible
- simple verb tenses
- consistent language
- short sentences

Although ASD Simplified Technical English was developed for the aerospace industry, companies in other industries have modified it or produced their own version.

## Assignment

Boeing has adopted ASD Simplified Technical English for its technical documentation and has modified this version for other, general types of technical communication. Boeing has also developed a Simplified Language Checker that can be modified for other types of technical communication. Learn more about Boeing's Simplified English Checker at www.boeing.com.

Search the Internet for at least one company (other than Boeing) that uses a version of Simplified Technical English. When you find one, provide the following information in an email to your instructor:
- name of the company
- version of Simplified English used by the company
- URL for the information you gathered

Source: www.boeing.com/phantom/sechecker/se.html.

# CASE STUDY ANALYSIS

## Why Clear Language Matters

### Background

In May 1996, SabreTech mechanics loaded five cardboard boxes of old oxygen generators into the forward cargo hold of ValuJet Flight 592. These oxygen generators had come to the end of their licensed lifetime; they had *expired* (meaning past their use-by date). ValuJet had provided SabreTech with a seven-step process for determining which generators be loaded into the cargo hold; the second step of this process instructed the workers as follows: *If generator has not been expended, install shipping cap on firing pins* (Stimpson 1998; Langewiesche 1998). This instruction required the 72 SabreTech workers to distinguish between generators that were *expired*—that is, most of the ones they were removing—and generators that were not *expended*—that is, many of the same ones, but still capable of exploding.

Some of these mechanics were temporary employees, and for some, Spanish was their native language. Working under a tight schedule, the mechanics did not clearly distinguish between *expired* and *expended* generators. In fact, many of the generators being loaded onto ValuJet 592 were expired but not expended; that is, they could still explode. Most of them should have had the shipping caps placed on the pins, but they did not. With five boxes of potentially explosive generators in the cargo hold, ValuJet 592 took off. Less than six minutes later, the plane crashed into Florida's Everglades Holiday Park. Two pilots, three flight attendants, and 105 passengers died in the crash.

The engineers who wrote the instructions clearly understood the distinction between *expired* and *expended*. This distinction, however, was not clear to all the mechanics.

### Assignment

Search the Internet for a disaster or problem created by unclear language. In a memo to your classmates and instructor

- Summarize the disaster or problem.
- Explain how language contributed (or caused) the disaster or problem.
- Tell your readers where you found the information.
- Document your sources.

# EXERCISES

DOWNLOAD A WORKSHEET FOR USING READER-FOCUSED LANGUAGE ONLINE AT
WWW.GRTEP.COM

1. Rewrite these sentences, substituting specific language for vague language. Add details and examples to make the language specific.
   a. The dryers in the laundry room are acting funny.
   b. The results of the survey will be available soon.
   c. Please turn in your project ASAP.
   d. The profits of our foreign offices increased significantly.

2. Rewrite these sentences to eliminate misplaced modifiers.
   a. A brochure about the scholarship program is enclosed with the application that gives complete details.
   b. The study suggests that we should continue the recycling program to the city and the council.
   c. The police shot the protesters with guns.
   d. The technician banged angrily on the flashlight in the laboratory that was dimly lighted.
   e. As a soccer mom, Mrs. Garcia's van was always full of soccer players.
   f. After returning to his office, Patrick's phone rang.
   g. Like Jessica, Sarah's automobile insurance went up after her speeding ticket.

3. Rewrite these sentences to eliminate dangling modifiers.
   a. After six months as an exchange student in Italy, the United States was a wonderful sight.
   b. Running to the meeting, her flash drive was lost.
   c. During discussions with the architect, it was determined that the building needed a new elevator shaft.
   d. After testing the new airbag, the new design was approved for delivery to the factory.
   e. At the age of 18, my parents bought me a new car.
   f. The software was upgraded in time for the December meeting by working overtime.

4. Rewrite these sentences to eliminate stacked nouns.
    a. The school district technology innovation committee meeting will begin at 6:00 p.m. in the district technology center.
    b. The report states that investigation modifications occurred after the study enrollment period.
    c. The teacher recommended that the students allow time for a writing center tutor analysis of their research papers.
    d. The human resources benefit task force will recommend a revised employee tuition reimbursement policy.

5. Rewrite these sentences to eliminate faulty word choices.
    a. After the town hall meeting, the citizens were revolting.
    b. The teacher was mad.
    c. The operators were held up in the briefing room.
    d. The tailor pressed his suit in court.

6. Revise these sentences to eliminate redundant words and phrases.
    a. This important and significant network upgrade should help each and every employee to work more efficiently and effectively.
    b. When you complete the programming, we will document the software fully and completely.
    c. To enhance the marketing of our new line of computers, we are offering free gifts to the first 100 shoppers.
    d. The pipe to the main generator rarely ever leaks.
    e. The designer plans to paint the auditorium walls green in color and to repeat the color again in the foyer.
    f. We have a very unique opportunity to see the future plans for the training center.
    g. It is my personal opinion that we should again repeat the study to determine the very latest enrollment trends.

7. Rewrite these sentences to eliminate unnecessary words and to condense wordy phrases. Correct any other style errors you find in the sentences.
    a. There are several scientists who are uneasy about the end results of the water quality tests.
    b. Preparedness for an attack involving biological agents is complicated by the large number of potential agents (most of which are rarely encountered naturally).

c. It is important that we turn in our applications by the required deadline.

d. As a matter of fact, we will be offering the vaccines again next month.

e. You should check the roof for damage on a yearly basis.

f. The majority of the citizens support the tax rebate, but have not taken into consideration the cost to educational programs.

g. With reference to the revised design, it is possible that not withstanding the fact that we have a good design, we should still conduct a discussion on ways to improve it.

h. It is interesting to note that at the conclusion of the council meeting, most of the opponents of the hands-free cell phone policy had left.

i. Until such time as the new health plan goes into effect, all employees should continue to file claims according to the current plan without further delay.

j. It is my understanding that the higher electricity rates will begin in August.

8. Revise these sentences, replacing fancy words with simple words. Correct any other style errors you find in the sentences.

a. The new tuition plan will commence for the fall semester of next year.

b. During this time of heightened national security alerts, bomb threats are proliferating nationwide.

c. To obtain optimum performance from your vehicle, you should endeavor to follow the maintenance program furnished in the owner's manual.

d. We are cognizant of the fact that you are attempting to facilitate our reimbursement for the damaged equipment that we purchased.

e. We will try to ascertain the opinions of the students through a survey.

9. Change the negative words to positive words in these sentences.

a. You should not treat any customer or coworker unprofessionally or discourteously.

b. Since the construction team did not know of the crack in the wall before they began their work, they could not repair the wall according to their original estimate.

c. Not many of the racers finished the triathlon because of the extreme heat and humidity.

d. Even though the plane was delayed because of thunderstorms, we were not late to the meeting.

e. Only ten percent of the students were not absent.

10. These sentences contain offensive language. Revise the sentences, replacing the offensive language with unoffensive language. You may change singular nouns to plural nouns when appropriate.
    a. Before the plane made an emergency landing, the stewardess checked the children's seatbelts.
    b. Each student should discuss his degree plan with his adviser at least two years before his planned graduation.
    c. The network operator should read instructions before she installs the updates.
    d. Many shoes contain man-made materials.
    e. The ramp will help handicapped students.
    f. The school district has a program for autistic children.

11. Assume that international readers or nonnative English speakers will read these sentences. Eliminate language these readers may not understand.
    a. Before the weekly meeting, our manager told us to stick to our guns when answering questions about what our employees need to complete the project.
    b. After the midterm exam, we walked to our apartment and crashed.
    c. The victims of the hurricane need medical supplies such as Band-Aids®, Kleenex®, and alcohol.
    d. After the meeting, the team needed to get their bearings.
    e. An iPad® was given to each member who completed the questionnaire.

chapter *nine*

# Building Persuasive Arguments

iStockphoto 2008.

Y ou have probably been in the position of having someone try to persuade you to do something, or you may have been the one doing the persuading. You might have tried to persuade someone to go out to eat or to help you with a volunteer project. You might have prepared a résumé and cover letter to persuade an employer to interview you. We use persuasion in our daily communication. *Persuasion* is the process of convincing others to act in a certain way or accept a viewpoint.

In the workplace, you will use persuasion both informally and formally. You may use persuasion for a situation as informal as convincing your manager to buy additional office supplies or as formal as convincing a client to hire your organization for some kind of service. You may also use persuasion to bring a group to consensus. Whether the persuasion is formal or informal, you use the same process and techniques for building persuasive arguments.

In this chapter, you will learn how to build a persuasive argument and how to deliver that argument effectively. At the end of this chapter, you will study samples of effective written persuasion. In the workplace, you will also be called on to deliver an effective verbal argument. This chapter will help you to build the argument, and Chapter 20 will help you to deliver that argument.

## IDENTIFY YOUR DESIRED OUTCOME

In building any argument, you begin by identifying the desired outcome: what you want to achieve. After you have determined this outcome, you need to consider how your audience might react.

### Consider How Your Audience Might React

Your audience may react positively to your desired outcome. On the other hand, they may resist or reject it. You should anticipate how your audience might react, so you can prepare an argument that addresses those potential reactions. Consider these guidelines:

- **Expect some audience members to disagree.** Regardless of the logic or the worth of your desired outcome, some audience members may disagree. Be prepared for your audience to see your desired outcome from a viewpoint different from yours. For example: You try to persuade your manager that your division needs an additional employee to share the workload because you and your coworkers have been working 50-hour weeks for the past six months. You know that your coworkers agree with you and that you can document the overtime. However, your manager could disagree because the company does not have the money to hire a new employee or your manager may not see a problem with working overtime.
- **Be prepared for resistance and for alternative ideas.** Prepare as though your audience will resist your desired outcome or will offer another idea. Be ready to listen, to consider the idea, and to be flexible. You don't have to accept a new idea; however, if the idea is reasonable and you can accept it, be flexible. Don't be defensive if some or all of your audience disagrees. Instead, listen sincerely.
- **Tailor your arguments to the audience.** Before you prepare your argument, research your audience and put yourself in your audience's shoes: If you were in their place, how would you see the desired outcome? Let's consider your request for an additional employee in your division. From your vantage point, your desired outcome is ideal. Now, look at the request from your manager's vantage point: How much will it cost? Where will the funds come from? Can you propose a more cost-effective way to reduce the employees' workload? To successfully persuade your manager, you need to consider these questions and then tailor your arguments to answer these questions.

- **Make sure your desired outcome is reasonable and appropriate.** You have a responsibility to offer reasonable arguments. Let's return to your request for another employee. You know that an experienced employee would be a good fit, but experienced employees come at a higher salary than less experienced ones. You also know that the company is cutting back in other divisions. Should you ask for the experienced employee at a higher salary, knowing that someone with less experience could do the job? You have to weigh these options in light of the company's situation and your manager's viewpoint. When you develop arguments, be sure they are reasonable and be willing to adjust your desired outcome when appropriate.

When you have considered how your audience may react to your recommendation, you can build an effective argument. Figure 9.1 illustrates the process of building a persuasive argument.

> Anticipate how your audience may react, so you can prepare an effective argument that addresses those reactions.

 ## CONSIDER THE CONSTRAINTS THAT COULD IMPACT YOUR ARGUMENT

Once you have determined your desired outcome and anticipated how your audience might react, you are ready to consider the constraints that could impact your argument. ***Constraints***

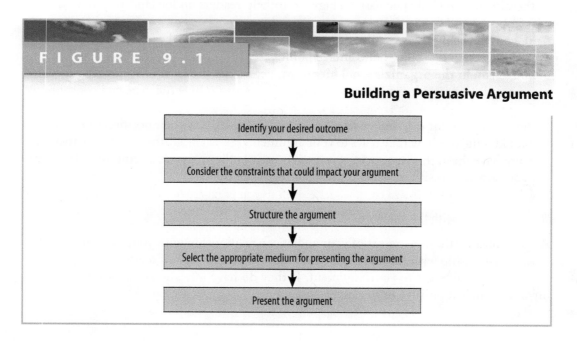

### FIGURE 9.1

**Building a Persuasive Argument**

Identify your desired outcome

↓

Consider the constraints that could impact your argument

↓

Structure the argument

↓

Select the appropriate medium for presenting the argument

↓

Present the argument

restrict or limit the actions of you and/or others. For example, if you plan to propose hiring an employee when your company has a hiring freeze, the freeze is a constraint that impacts your desired outcome. As you prepare your arguments, consider these constraints: the audience's situation and your workplace.

## Audience Constraints

Your audience will view your argument from their personal situation. They may react positively or negatively to your argument based on their situation. As you prepare your argument, consider how the following constraints could influence your audience members' reactions.

### Their Place in the Organizational Hierarchy

Whether your audience members are internal or external to your organization, their place in the organizational hierarchy influences how they will react to your argument. If you are trying to persuade *internal audience members* who are

- **below you in the organizational hierarchy,** they may feel pressured to agree with your argument. In this context, assure your audience that you want their honest reactions, and make them feel comfortable disagreeing with you. If you cannot change your argument, you could send a directive (see Chapter 14 to learn about writing directives). In the directive, include persuasive language to help readers understand why the directive is important to them.
- **at your level in the organizational hierarchy (your coworkers),** your job is easier because you understand their vantage point.
- **above you in the organizational hierarchy,** determine the level of formality and detail expected. Your argument is more persuasive when you follow the expected conventions.

If you are writing for *external audience members*, consider how their position in the hierarchy could influence how they react to your argument. For example, these audience members may not have the authority to accept your argument or they may feel uncomfortable accepting your argument without seeking the counsel of their peers.

### Your Relationship with the Audience

As you consider the constraints of your audience's relationship with you, ask yourself: Do I have a relationship with the audience? If not, how does that lack of relationship affect how the audience will react to your argument. If they do have a relationship with you or your organization, is it positive or negative?

When audience members don't know you or your organization, they may resist your argument because they don't know if you are trustworthy. You must persuade them that you are a qualified professional and that your organization is of high quality. If the audience members have a negative view of you or your organization, they may not have confidence in your argument or they may believe they cannot trust you or your organization. To persuade these audience members, spend time rebuilding that relationship and assuring them they can trust you.

### The Audience's Familiarity with the Topic

Your audience members might resist or reject your argument because they are unfamiliar with the topic. When we encounter a new topic, we may initially resist or reject it because we don't understand it. Your audience may react similarly. Find out what your audience knows about the topic. If they are unfamiliar with it, as part of your persuasive appeal, educate them about the topic.

## Workplace Constraints

These workplace constraints may impact both you and your audience:
- time and budget
- legal constraints
- ethical constraints
- political constraints

### Time and Budget

Time and especially budget are powerful workplace constraints. They could limit or block your audience from accepting your desired outcome regardless of its merit. You may have to adjust your desired outcome to accommodate your budget and time constraints or those of your audience. In other cases, you may have an excellent idea, but you may not have the time to prepare an effective argument—especially if you must present the argument in writing. As you prepare your argument, create a schedule by working backward from your document's due date. This schedule can help you determine if you have the time and resources to present an effective argument and if your audience has the time and/or resources to implement your proposal.

## Legal Constraints

Before you present your argument, be sure you are observing all the legalities. If you don't know if your desired outcome is legal, contact your organization's legal counsel. If your organization doesn't have legal counsel, find an attorney on your own. *If you doubt the legality of your desired outcome, don't present it.*

## Ethical Constraints

As with any workplace decision, ask yourself if your desired outcome and your means of achieving that outcome are ethical. Follow your professional code of conduct and your organization's ethical guidelines. If your profession or organization does not have established guidelines, follow those in Chapter 4. You have a responsibility to all involved to do the right thing.

## Political Constraints

What is the political climate at your workplace? For example, if you know your coworkers and manager disagree with your idea or that the idea has been proposed and rejected already, consider revising your idea or dropping it. You will gain credibility with your manager and coworkers when you do your homework before presenting an argument.

What are the chances your desired outcome will be rejected? You don't want to lose credibility or waste your time (or that of your coworkers and manager) by proposing something you know will be rejected. However, if by not presenting your idea you will violate legal or ethical guidelines, then you must present your argument as you intended (see Chapter 4 for information on legal and ethical guidelines).

## STRUCTURE A PERSUASIVE ARGUMENT

A persuasive argument has three elements:
- **claim:** your desired outcome
- **evidence:** what supports your claim
- **appeal:** why the audience should accept your claim

The *claim* is the outcome that you want your audience to accept. For example, your claim may be that your company should move to a four-day workweek. You want your audience (the company executives) to implement this idea.

The *evidence* is the information you use to support your claim. This evidence might be facts, statistics, examples, or testimonials. Let's consider your proposal for a four-day workweek. Your evidence might include the following:

- The company would save on janitorial services and energy costs.
- Two of our competitors, Design Ads and Pinnacle, have moved to a four-day workweek and have seen less absenteeism because employees schedule medical and personal appointments on their extra day off.
- Employees would spend less on gas and would have less wear and tear on their vehicles.
- Employees would drive to work one less day a week, reducing harmful emissions that cause ozone pollution.
- In a survey of our employees last month, 83 percent said they would prefer a four-day schedule. In that same survey, employees were asked if they would be willing to work a 10-hour day if they were to work four days a week; 87 percent said yes.

The *appeal* explains why the audience should accept the claim. Evidence alone may not be enough to persuade your audience members to accept your desired outcome or to change their minds. You must also appeal to their needs and values (Rottenberg 1991). Let's consider some possible appeals for your proposal for a four-day workweek:

- The company will save money.
- Employees will be more productive.
- The company will be more environmentally responsible.
- Employee morale will improve.
- Other companies have found this model successful.

These appeals link directly to the evidence, as shown in Figure 9.2.

## FIGURE 9.2

**Linking the Appeal to the Evidence for a Four-Day Workweek**

| Appeal | Evidence |
|---|---|
| Saving the company money | Reduced janitorial services<br>Reduced energy costs |
| Increased productivity | Lower absenteeism |
| Improved environmental responsibility | Reduced harmful emissions that cause ozone pollution |
| Improved employee morale | Survey results |
| Successful at other companies | Information from our competitors, DesignAds and Pinnacle |

## Types of Evidence

Evidence is a powerful piece of your argument. Without evidence, you will rarely persuade your audience to accept your claim. Audiences will also expect your evidence to be credible.

Your arguments are most effective when you use the following types of evidence:
- facts
- statistics
- examples
- expert testimony

### Facts

**Facts** are evidence that you or your audience can verify. A fact can be observed, demonstrated, or measured. For example, the statements below are facts that an audience can verify.

| Factual evidence | Hybrid cars use less gasoline than gasoline-only cars. |
| Factual evidence | With a four-day workweek, employees will spend less on gas and experience less wear-and-tear on their vehicles. |

## Statistics

*Statistics*, or numerical data, make your arguments highly persuasive. For example, look at the following statements.

| Statistical evidence | In a survey of employees last month, 83 percent said they would prefer working a four-day week. In that same survey, 87 percent said they would prefer working a 10-hour day if they worked four days per week. |

In these statements, the numerical information (83 percent and 87 percent) supports the claim to move to a four-day workweek. When possible, use statistics to support your argument; however, when you use such data, make sure that readers can understand it and that it is accurate and ethical.

### TIPS FOR PRESENTING PERSUASIVE EVIDENCE

- **Present credible, verifiable evidence.** Audiences expect you to present credible evidence that they can verify. If you present evidence that's unverifiable, you will quickly lose credibility with your audience.
- **Focus on the best evidence.** You may be tempted to present every possible piece of evidence, thinking you can persuade your audience with the quantity of evidence. However, your argument will be more convincing if you select the strongest evidence to support your claim. As one professional put it, "When presenting your argument, less is more."*
- **Cite your sources.** If you present your argument in writing, include a list of references and/or footnotes. If you present your argument orally, tell your audience where your sources came from and/or prepare a handout listing them.

* Source: W. Sims, personal interview.

## Examples

*Examples* help audiences to understand abstract information and to remember and identify with your argument. Examples, especially when coupled with statistics, make powerful arguments. The following example helps the audience understand what a four-day workweek could do for an employee and for the company.

> **Example**      Rachel Olsin takes off an average of four hours a week to assist her 92-year-old parents. As their only living child, Rachel is the sole caretaker and the only person who can take them to the doctor. If she was able to work four days a week, she could schedule the appointments on her extra day off and lessen her absenteeism.

## Expert Testimony

You are probably familiar with *expert testimony* from television shows and movies where an expert testifies at a trial. If unbiased, an expert's input lends credibility to your argument. However, if the expert is biased, his or her input can damage your argument and your credibility. If you decide to use an expert as part of your argument, make sure you select an expert(s) with credentials that the audience will recognize as valid. Let's look at an example:

> **Expert Testimony**      Vicki Peake, CEO of DesignAds, reports that since her company moved to a four-day workweek in 2009, employee absenteeism has dropped by 25 percent.

This expert testimony is credible because the writer includes her credentials, which this audience would recognize as valid.

## Types of Appeals

Use the following appeals to convince your audience to accept your claim:
- Appeal to shared goals and values.
- Appeal to common sense.
- Appeal by recognizing the opposing viewpoint/evidence.
- Appeal to the audience's emotion.

### Appeal to Shared Goals and Values

Our goals are shaped by our values. *Values* are characteristics that we live by (integrity, honesty, loyalty, friendship, fairness, etc.). Even though these values and goals do not constitute evidence, they do influence how audiences react to arguments. If, for example, an audience values fairness and integrity, use those values when you present your evidence. By identifying these shared goals and values, you structure a more effective argument. Shared goals and values are especially effective when trying to build consensus.

For example, if you are trying to convince employees that a four-day workweek is a good idea, you could appeal to the common goals of spending less money on gas and increasing time for personal activities. Most employees will share these goals. When presenting that same claim to company executives, you would appeal to their common goal of saving the company money.

## Appeal to Common Sense

For some arguments, you may not have evidence to support your claim, but you know the claim is sound. For those arguments, appeal to your audience's common sense. **Common sense** is a sound judgment based on a reasonable perception of the situation or facts. For example, common sense dictates that you register for classes early because you have a better chance of getting the classes you want. Or, you arrive at the theater early to get a better seat. In our argument for a four-day workweek, we might use the following appeal to common sense:

> A four-day workweek makes sense because gasoline prices have increased by almost 25 percent, negatively affecting employees' wallets.

If your audience members share your commonsense argument, you will communicate to them more persuasively. However, you cannot rely solely on commonsense appeals. You must augment your argument with sound evidence.

## Appeal by Recognizing the Opposing Viewpoint or Evidence

To gain credibility with your audience, recognize the opposing viewpoint or evidence. Many arguments fail because the person presenting the argument does not recognize and appropriately respond to opposing viewpoints and evidence. For example, an opposing viewpoint to the four-day workweek might be that employees will be less productive. You could respond to this viewpoint as follows:

> You may be concerned that with fewer workdays, employees will be less productive because of the 25 percent increase in work hours per day. I, too, was concerned with this potential productivity loss; however, the CEOs of both Design Ads and Pinnacle report that when their companies moved to this shorter workweek, employees were as productive as they were during the traditional five-day workweek. These executives report that in some departments, employees were more productive.

When faced with opposing viewpoints and evidence, address them by using these tactics.

- **Respectfully recognize the opposing viewpoint and evidence.** Be careful to treat an opposing viewpoint professionally and objectively. Avoid subjective statements such as This argument has no merit or I'm not sure how anyone could believe this so-called evidence.
- **Focus on the viewpoint, not on the person(s) holding that viewpoint.** You want to keep the good will not only of the person(s) with the opposing viewpoint, but also with the audience. If you appear to attack or act disrespectfully toward others, you will lose much of your power to communicate persuasively.
- **Address the merits of the opposing viewpoint or evidence.** To keep the good will and gain the trust of your audience, recognize the merits of opposing viewpoint—especially if your audience holds that viewpoint.
- **Explain the merits of your argument.** Focus on the merits of your argument, not on subjective statements such as This method is so much better. Instead, demonstrate why the method is better.

### Appeal to Emotion

Emotional appeals are effective when used responsibly. You use them responsibly when you combine them with appeals to shared goals and values and with sound evidence. An example of an emotional appeal appears in Figure 9.3. In this request for donations, Big Brothers Big Sisters appeals to the audience members' emotions with the photo and the second-person pronouns *you* and *your*. The writers combine the emotional appeal with an appeal to shared goals and values ("It's not just a donation. It's an investment in a child's future.")

## SELECT THE APPROPRIATE MEDIUM FOR PRESENTING YOUR ARGUMENT

Once you have structured and written or rehearsed your argument, you are ready to present it (see the chapters in Part IV for information on writing and presenting persuasive arguments). You begin by deciding on the best medium for that presentation. Will you present it orally? Will you present it in writing? Which format will you use? Once you have determined the medium, follow the Tips for Presenting Your Argument Persuasively on the next page to present an effective argument.

## TIPS FOR PRESENTING YOUR ARGUMENT PERSUASIVELY

- **Present yourself as a professional, reasonable person.** Many arguments are won or lost based on the presenter's *persona*. If you appear to be a professional, reasonable person, your audience will be more likely to listen to your arguments. In most cases, you will not win an argument based solely on your *persona*; however, if you present yourself as unreasonable and/or unprofessional, you will rarely win your argument.
- **Acknowledge the contributions, knowledge, and ideas of others.** If others have helped you develop your argument or idea, acknowledge their contributions. When appropriate, acknowledge the contributions, knowledge, and ideas of your audience. When you acknowledge these contributions you add power to your argument.
- **Don't oversell.** You can oversell in these ways: by using unsupported subjective language, by including too much evidence, or by continuing to push your idea when your audience members are no longer interested or are not going to change their minds. If you can't get your audience to agree, save your argument for a later time or, if appropriate, drop it.
- **Don't be defensive.** When someone in your audience disagrees with you, respectfully consider the argument. Keep an open mind. If you get defensive, your audience may assume that you lack the evidence to support your argument or that your argument is unsound.
- **Present well-designed documents and graphics.** Well-designed documents and graphics add credibility to your argument. Likewise, if the documents are sloppy and poorly designed, you lose credibility. Follow the guidelines in Chapters 10 and 11 as you prepare your documents and graphics.

 **SAMPLE DOCUMENTS**

The following sample documents illustrate how writers have crafted persuasive arguments appropriate to the situation and the audience. Figure 9.3 presents a page from a website for a nonprofit organization. Figure 9.4 presents a page from a website for a community-minded construction company. Figure 9.5 presents a page from a promotional brochure for an oven.

FIGURE 9.3

## Using Appeals to Emotion and to Shared Goals and Values to Persuade

### It's not just a donation. It's an investment in a child's future.

When you donate online to Big Brothers Big Sisters, you join our cause and directly support children in your community. No matter how little or big the amount, donating can start making a difference in the lives of young people around you.

### Donating pays dividends.

Research shows that our mentoring works. Children with a Big Brother or Big Sister show real differences in their personal and academic lives. They are more confident in their schoolwork performance, they get along better with their families and they're 52% less likely to skip school.[1]

### Your support goes far.

Your financial support helps us provide our programs and services nationally and in your local community—so we can develop more college grads, community leaders and entrepreneurs.

Roughly 90% of every dollar you give goes directly to making and supporting matches between Littles and Bigs. Great Nonprofits, a leading provider of reviews and ratings of nonprofit organizations throughout the U.S, has ranked Big Brothers Big Sisters of America as a top Children's and Families Nonprofit and awarded us a 5-star rating. This means you can rest assured that we are using donations wisely.

Your financial support starts lots of things, like:
• recruiting new Big Brother and Big Sister volunteers
• covering the costs of background checks, while ensuring trained professionals match Littles to responsible Bigs
• enabling ongoing supervision and relationship support for every Big, Little and Little's family
• providing cultural and social activities to enrich the opportunities for children

Become a part of the Big Brothers Big Sisters family today.      Donate now>

[1] Tierney, J.P., Grossman, J.B., and Resch, N.L. (1995) Making a Difference: An Impact Study of Big Brothers Big Sisters. Philadelphia: Public/Private Ventures

Source: Copyright © 2012 by Big Brothers Big Sisters. Reprinted by permission.

**Persuading Customers and Potential Employees about a Company's Commitment to Supporting the Community**

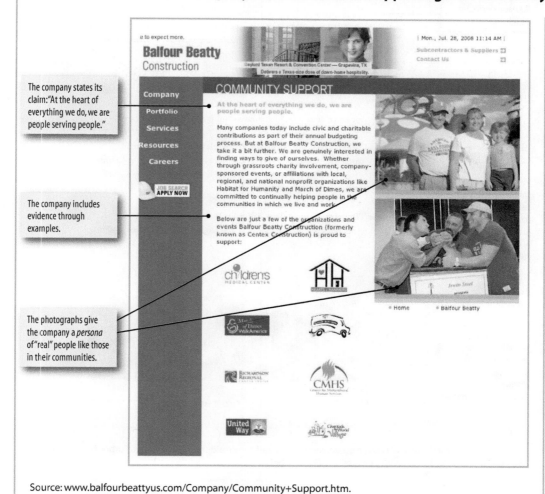

The company states its claim: "At the heart of everything we do, we are people serving people."

The company includes evidence through examples.

The photographs give the company a *persona* of "real" people like those in their communities.

Source: www.balfourbeattyus.com/Company/Community+Support.htm.

## FIGURE 9.5

**Persuading a Consumer**

The claim is implied in the title.

### An oven for *your* time.

A meal can say many things. It says welcome home, thank you, or relax. It says let's celebrate. And it always says you care.

Meals can make friends, nurture relationships, and create memories that last forever. But at today's busy pace – with our lives overflowing with daily tasks – finding time to serve great meals is a real challenge.

The claim is stated in the last line of the first page: "gives you the freedom to be the cook you want to be more often."

To help you meet this challenge, TurboChef introduces the oven that *gives you the freedom to be the cook you want to be more often.*

The writers use design and graphics to make the persuasion more effective.

turbochef.com  866.54ENJOY

Source: *TurboChef 30 Double Wall Oven Guide:* www.turbochef.com/residential/shared/pdf/TurboChef-30Double-Wall-Oven.pdf, page 1. Used with permission of TurboChef.

# FIGURE 9.5

**Persuading a Consumer** *continued*

## Our oven is designed around *you.*

TurboChef is dedicated to providing a real solution for your lifestyle. From the fashionable retro-modern styling to the easy-to-use controls to the amazing cooking performance, our oven gives you more freedom.

**Introducing the TurboChef 30" Speedcook Ovens – Single and Double Wall.**

The writers use statistics and examples as evidence.

Imagine cooking with a touch of magic. Steamed asparagus – perfectly al dente – in 45 seconds. A rack of lamb in 4 minutes. A 12 pound Thanksgiving turkey in 42 minutes. From family favorites to a gourmet dinner, our oven enables you to cook fresh, delicious food up to 15 times faster than conventional methods with the flavor and quality endorsed by four-star chefs. Meats are caramelized, moist and tender. Baked goods are golden and flaky. And, vegetables come out crisp, succulent and nutritious.

The writers use the appeal to shared goals and values: The audience is busy but still wants to serve great meals.

Whether it's dinner on a busy Wednesday night, a dinner party for friends on Saturday night, or a once-a-year special occasion, *the TurboChef oven gives you the freedom to be the cook you want to be more often.*

turbochef.com  866-548-8JOY

TAKING IT INTO THE *workplace*

## Persuasion and Leadership

Persuasion is an important component of every professional's toolbox. How you use that tool is important to your success in leading others in the workplace. As Lois Zachary, author of *Rekindling the Art of Persuasion* (2008), explains

> We live in a world where the command and control model of persuasion just doesn't work anymore. Achievement, money, and status no longer persuade but actually raise the level of skepticism. Positional power is slowly being replaced by personal power and new strategies are being used to connect and reconnect with the people with whom we do business. Getting someone to "buy in" to something and commit to it is a more effective approach than authority-based management.

If you want to persuade your coworkers, your managers, or your clients to "buy in" to your products and ideas, you have to convince them to take part in your vision (Zachary 2008). You must effectively lead them to not only go along with your ideas or product, but to want to be a part.

In the workplace, you may lead a team of coworkers or you may manage a large team. As a leader, you will need to persuade others. Use the techniques presented in this chapter to develop and present those arguments.

## Assignment

Interview a professional in your field (see Chapter 5 for information on interviews). You may conduct your interview in person, by phone, or by email. At the interview, ask the professional about (1) how he or she uses persuasion in informal meetings to convince others to accept his or her ideas as and (2) in these settings, what techniques has he or she found successful and unsuccessful.

Email a summary of your interview to your instructor.

# CASE STUDY ANALYSIS

## Persuading a City Council

### Background

In 1992, a solid majority of the New York City Council voted to approve a controversial garbage disposal plan. Interestingly, only one month prior to the vote, the measure was considered dead. What persuaded the council was "education," according to Bill Lynch Jr., the political lobbyist and mastermind for then-mayor David Dinkins.

City council members are reluctant to approve unpopular or unpleasant measures. In this case, garbage incineration was unpopular. To complicate matters, this garbage plan would have ramifications far into the future and would leave the door open for building more incinerators. No council member wanted to be responsible for putting an incinerator in their constituents' backyard.

The mayor and his associates began a program to educate the council. They used a variety of methods to persuade council members to support the plan: phone calls, discussions, action on local problems, and rewrites of the plan. Ultimately, the mayor dropped two incinerators and an ash landfill from the plan and agreed to include more future recycling.

Dinkins and Lynch were satisfied with the vote. Their success resulted from persuasion rather than strong-arm tactics.

### Assignment

1.  Imagine that you are Bill Lynch. Write a memo to the city council members, persuading them to support the mayor's garbage plan. Consider your readers' resistance to the plan, the constraints they face, and the relationship of the mayor's office to the council members. Turn in your memo to your instructor. For evidence to support your arguments, research the garbage incineration process using the techniques you learned in Chapter 5.

# EXERCISES

DOWNLOAD A WORKSHEET FOR BUILDING PERSUASIVE ARGUMENTS ONLINE AT
WWW.GRTEP.COM

1. Visit the website of a major company such as Dow (www.dow.com), Exxon (www.exxonmobil.com), or GE (www.GE.com). Evaluate how the company presents information about its commitment to its communities and the environment.
   a. Identify the stated or implied claim about the company's commitment to the environment and the community. If the claim is implied, what words and graphics does the site use to make the claim?
   b. Identify the types of evidence the company uses. Consider both the words and the graphics.
   c. Identify the appeals. Consider both the words and the graphics.
   d. Write a memo to your instructor. In your memo, use the information in Exercises 1a-1c to identify whether the company presented an effective argument. (For information on writing memos, see Chapter 12.)

2. Find a sales brochure for the same type of product from two companies. The purpose of these brochures must be to persuade a consumer to purchase the product.
   a. Write a memo to your instructor comparing and contrasting the persuasive evidence and appeals used in the two brochures. (For information on comparison and contrast, see Chapter 6.)
   b. Attach a copy of the two brochures to your memo.

## Understanding How Nonprofits Use Persuasion

Your community has many nonprofit organizations that work to improve lives and the environment. Identify one nonprofit organization in your community. You might consider animal shelters, food banks, or organizations that help children or senior adults. Once you have selected an organization, visit the organization's website or offices to look at how they persuade people to donate and to volunteer.

Write a memo to your instructor. In the memo
- Identify the appeals the organization uses. Consider both the words and the graphics.
- Identify the evidence the organization uses. Consider both the words and the graphics.
- Explain why the persuasion was effective. Consider whether you would volunteer or donate based on the appeals and evidence.
- Attach the documents you gathered and/or provide the URL for the organization's website.

## chapter *ten*

# Designing Reader-Focused Documents

eaders form an impression of your document before they begin to read it. They draw this impression in part from the design elements—or lack of them. These elements contribute to a favorable or unfavorable picture of your document and possibly you and your organization. Design elements such as headings, type size, color, page layout, and white space affect the readability, success, and effectiveness of a document. These elements also help readers locate information and motivate them to read. In this chapter, you will learn the principles of designing documents that will favorably impress your readers.

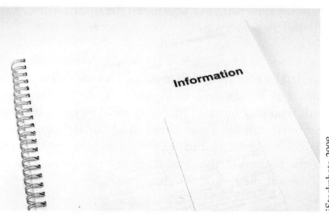

iStockphoto 2008.

## PRINCIPLES OF EFFECTIVE DESIGN

In *The Non-Designer's Design Book* (2008), Robin Williams suggests the following principles for designing effective documents:

- contrast
- repetition
- alignment
- proximity

In the following sections, you will learn about how to apply these principles.

## Contrast

You create *contrast* when two elements on a page are different. For example, when you put white text on a black background, you create contrast through color. For effective contrast the elements must be clearly different—not just sort of different (Williams 2008). For example, you cannot create contrast by making one element dark blue and one element black; the colors are too similar.

Contrast enables you to
- **create interest on the page.** When a page has visual interest, readers are more likely to pay attention to the page and read it.
- **show how you have organized the information.** Take advantage of contrast to reveal to readers the structure of your document.

Let's look at an example. Figure 10.1 demonstrates effective contrast. Notice the contrast created by the reversed type. *Reversed type* occurs when white or light-colored type appears on a dark background. In Figure 10.1, the reversed type beginning with "studies show that kids who play outside" contrasts with the green background. The figure also demonstrates contrast with the Texas Parks and Wildlife logo. The dark green logo contrasts with the lighter background. Finally, the colors in the photo of the girl contrast with the light green at the bottom of the document. See more examples of contrast in the sample document designs at the end of this chapter.

## Repetition

You use the principle of *repetition* when you repeat some aspect of the design throughout the document (Williams 2008). You might repeat a color, a graphic element, a logo, or an icon. You also create repetition by using the same layout and location for related elements. For example, the first-level headings in this book are consistent throughout; the repeated format distinguishes first-level headings from second-level headings and from the paragraphs. Repetition unifies a document and adds visual interest.

FIGURE 10.1

**A Document That Demonstrates Contrast, Repetition, Alignment, and Proximity**

Source: Downloaded from the World Wide Web, June 2009: www.tpwd.state.tx.us/publications/pwdpubs/media/pwd_lf_k0700_1660b.pdf. Texas Parks and Wildlife Department, "Life's Better Outside" poster, (PWD LF K0700-1660B).

Figure 10.1 demonstrates repetition through color. Light green appears three times: the background for the list, the foliage in the smaller photograph, and the grass in the upper left corner of the larger photo (look at the callouts on the figure).

## Alignment

Use the principle of *alignment* to unify elements on a page by visually connecting them. When you follow the principle of alignment, you don't simply place items wherever there happens to be room. Instead, you align every item with the edge of another item on the page. For example, in Figure 10.1, the heading—Studies show that kids who play outside—aligns with the list and the statement that begins Learn more. This alignment visually connects the text and leads the readers to scan the list. If the features were placed wherever the designer had space, readers would not know if or how the elements were related.

## Proximity

Use the principle of *proximity* to group related items. When related, or like, elements are closely grouped, they appear to be a cohesive group instead of a bunch of unrelated items (Williams 2008). Unrelated elements should not be in proximity. Proximity visually organizes information or graphic elements on a page. For example, in Figure 10.1, the list and its related heading are close together. Their proximity shows that the heading and list are related.

## ENVISION THE DOCUMENT DESIGN AS YOU PLAN YOUR DOCUMENT

To save yourself time and frustration, envision the design elements as you identify your readers and their purpose for reading. If you wait until you have written one or more drafts, you may not have time to incorporate the design elements you want or the readers need. Or, you may have to spend unnecessary time reformatting the text to fit your design. Before you begin writing, decide on the page size, page layout, typefaces, type sizes, and heading style. By deciding on these elements during the planning stage, you can format your document as you write; or you can build a template with your word processing or layout software to create consistent, effective page designs. Before we discuss planning the design elements, let's consider how readers' needs and expectations and your resources impact the design. Think about the following questions:

- **What design elements will help readers fulfill their purpose for reading your document?** Readers have a goal when reading your document. They may be reading to answer a question, to gather information, to complete a task or procedure, or to learn how to do something. For example, if a guest in a hotel room is reading instructions on what to do if the fire alarm goes off, what format would help the reader quickly identify the best escape route?

- **Where will readers use the document?** Think about the readers' environment (desk, laboratory, work site, etc.) and where they will use or read it. For example, if you are writing a manual for an auto mechanic, you would want pages made of durable material and text large enough to see while working on the vehicle.
- **Do readers have quality expectations?** For example, readers of a proposal for a multimillion dollar project would expect the material to have high-resolution color graphics printed on high-quality paper stock, with a professional layout. However, if you were proposing to buy a copier for your office, your readers probably would not expect the same level of quality.
- **Do readers have expectations for the presentation of the information?** Your readers may expect information to be presented in a particular format. For example, car owners would expect an owner's manual that fits easily into the glove compartment or console.

As you consider these questions, you will also want to reflect on and experiment with how and where you will place the text and the graphics. For ideas, look through layout books such as *Layout Index* (Krause 2001) and *Idea Index* (Krause 2000). These books provide you with idea starters for designing brochures, posters, websites, and other types of documents. As you plan your design, experiment with thumbnail sketches, prototypes, style sheets, and preformatted templates and styles.

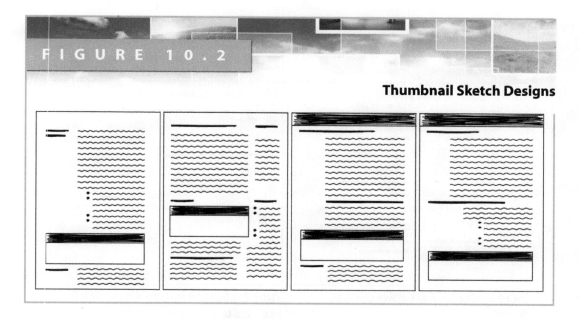

**FIGURE 10.2**

**Thumbnail Sketch Designs**

## Thumbnail Sketches

*Thumbnail sketches* are rough drawings of page layout possibilities (see Figure 10.2). Roger Parker and Patrick Berry (1998) recommend sketching your initial page layout ideas: "Try out a variety of ideas. When you finish one sketch, begin another. ... Don't bother with excessive detail—use thin lines for text, thick lines or block lettering for headlines [headings], and happy faces for art or photographs. Even simple representations such as these will give you a sense of which arrangements work and which don't" (5-6). As you sketch pages, consider different types of page layouts and sizes. Figure 10.3 illustrates some common layouts (sometimes called grids).

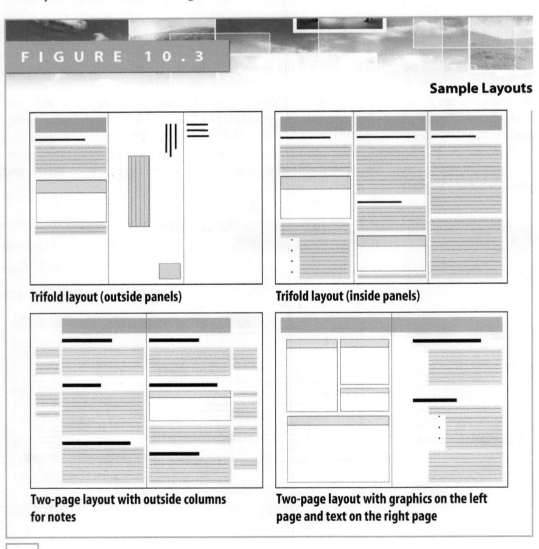

FIGURE 10.3

**Sample Layouts**

**Trifold layout (outside panels)**

**Trifold layout (inside panels)**

**Two-page layout with outside columns for notes**

**Two-page layout with graphics on the left page and text on the right page**

## Prototypes

*Prototypes* are similar to thumbnail sketches, except prototypes are the actual size of the paper you will use. For example, if you plan to design a bifold booklet with a page height of 8½ inches and a width of 6½ inches, you would take standard paper (8½ x 11 inches) and fold the document to create the bifold booklet. Then you sketch where the headings, text, and graphics would appear.

## Style Sheets

A *Style sheet* is a tool that helps writers and designers maintain consistency throughout a document and throughout the organization. A style sheet might include language choices such as those discussed in Chapter 8. It also can serve as a plan for designing a document. Figure 10.4 shows a simple style sheet for the design elements of a manual written by a team of students. A style sheet helps you maintain consistency throughout all elements of your document. When you work on a long document, a style sheet helps you remember the design decisions that you made at the start of the project. A style sheets also helps you maintain a consistent appearance for similar documents or for all documents written for an organization.

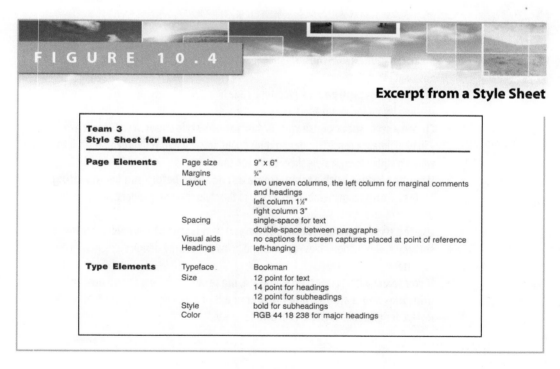

**FIGURE 10.4**

**Excerpt from a Style Sheet**

| Team 3 |||
| Style Sheet for Manual |||
|---|---|---|
| **Page Elements** | Page size | 9" x 6" |
| | Margins | ¾" |
| | Layout | two uneven columns, the left column for marginal comments and headings |
| | | left column 1½" |
| | | right column 3" |
| | Spacing | single-space for text |
| | | double-space between paragraphs |
| | Visual aids | no captions for screen captures placed at point of reference |
| | Headings | left-hanging |
| **Type Elements** | Typeface | Bookman |
| | Size | 12 point for text |
| | | 14 point for headings |
| | | 12 point for subheadings |
| | Style | bold for subheadings |
| | Color | RGB 44 18 238 for major headings |

Many organizations have their own style guides or specific design requirements for their documents. For example, a telecommunications company requires the company logo always to appear in the same typeface, type size, and color. This company also has specific page layout requirements for business letters and reports. As you prepare documents for your organization, find out whether it has a style sheet or specific design requirements.

When you are working as part of a team, use a style sheet to remind you to use the same design elements and to format consistently. Keep the style sheet as simple as possible so team members can easily follow it. The style sheet should specify at least these design elements:

- typefaces
- type sizes
- margins
- heading style
- line spacing

If team members follow the guidelines spelled out in the style sheet, the team can more easily incorporate each member's contribution to create a unified document.

**TIPS FOR PLANNING THE DOCUMENT DESIGN**

- **Make thumbnail sketches.** Thumbnail sketches help you to see multiple page design possibilities.
- **Create a prototype page.** A prototype page helps you to determine the appropriate size and layout for your readers and your purpose.
- **Create a style sheet or use your organization's style sheet.** A style sheet helps you to maintain a consistent design throughout document or your organization. If you're working with a team, a style sheet saves you time.
- **If you're working with a team, create a style sheet before you begin writing.** Make sure each team member has a copy of the style sheet and understands how to use the various elements.
- **Use the styles function (described below) that is part of your word processing software.** This fuction saves you time and helps you use the design elements consistently.
- **If you select a preformatted template, make sure it follows good design principles and is appropriate for your needs.** If it isn't right for your situation, review design books or create your own template.

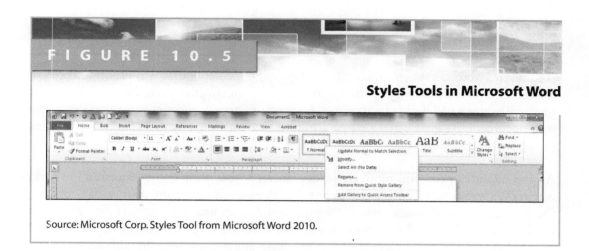

**FIGURE 10.5**

**Styles Tools in Microsoft Word**

Source: Microsoft Corp. Styles Tool from Microsoft Word 2010.

## Preformatted Templates and Styles

You can select a preformatted template available in most word processing or layout software. These templates provide page layouts for many document types. If you decide to use a preformatted template, think through the possible problems. Preformatted templates often

- don't fit the purpose of your document
- don't follow good design principles
- omit key conventional elements required in some documents
- are commonplace (many writers use these templates, so your document could look like many other documents)
- include inappropriate graphics or design elements

Instead of using a preformatted template, you could use the styles function of your word processing software to create a custom template you can apply to headings, paragraphs, lists, etc. By using the styles function, you save time and achieve a consistent look in one or among several documents. The styles function lets you customize the type, type size, color, and spacing of text, headings, etc. Figure 10.5 shows the Styles tool in Microsoft *Word*. For example, before you begin to write your document, you define the characteristics of your heading style. By doing that, you only have to format a heading once, then apply that style to every headline as you write. After you type a heading, you apply the heading style by positioning the cursor in the heading text and selecting the appropriate style for that heading tag under the Styles menu.

As you plan your document, think about the design elements that will prompt people to read and use your document. Readers may not notice an effective design or appearance but they will notice a bad design or appearance. Good design will encourage them to delve into your document. Readers often are first attracted to a document by its packaging: the cover, paper, binding and layout.

As you consider what will motivate readers to read, you must also understand how and where the readers will use your document. For example, if you know your readers will use the document in a laboratory where they use liquids, laminate the pages. If they work in a confined space, design a document that will take up less space (such as 6 by 9 inches instead of the standard 8½ by 11 inches). If you are designing a document that drivers will carry in their delivery vans, the standard paper size would be awkward whereas as a page size of 4½ by 5 inches would better meet their needs. The following sections will give you guidelines for designing the "packaging" elements that will motivate readers to read your document and will work in their environment.

## TIPS FOR DESIGNING DOCUMENT COVERS

- **Use color to draw the readers to the page.** You will find more information about color later in this chapter.
- **Use ample white space, or empty space, to highlight and unify the information you want to emphasize.** Be sure to surround the name of the document or organization with ample white space. The white space creates a frame that keeps related information together.
- **Include information about the contents of the document.** You might use appropriate graphics that relate to the contents and invite readers to look beyond the cover.
- **Remember that less is more.** A clean, simple cover will attract more readers than one filled with excessive text or graphics. When you use too many graphics, your readers don't know what is most important and they may miss important information.

## An Engaging, Appropriate Cover

The cover is the part of a document that readers see first. An effective cover makes a good first impression and invites readers to open and use the document. It should feature a clear, legible title. If, for instance, you use graphics, select ones that do not detract from

## TIPS FOR SELECTING PAPER

- **Select paper with a lower weight and lower brightness for most internal, everyday documents.** If you are printing a memo to your coworkers, you can use a lower weight paper with a brightness in the 80s (brightness is measured on a scale of 1 to 100). This paper is the type of paper used in most photocopy machines.
- **Select a 20- or 30-pound bond paper for external and formal internal documents.** This weight gives your documents a more professional feel and appearance. On a practical note, it doesn't tear as easily. If you select a lower weight paper, the document could look flimsy and unprofessional. If you print the document on both sides on a lower weight paper, the print will bleed through the paper.
- **For external and formal internal documents, especially documents with color graphics, use paper with a high brightness number.** High-quality paper has a brightness number in the 90s. Some paper manufacturers simply use terms such as "bright white" or "ultra bright" instead of a number. On paper with a lower brightness, colors are darker and less vibrant. On paper with a highter brightness, colors are more vibrant.
- **If you will be doing two-sided printing, make sure the printing will not bleed through from one side to the other.** Select at least a 20- or 30-pound paper so the printing will not bleed through.
- **Use coated paper to increase the paper's durability and the print resolution.** Coated paper is more expensive, but print resolution is much higher on this paper. Coated paper also projects a sharper, more professional look. If you select coated paper, use an off-white or ivory paper to decrease glare.
- **For formal documents, select a white, ivory, or off-white paper.** Select colored paper only when appropriate for the tone, formality, subject, and readers. For example, if you are writing a proposal to a client, select a white, ivory, or off-white paper. However, if you are inviting that same client to a Mardi Gras celebration of your winning proposal, you might use light-purple paper with green accents. Regardless of the color, make sure your readers can easily read the print.

or overpower the title. Select a cover material and style that are appropriate for and will enhance your document. If you have the budget, have the cover professionally printed on special stock or have it laminated. To design an effective cover, look at Tips for Designing Covers.

## Appropriate Paper

Choose the best type of paper for your readers' purpose and environment. Paper comes in different weights, brightness, and coatings: the higher the weight and the brightness, the higher the quality (and the more expensive). Review the Tips for Selecting Paper.

## Appropriate Binding

Several types of binding are available for long documents:

- **Loose-leaf binders.** With these binders, users can open the rings and remove or insert pages. This type of binding works well if you or your readers will be updating a document. This binding is excellent if the document needs to lie flat or stay open to a specific page.

**TIPS** FOR CREATING A CONSISTENT PAGE LAYOUT

- **Use the same top, bottom, left, and right margins on every page.** Inconsistent margins make the document look unorganized and unprofessional.
- **Use typefaces, type sizes, and type styles for headings and text consistently throughout the document.** For example, if you use a 14-point bold sans serif typeface for the first-level headings in the first chapter, use the same typeface throughout. Use Word's Styles tool or the equivalent function of your word processing software to ensure a consistent layout.
- **Use consistent paragraph indents and spacing between columns, within lists, and before and after headings.** You can set up all these elements in the Paragraph tool in Word or its equivalent.
- **Put the page numbers in the same position on every page except the first.** You can pre-set the page numbers using Word's Header and Footer function (or its equivalent in your word processing software).

- **Wire or plastic spiral binding.** With this type of binding, users cannot remove or insert pages. It also is less durable because the wire and plastic coils are easily crushed and broken. On the other hand, coils are excellent when the document needs to lie flat or stay open to a specific page. This binding is less expensive than most loose-leaf binders.
- **Saddle stitch binding.** Saddle stitch binding uses large staples through the centerfold to bind the pages. This binding is practical for documents of up to 64 pages (32 sheets of paper). However, the document is difficult to lay out using word processing software.

- **Perfect binding.** Perfect binding is how most books are bound: The pages are glued together along the spine, to which a cover is usually added to cover the glued spine. This type of binding produces a formal appearance, but pages can easily fall out and the document does not lie flat.

## Consistent Page Layout

As readers move beyond the external packaging, they look at the page layout to decide whether to continue reading and what to read. Page layout can attract readers to your document and present a "picture" of you and your organization. A consistent page layout helps readers locate information. To create consistent page layouts, review Tips for Creating Consistent Page Layout.

## CHOOSE DESIGN ELEMENTS THAT HELP READERS LOCATE INFORMATION

As you design the page layout, remember that most readers have a goal when reading your document. They may be reading to
- answer a question
- gather information
- complete a task or procedure
- learn how to do something

To help readers achieve their goals, include design elements that help readers locate information at the document's division, chapter, section, or page level.

## Division- or Chapter-Level Locating Tools

For longer documents, you will need to create divisions, chapters, and sections. For example, a document of two or more divisions could use tabs to indicate the division level. Within each division, divider pages could indicate two or more chapters or sections.

### Tabs

Frequently used in manuals, reports, and proposals, tabs help readers identify divisions, chapters and sections. Tabs are often color-coded and follow the design principle of contrast. They extend beyond the paper's edge so readers can go to specific parts of a document.

If you use tabs in your documents, select tabs with a professional appearance and print a shortened version of the chapter or division title on the tab. Figure 10.6 shows an example of tabs.

## Divider Pages

Divider pages help readers locate chapters within divisions and even major sections within chapters. ***Divider pages*** appear before chapters or sections. These pages list the chapter's or section's title and often include a table of contents for that chapter or section. They are usually a different color than the chapter or section pages. In this book, for example, divider pages list the division title and the chapters within the division.

> Locating tools make your document more usable by helping readers scan and locate the information they need.

## Page-Level Locating Tools

Page-level tools that help readers locate information include
- headers and footers
- page numbers
- headings
- color
- white space
- icons

### Headers and Footers

***Headers*** and ***footers*** are design elements that appear at the top (header) and bottom (footer) of the page (although not all documents necessarily have both). They contain information that does not change with every page such as the title of the document, division, or chapter, in an abbreviated version if the title is too long. They may also include the author's or the organization's name. Figure 10.7 shows a header and footer.

### Page Numbers

The page number appears in either the header or the footer. Position the page number at the outside margin of the page so readers can easily see and use them. Use the Tips for Numbering Pages.

FIGURE 10.6

**A Document with Tabs**

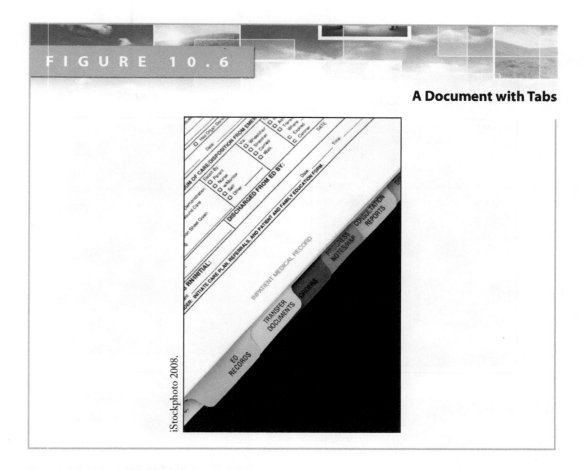

iStockphoto 2008.

## Headings

*Headings* are subtitles that show readers how you have grouped the information in your document. When information is grouped, or "chunked," readers can easily locate the information they need. In the absence of headings, readers must read or skim every page until they find the information they want. Figure 10.8 shows three ways to position headings. Follow the Tips for Creating Effective Headings.

## Color

Color is an effective tool for organizing information. Color is usually the most prominant element on a page. Use color to highlight important information, to guide readers, and to

**FIGURE 10.7**

**Headers and Footers**

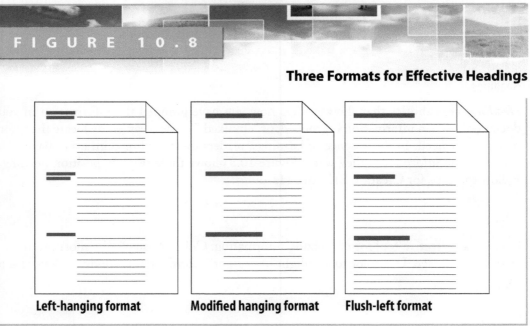

**FIGURE 10.8**

**Three Formats for Effective Headings**

**Left-hanging format**  **Modified hanging format**  **Flush-left format**

- **For one-sided pages, put page numbers in the top or bottom outer corner.** Be consistent: Place the page number in the same position on every page. If you insert a header or footer with the page numbers in a header or footer, use the same style of header or footer on every page. (See Figure 10.7.)
- **For two-sided pages, put the page numbers in the outer top or bottom corners.** If you put the page numbers in the center or on the inside margin of the page, readers may not see them as they thumb through your document.
- **As a rule, do not print the page number on the first page of a document or chapter.** Include the first page in your page count, but don't print the number on the first page.
- **For longer and more complex documents, use a different number sequencing for the front matter.** Use lowercase Roman numerals (i, ii, iii, iv, etc.) for the front matter. Use Arabic numerals (1, 2, 3, etc.) for the body. Chapter 15 will give you more information on numbering the front matter.
- **For documents that will be updated, number the pages by section.** By numbering each section separately, you will only have to reprint the sections that change. If you number by section, the page numbers should have two parts: section number – page number. That is, for section 2, page 4, the page number would read 2–4 or 2.4.

organize the information. Figure 10.10 illustrates how color highlights information in a cell phone user guide. Color highlights the header, page numbers, and first-level headings. Because color creates contrast, combine color with these locating tools:

- headings
- tabs
- divider pages
- headers and footers

Figure 10.11 illustrates how you can
- use colored bullets to highlight a list
- put key words in color to indicate links in online documents
- use horizontal rules to highlight blocks of text or sections of a document
- use shading within or colored rules around boxes to highlight a warning or special note

When you use color, follow the Tips for Using Color.

FIGURE 10.9

## A Floating Heading

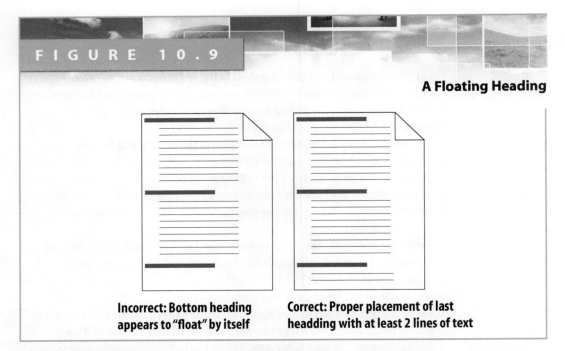

**Incorrect: Bottom heading appears to "float" by itself**

**Correct: Proper placement of last headding with at least 2 lines of text**

FIGURE 10.10

## Effective Color Use

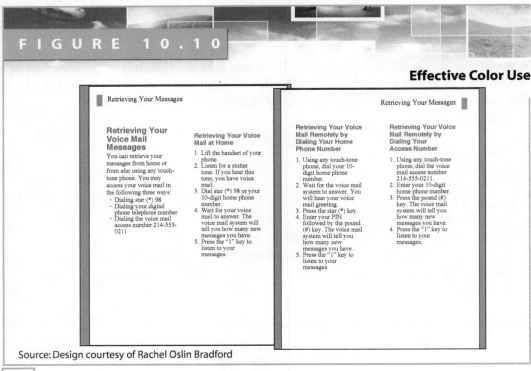

Source: Design courtesy of Rachel Oslin Bradford

- **Put the headings flush with the left margin.** Readers can more easily locate a heading if you align it flush against the left margin. Avoid centering headings because readers can't locate centered headings as quickly as flush-left headings; centered headings violate the principle of alignment.
- **Use no more than four levels of headings in most documents.** Too many levels clutter a document and confuse readers.
- **Allow more space above your headings than below.** For instance, in a double-spaced document, use three lines of space above the heading and two lines after. In a single-spaced document, use two lines of space above and one line after. Word processing software allows you to adjust the spacing.
- **Include at least two lines of text below a heading.** Don't leave a heading floating at the bottom of a page. Headings without these lines appear to "float" at the bottom of a page (see Figure 10.9).
- **Use different type sizes and styles (such as bold or color) to indicate levels of headings.** Readers associate size of type with importance—the larger the type, the more important the information (White 1988). You will find more information about type size and headings later in this chapter.

## White Space

Readers look for relationships among the text, graphics, and headings on a page. These elements should look as though they belong together; otherwise, readers will be confused about how one element relates to another. To create a unified layout, frame the elements with white space (Lay 1989; Yeo 1996). *White space* is the space on the page not occupied by text or graphics. As Williams (2008) explains, many novice designers tend to avoid white space. They feel they must fill the entire page. However, effective designers use ample white space. Use white space to take advantage of two design principles: proximity and contrast. When related items are in proximity, use the surrounding white space to show readers which items are related. White space creates contrast. For example, Figure 10.12 has excellent contrast around "Zero Harm."

## TIPS FOR USING COLOR

- **Use the same color throughout the document for the same type of information.** For example, if you use green for the first-level headings in the first chapter, use green for the first-level headings in all chapters. If you use colors inconsistently, they are merely decoration rather than an aid to readers.
- **Use color in combination with other devices, such as white space, bold type, or type size.** Colorblind readers need other clues to help them locate information. If you use only color as a locating device, some readers will not be helped.
- **Use colors to communicate, not to decorate.** Color attracts the readers' eyes. If the color merely decorates, it will distract (or confuse) them from the information you are trying to communicate.
- **Consider your readers' culture when selecting colors.** Colors have different meanings in different contexts (Horton 1993). For example, when U.S. readers see instructions printed in red, they associate the red with danger. However, when they see red while driving, they know to stop. In business, red is associated with financial loss and black connotes formality and power. In the U.S. and other Western cultures, people associate black with death and mourning; but in China, white is associated with death. As you select colors for your document, consider what the color might indicate to your readers, especially readers from other cultures.
- **Use color to unify a document or a series of documents.** Used consistently, color unifies a document or a series of documents. Throughout one document or a series, use the same color for the same types of information, design elements, or visuals. For example, if you use blue for the headers, footers, and bullets in the first document in a series, use the same shade of blue in all other documents in the series.

## Icons

*Icons* are graphics that symbolize an action or a concept. You see and use icons daily on your cell phone and your computer. Icons operate on the design principle of repetition. For example, when you see the scissor icon in a software program, you know it indicates "to cut." Figure 10.13 shows icons commonly used on smart phones. When users see these icons, they know what applications are available.

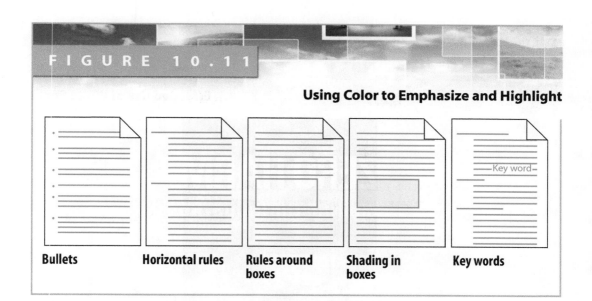

**FIGURE 10.11**

**Using Color to Emphasize and Highlight**

Key word

| Bullets | Horizontal rules | Rules around boxes | Shading in boxes | Key words |

**TIPS FOR USING WHITE SPACE**

- **Push related elements together with white space.** Use white space to "push" page elements together (Lay 1989), helping readers to see what elements belong together. For example, when you leave more white space before than after a heading, you help readers clearly see to which text the heading belongs.
- **Use white space to surround elements you want to emphasize.** By surrounding elements with white space, you emphasize them. For example, surrounding your company's logo with white space draws the reader's eye to the logo.
- **Set off elements such as headings, bullets, and graphics with white space.** The white space increases visibility and readability. For example, notice that white space highlights the bullets in this textbook. The text aligns to the right of the bullet not under it, and the white space reduces clutter and increases readability. If the text aligned under the bullet (see Figure 10.14), the bullets would be less visible.

FIGURE 10.12

**Effective Use of White Space**

Source: Balfour Beatty Construction. Reprinted with permission.

FIGURE 10.13

**Smart Phone Application Icons**

© 2012 by koya979. Used under license of Shutterstock, Inc.

**FIGURE 10.14**

**Using White Space to Highlight Bullets**

**White space doesn't highlight the bullets**

**White space highlights the bullets**

**FIGURE 10.15**

**Examples of Serif and Sans Serif Typefaces**

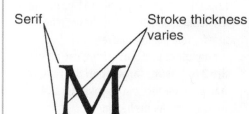

Serif

Stroke thickness varies

**Serif Type**
Times Roman
Bookman
Rockwell

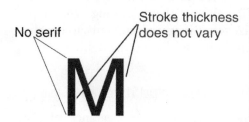

No serif

Stroke thickness does not vary

**Sans-Serif Type**
Tahoma
Gill Sans
Helvetica

As you plan, select design elements to enhance the readability of your documents. When you select the type in which your text will appear, think about the typeface, type size, and type style of each text element. You also need to "set" the margins and line spacing using your word processing tools.

## Appropriate Typefaces

A *typeface* is a set of letterforms (letters, numbers, punctuation marks, and other symbols) with a coherent design. In word processing software, typefaces are often referred to as *fonts*. You can select from two kinds of typefaces: serif and sans serif (see Figure 10.15). A *serif* is a short stroke, or line at the top and/or bottom of a letterform. In serif type, the thickness of letters' strokes varies, helping readers to distinguish the shapes of different letters. In a *sans serif typeface*—type without serifs (*sans* means "without" in French)—no small strokes project from the top or bottom of the letter, and generally, the thickness of the letters' strokes are uniform. Note that we have used a sans serif font for headers and a serif font for the text in this book. As you select fonts for your documents, follow the Tips for Selecting Typefaces on the next page.

## Appropriate Type Sizes for Text and Headings

Type size is measured in points: 72 points equal 1 inch. Most word processing and desktop-publishing programs allow you to adjust the type size up to 72 points. When deciding what type size to use in your documents, follow the tips in the sidebar on the right.

## Appropriate Type Styles and Case

By modifying the appearance of the type, you create different looks in your document. With word processing software, you can vary the style (often referred to as *effects*) of a typeface. For example, the most commonly used styles are bold and italics. Underlining is rarely used in text; instead use italics (the exception to this rule applies

**TIPS** FOR SELECTING THE APPROPRIATE SIZE TYPE

- **For text, use 10-, 11-, or 12-point type.** Type sizes are not the same for all fonts. For example, the approximate equivalent of a 12-point serif font might be an 11-point sans serif font. Experiment to find the optimum sizes for your purpose and readers.
- **For headings and most titles, use a type size 2 to 4 points larger than the text.** For example, if the text is in 12-point, use a 14- or 16-point type for the headings.
- **For footnotes, use a type size 2 points smaller than the text.**

- **As a rule, use serif typefaces for body text.** Serifs guide readers' eyes from letter to letter; they help readers see the text "in terms of words and sentences instead of as individual letters" (Parker and Berry 1998, 60). Serifs and the variations in stroke thickness help readers distinguish among letters with similar shapes (such as the numeral 1 and a lower case l [L]) and to recognize the shapes of all letters.
- **As a rule, use sans serif typefaces for titles and headings.** Sans serif type is difficult to read in long blocks of text and in small sizes, but small amounts of it add impact to a document, especially when white space surrounds the elements (Parker and Berry 1998). The key is contrast: If you want to use different typefaces for headings and text, use fonts that are noticeably different from each other. For example, if your text is Times Roman (a serif typeface), don't select Garamond—a similar serif typeface—for the headings. Instead, select a sans serif type, such as Tahoma or Arial.
- **Limit the number of typefaces in your documents to two: a serif typeface for the text and a sans serif typeface for the titles and headings.** You can use a different, perhaps decorative typeface for title pages, chapter titles, covers, or divider pages. Otherwise, limit yourself to two typefaces.
- **Select a typeface that is easy to read. Script and decorative typefaces are inappropriate for text or headings in technical documents.** These typefaces are hard to read and appear unprofessional. You might use these typefaces in logos, party invitations, title pages, divider pages, or covers. If you decide to use a script font, use a large size. The smaller the script font, the harder it is to read.
- **Use a sans serif typeface for reverse type.** When you place white (or light) type on a dark background, you are using reverse type. Reverse type should always be sans serif.

to Internet links). If you want to emphasize a limited block of text, you can use reversed type, which is light-colored text on a dark background. Because reversed type is difficult to read for long passages and because it uses a lot of copier ink, limit your use of this feature. Unless you are designing a party invitation, for example, you will not have occasion to use shadowing or outlining type as they are distracting and difficult to read. Some styles can improve your documents' appearance by providing "visual relief in an otherwise uniform page of text" (Felker et al. 1981, 72). However, some styles make type almost unreadable, create an unprofessional appearance, clutter the page, and distract readers from what you want to communicate.

Text in upper- and lowercase letters is easier to read than text in all uppercase letters. Lowercase letters take up less space, so readers can "take in more words as they scan a line of text" (Benson 1985, 41); lowercase letters give each word a distinct shape. Shape helps readers distinguish letters and identify words (Felker et al. 1981). As Figure 10.16 shows, words set in uppercase letters have the same basic shape or outline, but words set in lowercase or in both upper- and lowercase letters have different shapes. The uniform shape of words set in uppercase letters slows readers' ability to recognize each word. To use case and type style effectively, follow the tips in sidebar to the right.

## Appropriate Margins and Line Lengths

When selecting the margins for your pages, balance the length of your lines against the width of the margins.

When lines of text are of different lengths and do not align on the right, the text is *unjustified* or *ragged* such as the text in the sidebar. When lines of text are equal in length, the text is said to be *justified* such as this text (see Figure 10.17). Readers find text with unjustified right margins easier to read (Bensen 1985). When line lengths vary, readers' eyes move more easily from the end of one line to the beginning of the next. When text is justified, all the lines look the same, and readers can't easily distinguish one line from the next; hence, they find their eyes moving to the wrong line as they read.

**TIPS** FOR SELECTING TYPE STYLES AND CASE

- **Use bold type to add emphasis.** Bold type increases the visibility of headings and individual words and phrases. Use bold type for headings and, sparingly, to emphasize individual words in blocks of text; do not use it for entire paragraphs or for more than two or three lines of type.
- **Use italics to add emphasis.** Italics effectively emphasize individual words and short phrases, though less dramatically than bold type. Use italic type for isolated words and short phrases, such as for non-English words, not for entire paragraphs or large blocks of text.
- **Use reverse type sparingly.** If you use reverse type, use a large sans serif typeface.
- **Avoid outlined or shadowed type.** These type styles are especially hard to read in small sizes and in uppercase letters (Parker and Berry 1998). These type styles make your documents appear unprofessional.
- **Avoid underlining.** Underlining interferes with readers' ability to recognize the shapes of some letters. It can distort letters with descenders (letters that descend below the base line of the text)—$y, j, p, q, g$—and punctuation marks such as commas and semicolons. Instead of underlining, use boldface, italics, or color.
- **Avoid text in all uppercase (capital) letters.**

**FIGURE 10.16**

**Text Set in Uppercase Letters and in Lowercase and Uppercase Letters**

Because readers recognize words by their shape, text in

UPPERCASE LETTERS IS HARDER TO READ.

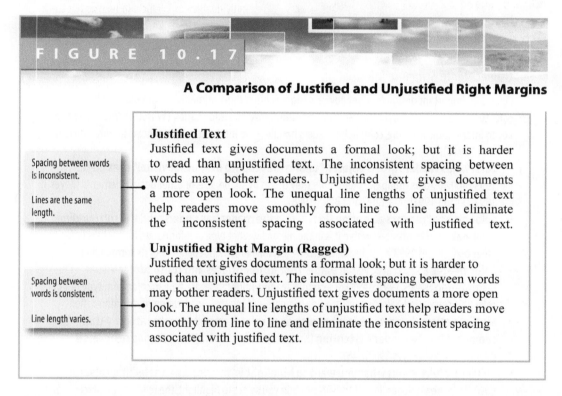

**FIGURE 10.17**

**A Comparison of Justified and Unjustified Right Margins**

Spacing between words is inconsistent.

Lines are the same length.

**Justified Text**
Justified text gives documents a formal look; but it is harder to read than unjustified text. The inconsistent spacing between words may bother readers. Unjustified text gives documents a more open look. The unequal line lengths of unjustified text help readers move smoothly from line to line and eliminate the inconsistent spacing associated with justified text.

Spacing between words is consistent.

Line length varies.

**Unjustified Right Margin (Ragged)**
Justified text gives documents a formal look; but it is harder to read than unjustified text. The inconsistent spacing berween words may bother readers. Unjustified text gives documents a more open look. The unequal line lengths of unjustified text help readers move smoothly from line to line and eliminate the inconsistent spacing associated with justified text.

The amount of space between words in justified text is inconsistent. From one line to the next, the space between words varies so that all lines will align evenly on the right. This inconsistent spacing can slow reading. In the justified example in Figure 10.17, note the inconsistent spacing between words and the uniformity in line lengths. In the unjustified example, note the uniform spacing between words that results when the right margin is ragged.

**TAKING IT INTO THE** *workplace*

## Using Color to Structure Information

Color is an important design tool, yet novice designers often think primarily about what and how much color to use, rather than how color can "enhance and clarify" the information (Wilson).[1] When used as a key to information structure, color helps readers handle more information and process it more efficiently (Horton 1991b).

- **Color helps readers group objects, "taking precedence over other visual" cues** (Keyes 1993, 647). Readers group by color before they group by shape, size, or other design elements (Keyes 1993; Horton 1991b; Martinez and Block 1988).
- **Color grabs a "reader's attention first,** *before* **the reader has understood the surrounding informational context**—where it is in the hierarchy, what type of information it is, or its relation to other text" (Keyes 1993, 647). Readers perceive a color element independent of its surrounding text.
- **Color creates a separate "visual plane" that differentiates and consolidates visual information** (Keyes 1993, 649). For example, readers might separate type in color from type not in color. This separation helps readers scan documents and see the organization of the information.
- **Multiple colors distract readers because each color forms a separate category that competes for the reader's attention** (Krull and Rubens 1986). When selecting color, "less is definitely more" (Keyes 1993, 648).
- **Think carefully about what you want to highlight with color when selecting color for your document.** Regardless of the information you select to highlight, the readers will perceive that information first.

[1] Personal communication (2001).

## Assignment

Visit a local business or nonprofit organization and gather a color document that the business or organization produced.

- Ask an employee, manager, or owner the following questions:
  - How much did you spend to produce the document?
  - Why did you select the color(s) used?
- Write a memo to your instructor:
  - summarizing what you learned about the cost of producing the document in color and why the organization selected the color(s) used
  - explaining whether the color is used effectively to structure and highlight information and if the color detracts from or reinforces the message.

## SAMPLE DOCUMENT DESIGNS

Figures 10.18, 10.19, and 10.20 illustrate how writers have effectively designed documents.

# FIGURE 10.18

**Effective Use of Typeface and Color**

The designer uses a sans serif typeface for the headings.

The designer creates repetition by repeating the red twice: in the flowers and in the red background on the facing page.

**Getting better all the**

**Effective Use of Typeface and Color** *continued*

The designer selected a sans serif typeface because the text is white on a dark background.

The designer creates contrast by using white (blank) space.

The designer creates effective alignment by aligning the heading with the text, the Texas Parks and Wildlife logo, and the publication information.

**CONTENTS**

3    New Agency Leadership

4    Access to Outdoor Recreation

6    Getting Families and Kids Outdoors

8    Land and Wildlife Conservation

12   Water and Fisheries Conservation

14   Hurricane Ike

16   Protecting People and Resources

18   Sites and Infrastructure

20   Streamlining Business Operations

21   Valuing Employees

22   Employee Recognition Awards

24   TPWD Leadership Team

25   TPW Commissioners

26   Accountability Measures

Source: Downloaded from the World Wide Web, June 2009: www.tpwd.state.tx.us/publications/pwdpubs/
media/pwd_bk_e0100_003_01_09.pdf.   Texas Parks and Wildlife Department, 2008 Annual Report, pp. 2-3,
(PWD BK E0100 003).

## A Document That Demonstrates Effective Contrast, Alignment, and Proximity

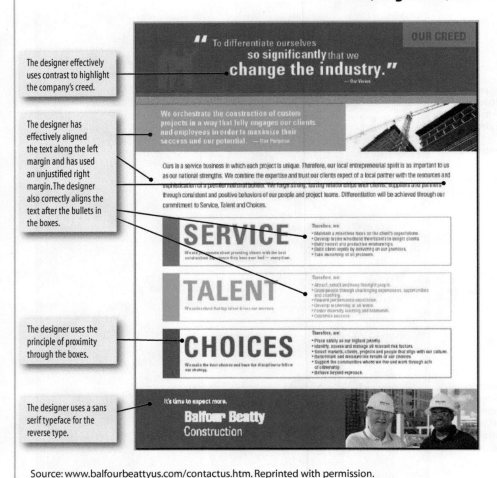

The designer effectively uses contrast to highlight the company's creed.

The designer has effectively aligned the text along the left margin and has used an unjustified right margin. The designer also correctly aligns the text after the bullets in the boxes.

The designer uses the principle of proximity through the boxes.

The designer uses a sans serif typeface for the reverse type.

Source: www.balfourbeattyus.com/contactus.htm. Reprinted with permission.

**Effective Use of Color, Headings and Typeface**

### Chapter 3
### Keeping the Participants Interested

Once you have your equipment in place and you have planned and rehearsed your presentation, you're almost ready. However, you can improve your chances for a successful presentation by understanding ways to keep your participants interested (and awake). In other words, put yourself in your participants' seat! This chapter will present some strategies to help you keep participants interested:

- Give participants only the information they need.
- Anticipate participants' needs and questions.
- Provide participants with a "road map" and examples.
- Help participants enjoy your presentation.

### Strategy 1: Give Participants Only the Information They Need

Keep your presentation short and simple. Participants want to hear only the information they need and no more. As you prepare for your presentation, consider the following:

- **Listening to information takes twice as long as reading that same information.** Thus, if you can read 10 pages in 8 minutes, your participants can comprehend the same information in about 16 minutes.
- **Condense your presentation into a few points.** Don't try to give participants every bit of information you have about a topic or all the tiny details. Instead, select the key points and present those. If necessary, you can refer your participants to the quick reference cards or to other printed handouts.
- **Plan the presentation to take slightly less then the allotted time.** Look for ways to tighten your presentation, so you have time for the participants to ask questions. Your participants will prefer a presentation that is a couple of minutes short rather than a presentation that exceeds the allotted time.

### Strategy 2: Anticipate Participants' Needs and Questions

As you are preparing and even as you are speaking, think about what participants already know and what they will want to know about the topic.

- **Customize your presentation according to what you know about your participants.** You will always begin your presentation with the same four databases: Project Description, Project Contacts, Specifications, and

Modified hanging headings help readers locate Information.

The designers effectively use color to emphasize the headings. Notice that a colorblind reader could still easily locate the headings because they appear in boldface type as well as color.

The text aligns after the bullets.

The designers have used a sans serif typeface for the headings and a serif typeface for the text.

Source: Reprinted courtesy of Balfour Beatty Construction Company.

# CASE STUDY ANALYSIS

## Why Aren't Students Using the Career Center?

### Background

You manage the Career Center at a large university. You began only a couple of months into the semester. The university president has charged you with improving the employment rate of students who graduate from the university. You know that the current unemployment rate for new college graduates is 53 percent across the U.S.

You begin by looking at the unemployment rates for graduates from your university. Although it is lower than the national average, it is still high. You notice that in the past two years only 20 percent of graduating seniors visited the placement center and applied for jobs through the center. You decide to investigate why students aren't taking advantage of the services offered by the career center. You begin by looking at documents created by the center to introduce students to the center and its services. You find several flyers like the one in Figure 10.21. You believe the flyer's contents and design would turn off students and discourage them from using the center and its services.

### Assignment

- Evaluate the document in Figure 10.21. Does the figure follow the design principles presented in the chapter? Does the flyer present a positive image of the center? Be prepared to discuss your answers in class.
- Visit the career placement center at your college or university. Find a document that provides information about the center's services. You may locate this document in person or online. Be prepared for a class discussion on the document's design.

**FIGURE 10.21**

**Document for Case Study Analysis**

# Job Search Overview

Interested in internships, part-time employment, or full-time employment? Access your student network account to search for jobs!

Part-time Employment or Full-time Employment
  To access your student network account:
  Login to your account and click on the student resource tab
  Next look for the network logo
  Click on the "student employment or career center" button (be sure to disable any popup blockers)
  Complete your profile and upload your resume

Internships & Co-op Positions
  To access your student network account:
  Login to your account and click on the student resource tab
  Next look for the network logo
  Click on the "internships" button (be sure to disable any popup blockers)

## Resumes & Cover Letters

To apply for jobs, you must upload at least one resume to your account. You can upload resumes, cover letters, and other documents by holding the mouse pointer over the "my account" tab at the top of the home page. Scroll down and click on "My Documents." To add a new resume, cover letter, or application, click on the upload file link. Once you name and upload your documents you can start applying for positions available through the career center. You may view resume and cover letter samples at http://careercenter.youruniversity.edu/students/resouces/html

## Applying for Jobs Advertised through the Career Center

*ATTN: You must upload a resume before you can apply for jobs.*
1. From your search results page, select the position you want to view by clicking on either the job ID# or the Position title.
2. Click on the "submit my resume" button to have your resume sent to the employer.
3. In the new window, select the documents that you want to send to the employer. You may select from any documents such as resumes and cover letters that you have uploaded to your account.
4. Click the "submit" button.

## Saved Job Searches

The career center allows you to save your job search criteria to help you simplify your job search activities. From the job search results screen, click on "save search." In the pop-up window, name your saved search and click in the check-box if you want to be emailed jobs that fit your search criteria.

## International Job Opportunities

Use "Global Opportunities" to search for jobs with international companies in the U.S. and abroad. Click the "Jobs" tab. Then scroll down to the "Global Opportunities" link.

## Resources Available Through the Career Center

The "Jobs" link section gives you additional job search resources: Vault, Global Opportunities, AfterCollege.com, Monster Trak, Wet Feet
The "Resource Library" link provides job search and career development resources. To access the "Resource Library," scroll down on your home page to the library window. Select the +/- next to the folders you want to view. Then, select the items you want to view by clicking on the document titles:
- Career center presentations
- Job search resources
- What can I do with my Major?
- Interview tips

# Questions?

Contact the Career Center at Union Hall, Suite 116 * careercenter.youruniversity.edu* (555) 575-8999 *
careercenter@myuniversity.edu

# EXERCISES

DOWNLOAD A WORKSHEET FOR DESIGNING READER-FOCUSED DOCUMENTS ONLINE AT
WWW.GRTEP.COM

1. Redesign the flyer in Figure 10.21. Correct the design problems you identified in your evaluation.

2. Find a one- or two-page document that has an ineffective design. Look for these documents on the Internet, on your college or university campus, at home, at work, or in your community.
   a. Write a memo to your instructor explaining the document's design problems. For information on writing memos, see Chapter 12.
   b. Attach a copy of the document to your memo. If you found the document online, include the URL in your memo.

3. Redesign the document you found for Exercise 2. Correct the design problems that you identified in your memo.

4. Write a memo to your instructor evaluating the design of Guest Safety Tips in Figure 10.22. In your memo, comment on how effectively the document
   • follows the design principles of contrast, repetition, alignment, and proximity
   • uses type
   • uses white space
   • uses color
   For information on writing memos, see Chapter 12.

5. Write a memo to your instructor evaluating the design of the guide on bear safety in Figure 10.23. In your memo, comment on how effectively the document
   • follows the design principles of contrast, repetition, alignment, and proximity
   • uses type
   • uses white space
   • uses color

6. Assume that you work for the National Park Service. Your manager has asked you to create a document that park visitors can carry as they explore Grand Teton National Park. This document will be used in addition to the document in Figure 10.23. Your document must
   - fit easily into a backpack or pocket
   - include safety information and park regulations
   - include at least two color graphics

FIGURE 10.22

**Document for Exercise 4**

## AMERICAN HOTEL & LODGING ASSOCIATION

# GUEST SAFETY TIPS

**1** Don't answer the door in a hotel or motel room without verifying who it is. If a person claims to be an employee, call the front desk and ask if someone from their staff is supposed to have access to your room and for what purpose.

**2** Keep your room key with you at all times and don't needlessly display it in public. Should you misplace it, please notify the front desk immediately.

**3** Close the door securely whenever you are in your room and use all of the locking devices provided.

**4** Check to see that any sliding glass doors or windows and any connecting room doors are locked.

**5** Don't invite strangers to your room.

**6** Do not draw attention to yourself by displaying large amounts of cash or expensive jewelry.

**7** Place all valuables in the in-room safe or safe deposit box.

**8** When returning to your hotel or motel late in the evening, be aware of your surroundings, stay in well-lighted areas, and use the main entrance.

**9** Take a few moments and locate the nearest exit that may be used in the event of an emergency.

**10** If you see any suspicious activity, notify the hotel operator or a staff member.

© Copyright 2003 The American Hotel & Lodging Association
1201 New York Avenue, NW, #600
Washington, DC 20005-3931
www.ahla.com

American Hotel & Lodging Association

COM001727

Source: Copyright © 2003 by The American Hotel & Lodging Association. Reprinted by permission.

FIGURE 10.23

**Document for Exercises 5 and 6**

# Grand Teton

National Park Service
U.S. Department of the Interior

Grand Teton National Park
John D. Rockefeller, Jr.
Memorial Parkway

## Bear Safety

**Exploring Bear Country**

Black bears and grizzly bears thrive in Grand Teton National Park and the John D. Rockefeller, Jr. Memorial Parkway. You may encounter a bear anywhere at anytime. Some of the most popular trails pass through excellent bear habitat. Bears will usually move out of the way if they hear you approaching.

Your safety is important to us. Please review the following bear safety information before hiking or camping in the park.

**Make Noise**

Do not surprise bears! Make noise when you are hiking or away from your vehicle. Bears will usually move out of the way if they hear you approaching. Calling out (such as 'Hey Bear') and clapping your hands at regular intervals are the best ways to make your presence known. Bear bells are not sufficient.

Some trail conditions make it difficult for bears to hear, see, or smell approaching hikers. Be particularly careful near streams, when it is windy, in dense vegetation, or in any circumstance that limits line of sight (such as a blind corner or rise in the trail). Be aware of your surroundings. The use of portable audio devices is strongly discouraged.

**Hike in Groups**

If possible, hike in groups of three or more people. Typically, larger groups of people make more noise and appear more formidable to bears. Keep your group together and make sure your children are close to you at all times. Avoid hiking when bears are more active; early in the morning, late in the day or when it is dark. Trail running is strongly discouraged; you may startle a bear.

**Bear Spray**

Bear spray is extremely effective to deter bear attacks. Bear spray is a non-toxic and non-lethal means of warding off aggressive bears. It temporarily affects the bear's respiratory system and mucus membranes.

Keep bear spray immediately available on your belt or your pack's waist strap, not in your pack. Use only bear spray; personal self-defense pepper spray is not effective. Bear spray is not a repellent. Bear spray should never serve as a substitute for standard safety precautions in bear country. Follow the manufacturer's instructions. Know how to use it, and be aware of limitations, including the expiration date.

For your protection, do not remove the safety clip unless you are preparing to use the spray. It may accidentally discharge. Never store the bear spray in a vehicle. It may explode due to heat. Keep out of reach of children. Ask a ranger for additional information.

**Stay with Your Food**

DO NOT leave backpacks, coolers, or anything with an odor unattended for ANY length of time. Your food should always be within arm's reach or properly stored.

DO NOT allow bears to obtain human food. Allowing a bear to obtain human food, even once, often results in aggressive and dangerous behavior. The bear is then a threat to human safety and must be relocated or killed.

If approached by a bear while eating, put food away and retreat to a safe distance. Never abandon food because of an approaching bear. Always take the food with you.

Never throw your pack or food at a bear in an attempt to distract it.

Source: National Park Service. U.S. Department of the Interior.

# REAL WORLD EXPERIENCE

## Designing Documents for a Nonprofit Organization

Working with a team assigned by your instructor, redesign or create documents for a campus or community nonprofit organization.

**Step 1: Organize the team.**
- Select a team leader to serve as the project's *managing editor*. The managing editor is responsible for communicating with your instructor, handing in the final documents, assigning tasks when necessary, and proofreading the final documents.
- Exchange telephone numbers and email addresses.

**Step 2: Identify a nonprofit organization and identify the documents you will redesign or create.**
- Ask the nonprofit organization if it has documents that you can update or redesign.
- Obtain enough copies or make enough copies of the documents for each team member. Work with your instructor to determine which documents your team will update and/or redesign.
- If the organization doesn't have documents, determine what documents they need written and designed. Gather any needed information. Work with your instructor to determine the appropriate number and type of documents your team will write and design.

**Step 3: Plan the designs.**
- Create thumbnail sketches or prototypes for possible page designs.
- When you have decided on a sketch or prototype, determine the page size appropriate for your design.
- Create a style sheet for the redesigned or new documents.

**Step 4: Write or rewrite and revise the documents.**
- If you are creating documents from scratch, organize and write the documents.
- If you are revising existing documents, make sure you have up-to-date information.
- Follow the guidelines in Chapters 6, 7, and 8.

**Step 5: Hand in your documents to your instructor.**
- Attach copies of the original documents if there were any.

# chapter *eleven*

## Creating Effective Visual Information for Your Readers

ou've probably heard the expression A picture is worth a thousand words. Indeed, you can often convey information in technical documents more effectively and efficiently with pictures than with words. Pictures, or graphics, can explain abstract ideas or summarize concepts that are difficult for readers to grasp by text only. How can visual information, graphics, help readers?

iStockphoto 2008.

- Graphics support and supplement the text. Graphics are especially helpful to readers who are unfamiliar with concepts or details or who want to gather information at a glance.
- Graphics summarize information in the text and clarify or present it differently for readers who may not have understood the text.
- Graphics help readers understand how something works or how to do something.
- Graphics present some types of information more quickly and efficiently than words. For instance, a map more effectively conveys the locations of coral reefs than can words. A hotel guest can read a line drawing map showing how to evacuate the hotel in an emergency better than he or she could understand the same information in words.

We are bombarded with visual information through television, advertisements, and the Internet. Because we are so accustomed to receiving information visually, we often look first to graphics to obtain information. Many of your documents will be more effective and complete when you add graphics to a written text that describes concepts or data. Without the graphics, many readers may abandon a document or miss important information because they do not want or lack the time to read page after page of text.

In most documents, however, you can't rely solely on graphics to communicate all the information. For example, in Figure 11.1 the writers rely primarily on line drawings to instruct readers on how to tie a Windsor knot. Brief step-by-step instructions accompany the graphics to provide more information. The graphics alone convey the primary message, but the written instructions provide the details.

To balance the visual and textual information, consider the needs of your readers and what you want to communicate. This chapter will help you choose the most appropriate graphics for documents and strike the proper balance between visual and textual information.

##  WHY USE VISUAL INFORMATION?

Effective visual information helps you convey part or all of a message. Visual information helps you

- show how to follow instructions or visualize a process
- show what something looks like
- show and summarize relationships among data
- emphasize and reinforce information
- show how something is organized
- simplify complex concepts, discussions, processes, or data
- add visual interest

### Show How to Follow Instructions or Visualize a Process

Graphics are excellent devices for giving readers instructions or helping them visualize a process. Instructions without graphics are often hard to follow. For example, imagine trying to tie a Windsor knot for the first time without a visual aid. Without graphics, most of us would not be able to tie the knot; however, with drawings, as in Figure 11.1, you can visualize the process and tie the knot. Notice that the drawings mirror the process: The drawings appear as if the reader were looking in a mirror.

FIGURE 11.1

**Graphics Help Readers Visualize a Process**

*The Half Windsor*

YOUR MIRROR REFLECTION

**1**
Start with wide end of tie on your right
and extend a foot below narrow end.

**2**
Cross wide end over narrow end and
back underneath.

**3**
Bring up and turn down through loop.

**4**
Pass wide end around front from
left to right.

**5**
Then, up through the loop, and...

**6**
...down through knot in front.
Tighten carefully and draw up to collar.

Source: Taken from *How to Tie a Tie* brochure, distributed by The Men's Wearhouse, Inc. Permission granted by Kim Owens via email June 5, 2009.

## Show What Something Looks Like

Graphics, such as photographs and drawings, are excellent tools for helping readers to see what something looks like. They help readers visualize a concept, theory, or object. For example, the photo in Figure 11.2 shows readers what a coral reef looks like.

## Show and Summarize Relationships among Data

For some readers, you will display numerical data or show how one set of data relates to another. Perhaps you want to show the results of changes over time for a laboratory test, a survey, or a trend. Graphics help readers quickly see relationships or trends.

You have many types of graphics available to you to show relationships or trends among numerical data. The line graph in Figure 11.3 compares the change in gasoline and diesel prices from 1994 to 2012. The same numbers presented in a paragraph would not adequately convey the scope of the change. The table in Figure 11.4 shows the relationship between mined acres of land and reclaimed acres of land. The table also summarizes the total acres mined and reclaimed.

**FIGURE 11.2**

**Photo That Shows What Something Looks Like**

iStockphoto 2008.

## FIGURE 11.3

### Line Graph That Shows Relationships

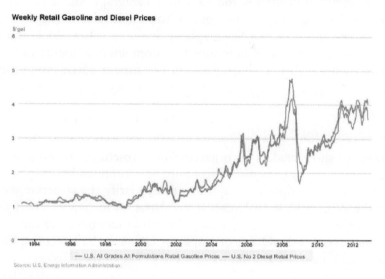

Weekly Retail Gasoline and Diesel Prices

$/gal

— U.S. All Grades All Formulations Retail Gasoline Prices — U.S. No 2 Diesel Retail Prices

Source: U.S. Energy Information Administration

Source: U.S. Energy Information Administration.

## FIGURE 11.4

### Table Summarizing Numeric Data

| Mining and Reclamation | | | | |
|---|---|---|---|---|
| Acres of Mined and Reclaimed | Oh My Mine | Darling Mine | Clemintine Mine | Total (in acres) |
| Mined in 2010 | 210 | 745 | 643 | 1,598 |
| Mined Since 2000 | 13,465 | 20,442 | 13,456 | 47,363 |
| Reclaimed Since 2010 | 268 | 1,875 | 897 | 3,040 |
| Reclaimed Since 2000 | 15,601 | 21,465 | 14,575 | 51,641 |

## Emphasize and Reinforce Information

You can use many types of graphics to convey information presented in the text. Your choice will depend on your objectives and the information you want to emphasize or reinforce. For example, if you want to emphasize the findings of a series of air-bag tests, you might first discuss the data in a paragraph and then reinforce the data with a horizontal bar graph or a line graph You might also display the data in a table and then reinforce the data in a bar graph or line graph. Let's look at a specific example: To reinforce the concept of how investing even small amounts of money over time helps individuals reach their savings goals, an investment advisor might use the table in Figure 11.5.

## Show How Something Is Organized

You may need to show readers an organizational structure. For example, investors may need to understand the organizational structure of a company, but they are having trouble grasping the textual description. Graphics quickly clarify the structure. For example, the website for the National Credit Union Administration includes a chart that shows how the agency is organized (see Figure 11.6). This chart identifies the three offices that the board and chair oversee: the Office of Inspector General, the Executive Director, and the General Counsel. The chart also shows that the Office of the Executive Director oversees

**FIGURE 11.5**

### Table That Reinforces Information

| Investing Your Money Over Time[1] | | | | |
|---|---|---|---|---|
| When you contribute monthly[2] | In 5 years, *you could have* | In 10 years, *you could have* | In 20 years, *you could have* | In 30 years, *you could have* |
| $50 ($600) | $3,698 | $9,208 | $29,647 | $75,015 |
| $100 ($1,200) | $7,397 | $18,417 | $59,295 | $150,030 |
| $150 ($1,800) | $11,095 | $27,625 | $88,942 | $225,044 |

[1] Assumes an 8% annual return, compounded monthly
[2] Number in parentheses shows the total annual contribution

two types of offices: central and regional. Under regional offices, the chart includes a U.S. map showing the regions. Notice also how the chart is designed to fit on the screen of a small, as well as a large, monitor. The chart uses color to show that all the central offices belong in the same group and are equal in the hierarchy. Traditional organizational charts use a horizontal layout to show equal rank; however, the chart wouldn't fit on a screen if the central offices appeared horizontally.

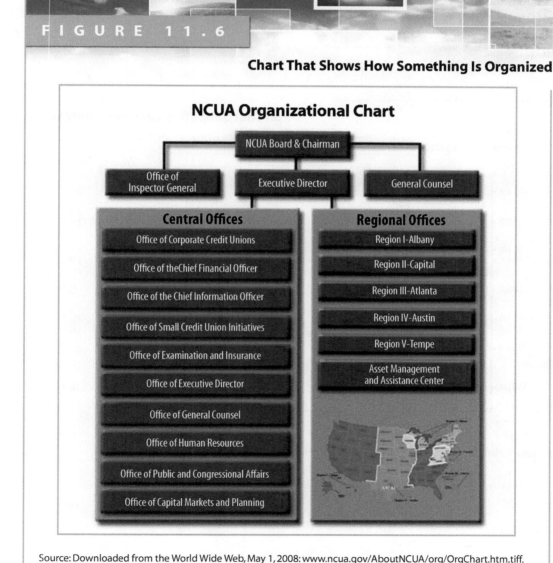

**FIGURE 11.6**

**Chart That Shows How Something Is Organized**

Source: Downloaded from the World Wide Web, May 1, 2008: www.ncua.gov/AboutNCUA/org/OrgChart.htm.tiff.

## Simplify Complex Concepts, Discussions, Processes, or Data

Readers may have difficulty understanding and analyzing complex information presented in words. When complex information is presented visually, readers understand that information more quickly and easily. For example, the scientists working on the Galileo mission wanted to show the stages of a probe's descent into Jupiter's atmosphere after being launched from the Galileo satellite. They used a graph to plot and briefly describe the probe's decent (see Figure 11.7). Even though the graphic is complex, it still simplifies information that would be difficult to follow without a graphic.

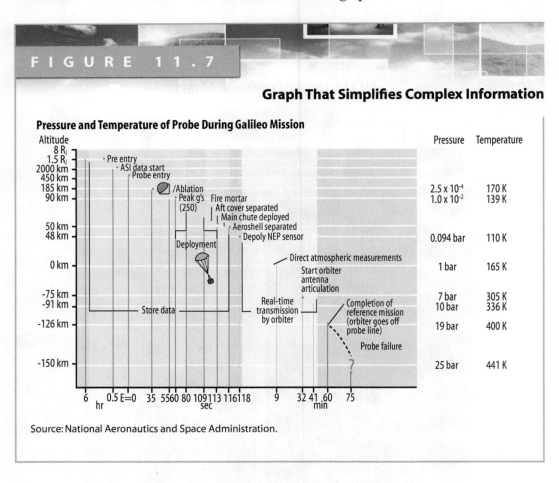

**FIGURE 11.7**

### Graph That Simplifies Complex Information

Source: National Aeronautics and Space Administration.

## Add Visual Interest to a Document

When used appropriately, graphics such as photographs and pictographs add visual appeal to your documents. For example, when scientists discuss volcanic eruptions, they use graphics—especially photographs—to show the eruptions and lava flows such as the eruption photo in Figure 11.8.

Some graphics not only add interest, but they also convey important information. For example, Figure 11.9, compares the amount of beef comsumed in the U.S. between 1950 and 2011. This pictograph clearly adds interest to the document, and it also informs.

FIGURE 11.8

**Photo That Adds Interest**

iStockphoto 2008.

Think about the documents that you have read or that you might write at work. Many of them probably contain graphics. Effective graphics help you convey part or all of a message. Before you select a graphic, ask yourself what readers expect from your document and what they know about the topic. As you plan, answer these questions:

- **Will visual information help you to achieve your purpose?** For example, if your purpose is to show what something looks like, a visual is essential to achieving your purpose.
- **Who are my readers and will they need or expect information to be presented visually?** For example, expert readers may expect more detailed graphics such as numerical tables or complex drawings, whereas general readers may prefer a less detailed graphic where the key points are extracted and easily viewed.
- **What types of graphics are appropriate for the information and the readers?** For example, how will your readers' culture or language affect the types of graphics you select? Can you best present the information in a drawing or a photo? Will the readers' level of knowledge about the topic affect the types of graphics you use?

Plan the graphics early in the writing and designing process. Think about them as you decide what information to include in the document. If you wait too long, you may not have the time or resources to create the graphics, you may not have enough time to obtain permission to reproduce someone else's graphics, or you may find that adding graphics will require reformatting the document.

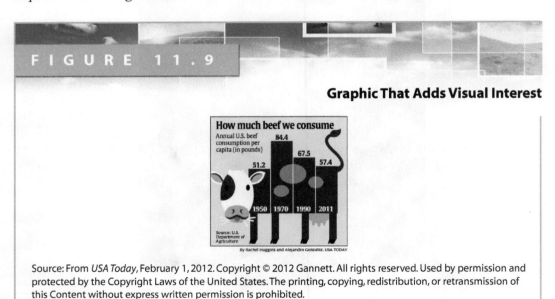

## FIGURE 11.9

### Graphic That Adds Visual Interest

To determine the appropriate graphic, ask yourself, What do I want to illustrate with the graphic. "What is the purpose of the graphic?" Use graphics for these purposes:

* to illustrate quantitative information
* to show relationships
* to illustrate instructions and processes
* to show what something looks like

Figure 11.10 summarizes the types of graphics and the most appropriate uses for each.

## Bar Graphs

*Bar graphs* compare relationships among numerical data. Bar graphs display approximate—not specific—values. They let readers see relationships and trends at a glance. You can orient bar graphs vertically or horizontally; you can use single bars, stacked bars, or multiple bars. Bar graphs are excellent choices when you want to

* **Compare values.** Use a simple bar graph to compare values. For example, Figure 11.11 shows the percentage of revenue possible from five fundraising programs.
* **Show the values that make up a total.** For example, Figure 11.12 shows the distribution of fall undergraduates enrolled full time and part time in degree-granting institutions. Each bar is subdivided by type of institution.
* **Show two or more relationships.** Show relationships with a multiple-bar graph. The multiple bar graph in Figure 11.13A shows the percentage of high school seniors who participated in extracurricular activities in 2010. The graph compares seniors who planned to attend college with those who did not.
* **Show trends over time.** Figure 11.13B compares the number of degrees granted by post-secondary institutions between 1999-2000, 2004-2005, and 2009-2010. For example, the bar graph shows that in 2009-2010, the number of Bachelor's degrees awarded was higher than the number of Associate's degrees.
* **Show positive and negative values.** With some data, you need to indicate both positive and negative values. You do that with a deviation bar graph like the one in Figure 11.14.

Read the Tips for Creating Bar Graphs for a quick review.

FIGURE 11.10

**Selecting the Appropriate Graphic**

| Purpose | Types of Graphic | Best Use of the Graphic |
|---|---|---|
| **Illustrate quantitative (numerical) information** | Bar graphs | • show comparisons of approximate values<br>• summarize relationships among data |
| | Line graphs | • show trends (changes) over time, cost, or other variable |
| | Pie charts | • show the relationship of the parts to a whole |
| | Pictographs | • summarize statistical information for general readers |
| | Tables | • summarize and categorize large amounts of numerical data |
| **Show relationships of qualitative (not numerical) information** | Organizational charts | • show the hierarchy in an organization or company<br>• show how something is organized |
| | Diagrams | • show a sequence of events |
| | Tables | • show relationships and summarize data |
| **Show instructions and processes** | Flow charts | • explain a process or a sequence of events or steps |
| | Tables | • organize information<br>• indicate troubleshooting and frequently asked questions with answers |
| | Line drawings | • show a realistic, but simplified view of what something looks like |
| | Diagrams | • demonstrate how to do something<br>• show where something is located to complete a task or understand a process |
| **Show what something looks like** | Line drawings | • show a representation of what something will or does look like |
| | Photos | • give a realistic picture<br>• show exactly what something looks like |
| | Screen shots | • show what appears on a computer monitor |

**Simple Bar Graph**

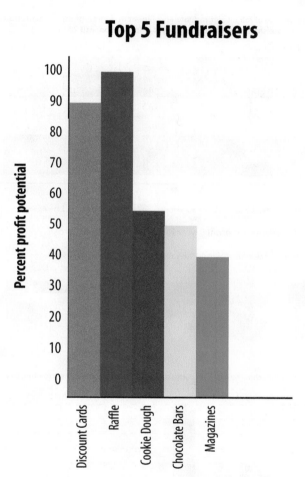

**Top 5 Fundraisers**

# FIGURE 11.12

## Divided Bar Graph

Percentage distribution of fall undergraduate enrollment in degree-granting institutions, by student attendance status and control and level of institution: Fall 2010

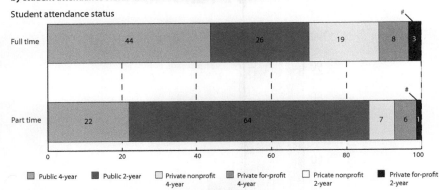

Student attendance status

| Full time | 44 | 26 | 19 | 8 | 3 | # |
| Part time | 22 | 64 | 7 | 6 | 1 | # |

Legend:
- Public 4-year
- Public 2-year
- Private nonprofit 4-year
- Private for-profit 4-year
- Pricate nonprofit 2-year
- Private for-profit 2-year

The percentage share for private nonprofit 2-year institutions rounds to zero.

SOURCE: U.S. Department of Education, National Center for Education Statistics.

# FIGURE 11.13A

## Multiple-Bar Graph

Percentage of high school seniors who participated in various extracurricular activities, by college plans: 2010

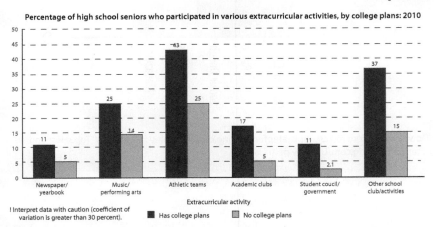

| Extracurricular activity | Has college plans | No college plans |
|---|---|---|
| Newspaper/yearbook | 11 | 5 |
| Music/performing arts | 25 | 14 |
| Athletic teams | 43 | 25 |
| Academic clubs | 17 | 5 |
| Student coucil/government | 11 | 2.1 |
| Other school club/activities | 37 | 15 |

! Interpret data with caution (coefficient of variation is greater than 30 percent).

Source: Downloaded from the World Wide Web, December 12, 2012: http://nces.ed.gov/programs/coe/figures/figure-exa-2.asp

**Multiple-Bar Graph** *continued*

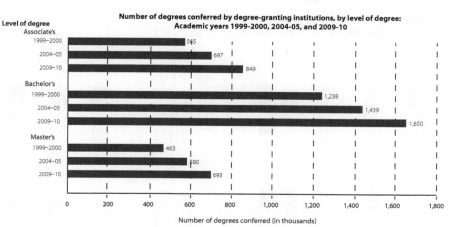

Number of degrees conferred by degree-granting institutions, by level of degree: Academic years 1999-2000, 2004-05, and 2009-10

Level of degree

Associate's
- 1999–2000: 565
- 2004–05: 697
- 2009–10: 849

Bachelor's
- 1999–2000: 1,238
- 2004–05: 1,439
- 2009–10: 1,650

Master's
- 1999–2000: 463
- 2004–05: 580
- 2009–10: 693

Number of degrees conferred (in thousands)

Source: Downloaded from the World Wide Web, May 1, 2008: www.nsf.gov/statistics/seind08/pdf/c07.pdf.

## TIPS FOR CREATING BAR GRAPHS

- **Use an appropriate scale.** Extend the longest bar nearly to the end of its parallel axis, as in Figure 11.11. Make sure the scale appropriately and ethically conveys the differences in values. Read the section "Presenting Visual Information Ethically" for more information on appropriate scale.
- **Begin the scale at 0 if possible to ensure that bars accurately represent values.**
- **Make all the bars the same width**—unless you overlap them.
- **Make the space consistent between bars.**
- **Label the bars.** Label each bar at its base. For multiple- or divided-bar graphs, include a key to indicate what the bars or divisions represent, as in Figure 11.12.
- **Put tick (or hash) marks at regular intervals on the appropriate axis.** The tick marks should indicate quantities, such as percentages or amounts of money.
- **Use a different pattern or color for each bar in a divided- or multiple-bar graph.**
- **Cite the source of your data below the graph** if you do not generate the data yourself. If you use a graph from another source, obtain written permission for using it and cite the source below the graph.

FIGURE 11.14

## Deviation Bar Graph

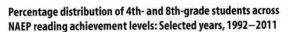

**Percentage distribution of 4th- and 8th-grade students across NAEP reading achievement levels: Selected years, 1992–2011**

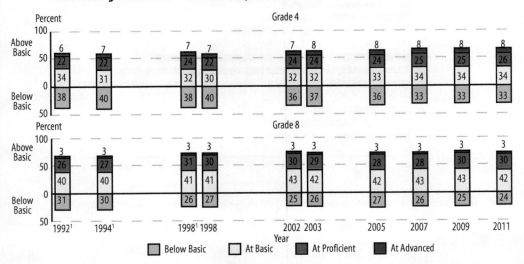

¹ Testing accommodations (e.g., extended time, small group testing) for children with disabilities and English language learners were not permitted during these assessments. Students were tested with and without accommodations in 1998.

NOTE: Achievement levels define what students should know and be able to do: *Basic* indicates partial mastery of fundamental skills, *Proficient* indicates demonstrated competency over challenging subject matter, and *Advanced* indicates superior performance. Detail may not sum to totals because of rounding. For more information on the National Assessment of Educational Progress (NAEP), see Appendix B – *Guide to Sources*.

SOURCE: U.S. Department of Education, National Center for Education Statistics.

## Diagrams

***Diagrams*** illustrate a sequence of events or actions. For example, the diagrams in Figure 11.15 show the relationship between beach erosion and seawalls. As you create diagrams, follow the Tips for Creating Diagrams.

## TIPS FOR CREATING DIAGRAMS

- **Sketch rough drafts of the diagram.** Try several drafts to determine exactly what you want in the diagram. Diagrams take a lot of time to create, so before you begin the final draft, make sure you have a clear idea of what information you want the diagram to communicate.
- **Label the diagram and explain the process.** Labels should be easy to read. Place explanations in the diagram if they won't interfere with or cause clutter. If the explanation will be more confusing than helpful, put it in the paragraph that precedes or follows it.
- **Use graphics software to produce the diagram.**
- **Cite the source of any data that you did not generate.**

**Diagrams**

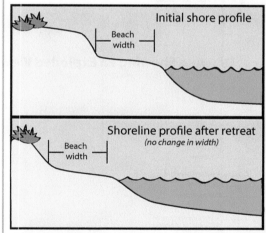

A beach undergoing net long-term retreat will maintain its natural width.

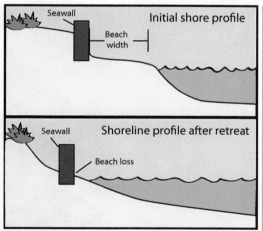

Beach loss eventually occurs in front of a seawall for a beach experiencing net long-term retreat.

Source: Downloaded from the World Wide Web, May 1, 2008: www.mothernature-hawaii.com/images/beach%20erosion_diagram.

FIGURE 11.16

## Drawing Showing a Cross Section

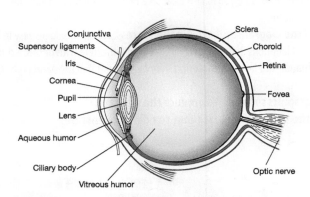

Conjunctiva
Supensory ligaments
Iris
Cornea
Pupil
Lens
Aqueous humor
Ciliary body
Vitreous humor

Sclera
Choroid
Retina
Fovea
Optic nerve

FIGURE 11.17

## Drawing Showing an Exploded View

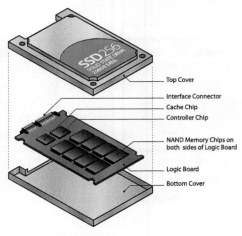

SSD256
SOLID STATE DRIVE

Top Cover
Interface Connector
Cache Chip
Controller Chip
NAND Memory Chips on both sides of Logic Board
Logic Board
Bottom Cover

## Drawing Showing a Cutaway

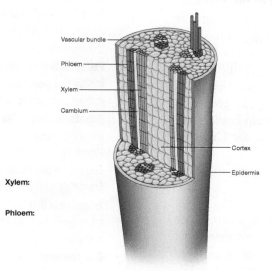

Vascular bundle

Phloem

Xylem

Cambium

Cortex

Epidermis

**Xylem:**

**Phloem:**

Source: Downloaded from the World Wide Web, November 2008: www.imagedatabase.bent treepress.com/db.bioart.asp. Bent Tree Press Biology Lab Database.

## TIPS FOR CREATING DRAWINGS

- **Present professional-looking drawings.** Use software to create your drawings, giving yourself time to learn the software. If you plan to create your your own drawings, make sure that you have the tools and training to create drawings with a professional appearance.
- **Render your drawing from the same angle that readers will have when they work with or observe the object in the drawing.** Figures 11.16–11.18 illustrate three angles or vantage points: a cross section, an exploded view, and a cutaway.
- **When appropriate, make the feature or detail you want to emphasize larger than it really is.** The larger size emphasizes the feature or detail, as in Figures 11.16 and 11.18.

## Drawings

*Drawings* are excellent graphics for instruction and showing readers what something looks like. Many writers select drawings instead of photographs to help readers see how something is put together. Drawings emphasize important details or parts that are not apparent in a photograph. They also allow you to explode (make larger) a particular detail. Figures 11.16–11.18 present drawings that help readers see details. Review the Tips for Creating Drawings.

## Flow Charts

Use *flow charts* to explain a process or to show a sequence of steps or events. Flow charts are especially useful for explaining a complex process that has conditional (if/then) steps. Flow charts generally work best for processes that have a definite beginning and a definite end (use diagrams for ongoing processes, such as recycling).

Flow charts usually consist of circles, rectangles, diamonds, and other geometric shapes that indicate the steps of a process or event. In some fields, various geometric shapes have specific meanings, and people in those fields understand what the shapes represent. If the shapes you use in your flow chart have specific meanings, ensure your readers understand what the they represent or use a key (see Figure 11.19). As you create your flow charts, follow the Tips for Creating Flow Charts.

## Line Graphs

*Line graphs* show relationships among data with more precision than bar graphs. Like bar graphs, line graphs use a horizontal and a vertical axis; but line graphs use lines and sometimes bands instead of bars to indicate relationships. Line graphs emphasize changes and trends. They are especially effective when you want to compare information.

**Flow Chart That Illustrates a Process**

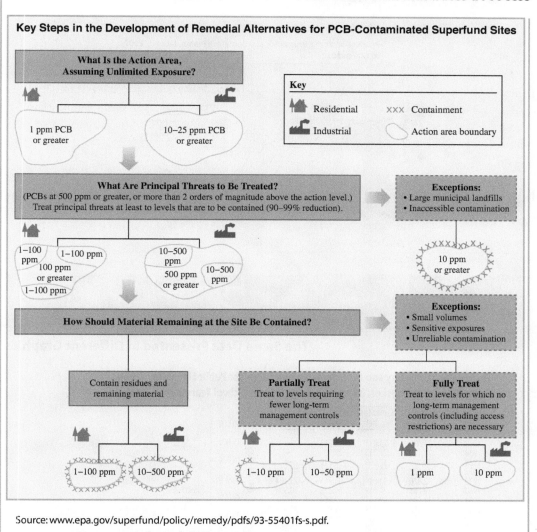

Key Steps in the Development of Remedial Alternatives for PCB-Contaminated Superfund Sites

**What Is the Action Area, Assuming Unlimited Exposure?**

1 ppm PCB or greater

10–25 ppm PCB or greater

**Key**

Residential    xxx Containment

Industrial    Action area boundary

**What Are Principal Threats to Be Treated?**
(PCBs at 500 ppm or greater, or more than 2 orders of magnitude above the action level.) Treat principal threats at least to levels that are to be contained (90–99% reduction).

**Exceptions:**
• Large municipal landfills
• Inaccessible contamination

1–100 ppm
1–100 ppm
100 ppm or greater
1–100 ppm

10–500 ppm
500 ppm or greater
10–500 ppm

10 ppm or greater

**How Should Material Remaining at the Site Be Contained?**

**Exceptions:**
• Small volumes
• Sensitive exposures
• Unreliable contamination

Contain residues and remaining material

**Partially Treat**
Treat to levels requiring fewer long-term management controls

**Fully Treat**
Treat to levels for which no long-term management controls (including access restrictions) are necessary

1–100 ppm    10–500 ppm

1–10 ppm    10–50 ppm

1 ppm    10 ppm

Source: www.epa.gov/superfund/policy/remedy/pdfs/93-55401fs-s.pdf.

## FIGURE 11.20

### Line Graph That Shows Change Over Time

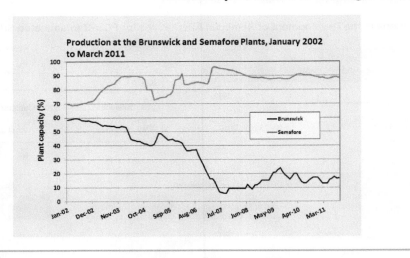

Production at the Brunswick and Semafore Plants, January 2002 to March 2011

## FIGURE 11.21

### The Same Data Presented in Different Graphics

**Average Annual Salary and Average Beginning Salary for Public Elementary and Secondary School Teachers (in 1993 Dollars): Selected School Years Ending 1960–93**

| School year ending | All teachers | Elementary teachers | Secondary teachers | Beginning salary* |
|---|---|---|---|---|
| 1960 | $ 24,599 | $ 23,712 | $ 25,983 | — |
| 1964 | 28,127 | 27,235 | 29,398 | — |
| 1968 | 31,584 | 30,669 | 32.729 | — |
| 1972 | 34,127 | 33,138 | 35.273 | $ 24,128 |
| 1976 | 32,876 | 32,041 | 33.755 | 23,104 |
| 1980 | 29,766 | 29,019 | 30.678 | 20,504 |
| 1984 | 31,184 | 30,547 | 32.064 | 21,562 |
| 1988 | 35,017 | 34,373 | 35.974 | 23.968 |
| 1992 | 34,618 | 34,053 | 35.421 | 24,001 |
| 1993 | 35,873 | 35,308 | 36.609 | 23,969 |

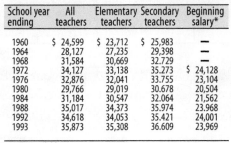
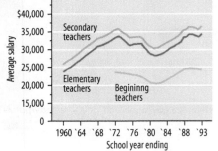

— Not available
\* Beginning teacher salary is for the calendar year.

Source: U.S. Dept. of Education.

FIGURE 11.22

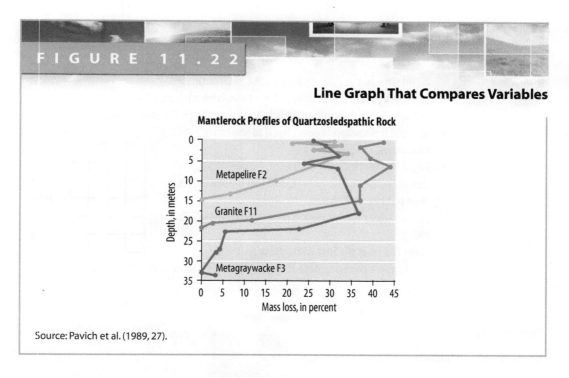

**Line Graph That Compares Variables**

Mantlerock Profiles of Quartzosledspathic Rock

Source: Pavich et al. (1989, 27).

Use line graphs to

- **Show or compare trends.** Line graphs show patterns of change over time. Figure 11.20 shows the change in production at two manufacturing plants between 2002 and 2011. Tables can present the same numerical data as line graphs, but, as Figure 11.21 shows, readers can identify trends from a line graph more easily than from a table of numbers. The table in Figure 11.21 contains the same numerical data as the line graph in Figure 11.21, but trends are easier to spot in the line graph.
- **Compare variables.** Line graphs show readers how two or more variables compare under similar situations. For example, the line graph in Figure 11.22 compares the rocks at various depths in the Virginia Piedmont.

Line graphs generally show how changes in one variable (the ***independent variable***) affect changes in another variable (the ***dependent variable***). For example, Figure 11.22 shows how three dependent variables are affected when the percentage of mass loss (the independent variable) varies. The independent variable always appears on the horizontal axis. Once you have determined the dependent and independent variables, follow the Tips for Creating Line Graphs.

## TIPS FOR CREATING LINE GRAPHS

- **When time is a variable, put it on the horizontal axis.**
- **Place tick (hash) marks at regular intervals on each axis.** Use the appropriate scale for each interval. Generally, make tick marks short; longer tick marks add clutter.
- **Use grid lines when readers need to see exact quantities.**
- **Begin the vertical axis with zero.** If it doesn't begin with zero, use breaks to show your readers that the axis begins at some point other than zero.
- **Label each axis.** Most readers prefer labels centered along each axis.
- **Make the lines distinct** with color or symbols.
- **Cite the source of any data that you did not generate.**

*Grid lines*

## Organizational Charts

*Organizational charts* are an efficient way to show

- an organization's hierarchy of people and departments
- an organization's lines of responsibility

The same relationships explained only with words may be difficult for readers to envision. Without a visual representation of the organizational hierarchy, readers may misunderstand the relationships within the organization.

The chart in Figure 11.23 shows the organization and lines of responsibility for a university. The person or department with the most responsibility is at the top, and those with the least responsibility are at the bottom. Figure 11.23

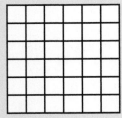

## TIPS FOR CREATING ORGANIZATIONAL CHARTS

- **Use color to indicate divisions within the organization.** For example, in Figure 11.23, the divisions under the Vice President of Accounting are one color and the divisions under the Vice President of Academic Affairs are another. Colors help the readers distinguish the divisions of the university.
- **Remember that you don't have to include every person or division in the organization. Include only those people or divisions that the readers need to see.** Figure 11.23, for example, does not show people and divisions in the College of Sciences or the College of Engineering.

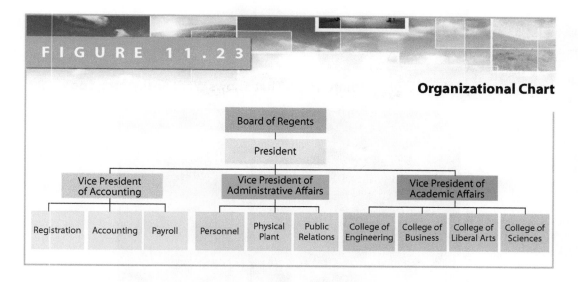

FIGURE 11.23

**Organizational Chart**

Board of Regents

President

Vice President of Accounting

Vice President of Administrative Affairs

Vice President of Academic Affairs

Registration | Accounting | Payroll

Personnel | Physical Plant | Public Relations

College of Engineering | College of Business | College of Liberal Arts | College of Sciences

indicates that the Board of Regents and the greatest responsibility and that the heads of Payroll, Public Relations, and the College of Sciences, for example, have less responsibility. The chart also uses titles instead of names, so it will be relevant despite personnel changes. Follow the Tips for Creating Organizational Charts.

## Photos

*Photographs* are excellent graphics when you want to

- **Show what something looks like.** Often, words are not enough to help readers know what something looks like, especially if they have never seen what you are describing. For example, if you are describing a piece of equipment that readers may need for an experiment, a photo is an effective tool. If you are cataloging types of sea life, you might use photos (see Figure 11.24). Photos are a practical way to help readers recognize sea life.
- **Show where something is located on a machine, a piece of equipment, and so on**. For example, a car manufacturer uses a photo with labels to help readers locate and identify car's lights, gauges, and warning indicators (see Figure 11.25).
- **Show how something is done.** For instance, you might use a photo to show readers how to plant seeds (see Figure 11.26).

To create and use photos effectively, follow the Tips for Creating Effective Photos.

**Photograph That Shows What Something Looks Like**

iStockphoto 2008.

**Photo That Shows Where Something Is Located**

### LIGHTS, GAUGES AND INDICATORS

1. Lamps On Reminder
2. Fog Lamp Light
3. Tachometer
4. Cruise Control Light
5. High Beam On Light
6. Speedometer/Odometer
7. Winter Driving Mode Light

8. Malfunction Indicator (Check Engine) Lamp
9. Sport Mode light
10. Air Bag Readiness Light
11. Safety Belt Reminder Light
12. Fuel Gauge
13. Charging System Light
14. ABS System Warning Light

15. Traction Control Warning Light
16. Brake System Warning Light
17. Engine Coolant Temperature Warning Light
18. Security Light
19. Temperature Gauge
20. Oil Pressure Light

Source: Cadillac Motor Car Division, www.cadillac.com. *CTS Owner's Manual.* Used with permission.

**Photo of How Something Is Done**

iStockphoto 2008.

## TIPS FOR CREATING EFFECTIVE PHOTOS

- **Eliminate unnecessary detail and clutter.** Show only what you want readers to see.
- **Use an appropriate angle.** Take photos from the angle at which readers will actually view the object.
- **Crop the photo to focus on the information you want the reader to see.** For example, see Figure 11.27. In the photo on the left, the flower is off center and too small; however, in the photo on the right, the focus is on the flower. It is larger and framed within the image boundaries.
- **Use software to edit your photos.** Use software to size or eliminate distracting elements.
- **Do not unethically manipulate photos.** You can ethically crop a photo to eliminate excess background or to draw attention to a particular detail; however, if you airbrush a photo to take out essential detail, you are unethically manipulating it.
- **If you did not take the photo yourself, cite the source of your photo and obtain permission to use it.**

**Cropping Photos Effectively**

iStockphoto 2008.

## Pictographs

*Pictographs* are similar to bar graphs but use pictures or drawings instead of bars to depict statistical information. Pictographs make your document visually interesting. For example, in Figure 11.28 a person's hand replaces the bars. As with bar graphs, pictograph measurements are not as exact as line graphs. Many pictographs lack a visible vertical or horizontal axis or tick marks, as in Figure 11.28. As you create pictographs, follow the Tips for Creating Pictographs.

## Pie Charts

*Pie charts* are circles divided into wedges—like pieces of pie. Each wedge represents a part of the whole. The pie chart in Figure 11.29 illustrates how a county spends tax dollars. Use pie charts to effectively support oral presentations and to summarize information in your documents.

Pie charts are easy to create with graphics software. For a professional look, make them three-dimensional or rotate them. As you create pie charts, follow the Tips for Creating Pie Charts.

FIGURE 11.28

**Pictograph**

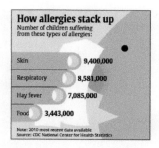

How allergies stack up
Number of children suffering
from these types of allergies:

| | |
|---|---|
| Skin | 9,400,000 |
| Respiratory | 8,581,000 |
| Hay fever | 7,085,000 |
| Food | 3,443,000 |

Note: 2010 most recent data available
Source: CDC National Center for Health Statistics

## TIPS FOR CREATING PICTOGRAPHS

- **Use pictures and drawings that are meaningful and appropriate to the readers, the tone, and the purpose.** Create pictographs that fit your purpose and your readers' expectations. Pictographs should fit the tone of your document. For example, if you are preparing a proposal to the U.S. Department of Defense to build a new aircraft carrier, a pictograph would be inappropriate not only for the purpose, but also for the formal tone of the document.
- **Use drawings rather than photos.** Photos contain too much detail and are too realistic for most pictographs.
- **Use color to enhance pictographs.** Color adds visual interest.
- **Label pictographs.** Even though pictographs are less exact than other graphics, they are not merely decorative. Pictographs need appropriate, readable labels, as in Figure 11.28.
- **Use pictographs primarily for general readers.** If you want to use pictographs for experts or decision makers, use them in oral presentations or for less formal situations. Make sure the pictograph is appropriate for the occasion.
- **Cite the source for any data that you did not generate.**

**Pie Chart**

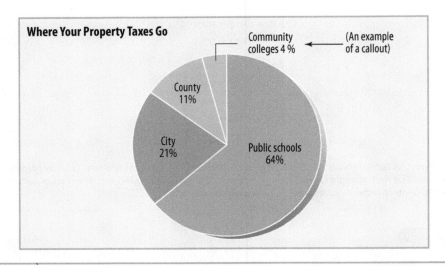

Where Your Property Taxes Go

Community colleges 4 %

(An example of a callout)

County 11%

City 21%

Public schools 64%

## TIPS FOR CREATING PIE CHARTS

- **Label each wedge of the pie chart and place the labels inside the wedge.** If the labels won't fit inside the wedge, use *callouts*—lines drawn from the label to the appropriate pie section. Depending on the graphics software, you may be able to pull out or explode some of the small wedges so the labels will fit inside them.
- **Place the labels horizontally inside the wedge, not diagonally.** In Figure 11.29 notice how the words Public schools, City, and County are placed horizontally inside the wedges.
- **Sequence the wedges from the largest to the smallest.** Place the largest wedge in the 12 o'clock position, and move from largest to smallest as you work around the "clock," as in Figure 11.29.
- **Make sure that the wedge percentages add up to 100 or that the size of each piece is proportionate to its share of the pie.**
- **Use contrasting colors to emphasize each section.** For example, in Figure 11.29, the Public schools wedge contrasts with the lighter-colored wedges.
- **Use color to make pie charts visually interesting and to differentiate wedges.**
- **Cite the source for any data that you did not generate.**

## Tables

*Tables* present quantitative (numerical) information arranged in columns and rows. With tables, you can present dense quantitative information in a format that readers can review and understand more easily than text alone. To create a table, put the information into vertical columns topped with appropriate headings, as in the table shown in Figure 11.30. Although tables usually display numerical data, they are also effective for presenting information in words. You can summarize quantitative information and show relationships among the information. Confronted with paragraphs of text, readers have to keep on reading until they find the information they need; in contrast, a table lets readers locate key words and information more easily. The table in Figure 11.31 provides information on safely storing egg products.

Whether your tables consist of words or numbers, they are likely to be more effective when you want to

- **present detailed information in a concise, readable format**. With tables, you can present dense information in a format that readers can scan and understand.

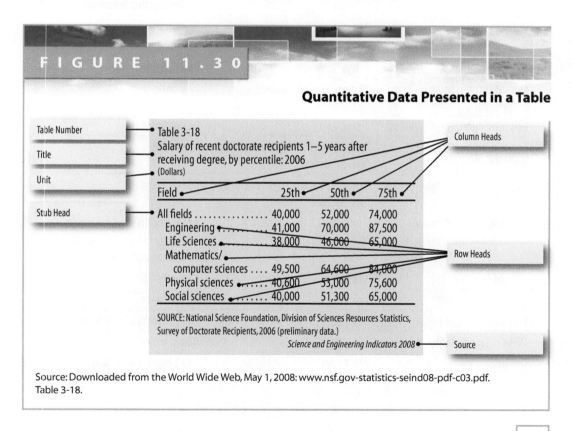

**FIGURE 11.30**

**Quantitative Data Presented in a Table**

Table Number
Title
Unit
Stub Head

Column Heads
Row Heads
Source

Table 3-18
Salary of recent doctorate recipients 1–5 years after receiving degree, by percentile: 2006
(Dollars)

| Field | 25th | 50th | 75th |
|---|---|---|---|
| All fields | 40,000 | 52,000 | 74,000 |
| Engineering | 41,000 | 70,000 | 87,500 |
| Life Sciences | 38,000 | 46,000 | 65,000 |
| Mathematics/ computer sciences | 49,500 | 64,600 | 84,000 |
| Physical sciences | 40,600 | 53,000 | 75,600 |
| Social sciences | 40,000 | 51,300 | 65,000 |

SOURCE: National Science Foundation, Division of Sciences Resources Statistics, Survey of Doctorate Recipients, 2006 (preliminary data.)

*Science and Engineering Indicators 2008*

Source: Downloaded from the World Wide Web, May 1, 2008: www.nsf.gov-statistics-seind08-pdf-c03.pdf. Table 3-18.

- **help readers locate information.** Confronted with paragraphs of prose, readers have to read until they find the information they need; in contrast, a table allows readers to locate keywords and information more quickly.

As you create tables, follow the Tips for Creating Tables.

FIGURE 11.31

**How to Store Egg Products Safely**

| Type of egg product | How long can you store the product in the refrigerator? | How long can you store the product in the freezer? |
|---|---|---|
| Raw eggs in shell | 3 to 5 weeks | Do not freeze. (Beat yolks and whiles together before freezing) |
| Raw egg whites | 2 to 4 days | 12 months |
| Raw egg yolks | 2 to 4 days | Do not freeze |
| Hard-boiled eggs | 7 days | Do not freeze |
| Egg substitutes, liquid (unopened) | 10 days | 12 months |
| Egg substitutes, liquid (opened) | 3 days | Do not freeze |
| Egg substitutes, frozen (unopened) | 7 days after thawing or refer to the "use-by" date | 12 months |
| Egg substitutes, Frozen (opened) | 3 days after thawing or refer to the "use-by" date | Do not freeze |
| Casseroles containing eggs | 3 to 4 days | 2 to 3 months after baking. Do not freeze unbaked casseroles containing eggs |
| Eggnog (commercial) | 3 to 5 days | 6 months |
| Eggnog (homemade) | 2 to 5 days | Do not freeze |
| Pies-Pumpkin and pecan | 3 to 4 days | 1 to 2 months after baking |
| Pies-Custard and chiffon | 3 to 4 days | Do not freeze |
| Quiche | 3 to 4 days | 1 to 2 months after baking |

Source: Data adapted from FoodSafety.gov

- **Put the table number and title at the top.** Readers view tables from the top down.
- **Label the column, stub, and row heads to orient your readers.** See Figure 11.30 to locate the column, stub, and row heads.
- **Use horizontal rules above the column heads to separate them from the table number and title and below the column heads to separate them from the data in the body.** The rules help readers locate the column heads.
- **Use rules to help readers to read across a table to find specific information.** For example, you might place rules after each grouping of information or after every five rows of information.
- **Use shading to help readers distinguish columns or rows.** For example, you might shade the first, third, and fifth columns in a table with six columns. Or you might shade every other row.
- **Note all units of measure.** In Figure 11.30 the unit (dollars) is noted in the title. You can also label the units in the column and row heads. If all the data are in the same unit of measure, include the unit in the title. If the data in the columns vary, label the unit in the column heads. For example, in a table summarizing data related to reclaiming land from mining operations, the columns would have different units:

| Amount spent reclaiming (in millions of dollars) | Total area reclaimed (in acres) |

- **Use X, NA, or a long dash to indicate omitted or unavailable data.** NA indicates *not available*.
- **Align the numbers and words correctly.** Vertically align columns of numerical data at the right or on the decimal points. Align words to the left.

| Right-aligned column | Decimal-aligned column |
|:---:|:---:|
| 7 | 0.23 |
| 11,890 | 203.78 |
| 789 | 33.90 |
| 318,900 | 3.00 |

- **Use footnotes for information you did not generate.** Use letters instead of numbers for table footnotes if numbers could confuse readers ($14^b$ instead of $14^2$). Readers can mistake footnote numbers for mathematical notation. For example, $14^2$ could mean *14 squared* rather than *footnote 2*.
- **Check the data.** Make sure the data are accurate. Double-check your math and make sure you have entered it correctly.

**FIGURE 11.32**

Source: Downloaded from the World Wide Web, August 8, 2012: www.irs.gov.

## Screen Shots

A *screen shot* is a picture—snapshot—of what appears on a computer monitor (screen). Screen shots help readers who are using or learning to use computer software. The screen shot shows readers what the screen looks like as they use the software. To create a screen shot, use the Print Screen function of your computer or graphics software. Figure 11.32 shows a screen shot.

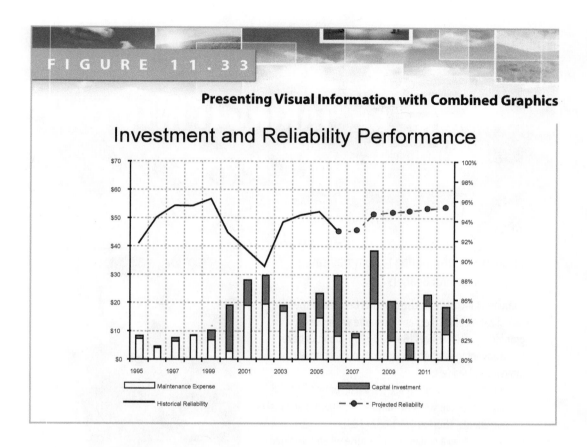

**FIGURE 11.33**

**Presenting Visual Information with Combined Graphics**

Investment and Reliability Performance

Legend:
- Maintenance Expense
- Capital Investment
- Historical Reliability
- Projected Reliability

## Combined Graphics

At times, you may have two purposes for presenting visual information; for example, you may want to contrast the information while also showing a trend. One type of graphic may not accomplish both goals, so you could use two types of graphics together. If you decide to use this approach, make sure

- your readers can understand both graphics
- the graphic remains uncluttered
- the relationship between the graphics is clear
- labels are included to clearly identify the information

Figure 11.33 shows a graphic that combines a line graph with a bar graph.

# TAKING IT INTO THE *workplace*

## Using Visual Information to Communicate with Intercultural Readers

Companies increasingly use graphics because of the globalization of markets and the more widely used graphical user interfaces (Bosley 1996). Graphics have these advantages when you are communicating with intercultural readers:

iStockphoto 2008.

- Graphics can "fit into space too small for text" (5) and can "reduce the size and number of editions [versions] of documents" (Horton 1993, 682–683).
- Graphics help a reader learn because when combined with text they are clearer than text alone. Readers find it "easier to see and understand than to see, translate, and then understand" (683).
- Graphics improve reader comprehension (Horton 1993).
- Graphics can replace technical terms that readers find difficult to understand (Bosley 1996).

## Assignment

Find a graphic from a company that markets its products or services internationally. After you find the graphic, answer these questions in an email to your instructor:

- Does the graphic have a neutral appearance? Explain your answer.
- Is the graphic simple? Does it use too many words? Explain your answer.
- Does the graphic make the concept, process, instruction, etc., easier to understand? If so, how? If not, how would you improve it?

DESIGN GRAPHICS THAT ARE CLEAR

When you have determined where visual information will help you achieve your purpose and you have determined the most appropriate graphics, you can begin to design them. As you design, follow these guidelines:

- Use simple, uncluttered graphics.
- Give each graphic a number and a descriptive title.
- Find out if international readers will see your graphics.
- Use color to enhance and clarify your graphics.

## Use Simple, Uncluttered Graphics

Your graphics will be effective if your readers can understand them. Cluttered graphics have too much information for the space or contain unnecessary detail. To create simple, uncluttered graphics follow the Tips for Creating Simple, Uncluttered Graphics.

**TIPS** FOR CREATING SIMPLE, UNCLUTTERED GRAPHICS

- **Include only the information your readers need.** Don't clutter graphics with unnecessary information or visual details.
- **Create two or more graphics if you have too much information for one.** If you use two, each one should serve a purpose and enhance your document.
- **Use diagrams and drawings to eliminate unnecessary detail.** Photos often have too much detail and clutter.
- **Exclude distracting visual information in photos.** Compare the photos in Figure 11.34A and 11.34B. Photo A is ineffective because it includes distracting information. Photo B is more effective because the distracting information is eliminated.
- **Don't crowd graphics into tight spaces.**

## Find Out If International Readers Will See the Graphics

Visual language, like verbal language, differs from nation to nation and culture to culture. A graphic that is effective for U.S. coworkers may be inappropriate for international readers. For example, British software designers used a wise old owl as an icon for online Help. The designers assumed that this image would work in the international community. However, in Hispanic countries, the owl symbolizes evil. In India, if someone calls you an owl, it means you are crazy (Barthon 2007).

The writers and designers assumed that intercultural readers would interpret the pictures as western readers would interpret them.

**Comparing Backgrounds in Photographs**

**A**

iStockphoto 2008.

**B**

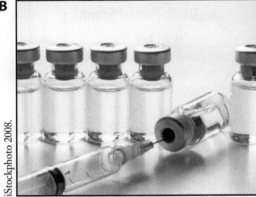

iStockphoto 2008.

Before you put graphics into a document, find out how readers in other countries and cultures will *read* them. When feasible, ask people native to that culture to look at the graphics you plan to use. They might be able to suggest changes that will make them better suited for international readers. As you design graphics for international readers, follow the Tips for Creating Graphics for International Readers.

## TIPS FOR CREATING GRAPHICS FOR INTERNATIONAL READERS

- **Give graphics a neutral look** (Horton 1993). For example, use a simple line drawing of a hand; the hand shouldn't appear to be masculine or feminine. Use outlines or neutral drawings, such as stick figures, to represent people (Bosley 1996).
- **Use simple graphics.** Eliminate unnecessary details (Bosley; Horton).
- **Use only colors that will convey the correct impression and/or meaning to your intercultural readers.** Colors have symbolic meanings and they vary among cultures. For example, in Japan blue symbolizes *villainy*, whereas in Arabic countries blue symbolizes virtue, faith, and truth. Bosley suggests using black and white, or gray and white for international graphics; but Horton suggests that "color can prove especially valuable" (687) if the designer carefully considers symbolic meanings when selecting colors.
- **Avoid culture-specific language and symbols.** For example, don't use a red, octagonal shape to indicate stop; not all countries use that shape in that way (Bosley).
- **Consider the reading direction of your readers** (Horton). In some countries, readers read graphics from left to right and clockwise. In other countries, they read them from right to left in a counterclockwise direction (Bosley). Horton suggests designing intercultural graphics that readers can read from top to bottom, or the graphic can include an arrow to direct readers.

## Use Color to Enhance and Clarify Graphics

Color is a powerful tool. When considering color, begin by asking yourself not how to use it, but whether to use it all (Parker and Berry 1998). As Parker and Berry explain, most documents can benefit from color, but only if it is applied correctly. As you consider whether to use color, ask yourself these questions:

- **Can you afford to use color?** Color printing costs are higher than black-and-white printing costs. If color will enhance your graphics, make sure you have money in your budget for it.
- **Will color enhance the graphic or add to its impact?** Some graphics will not lose their impact if you use black and white. For example, most line drawings don't need color.

- **Don't overuse color** (Parker and Berry 1998). If you use too many colors in a document or on one page, you won't impress your readers and you may confuse them. Make sure each color has a purpose.
- **Choose colors that will give your documents a unified look.** Use a color wheel such as the one in Figure 11.35. When selecting colors for a document, pick corresponding colors—three or four adjacent colors on the wheel (Parker and Berry). For example, you might select blue, green, and yellow.
- **Choose a triad of colors to create contrast in your graphics.** A triad of colors is three colors that are relatively equidistant from each other on the color wheel—such as yellow, red, and blue (Parker and Berry).
- **To create an effective contrast, choose colors that stand out against the background.** For example, don't use a shade of red on a red background; not all readers can easily distinguish among shades of red (see Figure 11.36). Use contrasting colors such as black and red.
- **If your readers associate a color with a particular meaning, use that color as your readers expect.** For example, U.S. readers associate red with danger or warning and yellow with caution. However, for readers outside the United States, these colors have different meanings.
- **Use bright colors to make objects look bigger.** For example, look at the stars in Figure 11.37. The stars are the same size; however, the yellow star looks larger than the blue star.
- **Make sure the text stands out from the background.** If you use a dark background, make the text white or another light color (see Figure 11.38).

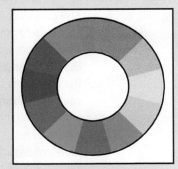

**Figure 11.35 The Color Wheel**

**Figure 11.36 Using Color to Create Contrast**

**Figure 11.37 Bright Colors Make Objects Look Larger**

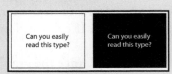

**Figure 11.38 Make Sure Text Stands Out**

- **Will my document look complete without color?** If your readers expect color graphics, the absence of color could become a liability (Parker and Berry 1998). However, color will not compensate for a poorly designed, inaccurate, or unclear graphic.

If you decide that color will enhance your graphics, follow the Tips for Using Color to Enhance and Clarify Graphics.

## ETHICS NOTE

### Presenting Visual Information Ethically

You have a responsibility to present visual information ethically. The visual information you include in your documents should be accurate, complete, and honest. To ensure that you use visual information ethically, follow these guidelines:

- **Present an accurate representation of the information.** For example, don't use a table to hide an unfavorable data point when that same data point would stand out in a bar or line graph.
- **Edit photos ethically.** Airbrushing is ethical and legitimate when used to highlight essential or important information in a picture; airbrushing becomes unethical when it removes information to deceive or mislead readers.
- **Use an accurate scale.** As you create graphics requiring scales, the graphics must accurately and honestly present the data and differences among the data. The scale you select affects how readers perceive your data. If you use inappropriate scales, you exaggerate the differences in data when differences are minor; or you make differences in data look small, even though they really are large. Figure 11.39 uses an inaccurate scale. The difference between Burgert, the most recommended, and Raign, the least recommended, is only 1.34 percent. The bar graph, however, makes the difference between Burgert and Raign look dramatic—certainly more than 1.34 percent. The scale misleads and distorts. The graph needs a smaller scale and size to ethically represent the difference between Burgert and other builders (see Figure 11.40).
- **Begin the axis at zero.** If you can't practically begin at zero, clearly indicate that the axis does not begin at zero.
- **Don't omit relevant information.** For example, even if you have values that you can't explain, don't leave them out. You must somehow account for them.
- **Cite the source of any data or information that you did not generate.**

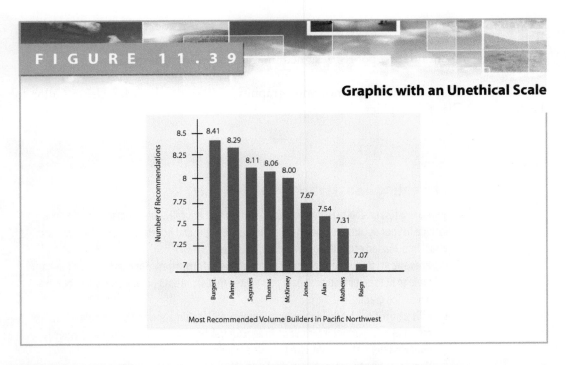

## FIGURE 11.39

**Graphic with an Unethical Scale**

Most Recommended Volume Builders in Pacific Northwest

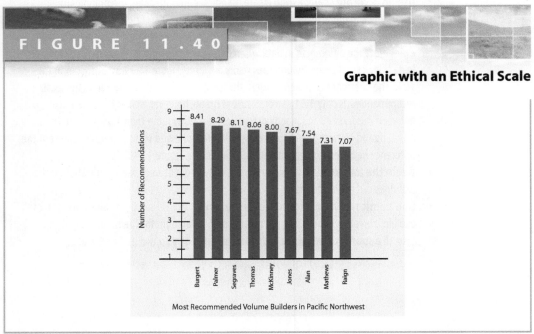

## FIGURE 11.40

**Graphic with an Ethical Scale**

Most Recommended Volume Builders in Pacific Northwest

When you have designed and created your graphic, integrate it into the text of your document. Think about how the graphic supports and reinforces the text to create a meaningful statement, assertion, etc. To effectively integrate graphics into the text

- Give each graphic a number and an informative title.
- Introduce and refer to each graphic by number.
- Tell readers what is important about each graphic.
- Place each graphic as close as possible to its related text.

## Give Each Graphic a Number and an Informative Title

Include a number (such as Table 2.15 or Figure 3.4) and a title with every graphic. Numbers help readers locate graphics. The titles and captions should be brief yet informative phrases that describe the content of the graphics.

### TIPS FOR NUMBERING GRAPHICS

- **Number graphics consecutively within each document.** If you don't divide your document into chapters, number the graphics consecutively from the beginning to the end of the document.
- **If you divide your document into chapters or sections, give each figure a two-part number: chapter number first and figure number second.** For example, you would number the graphics in Chapter 2 as 2.1, 2.2, 2.3, and so on; and those in Chapter 3 as 3.1, 3.2, 3.3, and so on, as in this book. Alternatively, number tables and figures separately: Chapter 1 figures would be numbered Figure 1.1, Figure 1.2, etc. Chapter 1 tables would be numbered Table 1.1, Table 1.2, etc.
- **Put the number and title where the reader would begin viewing the graphic.** For example, readers generally read bar graphs from the bottom to the top, so the number and title should appear at the bottom. However, readers read tables from the top to the bottom, so the number and title should appear at the top.
- **For some documents, use Arabic numbers (1, 2, 3, etc.) for figures and Roman numerals (I, II, III, etc.) for tables.** For some technical documents, readers may prefer or even expect separate numbering sequences for figures and tables. Figures are all visual aids that aren't tables. If you are unsure what your readers expect, look at similar documents written by your coworkers or by others in your field. If you don't see a separate numbering sequence, use Arabic numerals for all visual aids, including tables.

Compare these titles:

**Vague title**    Figure 6.1 A Figure Showing Inflation

**Specific title**  Figure 6.4 Comparison of Inflation Rates 2000–2012

The vague title needlessly repeats Figure. The specific title uses Comparison to indicate what the graphic shows about inflation. The specific title also identifies the years the graphic covers and gives readers the information they need to locate a specific graphic and identify the information in it. When numbering your graphics, follow the Tips for Numbering Graphics.

## Introduce and Refer to Each Graphic by Number

Introduce and refer to graphics by number. Many readers will only know that you want them to look at a graphic or what you expect them to learn from it if you refer them to it. Introduce and refer to graphics in one or two sentences or in a parenthetical reference:

**One-sentence introduction**   As Figure 7.3 illustrates, heart disease kills more U.S. women than the next four causes of death combined.

**Two-sentence introduction**   Heart disease kills more U.S. women than the next four causes of death combined. Figure 7.6 shows the five leading causes of death among U.S. women.

**Parenthetical reference**   Heart disease kills more U.S. women than the next four causes of death combined (see Figure 7.9).

In each example, the writer introduces the figure by number and by content.

Sometimes you will need to tell readers how to use or read a graphic or give them information to understand it. The following introduction tells readers when and how to use a table:

> If you receive an error message when installing the software, refer to Table 16.2. Read down the first column of the table until you find the error message that you received. When you find the message, go to the second column labeled What to do when you receive this message.

## Tell Readers What Is Important about Each Graphic

Briefly explain the purpose of each graphic or tell readers what they should notice in each one. Readers may not draw the conclusions you drew, so state your conclusions to ensure sure that readers understand the purpose and meaning of the graphic.

For example, the writers of a scientific paper on women and cardiovascular diseases wanted readers to understand the urgency of studying these diseases specifically in women, so they wrote the following explanation of two bar graphs, one showing the causes of death among U.S. women and the other showing the causes among U.S. men:

> Once a neglected field of research, cardiovascular diseases in women have rapidly become a major topic of scientific investigation. In 2006, cardiovascular disease killed more U.S. women than U.S. men and was the leading cause of death among women. Cardiovascular disease kills more U.S. women than the next four causes of death combined.[1]

The writers clearly state two important pieces of information that they want readers to understand after reading the bar graphs: Cardiovascular diseases kill more U.S. women than men, and the diseases kill more U.S. women than the next four causes of death combined.

## Place Each Graphic as Close as Possible to Its Related Text

Graphics are most effective when they appear either on the same page as the text that refers to them or on a facing page. Readers may ignore a graphic if they have to flip from the discussion to hunt for the graphic elsewhere in the document. If you must place a graphic some distance away from its text discussion, refer to the graphic and tell readers where to find it. For example, if a graphic appears in an appendix, you might write

> A large-scale map of the Bobwhite Quail habitat in Louisiana appears in Figure 26 in Appendix C (see page 51).

If you want readers to take another look at a graphic that you discussed earlier in your document, you might write

> The nonspinning portion of the Galileo orbiter, discussed earlier, provides a stable base for four remote sensing instruments (see Figure 3.2, page 120, for a diagram of the orbiter).

A note of caution: If you refer to graphics by page number, you must double check the page numbers every time you change and reprint your document. Page numbers can change, even with very small alterations to the text. If you expect your document to change or be revised later, omit the page number so you do not inadvertently give incorrect page numbers. In the previous two examples, you might say:

> Example 1... in Appendix C.
> Example 2... base for four remote sensing instruments (see Figure 3.2 for a diagram of the orbiter)

---

[1] Adapted from Beil 1995, 6D.

When possible, use software to produce professional-looking, high-quality graphics and images. For example, use the following types of software to produce graphics:

- Graphics software, such as Adobe Illustrator® or Adobe Photoshop®, allows you to create and edit flow charts, diagrams, drawings, and organizational charts.
- Photo editing software lets you crop and edit digital photos.
- Presentation software, such as Microsoft PowerPoint®, allows you to create slides.
- Spreadsheet software, such as Microsoft Excel®, makes it easy to enter data that you can use to create tables, charts, and graphs.
- Desktop publishing software, such as Adobe InDesign®, lets you integrate graphics into the text.

You can download many ready-to-use graphics. Hundreds of websites offer downloadable photos, and images. Some graphics are available at no cost while others may cost hundreds of dollars. If you download an image, make sure you

- get permission to use the graphic. Even if the graphic is free, you must have permission to use it. If you cannot get permission, don't use it.
- follow the copyright law (see Chapter 4).

EVALUATE THE DESIGN OF A GRAPHIC IN THE INTERACTIVE STUDENT ANALYSIS ONLINE AT
WWW.GRTEP.COM

## Forest Service Accused of Using Misleading Photos to Promote Forest Management[2]

### Background

In 2005, the U.S. Forest Service printed 15,000 copies of a brochure entitled Forests With a Future to promote old-growth forest management (see Figure 11.41). The cost was $23,000 for printing and production, paid to a private public relations firm. The brochure featured a series of six photos, dating from 1909–1989, showing a thickening progression of growth in what was portrayed as the Sierra Nevada Forest.

Shortly after the brochure was released, it came under attack from Chad Hanson, director of the John Muir Project in Cedar Ridge, California, and Timothy Ingalsbee of the Western Fire Ecology Center in Eugene, Oregn, organizations that work to preserve public forest lands. Hanson said he recognized the photos in the brochure from a similar publication released in Montana. The photos were not taken in the Sierra Nevada Forest, but in the Bitterroot National Forest in Montana. Hanson also closely examined the series of six photos and realized that the 1909 photograph showed an area of forest that had been logged; piles of slash and stumps appeared in the background. The Forest Service had depicted the lightly forested area in the 1909 photograph as proof that forests have grown increasingly thick over time, resulting in an increased threat of wild fire.

After receiving complaints about the brochure, Forest Service spokesperson Matt Mathes defended the photos. He said the Montana forest photographs appeared in the Sierra Nevada brochure because "it is difficult to find a good series of repeat photographs of the same place over almost 100 years." He said the photos were used only to show a progression of growth through the years. "Our goal here," Mathes said, "was to ... increase the clarity and understandability of our message. We needed to be accurate, but not necessarily precise to the 99th degree."

### Assignment

- Do you agree or disagree with Mr. Mathes's statement that the U.S. Forest Service "needed to be accurate, but not necessarily precise to the 99th degree." Be prepared to defend your answer.
- Write a memo to your instructor recommending how organizations such as the Forest Service can ensure that photos are used accurately. Recommend ways to archive and label photos. State how your recommendations might have prevented the Forest Service from using misleading photos in its brochure. (For information on writing memos, see Chapter 12.)

[2] Compiled from www.msnbc.msn.com/id/4722630/

# FIGURE 11.41

**Brochure for Case Study**

## Forests With A Future Campaign

This campaign expects to reduce acres lost to catastrophic wildfires more than 30% within the next fifty years. We also expect the habitat of wildlife, such as the spotted owl, and old growth forest areas to double in the same period.

*Increasing Density*

### Methods to reduce fire damage

Fire itself is a method to reduce the highly flammable dense brush and trees in forests – although in many areas now fire is too risky to use. Even a small fire can explode out of control, where vegetation is dense. Prescribed burns can only be used with extreme care.

Thinning some trees and clearing underbrush and "slash" (small branches left after tree thinning) is expensive but must be done in key areas. Around homes and communities, is the top priority. Clearing brush and thinning trees in strategic sites where wildfires are most likely due to the density of vegetation, terrain, and wind patterns, will slow down these fires.

There are about 90 million trees measuring 20 to 30 inches in diameter in the Sierra Nevada. About 183,000, or 0.2%, of these will be thinned each year as part of an approach tailored to the requirements of each local forest. Thinning these trees serves two purposes –

reducing biomass in strategic locations and selling this timber to offset some of the costs of making the forests more fire safe.

The campaign will adapt these and other methods to meet the specific needs of each forest watershed, with scientists and professional foresters monitoring the effect on old growth trees, wildlife, and wildfires.

### Focusing the Sierra Nevada Forest Plans

Sierra Nevada forest plans, which provided the basis of this campaign, have evolved over the last decade with the input of hundreds of scientists, forest professionals, and the public, as knowledge and practical experience has deepened. After the Sierra Nevada Forest Plan Amendment was released in 2001, Forest Service District Rangers, responsible for managing the forest to prevent catastrophic wildfires, found that the amendment needed to be improved because they were not able to accomplish the necessary

# EXERCISES

DOWNLOAD A WORKSHEET FOR CREATING VISUAL INFORMATION

WWW.GRTEP.COM

1. Visit the computer labs on your campus. Find out the following:
   a. What graphics software is available to students, and what types of graphics can you create with the software?
   b. What drawing software is available to students, and what graphics can you create with the software?
   c. If your campus doesn't have labs or graphics and drawing software, visit a computer or office supply store (in person or online) to gather information about graphics software. After you have gathered information on the software,
      • Create a table summarizing the information you gathered.
      • Write a memo to your instructor reporting what you found.
      • Incorporate the table into your memo. (For information on writing memos, see Chapter 12.)

2. Examine several technical publications or journals in your field.
   a. Find examples of effective and ineffective photos, diagrams, and drawings.
   b. Write a memo to your instructor analyzing the photos, diagrams, and drawings that you selected. (For information on writing memos, see Chapter 12.)
   c. Include a copy of the graphics at the appropriate place in the memo. Number the graphics and give them titles.

3. Create a drawing that you might use in a manual for a piece of equipment. You could select a household appliance, a piece of equipment used in your field, or a piece of equipment for which you are writing instructions in your technical communication class. Label the appropriate parts of the equipment, and give your drawing a number and a descriptive title.

4. Create an organizational chart for an organization or company. The chart must include at least four levels of management, divisions, or departments. Use one of these organizations:
   a. a civic organization such as Boy Scouts, Little League, or Girl Scouts
   b. the company you work for
   c. a campus or student organization, such as a fraternity, sorority, or a service organization
   d. a city department, such as the fire or police department

5. Prepare a flow chart illustrating one of these processes. Include readable labels, a descriptive title, and a number.
   a. how to apply for a passport
   b. how to apply for financial aid at your college or university
   c. how to explain a process or procedure common in your field or at your place of employment
   d. how to complete a degree plan at your college or university

6. Find a graphic that you consider unethical.
   a. Write a paragraph explaining why you think the graphic is unethical.
   b. Print a copy of the graphic.
   c. Revise the graphic so it presents the information ethically.
   d. Be prepared to show your revised graphic in class.

7. The table in Figure 11.42 gives salary and unemployment information for science and engineering graduates up to 5 years after graduating from college. Study this data and create
   a. two graphics that compare salary information for bachelor's, master's, and doctorate graduates
   b. two graphics that compare the unemployment rates for each of the fields listed in the column heads
   c. a graphic that compares the involuntary out-of-field rate to the unemployment rate by degree and by field

8. **Collaborative exercise:** Figure 11.43 contains information that would be more effective if presented with graphics. You and your team should complete the following tasks:
   a. Determine what types of graphics will best convey the information.
   b. Determine what colors would add contrast.
   c. Revise the document to include two or more graphics.
   d. Select the best layout for the information.

FIGURE 11.42

**Table for Exercise 7**

**Labor market indicators for recent S&E degree recipients up to 5 years after receiving degree, by field: 2008**

| Indicator and degree | All S&E fields | Highest degree field | | | | |
|---|---|---|---|---|---|---|
| | | Computer/ mathematical sciences | Biological/ agricultural/ environmental life sciences | Physical sciences | Social sciences | Engineering |
| Unemployment rate (%) | | | | | | |
| All degree levels | 4.6 | 3.2 | 5.1 | 3.4 | 6.1 | 2.0 |
| Bachelor's | 5.3 | 3.2 | 6.0 | 3.9 | 6.7 | 2.1 |
| Master's | 2.9 | 3.5 | 2.4 | 2.5 | 3.5 | 2.0 |
| Doctorate | 1.5 | 0.3 | 2.1 | 2.5 | 1.2 | 1.0 |
| Involuntary out-of-field rate (%) | | | | | | |
| All degree levels | 7.9 | 4.0 | 7.6 | 5.6 | 12.0 | 2.4 |
| Bachelor's | 9.7 | 5.4 | 9.1 | 7.6 | 13.6 | 2.5 |
| Master's | 3.5 | 0.7 | 4.1 | 1.8 | 6.1 | 2.6 |
| Doctorate | 1.5 | 0.9 | 1.2 | 3.1 | 1.9 | 0.8 |
| Median annual salary ($) | | | | | | |
| All degree levels | 42,000 | 55,000 | 34,000 | 40,000 | 36,000 | 63,000 |
| Bachelor's | 39,800 | 51,000 | 30,000 | 32,000 | 34,000 | 59,000 |
| Master's | 57,000 | 72,000 | 44,000 | 47,000 | 43,000 | 70,000 |
| Doctorate | 65,000 | 80,000 | 50,000 | 67,000 | 60,000 | 86,000 |

NOTES: Median annual salaries are rounded to nearest $1,000. All degree levels includes professional degrees not broken out separately. Includes degrees earned from October 2003 to October 2008. Involuntarily out-of-field rate is proportion of individuals employed in job not related to field of highest degree because job in that field was not available.

SOURCE: National Science Foundation, National Center for Science and Engineering Statistics, Scientists and Engineers Statistical Data System (SESTAT) (2008), http://sestat.nsf.gov.

*Science and Engineering Indicators 2012*

Source: www.nsf.gov/statistics/seind12/c3/tt03-18.htm.

**FIGURE    11.43**

**Document for Exercise 8**

### Backpack-related injuries in children

Overloaded backpacks used by children have received a lot of attention from parents, doctors, school administrators and the media in the past several years. According to the U.S. Consumer Product Safety Commission there were more than 21,000 backpack-related injuries treated at hospital emergency rooms, doctors' offices, and clinics in the year 2003. Injuries ranged from contusions, to sprains and strains to the back and shoulder, and fractures.

"Back pain in children is not so uncommon anymore," according to John Purvis, MD, pediatric orthopaedic surgeon. "Orthopaedic surgeons nationwide have seen an increase in children visiting their offices complaining of back and shoulder pain. If a child complains of back pain, parents should consider that it might be due to the backpack or perhaps something more serious. Back pain that persistently limits a child's activities, requires medication or alters sleep patterns warrants investigation."

The American Academy of Orthopaedic Surgeons recommends that a child's backpack should weigh no more than 15 to 20 percent of the child's body weight. This figure may vary, however, depending on the child's body strength and fitness.

While some experts disagree on whether heavy backpacks are the source of back pain in children, most agree that using good judgment when wearing one will reduce the risk of backpack-related injuries. It is important to partner with your child on the selection, packing and caring of the backpack.

### Warning signs a backpack is too heavy
- Change in posture when wearing the backpack
- Struggling when putting on or taking off the backpack
- Pain when wearing the backpack
- Tingling or numbness
- Red marks

*Part 3*

# Using the Writer's Tools to Correspond with Your Reader

# chapter *twelve*

## Writing Reader-Focused Letters, Memos, and Emails

ike most professionals, you will use letters, memos, and emails to correspond with coworkers and people outside your organization. Memos, letters, and emails are the everyday communication tools of the workplace. In some workplace situations, your coworkers, clients, and others will know you only through your emails. Especially in a virtual workplace, others will develop impressions of you through your email. You need to think about how your correspondence represents you and your organization.

iStockphoto 2008.

### DETERMINE THE OBJECTIVES OF YOUR LETTER, MEMO, OR EMAIL

Before writing a letter, memo, or email, decide what you want it to accomplish. Do you want readers to take a particular action after reading your correspondence? Do you want readers to give you information? Do you want to inform readers about good or, perhaps, bad news? Your objective may be to maintain or establish a positive relationship with the reader.

As you write your correspondence, ask yourself these questions:

- **What is the purpose of the correspondence? What do you expect it to accomplish?** Your correspondence frequently will have more than one objective. For example, the primary objective of the letter shown in Figure 12.1 is to inform the reader of the new customer comment cards. The secondary objective is to mend a damaged relationship with the reader and ensure the continued business and goodwill of that reader.
- **What action, if any, do you expect the reader to take after reading the correspondence?** If you decide that you want the reader to do something, clearly and directly state what you want him or her to do. Much correspondence is ineffective because the writer doesn't clearly and directly state what the reader should do. Many writers assume that the reader will know what to do. If you assume incorrectly, you may not get the response you expect.
- **What do you expect the reader to know after reading the correspondence?** If you don't clearly understand and clearly state all that you wish to convey, your reader will miss your point. Informally list what you want your reader to know. This list can help you spot irrelevant or unclear information.

 ## FIND OUT ABOUT YOUR READER AND HOW HE OR SHE WILL PERCEIVE YOUR MESSAGE

Effective letters, memos, and emails demonstrate the following characteristics (see Figure 12.1):

- **They are reader-focused.** When your correspondence focuses on the reader, it contains all the information the reader needs to understand the message. It doesn't contain more information than is needed and it doesn't omit the reason why you sent the correspondence. It also respects the reader's time.
- **They are helpful.** When your correspondence is helpful, it anticipates and answers your reader's questions.
- **They are tactful and professional.** When your correspondence is tactful and professional, it is courteous and, when possible, positive. It maintains or gains the reader's goodwill by using a professional tone.

To ensure that your correspondence focuses on the reader and is helpful, tactful, and professional, find out as much as possible about your reader. For much of the correspondence that you will write, this task will be simple because you will know the reader. However, you may write to people whom you don't know. Use these questions to gather information about your reader. (You can find additional information about writing for your readers in Chapter 2.)

## Letter Demonstrating the Characteristics of Effective Correspondence

 **Computers on Wheels**

February 6, 2012

Mrs. Wanda Perrill
902 Indian Creek
St. Paul, MN 57904

Dear Mrs. Perrill:

*This letter focuses on the reader by acknowledging the writer's conversation with the reader.*

After our conversation last month about the quality of service in your home, we created a Customer Care Card. To improve our service to you, your computer team will now leave this card on each visit. The purpose of the card is to solicit your comments about our service on each visit. These cards resulted directly from our conversation, and we thank you for the suggestion.

*The writer anticipates the reader's questions.*

The comment cards will help us maintain and monitor the quality of service that we provide in your home. They also are part of a new incentive program for our employees, so please take a moment after each maintenance visit to fill out the postage-paid card and drop it in the mail. You may also visit our website at www.computersonwheels.com to complete the online comment card. Your comments will help us to provide the service you deserve and expect.

*This letter is tactful and professional.*

Thank you, Mrs. Perrill, for your comments that led to these new cards. We appreciate the confidence you have placed in Computers on Wheels.

Sincerely,

*Bob Congrove*

Bob Congrove
Owner

*"Serving you so you can work at home."*

- **Who will read the correspondence? Will more than one person read it?** If you will have more than one reader, prepare to meet the needs and expectations of all your readers. If their needs and expectations vary substantially, consider writing separately to each person or group.
- **What are the positions and responsibilities of the readers? How might their positions and responsibilities affect how they will perceive your message?** If you have this information, you can better determine what they know about you, your responsibilities, and possibly, about the subject of your message. This information about your readers also helps you anticipate how they will perceive and react to your message. Suppose your purpose is to inform them about the company's new cell phone policy. Under this policy, they will no longer receive a company cell phone. Instead, they will use their personal cell phones, and the company will pay each employee a monthly stipend for their personal cell phones. For readers who use their current company cell phone for both business and personal needs, you know this new policy will upset them. With this information, you can address their concerns and potential questions.
- **If your readers are external, what is their relationship to you and your organization? How will this relationship affect how they will perceive your message?** Find out as much as possible about past interactions among the readers, their organization, and your organization. This information will help you understand how readers may perceive you and your organization; and it will help you select an appropriate approach and language.
- **What do your readers know about the subject of the correspondence?** If you can find out what your readers know about your subject, you are more likely to include the appropriate amount of background and detail.

## USE THE APPROPRIATE FORMAT

Letters, memos, and most emails have basic formats that are appropriate in any workplace. The format depends on whether the reader is internal or external and whether your communication needs to be formal or informal. A letter is more formal than a memo or email.

Letters are used primarily to communicate with people outside the organization. Letters are also used inside the organization to handle confidential matters, such as personnel and salary issues, or when you are sending a formal communication. You write memos to communicate with people within the organization, for routine correspondence, or for an informal report.

Email is especially effective for taking care of routine business and for working with people in different time zones. However, it is inappropriate for confidential or sensitive business; you can never assume an email is private. Your email may be forwarded to someone whom you did not intend to receive the correspondence.

> You can never assume an email is private. Your email may be forwarded to someone whom you did not intend to receive the correspondence.

## Letters

The three basic formats for letters are *block style* (Figures 12.2 and 12.3), *modified block style* (Figures 12.4 and 12.5), and AMS simplified style (Figure 12.6). Figure 12.7A describes the elements of a letter and Figure 12.7B gives an example.

The *AMS simplified style* omits the salutation, complimentary closing, and signature. This format is useful when you don't know the reader's name or courtesy title (Ms., Mrs., Mr., Dr., etc.). The AMS simplified style may strike some readers as impersonal; therefore, whenever possible, take the time to find the recipient's name and title.

The three letter formats differ in the following ways:
- **Position of the date, the complimentary closing, and the signature block.** In letters set up in block or AMS simplified formats, place these elements flush against the left margin. In letters set up in modified block format, indent these elements from one half to two thirds of the width of the page. Be sure to indent all three elements the same distance from the left margin, so they align on the page (see Figures 12.4 and 12.5).
- **Paragraph indentation.** Indenting paragraphs is optional in the modified block format. Do not indent paragraphs in block or AMS simplified formats.
- **Use of salutation and complimentary closing.** Omit these elements from letters in AMS simplified format.

### Using Letter Templates

Your word processing software offers letter *templates*, predesigned letter formats. These templates provide fields in which you insert the heading information, date, your name, etc. Some templates provide decorative elements that may be inappropriate for professional correspondence. Unless the context calls for an informal, decorative template, go with a simple, conventional format. If you cannot find an appropriate template, work from a blank page.

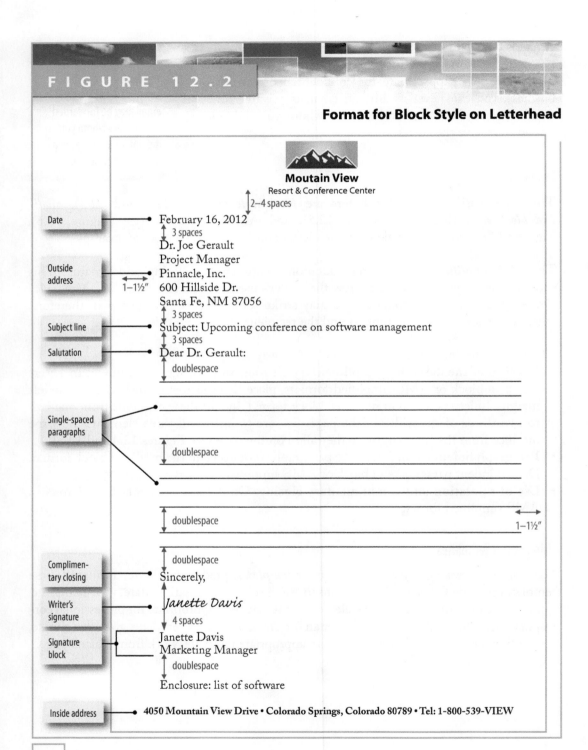

**FIGURE 12.2**

**Format for Block Style on Letterhead**

**Moutain View**
Resort & Conference Center

2–4 spaces

**Date** → February 16, 2012

3 spaces

Dr. Joe Gerault
Project Manager
**Outside address** → Pinnacle, Inc.

1–1½″

600 Hillside Dr.
Santa Fe, NM 87056

3 spaces

**Subject line** → Subject: Upcoming conference on software management

3 spaces

**Salutation** → Dear Dr. Gerault:

doublespace

**Single-spaced paragraphs**

doublespace

doublespace

1–1½″

doublespace

**Complimentary closing** → Sincerely,

**Writer's signature** → *Janette Davis*

4 spaces

**Signature block** → Janette Davis
Marketing Manager

doublespace

Enclosure: list of software

**Inside address** → 4050 Mountain View Drive • Colorado Springs, Colorado 80789 • Tel: 1-800-539-VIEW

# FIGURE 12.3

## Format for Block Style without Letterhead

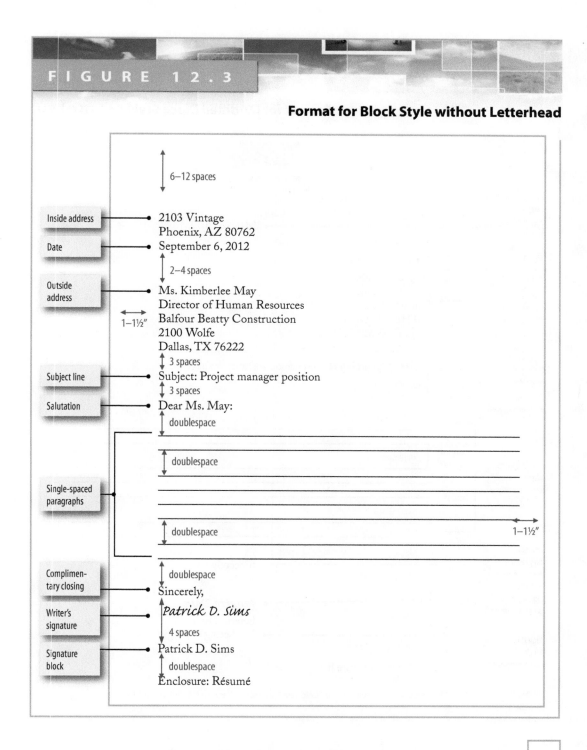

6–12 spaces

Inside address
2103 Vintage
Phoenix, AZ 80762

Date
September 6, 2012

2–4 spaces

Outside address
Ms. Kimberlee May
Director of Human Resources
Balfour Beatty Construction
2100 Wolfe
Dallas, TX 76222

1–1½″

3 spaces

Subject line
Subject: Project manager position

3 spaces

Salutation
Dear Ms. May:

doublespace

doublespace

Single-spaced paragraphs

doublespace

1–1½″

doublespace

Complimentary closing
Sincerely,

Writer's signature
*Patrick D. Sims*

4 spaces

Signature block
Patrick D. Sims

doublespace

Enclosure: Résumé

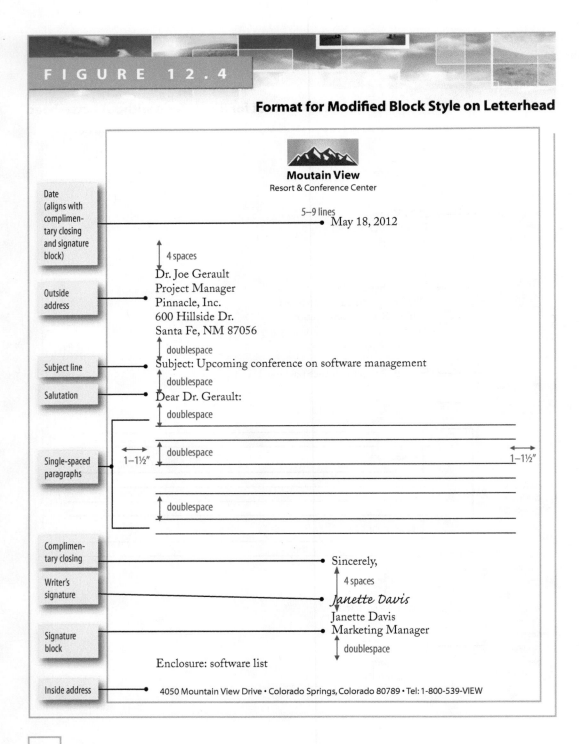

FIGURE 12.4

**Format for Modified Block Style on Letterhead**

**Moutain View**
Resort & Conference Center

Date
(aligns with
complimen-
tary closing
and signature
block)

5–9 lines
May 18, 2012

4 spaces

Outside
address

Dr. Joe Gerault
Project Manager
Pinnacle, Inc.
600 Hillside Dr.
Santa Fe, NM 87056

doublespace

Subject line

Subject: Upcoming conference on software management

doublespace

Salutation

Dear Dr. Gerault:

doublespace

doublespace

1–1½"                                                              1–1½"

Single-spaced
paragraphs

doublespace

doublespace

Complimen-
tary closing

Sincerely,

4 spaces

Writer's
signature

*Janette Davis*
Janette Davis

Signature
block

Marketing Manager

doublespace

Enclosure: software list

Inside address

4050 Mountain View Drive • Colorado Springs, Colorado 80789 • Tel: 1-800-539-VIEW

**FIGURE 12.5**

**Format for Modified Block Style without Letterhead**

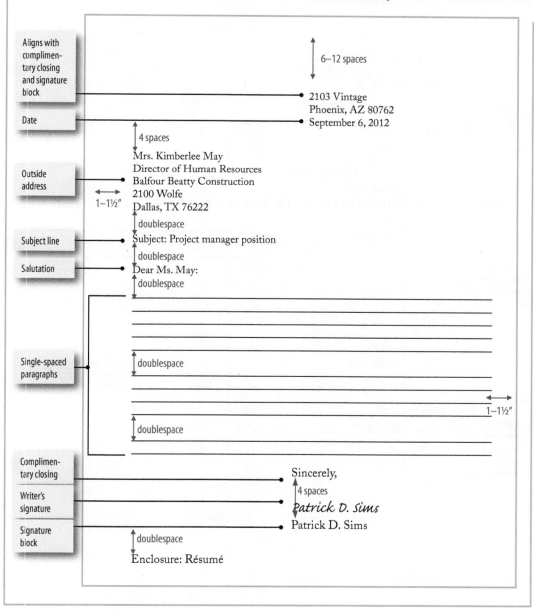

Aligns with complimentary closing and signature block

6–12 spaces

2103 Vintage
Phoenix, AZ 80762

Date

September 6, 2012

4 spaces

Outside address

Mrs. Kimberlee May
Director of Human Resources
Balfour Beatty Construction
2100 Wolfe
Dallas, TX 76222

1–1½"

doublespace

Subject line

Subject: Project manager position

doublespace

Salutation

Dear Ms. May:

doublespace

Single-spaced paragraphs

doublespace

1–1½"

doublespace

Complimentary closing

Sincerely,

4 spaces

Writer's signature

*Patrick D. Sims*

Signature block

Patrick D. Sims

doublespace

Enclosure: Résumé

**Format for AMS[1] Simplified Style**

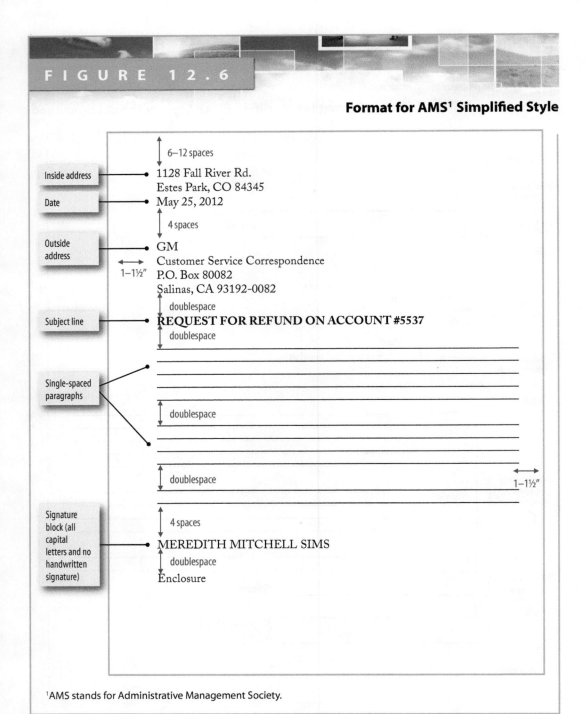

6–12 spaces

Inside address — 1128 Fall River Rd.
Estes Park, CO 84345

Date — May 25, 2012

4 spaces

Outside address — GM
Customer Service Correspondence
1–1½″ — P.O. Box 80082
Salinas, CA 93192-0082

doublespace

Subject line — **REQUEST FOR REFUND ON ACCOUNT #5537**

doublespace

Single-spaced paragraphs

doublespace

doublespace

1–1½″

Signature block (all capital letters and no handwritten signature)

4 spaces

MEREDITH MITCHELL SIMS

doublespace

Enclosure

[1]AMS stands for Administrative Management Society.

## Memos

Although most companies use email for internal correspondence and for some informal reports, they use memos for more formal communications. You may frequently use memos for informal reports such as a sales call report to your manager or a recommendation to advertise in a new medium (see Chapter 14 on writing informal reports). Like letters, memos have a conventional format. Unlike letters, memos do not include a salutation, complimentary closing, or writer's signature. Most memos are printed on plain paper, not letterhead. You may also attach these memos to or paste them in an email. Figure 12.8 presents three typical memo formats.

### Using Memo Templates

Your word processing software offers memo *templates*, predesigned memo formats or your organization may have predesigned (and expected) memo templates. If your organization has such a template, use it. If you decide to use a template from your word processing software, select a simple, conservative format.

## Emails

Use email for both interoffice and external communications. Although email software formats the heading of your email, you need to add some elements and follow proper email *netiquette* (*network etiquette*). Your workplace email should include the following:

- **Informative, specific subject line.** The subject line should inform readers of the purpose of your email. Readers use the subject line to decide whether to open an email. If the subject line isn't informative, specific, or clear, many readers ignore the email. Always include specific information in the subject line; don't leave it blank.
- **Optional greeting.** Include an optional greeting, such as:
      Dear Jim:
      Jim,
      Dear Mr. Jackson:
- **Signature block.** Usually called a *signature* in email software, this element includes the following information:
      Your name and position
      Company
      Location (optional)
      Phone number
      Fax number (optional)
      Email address

**FIGURE 12.7A**

1. **Inside address**
   The **inside address** consists of your organization's address or your personal address. Most organizations have pre-printed (or digital) letterhead that includes the organization's logo and address. If you are not using letterhead, include your address without your name as the inside address.
2. **Date**
3. **Outside address**
   The **outside address** is that of the person who will receive your letter. The outside address has these elements:
   - Name and position. If the person has a professional title, include that title; for example, if you are writing to a physician, use Dr. John Smith, Director of Medical Services
   - Organization
   - Street address or Post Office box
   - City, state, and ZIP code
4. **Subject or reference line**
   A **subject line** tells readers what the letter is about. A **reference line** refers readers to the date of previous correspondence or to the project, order, or account mentioned in the letter. Subject lines begin with *Subject* and reference lines with *Re*. These lines are optional in the block and modified block styles; a subject line is required for the AMS simplified style.
5. **Salutation (a greeting)**
   Use Dear followed by the reader's name (or official title if you don't know the reader's name) and a colon (not a comma).
   - Dear Mr. Sampson:
   - Dear Personnel Director:
   Always use a nonsexist salutation. When you don't know the reader's name or gender *Dear Sir* or *Dear Madam* is inappropriate. Instead, use the AMS simplified style and omit the salutation (see Figure 12.6), or use the reader's title in the salutation. Do not use To whom it may concern because it is vague and impersonal.
6. **Body**
   The body usually consists of at least three paragraphs. (See Organize Your Correspondence to Meet Your Readers' Needs)
7. **Complimentary closing**
   Select from traditional closings such as
   - Sincerely,
   - Best wishes,
   - Warm regards,
   - Cordially,
   - Best,
8. **Signature**
   Type your full name and your position. Sign your name above your printed name and position.
9. **Enclosure line**
   If you will be enclosing documents with the letter, include an enclosure line one line below your printed title. The enclosure line indicates the number of enclosures (if more than one). Some writers also identify the enclosure.
   - Enclosures (2): Proposal
     Drawings of Proposed Renovation
10. **Copy line**
    If you are sending copies of the letter to others, include their names in a copy line. Use the lowercase *cc* for copy, followed by a colon and the name, and possibly position, of those receiving a copy.
    - cc: Norma Rowland, Director of Sales

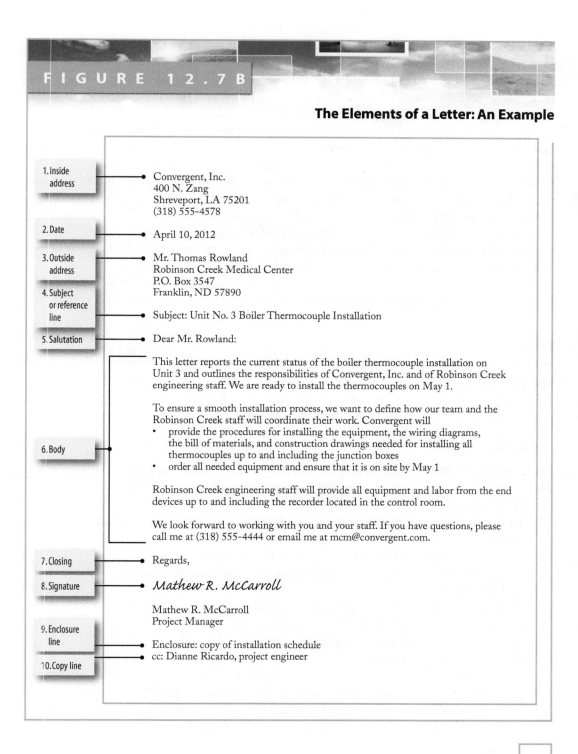

**F I G U R E   1 2 . 7 B**

## The Elements of a Letter: An Example

**1. Inside address**

Convergent, Inc.
400 N. Zang
Shreveport, LA 75201
(318) 555-4578

**2. Date**

April 10, 2012

**3. Outside address**

Mr. Thomas Rowland
Robinson Creek Medical Center
P.O. Box 3547
Franklin, ND 57890

**4. Subject or reference line**

Subject: Unit No. 3 Boiler Thermocouple Installation

**5. Salutation**

Dear Mr. Rowland:

**6. Body**

This letter reports the current status of the boiler thermocouple installation on Unit 3 and outlines the responsibilities of Convergent, Inc. and of Robinson Creek engineering staff. We are ready to install the thermocouples on May 1.

To ensure a smooth installation process, we want to define how our team and the Robinson Creek staff will coordinate their work. Convergent will
- provide the procedures for installing the equipment, the wiring diagrams, the bill of materials, and construction drawings needed for installing all thermocouples up to and including the junction boxes
- order all needed equipment and ensure that it is on site by May 1

Robinson Creek engineering staff will provide all equipment and labor from the end devices up to and including the recorder located in the control room.

We look forward to working with you and your staff. If you have questions, please call me at (318) 555-4444 or email me at mcm@convergent.com.

**7. Closing**

Regards,

**8. Signature**

*Mathew R. McCarroll*

Mathew R. McCarroll
Project Manager

**9. Enclosure line**

Enclosure: copy of installation schedule

**10. Copy line**

cc: Dianne Ricardo, project engineer

With most email software, you can create an electronic signature to insert into your messages. The software allows you to customize the signature. For example, some software allows you to insert your business card into an email. For email correspondence with coworkers, you may want to leave off the signature block, simply ending with your name.

Because email is perceived as less formal, you may be tempted to abandon some conventions expected in workplace correspondence. When writing email, remember to follow these rules:

- **Follow the rules of capitalization.** Don't use all uppercase letters or all lowercase letters.
- **Avoid abbreviations.** You probably use abbreviations or shortcuts when sending a text message or communicating via Instant Messenger or Twitter™. However, these abbreviations and shortcuts are unappropriate for workplace correspondence.
- **Limit the email to business issues.** When using email to conduct business, focus on the business and avoid discussing personal issues.

For more information on following email etiquette, see Taking It into the Workplace.

 ## ORGANIZE YOUR CORRESPONDENCE TO MEET READERS' NEEDS

You may present the main message of your correspondence either directly or indirectly (Dragga 1991).

### The Direct Approach

For most of your letters, memos, and email, you will use the direct approach. This approach enables readers to quickly grasp the gist of your correspondence. The direct approach has three sections, as follows:

1. **In the first paragraph, present the main message.** Tell readers the reason you are writing.
2. **In the middle paragraph(s), explain the main message.**
   - Explain the main message (your purpose for the correspondence) presented in the first paragraph.
   - Present necessary details about the main message.
3. **In the final paragraph, close the correspondence.**
   - Tell readers if and when they or you will act next.
   - Tell readers, if necessary, what you want them to do.
   - Tell readers how to contact you (your phone number, fax number, email address, or mailing address). Tell readers where or how you would prefer to be contacted. For example, if you prefer that readers email you, give your email address. If you prefer they call you on your cell phone, include only your cell phone number.

## Typical Memo Formats

**Your name, your position or department (optional), and your handwritten initials**

**P.S. Communications
Interoffice Communication**

To:        Jill Byrd
From:      Nneka Leon, Project Manager *NL*
Subject:   Recommendation for new safety glasses
Date:      April 10, 2012

**List the name (and possibly the position or department) of each reader**

**Memo**

Date:      September 16, 2012
To:        John Garcia
           Haj Ross
           Heather Huggett
From:      Sean Thompson *ST*
Subject:   Trip report—EUCG conference

**Date**

**Specifically states the topic of the memo**

**Interoffice**

Date:      March 20, 2012
To:        Meredith Mitchell, Communications Division
From:      Hope McCarroll, Director of Marketing *hm*
Subject:   Update on plan to relocate the communications
           division

You can adapt a direct approach for most correspondence. The letter shown in Figure 12.9 illustrates the direct approach.

## The Indirect Approach

When you use the indirect approach, you delay or buffer the main message until you have graciously opened the correspondence and explained the message. The indirect approach has three sections, as follows:

1. **In the first paragraph, buffer the main message.** A *buffer* is a positive or neutral statement. The buffer helps readers be more receptive to your message, especially if it is negative.
2. **In the middle paragraph(s), explain and then state the main message.**
   - Explain the main message. For instance, state the reason for a refusal or rejection. By first explaining the message, you prepare readers for the negative news.
   - State the message.
   - When the message is negative, if possible, suggest an alternative or remedy. By suggesting an alternative or remedy, you may be able to keep the goodwill of your readers or show that you want to meet their needs.
3. **In the final paragraph, close the correspondence.** End it with a gracious statement.

Writers rarely use this approach, but it is appropriate when the news is not urgent or doesn't require readers to respond or act. This approach is also appropriate in correspondence with international readers who may be accustomed to a less direct approach than is common in American business (Sims and Guice 1992). The letter shown in Figure 12.10 illustrates the indirect approach.

> ### ETHICS NOTE
>
> #### Ethics and the Indirect Approach
>
> Before you use the indirect approach, ask if it is an ethically appropriate choice for the situation. The indirect approach can inappropriately obscure information. It also can mislead readers into thinking that the message is good because the gracious, usually positive, opening delays the bad news. Readers who see only the opening may misinterpret the purpose of the correspondence. Before using the indirect approach, carefully consider your readers and how they are likely to read the message.

FIGURE 12.9

## Letter Using the Direct Approach

402 Summer Court
Carrollton, TX 75007
June 11, 2012

Mrs. Norma Rowland
Denton County Appraisal District
3911 Morse Street
Denton, TX 76202-3816

Subject: Appraisal of block 5, lot 15, in Villages of Indian Creek phase 1

Dear Mrs. Rowland:

The writer tells the reader why he is writing.

I am requesting that you reconsider the 2012 appraisal of my home, 402 Summer Court in Carrollton. I have included information from the 2012 Dallas County appraisal and a market analysis by a local realtor. Based on this information, I request that you consider appraising the home between $101,300 and $105,352.

The writer explains the main message presented in the first paragraph. He also presents details about the message.

**The Dallas County Appraisal**
Dallas County appraised my home as follows in 2011 and 2012.

|      | Total Value | Improvements | Land     | Sq. ft. | $ per sq. ft. |
|------|-------------|--------------|----------|---------|---------------|
| 2011 | $103,220    | $86,220      | $17,000  | 2,030   | 51            |
| 2012 | $ 99,820    | $84,820      | $15,000  | 2,030   | 49            |

Denton County appraised my home as follows in 2011 and 2012.

|      | Total Value | Improvements | Land     | Sq. ft. | $ per sq. ft. |
|------|-------------|--------------|----------|---------|---------------|
| 2011 | $106,896    | $72,896      | $34,000  | 2,170   | 49            |
| 2012 | $122,931    | $83,831      | $39,100  | 2,170   | 56            |

As the above tables show, Denton County increased the appraisal by $16,035 while Dallas decreased the appraisal by $3,400. This increase in the appraised value concers me because similar homes in our neighborhood have not sold for more than $98,000.

**The Market Analysis**
A local realtor with Providence Realty, Ms. Ellen Babcock, reports that the price per square foot should be between $48 and $52 for our home. Ms. Babcock reports that similar homes in this neighborhood have not sold for more than $52 per square foot. As the tables in the above section show, the 2012 Denton County appraisal is $4 more per square foot than the upper end of the range reported by Ms. Babcock.

The writer closes by offering to supply documents or to answer questions. The writer tells the reader how to contact him.

I will be happy to supply documents from the Dallas appraisal or the realtor. If you would like these documents or have questions, please contact me at (972) 555-5555 or at the above address.

Sincerely,

*William W. Sims*

William W. Sims

## Letter Using the Indirect Approach

**Independent's Research, Incorporated**

1010 West Main • Los Alamos, New Mexico 87890 • (505) 565-3000

May 16, 2012

The first paragraph includes a positive statement about the reader.

Ms. Lisa Jackson
402A Summer Court
Edwardsville, IL 67843

Dear Ms. Jackson:

Last week, we told you that we were recommending you for a summer intern position with our Research and Development Department. Your excellent background and education would benefit you and us.

The writer explains the main message in the first sentence and then states the message in the second and third sentences. The final sentence suggests an alternative.

Last week, the board of directors announced a hiring freeze for all positions until the end of the year. We hoped this freeze would not include the internship positions, but sadly, it does. Therefore, we cannot offer you an internship this summer. The board feels certain that these intern positions will once again be available next summer. Because you are currently a sophomore, please reapply next year.

The letter concludes with a gracious statement.

We appreciate your interest in our company and look forward to your application next year.

Sincerely,

*Peggy Fagner*

Peggy Fagner
Manager, Recruitment

## CREATING A PROFESSIONAL IMAGE THROUGH YOUR CORRESPONDENCE

You create a professional image through your correspondence when you
- Put yourself in the readers' shoes.
- Use a tactful, professional tone.
- Avoid overused phrases.
- Use specific language.
- Follow grammar and punctuation rules.

### Put Yourself in the Readers' Shoes

When you open an email from your instructor or your university, you want to know how the information will affect you or what you will have to do. Similarly, in the workplace, your readers want to know how your letter, memo, or email will affect them. Particularly with email, readers may ask these questions:
- Why should I read this correspondence?
- What, if anything, do I have to do after reading this correspondence?
- How does this correspondence affect me?

**Writer-Focused Letter**

# C**O**UTFITTERS

1212 canyon drive
boulder, co 67899
(303) 555-4986
drr@co.com

May 18, 2012

Mrs. Annie Shepard
1244 Fork Road
Socorro, NM 54233

Dear Mrs. Shepard:

We here at Colorado Outfitters are always glad to hear from our customers. We try to please our customers with quality recreational gear and equipment. Our newest feature for customers is our Colorado Outfitters Catalog, a way to shop by telephone, email, or the Internet. However, this feature does have one drawback—our mailing list for the catalog is incomplete.

Recently, we received your letter about a problem with our service. Your neighbor purchased a Flashmagic 2-person tent for $250 during our spring catalog sale, but you bought the same tent at the full price of $350 during January.

It is a shame that you weren't on our mailing list, so we could have offered you the Flashmagic 2-person tent for $250. We will put you on our mailing list today, so you won't miss any more of our sales. If we can serve you in any way, please call, write, or email us—Colorado Outfitters is here to make your recreational activities safe and fun.

Happy camping,

*David R. Rowland*

David R. Rowland
Manager

FIGURE 12.12

# C**O**UTFITTERS

1212 canyon drive
boulder, co 67899
(303) 555-4986
drr@co.com

May 18, 2012

Mrs. Annie Shepard
1244 Fork Road
Socorro, NM 54233

Dear Mrs. Shepard:

Your recent letter about your purchase of a Flashmagic 2-person tent in January concerned us. You explained that a neighbor had purchased the same tent during the spring catalog sale; however, you paid $100 more than your neighbor. We understand your concern, so we have enclosed a 50% discount coupon good on your next purchase from Colorado Outfitters.

You must wonder why you didn't receive a catalog. The spring catalog is the first one sent to our customers as part of our new shop-at-home service. Because this service is new, we are still adding long-standing customers to the mailing list. We have added your name and address to the mailing list. You will receive future catalogs and sales notices. Soon, you—like your neighbor—can shop at home and take advantage of sales available exclusively to customers on our mailing list.

Mrs. Shepard, please let us know if we can serve you further. You are a valued customer.

Happy camping,

*David R. Rowland*

David R. Rowland
Manager

Enclosure: discount coupon

To help readers answer these questions, consider how your message affects the readers not how it affects you. You must *put yourself in the readers' shoes.*

To put yourself in the readers' shoes, think about how readers will respond to your message. Compare the letters shown in Figures 12.11 and 12.12. The writer of the letter in Figure 12.11 didn't carefully consider his letter's tone. He uses language focused on himself and on his company. This writer-focused, *we* tone is evident in the pronouns that refer to him and his company (*we* and *our*) and the way he focuses on company actions and policy instead of on the reader and her problem. In the final paragraph of his letter, he implies that the reader was negligent.

In the letter in Figure 12.12, the writer achieves a reader-focused, *you* tone. He focuses on the reader and her interests instead of on the company. He uses a positive tone and refers to the reader frequently by name and with second-person pronouns (*you* and *your*).

## Use a Tactful, Professional Tone

Readers resist messages that carry bad news or point out their mistakes. Just as you prefer to receive positive news, so do your readers. They will respond more favorably if a message concentrates on the positive, deemphasizes their mistakes, and when possible, focuses on how to do better. Even when you can't focus on the positive, use a tone that creates goodwill for you and your organization by focusing on the information, not on the reader.

### Focus on the Information, Not on the Reader

Compare the impression made by the following messages:

| | |
|---|---|
| **Focuses on the reader's actions** | You failed to read the instructions at the top of the form. If you had read them, you would have signed the back of the form on the appropriate line. Without your signature, your application for an account cannot be processed. |
| **Focuses on the information** | We will gladly process your account application. Please sign the back of the enclosed form on line 28 and return it to us. |

- **Avoid words and phrases that point out readers' mistakes in a negative tone or a tone that makes them feel inferior or ignorant.**

> You neglected to ...
> You failed to ...
> You ignored ...
> We fail to see how you could possibly ...
> We are at a loss to know how you ...
> We cannot understand how you ...

- **Avoid phrases that *inappropriately or unnecessarily* demand or insist that readers act.** These phrases may cause readers to resist or ignore your perceived demand.

> You should ...
> You ought to ...
> You must ...
> It is imperative that you ...
> We must insist that you ...
> We must request that you ...

- **Avoid ambiguous words and phrases that may sound fine to you but may make readers feel inferior.**

> No doubt ...
> Obviously ...
> Of course, you understand ...

- **Avoid implying that your readers are lying.**

> You claim that ...
> Your letter (memo, email) implies that ...

- **When possible, avoid negative words when referring to readers, their actions, or their requests.**

| | | |
|---|---|---|
| impossible | deny | unable |
| will not | inferior | fail |
| neglect | inconvenient | difficulty |
| incorrigible | complaint | wrong |

- **Don't click Send when you are angry or upset. Instead, click Save as Draft and wait until you have cooled down.** When you are angry or upset, you may write a message that includes inappropriate information or tactless or unprofessional language. If you are angry or upset, wait to send the email or ask a coworker to read it before you click Send.

| | |
|---|---|
| **Focuses on the reader's actions** | Your frivolous responses below clearly illustrate why we have been having problems with your company's transactions. Your responses demonstrate a profound lack of attention to simple details. |
| **Focuses on the information** | Thank you for responding to our questions. We have some additional questions about the following transactions. |

In the passages that focus on the reader's actions, the writer does not create goodwill. These statements focus on what the reader has done (or not done) rather than on the information. These passages point out the reader's mistakes instead of offering a way to correct them. mistakes. Follow the Tips for Creating a Tactful, Professional Tone when choosing words and phrases to help readers perceive your messages as you intend them.

## Avoid Overused Phrases

Over the years, many phrases have become associated with correspondence; you have probably read and possibly used some of these phrases. These phrases are overused, insincere, and inflated. Figure 12.13 lists overused phrases.

## Use Specific Language

To create a professional image through your correspondence, use specific language. When you use specific language, you eliminate questions that readers may ask when the language is ambiguous or vague and you lessen the chance of miscommunication.

When the language is not specific, your readers must guess at your intentions and they may guess incorrectly. Let's look at an example:

**Not specific**   Please send your revised report ASAP.

The writer does not give the reader a specific date for sending the revised report. By using *ASAP*, the writer expects the reader to send the revised report very soon. However, *ASAP* (short for as soon as possible) is vague. The writer means *send the report immediately*. However, the reader may read *ASAP* as *as soon as possible for me*. The reader will send the revised report when convenient. The writer should have included a date:

**Specific**        Please send your revised report by April 11.

In this version, the reader knows exactly when to send the report.

**FIGURE 12.13**

## Overused Phrases Common in Correspondence

Your cooperation in this matter is greatly appreciated
Any assistance would be appreciated
Attached please find …
Enclosed please find …
Enclosed you will find the information you requested
Pursuant to our agreement
To Whom It May Concern
Dear Sir or Madam
Thanks in advance
Thank you for your assistance in this matter
Please do not hesitate to call
Feel free to call me any time

## Follow Grammar and Punctuation Rules

Your correspondence should present a positive, professional picture of you and your organization. When your correspondence contains grammar, punctuation, or spelling errors, you and your organization look sloppy.

Your correspondence says a lot about you: It tells readers how well you pay attention to details—or how you **_overlook_** details. Take time to proofread your correspondence.

TAKING IT INTO THE *workplace*

## Email Etiquette at Work

Like face-to-face conversations, email allows for spontaneous responses and feedback (Lakoff 1982; Ong 1981). Email writers misuse this spontaneity when they misspell words and incorrectly use lowercase or uppercase letters. When you work for an organization, read the email of others before you send your own. Determine the level of formality. Find out the organization's guidelines for email. For example, does the organization allow you to send and receive personal email?

To be sure you follow proper email etiquette, follow these guidelines:

- **Make your messages easy to read and keep the paragraphs short.** Follow the standard rules for capitalizing letters, and add a line between paragraphs. Use a readable type.
- **Get to the point.** Put the main message in the first paragraph and make the Subject line specific.
- **Cut the clutter.** Eliminate words or information the readers do not need. Don't make the reader scroll through irrelevant information to find the main message.
- **Use a polite tone—don't flame.** *Flaming* is sending rude or angry emails. Before sending an email when you are angry or upset, step away from it before pressing Send. Later, reread your email from the readers' perspective. Does it present a professional picture of you and your organization?
- **Send messages only when you have something to say—don't send junk mail.** Unnecessary or uninformative email wastes readers' time.
- **Remember that email is permanent and that it is not private.** Most organizations archive all email written by their employees, so don't write anything in an email that you wouldn't put in print or want others to read. The organization may also scan emails for inappropriate language or topics.
- **Don't copy or forward email unless someone needs to see it.** When you copy or forward email to people who do not need it, you are *junking* their inboxes and creating work for them.
- **Proofread!** Before sending your email, proofread it for grammar, spelling, and clarity.

## Assignment

Most colleges, universities, and organizations have policies regarding email.

- Contact a faculty or staff member at your college or university and ask for a copy of the policy that governs how they use email. (If your university does not have a policy, contact a company in your area and ask for a copy of their policy—or ask them to summarize the policy for you.)
- Summarize the policy in an email to your instructor.

## CASE STUDY ANALYSIS

### When Email Becomes Public:
### How Microsoft Learned an Embarrassing Lesson

## Background

To protect itself against potential legal scrutiny several decades ago, Microsoft implemented a system for documenting internal communications between key employees and project managers in the company. Approximately every 30 days, IT experts would download and make copies of key employees' computer hard drives and email archives. Then the files would be sent to outside law offices to be reviewed for potential lawsuits. Any material deemed pertinent to ongoing cases was immediately turned over to the U.S. Department of Justice or to companies that had filed suit against Microsoft.

Because these files became part of legal actions, many of the private email correspondence became public evidence in trial. In an Iowa antitrust lawsuit, one company executive's email read, "If I didn't work here, I'd buy a Mac." The Microsoft executive, Jim All, made the statement to be "purposefully dramatic" to make a point (All 2006). However, the statement, taken out of context, did not portray a positive image of Microsoft or Mr. All. In another email, a Microsoft senior executive harshly criticized Bill Gates's leadership.

In addition to the scrutiny Microsoft was under due to the 20+ antitrust suits it faced, the company also suffered public embarrassment when these supposedly internal, *private* communications became public. As these Microsoft executives learned, do not write anything in your email that you don't want read publically.

## Assignment

1. Imagine that you are a Microsoft executive. Draft a memo to company employees advising them of the rules they should follow when drafting internal memos and email. Refer to the antitrust cases and the exposure of previous internal memos. Send your memo to your instructor.
2. Imagine that you are Bill Gates. Draft a letter to investors addressing the controversial email that was released in the antitrust suits. Reassure investors that the corporate atmosphere at Microsoft is still strong and that rifts between key executives have been mended. Turn in your letter to your instructor. Add a page of notes that discusses which approach you used in your letter—direct or indirect—and why you selected that approach.

# EXERCISES

1. Revise these sentences to improve their tone. If the sentence contains vague or ambiguous language, make the language specific.
   a. We are sorry that we cannot fill your order for our product. We get so many orders that we find it utterly impossible to fill them all.
   b. You understand, of course, that we cannot credit your account for the price of the opened software.
   c. We are searching for the revised report that you claim to have mailed to us on September 17.
   d. Your cooperation in this matter is greatly appreciated.
   e. We cannot understand how you could have left out your quarterly check when you mailed your copy of the statement.
   f. If you paid attention to simple details, you would notice that I sent that email at 4:38 p.m. yesterday.
   g. In filling out your warranty information, you failed to fill in the serial number of the printer.
   h. On the mechanical drawings, you do not indicate the size of the windows— as the drawings should. Please specify a size for the windows.
   i. The following submittals are way overdue and are now urgent for completion. Please submit these submittals immediately.
   j. After reviewing the dimensions for the elevator shaft, it seems you made an error.

2. Write an email or memo to your instructor explaining how the direct and indirect approaches differ. Suggest three specific writing situations where you would use the direct approach and three where you would use the indirect approach. Explain your suggestions.

3. You manage several project teams for an environmental engineering firm. Recently many team members have been charging personal expenses to their corporate credit cards. Several of them have been unable to cover their expenses when the payments are due. When the employees pick up their corporate credit cards each year, they

receive a copy of the company policy on using these cards on personal expenses. The policy reads as follows:

> You may use your corporate credit card for travel and other business-related expenses. You may not use your card for personal expenses such as meals, gifts, and personal travel.

Write a memo to your project teams restating the policy and explaining that the firm will take cards away from employees who misuse the cards and that these employees may lose their jobs if they violate the policy.

4. Think of a service, procedure, or policy that your college or university should change. Write a letter or email message to the appropriate school official and suggest the change.

5. Think of a service or product with which you have recently experienced a problem. Write a letter to the appropriate person about the problem and ask for an appropriate solution or remedy. If you cannot find the name of the appropriate person, use the AMS simplified letter style (see Figure 12.6).

6. Find the email address of a company, nonprofit organization, or government agency that has sample materials or information that you need for a class project. Write an email to this organization and request the information or materials you need. Send a copy of the email to your instructor.

7. You are the network manager for your company's computer network. Over the past few weeks, many employees have tied up the network by downloading graphics for personal use during peak business hours, sending large files to their home computers, and surfing the Internet for personal business during regular business hours. The downloaded graphics and surfing consume enormous amounts of memory on the network server, slowing network response time. You have sent several emails to all network users about this problem, but the number of users who continue to download graphics and surf the Internet for personal use has not decreased. Yesterday, you confiscated a downloaded and printed graphic of Mickey and Minnie Mouse and one of the President's dog. Today, two senior managers could not log on to the Internet between 11:30 a.m. and 1:00 p.m. because employees were downloading graphics and surfing the Internet. You are frustrated and angry. You write the email in Figure 12.14 to all network users. The message is direct, abrupt, and writer focused. You mean the threat humorously; however, your message offends several employees.

**Email Message for Exercise 7**

Today, two senior managers could not take care of company business between 11:30 and 1:00 because the network was saturated with users surfing the Internet and downloading and printing graphics for personal use. During the past week, during regular business hours, I have confiscated printouts of the President's dog and of Mickey and Minnie Mouse, among others. I have also watched groups of employees watching YouTube videos. I will say it again: IT IS AGAINST COMPANY POLICY TO SURF THE INTERNET AND TO DOWNLOAD GRAPHICS FOR PERSONAL USE DURING BUSINESS HOURS. IT IS ALSO AGAINST COMPANY POLICY TO WATCH INTERNET VIDEOS. In the future, IT will report all employees who use their computers for personal use to their supervisors and to senior managers.

a. Write an email to all employees retracting your "humorous" threat and explaining the company's Internet policies. Make the message reader focused and, when possible, positive.

b. Write a memo to your manager explaining the problems the network users are creating and the "threatening" email message you sent to all network users. Explain to your manager how you are smoothing out the turmoil caused by the email and ask your manager for suggestions for solving these network problems.

8. You are the regional manager for a chain of electronics stores. You have received a letter from a customer, Ms. Meredith Sims (3567 Rockcreek, Tampa, FL 10067). Ms. Sims writes that she purchased a new computer and monitor from the Tampa store a month ago. Two days after she purchased the computer, the monitor quit working. She immediately returned the monitor to the Tampa store and asked for a replacement. The store manager refused to replace the monitor and instead offered to repair it. Your company doesn't offer replacements—only repairs. Ms. Sims doesn't want the monitor repaired because a clerk at the Tampa store told her that several customers had returned monitors like hers.

Determine the best solution to Ms. Sims's situation and write a letter to her explaining the company's policy and your solution. Your solution should follow company policy and your letter should keep her goodwill.

## A 'Mixed-Up Situation'

You are the customer service manager for Kitchen Wizard, Inc. Your company manufactures small kitchen appliances such as blenders, food processors, and mixers. Yesterday you received a letter and package from Joanna Logan. The text of her letter appears in Figure 12.15. Ms. Logan apparently has not read her warranty or the owner's manual that she received with her mixer.

- The manual clearly states that users should not allow food to get into the motor housing. The company expects that some dust from flour and powdered sugar and dried dough on occasion to creep into the housing. However, the mixer was not designed to function if dough works its way into the motor housing.
- The manual instructs users not to immerse the motor in water. This warning is restated on the mixer. By immersing the mixer in water, users not only damage the motor, they could also electrocute themselves if the mixer is plugged into an electrical socket.

You want to keep Ms. Logan's business—after all she sent you cookies (and they were tasty!). However, her warranty is now invalid because she immersed the mixer in water and she used the mixer when letting bread dough rise. You now must write to her and explain that you will not repair the mixer—it can't be repaired—and that you can't give her a new mixer. However, you have decided to give her a coupon for 35 percent off a new mixer.

## Assignment

Write a letter to Ms. Logan explaining that you cannot repair or replace her mixer. Remember to tell her about the coupon and to use an appropriate tone.

**Real World Experience: Broken Mixer Letter**

October 15, 2012

Customer Service Manager
Kitchen Wizard, Inc.
36789 Industrial Blvd.
Houston, TX 77843

Dear Customer Service Manager:

I have enclosed my Kitchen Wizard mixer, model 69B. I bought the mixer 3 years ago at Smith Hardware in Ennis, Texas. I have enclosed the registration card and warranty for the mixer. Last week, the mixer stopped working. I took the cover off the motor to see if it was clogged from flour, powdered sugar, or bread dough. (When I make bread, I let the bread dough rise in the mixing bowl on the mixer stand. When the bread rises to the motor casing, I know that it has doubled. Sometimes I get to talking on my cell phone and let the bread rise too high and a little bread dough gets into the motor.) The motor had a lot of dried bread dough and powdered sugar in it. (I also make a lot of cookies that call for powdered sugar. Sometimes when I dump 6 cups of powdered sugar into the mixing bowl and turn on the mixer at high speed, the powdered sugar gets into the motor and on the ceiling and walls. It makes a big mess, but the cookies are great. I also enclosed some of these cookies for you to sample.)

I cleaned the motor well. I soaked it in hot soapy water for several hours and then dried the motor with my hairdryer. However, now the mixer won't turn on. Please repair the mixer since it is still under warranty and return it to me in the same box. If you can't repair it, I will happily accept a new mixer. Enjoy the cookies.

Best regards,

Joanna Logan
Expert Baker

P. S. If you like the cookies, let me know and I'll send you the recipe.

Enclosure

# chapter *thirteen*

## Writing Reader-Focused Job Correspondence and Résumés

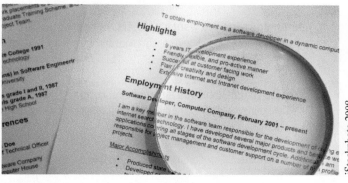

*iStockphoto 2008.*

icole will graduate from college in three months. She is excited about finding a job in her chosen field and beginning her career, but first she has to find that job. Nicole realizes that all the jobs she applies for will require a résumé—even those that she learns about at her university career placement center. For jobs that she discovers for herself, she will also need to write a letter of application, or cover letter, to accompany her résumé.

Like Nicole, you soon will graduate and look for a job. You might also want to apply for an internship and will need a cover letter and résumé. This chapter presents principles to help you locate job opportunities and then to write appropriate job correspondence before and after the interview.

**The Stages of an Effective Job Search**

**Plan your search.**
- Determine the type of job you want.
- Learn about organizations where you would enjoy working.
- Conduct a personal inventory.

**Decide how you will locate jobs.**
- Use more than one resource to locate jobs.
- Use your career placement center on campus, published ads, company websites, and online job boards.

**Find out about organizations where you will apply.**
- Do your homework.
- Follow the guidelines presented in Chapter 5 for researching information.

**Determine what you want employers to know about you.**
- Think about your skills and qualifications and what you want employers to know about you after reading your résumé and cover letter.

**Prepare your résumé and letter of application.**
- Determine the best résumé organization for your information and employment history (chronological or skills-based).
- Prepare a paper and a scannable résumé.
- Write a letter of application tailored to the specific job for which you are applying.

**Proofread your résumé and letter of application.**
- Make sure your résumé and letter of application are free of grammar and style errors.
- Remember that errors can cost you an interview.

**Prepare for the interview.**
- Do your homework.
- Find out about the organization and prepare appropriate questions.
- Practice answering possible questions.

**Write a follow-up letter.**
- Write a letter thanking the employer after the interview.

Many students believe that a job search is simply posting your résumé on a website and waiting for employers to contact you. However, an effective job search takes planning and time. Figure 13.1 presents the stages of an effective job search.

## What Type of Job Do You Want?

Eli Davidson, business coach, reports that many job searchers don't do their homework and they send applications simply to apply. Instead, apply only for jobs and to organizations that interest you. Don't waste your time or that of an employer by sending out résumés for jobs you don't want or that don't match your qualifications. Davidson adds, "The best way to get a great job is to have a laser beam focus. The more targeted and specific you are, the more powerful your job search will be" (Davidson, quoted in Zupek 2007, 1).

To determine the type of job you want, conduct a personal inventory by asking yourself the following questions:

- **What kind of organization appeals to you?**
    - Do you want to work for a large or a small organization?
    - Do you want a government position or an industry position?
    - Do you want to work for a nonprofit organization?
- **Where do you want to live?**
    - Do you want to stay in your current location?
    - Can you or do you want to commute?
    - Do you want an international position?
- **What are your strengths and weaknesses, and how do they affect the type of job you want?**
- **Do your skills and education match the jobs you want?**

To learn more about the kind of job you want, attend job fairs and find out about trends in your field. Visit with professors in your field and with the people in the career placement center at your college or university. These people can help you learn about jobs available in your field.

## How Will You Locate Job Opportunities?

After you have determined the type of job you want, look for that job using the methods described in this text. To ensure that you find the right job for you, use more than one method.

- **Contact your college or university placement center.** Most colleges and universities have career planning and placement centers that help graduating seniors and recent graduates. These placement centers link organizations and their recruitment officers with qualified applicants. Most placement centers require you to register with them before you can interview. As part of the registration procedure, you probably will need to create a file (sometimes called a *dossier* or *electronic portfolio*) that includes an information sheet about you and your job interests, your résumé, and your college or university transcripts. In your file, you also may include samples of your work and other information that might interest potential employers. After receiving your dossier, the placement center will give copies of it to recruiters from businesses, government agencies, and industry; these recruiters will use the placement center to set up campus interviews. Visit your campus placement center to find out how to set up a file and schedule interviews. The placement center is an excellent way to begin your job search; it's free, simple, and convenient.

> To ensure that you find the right job for you, use more than one search method for discovering employment opportunities.

- **Respond to ads published on an organization's website.** Most organizations post job ads on their websites. Most of these sites will ask you to complete an online application and upload your résumé. When responding, carefully follow their instructions. You don't want your application thrown out simply because you did not follow instructions.
- **Use an online job site.** Search for jobs online through websites sponsored by federal agencies, professional organizations, and private organizations. These sites are called *job boards*. You will find two types of job boards:
  - Some job boards only list positions. You apply for those positions by mailing or emailing your résumé and letter of application.
  - Some job boards let you submit your résumé electronically so employers can search for qualified candidates and contact them directly.

  If you decide to post your résumé to a site, you have no control over it—who sees it, who uses it, or how it is used. Before you post your résumé, read the Tips for Using an Online Job Board.
- **Network with others in your field, with people whom you know, and with your professors.** When you begin your job search, tell people in your field, your professors, and your personal and family friends that you are looking for a job. Send them a copy of your résumé. These people may have contacts to help you locate job opportunities.
- **Send out unsolicited application letters.** If you are interested in working for a specific organization, send an unsolicited letter. Many organizations do not advertise job opportunities, so unsolicited letters can be effective. Unsolicited letters do have a disadvantage:

- **Determine if the online job board meets your needs.** Before you post your résumé or any information on a job board, ask yourself these questions:
  - **Who will have access to your résumé?** If the site is not secure and anyone can view your résumé, decide if you want to post it. If you do post it on an unsecured website, remove your phone number and address.
  - **Will the job board charge you a fee to post or to update your résumé?** Some job boards charge a fee for posting your résumé, and some charge a fee each time you update it. Make sure you know about the charges upfront. If a job board charges to update your résumé, use a free site.
  - **Can you update your résumé?** If not, maybe you should use other job boards.
- **Find out how you will be notified when an employer requests your résumé.** Some job boards will notify you while others will not. If you know an employer has requested your résumé, follow up to find out about potential job opportunities.
- **Find out whether your current employer or manager will see your résumé.** Depending on your employer or manager, you may jeopardize your current job if he or she finds out you are searching for another position. If your manager knows you're looking, use the job board. If not, look into other ways to find job opportunities.
- **Use more than one online job board.** A potential employer may not see your résumé or personal information if you use only one job board. Post your résumé on boards specifically for your field. Some of the more popular job boards are
  - Monster
  - CareerBuilder
  - AfterCollege

The organization may not have any openings. However, if you are truly interested in working for a particular organization, an unsolicited application letter might be worth your time.

- **Use professional placement agencies.** Professional placement agencies present your résumé to potential employers. These agencies work much like a college placement center but often charge a fee paid either by the employers or the job seeker. Most of these agencies cater to experienced job seekers.

## What Do You Want Employers to Know About You?

Before you put together a résumé or send out letters of application, think about what information you want employers to know about you and what information employers want to know about potential employees like you. The information you provide should give employers a positive, accurate picture of you and what you can offer their organization.

> To ensure that you find the right job for you, use more than one way to find employment opportunities.

Begin by determining what information is likely to interest prospective employers. Concentrate on these categories: education, work experience, activities, goals, and skills. After selecting your categories, brainstorm to create lists of information about yourself in each category. Write down any information you think will help an employer understand you and your qualifications, as well as information that might impress an employer. For instance, under education, list the degree you will receive when you graduate, the date you will receive the degree, your major, and significant projects you completed in your major field of study. Figure 13.2 shows the brainstorming list that Nicole created. Although she may not use all the information on her list, it gives her something to work with when she prepares her résumé and letter of application.

Think about what employers might want to know about you. If you are applying for several jobs at the same time. Prepare a résumé first, concentrating on information that will demonstrate what you can offer an employer. Later, you can customize your application letter and your résumé for each employer, including information that will particularly interest each employer or that relates directly to a specific job opportunity.

## PREPARE AN EFFECTIVE PAPER RÉSUMÉ

Robert Greenly of Lockheed Martin writes that "your résumé is the first impression you make. It should be eye-catching, clearly written, and easy to read" (1993, 47). Your résumé and letter of application generally are the first information an employer sees about you, so you want these documents to persuade an employer to interview you. To write an effective résumé,

- Organize your résumé to highlight your qualifications.
- Use dynamic, persuasive language that demonstrates what you can do.
- Proofread and remove errors.
- Create an eye-catching, accessible design for paper résumés.

FIGURE 13.2

**Education**
>B.S. in mechanical engineering from University of Washington
>Expect to graduate in December 2012
>Dean's list three semesters—fall 2010, spring 2010, spring 2011
>GPA 3.45

**Work Experience**
>Internship at General Dynamics
>Helped design robotics machinery for automated assembly lines; used CAD in refining designs
>Learned to work as a team member

**Trinity Pharmacy**
>Pharmacy technician since January 2010
>Began as cashier and did general cleanup of store
>Operate the cash register
>Enter prescription information into the computer system
>Help customers needing information about over-the-counter drugs and other items in the pharmacy area
>Deal with confidential customer information

**Lifeguard and Swimming Instructor**
>Summers since high school
>Know CPR
>Certified Red Cross lifeguard at YMCA pool at home
>Received Lifeguard of the Month award four times (get years and months)
>Certified Red Cross swimming instructor
>Taught private, semiprivate, and group swimming to children through the YMCA

**Skills**
>Java
>Have designed Web pages for Trinity Pharmacy—however, not experienced here
>Know statistics packages, spreadsheets, CAD, and Dreamweaver
>People skills—have learned to interact with customers and to be a team player
>Work well with children

**Activities**
>Mortar Board, senior year
>American Society of Mechanical Engineers
>Did volunteer work for Habitat for Humanity

**Career Goal**
>To find an engineering position in robotics

One of the most commonly asked questions about résumés is how long should my résumé be? Your résumé should be long enough to provide employers with the information they need to understand what you can offer their organization, but not so long as to irritate them. Davidson writes that "sending a 10-page résumé is a mammoth error" (2007, 2); instead, highlight your abilities on one page. If you're having trouble, invite someone to help you. Remember that "the person reviewing résumés has 15 seconds to decide to bring you in" (in Zupeck, 2007, 2). If you have less than 10 years of experience in your field, keep your résumé to one page.

## Organize Your Résumé to Highlight Your Qualifications

Once you have determined what you want employers to know about you, organize your résumé. Use two levels of organization: (1) the overall organization of the major categories of information (education, work experience, skills, etc.), and (2) the organization within those categories.

For the overall organization, decide what category of information you want the employer to see first. Many recent college graduates begin with their education—including college-related activities or honors—and move to work experience or skills.

After determining the overall organization, think about how you will organize the information within each category. For example, work experience is often the longest category in the résumé and, for experienced job seekers, the most important. For this category, use one of two organizational patterns: chronological or functional (sometimes called skills-based).

If you organize your résumé *chronologically*, you present the information in both the work experience and the education categories in *reverse chronological order;* that is, you begin with your most recent or current job or degree and end with the oldest. The résumé in Figure 13.3 illustrates chronological style. In the Education category, the writer begins with her most recent college work and ends with her oldest. In the Work Experience category, she begins with her current work at the University of North Texas and ends with her first work as a server at Red Lobster. Figure 13.4 shows a chronological résumé for a nontraditional student.

FIGURE 13.3

## Chronological Résumé from a Traditional Student

The writer uses 16-point type to emphasize her name.

**Leigh Andrea Thompson**
204 Oak Street • Denton, TX 76205 • (817) 555-5555 • lthomas@unt.edu

**Objective**     Entry-level position in programming where I can use my technical communication skills

Headings and subheads allow employers to easily locate categories of information.

**Education**

**University of North Texas, Denton, Texas**
Bachelor of Arts in Professional and Technical Communication
August 2012
GPA 3.6/4.0

**Advanced Courses**
- Commercial Publications
- Online Publications
- Advanced Technical Writing
- Manuals and Procedures

**Baylor University, Waco, Texas**
Foundation Courses

The writer includes information on her part-time work to let the employer know she has maintained a good GPA while working to pay for her education.

Worked part-time to finance my education

**Work Experience**

**University of North Texas, Denton, Texas**
Department of Linguistics and Technical Communication
Student Assistant
September 2010 to 2012 (fall and spring semesters)

The writer puts information in reverse chronological order in the work experience section.

Bulleted lists highlight information.

- Assisted the office manager and the department chair
- Designed recruitment brochures for new undergraduate major in Professional and Technical Communication
- Created an online system for faculty to order books

**Sabre Airline Solutions, Southlake, Texas**
Technical Writing Intern
May 2011 to September 2011
- Worked with subject matter experts to create training manuals
- Edited and proofread online training materials

Ample white space helps employers easily see the headings.

**Red Lobster, Denton, Texas**
Server
June 2005 to December 2005
- Earned awards for service in August and October

The writer uses verbs in the work experience section to demonstrate what she did rather than to describe her work.

**Organizations**

Society for Technical Communication
Freshman Council (a leadership organization)
Baylor President's Council (a leadership and service organization)
Volunteer for Habitat for Humanity

*References available upon request*

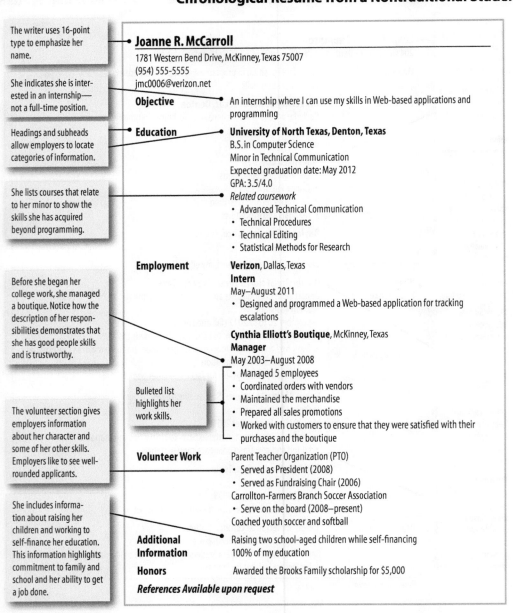

## FIGURE 13.4

### Chronological Résumé from a Nontraditional Student

The writer uses 16-point type to emphasize her name.

She indicates she is interested in an internship—not a full-time position.

Headings and subheads allow employers to locate categories of information.

She lists courses that relate to her minor to show the skills she has acquired beyond programming.

Before she began her college work, she managed a boutique. Notice how the description of her responsibilities demonstrates that she has good people skills and is trustworthy.

Bulleted list highlights her work skills.

The volunteer section gives employers information about her character and some of her other skills. Employers like to see well-rounded applicants.

She includes information about raising her children and working to self-finance her education. This information highlights commitment to family and school and her ability to get a job done.

**Joanne R. McCarroll**

1781 Western Bend Drive, McKinney, Texas 75007
(954) 555-5555
jmc0006@verizon.net

**Objective**  An internship where I can use my skills in Web-based applications and programming

**Education**  **University of North Texas, Denton, Texas**
B.S. in Computer Science
Minor in Technical Communication
Expected graduation date: May 2012
GPA: 3.5/4.0
*Related coursework*
- Advanced Technical Communication
- Technical Procedures
- Technical Editing
- Statistical Methods for Research

**Employment**  **Verizon**, Dallas, Texas
**Intern**
May–August 2011
- Designed and programmed a Web-based application for tracking escalations

**Cynthia Elliott's Boutique**, McKinney, Texas
**Manager**
May 2003–August 2008
- Managed 5 employees
- Coordinated orders with vendors
- Maintained the merchandise
- Prepared all sales promotions
- Worked with customers to ensure that they were satisfied with their purchases and the boutique

**Volunteer Work**  Parent Teacher Organization (PTO)
- Served as President (2008)
- Served as Fundraising Chair (2006)
Carrollton-Farmers Branch Soccer Association
- Serve on the board (2008–present)
Coached youth soccer and softball

**Additional Information**  Raising two school-aged children while self-financing 100% of my education

**Honors**  Awarded the Brooks Family scholarship for $5,000

*References Available upon request*

FIGURE 13.5

## Skills Résumé from a Nontraditional Student

The writer uses 16-point type to emphasize her name.

Headings and subheads allow employers to easily locate categories of information.

Bulleted lists highlight skills.

Skills and accomplishments appear before education and employment. The accomplishments demonstrate how she has developed and used her skills.

Ample white space helps employers easily see the headings.

The employment section lists jobs; it omits descriptions of responsibilities. Compare this résumé with the chronological style in Figure 13.4.

**Joanne R. McCarroll**

1781 Western Bend Drive, McKinney, Texas 75070
(954) 555-5555
jmc0006@verizon.net

**Objective** — A position where I can use my programming skills along with my management and communication skills

**Skills and Accomplishments**

**Programing Skills**
Java, PHP, C++
- Designed and programmed a Web-based application for tracking escalations for Verizon, using Java, Tapestry, MySQL, and Hibernate
- Designed and programmed a Web-based test generator for McKinney ISD

**Communication Skills**
- Prepared a business plan for an intranet concept juried by senior executives at Balfour Beatty Construction, Dallas, Texas
- Prepared a website for a dog rescue group in Grand Prairie, Texas
- Wrote a handbook for parents in the wrestling program
- Have taken 12 hours of technical communication courses

**Management and Leadership Skills**
- Managed all aspects of a boutique, including staff, inventory, and payroll
- Led the Parent Teacher Organization for a high school of 2,000 students

**Education**
**University of North Texas**, Denton, Texas
B.S. in Computer Science
Minor in Technical Communication
Expected graduation date: May 2012
**Related coursework**
- Advanced Technical Communication
- Statistical Methods for Research
- Technical Procedures
- Technical Editing

**Employment**
**Verizon**, Dallas, Texas
*Intern* (May –August 2011)

**Cynthia Elliott's Boutique**, McKinney, Texas
*Manager* (May 2003–August 2008)

**Volunteer Work**
**Parent Teacher Organization** (PTO)
McKinney High School Wrestling Boosters
Coached youth soccer and softball

**Additional Information**
Raising two school-age children while self-financing 100% of my education

**Honors**
Awarded the Brooks Family scholarship for $5,000

*References Available upon request*

Most job seekers "prefer the logical progression of a chronological résumé" (Greenly 1993, 44). For recent college graduates or for job seekers looking for their first career job, skills-based résumés are generally less effective than chronological résumés. Some job seekers, however, need a ***skills-based résumé***—one that focuses the reader's attention on the writer's marketable job skills and accomplishments rather than on a chronological listing of work experience. A skills-based résumé is especially effective in two situations:

- when you want to present your most important accomplishments or skills early in the résumé or at least in a lead-off position within categories
- if you want to change careers and a chronological organization might undermine your search (Greenly 1993)

The résumé in Figure 13.5 is skills-based. The major accomplishments category focuses on the job seeker's skills and accomplishments in two areas: financial planning and financial analysis. The résumé includes work experience, but simply lists the jobs; it does not list the corresponding responsibilities and duties.

Whether you use the chronological or the skills-based style, select information that highlights your qualifications and prompts employers to interview you. Include the first three sections in all résumés and the last two whenever you can.

- career objective
- education
- work experience
- skills and specialized training
- personal information

## Career Objective

A ***career objective*** states the kind of work you are seeking in the form of a brief phrase. For example, you might write the following for your objective: Entry-level position in commercial building construction. Many hiring managers consider these statements important because they indicate that the writer has goals. However, other managers find these statements vague, especially if the statements are general or don't relate directly to the advertised job. The following career objective could cause a manager to pass over a qualified job applicant: An entry-level position in computer programming with the opportunity to advance into management. A broad statement like that can have unintended consequences. After reading such a statement, a potential employer might decide not to consider the applicant for a job that will not quickly lead to a management position. Résumés that omit an objective give employers "greater flexibility in considering you for any number of peripheral

positions that your experience and training qualify you for, perhaps even future openings that do not yet exist" (Greenly 1993, 43). If you include a career objective, follow these guidelines:
- Use brief, specific statements directly related to the job for which you are applying.
- Include only the position, goals, or tasks specifically stated in the job advertisement.
- Avoid general, broad statements such as A position where I can use my programming skills.

## Education

In the Education section, give employers information about your degree(s). In this section, you identify
- your college or university degree
- the institution awarding the degree
- the location of the institution
- the date you received or will receive the degree

If you haven't yet graduated, list the colleges or universities you have attended beyond high school, their location, and the expected date of your degree. For example, a senior at San Diego State University might write the following:

San Diego State University, San Diego, California
B.S. in Mechanical Engineering
Expected graduation, May 2013

In addition to listing your degree(s), include information such as
- courses that qualify you for the type of job you are seeking
- minors or double majors
- academic (merit-based) scholarships or fellowships you received
- a high grade-point average (above 3.0 on a 4-point scale)
- academic (merit-based) honors or awards you received as a college or university student
- outstanding accomplishments, such as special projects or research that you did as a student

If you list courses related to the work you are seeking, include primarily upper-level courses in your major. List courses by title, not number. For example, if you want to mention a course in advanced automated systems, write Advanced Automated Systems, not MECH 4302. Figure 13.4 shows how you could list courses in the Education section of your résumé.

The Education section shown in Figure 13.6 includes several optional items, along with the writer's degree information. The writer lists his grade-point average (3.7) along with a reference point (4.0). He also mentions his academic honors. Notice that he states in this section that he worked part-time to help finance his education. With this format, he highlights his impressive achievement of earning a high grade-point average and honors while holding a job.

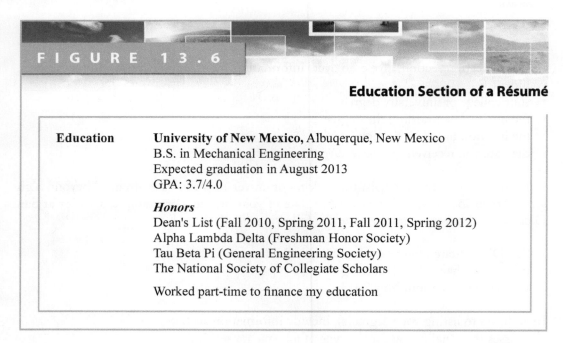

**FIGURE 13.6**

**Education Section of a Résumé**

| Education | **University of New Mexico,** Albuqerque, New Mexico |
|---|---|
| | B.S. in Mechanical Engineering |
| | Expected graduation in August 2013 |
| | GPA: 3.7/4.0 |
| | |
| | *Honors* |
| | Dean's List (Fall 2010, Spring 2011, Fall 2011, Spring 2012) |
| | Alpha Lambda Delta (Freshman Honor Society) |
| | Tau Beta Pi (General Engineering Society) |
| | The National Society of Collegiate Scholars |
| | |
| | Worked part-time to finance my education |

## Work Experience

In the Work Experience (or Employment) section, include information on jobs you've held. List them in *reverse chronological order*, beginning with your most recent experience. For each job, include

- the name and location of the organization for which you worked
- the years (or months, if less than a year) of your work with that organization
- your job title
- verb phrases describing the work you did (your job responsibilities)

FIGURE 13.7

**Work Experience Section for a Job Seeker with Experience**

| | |
|---|---|
| **Employment** | **Texas Instruments, Inc.,** Dallas, Texas (2000–present) |

**Manufacturing Facilitator** (2005–present)
- Facilitated two self-directed work teams of 26 team members performing screen printing and printing operations
- Led screen printing team to win Gold Teaming for Excellence Award
- Converted coating system to low VOC formulations that comply with existing air-quality standards

**Reengineering Team Leader** (2002–2005)
- Reengineered screen printing work flow to eliminate non-value-added effort and reduce task handoffs from one person to another
- Reduced cycle time from 5 days to 2 days, increased productivity by 25%, and saved $250,000 annually
- Received two Site Quality Improvement Award for reducing cycle time and improving quality (2003, 2004)

**Process Improvement Engineer of Finish and Assembly Areas**
(2000–2002)
- Designed and installed custom equipment and machine upgrades that reduced manual labor required, saving $100,000 annually
- Improved part racking on plating line, reducing scrap, saving $20,000 annually

As you describe your responsibilities, show how well you did your job and demonstrate that you can produce results. "The most qualified people don't always get the job. It goes to the person who presents himself [or herself] most persuasively in person and on paper. So don't just list where you were and what you did ... tell how well you did. Were you the best salesperson? Did you cut operating costs? Give numbers, statistics, percentages, increases in sales or profits" (Simon 1981).

Figures 13.7 and 13.8 illustrate how two writers describe their work experience. In Figure 13.7, instead of using vague, unimpressive language, the writer, an experienced job seeker, uses specific information to demonstrate how well he did his job:

Vague and unimpressive    Facilitated work teams
Improved production

| Specific and impressive | Facilitated two self-directed work teams of 26 team members |
|---|---|
| | Reduced cycle time from 5 days to 2 days |
| | Saved $250,000 annually |

The writer doesn't simply tell prospective employers he saved the company money or reduced the cycle time. He states the specific reduction in days and the amount saved in dollars.

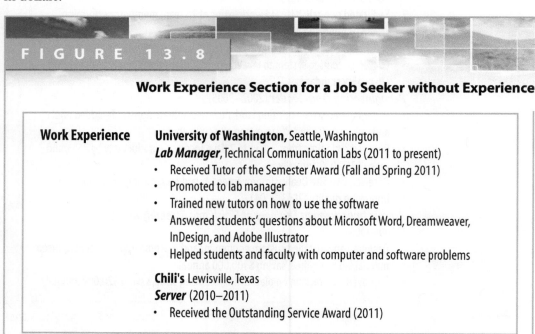

**FIGURE 13.8**

**Work Experience Section for a Job Seeker without Experience**

| Work Experience | **University of Washington,** Seattle, Washington |
|---|---|
| | *Lab Manager*, Technical Communication Labs (2011 to present) |

- Received Tutor of the Semester Award (Fall and Spring 2011)
- Promoted to lab manager
- Trained new tutors on how to use the software
- Answered students' questions about Microsoft Word, Dreamweaver, InDesign, and Adobe Illustrator
- Helped students and faculty with computer and software problems

**Chili's** Lewisville, Texas
*Server* (2010–2011)
- Received the Outstanding Service Award (2011)

The experience section in Figure 13.8 is an excerpt from a college student's résumé. This student is looking for her first job in her field. She doesn't have the extensive work experience of the writer in Figure 13.7. However, she demonstrates how well she did the jobs she held as a student at the University of Washington. She lists her award for service at Chili's restaurant, along with the year she received the award. She also lists her Tutor of the Semester award. These awards and her promotion demonstrate that she did her jobs well.

Like the writer in Figure 13.8, you may not have work experience in your field. However, you should list your summer or part-time jobs. If you were promoted or received awards while in these jobs, include this information so potential employers see that you are reliable and hardworking.

## Skills and Specialized Training

Some writers include a section listing their skills or specialized training or education they received. These sections are most common in skills-based résumés. In a skills-based résumé, this section usually appears prominently near the beginning and can have various headings such as Major Accomplishments or Skills. Figure 13.9 shows the skills section from the résumé of a job seeker wanting to change careers. Many job seekers in computer science list their programming languages in a skills section. Figure 13.10 shows a specialized training section. If you decide to use these sections in your résumé, include only information relevant to the type of job you are seeking.

## Personal Information

You may want to include personal information that gives readers "a glimpse of the personal you" and furthers "the image you've worked to project in the preceding sections" of the résumé (Simon 1981). List any of the following information if it will enhance a prospective employer's picture of you:

- volunteer work (such as work for charitable [nonprofit] organizations, membership in community service organizations, or leadership or work with community youth organizations)
- college activities (such as membership on teams and in organizations, offices held, and awards won)

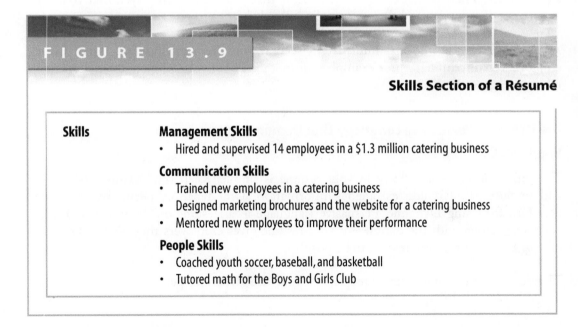

**FIGURE 13.9**

**Skills Section of a Résumé**

| Skills | **Management Skills** |
|---|---|
| | • Hired and supervised 14 employees in a $1.3 million catering business |
| | **Communication Skills** |
| | • Trained new employees in a catering business |
| | • Designed marketing brochures and the website for a catering business |
| | • Mentored new employees to improve their performance |
| | **People Skills** |
| | • Coached youth soccer, baseball, and basketball |
| | • Tutored math for the Boys and Girls Club |

**FIGURE   13 . 10**

**Special Training Section of a Résumé**

| | |
|---|---|
| **Special Training** | • Business Process Engineering (reengineering) |
| | • Statistical Process Control (design of experiments and Six Sigma quality) |
| | • Structural Steel Design |

- professional memberships (such as in organizations in your field, including leadership positions you've held). You can put professional membership information in a separate section
- personal interests and hobbies, especially if they relate to your qualifications
- sports or recreational activities that you enjoy

Perhaps you've been a Girl Scout or Boy Scout leader in your community; you've organized a blood drive for your college or university campus; or you've won awards for your leadership abilities. These activities and awards show that you are a team player, that you care about your community, and that you are disciplined.

As you prepare the personal information section, omit information that might invite employers to discriminate—for example, information about your religion, ethnicity, marital status, age, or health.

## Use Dynamic, Persuasive Language That Demonstrates What You Can Do

The guideline for word choice in your résumé is simple: Keep your writing style clear and uncluttered. Exclude extraneous information. Use dynamic, persuasive language (see Tips for Using Dynamic, Persuasive Language in a Résumé on the next page). The language—along with the design—of your résumé gives employers their first impression of you. You want that impression to be positive.

The following examples illustrate phrases that use dynamic, persuasive language (the dynamic action verbs appear in bold type):

## TIPS FOR USING DYNAMIC, PERSUASIVE LANGUAGE IN A RÉSUMÉ

- **Keep the information and language simple and direct.** The employer reading your résumé may be reading hundreds of others for the same job.
- **State your information or qualifications directly; omit unnecessary information.** Be brief. Give employers the information they need to know about your abilities and background—and then stop.
- **Use dynamic action verbs.** Use verbs such as *saved, designed, supervised, directed,* and *designed*. Avoid words and phrases that don't describe action or demonstrate what you have achieved and can achieve. Avoid phrases such as *my responsibilities included* or *my tasks and duties were*.
- **Use specific language that emphasizes your accomplishments and what you can do.** When possible, use statistics and numbers to show rather than to describe. Statistics and numbers effectively demonstrate your accomplishments.
- **Use verb phrases, not sentences.** Because you want to focus on what you have accomplished, use verb phrases, not full sentences.

| | |
|---|---|
| Not Dynamic/Persuasive | Created a computer program for students logging into the lab |
| Dynamic/Persuasive | **Designed** and **programmed** software that **reduced** the number of employees needed in the student computer labs and **saved** the university $16,640 annually |
| Not Dynamic/Persuasive | In charge of charity gala for my sorority |
| Dynamic/Persuasive | **Coordinated** the Red Dress charity gala that **raised** $8,600 for the American Heart Association |
| Not Dynamic/Persuasive | Was responsible for designing and installing custom equipment and upgrading machines |
| Dynamic/Persuasive | **Designed** and **installed** custom equipment and machine upgrades that **reduced** the manual labor required by $100,000 annually |

## Create an Eye-Catching, Accessible Design

Design your résumé so an employer can quickly get a good idea of your qualifications (Greenly 1993). You want to design your résumé so that "employers don't have to hunt for your qualifications"; employers should be able to quickly locate your qualifications without "playing detective" (Parker and Berry 1998, 318). If they have to play detective, they may overlook something important or ignore your résumé. To help employers, create visual categories with white space, headings, varied type sizes, and bulleted lists.

In the résumés shown in Figures 13.3, 13.4, and 13.5 employers can easily spot the categories because the headings are surrounded by white space, making them stand out. These headings help employers quickly locate information about the writer's qualifications. The writers use bold type and different type sizes within the categories to highlight and prioritize information. The writers also use bulleted lists to help employers read the résumé. As you design your résumé, follow the Tips for Designing Effective Résumés.

## ETHICS NOTE

### Honesty in Your Résumé

Good jobs are competitive. Only 1 of 1,470 résumés put into circulation actually results in a job offer (Bolles 2009). Given such odds, young professionals are often tempted to embellish their résumés. According to Steven Levitt, coauthor of *Freakanomics* and a professor at the University of Chicago, more than 50 percent of résumé writers lie on their résumés (quoted in Issacs 2012).

Such deception occurs at the most elite levels: Jean Houston, an infamous psychologist who counseled Hillary Rodham Clinton to imagine herself in dialogue with deceased luminaries like Eleanor Roosevelt, reported on her résumé having received a doctorate in the philosophy of religion from Columbia University. However, Joseph Berger (1996), a writer for the *New York Times*, reported that Houston had never completed her dissertation, a requirement for the doctorate. Houston lied on her résumé.

Houston claimed that an aide had selected a résumé from the "bottom of the barrel" of résumés she kept on file. Her ethical lapse—falsifying her credentials—is the kind that some résumé writers deliberately make. Other common résumé deceits include inflating one's

iStockphoto 2008.

title or responsibilities. Employers are more savvy about the probable areas of deception and double-check advanced degrees, unexplained gaps in employment history, and job titles.

Here's the bottom line: *Your résumé must be honest and accurate.*

 PREPARE EFFECTIVE DIGITAL RÉSUMÉS

Most employers use an applicant-tracking system to post job openings, screen résumés, and generate interview requests to potential job candidates. These employers expect you to submit your résumé in a digital format. A digital résumé can be used by search engines, searched by keywords, converted into other electronic file types, such as a database, and printed. You can send your digital résumé in three ways:

- as an email attachment (as a PDF)
- as a text-based, scannable résumé
- as an Internet résumé

The email and Internet résumé formats are similar to a paper résumé. The Internet-based résumé contains links to items such as documents in your electronic portfolio.

## Email Attachment

For many employers, you can attach your résumé as a PDF file. With a PDF, your résumé appears as you formatted it, regardless of the employer's Internet browser. This file type ensures that your formatting does not change when an employer opens your résumé.

If the employer requests a plain-text document sent in the body of an email, do not attach the file. Follow the guidelines in the next section for creating a text-based, scannable résumé and add it to the body of your email to the employer.

## Text-Based, Scannable Résumé

A text-based, scannable résumé has the same information and major categories as a paper résumé. However, it has no indentations or graphic elements, such as lines, bullets, or symbols. In your text-based, scannable résumé, you use a simpler design and focus on keywords (usually nouns) to accommodate applicant-tracking scanning software. When you incorporate the right keywords, you have a better chance of having your résumé selected by the system. Use words that were included in the job posting—these words are likely to be programmed keywords. Most keywords are nouns that signal job titles, skills, and levels of experience. For example, if you are applying for a job that requires good oral and written communication skills, include *writing*, *public speaking*, *editing*, and *presentations* in your résumé. If you are seeking a job in health management, include keywords such as *health science*, *management*, *interpersonal communication skills*, *public health*, and *health care management*.

Figure 13.11 is a text-based, scannable version of a paper résumé shown in Figure 13.3. The writer has used no formatting (only letters, numbers, and basic punctuation marks) and has eliminated all bold, bullets, italics, and horizontal lines. The writer has also included a list of keywords in a section at the end of the résumé.

## WRITE A READER-FOCUSED LETTER OF APPLICATION

You will need a letter of application, or cover letter, to send with your résumé. If you send your résumé in digital format, also include a letter of application as a cover email or if possible as an attachment. With this letter (and your résumé), employers want to know as quickly as possible who you are and what you can do. The employer does not want to "wade through lots of text to find out" (Hansen, 2009). Put yourself in the employer's position: Ask yourself what you can do for the employer—not what the employer can do for you.

FIGURE 13.11

## Text-Based, Scannable Résumé

The writer uses a sans serif type for easy scanning.

Headings and subheads allow employers to easily locate categories.

The writer has deleted all special characters, indenting, bold, italics, bullets, and formatting

The writer has included a keywords section.

Leigh Andrea Thompson
204 Oak Street
Denton, TX 76205
(817) 555-5555
lthomas@unt.edu

Objective
Entry-level position in programming where I can use my technical communication skills

Education
University of North Texas, Denton, Texas
Bachelor of Arts in Professional and Technical Communication
August 2012
GPA 3.6/4.0

Baylor University, Waco, Texas
Foundation Courses
Advanced Courses
Commercial Publications
Online Publications
Advanced Technical Writing
Manuals and Procedures

Worked part-time to finance my education

Work Experience
University of North Texas, Denton, TX
Department of Linguistics and Technical Communication
Student Assistant
September 2010 to 2012 (fall and spring semesters)
Assisted the office manager and the department chair
Designed recruitment brochures for new undergraduate major in Professional and Technical Communication
Created an online system for faculty to order books

Sabre Airline Solutions, Southlake, TX
Technical Writing Intern
May 2011 to September 2011
Worked with subject matter experts to create training manuals
Edited and proofread online training materials

Red Lobster, Denton, Texas
Server
June 2005 to December 2005
Earned awards for service in August and October

Organizations
Society for Technical Communication
Freshman Council (a leadership organization)
Baylor President's Council (a leadership and service organization)
Volunteer for Habitat for Humanity

Keywords
Communication, volunteer, award, technical writing, editing

References available upon request

A letter of application introduces your résumé and gives the employer additional information about you and your experience. Address the letter personally to the executive or manager most likely to make the hiring decision (Greenly 1993; Simon 1981). Before writing your letter, do your homework; find out where to send the letter and who will read it.

## TIPS FOR PREPARING TEXT-BASED, SCANNABLE RÉSUMÉS

- **Include keywords an employer is likely to use to search for qualified candidates.** For example, if an employer is looking for someone who has experience designing websites, you would include keywords such as *website, Web pages, Java, Web-based applications,* and *HTML.* Also include industry-specific language that an employer might search for in a résumé database. Include keywords only if they refer to skills you actually have: Never lie or mislead on a résumé. If caught, this lie usually leads to an automatic dismissal. Add a keywords section, as did the writer in Figure 13.11.
- **Include nouns as keywords.** While action verbs are important, use key phrases and nouns that a potential employer might use as search terms. Try using terms that the employer has included in the job advertisement.
- **Use a 10, 11, or 12-point sans serif type.** You could use Gil Sans, Arial, or Tahoma. Omit all bold, italics, underlining, special characters, and formatting, such as horizontal or vertical lines and graphics.
- **Align all text at the left margin.** Don't indent, center, or use columns.
- **Use a line length of no more than 65 characters.** If you use longer lines, they may not appear as you intend.
- **Use spaces, not tabs.** Readers may have their default tabs set differently than yours.
- **When you save your résumé file to post online, save it as plain text.**
- **Open your résumé in a text editor, such as Notepad®, or email your résumé to yourself before sending it to an employer.** Make sure it appears as you intend. For example, if you use Google mail as your email provider, send your résumé to someone who uses Yahoo! mail or Hotmail to see how well it transmits. You may have to adjust its design.
- **When sending a scannable résumé on paper, use a high-quality laser or inkjet printer and use only white, 8½ x 11-inch paper.**

- Address your letter to a specific person, and spell the addressee's name correctly.
- If you don't know who should receive your letter, don't address it to Dear Sir or Madam, To Whom It May Concern, a department, or a person's job title unless the advertisement says to address the letter that way.
- Call the organization to find out who will receive your résumé. If you can't find out by phone, address the letter to an executive, such as the president or CEO, and use the person's name.

Once you have determined who will read your application letter, customize it for that reader and appeal directly to his or her needs (Greenly 1993, Hansen, 2009). For example, if you have classroom, internship, or employer experience relevant to the job for which you are applying, discuss that experience or classwork in the body of your letter. Remember, employers want to know

- what you can do for the organization
- how you and your skills and qualifications would benefit the organization
- how you would fit into the team

Your customized, generally one-page letter, should have three sections:
1. **your purpose for writing:** the introductory paragraph
2. **your qualifications:** the education and experience paragraphs
3. **your goal** (what you want from the employer): the concluding paragraph

## Your Purpose for Writing: The Introductory Paragraph

In the introductory paragraph, tell the employer why you're writing. As you write, follow these guidelines:

- **Identify the position you are applying for.** Employers receive many letters of application for several jobs at the same time, so identify the specific job you are seeking.
- **Tell the employer where you found out about the job.** Because employers may be soliciting résumés in more than one place, they often want to know where you found out about the job. This information is especially important if you learned of the job from an employee, coworker, or acquaintance of the employer. This information may lead the employer to show more interest in your résumé, if they can confirm your talent, experience, etc. If you are writing an unsolicited letter, state why you are contacting the company, and then ask whether a job is available (Simon 1981).

Figure 13.12 presents three introductory paragraphs. Each specifically identifies the job and the writer's purpose for writing. The first writer uses a personal contact (Kathryn Raign) to open the paragraph and get the employer's attention. The second writer mentions a specific job advertisement. The third writer is sending an unsolicited letter. That writer is not responding to a specific job advertisement and doesn't know whether the company has any current openings.

As these introductory paragraphs below illustrate, the tone of your letter must be positive and confident—not tentative or boastful. State your qualifications in a positive manner without focusing on your weaknesses, but be careful not to sound arrogant. You want to appear confident about your education, experience, and abilities while indicating that you know you have much to learn and are eager to work in your profession.

**FIGURE 13.12**

### Introductory Paragraphs

**Using a personal conact**

Dr. Kathryn Raign suggested that I contact you about the project engineer position you currently have open in the Orlando office. My experience as an intern for Balfour Beatty provides me with the qualifications you are seeking. Please consider me for this position.

**Using a job advertisment**

My coursework in computer science and my experience as an intern for Microsoft qualify me for the Web applications designer position that you posted on CareerBuilders.com on May 16. Please consider me for this position.

**Sending an unsolicited letter**

My experience as an intern at BlueCross/Blue Shield, my work as a health technician at Parkland Hospital, and my degree in health management give me a solid foundation in health management. Please consider me for a position in your management training program.

## Your Qualifications: The Education and Experience Paragraphs

After you have told the employer why you are writing, present information about your education and experience. As you write the education and experience paragraphs, follow these guidelines:

- **Follow the order of your résumé when discussing your education and work experience.** If your résumé presents your education first, then in your letter you discuss your education first. If your résumé gives information about your work experience or skills first, then do the same in your letter. When you have many years of work experience, you can eliminate the education paragraph and include two or more experience paragraphs.
- **Highlight, add to, or expand on the information in your résumé.** Don't simply repeat the information in your résumé or give the details of your education and experience in chronological order. Instead, highlight or add to information that may especially interest the employer or that is particularly relevant to the job for which you are applying. For example, in your résumé, you may have stated that you had an internship; therefore, in the letter, expand on that internship information by including a project on which you worked or by detailing some of your responsibilities.
- **Create a unified theme in these paragraphs.** Avoid the temptation to simply list (often unrelated) information about your education or work experience. Instead, begin each paragraph with a topic sentence and develop that topic in the sentences that follow. As you discuss your education, consider how it qualifies you for the job you seek. For instance, if the advertisement says that applicants should write well, discuss projects where writing was a significant component.
- **Think about how your experience qualifies you for the job.** This task is challenging if your experience does not directly relate to the job you are seeking. For example, Rodney is a new college graduate looking for an engineering job. He has never worked in the engineering field, but he worked as a tutor in a computer lab for three years and was promoted to student manager of the lab. He has several skills that will impress employers. He was promoted because of his ability to work well with others and his ability to supervise his peers. In addition, the lab implemented several of his ideas, such as putting a flat-screen monitor outside the lab to display with the weekly schedule of classes, so students would know when their classes met in the lab and when the lab was open for general access. This idea saved the lab $400 a year in paper costs. Although Rodney's experience is not directly related to engineering, he can write a paragraph focusing on his abilities to work with others and to be a team player by suggesting money-saving ideas. As Katherine Hansen, author of "Powerful New Grad Résumés and Cover Letters" (2009), explains,

> Experience is experience. It doesn't have to be paid. Anything you've done that has enabled you to develop skills that are relevant to the kind of job you seek is worth consideration for résumé and cover letter mention. That's especially true if you don't have much paid experience. The key … is relevance. Consider the following in evaluating what experience and skills you've gained that are relevant to what you want to do when you graduate: internships; summer jobs; campus jobs; sports; entrepreneurial/self-employed jobs; temporary work; volunteer work. (3)

Hansen also suggests that you include your research papers or projects, your campus activity positions, fraternity/sorority/social club positions, and any extracurricular or sports leadership positions.

Figures 13.13 and 13.14 illustrate how two writers approached the experience and education paragraphs for an application letter. The writer of the paragraphs shown in Figure 13.13 has no work experience in her field. The writer of the paragraphs shown in Figure 13.14 has work experience. The writer with experience begins with his experience and moves to education because his résumé follows that order. This writer also includes his major, degrees received, and school in the education category. The tone of both writers is confident as they mention facts about their education and experience and state qualities and experiences that are relevant to potential employers.

## Your Goal: The Concluding Paragraph

In the concluding paragraph, directly state what you want from the reader: an opportunity to meet with the employer and discuss your qualifications. In the paragraphs preceding

**FIGURE 13.13**

**Experience and Education Paragraphs Written by a Job Seeker without Experience**

At Chambers University, I took many courses requiring writing. In an advanced technical communication course, I used InDesign to produce a 40-page user's manual for inventory software used by Minyards, Inc. (a regional grocery store chain). Currently, all Minyards stores use the manual to train new employees on the inventory system and as a reference guide for employees after initial training.

For the past three years, I have worked in the Technical Communication Lab at Chambers University. I began as a lab tutor, assisting students with software questions, especially related to Microsoft Word, Adobe InDesign, and Microsoft PowerPoint. After 18 months, I was promoted to student lab manager. As manager, I work with the faculty to schedule lab classes, work with the lab tutors to set up their schedules, and conduct meetings each week with the tutors. Most recently, I set up a scheduling system that uses email instead of paper. This system saved $400 in annual paper costs. As manager and tutor in the lab, I have developed interpersonal skills that would benefit Writers, Inc.

**Experience and Education Paragraphs Written by
a Job Seeker with Experience**

While at Texas Instruments, I worked as an innovative design engineer. I have more than 15 years of research, production, and manufacturing experience, especially in the areas of machine design, power transmission, and structural analysis. I began as a process improvement engineer and was promoted to reengineering team leader and then to manufacturing facilitator. As manufacturing facilitator, I supervised two self-directed work teams of 26 team members. I led one of these teams, the screen printing team, to win the Gold Teaming for Excellence Award. I also received the Site Quality Improvement Award in 2010 and 2011 for increasing productivity by 25% annually.

Along with my experience as a design engineer for Texas Instruments, I have a Bachelo's degree and a Master's degree in agricultural engineering from Texas A&M University. As part of my academic experience, I worked as a research assistant in the agricultural engineering department. I designed and constructed custom equipment and instrumentation used in energy conservation research.

the conclusion, you provide specific, detailed information about yourself—information to convince the employer to invite you for an interview. In the concluding paragraph, do the following:

• **Refer the employer to your résumé.**
• **Request an interview.**
• **Tell the employer how to contact you by phone, text messaging, and email.** Give the employer your phone number, and mention the best time to call. You encourage the employer to act by including this specific information in the concluding paragraph. As Katherine Hansen suggests, powerful letters of application "do no good if the employer can't reach you" (2009, 6). This information should appear both in the résumé and the letter.
• **Make sure your email address and outgoing message on your cell phone are professional.** Your email address and outgoing message say something about you. Bill Behn, a national director of staffing for Solomon Edwards Group, reports that "I actually had an interviewee tell me to contact her via email at likes2party@aol.com. Needless to say, that person was not offered the job" (2007, 1).

Use specific language in the concluding paragraph. Avoid vague language as in the following examples. These writers don't confidently state the goal of meeting the employer or encourage the employer to contact them:

| Vague | I look forward to hearing from you soon. Thank you for considering my résumé. |
| Vague | If possible, may I meet with you or someone in your company to discuss my résumé and qualifications? |

The writers of the following paragraphs refer the employer to their résumé and directly ask the employer to contact them for an interview. (For more information on tone, see Chapter 12.) These writers use a polite, respectful, confident tone:

| Specific | My résumé provides additional information about my education and work experience. I would enjoy discussing my application with you. Please write me at Kathryn.Raign@gmail.com or call or text me at (307) 555-9061. |
| Specific | You can find more information about my education and experience in the enclosed résumé. I would appreciate the opportunity to discuss it with you at your convenience. Please email or text me at jscott@verizon.net or call me at (505) 555-9033. |

Figures 13.15 and 13.16 illustrate effective application letters. The writers use a respectful, yet confident tone and include specific information to persuade the employer to invite them for an interview.

 ## PREPARE FOR A SUCCESSFUL INTERVIEW

You've written a successful résumé and letter of application, and now you have an interview. As when writing your résumé and letter, you need to prepare for the interview. Successful job seekers do their homework before the interview. Follow the Tips for a Successful Job Interview to ensure your job interview is successful.

 ## USE LETTERS TO FOLLOW UP

Follow-up letters are important to your job search. Write a follow-up letter in these situations:

- **when you have sent an application letter and résumé and have not received a response within three or four weeks.** If you have not received a response, write a brief, polite letter.

## Letter of Application Written by a Graduating Senior

204 Oak Street
Denton, TX 76205
August 6, 2012

Dr. Brandon McCarroll
Ericson Technology
2221 Lakeside Boulevard
Raleigh, NC 75082

Dear Dr. McCarroll:

*The writer tells the employer where she found out about the job.*

I am writing in response to your advertisement posted with University of North Texas career center. Would you please consider me for the entry-level position in technical documentation? I believe that my experience as an intern with AT&T, along with my education in technical communication and computer science from University of North Texas, qualify me for this position.

*The writer identifies the position for which she is applying.*

My education has given me a strong background in technical communication and computer science. I have concentrated on the design, programming, and documentation of Web-based applications. For a senior-level course, with two students in computer science, I designed an intranet site for Texas Instruments. The site describes corporate history and culture at Texas Instruments. For my senior project, I designed a website for the dual degree program between a university in Toluca, Mexico and the University of North Texas. I conducted usability testing for this site. You may view the site at www.ltc.unt.edu/uaem.

*The writer highlights and expands on information in her résumé.*

While working as an intern for AT&T, I applied my classroom learning in a workplace environment. For one of my projects, I used my experience in designing online documents to develop a Web-based application for wireless services offered by AT&T. More than 2,000 employees and customers use this application each week. During my second summer with AT&T, I updated this application. I also edited and proofread customer documentation for wireless service.

*The writer refers to her résumé and tells the reader how to contact her.*

My résumé provides further information about my education and work experience. Dr. McCarroll, I would enjoy the opportunity to meet with you to discuss my qualifications and résumé. You can reach me at (972) 555-5555 or at jdowdie@unt.edu.

Sincerely,

*Jessie Dowdie*

Jessie Dowdie

*The writer uses a professional email address.*

Enclosure

FIGURE 13.16

## Letter of Application Written by a Job Seeker with Extensive Work Experience

310 North Edna
Lewisville, TX 75057
December 12, 2012

Mr. Barry Boswell
AMC Engineering, Inc.
26789 Westfall Road
Portland, OR 97501

Dear Mr. Boswell:

*The writer uses a personal contact to introduce himself.*

Mr. Jon Botsford of your research and development department suggested that I contact you. He believes that my experience as a design engineer for Texas Instruments qualifies me for the manufacturing engineer position that you currently have open in your production division. My experience and education in reengineering and in supervising work teams provide me with the qualifications that you are seeking.

*The writer identifies the position for which he is applying.*

While at Texas Instruments, I worked as an innovative design engineer. I have more than 15 years of research, production, and manufacturing experience, especially in the areas of machine design, power transmissions, and structural analysis. I began as a process improvement engineer and was promoted to reengineering team leader and finally to manufacturing facilitator. As manufacturing facilitator, I supervised two self-directed work teams of 26 team members. I led one of these teams, the screen printing team, to win the Gold Teaming for Excellence Award. I also received the Site Quality Improvement Award in 2010 and 2011 for increasing productivity by 25% annually.

*The writer expands on information in his résumé.*

Along with my experience as a design engineer for Texas Instruments, I have a Bachelor of Science and a Master of Science degree in agricultural engineering from Texas A&M University. As part of my academic experience, I worked as a research assistant in the agricultural engineering department. I designed and constructed custom equipment and instrumentation used in energy conservation research.

*The writer refers to his résumé and includes contact information.*

The enclosed résumé provides further information about my experience and my education. Mr. Boswell, I would like to meet with you to discuss my qualifications for this position. Please call or text me at (972) 555-7893. I look forward to visiting with you.

Sincerely,

*C. Randall Harrison*

C. Randall Harrison

Encl.: résumé

Mention your previous letter and its date, and include another copy of your résumé. To know when to write such letters, keep copies of all the application letters you send, and keep a file of the responses you receive from employers. Without these copies and a detailed file, you may not know when to send follow-up letters.

- **after an interview.** Within two days following an interview, write a brief thank-you letter addressed to the manager who will decide whether to hire you. If you interviewed with more than one person, write to all those who interviewed you. In your letters, state your interest in the job and the organization. Use these letters to reinforce what you can offer—what you can bring to the job. Mention the organization by name, and mention the names of people in the organization with whom you met.
- **when you accept a job.** When you accept a job, write a brief letter confirming your acceptance. In this letter, you can confirm details such as when you will begin work.
- **when you reject a job offer or no longer want an employer to consider you for a job.** When you accept a job, don't forget to write the other organizations that seriously considered you for a job. You may want to work for or with one of those organizations in the future, so do them the courtesy of writing a brief letter. Thank the organization and the people who interviewed you for their interest in you. State that you have taken a job with another organization. You don't have to identify the specific job offer that you accepted; instead, write, "I have decided to accept another offer." Include only positive comments about the organization and your experiences with the interviewer. End your letter with a brief statement of goodwill, such as "Thank you for the interest you showed in my application."

Follow-up letters are most effective after an interview. Post-interview letters offer an excellent opportunity to restate your qualifications and add information about your application that you didn't have the opportunity to discuss during the interview (Simon 1981). Figure 13.17 illustrates the kind of follow-up letter you should send after an interview.

 ## PREPARING AN ELECTRONIC CAREER PORTFOLIO

An *electronic career portfolio* (*or e-portfolio*) is a Web-based collection of materials related to your job search and your career. As a first-time job seeker, use the portfolio to provide employers with a traditional résumé along with other materials that enhance your job search. After you have a job, use a career portfolio to show your skills, experiences, and accomplishments to your coworkers, your supervisors, and potential employers.

An electronic portfolio usually includes these sections
- introductory page
- web-based, searchable résumé
- references (letters of recommendation)
- transcripts
- skills
- samples of your work (sometimes called artifacts)

FIGURE 13.17

**Post-Interview Follow-Up Letter**

402 Spring Avenue, Apt. 6C
Alexandria, VA 23097
May 4, 2012

Mr. Dwight Wilson
Senior Production Engineer
I-2 Technology, Inc.
1111 Jorge Mendoza Blvd.
San Diego, CA 92093

Dear Mr. Wilson:

Thank you for taking time from your busy schedule yesterday to show me I-2 Technology's facilities and to discuss the quality control job. I especially enjoyed meeting many of your coworkers. Please thank Ms. Johnson in the quality control division for the tour she gave me of the facility.

As a result of our visit, I have a good understanding of I-2 Technology and appreciate its progressive approach to maximizing production without sacrificing quality control. I feel confident that my work as an intern at Boeing provides the experience you are looking for in your team.

I-2 Technology's place in the semiconductor industry and your colleagues in the quality control division confirm my impression that I-2 Technology would be an exciting place to work. If I can answer further questions, please call me at (703) 555-0922.

Best regards,

*Cynthia Demsey*

Cynthia Demsey

## TIPS FOR A SUCCESSFUL JOB INTERVIEW

### Before the Interview

- **Do the research necessary to understand the position and the company with which you are interviewing.** Kip Hollister, founder and CEO of Hollister, Inc. staffing, explains that "one of the biggest turn-offs for a hiring manager is when an interviewing candidate has not done the research necessary to understand both the position and the company" (Hollister, in Zupek, 2007, 1). Find out what products the company produces or what services it provides. Visit the company's website; read its mission statement, find out about its locations, etc.

- **Create a list of solid questions to ask.** Near the end of the interview, the interviewer will probably ask you if you have questions for him or her. If you do not ask questions or if you do not ask good questions, the interviewer may assume you are uninterested in the position or that you are unprepared. Rachel Zupek of CareerBuilder.com recommends asking *open-ended questions*—questions that require more than a one- or two-word response. For example, ask, "How do you see me fitting in at your company?" or "What will make the person who takes this position successful?" (Zupek 2007, 2).

- **Study lists of common interview questions.** Visit job boards and your college or university placement center for lists of common interview questions. These questions will help you prepare for what an interviewer may ask you.

- **Hold a mock interview.** Rehearse the interview by asking a friend, family member, or professor to hold a mock interview with you. Your college or university placement center may also conduct practice interviews.

- **Decide what you will wear.** Don't neglect your appearance. Bill Behn, a national director of staffing for Solomon Edwards Group, recommends that you "dress for the position you want to have" (Behn, in Zupek, 2007, 1). Dress conservatively; avoid clothing that is too revealing, too casual, or too outrageous. Don't wear too much jewelry or cologne, and don't chew gum.

- **Make sure you know where you are going for the interview.** If you will drive to the interview, make sure you know how to get there. If you are unfamiliar with the location, drive to the location a day or two before the interview so you are sure how to get there, where to park, and how long it will take to get there.

### The Day of the Interview

- **Look over your list of questions.**
- **Arrive early.** If you arrive late, the interviewer may assume you have sloppy work habits.

### At the Interview

- **Shake the interviewer's hand firmly and look him or her in the eyes.**
- **Use the interviewer's title, such as Mr., Dr., or Ms.** unless the interviewer says something like "Please call me Brenda."
- **Give more than *yes* or *no* responses to questions when appropriate.** Hollister says that interviewers want you to answer directly, but "it is OK to support your point with specific examples that are relevant to your work experience" (Hollister, in Zupek 2007, 1–2). For example, if an interviewer asks if you had courses in technical communication, you might respond, "Yes, and in my technical communication class, I completed a volunteer's handbook for the local Boys and Girls Club."
- **Avoid speaking negatively about past employers (Zupeck 2007).** If the interviewer asks you about a previous job, be prepared to show how you valued the experience. For example, say, "I learned how to solve problems" or "The job taught me how to work with people with various work styles."

Figure 13.18 shows a sample electronic portfolio. Your university may require standard templates for students who use the career placement center. If your university does not require or have such templates, create your own. As you plan your electronic portfolio, follow the design guidelines for building effective websites in Chapter 19.

**FIGURE 13.18**

**Electronic Portfolio**

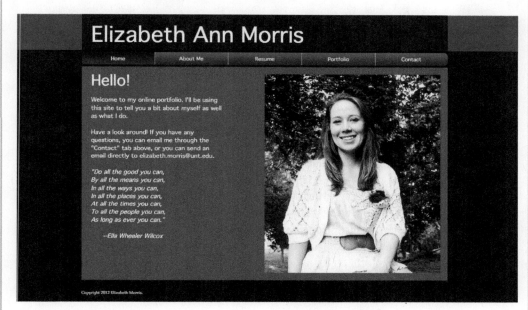

Courtesy of Elizabeth Morris.

TAKING IT INTO THE *workplace*

### Designing Your Résumé to Land an Internship

You can enhance your work experience and learn about your field by landing an internship. With an internship, you can take what you are learning in the classroom and apply it in the workplace. To obtain an internship, you will need an up-to-date résumé. For your internship résumé, you will use the chronological style with these modifications adapted from Marianne Green of JobWeb.com:

- **In the objective category, include the word internship and your field of interest.** For example, you might write "Internship in health management."
- **Include details about your academic background, including relevant courses, GPA, honors, scholarships, and projects.**
- **Include high school information, if helpful.** Most job seekers leave out high school activities. However, if you are a sophomore or junior in college, you could include high school information if it will give employers relevant information about you.
- **Include your expected graduation date.**
- **Include detailed information about activities:** volunteer work, research, and leadership.
- **List all your jobs, even though they probably do not relate to your career goals.** These jobs can communicate a strong work ethic and demonstrate some of your skills and accomplishments.
- **Identify your skills.** Put yourself in the hiring manager's place. What skills would he or she expect in an intern?
- **Limit your résumé to one page.**

### Assignment

1. Visit your college or university placement center and find an internship for which you are qualified. If your placement center does not post internships or you can't find one, visit an online job board and search for internships in your field.
2. Prepare a résumé for applying for the internship.

## Will Your Social Networking Sabotage Your Job Search?

### Background

Millions of us log on to the Internet each day to network with friends and families through social networking sites such as Facebook. But, could you pay a price for the information or the lack of information on your social networking profiles?

Many job seekers have discovered that putting the details of their lives on social media sites has a downside (Metro 2009). Job seekers aren't alone in paying a price for information on their social media sites. In March 2009, Dan Leone, a longtime employee and fan of the Philadelphia Eagles football organization, was fired over a Facebook posting. In the posting, he criticized the team for not resigning a player. Even though Leone had a long history of employment with the Philadelphia Eagles, his post got him fired (2009). You may think that the decision to fire a long-time employee was harsh; however, the Philadelphia Eagles aren't alone in scanning social media sites to monitor employees' posts and to act on negative postings. Employers also review the postings of potential employees for clues to behavior, maturity, abilities, etc.

The social media monitoring service Reppler surveyed more than 300 hiring professionals. Reppler found that more than 90 percent of recruiters and hiring managers have visited a potential job candidate's profile on a social networking site as part of the screening process (Swallow 2011). Of these recruiters and hiring managers, 69 percent had rejected a candidate based on the content on his or her social networking profile and 68 percent had hired a candidate based on his or her presence on those sites (Swallow 2011).

As you review your social networking profile, follow these guidelines adapted from Metro Creative Communications (2009):

- **Use the "grandmother rule."** If the information or photograph you want to post is something that your grandmother would disapprove of, then most likely a job recruiter would frown on it—so don't post it.
- **Promote yourself.** Your social networking profile can benefit your job search. Post images of yourself doing positive activities such as volunteer work.
- **Don't "mug" for the cameras.** Images of you can appear on other people's profiles. Ask your friends and family to limit photo postings of you on their profiles. Remember that someone can snap a picture of you at any time.
- **Keep your opinions to yourself.** You may feel that recruiters and hiring managers do not have the right to use social networking sites to determine the worthiness of a prospective employee. Nonetheless, successful job seekers understand how recruiters and hiring managers use social networking, and those job seekers adjust their online profiles to avoid controversial topics. Regardless of how strongly you feel about politics, religion, or any other topic that might invite controversy, keep those opinions off your social networking profiles.

## Assignment

1. Evaluate your social networking profiles on all platforms you use. If you don't have a profile, select a networking site such as Facebook, Twitter, or LinkedIn and create one.
2. Write an informal memo report to your instructor about your profile. Your report should answer these questions:
   a. What information on the profile might cause hiring managers and recruiters to reject you?
   b. What information on the profile might encourage hiring managers and recruiters to hire you?
   c. What can you do to improve your social networking profiles?

1. Find a job opportunity in your field for which you are or will be qualified when you graduate. Look for an opportunity on online job boards or at your college or university placement center. You can also locate job opportunities by talking to family and friends in business and industry. After you have located a job opportunity, complete one of these steps:
   - If you located the job through a print publication, copy or cut out the advertisement.
   - If you located the job on an online job board, print a copy of the advertisement.
   - If you talked to someone about the job, ask for a business card from that person or get a copy of the job announcement.

2. Decide on the sections such as Education, Work Experience, etc. that you might include in your résumé for the job you located in Exercise 1. Create a list of the information you could include in each of these sections. Your list might look like the brainstorming list in Figure 13.2.

3. Using some or all of the information from the list you created in Exercise 2, prepare a paper résumé. Use the questions in the online Worksheet for Writing Reader-Focused Job Correspondence and Résumés as you write your résumé.

4. Create a text-based, scannable version of the résumé you created for Exercise 3. Remember to follow the tips for creating text-based, scannable résumés. Send your résumé to your instructor as an email attachment.

5. Write a letter of application for the job you located in Exercise 1. Use the online Worksheet for Writing Reader-Focused Job Correspondence and Résumés as you write your letter.

6. Using the questions in the online Worksheet for Writing Reader-Focused Job Correspondence and Résumés, evaluate your paper résumé, your text-based, scannable résumé, and your letter of application. Your instructor may ask you to use these questions to evaluate the résumés and application letters of two classmates.

7. Write a paragraph evaluating the follow-up letter below. Use the questions for follow-up letters in the online Worksheet for Writing Reader-Focused Job Correspondence and Résumés to guide you as you evaluate the letter.

> Dear Penny:
>
> Meeting you and all your coworkers was great fun. The company seems to be a wonderful place to work. Thanks for showing me the facilities and for taking me to lunch. I would love to become one of your coworkers.
>
> Again, I would enjoy working with you and your coworkers. And I believe that I have a lot to offer your company. Have a great week.
>
> Best,
>
> Gretchen Delpero

8. Rewrite the follow-up letter in Exercise 7.

# Part 4

# Using the Writer's Tools to Create Effective Documents and Presentations

# chapter fourteen

# Writing Reader-Focused Informal Reports

*iStockphoto 2008.*

You will give many reports during the course of your career. These reports will be both oral and written. You've given reports during much of your school life. For example, in elementary school you probably wrote or presented a book report. In middle school you might have reported on a historical figure; and in high school, you may have written a lab report for your chemistry class. If you have a job, your manager may have asked you to complete a project and you might have reported on the project's status. Even though each report probably had a different format and subject matter, they were all reports. **Reports** are oral or written communications that help people to understand, to analyze, to act, or to make a decision. Reports can be formal or informal. In this chapter, we will discuss informal reports. In Chapter 15, we will discuss formal reports.

An *informal report* communicates information about routine, everyday business. Informal reports cover any number of topics, from a memo clarifying a travel policy to a memo requesting that your manager approve $2,500 to buy a laptop and software. You might present an informal report via memo, email, letter, or oral presentation. Even though we use the word informal, it doesn't mean that the information or purpose of the report is insignificant. For example, an informal report informing the architect of a problem in a bridge design could save lives.

How do you know if a report is formal or informal? Your readers and your organization may give you some clues. Your readers may require that the report be formal or informal. In some organizations, a report might be formal while in another organization, the same report might be informal. For instance, a field report in most companies is an informal report; yet at a nearby energy company, these reports generally are formal reports. To determine if a report is formal or informal, find out what your organization and your readers expect. Look also at similar reports written by your coworkers. After you analyze these expectations and review similar reports, you may still be uncertain about whether to treat your report as formal or informal. Generally, you use informal reports to communicate about everyday business.

In this chapter, you will first learn three guidelines to apply to any informal report. Use these guidelines as a problem-solving framework. After we've discussed these guidelines, we'll consider the formats you could use for these reports and apply the guidelines to five common types of informal reports:

- directives
- progress reports
- meeting minutes
- field and lab reports
- trip reports

##  FIND OUT ABOUT YOUR READERS

Before you can decide on the format (or whether the report is formal or informal), find out about your readers. This task is easy for some reports. For example, if you are writing a progress report on your monthly activities for your manager, you know what your reader expects. You also know the report format that he or she prefers because you routinely turn in this report. However, if you are reporting progress on a project for external readers, you may be writing to more than one person and you may know little about your readers' needs and expectations. Because you don't routinely write for these external readers, your task may be more challenging.

As you analyze the readers, ask yourself these questions:
- What do your readers know about the topic of your report?
- Why are they reading your report. To gather information? To complete a task? To make a decision?
- What questions will they ask as they read the report?
- Are they internal or external?
- What positions do they hold in the organization? If they are internal readers, where are their positions in relation to yours in the organizational hierarchy?
- Will more than one group read the report?
- What do they know about you or your organization? Have their previous experiences with you or your organization been positive? If not, why not?

Once you know the purpose of the report and your readers' needs, you can better prepare an effective report. Whether you're writing a report that presents the progress of your work or the minutes of a meeting, your report will succeed only if you meet your readers' needs and expectations.

##  ANTICIPATE AND ANSWER YOUR READERS' QUESTIONS

To help your readers understand your report, gather the information necessary to answer their questions. This task may be as simple as printing a spreadsheet or as complex as using primary and secondary research techniques (see Chapter 5 for research guidelines). For some reports, once you have gathered the information, you need to analyze it and make recommendations or draw conclusions.

> Your readers want to know the purpose of your report, why they are receiving it, and how your report affects them or their organization.

Although the specific questions will vary with the topic and purpose, your readers expect you to answer these basic questions:
- What is the purpose of your report?
- Why are they receiving the report?
- How does the report affect them or their organization?

For each of the informal reports described in this chapter, you will find a figure that lists specific questions that readers may ask as they read that type of report. These questions will help you prepare your informal reports.

## SELECT THE APPROPRIATE FORMAT

Once you find out about your readers, determine the most appropriate format. Use any of the following formats for informal reports:

- **Memos.** Use the memo format for most informal reports. Some organizations call informal reports memo reports. Use memos for informal, internal correspondence to people within your organization. You might, for example, send a memo about the status of a project to your manager; however, you would send a letter to report that status to a client who is external to your organization.
- **Letters.** Most organizations expect you to use the letter format for informal reports with people outside the organization. However, if you are sending an informal report to someone several levels above you in your organization, it might be better to use the letter format. Check with your coworkers to determine what your organization prefers in this situation.
- **Email.** Many organizations send informal reports via email because of its speed and convenience. When you email an informal report, readers and writers can easily edit it. For example, if you are writing meeting minutes for your team, you can send a draft to all the meeting participants. They can examine the draft, insert comments, and email the revised draft back to you. Then you can revise the minutes and save time at the next meeting because participants have already seen a draft.
- **Forms and templates.** Some organizations have forms and templates for informal reports. The form or template may simply be a cover sheet for the report, or it may be a format for the entire report. For example, Balfour Beatty, a construction company, has templates for meeting minutes. Employees use this template to write and archive the minutes. The template prompts the writer to insert the project name, project number, date, etc. Another company uses an Examination Action Item List template to accompany field reports. This template includes sections for the observations, recommendations, and engineer's comments. Before you select the format for your informal reports, find out if your organization has forms and templates for these reports. These forms and templates may save you time.

When you have determined the appropriate format for your readers and your organization, you are ready to draft your report. If you are writing an informal report that doesn't fit into one of the categories discussed above, use one of the standard patterns of organization presented in Chapter 6 or the direct approach for correspondence presented in Chapter 12.

## WRITING DIRECTIVES

*Directives* explain a policy or procedure that readers are expected to follow. For example, you might write a directive about required procedures for submitting receipts for business expenses. You might receive a directive on procedures for purchasing safety equipment. When writing a directive, you have two purposes: (1) to inform or remind readers of the policy or procedure, and (2) to explain why the policy or procedure is important to the readers and the organization.

Pay particular attention to the directive's tone. Although you can require readers to follow a directive, you want to convince them that the policy or procedure is desirable or, at least, necessary. The questions in Figure 14.1 will help you include the information needed to convince readers of the importance of the policy or procedure. The directive in Figure 14.2 discusses the reasons for a company dress code.

**FIGURE 14.1**

**Readers' Questions about a Directive**

- Why am I receiving this directive?
- Why is this directive important to me?
- Why is this directive important to the organization?
- How will the directive impact me or my job?

**FIGURE  14.2**

**Directive**

## Tech Ad, Inc.

**Memo**

May 19, 2012

To:       All office employees
From:    Kimberlee May, Vice President, Human Resources
Subject:  Business Casual Fridays

The writer explains why the policy is important.

The writer uses a positive tone to recognize those employees who are following the guidelines.

Recently I have noticed that some employees are dressing too casually on Fridays. This dress creates problems for managers and presents an unprofessional image to our clients. Because the company has not clearly defined "casual" dress, we have developed a dress code that will help all employees maintain a professional appearance on business casual Fridays. Many of you follow the guidelines of the new dress code for business casual Fridays. For others, the policy will clearly define what is and is not acceptable for business casual dress.

The writer clearly states the policy that the employees are expected to follow.

**The Dress Code for Business Casual Fridays**

Business casual dress will be attractive, comfortable, and professional. You may not wear the following clothing items on Fridays, or any other day.

- Shorts
- Athletic shoes
- Spandex
- Clothing of any kind that promotes the products or services of competitors
- Hats
- Clothing with cartoons or drawings
- Ultra low-rise pants or shorts
- Bare feet
- Noticeably missing or exposed undergarments
- T-shirts

The writer explains the consequences of not following the policy.

If employees do not follow the dress code, managers may send those employees home to change clothes. The time spent away from work for this reason will be treated as vacation or leave without pay. When an employee's clothing is questionable, the manager will decide whether the employee must go home and change.

*Progress reports* describe the current status of an ongoing project or the activities of a department or division. Progress reports may also be called status reports or activity reports. Progress reports are often the intermediate document between a proposal and the end of a project. Readers of progress reports may be managers, clients, coworkers, or project sponsors. Progress reports have three primary purposes:

- to describe progress on one or more projects—or to describe the activities of a department or division—so readers can monitor the work over a period of time
- to provide a written record of progress
- to document problems with and changes to a project.

These reports not only give you the opportunity to inform readers of the project's progress, but also to provide a written record of that progress. Suppose your manager decides to postpone work on your project for one year. The monthly progress reports you wrote before the delay will provide a record of completed work, so when the project restarts, you or your coworkers can refer to the reports to determine where to resume work. The reports could prevent you or your coworkers from duplicating work completed before the company postponed the project.

## ETHICS NOTE

### Reporting Your Progress Ethically

Readers want to know the project's status. If the project is not progressing as planned, they want to know what specific problems you have encountered, the problems' effect on the project, and your recommendations for handling these problems. For example, if your construction project is behind schedule because of excessive rain, specifically state the number of days that rain impacted the schedule and how you expect the overall schedule to be affected. As you report problems with the project

- **Use an objective tone.** Don't make excuses.
- **Be specific.** Provide details that led to the problem.
- **Realistically estimate how the problem will affect the schedule and the budget.**

You may be tempted to withhold bad news about the project's status because you hope it will improve before the next report. However, when you withhold information, you mislead your readers. You have an ethical responsibility to report the progress as it is—not as you want it to be or expect it to be.

As you write your progress reports, ask yourself:
- Why will readers read your report?
- How will they use it?
- What questions will they want it to answer?

Readers will ask questions about the project or work that the report covers, your progress (and how that progress may affect the deliverable), future work, and the overall project's status. Readers will be interested in your specific accomplishments during the reporting period to understand whether your work is progressing as planned. They will want to know your schedule and, possibly, your budget for the next reporting period or for the remainder of the project, especially if you will not be writing additional progress reports. They will also want to know what results they can expect during the next reporting period.

## The Conventional Sections of Progress Reports

Most progress reports contain these conventional sections:
- Introduction
- Progress discussion
- Conclusion

Figure 14.3 on the next page lists questions that readers may ask and relates those questions to the conventional sections of a progress report.

### Introduction

The *introduction* identifies your project and the purpose of your report. In the introduction, you
- identify the project(s) the report covers
- state the time the report covers
- state the project's objectives (if readers need this information)

You can usually identify a project and the time covered in one sentence, such as "This report covers progress on the Midwest Relocation project from January 1 through March 31, 2012." You would explain the project's objectives to help readers put your report in context or to remind them of its purpose. You also can state the objectives as you defined them in the project proposal. Figure 14.4 presents a paragraph in which the writer states the project's objectives and identifies the project and the time the report covers.

FIGURE 14.3

**Readers' Questions about the Conventional Sections of a Progress Report**

| Section | Readers' Questions |
|---|---|
| Introduction | • What project does the report discuss?<br>• What time does the report cover?<br>• What are the project's objectives? |
| Progress Discussion | • What work have you accomplished since the project's start or since the last progress report?<br>• Is the project progressing as planned?<br>• What work is planned for the next reporting period or for the remainder of the project?<br>• What are the results of the work to date?<br>• What problems, if any, have you encountered?<br>• How do you plan to fix the problems? |
| Conclusion | • What changes, if any, do you recommend?<br>• How will these changes affect the project?<br>• How will these changes affect the project's budget?<br>• What is the overall status of the project? |

FIGURE 14.4

**Introduction to a Progress Report**

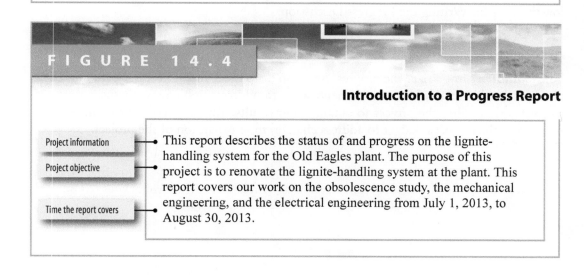

Project information
Project objective
Time the report covers

This report describes the status of and progress on the lignite-handling system for the Old Eagles plant. The purpose of this project is to renovate the lignite-handling system at the plant. This report covers our work on the obsolescence study, the mechanical engineering, and the electrical engineering from July 1, 2013, to August 30, 2013.

## Progress Discussion

The *progress discussion* answers readers' questions about how the project is proceeding and what work is planned for the next reporting period or for the remainder of the project (see Figure 14.3). Readers will be especially interested in

- how your progress compares with what you planned to accomplish during the reporting period
- problems you have encountered
- your results to date

You can organize the progress discussion in one of two ways:

- **By the progress made during the reporting period and the progress expected during the next period** (see Figure 14.5). This pattern emphasizes the total amount of progress you have made as well as the work you expect to do during the next reporting period.
- **By the tasks that remain to be completed** (see Figure 14.6). This pattern emphasizes the tasks, not the progress made or not made.

Using the progress-made/progress-expected pattern (shown in Figure 14.5), you organize the discussion around the progress made on one or several tasks during the reporting period and the progress expected during the next reporting period. Using the task pattern (shown in Figure 14.6) you organize the discussion around one or several tasks, discuss the progress made and expected on task 1, and then move to task 2, and so on. As you write the discussion of your progress, follow the Tips for Writing the Progress Discussion.

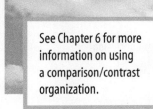

See Chapter 6 for more information on using a comparison/contrast organization.

## Conclusion

The *conclusion* summarizes the progress made on the project and, if necessary, recommends changes. In this section, you recommend ways to address problems with the project or suggest ways to alter the project to obtain better results. You may have to recommend an increase in the project's budget to address changes to or expansion of the project.

## FIGURE 14.5

### Progress-Made/Progress-Expected Pattern

**Progress made during the current reporting period** (the work you accomplished during the time covered by the progress report)
a. Task 1
b. Task 2
c. Task 3*
**Progress expected during the next reporting period** (the work you expect to complete during the next reporting period)
a. Task 1
b. Task 2
c. Task 3*
* You may have more or fewer than three tasks.

## FIGURE 14.6

### Task Pattern

**Task 1**
a. Progress made during the current reporting period (the work you accomplished during the time covered by the progress report)
b. Progress expected during the next reporting period (the work you expect to complete during the next reporting period)
**Task 2**
a. Progress made during the current reporting period
b. Progress expected during the next reporting period
**Task 3***
a. Progress made during the current reporting period
b. Progress expected during the next reporting period
* You may have more or fewer than three tasks.

In the conclusion, report the overall status of your project by
- summarizing the progress made on the project
- summarizing problems experienced during the reporting period
- evaluating the project's overall progress
- recommending ways to improve or change the project or future work, if necessary

The two sample progress reports presented in this chapter illustrate the conventional sections. In Figure 14.7, a student reports on her progress on a manual for the Double Oaks Golf Shop. She uses the progress-made/progress-expected pattern. In Figure 14.8, an engineering company reports its progress on a lignite-handling system. It uses the task pattern.

**TIPS** FOR WRITING THE PROGRESS DISCUSSION

- **Explain how your progress compares with what you planned to accomplish during the reporting period.** Readers want to know if your project is on schedule.
- **Report problems that you have encountered.** Explain how these problems affected your progress and the project's status. Will these problems affect the budget, the schedule, or the personnel? If so, explain how.
- **Include the major results of your work and any problems.** Readers need information about results and problems so they can approve or change the project, budget, schedule, or personnel. By documenting the problems, you lay the foundation for potential changes to the project.
- **Use either the progress-made/progress-expected pattern or the task pattern.** The progress-made/progress-expected pattern emphasizes the amount of progress you have made as well as the work you expect to complete during the next reporting period. The task/project pattern emphasizes the tasks of the project, not the amount of progress made or not made.
- **If your progress report is long, put the results and problems in a separate section.** Title that section Results and Problems or Evaluation of the Progress.

**FIGURE 14.7**

## Progress Report Using the Progress-Made/Progress-Expected Pattern

*The writer uses the memo format for her internal readers.*

**MEMO**

March 5, 2012

To:       Professor Patricia McCullough
From:     Nicole Sanders
Subject:  Progress report on the employee manual for Double Oaks Golf Shop

*The introduction lists the project and time period.*

This report covers my progress on an employee manual for the Double Oaks Golf Shop since February 15. This manual will include up-to-date procedures for opening, maintaining, and closing the shop, and for maintaining the inventory. It will also include the current employee policies. Although my work is progressing satisfactorily, I have experienced some problems in gathering information from the shop's manager.

*The writer uses the progress-made/progress-expected pattern.*

### My Progress during the Past Three Weeks

Over the last three weeks, I had planned to interview the sales staff and the manager and to update and revise the shop's procedures and policies. I have completed the interviews. Based on the information gathered in these interviews, I have updated the written procedures. However, I have not updated and revised all procedures and policies because my interviews revealed that many of them are not documented. To write the remaining procedures and policies, I need information from the manager and from the managers of other small golf shops.

#### Interviews with the Sales Staff and the Manager

I interviewed five members of the sales staff: Bart Thompson, Stella Smith, Melissa Connors, Dan Sandstedt, and Bradley Davis. Bart and Melissa explained that few of the current procedures and policies are documented. Before the interview, I assumed that the current employee manual contained most of the procedures and policies but that they were out of date. However, Bart and Melissa explained that the manual did not contain the inventory procedures—a major responsibility of the sales staff.

*The writer describes the project, including the progress made.*

I also interviewed the shop manager, Donna Shoopman. She explained how the manual differed from current shop policies. She also confirmed that the procedures for maintaining the inventory and closing the shop were not documented.

FIGURE 14.7

**Progress Report Using the Progress-Made/Progress-Expected Pattern** *continued*

### Updating and Revising the Policies and Procedures

I have updated and revised the policies on employee dress, customer satisfaction, substance abuse, disciplinary issues, and work schedules based on information from the shop manager. I have also updated and revised the opening procedures for the shop. These were all the written procedures.

*The writer includes the problems she has encountered.*

### Problems with Updating and Revising the Procedures

I cannot completely update the procedures for maintaining the inventory and for maintaining and closing the shop because they are not documented. By March 12, Donna plans to give me the notes she has made regarding maintaining the inventory, closing the shop, and maintaining the shop. These notes will serve as a foundation for the manual's procedures section. I cannot finish that section until I receive her notes.

### Progress Expected during the Next Three Weeks

During the next three weeks, I will
- interview managers of other small golf shops
- finish updating and revising the procedures
- prepare a completed draft of the manual

*The writer includes specific information on work she has planned.*

### Interviewing Managers of Other Golf Shops

I will interview Don Price, manager of Briarwood Golf Shop, and Bonnie Barger, manager of Brentwood Golf Shop. These interviews will help me appropriately revise the procedures for maintaining the inventory and the shop.

### Finish Updating and Revising the Procedures

I will update and revise the procedures for maintaining inventory and for maintaining and closing the shop after receiving the notes from Donna. I will also use the information from the interviews with the managers of Brentwood and Briarwood Golf Shops to help me appropriately revise these procedures.

*In the conclusion, she reports on the project's status.*

### Conclusion

My interviews with the sales staff and with the manager gave me valuable information for writing the manual. Even though I am behind schedule, I can complete a first draft of the manual by March 30 if Donna gives me her notes by March 12.

FIGURE 14.8

**Progress Report Using the Task Pattern**

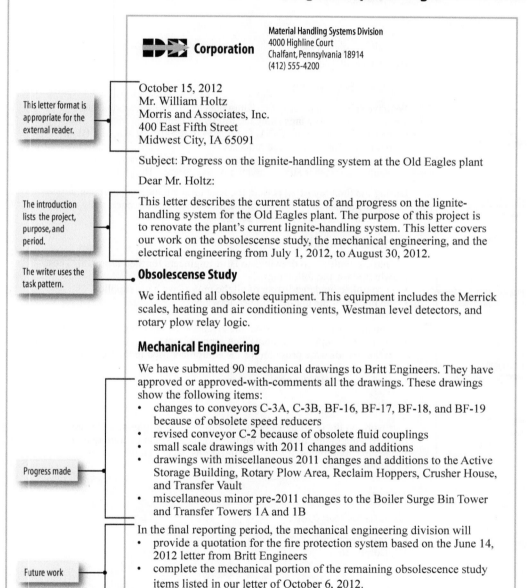

**Material Handling Systems Division**
4000 Highline Court
Chalfant, Pennsylvania 18914
(412) 555-4200

**Corporation**

This letter format is appropriate for the external reader.

October 15, 2012
Mr. William Holtz
Morris and Associates, Inc.
400 East Fifth Street
Midwest City, IA 65091

Subject: Progress on the lignite-handling system at the Old Eagles plant

Dear Mr. Holtz:

The introduction lists the project, purpose, and period.

This letter describes the current status of and progress on the lignite-handling system for the Old Eagles plant. The purpose of this project is to renovate the plant's current lignite-handling system. This letter covers our work on the obsolescense study, the mechanical engineering, and the electrical engineering from July 1, 2012, to August 30, 2012.

The writer uses the task pattern.

### Obsolescense Study

We identified all obsolete equipment. This equipment includes the Merrick scales, heating and air conditioning vents, Westman level detectors, and rotary plow relay logic.

### Mechanical Engineering

We have submitted 90 mechanical drawings to Britt Engineers. They have approved or approved-with-comments all the drawings. These drawings show the following items:

Progress made

- changes to conveyors C-3A, C-3B, BF-16, BF-17, BF-18, and BF-19 because of obsolete speed reducers
- revised conveyor C-2 because of obsolete fluid couplings
- small scale drawings with 2011 changes and additions
- drawings with miscellaneous 2011 changes and additions to the Active Storage Building, Rotary Plow Area, Reclaim Hoppers, Crusher House, and Transfer Vault
- miscellaneous minor pre-2011 changes to the Boiler Surge Bin Tower and Transfer Towers 1A and 1B

In the final reporting period, the mechanical engineering division will

Future work

- provide a quotation for the fire protection system based on the June 14, 2012 letter from Britt Engineers
- complete the mechanical portion of the remaining obsolescence study items listed in our letter of October 6, 2012.

# FIGURE 14.8

**Progress Report Using the Task Pattern** *continued*

Page 2
W. Holtz
October 15, 2012

## Structural Engineering

*Progress made*

We have submitted 82 structural drawings to Britt Engineers for their approval. These drawings show the following items:
- changes to conveyors C-3A, C-3B, BF-16, BF-17, BF-18, and BF-19 because of obsolete speed reducers
- miscellaneous 2011 changes and additions to conveyor C-2, the Transfer Vault, the Crusher House, and the Active Storage Building

*Future work*

During the final reporting period, the structural engineering division will complete the structural portion of the remaining obsolescence study items listed in our letter of October 6, 2012.

## Electrical Engineering

*Progress made*

We have submitted 16 drawings to Britt Engineers for their approval. These drawings show the following:
- a complete, updated listing of all the motors we have supplied
- an update of the one-line power drawing

*Future work*

During the final reporting period, the electrical engineering division will
- design I/O (input and output) rack arrangements
- write the software program for the equipment used in the lignite-handling system
- simulate and document the program

## Conclusions

*The conclusion includes the project's status.*

Our work on the Old Eagles project is progressing as planned. We are now working on the final tasks for the project and plan to complete them in the next six months. If you have questions, please contact me at (123) 456-7890.

Sincerely,

*Cynthia Dempsey*

Cynthia Dempsey
DE Corporation

*Minutes* are the official record of a meeting. The meeting could be as informal as a meeting of your product development team or as formal as a city council meeting. You may read or write minutes from meetings at your organization or meetings between representatives of your organization and another organization. For example, construction company representatives may meet with the owners of a project the company is managing. The company representatives will keep minutes of meetings with the owners to provide a record of what occurred. Meeting minutes are sent to those who belong to the group or organization represented at the meeting. They may also be made public as in the minutes of a city council meeting. Minutes may be made available in paper form or online for anyone to read.

## Informal Meeting Minutes

The type of meeting will dictate what you put in the minutes. For example, if the meeting is informal, you might simply send an email to those who attended. The email would
• summarize what was discussed
• summarize agreements
• identify action items

*Action items* identify what the group decided to do, who is responsible, and what deadlines were set.

## Formal Meeting Minutes

As discussed in Taking It into the Workplace, the minutes from a formal meeting actually begin with the agenda for what is planned at the meeting. (An *agenda* is an outline for what is planned at the meeting.) An effectively written agenda gives you an outline for the minutes. An agenda includes the following information:
• time and date of the meeting
• location of the meeting
• items to be discussed

As you prepare the agenda items to be discussed
• Consider including desired outcomes for each item.
• Start with the most important items. (If you run out of time, the items not discussed will be the less important ones.)
• Consider including times for each item.
• Identify the person(s) responsible for each item.

The following section provides guidelines for the conventional sections of formal minutes:
- information about the meeting and the attendees
- items discussed
- action items
- recorder's information

Figure 14.9 presents the questions that readers may ask as they read meeting minutes.

## Information about the Meeting and Attendees

Because the minutes serve as the meeting's official record, they should include the following information:

1.  **name(s) of the group(s) involved in the meeting.** Identify the name of the division, committee, companies, etc.
2.  **location, date, and time of the meeting.** Only note the beginning time (not the ending time).
3.  **type of meeting.** Was it a regularly scheduled meeting or a one-time or special meeting?
4.  **attendees.** List the first and last names of those who attended, those who were absent, and any guests who were present. At a large public meeting, such as a city council meeting, you may have an auditorium filled with guests. For these situations, you only need to list those who spoke or participated directly in the meeting.
5.  **time the meeting adjourned.**
6.  **name and title of the person who recorded and wrote the minutes.**

The first three pieces of information appear in a heading for the minutes. The list of attendees generally appears in a sentence or paragraph immediately after the heading, and the time the meeting adjourned appears as the last item of business in the minutes.

## Items Discussed and Action Items

If the meeting is a recurring meeting, organize this section by old business and then new business. If it is a one-time meeting, organize the minutes by the order in which the items were discussed. In either case, use the agenda to organize your minutes, unless the order of business is altered. In that case, you follow the order of business.

If the meeting is not the first one of your group or committee, you will have *old business*. For many meetings, old business is simply approving the minutes of the previous meeting. In some meetings, however, the attendees may discuss, update, or amend items introduced at a previous meeting. For example, at a previous meeting, a member of the group may

FIGURE 14.9

**Readers' Questions on the Conventional Sections of Meeting Minutes**

| Section | Readers' Questions |
|---|---|
| Information about the meeting and the attendees | • What is the name of the group(s) involved in the meeting?<br>• Where did you meet?<br>• What was the date and time of the meeting?<br>• Was the meeting a regularly scheduled or one-time (special) meeting? |
| Items discussed and action items | • Did you act on business discussed at a previous meeting?<br>  • If so, what did you do or discuss?<br>• What major topics did the group discuss?<br>• What motions, if any, were introduced?<br>  • Did the motions pass or fail?<br>• What actions did the groups agree to take?<br>  • Who is responsible for the action item?<br>  • What is the deadline for completing the action? |
| Information on the recorder of the minutes | • Who prepared the minutes? |

have initiated a discussion on getting approval from the Department of Transportation to install traffic lights near a commercial development. At the next meeting, the group may want to discuss whether they received approval or when the lights will be installed. This business would be old business. The group would put these items on the agenda before *new business*. For old business, you record what action was taken on the minutes of the previous meeting or on any previously introduced business item. For example, you might write, "Johnson moved to approve the minutes of the last meeting. Smith seconded the motion. The motion passed by a vote of 6 to 0." (Or you could write, "The motion carried by a vote of 6 to 0.")

To write effective minutes, you record the major topics discussed and any action taken. In a perfect meeting, the group would discuss the items in the order listed on the agenda.

However, meetings often deviate from the agenda, in which case you record the discussions and actions taken in the order the discussions and actions occurred. Your goal is to create a *snapshot* of items discussed in the meeting, not to record every word. For action items, you should identify

- the specific action
- who will complete the action
- the deadline for completing the action

The Tips for Writing Accurate Meeting Minutes will help you write accurate meeting minutes.

### Your Information

As the recorder and writer of the minutes, you end the minutes with information about you. As part of your contact information, you may give readers the opportunity to amend the minutes. You might end the minutes as follows:

> Respectfully submitted,
> John Smith, Senior Project Engineer

Figure 14.10 illustrates complete meeting minutes. Notice how the writer has included the conventional information and used a format to help readers locate information.

## WRITING FIELD AND LAB REPORTS

You may write a field or lab report after you complete an experiment or after you inspect some machinery or other equipment. You might also write a field report after you examine a site. For example, your company may be planning to buy a manufacturing plant. Your managers send you to the plant to inspect the equipment. When you return, you would write an informal report recording what you found during your inspections and listing your recommendations.

### The Conventional Sections of Field and Lab Reports

A field or lab report has the following conventional sections:

- **Introduction.** State the purpose of your report and the problem addressed in the report.
- **Methods.** Describe the methods you used. Because this report is informal, you only need to briefly describe them. In field and lab reports, most writers deemphasize the methods.

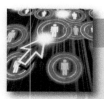

## TIPS FOR WRITING ACCURATE MEETING MINUTES

- **Include each major topic discussed.** For most meetings, especially formal ones, you will have a list of these topics on the agenda. If the meeting is less formal, include the major topics or items discussed.
- **Record the motions made, who made them, and the vote on each motion.** Include whether the motion was passed, defeated, or tabled. Include the vote count— "The motion passed by a vote of 7 to 2." If the group amended the motion, record specifically how the motion was amended and who offered the amendment.
- **Record the names of people who read reports, introduced action items, and so on.** Exclude the names of people who simply participated in the discussion; you record those names when you list the attendees in the first part of the minutes.
- **Summarize the discussions.** Effective meeting minutes summarize the discussions. Minutes aren't transcripts, but you should include enough information to create an accurate record, but omit information readers do not need.
- **Focus on the actions, not on the emotional exchanges.** Because minutes aren't a transcript, separate the actions from the emotional exchanges. For example, if the group argues, don't write, "The motion to paint the new office space taupe with hunter-green accents passed 6 to 1 after Garcia and McCarroll argued about the color. At one point, McCarroll said that 'the organization had no taste when it comes to interior decorating.'" Instead, simply write, "After discussion, the motion to paint the new office space taupe with hunter-green accents passed 6 to 1."
- **Include enough detail on an issue or action item so readers will understand the item,** especially those readers who had not attended the meeting.
- **If the discussion moves too quickly or you didn't hear and understand something, interrupt the discussion and ask the group to clarify.** Your job is to create an accurate record. If you don't understand something or you need someone to repeat a motion or action item, ask that person to clarify or repeat the information.
- **Ask someone to write the minutes and/or take notes if you are in charge of the meeting.** You cannot take accurate minutes if you are running the meeting.
- **Proofread the minutes before distributing them.**

**Meeting Minutes**

The writer identifies the group, date, time, and attendees.

The writer uses headings to help readers locate information.

The writer numbers each major topic in the order on the agenda or the order discussed.

The writer identifies the persons introducing and seconding motions.

The writer identifies the persons introducing new business.

The writer identifies action items— including the person responsible and the deadline.

The writer identifies the recorder of the minutes.

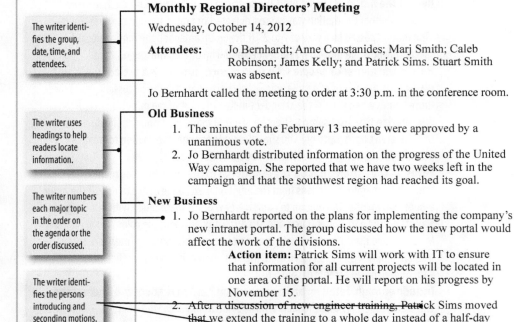

## Monthly Regional Directors' Meeting

Wednesday, October 14, 2012

**Attendees:** Jo Bernhardt; Anne Constanides; Marj Smith; Caleb Robinson; James Kelly; and Patrick Sims. Stuart Smith was absent.

Jo Bernhardt called the meeting to order at 3:30 p.m. in the conference room.

### Old Business

1. The minutes of the February 13 meeting were approved by a unanimous vote.
2. Jo Bernhardt distributed information on the progress of the United Way campaign. She reported that we have two weeks left in the campaign and that the southwest region had reached its goal.

### New Business

1. Jo Bernhardt reported on the plans for implementing the company's new intranet portal. The group discussed how the new portal would affect the work of the divisions.

   **Action item:** Patrick Sims will work with IT to ensure that information for all current projects will be located in one area of the portal. He will report on his progress by November 15.

2. After a discussion of new engineer training, Patrick Sims moved that we extend the training to a whole day instead of a half-day session and that we ask some engineers to join Human Resources in planning the training. Anne Constanides seconded the motion. The motion carried by a vote of 5 to 1.

   **Action item:** Jo Bernhardt will contact Human Resources and ask the project managers to suggest engineers to participate in the planning. She will ask the managers to send their suggestions to Human Resources by October 31.

3. James Kelly introduced information on the new hotel and convention center project. He requested that the engineers receive a briefing on the project. After discussion, James changed his request to a motion. Caleb Robinson seconded the motion. The motion passed unanimously.

   **Action item:** James Kelly will set up a date, time, and location for the briefing.

4. Jo Bernhardt adjourned the meeting at 4:45 p.m.

Respectfully submitted by Anne Constanides, project engineer

**Readers' Questions about the Conventional Sections of Lab and Field Reports**

| Section | Readers' Questions |
|---|---|
| Introduction | • What is the purpose of your report?<br>• Why did you conduct the inspection, experiment, etc.?<br>• What led to the inspection, experiment, etc.? |
| Methods | • What method did you use for your inspection, experiment, etc.? |
| Results | • What were the results?<br>• What did you learn?<br>• What problems, if any, did you observe? |
| Conclusions | • What do the results mean?<br>• Are the results conclusive?<br>• If you observed problems, are these problems major or minor? |
| Recommendations (optional) | • What do you recommend?<br>• If you observed problems, how do you recommend solving them? |

- **Results.** State the results of your experiment, inspection, etc. If the results are preliminary, state that in the minutes.
- **Conclusions.** Tell readers what you learned from the results.
- **Recommendations.** If your readers expect recommendations, include them in the report.

In many field and lab reports, you may not have a heading for all the conventional sections. Figure 14.11 presents questions that readers might ask as they read the field or lab report. The field report in Figure 14.12 illustrates how a writer uses the conventional structure to report on his inspection of a chimney at a power plant.

## WRITING TRIP REPORTS

You may write a trip report after you return from a business trip. You might, for example, attend a seminar on new software for project management. When you return, your manager may want you to report on the seminar. Your manager will want to know what you learned and what you recommend. Your manager will not, however, be interested in a minute-by-minute itinerary of what you did and what occurred at the seminar. You may also write a trip report after you visit with customers. Your report might include information on how your organization must follow up with these customers to best serve them. You might also write a trip report after you visit with employees who work away from the home or regional office. For instance, if you supervise field representatives who work in regional offices, you may visit them to find out about their work. After such a trip, you might write a report about how their work is proceeding or how the company can improve their work environment.

## The Conventional Sections of Trip Reports

When you write trip reports, use these conventional sections:
- **Introduction**. Include the place, date, and purpose of your trip.
- **Summary.** Summarize what you observed and learned, and what you recommend.
- **Discussion.** Present the gist of the important information you gathered during the trip. Your readers aren't interested in reading, "First, I did this; then, I did that." Instead, they want to know what you learned and why that information is important to them and the organization.
- **Recommendations.** State and explain your recommendations.

Because you will usually write a trip report to an internal reader, most trip reports take the format of a memo. Figure 14.13 presents the questions that your readers might ask as they read a trip report. Figure 14.14 presents a trip report written after an employee attended demonstrations of hands-free cell phone systems.

## SAMPLE INFORMAL REPORTS

In this chapter, you have read samples of the following types of informal reports:
- Directives (Figure 14.2)
- Progress reports (Figures 14.7 and 14.8)
- Meeting minutes (Figure 14.10)
- Field and lab reports (Figure 14.12)
- Trip reports (Figure 14.14)

Your organization or manager may have a specific format or template for these informal reports. Ask your coworkers or your manager if your organization has a preferred or an expected format. If so, use that format or template. If not, use these sample reports to guide you.

**FIGURE 14.12**

**Field Report**

**Structural Safety Engineering**
1545 Steam Road
Brazelton, KY 75609
(663) 555-9001

May 20, 2012

Ms. Joyce Carr, Plant Manger
Big Brown Steam Electric Plant
New Power
Santa Fe, NM 86090

Re: Examination of Chimney in Unit 3

Dear Joyce,

We performed a level 5 examination and structural assessment of the concrete chimney, brick liner, and associated components at Big Brown Electric Plant, Unit 3. Our examination follows up the baseline assessment performed in 2010. We will use the findings of this follow-up to update the database for future examinations and to plan maintenance and possible repairs.

**Methods**

We conducted the examination from April 20 through May 8, 2012. To examine the chimney and brick liner, we used five vertical drops (one in the interior of the brick liner, two in the annular space, and two along the exterior surface of the concrete shell). To examine the chimney components, we visually inspected the breeching duct, seals, platforms, ladders, lightning protection system, and other related appurtenances.

**Results of the Examination and Assessment**

The overall condition of the chimney is good. However, our examination and assessment revealed the following moderate structural deficiencies:

- Part of the brick liner that passes through the breeching duct is missing.
- The three aviation obstruction lights at the upper gas monitory platform are not working.
- The handrail around the perimeter of the top platforms does not continue between grating sections. This defect causes loose handrails and excessive lateral deflections.

We also found these safety issues:
- nonconforming safety chains across the openings
- inadequate safety rail clamps on the ladder

**Conclusions and Recommendations**

Except for the safety items and the missing liner bands in the breeching duct, the chimney is in good condition. However, we recommend repairing the following items to minimize the potential for structural problems:

---

The writer uses a letter format because he is writing to an external reader.

The writer identifies the purpose of the report.

The writer identifies the methods used.

The writer uses lists to highlight the results.

The writer includes recommendations.

## FIGURE 14.12

**Field Report** *continued*

- Replace the missing brick liner bands in the breeching duct. The severe environment requires that the replacement rods be coated with coal tar epoxy and encased in 316L stainless steel pipe.
- Replace the aviation obstruction lights.
- Add a handrail section to minimize excessive lateral deflections and to meet OSHA directives.
- Correct all safety items noted in this report.

The writer politely closes by offering to answer questions.

If you have questions, please call me at (305) 555-5555.

Regards,

*Mathew McCarroll*

Mathew McCarroll
Structural Engineer

## FIGURE 14.13

**Readers' Questions about the Conventional Sections of Trip Reports**

| Section | Readers' Questions |
|---|---|
| Introduction | • Where did you go? <br> • When did you go? <br> • What was the purpose of your trip? |
| Summary | • What did you observe or do? <br> • What, briefly, did you learn? <br> • What, briefly, do you recommend? |
| Discussion | • What did you learn? <br> • Why is the information important to the organization? |
| Recommendations | • What do you recommend? <br> • Why? |

**FIGURE 14.14**

**Trip Report**

<table>
<tr><td colspan="2">

The writer uses a memo format because he is writing to an internal reader who is a peer.

</td></tr>
</table>

**Memo**

| | |
|---|---|
| **Date**: | September 21, 2012 |
| **To**: | Robert Congrove, Director of IT |
| **From**: | Meredith Mitchell |
| **Subject**: | Trip to InFocus, Inc. |

This memo summarizes the information I gathered from a trip to InFocus, Inc. in Chicago on September 18, 2012. The purpose of my trip was to attend demonstrations of projectors for our account managers and our training staff.

The writer summarizes what he observed and what he recommends.

**Summary**

I recommend the Optoma ML 500 portable projector because of its warranty, maintenance cost, portability, and internal 2GB memory. The Optoma also has a carrying case included in the cost.

**Discussion**

InFocus offers portable and mounted projectors. For the portable projectors, they offer the following options that are within our budget:

- Hitachi CP-X2020 for $525
- Optoma ML 500 for $594
- Acer K330 for $548

The writer presents detailed information about what he learned. He selects only the information that is important to his reader.

The Hitachi CP-X2020 retails for $525. It has a three-year warranty and an expected lamp life of 3,000 hours in normal mode and 4,000 hours in economy mode. The replacement lamp costs $365. It weighs 2.6 pounds; however, it was hard to carry. It can read files directly from SD cards and USB memory keys. It does not have internal memory available for storing files.

The Optoma ML 500 retails for $594. It has a three-year warranty and an expected lamp life from 2,000 to 3,000 hours. The replacement lamp costs $200. It weighs 2.6 pounds, is easy to carry, and comes with a carrying case. It can read files from its internal memory, SD cards, and USB memory keys.

The Acer K330 retails for $548. It has a two-year warranty and an expected lamp life of 2,000 to 3,000 hours. The lamp replacement costs $250. It weighs 2.9 pounds and was easy to carry. It can read files from an SD card, USB memory key, or video source.

The writer presents and explains his recommendations.

**Recommendations**

I recommend that we purchase six Optoma ML 500 portable projectors for the account managers and training staff. The Optoma has the advantage of 2GB of internal storage, a low maintenance cost, and portability. It also is the only option that includes a carrying case.

I would like to talk with you and Gene about this recommendation. Please call me at x 7980 to set up a time to talk.

**TAKING IT INTO THE** *workplace*

## Conducting Effective Meetings

Meetings are a regular part of the workplace; yet meetings are often unpopular, in part because people see them as a waste of time or poorly run. GovLeaders (2012) suggests six "Golden Rules" for conducting an effective meeting:

1. Run your meetings as you would have others run meetings that you attend.
2. Be prepared and ensure that all participants are prepared as well.
3. Stick to a schedule.
4. Stay on topic.
5. Don't hold unnecessary meetings.
6. Wrap up meetings with a clear statement of the next steps and who is to take them (GovLeaders 2012).

### BEFORE THE MEETING

To observe these Golden Rules, follow these guidelines before the meeting:

- **Ask yourself, Is this meeting necessary?** Can you accomplish your goals by sending an email or memo or by simply making the decision on your own? If you can make the decision alone, don't call a meeting. If you want to explain your decision, a meeting might be a good way to do so.
- **Pick an appropriate time and location before announcing the meeting.** Efficiency experts suggest holding meetings on Tuesdays, Wednesdays, and Thursdays at 3:00 p.m. (Sozo 2010). Pick a location where you will not be distracted.
- **Prepare an agenda.** An agenda helps you organize the meeting, tell others why the meeting is important, and stay on task during the meeting. An agenda answers the question, Why should I come to this meeting? An agenda helps you accomplish your objectives. During the meeting, if the conversation drifts away from the topic, an agenda provides a road map to guide the conversation back on track.
- **Announce the meeting.** Attach the agenda to your meeting notification.

## DURING THE MEETING

Once you have notified participants of the meeting and distributed the agenda, you are ready to hold the meeting.

- **Start on time.** When you don't start on time, you waste everyone's time and encourage people to assume the meeting is unimportant.
- **Tell people why they are there.** Start with a brief, clear statement of the meeting's purpose. If you know the purpose, you will know when you've achieved the goal or met your objectives.
- **Follow the agenda and keep people on track.** You help people stay on track by recapping frequently. If the discussion gets off track, politely interrupt with a reference to a specific point under discussion and recap previous conversations.
- **Know when to move to the next agenda item and how to deal with side issues.** Side issues occur when some or all of the participants discuss issues not on the agenda. These issues waste time and distract everyone. To politely deal with side issues, use these techniques:
  - Ask specific questions of the person(s) discussing the side issues.
  - Use the person's name(s) when asking the questions. For example, you might say, "John, how would you suggest handling the training for the new software?"
  - Know when to move to the next agenda item. Side issues/conversations may occur because an item has been fully discussed.
- **End on time.** Respect your participants' time. If you announced that the meeting will end at 4:30, then end at 4:30. If you did not complete the agenda, schedule another meeting.

## AFTER THE MEETING

Once your meeting is over, follow up:

- **Send minutes to all the participants.**
- **Ask for their comments or corrections.**
- **Remind participants of action items they are responsible for completing.**

## Assignment

1. Attend a meeting at a local business, school board, city council, campus organization, or nonprofit organization. Take notes on the effectiveness of the meeting.
2. Write a trip report to your instructor on what you learned from the meeting and recommend ways that the leader of the meeting could have more effectively conducted the meeting. If the meeting was effective, recommend that the leader continue to conduct meetings in the same way. In your report, give specific examples of what was effective and what was ineffective.

# CASE STUDY ANALYSIS

## The Mailbox Problem

### Background

As the manager of Gotta Get Clean, a home cleaning service, you have received complaints that members of your staff are parking in front of mailboxes. When they park in front of mailboxes, mail carriers will not deliver the mail. The policy of the U.S. Postal Service is that mail carriers are not to deliver the mail if a vehicle is blocking the mailbox. Instead, the mail carrier is to place a note on the vehicle saying: "The Postal Service will not deliver mail to any mailbox that is obstructed by a vehicle or other item. If you wish to receive mail, do not obstruct the mailbox." Homeowners get irritated or angry when they do not get their mail. You are tired of the complaints.

### Assignment

1. Imagine that you are the manager of Gotta Get Clean. You decide you must send a directive to staff members who drive company vehicles instructing them not to park near mailboxes and explaining the consequences of ignoring the policy.
2. Determine the consequences of ignoring the policy.
3. Write the directive in memo format for the staff.
4. Send your directive to your instructor.

# EXERCISES

VIEW THE INTERACTIVE DOCUMENT ANALYSIS ONLINE AT

WWW.GRTEP.COM

1. Analyze the progress report in the interactive document analysis. In an email to your instructor, recommend ways to improve the report.

2. Revise the progress report you analyzed in Exercise 1. Incorporate your recommendations and include the conventional sections. Turn in the revised report to your instructor.

3. If you are working on a collaborative project in one of your classes, write the minutes of one of your meetings. Email the minutes to each team member and to your instructor. Follow the conventional structure and answer the readers' questions in Figure 14.9.

4. Visit a nonprofit organization in your community to learn about the work it does and about volunteer opportunities. Ask about the requirements for volunteers, if any, and how to apply for a volunteer position. After your visit, write a trip report for your instructor. Use the conventional sections and answer the readers' questions in Figure 14.13.

DOWNLOAD A COPY OF THE WORKSHEET FOR WRITING READER-FOCUSED INFORMAL REPORTS AT

WWW.GRTEP.COM

## Writing a Field Report

Like many college campuses and communities, your campus or community most likely has an inconvenient or dangerous situation. For example, your campus may have an intersection where traffic accidents frequently occur, or your community may have an area where pedestrians don't have a sidewalk and need one. Work with a team to identify an inconvenient or dangerous situation on your campus or in your community. Once your team has identified a situation to study, complete the assignment below.

### Assignment

1. Observe the situation or inspect the area on two or three consecutive days. (Be sure to observe during peak time; for example, don't observe the intersection at 2:00 a.m.)
2. Write a field report to the appropriate school administrators or city officials. Be sure to use the conventional sections and to answer the readers' questions in Figure 14.11.
3. Include a specific recommendation in your report.
4. Send your report to your instructor.

# chapter *fifteen*

## Writing Reader-Focused Formal Reports

assie and Jon are technical writers employed by an engineering firm that renovates and rebuilds manufacturing plants. Cassie's group is working with a client company to find out why a tower collapsed at one of its plants. Cassie will write a report discussing possible reasons for the collapse. Jon is working on a report recommending ways to repair the tower. Cassie and Jon are working on the same project, but are preparing different types of reports. Both Cassie and Jon will prepare a formal report, but their purposes for writing are different. Cassie will present the results of her research and draw conclusions based on those results. Jon will present results, draw conclusions, and make recommendations based on those conclusions.

Like Cassie and Jon, you may write formal reports for a class or in the workplace. A *formal report* communicates less routine business than an informal report. Like an informal report, a formal report can cover any number of topics. Unlike an informal report, a formal report,

iStockphoto 2008.

in most cases, has both front and back matter. A formal report might be the final step in a series of documents. This series might begin with a proposal, continue with progress reports, and end with a formal report. You might write a formal report that isn't preceded by a proposal or a progress report. For example, your manager asks you to evaluate telecommuting. You might examine whether telecommuting improves employee productivity. For this project, you would research telecommuting using both primary and secondary sources and write a report presenting the results of your research, possibly making recommendations. It is a type of research report (sometimes called a recommendation report) that workplace professionals frequently write.

In this chapter, you will get some guidelines for writing reader-focused formal reports. This chapter discusses a frequently written formal report, the feasibility report (sometimes called a recommendation report).

##  TYPES OF FORMAL REPORTS

You've heard the word report since you were in grade school. When you enter the workplace, you will be asked to write reports. *Report* is a term for a document that informs, analyzes, or recommends. To meaningfully discuss reports, we need some standard terminology; however, the workplace and many fields don't have standard terminology for reports. For example, some terms refer to the report's topic, such as *meeting minutes*, *lab reports*, or *field reports*. Other terms refer to the phase of the research or project, such as *progress reports* or *completion reports*. Still other terms refer to the report's purpose, such as *recommendation reports*.

If you are new to your organization and your manager asks you to write a report, talk with your manager to determine what type of report and format he or she expects. You might ask: "What is the purpose of the report?" "Do you have a preferred format for the report?" Look at similar reports written by coworkers.

For this chapter, we use the report's purpose to categorize formal reports into:
- information reports
- analytical reports
- recommendation reports

### Information Reports

*Information reports* present results so readers can understand a particular problem or situation (see Figure 15.1). For example, the manager of a city's website might prepare an

FIGURE 15.1

## Types of Reports Categorized by Purpose

| Type of Report | Presents Results | Draws Conclusions | Makes Recommendations |
|---|---|---|---|
| Information | ✓ | | |
| Analytical | ✓ | ✓ | |
| Recommendation | ✓ | ✓ | ✓ |

information report for the city council with analytics on the number of people who visit the site, the number who pay their city water and sewage bills online, the number of links to city-related websites, and the number of city departments that use the site to provide information to residents. The purpose of this type of report is to present facts—often called results—not to analyze the facts or draw conclusions.

As you learned in Chapter 14, a report can be formal or informal. When you determine the formality of the report, you know what format to use and whether to include front and back matter. *Formal* and *informal* refer to the format, not the purpose or significance of the report or the organization of the report's body. To decide if an information report should be formal or informal, determine whether the report is routine. For example, think about the city website manager. He or she might write an information report to the city's public information officer providing site analytics for the month. This report is routine and would be informal. The report to the city council, however, is not routine because the Web manager doesn't routinely present reports to the city council. The council might request such a report because it wants to know if the city is devoting too many or too few city resources to the site, and if current practices are improving communications to city residents. Because it is not routine, this report would be formal.

Information reports:
- **Present information on the status of current research or of a project.** For example, you might report on the status of a project to construct a new airport runway.
- **Present an update of the operations in your division.** For example, the website report for the city council might present an update of work done by the city's public information division.
- **Explain how your organization or division does something**. For example, you might report on how your division tracks the work of subcontractors.
- **Present the results of a questionnaire or research.** For example, you might present the results of an employee questionnaire to gather information on their daily commute: How far do they drive? Do they carpool? Do they or would they use public transportation?

These are only examples of the kind of information you might present in an information report.

## Analytical Reports

Analytical reports go a step beyond presenting results. Analytical reports present results, analyze those results, and draw conclusions based on those results (see Figure 15.1). Analytical reports analyze and interpret the information or data in the results. They answer the question, What do the results mean? These reports describe why or how something happened and then explain what the findings mean. For example, let's again consider the Web manager's report to the city council. Along with presenting the results, the manager might analyze those results and present conclusions. Based on the low percentage of city residents who use the site to pay their water and sewage bills, the manager might conclude that either the residents don't know the service is available or that they can't easily find the service. The manager's purpose in the report is only to draw conclusions based on the results, not to make recommendations.

Like information reports, analytical reports can be formal or informal and can present and analyze a variety of results. They can:
- **Explain what caused a problem or situation.** For example, you might present the results of a traffic study of an intersection where many accidents have occurred. In the report, you would draw conclusions about why the accidents occurred based on the study results.
- **Explain the potential results of a particular course of action**. For example, based on the results of your research, you might conclude that opening a new office branch will increase business for your organization. You might then present conclusions on whether the potential income will offset the cost of running the new office.

- **Suggest which option, action, or procedure is best**. For example, you might present options for treating people with diabetes and report which treatment has the best outcome. However, you would not recommend a treatment.

These are only a few examples of the conclusions you might present in an analytical report.

> Analytical reports analyze and interpret the information or data in the results. They answer the question, What do the results mean?

## Recommendation Reports

*Recommendation reports* suggest a course of action. These reports may seem to be the same as analytical reports, so how do you differentiate between them? Think of it this way: You might conclude that treatment X is more effective than treatments Y and Z. This statement is your conclusion, but it is not necessarily a recommendation to use treatment X. You might, for example, recommend using treatment Z because of cost; or you might recommend not using any treatment. Consider the Web manager's report again. Even though the percentage of city residents using the site to pay their water and sewage bills is low, the manager might recommend that the city council do nothing to increase the activity on the site because the public information division doesn't have the money to increase publicity.

Like information and analytical reports, recommendation reports may be formal or informal. Recommendation reports might address any of the following situations and advocate a specific course of action.

- **What should we do about a problem?** You might recommend a course of action for dealing with a problem. For example, you might answer the questions: What should we do about the problem of excessive absences in the manufacturing division? What should we do about the growing number of plastic bags in our landfills?
- **Should we or can we do something?** You might look at whether your organization can or should do something. For example, you might answer the question, Even though we currently have two engineers working on the airport runway projects, should we hire another project engineer to work on the new construction project that we will begin next year?
- **Should we change the method or technology we use to do something?** You might examine whether a change would benefit your organization. For example, your organization currently sends all printing to an outside vendor. You might answer the question, Should we continue to use an outside vendor or move all printing in-house?

**Plan for Preparing a Formal Report**

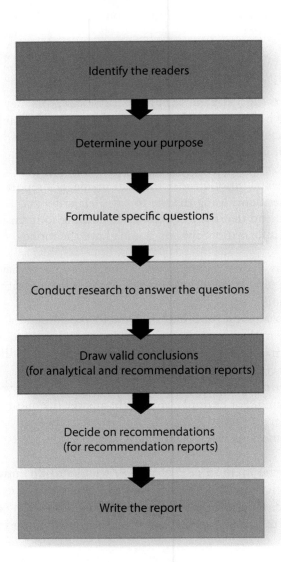

Identify the readers

Determine your purpose

Formulate specific questions

Conduct research to answer the questions

Draw valid conclusions
(for analytical and recommendation reports)

Decide on recommendations
(for recommendation reports)

Write the report

Although the report categories—information, analytical, and recommendation—make report writing seem easily defined, you will find the categories overlap. As you write reports, be flexible and ask questions. Seek help from people senior to you.

## IDENTIFY THE READERS AND PURPOSE OF YOUR REPORT

Before you begin to write your report, identify the readers and the report's purpose (see Figure 15.2). With most reports, you will know the purpose; with others—especially reports that you're writing for the first time or that someone asks you to write—you will need to first define the purpose. These questions will help you define the purpose:
- What do you want readers to know, do, or learn from the report?
- Do you only want to present results?
- Do you want to draw conclusions?
- Do you want to make recommendations based on those conclusions?
- Is the report routine?

As with informal reports, find out as much as possible about your readers. To help you analyze your readers, ask these questions:
- What do your readers know about your field or your report's topic?
- Why are they reading your report? To gather information? To complete a task? To make a decision?
- How much detail do readers need or expect? Does this need or expectation differ among your readers? If so, how?
- Do your readers expect an informal or formal report?
- Are your readers internal or external?
- What positions do your readers hold in the organization? If they are internal readers, where are their positions in relation to yours in the organizational hierarchy?
- Will more than one group read the report?
- What do your readers know about you or your organization? Have their previous experiences with you or your organization been positive? If not, why?

### Writing for Readers with Varied Knowledge and Purposes

Pay particular attention to two important factors that will help you uncover what readers need or expect: their familiarity with the topic and their purpose for reading (Holland, Charrow, and Wright 1988). Readers familiar with your topic will "find it easier to grasp new material about the topic than readers" who are unfamiliar with it (ibid., 30). If readers are unfamiliar with, or do not understand your field, include adequate detail and explain technical terms and concepts. If you know the knowledge level will vary among your readers, consider these three options:

- Write separate reports.
- Direct the language and detail to readers with the lowest level of knowledge.
- Compartmentalize the report (ibid.).

You will rarely write separate reports because it is time-consuming and expensive. If you direct the language and details to readers with the lowest level of knowledge, readers well versed in the topic may become impatient with what they see as simplistic and tedious explanations. Thus, compartmentalizing the report is the most efficient and effective way to write for varied readers. When you compartmentalize, you create a separate section for each group of readers. You compartmentalize by using headings, tables of contents, summaries, and indexes to help readers find the sections that interest them (ibid.). You also can place definitions and explanations of technical terminology and concepts in footnotes, glossaries, appendixes, or other sections within the report (ibid.).

After you have a sense of what your readers know about the topic and what they expect, think about these basic questions that your readers may also have:

- What is the purpose of this report? To present results? To draw conclusions? To make recommendations?
- Why are we receiving the report?
- How does this report affect us and our organization?

Once you know your purpose and understand your readers and what they expect, you can prepare to meet their needs and ensure that your report achieves its intended purpose.

##  FORMULATE QUESTIONS AND DO RESEARCH WHEN NEEDED

Have you ever asked a question and gotten the wrong response? Have you ever been asked a question and you didn't understand what you were being asked? If you ask vague questions, you may not receive the answer you need or expect. Likewise, if you use vague questions when researching your topic, you may not find the answers you are seeking or you may use the wrong research techniques or sources to find information. When you ask clear, specific questions, you do more effective research, you meet the readers' expectations, and you achieve your purpose. In some cases, these questions may be defined for you, especially if someone asks you to write a report. If the questions aren't defined, spend some time formulating specific questions.

Effective report writers tend to spend more time on macrowriting—big picture—issues (Baker 1994). These writers formulate questions and determine the best way to answer them. Less effective writers spend little time formulating good questions and doing the necessary research. Consider these questions for an analytical report on the health risks of electric and magnetic fields:

Vague          Do electric and magnetic fields cause health problems?

Specific       What are the health risks of exposure to low-strength, low-frequency electric and magnetic fields produced by power lines and cell phones?

The first question is vague because it does not specify the strength, frequency, or origin of the electric and magnetic fields. The second question gives the writer specific information to use when researching the topic.

When you have formulated specific questions, you're ready to determine what primary research techniques and secondary research strategies are appropriate for answering your questions. (For information on research techniques, see Chapter 5.)

## MAKE CONCLUSIONS AND RECOMMENDATIONS BASED ON SOUND RESEARCH

After you have formulated specific questions and researched your topic, you're ready to draw conclusions and make recommendations. For many reports, drawing valid conclusions is relatively simple if you have thoroughly researched your topic and gathered sufficient information or data. If you haven't done adequate research, you may have difficulty drawing sound conclusions or you may draw invalid conclusions. Depending on your report's topic, these invalid conclusions could put you, your organization, or your readers at risk. You have an ethical responsibility to conduct sufficient research to draw valid conclusions. See Tips for Drawing Valid Conclusions.

If you have thoroughly carried out the research plan to this point, you will more easily see the recommendations that the conclusions suggest. For example, if your conclusions indicate that customers are bringing in their cars for service because of faulty ignition systems, the clear course of action would be to send a recall notice to each customer who purchased that model car. The company would then repair the ignition systems at no charge to the customer. This recommendation is probably not the one you would have wanted, but your research results should dictate your recommendation, not your desires for a particular outcome or recommendation. Even if you don't like it, this recommendation is ethical and in the long run will protect you, the company, and most important, the customers who drive the cars.

## TIPS FOR DRAWING VALID CONCLUSIONS

- **When examining the results of your research, look for cause-and-effect relationships.** When you find these relationships, you may be able to draw valid conclusions. Or these relationships may indicate that you need to conduct further research. For example, if you are answering the question, Does drinking eight ounces of skim milk increase weight loss when combined with exercise? you may find that women who included six ounces of low-fat yogurt, but didn't drink skim milk, lost the same amount of weight as women who drank milk. You might assume that the relationship between dairy products—not only skim milk—and weight loss is an important cause-and-effect relationship.

- **Be wary of results that seem to point to the same conclusions.** In most projects, you want more than one or two results that point to the same conclusion. You typically need more evidence than only one or two results to draw a valid conclusion. Let's consider the question about skim milk and weight loss: In a six-month study of 150 women, you find women who drank milk and exercised lost an average of 10 pounds or more and women who did not drink milk lost an average of four pounds. Both groups performed 30 minutes of aerobic exercise each day. With these results, you can reasonably conclude that drinking skim milk, when combined with exercise, may cause women to lose more weight.

- **Watch for areas where you have used illogical or unsupported arguments.** For example, you may find that 10 percent of the study participants did indoor cycling for their 30 minutes of aerobic exercise and these participants lost a larger amount of weight. You might, then, conclude that indoor cycling when combined with drinking eight ounces of skim milk causes women to lose more weight. This conclusion would be invalid because not all the women included indoor cycling in their exercise routine. These women may have lost the same amount of weight if they had used other forms of aerobic exercise.

## THE CONVENTIONAL SECTIONS OF FORMAL REPORTS

When you have drawn your conclusions and determined the recommendations you will make (if required), you're ready to write the report. Unlike informal reports, most formal reports have common conventional sections and front and back matter (see Figure 15.3). This discussion presents guidelines for using the conventional sections of formal reports. We begin with the conventional sections because, even though your readers will see the front matter before the body, you write the body of the report before you can prepare the front matter.

**FIGURE 15.3**

## Conventional Sections and Front and Back Matter of Formal Reports

| Front Matter | Conventional Sections | Back (End) Matter |
|---|---|---|
| Letter of Transmittal<br>Cover<br>Title Page<br>Table of Contents<br>List of Illustrations<br>Executive Summary<br>  (or Abstract) | Introduction<br>Methods<br>Results<br>Conclusions<br>Recommendations | Works Cited or List of References<br>Glossary<br>List of Abbreviations or<br>  Symbols<br>Appendices<br>Index |

The type of your report (information, analytical, recommendation) determines what sections you will include. For example, an information report would not include a recommendations section. The questions in Figure 15.4 will help you decide what sections to include.

## Introduction

The *introduction* prepares the reader for the information presented in the report. The introduction
- identifies the purpose of the report
- identifies the topic of the report
- indicates how the report affects or relates to readers
- presents background information
- presents an overview of the report

The sample document in Figure 15.26 presents an effective introduction to a formal report from a telecommunications company. In the first paragraph, the writer introduces the general topic of the report: changing procedures in the proposal centers to improve productivity. The first paragraph also tells how the report affects the reader—the regional manager overseeing the proposal center. The first and second paragraphs give the reader background about the need to increase productivity without increasing costs. The third paragraph states the specific topic and purpose of the report: to evaluate three options for improving productivity. In paragraph four, the writer informs the reader that he will recommend one

- **State clearly the topic of the report.** If a proposal or progress report has preceded the report, you can most likely "cut and paste" the information on the topic directly from one of those documents.
- **State the purpose of your report.** Clearly state the purpose of the report, not the purpose of the project. For example, you might write, "In this report, we recommend the most cost-effective option for increasing our productivity without sacrificing quality and client satisfaction."
- **Identify how the report affects or relates to the readers (optional).** In the introduction, you may want to explain why readers should read the report.
- **Present the background that readers need to understand the report.** If other researchers have examined your research question, include a review of the current research to demonstrate that you have done your homework. Readers are more likely to accept your conclusions and recommendations if they know you have looked at other research on your topic. For some topics, little, if any, research is available; if that is the case, tell your readers.
- **Present an overview of the report.** Tell readers what follows in the report.

of these options later in the report. The introduction doesn't include the conclusions and recommendation. Those appear in an executive summary. The introduction also tells the reader what follows in the report. To help you write an effective introduction, follow the Tips for Writing the Introduction.

## Methods

The *methods* section answers the question, How did I do the research or conduct the study? Readers want to know exactly how you gathered your information. Some readers may be as interested in your methodology as in your results, so use specific, detailed language when describing your methodology. If readers will duplicate your methods, use language specific enough for others to reproduce your research methods.

Figure 15.27 illustrates a report with a methods section where the writers use specific language to describe their procedures. As you write your methods section, follow these tips. This report in Figure 15.27 was prepared for the U.S. Department of Energy by scientists at the Oak Ridge National Laboratory in Tennessee. The report presents the results of a

## FIGURE 15.4

**Questions Readers May Ask When Reading the Conventional Sections of a Formal Report**

| Section | Questions Readers May Ask |
|---|---|
| Introduction | • What is the topic of the report?<br>• What is the purpose of the report?<br>• How does the report affect me and/or my organization?<br>• What is the background of the report?<br>• Have others researched similar topics? If so, how does that research relate to this report?<br>• What follows the report? |
| Methods | • How did you conduct the research?<br>• How did you gather the information that led to your conclusions and/or recommendations?<br>• If you conducted an experiment or study, how did you design it? |
| Results | • What did you find out? |
| Conclusions | • What do the results mean? What do they tell you? |
| Recommendations (optional) | • Based on the results and the conclusions, what do you recommend? What should be done? |

study of macroinvertebrates and fish in streams near two oil retention ponds. This methods section includes specific references to the procedures used to collect water samples, and to identify and quantify benthic macroinvertebrates.

## Results

**Results** are the data you obtained from your research. The results section answers the question, What did you find out? When writing this section, only present the results; you will interpret them in the conclusions section. Readers are more likely to understand your logic and your conclusions if you present all the results before you present your interpretations. If you mix the results with the interpretations, you may confuse readers.

- **Tell your readers how you gathered your information.** Explain how you did the research or conducted the study. By giving readers this information, you add credibility to your results, conclusions, and recommendations.
- **Use clear, specific language.** If you use vague language, readers may think you didn't use clearly defined methods, and therefore, your results or conclusions may be invalid. Without specific language, readers can't duplicate your methods.

TIPS **FOR WRITING THE RESULTS SECTION**

- **Include only the results.** In the results section, report only the results—the data that you gathered. Interpret the results in the report's conclusions section.
- **Use a standard pattern of organization to arrange the results.** These patterns will help you present your results in an organized, logical manner.
- **Use graphics when appropriate.** If you have numerical data, use graphics such as tables, line graphs, or bar graphs to present the data. Be sure to introduce and explain any graphics you use.

The arrangement of a results section varies with the report's topic and purpose. For some reports, the results section may be a series of paragraphs and supporting graphics, such as tables and graphs. If you use a variety of methods in your research, organize the results section around those methods. You then structure your discussion of the results in the order in which you present the methods. For example, in the report presented in Figure 15.27, the writers first discuss the methodology for sampling benthic macroinvertebrates and then for sampling fish. In the results section, they discuss the results of the benthic macroinvertebrates sampling first. For other reports, you may use one of the standard organizational patterns for your results section (see Chapter 6). As you write the results section, follow the Tips for Writing the Results Section and study the results sections in the sample reports at the end of this chapter.

## Conclusions

The *conclusions* section answers the question, What do the results mean? In some reports, this section is titled Discussion of the Results. It interprets and explains the significance of the results. The conclusions and the recommendations sections are often the most important sections of a report.

When you have conducted sound research and adequately analyzed your results, you can state your conclusions clearly and confidently. To convey this confidence, avoid words and phrases that could undermine readers' confidence in your conclusions. For example, readers would think that the conclusion below indicates the writers lack confidence in their conclusion or perhaps the writers have not conducted sound research:

<table>
<tr>
<td>Lack of confidence</td>
<td>**We** believe that Option 1 will maintain current expense levels and may build on current expertise to reduce the time for writing the repurposed text. However, **we** think that Option 1 does not appreciably improve the quality of the text and could disrupt the work group.</td>
</tr>
</table>

The subject of both sentences in this conclusion is "we": We believe and we think. When the sentences focus on the options, not on the writers, the conclusions are more direct and confident (subjects appear in bold):

<table>
<tr>
<td>Confident</td>
<td>**Option 1** maintains current expense levels and builds on current expertise to reduce the time for writing the repurposed text. However, **Option 1** does not appreciably improve the quality of the text and could disrupt the work group.</td>
</tr>
</table>

When writing the conclusions section, you may discover that the results are inconclusive, that none of the options studied meet the criteria, or that the methodology was poor. The conclusions won't always fit into the neat categories that you expected. Nevertheless, you have an ethical responsibility to report clearly what the results mean, even when the conclusions are not what you or your readers expect or want. The sample report in Figure 15.26 includes a conclusions section that uses a clear, confident tone.

## Recommendations

The *recommendations* section answers the question, Based on the results and the conclusions, what do you recommend? In this section, you recommend a course of action (or perhaps, inaction) based on the results and the conclusions. The recommendations section may be shorter than the conclusions or results section. Some writers combine the recommendations and conclusions sections.

- **State the recommendations in clear, direct language.** Tell your readers what specific course of action you recommend. Even if your readers may not expect or may resist your recommendations, state them directly.
- **Make sure your recommendations clearly follow the conclusions and results.** If your readers have closely read your conclusions, they will understand why you are recommending a particular course of action.
- **Eliminate unnecessary explanations of the recommendations.** If you have drawn well-supported conclusions, the conclusions section will support and explain your recommendations. You don't need to restate the conclusions in the recommendations section.

The recommendations may not be what you or your readers expect. In one report, you might recommend more than one option if the results warrant such a recommendation; or, if none of the options meet the criteria set up in the research, you may be unable to make a recommendation. In another report, you might be able to make recommendations. In yet another report, you might recommend further research or a revised study because your results were inconclusive. Your readers may not expect such recommendations; but you have a responsibility to give them honest, well-supported recommendations.

The sample report in Figure 15.26 includes a recommendations section where the writer confidently states the recommendations in one sentence, offering little explanation because the recommendations clearly follow from the results and conclusions. The sample report in Figure 15.27 presents the recommendations section from the research report prepared for the Department of Energy. The writers recommend more studies and explain the issues the studies should address. See the Tips for Writing the Recommendations Section.

##  PREPARING THE FRONT MATTER

*Front matter* consists of the reference aids that come before the body of a document. Front matter has these primary purposes:
- To help readers locate information in the document. For example, the table of contents and list of illustrations help readers find information.

- To help readers decide whether they want to read the document. For example, the executive summary, abstract, and table of contents give readers the information they need to decide if the document has information they need or want to read.
- To summarize the document when readers may not have time to read the entire document. The executive summary may replace the document for executives and managers.

As you plan your report, you'll determine the type of front matter that best meets your purpose and your readers' needs. You may also find that your organization has standard formats and style guidelines, or even printed forms, for some front matter. Before preparing the front matter, find out if your organization has guidelines or templates for the front matter. If it does, follow those guidelines or use those templates. If it doesn't, find copies of successful reports written by others in your organization. These reports will show you how other employees formatted the front matter of similar reports and might reveal some of your organization's unwritten preferences. If your organization doesn't have guidelines or examples of front matter, you may choose the format.

Front matter consists of the following elements:
- Letter of Transmittal
- Cover
- Title Page
- Table of Contents
- List of Illustrations
- Abstract and Executive Summary

## Letter of Transmittal

The *letter of transmittal*—sometimes called a cover letter—has the following objectives:
- to summarize the subject and purpose of the document
- to identify the reason for preparing the document
- to emphasize information in the document of special interest to the readers, such as methods, conclusions, recommendations, or changes from the proposal or original plan for the document

As you write your letter of transmittal, follow the organization presented in the Tips for Writing the Letter of Transmittal. The letter of transmittal is the first part of your document that readers will see. Therefore, it should create a good impression of you and your organization. Attach the letter of transmittal to the document's cover, place it inside the cover before the title page, or send it separately. If you decide to send the letter separately, be sure it tells readers when you or your organization plan to send the document itself. Figure 15.5 shows a letter of transmittal written by a technical communications student. She prepared the report mentioned in the letter for the Louisiana Parks and Wildlife Department.

## Cover

The document's *cover* serves three purposes: (1) protect the pages, (2) identify the document, and (3) create a positive impression of the document (and possibly the organization).

Before you design a cover, check to see whether your organization has a standard cover design. If it does, use that design. The cover should spark readers' interest or establish a certain tone. For example, if you're preparing a proposal cover to customize telecommunications functions for a company, you might customize the cover by using the company's colors or displaying a picture of the company headquarters.

Use any of these methods to print the cover and attach it to the document:
- Print or copy the cover on card stock. Card stock can damage some printers, so you may want to print the cover on printer paper and then copy it onto card stock.
- Put a clear piece of plastic over the cover.
- Laminate the cover for durability and a more professional appearance.
- Use a binder with a clear pocket on the front to hold your report cover. For this type of binder, use printer paper.

### TIPS FOR WRITING THE LETTER OF TRANSMITTAL

**In the first paragraph ...**
- State the title or subject of the document.
- State the reason for preparing the document. For example, the reason might be to complete a class assignment, to respond to a request from a manager or client, or to complete a research project.

**In the middle paragraph(s) ...**
- State the purpose of the document. (Some writers include the purpose in the first paragraph.)
- Summarize your conclusions and recommendations.
- *Optional:* Include and explain any changes to your work or the document since you last corresponded with the readers.

**In the final paragraph ...**
- Offer to answer readers' questions about the document or its contents.
- *Optional:* Thank any person, group, or organization that helped you prepare the document.

FIGURE 15.5

**Letter of Transmittal**

**Louisiana State University**
Department of Biological Sciences
Choppin Hall
Baton Rouge, LA 70805

April 23, 2012

Dr. Louis Rowland
Director
Department of Wildlife and Fisheries
2000 Quail Drive
Baton Rouge, LA 70808

Re: Report on Black-Bellied Plover

Dear Dr. Rowland:

The first paragraph includes the title, the occasion, and the purpose of the document.

I am pleased to submit the accompanying report, "Black-Bellied Plover Habitat in Louisiana," in response to your request. The report examines black-bellied plover habitat in Louisiana as part of a program to prevent this species from becoming endangered.

The second paragraph includes the conclusion, the recommendation, and information that especially interests the reader.

For this report, I examined the literature about previous sightings of black-bellied plover in Louisiana and analyzed satellite images of those sighting locations. Based on this information, I have concluded that black-bellied plovers prefer pasture and shrub land. To protect the remaining black-bellied plover population, we must conserve and monitor the locations where the bird has been most frequently sighted.

In the third paragraph, the writer offers to answer questions.

If you have any questions, please call me at (225) 555-1234 or email me at dbrown@verizon.net.

Sincerely,

*Danielle Brown*

Danielle Brown
Research Assistant

These printing and binding options are inexpensive and give reports a professional appearance. Spiral or three-ring binders secure the document's pages more professionally than a binder clip or a file folder.

Most covers include some or all of this information:
- **Document title**
- **Your name and position** (If you are preparing a document for someone outside your organization, do not include your name or position on the cover. For some internal documents, you may also exclude this information. Look at other internal documents to determine whether the cover should include the writer's name and position.)
- **Your organization's name and/or logo**
- **Name of the organization or client for whom you prepared the document** (For documents for the general public, exclude this information.)
- **Date that you submitted the document to its intended readers.**

## ETHICS NOTE

### Present Honest, Well-Supported Recommendations

You have a responsibility to present honest, well-supported recommendations even if they are not what readers want to hear or what they expect. You may know, for example, that your readers want you to recommend a particular option because it will make your organization look good or they may want you to recommend the cheapest solution even if your research does not support that outcome. Instead, you should only recommend what your research and results can support.

You may be tempted to set up your research in a way that will lead you to the outcome your organization or your readers expect. This approach is dishonest; it could put you or your organization at risk for legal action. At worst, it could endanger a consumer.

As you set up your research and make your recommendations, ask yourself these questions:
- Is it legal?
- Is it consistent with company policy and my professional code of conduct?
- Am I doing the right thing?
- Am I acting in the best interests of all involved?
- How will it appear to others? Am I willing to take responsibility publicly and privately?
- Will it violate anyone's rights?

FIGURE 15.6

**Cover for a Student Report**

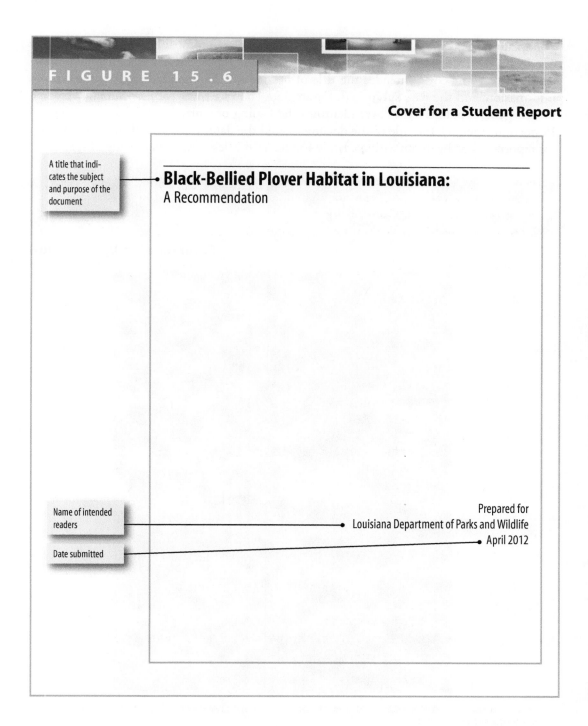

A title that indicates the subject and purpose of the document

# Black-Bellied Plover Habitat in Louisiana:
A Recommendation

Name of intended readers

Date submitted

Prepared for
Louisiana Department of Parks and Wildlife
April 2012

For documents prepared for your university courses, you will probably use a format like the one in Figure 15.6. This cover is for Danielle Brown's report for her technical communications class. The cover includes the title of her report, the intended readers, the writer's information, and the date submitted. Figure 15.7 shows a cover for a document prepared for the general public. This cover identifies the issuing organization (U.S. Environmental Protection Agency), the title of the document, and the date. This type of cover is common for reports issued by organizations, while Figure 15.6 is less common outside of school.

**FIGURE 15.7**

**Cover for a Workplace Report**

Source: Downloaded from the World Wide Web: http://cfpub.epa.gov/ncea/cfm/recordisplay.cfm?deid=190806. Environmental Protection Agency, *EPA's Report on the Environment 2008*

## Title Page

Some title pages look exactly like the cover; some repeat only certain parts of the cover; and some are completely different from the cover, having few, if any, graphics or color like the one in Figure 15.8. *Title pages* contain some or all of the following information:

- document title
- name of the organization or client for whom you prepared the document
- your name and position
- your organization's name and/or logo
- date you submitted the document to its intended readers

Many companies have a standardized format for title pages. These standardized formats may call for more information than generally appears on a title page. Figure 15.9 illustrates a title page from the U.S. Environmental Protection Agency's 2008 report on the environment. This title page lists not only the title of the report, but also the document number, a disclaimer, and information about the organization. Like many title pages in the workplace, this title page does not identify the writer's names or the names of the intended readers.

## Table of Contents

The *table of contents* identifies what is included in the document and helps readers locate specific sections of the document. An effective table of contents lists more than only the first-level headings. (If your document has only one level of headings, consider subdividing some sections to help readers locate information. Be sure to follow the guidelines for outlining presented in Chapter 6.) Figure 15.10 shows a table of contents that contains only first-level headings that convey no specific information about the document's subject matter. Readers curious about the Discussion section, for example, would have to search more than 15 pages to find a particular subsection or topic. To prepare an effective table of contents, follow the Tips for Preparing a Table of Contents.

Some word-processing software has a feature that generates a table of contents after you have typed your document. This same function can generate the list of illustrations (discussed in the next section). These functions can save you time and help you use the exact wording that appears in the body of the document.

FIGURE 15.8

Title Page from a Student Report

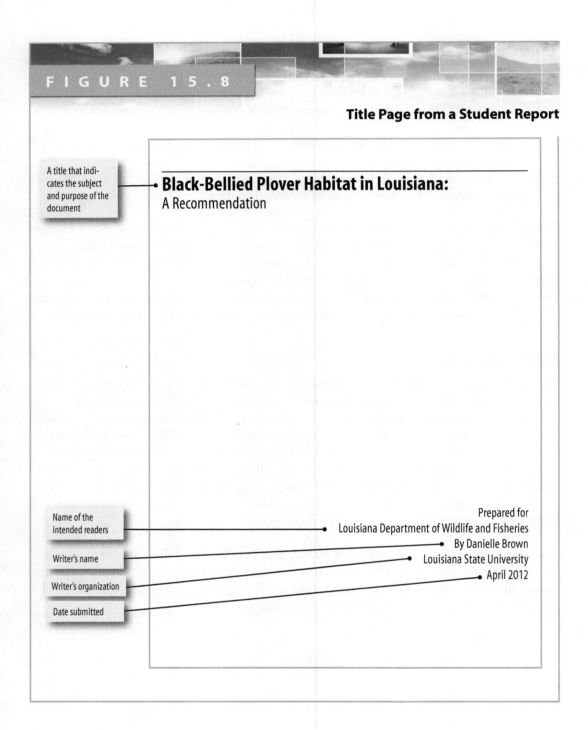

A title that indicates the subject and purpose of the document

**Black-Bellied Plover Habitat in Louisiana:**
A Recommendation

Prepared for
Louisiana Department of Wildlife and Fisheries
By Danielle Brown
Louisiana State University
April 2012

Name of the intended readers

Writer's name

Writer's organization

Date submitted

FIGURE 15.9

## Title Page from a Workplace Report

Name of the writer's organization

Document number

Date submitted

Title of the Document

Disclaimer

The writers do not include their names.

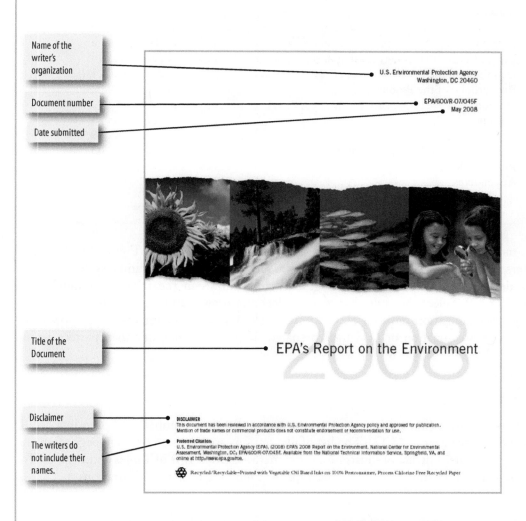

U.S. Environmental Protection Agency
Washington, DC 20460

EPA/600/R-07/045F
May 2008

2008

EPA's Report on the Environment

**DISCLAIMER**
This document has been reviewed in accordance with U.S. Environmental Protection Agency policy and approved for publication. Mention of trade names or commercial products does not constitute endorsement or recommendation for use.

**Preferred Citation:**
U.S. Environmental Protection Agency (EPA). (2008) EPA's 2008 Report on the Environment. National Center for Environmental Assessment, Washington, DC; EPA/600/R-07/045F. Available from the National Technical Information Service, Springfield, VA, and online at http://www.epa.gov/roe.

Recycled/Recyclable–Printed with Vegetable Oil Based Inks on 100% Postconsumer, Process Chlorine Free Recycled Paper

Source: Downloaded from the World Wide Web: http://cfpub.epa.gov/ncea/cfm/recordisplay.cfm?deid=190806. Environmental Protection Agency, *EPA's Report on the Environment 2008.*

**Uninformative Table of Contents**

**Contents**

The most commonly used style for the table of contents appears in Figure 15.11. Many writers and organizations, especially in the sciences, prefer a decimal system, which adds decimal numbers to the headings and subheadings in the table of contents (see Figure 15.12). Select the style that your readers and organization expect. If your readers and your organization have no expectations, look at similar documents to see how others in your organization or field have prepared the table of contents; then pattern yours accordingly.

## List of Illustrations

If you use graphics (illustrations) in your document, list their numbers and titles in a list of illustrations (see Figure 15.13). The list of illustrations appears on a separate page after the table of contents. The list of illustrations is sometimes titled List of Tables and Figures. To prepare a list of illustrations, follow the Tips for Preparing a List of Illustrations.

## Abstract and Executive Summary

The abstract and executive summary give an overview of the document's facts, results, conclusions, and recommendations. Without having to read the entire document, readers

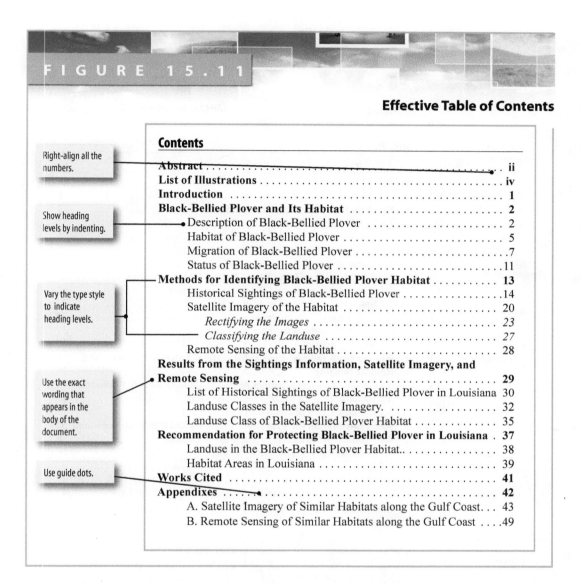

**FIGURE 15.11**

**Effective Table of Contents**

## Contents

Right-align all the numbers.

Show heading levels by indenting.

Vary the type style to indicate heading levels.

Use the exact wording that appears in the body of the document.

Use guide dots.

can use the information in these sections to decide whether they need to read the document. The abstract and executive summary appear before the body of the document. In this section, you will learn how to write an informative abstract, a descriptive abstract, and an executive summary.

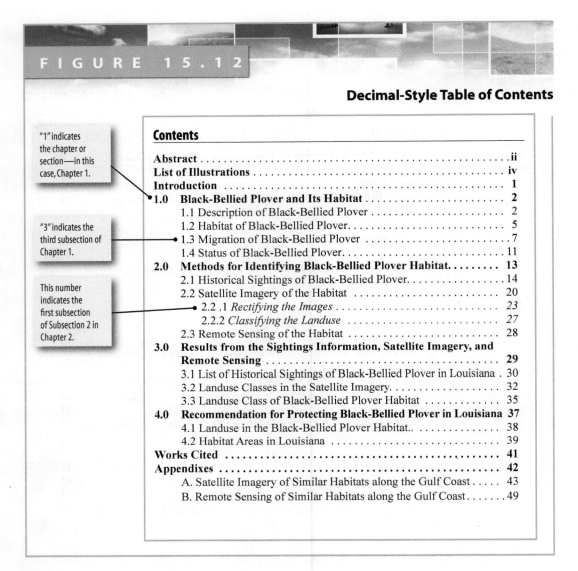

**FIGURE 15.12**

**Decimal-Style Table of Contents**

"1" indicates the chapter or section—in this case, Chapter 1.

"3" indicates the third subsection of Chapter 1.

This number indicates the first subsection of Subsection 2 in Chapter 2.

## Contents

## Writing Informative Abstracts

*Informative abstracts* are primarily for readers knowledgeable about the document's content. These abstracts must stand independent of the document. When writing an informative abstract, follow the Tips for Writing Informative Abstracts.

## TIPS FOR PREPARING A TABLE OF CONTENTS

- **Use the exact wording that appears in the headings and subheadings in the body of the document.** If the heading reads Habitat of Black-Bellied Plover, the wording in the table of contents should be the same, not a shortened version such as Habitat.
- **Show the heading levels by varying the style and indentation (see Figure 15.11).** By consistently varying the type style and indentation, you help readers locate first-level headings (or major sections). Then readers can locate related subheads.
- **List only the first three levels of headings if your document has more than three levels.** If you include four or more levels, the table of contents will be hard to read.
- **Use guide dots (. . . .), sometimes called dot leaders, to connect the headings and the page numbers (see Figure 15.11).** Some organizations use other graphic elements to help readers find the related page number of a heading in the table of contents. For example, some organizations will place lines above and below each table of contents entry, so readers can see the entry and corresponding page number.
- **Include the list of illustrations, abstract and/or executive summary, and other front matter.** Do not list the cover, title page, or letter of transmittal in the table of contents.
- **Use lowercase Roman numerals (i, ii, iii, etc.) for the page numbers of the list of illustrations, abstract, executive summary, and other front matter.**

## FIGURE 15.13

### List of Illustrations

**Illustrations**

Guide dots

## TIPS FOR PREPARING A LIST OF ILLUSTRATIONS

- **If you used separate numbering sequences for tables and figures, separate the tables from the figures in the list of illustrations.** You can title the entire list List of Illustrations or Illustrations.
- **If you used only one numbering sequence, title the list Illustrations or List of Illustrations.** If your document contains only tables, use List of Tables or Tables. If your document contains only figures, use List of Figures or Figures.
- **Use the exact wording and number that appears with the graphic.** If the graphic number and title is Figure 3.1. Migration Path of Black-Bellied Plover, the wording in the list of illustrations should match. Do not use a shortened version, such as Figure 3.1. Migration Path or Migration Path.
- **Use guide dots, sometimes called dot leaders, to connect the title of the graphic and the page number (see Figure 15.13).**

## TIPS FOR WRITING INFORMATIVE ABSTRACTS

- **Identify the document.** Because an informative abstract must stand independent of the document, writing Abstract above the abstract text will not give readers enough information. Instead, include the document title, your name, and perhaps the name of your organization.
- **State the topic and purpose of the document.** Don't assume that readers know what the document addresses. Instead, clearly state the topic and the purpose. With this information, readers can decide whether your document contains information they need or want to read.
- **Conclude with the key results, conclusions, or recommendations.** Because an informative abstract must be able to stand alone, include the key results, conclusions, or recommendations of your research or document. Exclude all examples and details. Include your methods only if they are new, unique, or vital to understanding your results, conclusions, or recommendations.

Generally, abstracts are one paragraph long. Figure 15.14 presents an informative abstract of the student report on the habitat of the black-bellied plover. The abstract identifies the report's title and author, and states the objective of the report in the first two sentences. It concludes with the key results of the writer's research and a recommendation. You can also find examples of informative abstracts in some professional journals. Many journals limit abstracts to 100–200 words.

## Writing Descriptive Abstracts

**Descriptive abstracts** are not a substitute for the document itself. Instead of reporting key results, conclusions, and recommendations, a descriptive abstract includes the major topics of the document. Its purpose is to help readers decide whether they want to read the document. Figure 15.15 presents a descriptive abstract for the student report on the habitat of the black-bellied plover.

## Writing Executive Summaries

**Executive summaries** present the conclusions and recommendations of a document. An executive summary provides information on which readers need to act or to make a decision. Many readers, such as decision makers, will only read the executive summary while other

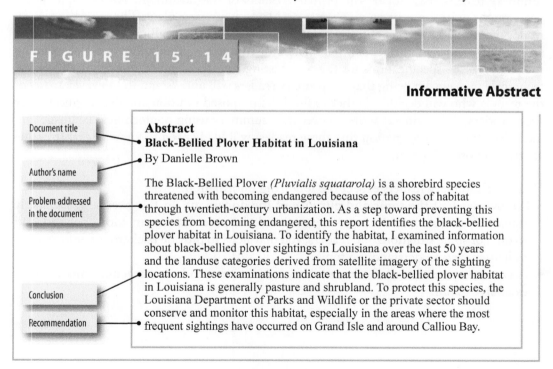

**FIGURE 15.14**

**Informative Abstract**

Document title →

Author's name →

Problem addressed in the document →

Conclusion →

Recommendation →

**Abstract**
**Black-Bellied Plover Habitat in Louisiana**
By Danielle Brown

The Black-Bellied Plover *(Pluvialis squatarola)* is a shorebird species threatened with becoming endangered because of the loss of habitat through twentieth-century urbanization. As a step toward preventing this species from becoming endangered, this report identifies the black-bellied plover habitat in Louisiana. To identify the habitat, I examined information about black-bellied plover sightings in Louisiana over the last 50 years and the landuse categories derived from satellite imagery of the sighting locations. These examinations indicate that the black-bellied plover habitat in Louisiana is generally pasture and shrubland. To protect this species, the Louisiana Department of Parks and Wildlife or the private sector should conserve and monitor this habitat, especially in the areas where the most frequent sightings have occurred on Grand Isle and around Calliou Bay.

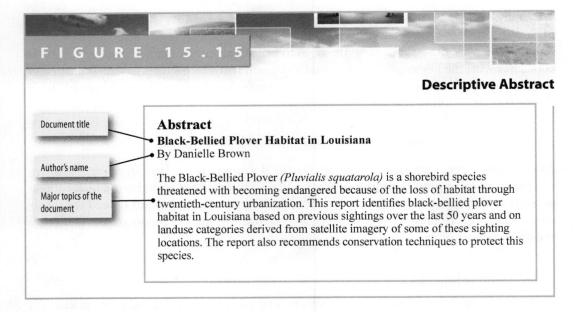

FIGURE 15.15

**Descriptive Abstract**

Document title

Author's name

Major topics of the document

**Abstract**
**Black-Bellied Plover Habitat in Louisiana**
By Danielle Brown

The Black-Bellied Plover *(Pluvialis squatarola)* is a shorebird species threatened with becoming endangered because of the loss of habitat through twentieth-century urbanization. This report identifies black-bellied plover habitat in Louisiana based on previous sightings over the last 50 years and on landuse categories derived from satellite imagery of some of these sighting locations. The report also recommends conservation techniques to protect this species.

readers may bypass the executive summary and read the body of your document. Executive summary readers may not be the primary readers of the document. For example, engineers might write a report on pipe stress problems at a power plant. The report's primary readers are other engineers and the plant operations manager—all experts in engineering and power plants. In the report, the writers discuss the methods they used to examine the problem, the specifications for the pipe testing, and the detailed test results. They use technical language, knowing that the primary readers will understand it. However, many of the readers who will decide whether to fund the proposed solution are non-engineers. For these readers, the engineers write an executive summary using nontechnical language and including only the information that these readers will likely need to knowledgeably evaluate the proposed solution.

Executive summary readers expect the following information:
- **An overview of the topic and purpose of the document**. In this overview, succinctly state the topic, such as the problem addressed, the procedure or situation analyzed, and so on. For some situations and readers, you may need to provide background information to help readers understand the topic.
- **A concise statement of the key results, conclusions, and recommendations without excessive detail.**

Put yourself in the readers' shoes and try to anticipate the questions they may ask as they read the executive summary:

- **What is the document about?** Specifically identify the document's topic and purpose. Readers will be especially interested in how the information directly affects them, their employees, their department, or their organization. They also will be interested in any costs related to the conclusions and recommendations.
- **How will the results, conclusions, and recommendations affect the department, employees, organization, and others?** Readers will be especially interested in costs and savings. Readers of executive summaries are less interested in details and evidence that support the findings than they are in the information that will help them make a decision or implement recommendations.
- **What are the key results, conclusions, or recommendations?** If you know that readers will understand the document's topic, include your key results. Such readers may expect you to summarize the significant data concerning the results. These readers will use this data to make decisions, not to conduct further studies. Some readers, in contrast, may not be experts in your field or may not want to read the results. For these readers, leave out the results and present only conclusions and recommendations. Such readers are interested in your recommendations based on your analysis or research—even if your recommendation is simply to study a situation or problem further or to "wait and see." The executive summary presented in Figure 15.16 focuses effectively on the conclusions and recommendations.

##  PREPARING THE BACK MATTER

*Back matter (or end)* appears after the body of a document. Back matter in technical documents generally includes the following:

- Works Cited or List of References
- Glossary
- List of Abbreviations or Symbols
- Appendices
- Index

## Works Cited or List of References

If you cite the works of others in your document, include a works cited list or a list of references after the body of your document. You might use MLA, APA, CSE, or a company-approved style of documentation. For information about documenting sources, see Appendix A.

FIGURE 15.16

## Executive Summary Focusing on Conclusions and Recommendations

Document title

**Executive Summary**
**Recommendations for Improving the Technical Communications Computer Lab**

Overview

The Technical Communications Computer Lab has outdated equipment. Specifically, the lab has 60 outdated personal computers. The personal computers have 14-inch, low-resolution monitors. These computers cannot support the latest version of Windows, graphics, or desktop publishing software. Although the lab does have 12 personal computers capable of running the latest version of Windows, faculty members cannot conduct classroom activities with only 12 computers. Because of our outdated computer equipment, many faculty members are not requiring their students to use computers to create their technical communications documents and are, therefore, not adequately preparing their students for the workplace.

We considered three options to deal with this problem:
1. Close the lab and require students to use their own personal computers and the open access labs in the library.
2. Request that the university spend $400,000 during the next fiscal year to upgrade all the personal computers and purchase current versions of Windows and desktop publishing software. With this request, the student fees would remain at the current level of $70 per technical communications class.
3. Raise the sudent fees to $98 per student in the next three fiscal years. With this fee, we can update 20 computers and buy Windows, graphics, and desktop publishing software for the computers the first year, and do the same for the remaining 20 computers the second year, and the final 20 computers the third year.

Conclusions and recommendations

We recommend the second solution. However, if the university will not provide the $400,000, then we recommend the third solution. We do not recommend the first solution because the technical communications faculty and students need a lab where they can hold class; the open-access labs are not set up for faculty members to conduct class. The second and third solutions would provide the faculty with a place to conduct class and students with up-to-date computers and software that they will encounter in the workplace.

## TIPS FOR WRITING THE EXECUTIVE SUMMARY

- **Include the title of your document.** Some writers in the workplace also include a subhead of Executive Summary with the title. Identify the summary in this way if the executive summary will circulate separately from the document.
- **Identify the topic and purpose of the document.** Include how the topic and purpose directly affect the readers, their employees, their department, or their organization.
- **Focus on the conclusions and recommendations, not on the details of your findings.** Exclude the details and evidence that support your conclusions. Include only information that helps readers make a decision or implement your recommendations.
- **Use nontechnical language.** Many executive summary readers may not be experts in your field. Even if the document is for technical readers, write the summary for decision makers who may not know the technical language of your field.
- **Give readers only the information they need to make a decision.** Eliminate, for example, information about your methods or about the theories behind your project.

## TIPS FOR CREATING A GLOSSARY

- **In the body of the document, identify all words that appear in the glossary.** Put these words in italic or boldface type, or place an asterisk next to them. Use the same system of marking throughout the document and explain to readers what you are doing—perhaps in the introduction or in a footnote accompanying the first glossary word that appears in the text. This footnote will explain that terms defined in the glossary appear in the body of the text in, for example, boldface italic type: This and all other terms appearing in boldface italic type are defined in the Glossary, which begins on page 77.
- **Define all terms that readers may not understand.** In the definition, use words that readers will understand and include cross references to other closely related terms defined in the glossary (see Figure 15.17).
- **List the glossary entries in alphabetical order.** Alphabetical order helps readers locate words.
- **Use phrases or clauses, not sentences, for the primary definitions.** After the primary definition, use sentences for secondary definitions. If you use words defined in the glossary, cross reference those words. For example, look at the definition of *continuous probability distribution* in Figure 15.17. In this definition, the writer uses *probability distribution*, which is also in the glossary; so the writer tells the reader to See probability distribution.
- **Include the glossary and its first page number in the table of contents.**

## Glossary

A *glossary* is an alphabetical list of specialized words unfamiliar to some readers and their definitions. Effective glossaries meet the needs of readers with different levels of expertise. While glossaries generally appear after the body of the document, they can appear immediately following the table of contents or list of illustrations. Figure 15.17 shows part of a glossary from a document on software used for forecasting. To create an effective glossary, follow the Tips for Creating a Glossary.

## List of Abbreviations or Symbols

If your document contains many abbreviations or symbols, include a list explaining their meaning (see Figure 15.18). This list usually appears at the end of a document before the appendix, although some writers put it in the front matter after the table of contents and list of illustrations. Follow the Tips for Creating a List of Abbreviations or Symbols.

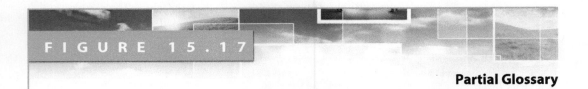

**FIGURE 15.17**

**Partial Glossary**

**Glossary**

**Assumption**
> An estimated value or input to a spreadsheet model.

**CDF**
> Cumulative distribution function representing the probability that a variable will fall at or below a given value.

**Certainty level**
> The percentage of values in the certainty range compared to the number of values in the entire range.

**Continuous probability distribution**
> A probability distribution that describes a set of uninterrupted values over a range. (See **Probability distribution**)

**Discrete probability distribution**
> A probability distribution that describes distinct values with no intermediate values. (See **Probability distribution**)

FIGURE 15.18

**Partial List of Abbreviations**

**Abbreviations**

| | |
|---|---|
| **ESS** | Electronic Still Store. The graphics box over the anchor's shoulder. |
| **NC** | News Conference. |
| **PREPS** | Preparations. Used in story descriptions. |
| **REAX** | Reactions. Used in story descriptions. |
| **SOT** | Sound On Tape. Used in a script to tell the editor where to place the sound on tape. |
| **VO** | Video Only. |

## Appendices

***Appendices (or appendixes)*** appear after the works cited, glossary, or list of symbols. Material in appendices supports information in the body of the document. Appendices contain information that

- is not essential for readers to understand the document
- may interest only a few readers
- would interrupt the flow of the document

An appendix might include maps, large diagrams or other graphics, a sample questionnaire, a transcript of an interview, or other supporting documents. Any of these items should supplement the body of the document. To prepare an effective appendix, follow the Tips for Preparing an Appendix.

## Index

An ***index*** lists terms used in a document and the page number where the terms appear. An index appears after all other items in a document in the back matter. The terms in an appendix appear in alphabetical order.

TAKING IT INTO THE *workplace*

## Smartphones and Protecting Company Information

In the 1990s, the personal computer, technology, and global communication revolutionized how companies conducted daily business and how they distributed information to their employees and to those outside the company. As the use of personal computers and the Web grew, so did the "user's expectation for information availability on or through that machine" and the Web (Foy 1996, 24).

Increasingly readers demand cell phones deliver information and services directly into their hands. For example, professionals must decide how to structure email messages and other documents so that readers can read and navigate them on smartphones. While this concept of providing universal access to information seems alluring to many readers and organizations, the real issue for companies is security. Because employees increasingly use their smartphones to deliver and receive reports and other sensitive information, companies face questions about how to keep confidential information secure and how to protect consumers' privacy rights. For example, many employees use their business phone for personal reasons while some employees use their personal phones for business. Either way, companies face the issue of employees installing and using programs that may open the door for hackers and the possibility of compromising company and client information.

## Assignment

- Locate two or more articles that discuss guidelines that companies should implement to safely manage information (such as reports and email) that employees can retrieve or deliver via their cell phones.
- Write a brief summary of each article and email the summaries to your instructor. Be sure to properly cite the article using APA, MLA, or CSE documentation style.

## TIPS FOR CREATING A LIST OF ABBREVIATIONS OR SYMBOLS

- **List the abbreviations in alphabetical order.** Alphabetical order helps readers locate abbreviations.
- **Use phrases or clauses to explain what the abbreviations or symbols mean.** You can write the words that an abbreviation or symbol represents or you can include other information readers may need to understand the abbreviation or symbol.

## TIPS FOR PREPARING AN APPENDIX

- **At the appropriate place in the body of the document, refer to each appendix.** For instance, if you summarize survey results in the body of the document and include the survey instrument and tabulated results in an appendix, you might write: Sixty-five percent of respondents reported that they used email more frequently than voice mail (see Appendix B for the tabulated results).
- **Put each major item into a separate appendix.** Identify each appendix with a letter or a title: Appendix A, Appendix B, and so on.
- **List each appendix in the table of contents.** If you've titled an appendix, include the complete title in the table of contents.
- **Put essential items in an appendix only when these items are so long or so large that putting them in the body of the document would interrupt the flow of information.** Otherwise, include only nonessential information in the appendix.

 NUMBER THE FRONT AND BACK MATTER CORRECTLY

As you prepare the front and back matter, follow these standards for numbering the pages:
- Use lowercase Roman numerals (i, ii, iii, etc.) for the front matter.
- Use Arabic numerals (1, 2, 3, etc.) for the body and the back matter.
- Put odd numbers on the right pages and even numbers on the left pages.
- Begin the body of the document on a right page, even if doing so means that the facing left page will be blank.
- Do not put a page number on the title page or any blank pages even though you will include them in your page count.

Figure 15.19 shows the page numbering of a formal document. In this document, the writer

- does not put a page number on the title page (even though the title page is actually page i)
- uses lowercase Roman numerals for all front matter
- begins the body on a right page

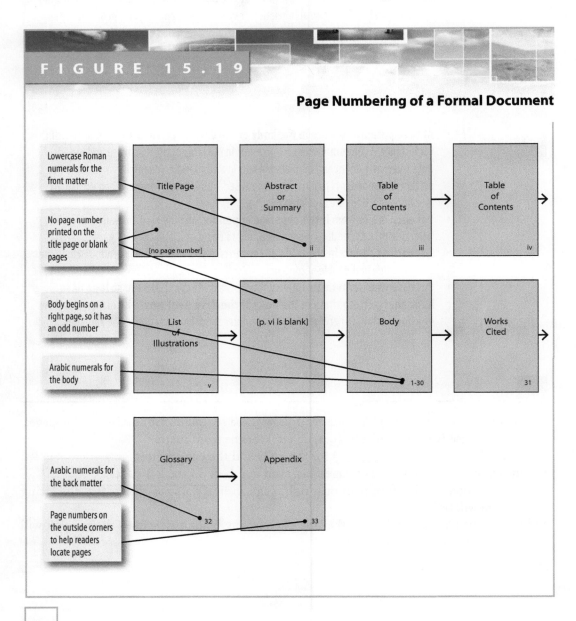

**FIGURE 15.19**

**Page Numbering of a Formal Document**

Lowercase Roman numerals for the front matter

No page number printed on the title page or blank pages

Title Page
[no page number]

Abstract or Summary
ii

Table of Contents
iii

Table of Contents
iv

Body begins on a right page, so it has an odd number

Arabic numerals for the body

List of Illustrations
v

[p. vi is blank]

Body
1-30

Works Cited
31

Arabic numerals for the back matter

Page numbers on the outside corners to help readers locate pages

Glossary
32

Appendix
33

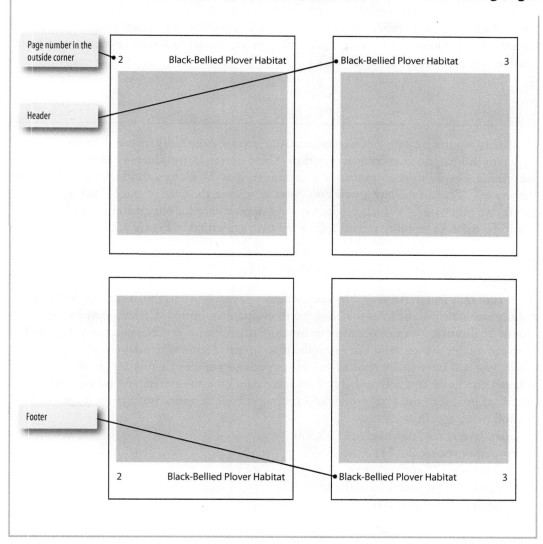

**FIGURE 15.20**

**Positions of Page Numbers and Headers or Footers on Facing Pages**

Page number in the outside corner

2      Black-Bellied Plover Habitat      Black-Bellied Plover Habitat      3

Header

Footer

2      Black-Bellied Plover Habitat      Black-Bellied Plover Habitat      3

You can put page numbers in two effective places on a page: the top or bottom outside corners (see Figure 15.20).
- On the left pages, place the page number in the top or bottom left corner.
- On the right pages, place the page number in the top or bottom right corner.

Page numbers in the outside corners are easier for readers to see as they flip through a document than are page numbers in the center of the top or bottom margins or in the inside corners. You could also place the page number in the header or footer. (For information on headers and footers, see Chapter 10.)

##  FOCUS ON FEASIBILITY REPORTS

Feasibility reports are a type of recommendation report. **Feasibility reports** document a study of two or more options or courses of action. These options are evaluated based on appropriate criteria. Feasibility reports answer questions such as "Which method is best for repairing the tower?" "Should we buy a new computer or update the current one?" "Which product should we purchase?" "Which product is most appropriate for our customers and our location?" To write a feasibility report, follow the plan presented in Figure 15.21.

### Establishing Criteria for Evaluating the Options

To ensure that you make sound recommendations, you must establish criteria. **Criteria** are requirements or benchmarks that you use to evaluate an option. Criteria may be quantitative or qualitative. You can quantify or measure quantitative criteria; you cannot qualify or measure qualitative criteria. For example, if you must decide which laptop to buy for your office, you will have many choices as well as perhaps company guidelines that affect what you can purchase. You will probably have minimum quantitative criteria (sometimes called specifications) for cost, size, speed, and memory. Your quantitative criteria might include the following specifications:
- **Cost**: lowest cost not to exceed $3,500
- **Processor speed**: 2 GHz
- **Display size**: 15 inches
- **Weight**: not to exceed 16 pounds
- **Hard drive size**: 200 GB

Qualitative criteria might be the reputation of the company that produces the laptop or the comfort of the keyboard. You cannot quantify a reputation or comfort.

FIGURE  15.21

**Steps for Completing a Feasibility Study**

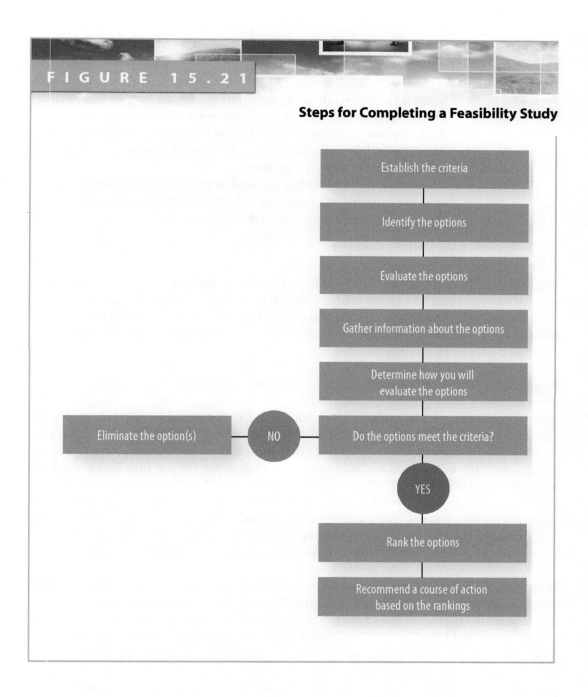

When you set up a feasibility study, you must specifically define the minimum criteria, so you can use those criteria to draw conclusions and recommend a course of action. If you are considering using a qualitative minimum criterion, how will you know if an option meets or exceeds this criterion? If you cannot define how an option will meet a criterion, you should revise or eliminate that criterion.

In setting up any feasibility study that involves cost, consider how you will factor in the other criteria. Cost is generally the overriding criterion. If the lowest cost option meets the minimum criteria, you must select that option unless you have established other overriding criteria. You should consider this situation as you set up your study. For example, you may decide (or your organization may decide) that you can consider criteria other than cost if the cost of the options are within 5 percent of each other. Or you may decide to factor in features that affect cost. Let's consider laptops: Option 1 is the least expensive laptop; however, you will have to pay for shipping and a three-year maintenance package if you recommend this option. Option 2 is the most expensive, but the shipping and the three-year maintenance package are free—making Option 2 the same cost as Option 1. You can then select the higher-priced option because you are factoring in other features that impact.

If someone has asked you to conduct a feasibility study, the criteria may be established for you. For example, if you are buying the laptop to use at your office, your manager may give you minimum criteria, such as a budget and a list of company-approved vendors. If the criteria aren't established for you, establish the criteria by researching your topic; you might interview subject matter experts, administer end-user questionnaires, or read journals and other technical documents related to your topic. For example, to determine the criteria for purchasing the laptop, you might interview people who work in information technology. Review the Tips for Establishing Criteria.

## TIPS FOR IDENTIFYING OPTIONS

- **Make sure you identify all available options.** If you miss an option or leave it out, you may eliminate the option that provides the best course of action. Your readers will assume that you identified all the options available that meet the minimum criteria. Therefore, you have an ethical responsibility to identify every option.
- **Research thoroughly.** Use a variety of primary and secondary research techniques to ensure that you identify all available options. (See Chapter 5 for information on primary and secondary research techniques.)
- **Avoid the temptation to simplify the study by unnecessarily eliminating some options.** You may feel tempted to eliminate options because you are on a tight schedule, you have a heavy workload, or you are unfamiliar with the subject. Remember, you may be eliminating the option that best meets the established criteria. For instance, you may be tempted to purchase a laptop when leasing one may actually cost the company less money in the long term because leasing keeps the hardware more current. You are ethically obligated to look at all the options that meet your criteria before you recommend the option that best meets (and possibly exceeds) your criteria.

## Identifying the Options

Once you have established the criteria, you can determine the options available. *Options* are possible solutions or courses of action. You should look for all options that meet your minimum requirements. If you find that you have too many options, narrow the criteria. Follow the Tips for Identifying Options.

## Evaluating Options

When you have established the criteria and identified the options, you're ready to evaluate them. You will need to gather information to determine how each option measures up to the criteria. You must ensure that you gather the same types of information for each option, so you can evaluate the options equally. Let's again consider the laptops: You might do secondary research by looking at consumer magazines that compare laptops or by talking to people who use each laptop. You might do primary research by going to stores and using the laptops or contacting vendors to see if they have additional features or packages that may exceed your minimum criteria—for example, features that may be incentives available only to corporate buyers.

Once you've gathered the information to evaluate your options, rank the criteria. How will you decide which option most closely meets or exceeds the criteria? You will need a way to eliminate as much subjectivity as possible. Some writers use a ranking system. While a ranking system will not ensure objectivity, it will ensure that you are looking at the same criteria for each option. For example, to evaluate the laptops, you might use a ranking system like that in Figure 15.22. You assign a value from 0–5, with 5 being the highest and 1 being the lowest.

## Drawing Conclusions and Making Sound Recommendations

After you have evaluated your options based on the criteria, you are ready to interpret the results of your evaluation. You may find that the conclusions and, thus, your recommendations are clear cut. However, the conclusions and the recommendation will not be apparent.

Let's look at the laptops in Figure 15.22. With this ranking system, the Micro Express and the Apple Macbook Pro have the same score. How do you decide which option to recommend? You could recommend both. However, because you can only purchase one laptop, this approach does not work. You must recommend only one laptop. You could use cost as the overriding factor; but the difference in cost is insignificant. The Micro Express costs $2,799 and the Apple costs $2,899. When you established your criterion, you determined that if the cost of the options was within $150, you could look at the other criteria to make a recommendation. Figure 15.23 compares these two options based on criteria other than cost. In this comparison, the Apple receives a higher total score. You can then recommend this option even though it has a slightly higher cost. In the workplace, cost is the overriding factor when evaluating options. If the difference in cost is not significant, you may be able to justify purchasing the higher-cost option using other criteria—especially if that option exceeds the minimum criteria. In this situation, you may also be able to use qualitative criteria that cannot be included in the ranking system. However, qualitative criteria generally cannot be the overriding criterion when cost is being considered.

You can present your recommendations in any of the following ways:
- **Recommend one option.** You might recommend that the company purchase the Apple MacBook Pro.
- **Rank order the options.** You might rank the laptops as follows: the Micro Express is the best option, the Apple Macbook Pro is the second-best option, the Dell Inspiron is the third-best option, and the Lenovo and HP Pavilion tie for the fourth-best option.
- **Categorize the options by their rankings based on certain criteria.** You might recommend the Apple as the best value or the Micro Express as the lowest cost.

FIGURE 15.22

**Table Used to Rank Options Based on Criteria (5 Is the Highest Rating)**

| Option | Cost | Processor Speed | Display Size (larger is preferred) | Weight (lighter is preferred) | Hard Drive Size | Total Points |
|---|---|---|---|---|---|---|
| Micro Express IFL9025 | 5 | 4 | 3 | 4 | 4 | 20 |
| Lenovo ThinkPad T61p | 2 | 4 | 3 | 5 | 1 | 15 |
| HP Pavilion HDX | 1 | 3 | 5 | 1 | 5 | 15 |
| Dell Inspiron 1720 | 3 | 3 | 4 | 2 | 4 | 16 |
| Apple Macbook Pro | 4 | 5 | 4 | 4 | 3 | 20 |

FIGURE 15.23

**Using Criteria Other Than Cost to Evaluate Two Closely Ranked Options**

| Option | Processor Speed | Display Size (larger is preferred) | Weight (lighter is preferred) | Hard Drive Size | Total Points |
|---|---|---|---|---|---|
| Micro Express IFL9025 | 4 | 3 | 4 | 4 | 15 |
| Apple Macbook Pro | 5 | 4 | 4 | 3 | 16 |

**FIGURE 15.24**

**Comparing by Criteria in the Results Section**

**Cost of Laptop (*criterion*)**
- Micro Express (*option*)
- Lenovo ThinkPad
- HP Pavilion
- Dell Inspiron
- Apple Macbook Pro

**Processor Speed (*criterion*)**
- Micro Express
- Lenovo ThinkPad
- HP Pavilion
- Dell Inspiron
- Apple Macbook Pro

**Display Size (*criterion*)**
- Micro Express
- Lenovo ThinkPad

- HP Pavilion
- Dell Inspiron
- Apple Macbook Pro

**Weight (*criterion*)**
- Micro Express
- Lenovo ThinkPad
- HP Pavilion
- Dell Inspiron
- Apple Macbook Pro

**Hard Drive Size (*criterion*)**
- Micro Express
- Lenovo ThinkPad
- HP Pavilion
- Dell Inspiron
- Apple Macbook Pro

## Organizing the Results Section of a Feasibility Report

In feasibility reports, you most effectively present the results by using a compare/contrast organization. Using this organization, you have two patterns from which to choose: comparing by criteria or comparing by options.

Compare by criteria (see Figure 15.24) if you are evaluating only a few options. If you are evaluating more than three options, compare by options (see Figure 15.25). When you compare by criteria, you focus the comparison on the criteria and the options are subsections of each criterion. When you organize by options, you focus on the options and the criteria are the subsections. When you use either organization, you can help readers understand your results by creating a chart or table that compares each option criterion by criterion.

FIGURE 15.25

**Comparing by Options in the Results Section**

**Micro Express (*option*)**
- Cost of the laptop (*criterion*)
- Processor speed
- Display size
- Weight
- Hard drive size

**Lenovo ThinkPad (*option*)**
- Cost of the laptop
- Processor speed
- Display size
- Weight
- Hard drive size

**HP Pavilion (*option*)**
- Cost of the laptop
- Processor speed

- Display size
- Weight
- Hard drive size

**Dell Inspiron (*option*)**
- Cost of the laptop
- Processor speed
- Display size
- Weight
- Hard drive size

**Apple Macbook Pro (*option*)**
- Cost of the laptop
- Processor speed
- Display size
- Weight
- Hard drive size

 TWO SAMPLE REPORTS

Figure 15.26 and Figure 15.27 present reports that met the readers' needs and expectations as well as the writers' purpose. Figure 15.26 is an internal feasibility report prepared for an executive director at a telecommunications company. The writer analyzes three options for writing single-sourced text for Select Business Account proposals. *Single-sourced* refers to any text that will be repurposed with little or no change. Figure 15.27 includes the body of a recommendation report prepared for the U.S. Department of Energy by scientists at the Oak Ridge National Laboratory. The report details a study of fish and benthic macroinvertebrates in streams near a landfill.

**Feasibility Report with Front Matter**

For internal format reports, you may use the memo form for the "letter" of transmittal.

## Memo

November 15, 2012

To:        Charlie Divine
              Executive Director

From:     Neil Cobb
              Regional Manager

Subject:  Feasibility report for hiring technical communications interns

I am pleased to submit the accompanying report, "Hiring Technical Communications Interns: A Feasibility Report," in response to your request. The report examines options for writing single-sourced text for our automated proposals.

For the report, I examined three options for writing single-sourced text: using the current proposal center staff, hiring professional technical communicators, and hiring graduate students as interns. I used the criteria of cost to produce the single-sourced text, the effect on proposal center productivity, the effect on the workplace, and the quality of the finished product. Based on my examination, I recommend hiring two technical communications interns in January 2013 to create single-sourced text for the automated proposals.

If you have any questions, please call me at (214) 555-5555.

Source: Courtesy of Neil Cobb

**FIGURE 15.26**

**Feasibility Report with Front Matter** *continued*

# Hiring Technical Communications Interns: A Feasibility Report

Prepared for
Charlie Divine, Division Manager, ISM

Prepared by
Neil Cobb, Account Manager, ISM

November 2012

**Feasibility Report with Front Matter** *continued*

iii

## Contents

# FIGURE 15.26

**Feasibility Report with Front Matter** *continued*

iv

The writer summarizes the report and states his recommendation.

## Executive Summary

I have investigated the feasibility of using current staff, hiring freelance technical communicators, and hiring student interns to generate low-cost single-sourced text for automated proposals. Because interns will work for low hourly wages with no benefits in exchange for experience, we can produce high-quality, low-cost single-sourced text. By using this text, the productivity of Proposal Specialists who serve the Select Business Accounts (SBA) will ultimately increase.

Universities in the Dallas, Houston, and St. Louis areas have programs that can provide these interns. Ninety percent of the students in these programs are looking for internship opportunities to compete their degree requirements. These programs will provide a continuous resource for capable writers to serve as interns.

I recommend hiring two technical communications interns in January 2013 to create single-sourced text for SBA automated proposals.

**FIGURE 15.26**

**Feasibility Report with Front Matter** *continued*

## Introduction

*The writer explains the background and the purpose of the report.*

Integrated Systems Marketing's proposal centers in Dallas, St. Louis, and Houston will publish more than 700 proposals in 2013 while keeping expenses at 2012 levels. In 2013, we will challenge our Account Managers and Proposal Specialists to double 2012 production without increasing costs. To meet this challenge and improve productivity, we must implement changes to our procedures early in 2013.

As a first step we have begun to automate the proposal process for Select Business Accounts. This preliminary work—writing client questionnaires, building graphics libraries, and developing price templates—is taking valuable resources from producing proposals. The most labor-intensive element of this work is pending—writing the single-sourced text for all our products. We estimate that writing the descriptions for each product will take 80 hours because the descriptions will identify several introductory scenarios for various industries and all potential problems and benefits that the product will address.

*The writer introduces the topic of the report.*

To complete the single-sourced texts while maintaining our current level of productivity and quality that our clients and their customers now expect, we have three options:

Option 1:   **Produce the single-sourced text as an overlap with current staff.** We assume that we can assign one of our three Dallas Proposal Specialists to write the text in lieu of producing proposals.

Option 2:   **Hire professional technical writers to produce the single-sourced text.** Freelance technical communicators who work on a contractual basis are readily available in the Dallas, Houston, and St. Louis areas.

Option 3:   **Hire graduate students as interns to produce the single-sourced text.** Students seeking Master's degrees are available from local universities.

*The writer tells the reader what follows in the report.*

In the report that follows, I examine these options and recommend the most cost-effective option that will allow us to increase our productivity without sacrificing quality or client satisfaction.

## Methods for Evaluating the Options

*The writer lists the criteria and explains the methods.*

To support my recommendations, I evaluate the feasibility of each option using four criteria.

- The cost of producing the single-sourced text
- The effect on proposal center productivity
- The effect on the workplace
- The quality of the finished product

## FIGURE 15.26

**Feasibility Report with Front Matter** *continued*

Results of the Evaluation 2

To gather information for the evaluation, I studied the proposal development process currently used in the proposal center for Select Business Account clients and the proposals for these and major account clients. I evaluated the quality of the proposals, especially the accuracy of the information and the quality of the writing. I interviewed Proposal Specialists and Account Representatives in the proposal center, and an Academic Specialist in technical communications. The two Proposal Specialists provided information on the workflow through the proposal center. The five Account Representatives gave me their perspectives on the proposal center's process and proposal quality. The Academic Specialist provided information on the availability, cost, and abilities of students from technical writing programs and of freelance professional technical communicators.

### Results of the Evaluation

To determine the feasibility of hiring interns, I evaluated the three options according to the criteria of cost, productivity, quality of the finished proposal, and effect on the workplace.

**Cost of Producing the Single-Sourced Text**

> The writer organizes the results by criteria.

Option 1, using the current staff, is the least expensive. Option 2, hiring freelance technical communicators, is the most expensive.

*Option 1: Overlap with Current Staff*

Proposal Specialists (SG-22) earn on average $48,700 per year. Their total compensation is equivalent to $72,000 per year, or $34.60 per hour. With Option 1, the initial text for a single product would cost approximately $2,800. Because salaries for the Proposal Specialists are an embedded cost, Option 1 would not affect expenses.

*Option 2: Hire Technical Communicators on a Contractual Basis*

> The writer uses specific figures to clearly explain the cost of each option. He tells the reader how he arrived at the figures.

Professional technical writers charge between $35 and $50 per hour, depending on their experience. With this option, the initial single-sourced text would cost between $2,800 and $4,000 and would raise our departmental expenses accordingly.

*Option 3: Hire Student Interns*

Graduate interns will work for $10–$15 per hour in exchange for on-the-job experience. These interns would be classified as parttime employees, so the company would not pay them benefits. With Option 3, the initial text for a single product would cost between $800 and $1,200 and would raise our expenses accordingly.

**Effect on Proposal Center Productivity**

Option 2, hiring freelance technical communicators, would be most productive. Option 1, using current staff, would be the least productive.

*Option 1: Overlap with Current Staff*

When Account Representatives fill out forms and pricing tables, Proposal Specialists can produce the proposal in 8 hours.[1] If we take Proposal Specialists from their

---

[1] I use an 80-hour estimate for development time to determine the cost of producing the single-sourced text.

**FIGURE 15.26**

**Feasibility Report with Front Matter** *continued*

Results of the Evaluation 3

The writer uses the same order for the options as in the introduction. The writer also uses the same order for the criteria throughout the results and clearly identifies each criterion and option in a heading.

regular proposal-writing tasks to write single-sourced text (80 hours of work), we would produce 10 fewer proposals every two weeks until the single-sourced text is complete. This option will reduce potential revenues. With this option, the proposal center will not meet the immediate needs of the Account Representatives and thus discourage them from using the center.

This option does have an advantage. Because the Proposal Specialists are familiar with our products and the proposal-writing process, they may be able to create the text for a product in less than the estimated 80 hours.

***Option 2: Hire Technical Communicators on a Contractual Basis***
Professional technical communicators should be able to produce text for a single product within the 80-hour benchmark. Some of these writers may require less time, depending on the writer's expertise in telecommunications and how long they work for us. Option 2 may be the most productive scenario overall because it will free Proposal Specialists to continue writing proposals while spending minimal time working with the hired writers to develop and edit the single-sourced text.

***Option 3: Hire Student Interns***
Like the professional technical communicators, the interns will lack experience with our products and proposal style. Because they are less experienced writers, we expect their productivity will be less than the professional communicators. However, student interns are professional writers in training. They will have considerable academic and practical experience from at least 20 hours of technical communications courses. Because much of their coursework is "real-world" oriented, the difference in productivity may not be significant. Like Option 2, Option 3 will free Proposal Specialists to continue producing proposals although the specialists may spend more time guiding the process.

## Effect on the Quality of the Finished Product

Options 2 (hiring freelance technical communicators) and 3 (hiring student interns) will provide the highest quality in the finished product.

***Option 1: Overlap with Current Staff***
Account Representatives praise the effectiveness of SBA proposals, especially the appearance of the documents. However, the quality of the text is presently inferior to that of proposals for major accounts. The content is technically correct—the Proposal Specialists know the products well—but they often write in passive voice and have difficulty writing clear prose. Because the Proposal Specialists know the material so well, they tend to let some difficult concepts and technical descriptions flow unedited into the final document.

***Option 2: Hire Technical Communicators on a Contractual Basis***
Professional technical communicators should greatly improve the quality of the SBA proposals. Their writing skills and a fresh perspective on our documents would ensure that the proposals meet the needs of nontechnical readers.

FIGURE 15.26

**Feasibility Report with Front Matter** *continued*

Conclusions 4

***Option 3: Hire Student Interns***

Interns would improve the quality of the written text for the same reasons discussed in Option 2. We would see work of higher quality because the interns' graduate advisers would evaluate the text. Their text would have to pass two layers of edits: edits from the advisers and from our Proposal Specialists.

**Effect on the Workplace**

Option 3, hiring student interns, could positively affect the workplace. Option 1, using current staff, and Option 2, hiring freelance technical communicators, could negatively affect the workplace.

***Option 1: Overlap with Current Staff***

Option 1 will affect the workplace negatively. By taking one Proposal Specialist from the group to write singled-sourced text, we will require others to do additional work and potentially turn away one out of three prospective clients. Neither result would be acceptable long term, and turning away clients could cripple the automation project before it starts. By choosing one Proposal Specialist to write the text, we might bruise the egos of the others. The choice could irreparably divide the group.

***Option 2: Hire Technical Communicators on a Contractual Basis***

Option 2 could help avoid the negative effects of Option 1, but could also cause problems. The Proposal Specialists might resent management hiring another writer to do "their" work, especially if the freelance writers receive higher wages.

***Option 3: Hire Student Interns***

Like Option 2, Option 3 should prevent the negative effects of Option 1. Interns could also help us to avoid the problems of Option 2 because the Proposal Specialists would more readily accept the interns as subordinates and take on the responsibility of supervising their work. The interns themselves also will more readily accept the role as subordinates.

The writer presents and justifies the conclusions.

## Conclusions

Each of the three options has advantages and disadvantages. Option 1 (produce the work as an overlap with current staff ) maintains current expense levels and builds on current expertise to reduce the time for writing single-sourced text. However, Option 1 fails to appreciably improve the quality of the text and could disrupt the work group. Option 2 (hire professional technical communicators to do the work) offers the highest quality text at the highest level of productivity, yet could cause the most friction in the workplace. It also carries the highest price tag on a "per-unit" basis. Option 3 (hire graduate students as interns to do the work) delivers improved quality and productivity at minimal cost with the most positive potential effect on the workplace. The quality of text written by interns and the speed at which they produce it will rival that of the professional writers if we screen the applicants properly.

**Feasibility Report with Front Matter** *continued*

Recommendations 5

Based on our evaluation of the options in light of the criteria, productivity and cost are secondary issues. The savings that we realize from automating the proposals will recover the up-front costs of creating the single-sourced text. Therefore, the center is primarily concerned with the quality of the text and the effect on the workplace.

**Recommendation**

The writer states and justifies his recommendations.

Because Option 3 offers the highest quality for the dollar with potentially no impact on morale, we recommend hiring two technical communications interns in January 2013 to write single-sourced text for Select Business Account (SBA) automated proposals.

**Recommendation Report**

Because the readers are biologists, the writers use technical terminology the readers will understand and expect.

# Biotic Characterization of Small Streams in the Vicinity of Oil Retention Ponds 1 and 2 Near the Y-12 Plant

## Introduction

This report provides data on the aquatic biota in the streams near the oil retention ponds west of the Y-12 place at Oak Ridge National Laboratory. Built in 1943, the Y-12 plant originally produced nuclear weapon components and subassemblies and supported the Department of Energy's weapon-design laboratories. In the production of the subassemblies, the plant used materials such as enriched uranium, lithium hydride, and deteride. The plant disposed of both solid and liquid wastes in burial facilities in Bear Creek Vally—approximately one mile west of the plant site. This report fulfills the Department of Energy's commitment to assess the aquatic biota near the man-made oil retention pond in the valley.

## Methods

The Environmental Sciences Division conducted quantitative sampling of benthic macroinvertebrates and fish at the following sites:

- Bear Creek above and below the confluence with Stream A, a small tributary that drains Oil Retention Pond 1 (Stations 1 and 2, respectively)
- Stream 1A just above the confluence with Bear Creek (Station 3)
- Stream 2, a small uncontaminated tributary of Bear Creek that flows adjacent to Bear Creek Road (Station 4, the control station)

We also conducted qualitative sampling at the following sites in the watersheds of Oil Retention Ponds 1 and 2:

- Stream 1A, immediately below Pond 1 (Station 5)
- The diversion ditch that carries surface runoff from portions of Burial Grounds B, C, D, and the area north of Burial Ground A to Stream 1A just below the pond (Station 6)
- Stream 1A above the diversion ditch (Station 7)
- Oil Retention Pond 2 (Station 8)

We could not sample above or below Pond 2 because of insufficient flows. We did not sample Oil Retention Pond 1.

### Methods for Sampling Benthic Macroinvertebrates

To sample the benthic macroinvertebrates at Stations 1B-4B (three samples per site), we followed these procedures:

1. Placed a 27 x 33 cm metal frame on the bottom of the stream in the riffle area.
2. Held a 363-m mesh drift net at the downstream end of the metal frame while agitating the stream bottom (within the frame) with a metal rod. The stream flow transported suspended materials into the net.
3. Washed the net three times with the stream water to concentrate the sample and remove fine sediments.
4. Transferred the sample to glass jars that contained approximately 10% formalin to preserve the sample.

In the laboratory, we followed these procedures to analyze the samples:

1. Washed each sample using a standard No. 35 mesh (500 m) sieve and placed the washed sample in a large white tray.

The writers list the specific sites studied.

The writers use lists and subheads to identify the methods for sampling benthic macroinvertebrates and fishes.

FIGURE    15.27

**Recommendation Report** *continued*

2

The writers use specific, detailed language so that readers can duplicate their methods. This language also helps to justify their conclusions and recommendations.

2. Examined large pieces of debris (e.g., leaves and twigs) for organisms and then removed the debris not containing organisms.
3. Covered the contents of the tray with a saturated sucrose solution and agitated the tray to separate the organisms from the debris.
4. Identified all organisms that floated to the surface by taxonomic order or family.
5. Collectively weighed (to the nearest 0.1 g) the individuals in each taxonomic group.

### Methods for Sampling Fishes

We used a Smith-Root Type XV backpack electro shocker to sample the fish community at Stations 1F-3F. This electroshocker can deliver up to 1200 V of pulsed direct current. We used a pulse frequency of 120 Hz at all times and adjusted the output voltage to the optimal value, based on the water conductivity at the site. We measured the conductivity with a Hydrolab Digital 4041. This instrument also concurrently measured the water temperature and pH.

At each of the sampling stations, we followed these methods to sample the fish community:
1. Made a single pass upstream and downstream using a representative reach. The length of the reach varied among sites (from 22 to 115 m).
2. Held captured fish in a 0.64-cm plastic-mesh cage until we completed the sampling.
3. Anesthetized the fish in the field with MS-222 (tricane methane sulfonate).
4. Counted the fish by species and collectively weighed the individuals of a given species to the nearest 0.5 g on a triple-beam balance.
5. Released the fish to the stream.

In a preliminary sampling we collected representative individuals of each species by seining and preserved the fish in 10% formalin. In the laboratory, we identified the fish using these methods:
1. Identified species using unpublished taxonomic keys of Etnier (1976).
2. Compared the mountain redbelly dace (Phoxinus Oreas) and the common shiner (Notropis Cornutus) with specimens collected from Ish Creek, a small stream on the south slope of West Chestnut Ridge, and identified as Phoxinus Oreas and Notropis Cornutus.

### Results

This section presents results of the sampling and analyzing of the benthic macroinvertebrates and of the fishes in the study sites.

The writers use parenthetical notes to refer readers to tables.

### Benthic Macroinvertebrates

Qualitative sampling at the sites near Oil Retention Pond 1 and in Pond 2 resulted in few samples (see Table I). We also found low densities in the quantitative samples taken from Stream 1A, which drains Oil Retention Pond 1, and in Bear Creek near the confluence with Stream 1A (see Tables II and III). Relatively high densities and biomass of benthic organisms appeared in Stream 2, a small uncontaminated tributary of Bear Creek (Station 4). Some of the differences in the composition of the benthic community between this site and others may have occurred because of sub-

**Recommendation Report** *continued*

3

strate differences (e.g., the large amounts of detritus in Stream 2 when compared to the predominately small rubble and gravel at Stations 1 and 2). However, a depauperate benthic fauna existed in Bear Creek and Stream 1A.

**Table I. Description of qualitative sampling conducted near oil Retention Ponds 1 and 2 west of the Y-12 Plant (previous study)**

The writers summarize results in tables.

| Station | Location | Method | Sampling Results |
|---|---|---|---|
| 5 | Stream 1A just below Oil Retention Pond 1 | Kick-seining | No organisms found |
| 6 | Diversion ditch just west of Oil Retention Pond 1 | Kick-seining | No organisms found |
| 7 | Stream 1A above the diversion ditch | Kick-seining | Few Isopoda; unidentified salamander |
| 8 | Oil Retention Pond 2 | Dip-netting; removal of sediment/litter from margins of ponds | No organisms found |

The writers use graphics to present the results.

**Table II. Total number and weight (g, in parentheses) of benthic macroinvertebrates in each of three 27 x 33 cm bottom samples collected from four sampling sites in the vicinity of Y-12 Oil Retention Pond 1**

| Sample no. | Sampling Station | | | |
|---|---|---|---|---|
| | 1B | 2B | 3B | 4B |
| 1 | 0 | 0 | 0 | 53 (0.8) |
| 2 | 0 | 2 (0.1) | 3 (0.1) | 46 (2.2) |
| 3 | 0 | 2 (0.1) | 0 | 25 (1.0) |
| Mean no./m$^2$ (g/m$^2$) | 0 | 14.9 (7.1) | 11.2 (0.4) | 501.3 (15.3) |
| Substrate | Coarse gravel embedded in sand and silt; leaf packs uncommon | Same as Station 1B | Sand, silt, mud, and detritus/leaves | Deep soft mud covered by leaves and woody debris |

**Recommendation Report** *continued*

4

**Table III. Density (mean no./m² ) of various benthic macroinvertebrate taxa in bottom samples collected from four sampling sites in the vicinity of Y-12 Oil Retention Pond 1. Biomass (wet weight, g/m² ) in parentheses. NC=None Collected.**

| Taxon | Sampling Station | | | |
|---|---|---|---|---|
| | 1B | 2B | 3B[a] | 4B |
| Amphipoda | NC | NC | NC | 67.3(0.6) |
| Annelida | NC | 7.5(0.4) | NC | NC |
| Chironomidae | NC | NC | NC | 273.1(0.7) |
| Decapoda | NC | NC | NC | 22.4(7.1) |
| Isopoda | NC | NC | NC | 86.1(1.9) |
| Oligochaeta | NC | NC | 11.2(0.4) | NC |
| Sialidae | NC | 3.7(1.5) | NC | NC |
| Tipulidae | NC | 3.7(5.2) | NC | 7.5(3.7) |
| Tricoptera | NC | NC | NC | 44.9(1.3) |

[a]Damselfly nymph collected by kick-seining.

*Fishes*

The four fish species collected at the four sample sites commonly inhabit small streams on the Department of Energy Oak Ridge Reservation. For example, these four species were the most abundant fishes found by electrofishing in Ish Creek, a small, undisturbed tributary of the Clinch River that drains the south slope of Chestnut Ridge. The presence of fish in the lower reaches of Stream 1A is consistent with the results of a bioassay conducted on the water from Oil Retention Pond 1. This bioassay showed no mortality to bluegill sunfish after 96 hours (Giddings). The high density and biomass of fish at Station 3F may relate to the abundant perphyton growth observed in the winter and to the chemistry of the effluent from Oil Retention Pond 1.

We found no aquatic species listed as threatened or endangered by either the U.S. Fish and Wildlife Service or the State of Tennessee. However, the Tennessee Wildlife Resources Agency has identified the mountain redbelly dace (Phoxinus Oreas) as a species which, though not considered threatened within the state, may not currently exist at or near their optimum carrying capacity (see Table IV).

**FIGURE 15.27**

5

Table IV. Density (mean no./m²) of various benthic macroinvertebrate taxa in bottom samples collected from four sampling sites in the vicinity of Y-12 Oil Retention Pond 1. Biomass (wet weight, g/m²) in parentheses. NC=None Collected.

| Species | Sampling Station | | |
|---|---|---|---|
| | 1F | 2F | 3F |
| Blacknose dace (*Rynichthys atratulus*) | 8(21.0) | 1(1.5) | 2(2.5) |
| Common shiner (*Notropis cornutus*) | 3(22.5) | 0 | 1(6.5) |
| Creek chub (*Semotilus atromaculatus*) | 42(204.5) | 4(76.5) | 10(64.0) |
| Mountain redbelly dace (*Phoxinus oreas*) | 39(64.0) | 1 (3.5) | 35(51.0) |
| Total (*all species combined*) Density (no./m²) Biomass (g/m²) | 0.30 1.00 | 0.03 0.41 | 1.68 4.33 |
| Physical characteristics of sampling site Length of stream sampled (m) Mean width (m) Mean depth (m) Conductivity (S/cm) Water temperature (*C) pH | 115 2.7 19 260 8.5 7.1 | 91 2.2 13 1005 0.5 7.6 | 22 1.3 10 477 1.5 7.5 |

**FIGURE 15.27**

The writers interpret the results.

6

## Conclusions

The Y-12 Plan operations have had an adverse impact on the benthic communities of Bear Creek and some of its tributaries. The low benthic densities at Station 2B just above the confluence with Stream 1A suggest that the source of impact is not limited to the effluent from Oil Retention Pond 1. The relatively low fish density at Station 2F also implies an upstream perturbation (such as the S-3 ponds).

Further evidence of upstream impact(s) is available from the results of a similar study conducted 10 years prior to this study. In this study, researchers sampled benthic macroinvertebrates and fish at two sites located 50 m about and 100 m below the Y-12 sanitary landfill site. The west end of the landfill is approximately 1.4 stream kilometers about the confluence of Stream 1A with Bear Creek. No benthic organisms or fish were collected at either of the two sites, and in situ fish bioassays conducted just about and 500 m below the landfill resulted in 100% mortality after 24 hours.

The results of the earlier study differ significantly from those of the present study. The current presence of fish at Station 2F, which is approximately 500 m below the site of the earlier bioassays, may indicate changes in water quality over the past 10 years. However, the occurrence of fish in this region of Bear Creek may only be a temporary phenomenon. In view of the information currently available, both explanations of the difference in results seem equally plausible.

The writers present only the recommendations here.

## Recommendations

We recommend additional studies to address several important issues:

- More extensive season sampling of the benthic macroinvertebrate and fish communities to obtain a complete inventory of the aquatic biota in Bear Creek watershed, to investigate the potential recovery of biotic communities downstream of the confluence of Stream 1A, and to identify specific sources of impact to aquatic biota in Bear Creek about the confluence with Stream1A.
- In situ and acute bioassays to assist with identifying potential sources of impact.
- Chronic bioassays to determine the effects on biota of long-term exposure to effluent sources.
- Studies of storms and their role in transporting contaminants downstream and in establishing and/or recovering the biotic communities in Bear Creek.

Source: Adapted from Loar, J. M. and D. K. Cox, *Biotic Characterization of Small Streams in the Vicinity of Oil Retention Ponds 1 and 2 Near the Y-12 Plant Bear Creek Valley Waste Disposal Area*. Jan. 31, 1984. Oak Ridge National Laboratory, Oak Ridge, TN.

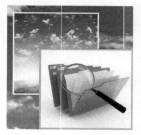

# CASE STUDY ANALYSIS

## Moving Front and Back Matter in Online Documents

The Internet is redefining traditional notions of what makes up front and back matter and what constitutes the appropriate format for documents. Effective online documents aren't mirror images of their paper counterparts. Gary Beason (1996) explains that when a computer company put its documents on the Web, the "boundaries between individual books [documents] began to disappear" (339); the books became more of a searchable database than a traditional book with chapters, a title page, and an index. Unlike traditional paper documents, online documents are dynamic and interactive. These online documents multiply into a set of documents, in part because a series of files make up the documents—files that are in flux (ibid.). Traditional paper documents, on the other hand, are static once they appear in print. However, does this dynamic, flexible nature of online documents suggest that we should put all documents online or that readers prefer online documents?

Online and paper documents each have distinct advantages. Online documents cost less than paper documents and provide instant access to information, especially with computer software and hardware. Paper documents, on the other hand, are easier to read; if a document is "more than a few sentences, print is easier to read than a monitor" (Bellis 1996, 21). How, then, do you decide what to put online and what to put on paper? How does the reader affect this decision? Bellis (1996) suggests a combination of both online and paper documents to take advantage of the strengths of each. As you seek this balance between online and paper, consider that the product will change as technology changes; but the change should not be arbitrary (Beason 1996). Thus, will documents in the future need the front and back matter of today's documents? That decision may be up to you and your coworkers.

### Assignment

- Find a document developed to be read online. This document should have front and/or back matter.
- Write an email to your instructor describing the front and back matter and include the URLs of each item you found. Discuss how readers could interact with the document through the front and/or back matter. For example, does the table of contents allow the reader to click on items and link to the associated text?

1. **Collaborative exercise:** Working with a team of peers in your major field, identify a problem to research and then decide how to approach the research. For example, you might identify the methods you would use to research the problem, the means for verifying your results, and so on. Write a memo to your instructor describing the problem and your approach to researching it.

2. Locate a formal report from a federal, state, or city government agency or organization; from a private organization; or from a department or group at your college or university. You can also ask reference librarians to help you locate a report. When you have located a report, analyze it and write a memo to your instructor about it. Identify the type of report (information, analytical, or recommendation) and the intended readers. Your memo should
   - evaluate the conventional sections of the body of the report
   - evaluate the front matter
   - evaluate the overall effectiveness of the report

   (For information on memos, see Chapter 12.)

3. Write a letter of transmittal for a report that you are writing. Follow the paragraph-by-paragraph outline in Tips for Writing the Letter of Transmittal.

4. Prepare a table of contents for a report you are writing. Include all first-level, second-level, and third-level headings.

5. Design a cover and title page for a report you are writing. As you design the cover, decide what materials and binding style you will use. When you have completed the cover and title page, turn in the following to your instructor:
   - a memo explaining the material you will use for the cover and justifying your design of the cover and title page: why you selected the graphical elements, what the graphical elements represent, whether the design is the organization's standard design (if applicable), and so on. (For information on memos, see Chapter 12.)
   - the cover printed on plain paper (indicate in the memo how you will present the final version of the cover: type of paper, binding, and so on)
   - the title page

6. Decide whether any material for a report that you are writing should appear in an appendix. Write a memo to your instructor explaining your decision. (For information on writing memos, see Chapter 12.) If you decide to include material in an appendix, answer these questions in your memo:
   • Why is the material better placed in an appendix than in the body of the document?
   • What readers are likely to be interested in or need the information in the appendix?
   • What is the purpose of the material that will appear in the appendix?

7. Decide whether the report you are writing should have an abstract or an executive summary. Write the abstract or the executive summary for your report.

8. Many organizations, websites, and consumer groups compare products and make recommendations. For each example, one of the better known such publications is *Consumer Reports*. This publication has established criteria for evaluating consumer products such as cars, electronics, appliances, and computers. The editors recommend the best option based on their established criteria. Visit the website of *Consumer Reports*, at www.consumerreports.org, or find a similar group. After visiting the site
   • select a product (it can be food, paper products, appliances, etc.)
   • establish criteria for evaluating options
   • identify the options
   • research the options
   • evaluate the options
   • write a feasibility report for consumers in your area recommending one of the options

DOWNLOAD A COPY OF THE WORKSHEET FOR WRITING READER-FOCUSED FORMAL REPORTS AT

WWW.GRTEP.COM

## Improving Your Community

Every day you encounter problems that, if solved, would improve the lives of the people who live in your community. You might face these problems on your campus. You may witness these problems and their impact on the people in your community. Working with a team of your classmates, identify a problem for which you can identify options to solve it.

### Assignment

Write a feasibility report addressed to the decision maker with the authority to implement your proposed solution. As your team works, follow these guideline:

- Make sure that all team members are familiar with the problem and can gather the needed information.
- Establish reasonable and appropriate minimum criteria for evaluating the options.
- Identify the options and decide what methods your team will use to gather the needed information to evaluate the options.
- Assign each team member an information-gathering task. For example, if your team decides to develop and distribute a questionnaire, decide who will write the questionnaire, who will prepare and distribute it, and who will tabulate the returned questionnaires.
- Use the online Worksheet for Writing Reader-Focused Formal Reports as you plan and evaluate your feasibility report. Follow the Tips for Establishing Criteria and Tips for Identifying Options.

# chapter *sixteen*

## Writing Persuasive Proposals

*iStockphoto 2008.*

**P**roposals are documents designed to persuade someone to follow or accept a specific course of action. Proposals usually offer to solve a problem, provide a service or product, or perform research. They suggest a specific plan for delivering that solution, service, or product, or for performing that research. An effective proposal is persuasive; it convinces readers to accept and possibly to pay for the work that it proposes. If you propose a project for a fee, you must persuade your readers that you can carry out the project within a reasonable time and at a reasonable cost. A proposal, then, is a *sales* document: It *sells* a proposed action and possibly your services or the services of your organization to carry out that action. If you are proposing to perform research, your proposal should convince the readers that your research is valid and that you have a sound plan for conducting that research.

You might write a proposal, sometimes called a bid, in response to several scenarios. Let's look at five scenarios and how the writers responded:

| Scenario 1 | Bill Martinez works for a large construction company that is building a new manufacturing plant. The manufacturing process will create large amounts of ash. According to EPA guidelines, the company must dispose of the ash properly. Bill is responsible for hiring a company to develop recommendations for ash disposal. Therefore, he sends out requests to several environmental service companies, inviting them to submit proposals to develop the recommendations. (The sample proposal in Figure 16.8 responds to Bill's request.) |
|---|---|
| Scenario 2 | A government agency in Wisconsin decides that it should renovate its office building. The building is 50 years old and has several problems: It doesn't meet current fire code regulations, the windows and outside doors provide little insulation from the weather, the bathrooms have plumbing problems, and the offices are not appropriately wired for current telecommunications technology. The agency wants to find a qualified construction company to renovate the building at a reasonable price. The agency advertises the proposed work in newspapers across Wisconsin and online. Companies interested in submitting proposals can request the project specifications. |
| Scenario 3 | The National Interagency Fire Center requests bids for providing non-perishable food for smokejumpers. The center put an IFB (information for bid) in the *Commerce Business Daily* (see Figure 16.1). The IFB describes the specifications for the food, gives the due date for the bid, and provides information on obtaining specifics of the request. |
| Scenario 4 | Susan Rowland writes software documentation. In recent months, her workload—as well as that of other technical writers in her office—has dramatically increased. Susan knows that her company currently has a hiring freeze, so she can't hire another writer. She believes the only way to get help with the increased workload is to update the computer software and hardware they use to write and produce documentation. She writes a proposal to her regional manager, requesting updated software and hardware for her department. |
| Scenario 5 | Nancy Griffin wants to determine whether the concentrations of mercury and lead allowed by the government are safe. She wants to know if people living in areas with allowable concentrations of mercury or lead have a history of health problems. To conduct this research, Nancy needs funds from a public or private agency, but she cannot find a specific request |

# FIGURE 16.1

## Information for Bid (IFB) from the *Commerce Business Daily*

A daily list of U.S. Government procurement invitations, contract awards, subcontracting leads, sales of surplus property and foreign business opportunities.

### Non-perishable food items for smokejumpers food boxes

**General Information**

| | |
|---|---|
| Document Type: | PRESOL |
| Posted Date: | Mar 19, 2008 |
| Category: | Subsistence |
| Set Aside: | N/A |

**Contracting Office Address**

BLM-FA NATIONAL INTERAGENCY FIRE CENTER3833 DEVELOPMENT AVE BOISE ID 83705

**Description**

The Bureau of Land Management, National Interagency Fire Center, will post Request for Quotation solicitation #RAQ083004 for non-perishable food items for smokejumpers fire food boxes, which will include, but not limited to canned soups, canned meats, candy bars, energy bars, and dried fruit. This solicitation falls under NAICS code 424410, and Product Service code 8970. This will be set a side totally for small businesses. Small business classification per SBA table is 100 employees. The solicitation will be made available electronically on March 12, 2008 from the Electronic Commerce site "http://ideasec.nbc.gov." Contractors must be registered and active at the Central Contractor Registration website at: www.ccr.gov to participate, receive notifications of amendment, award notification, and to faciitate payment. No hard copies will be sent. The anticipated solicitation closing is March 31, 2008. The Government reserves the right to make multiple awards, as a result of the solicitation responses. Questions regarding this announcement may be directed to Dawn Graham at (208)387-5544.

**Original Point of Contact**

POC Dawn Graham Purchasing Agent 208387554 Dawn_Graham@nifc.bim.gov

Source: Downloaded from the World Wide Web, November 2008: www.cbdweb.com/index.php/search/show/21773566.

related to her research topic. She prepares a proposal to send to several private and public agencies, hoping one of these agencies will fund her research.

These five scenarios illustrate the primary types of proposal situations: solicited and unsolicited, and internal and external.

*Solicited* proposals originate when a person, organization, or government agency requests qualified organizations or individuals to deliver a product and/or services or to perform research. In scenarios 1, 2, and 3, companies or government agencies are soliciting proposals or bids. In scenario 1, Bill Martinez is requesting proposals for a *service*: He wants companies to propose plans for ash disposal. He is not asking the companies to dispose of the ash, only to develop a comprehensive, feasible plan for ash disposal. Similarly, in scenario 2, the agency is requesting proposals for providing a service, in this case, renovating a building. In scenario 3, the National Interagency Fire Center is requesting bids for a *product*, in this case, nonperishable food. In each scenario, the organizations and individuals write proposals (or bids) in response to a specific request: an **RFP** (request for proposal) or **IFB** (information for bid).

> Both solicited and unsolicited proposals offer to solve a problem, to provide a service or product, or to perform research.

Scenarios 4 and 5 illustrate a situation requiring **unsolicited** proposals—proposals not requested by the organization, individual, or government agency that receives them. Unlike solicited proposals, unsolicited proposals must convince readers that a specific need or problem exists before explaining the plan, cost, or qualifications. You can write unsolicited proposals to people in your own organization, as in scenario 4, or you can write to people outside your organization.

Scenario 5, Nancy Griffin's proposal, is unsolicited because she is not responding to a request for proposals. This scenario is also different from the other proposals because Nancy is not proposing a service or product. Instead, she is proposing that an organization fund her research. Some research proposals are solicited because an organization may have posted a request for research proposals.

Susan Rowland's and Nancy Griffin's task—writing an unsolicited proposal or a research proposal—is more difficult than writing a proposal in response to a specific request. Susan and Nancy not only must convince readers that they have worthy projects and can carry out those projects at a reasonable cost, but they also must persuade readers that their projects are worthwhile and will fill a need. Susan wants to convince her readers that her department has an increased workload and that the computer software and hardware are preventing the technical writers from completing their work in a reasonable time and with the quality the company expects. Nancy wants to persuade her readers that the allowable levels of mercury and lead may be too high, and that a scientific study can determine if the levels actually are too high. Even if she is responding to a request for research proposals, she must convince her readers that her research proposal is reasonable and worth funding.

The five scenarios illustrate how proposals originate and where readers are located. Proposal readers can work in or outside your organization. If the readers work in your organization, as in Susan's scenario (scenario 4), the proposal is *internal*—written to someone in the writer's organization. If the readers work outside your organization, as in scenarios 1, 2, 3, and 5, the proposal is *external*. This chapter will help you write effective proposals, whether they are solicited or unsolicited, internal or external.

## FIND OUT ABOUT THE READERS

Before writing a proposal, find out about the people who are most likely to read it. You can write an effective proposal only if you understand your readers and have some idea about how they will respond to the work you propose. To find out about your readers, ask yourself these questions:

- **What positions do they hold in the organization? If they work in the organization that employs you, where are their positions in relation to yours in the organizational hierarchy?** When you know readers' positions in the hierarchy, you can more accurately determine who can approve your proposal, who will understand the topic and the background of your proposal, and who will be your primary and secondary readers. Are your readers above you, below you, or at the same level as you in the organization? If they are at a higher level than you, use a more formal approach or have your manager read a draft of your proposal before you send it to your primary readers. If you and your readers are at the same level in the organization or if you are at a higher level, they may expect a less formal approach.

- **Will more than one group read the proposal? If so, what sections of the proposal will each group read?** Several groups of readers may review a proposal. For example, managers or executives may read the summary to determine whether the proposal has merit. If they decide the project has merit, they may send the proposal to the accountants to look at the budget and to the technical experts to look at the proposed solution and plan of work.

- **What do your readers know about the problem or need that prompted your proposal?** If your proposal is unsolicited, readers probably will know little about the problem or need addressed in your proposal. If your proposal is solicited, readers will understand the problem.

- **What do your readers know about you or your organization? Have their previous experiences with your organization or with you been positive? If not, why not?** Find out whether your readers have had previous experiences with your organization. Was the experience extended or brief, positive or negative? What impression are the readers likely to have of you or your organization? When you know the answers to these

## TAKING IT INTO THE *workplace*

### Examining the Forms of Bids and Proposals

Organizations of all sizes use proposals and bids to evaluate projects. Some organizations require a formal procedure for submitting proposals and bids and specific formats for the proposal. Others have a less formal approach, expecting fewer details and requiring no specific format. However, most organizations expect a written proposal and bid to compare against others, select, and award contracts. By examining how proposals and bids are solicited, you can better understand the variety of forms that bids and proposals take.

### Assignment

Visit a department of your choosing on your campus. Consider a department associated with your degree, an administrative department, or a maintenance or food services department.
- Talk to the person in charge of accepting bids or writing proposals.
- Ask that person to show you an example of a recent bid or proposal received by his or her department.
- Discuss what aspects of the proposal or bid are the most important when considering the item, and which are the least helpful.
- Ask the person considering the proposal or bid what he or she liked or disliked about the item.
- Be prepared to make an oral presentation to your class about how real-world proposals and bids compare to what you learned in class. (See Chapter 20 for information on oral presentations.)

questions, you can better write the qualifications section of the proposal and lessen any negative concerns your readers may have about you or your organization.

If you are aware of the answers to these questions, you can more effectively write a proposal that meets your readers' needs and expectations. Once you have found out about your readers, you can determine what they may ask about your proposal.

## ANTICIPATE AND ANSWER READERS' QUESTIONS

The success of your proposal depends on

- how persuasively and logically you argue for your proposed solution, service, product, or research
- how convincingly you argue that you or your organization is best qualified to carry out the plan
- how persuasively you argue that you or your organization can complete the work within a reasonable time and at a reasonable cost

The questions in Figure 16.2 relate to three areas that will help you anticipate what readers expect from your proposal and what they may ask as they read it. The three areas are the problem or need addressed in the proposal; the proposed solution, product, or service; and the plan of work.

To answer readers' questions, you need to research the readers and their organization. Research the organization's history, its financial standing and goals, and its organizational hierarchy. Look into the organization's corporate culture to see how it might affect your readers' perspectives and ideas. With this information, you can better anticipate your readers' questions and provide persuasive answers.

In addition to anticipating readers' questions, consider what you and your organization can realistically propose and look at the strengths and weaknesses of your proposal. Figure 16.2 lists questions that you can consider as you evaluate your proposal. You must ensure that your proposal will appeal to readers, without overpromising what you and your organization can actually do.

 ## THE CONVENTIONAL SECTIONS OF PROPOSALS

As the five scenarios illustrate, you may write proposals in response to many situations. The proposal formats will vary with the situation. If your proposal is formal, you might choose to include front matter, such as a letter of transmittal, title page, table of contents, and executive summary (see Chapter 15). If your proposal is informal, you might select a letter or memo format. Whether you use a formal or an informal format, your proposal will have some or all of the conventional sections discussed in this chapter. From one organization to another, these sections may have different titles, but their purpose is the same. For example, instead of Problem Definition, some organizations may use the heading Scope of Work;

## Questions to Consider When Writing the Conventional Sections

| Conventional Section | Writer's Questions | Readers' Questions |
|---|---|---|
| **Introduction and Definition of the Problem** | • How can the proposal demonstrate that you understand the problem or need?<br>• Should you restate the problem or do you need to show readers that you understand the problem? | *If the proposal is solicited*<br>• What do readers expect from your proposal?<br>*If the proposal is unsolicited*<br>• Why should readers be interested in your proposal?<br>• What problem or need does your proposal address?<br>• Why is the problem or need important to the readers? |
| **Proposed Solution, Product, Service, or Research** | • How can you reasonably solve the problem or meet readers' needs?<br>• What are the strengths of your solution, product, service, or research?<br>• How can you emphasize those strengths?<br>• What are the weaknesses of your solution, product, service, or research?<br>• How can you ethically counter those weaknesses and readers' objections to them?<br>• How does your solution, product, service, or research meet readers' needs or those of the community or your field?<br>• Can you and/or your organization reasonably carry out what you propose?<br>• How can you make the solution, product, service, or research attractive to readers without overpromising what you and/or your organization can do? | • How will you solve the problem or satisfy the need?<br>• What do you specifically propose to provide or do?<br>• Are other solutions, products, services, or research methods possible? If so, why have you chosen the solution, product, service, or method presented in your proposal?<br>• How does your choice compare with other possibilities?<br>• How will readers view the solution, product, service, or research that you propose? |

## Questions to Consider When Writing the Conventional Sections *continued*

| Plan of Work | • What are the strengths of your plan?<br>• What are the weaknesses of your plan?<br>• How can you counter those weaknesses and the readers' possible objections to them?<br>• Can your organization reasonably carry out the plan?<br>• How can you ethically make your plan attractive to readers without overstating what you and/or your organization can do? | • What do you propose to do, make, or provide?<br>• How long will the plan take?<br>• Is the plan ethical and reasonable? |
|---|---|---|
| **Qualifications** | • How can you demonstrate that you and/or your organization are qualified and that the readers can depend on you to do what you propose? | • Why should readers believe that you and/or your organization have the expertise to do what you propose?<br>• Why should readers believe that they can depend on you and/or your organization to deliver what you propose? |
| **Budget** | • Does the budget reflect the actual cost of the plan?<br>• Have you justified your budget and anticipated readers' possible objections to it? | • How much will the proposed solution, product, service, or research cost?<br>• Is the cost reasonable? |

and instead of Budget, some organizations may use Cost Estimates. If your organization prefers certain titles for the sections or requires particular sections to appear in its proposals, use those titles and include those sections. If you are responding to an RFP or IFB, the request may specify the sections and the format you should follow. Follow the specifications of the requesters; otherwise, your proposal or bid may be rejected.

Most proposals contain the following sections:
- Executive Summary
- Description of the Proposed Solution, Product, Service, or Research
  - Introduction
  - Problem Definition
  - Proposed Solution
  - Plan of Work
- Qualifications
  - Personnel
  - Resources
- Budget
- Conclusion

For some proposals, you may not need all these sections—especially the qualifications and budget. Those two sections may be unnecessary based on your relationship with the readers and the proposal's purpose. For example, if you are writing an informal proposal to your manager, you wouldn't include a qualifications section because your manager knows your qualifications. However, if you are writing a formal proposal to external readers who are unfamiliar with you, include a qualifications section.

The following pages describe these conventional sections. They correspond to the questions that readers may ask and questions that you should ask (see Figure 16.2).

## Executive Summary

The *executive summary* is a powerful tool; it is a condensed version of your proposal. A well-written executive summary persuades readers to read more about your proposed project, while a poorly written executive summary may cause readers to ignore or reject your proposal.

Because readers look at the executive summary first, it is crucial to your proposal's success for these reasons:
- Many readers use the executive summary to decide whether to consider a proposal.
- Many readers may read only the executive summary.
- Readers who have received many proposals in response to one RFP may use the summaries to determine which proposals to consider seriously.

The executive summary contains essential information about the proposed solution, product, service, or research; the plan of work; and the cost. To write an effective summary, follow the Tips for Writing an Executive Summary.

Figure 16.3 presents the executive summary of an unsolicited proposal for a service-learning project. For this project, the student is proposing to write a training and reference manual for a university Office of Disability Accommodation.

## Description of the Proposed Solution, Product, Service, or Research

The description of the proposed solution, product, service, or research is the heart of the proposal. It presents detailed information about the problem or need; the proposed project, solution, product, or research; and the plan. The description may include an introduction, problem description, proposed solution, and plan of work.

### Introduction

The *introduction* briefly describes the problem, product, service, or research that you propose and tells why you are proposing it. For example, you state that you are writing in response to a request from readers or to a specific RFP. In the introduction, you tell readers what follows in the proposal. The writer of the example in Figure 16.4 combines the introduction and the executive summary; this combination is common in short, informal proposals. The writer identifies the problem being addressed: To develop a conceptual closure

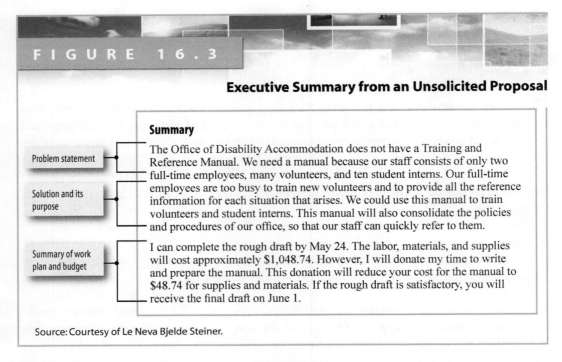

## FIGURE 16.3

**Executive Summary from an Unsolicited Proposal**

**Summary**

Problem statement

The Office of Disability Accommodation does not have a Training and Reference Manual. We need a manual because our staff consists of only two full-time employees, many volunteers, and ten student interns. Our full-time employees are too busy to train new volunteers and to provide all the reference information for each situation that arises. We could use this manual to train volunteers and student interns. This manual will also consolidate the policies and procedures of our office, so that our staff can quickly refer to them.

Solution and its purpose

Summary of work plan and budget

I can complete the rough draft by May 24. The labor, materials, and supplies will cost approximately $1,048.74. However, I will donate my time to write and prepare the manual. This donation will reduce your cost for the manual to $48.74 for supplies and materials. If the rough draft is satisfactory, you will receive the final draft on June 1.

Source: Courtesy of Le Neva Bjelde Steiner.

plan for the Caney Branch Ash Disposal Area. The writer then briefly explains how the plan will be developed and describes what follows in the proposal. As you write your introduction, follow the Tips for Writing the Introduction.

## Problem Definition

Once you have told readers what you are proposing, convince them that you understand the work that you are addressing and that you designed your solution and work plan after studying their needs. If the proposal is unsolicited, convince readers that your proposal addresses a significant problem or need and demonstrate how that problem or need affects them. If you are writing an unsolicited research proposal, persuade the readers first that a problem or need exists and that it is important to their field or their interests.

Anticipate and answer any questions that readers may have, so they know that you clearly understand their situation. (Figure 16.2 lists questions that readers might ask as they read a problem definition. Your readers may have other questions about the specific subject addressed in your proposal.) Depending on whether the proposal is solicited or unsolicited, the problem definition may do any of the following:

## TIPS FOR WRITING AN EXECUTIVE SUMMARY

- **Concisely state the problem or need addressed in the proposal.** Include only the information necessary for readers to understand the problem or need.
- **Summarize the proposed solution, product, service, or research.** Show how it meets the readers' needs or requirements and why your proposal is valuable to the readers, the community, or your field.
- **Describe your plan for carrying out the proposed solution, product, service, or research.** Exclude details about the plan of work. Present only the basics of the plan.
- **Summarize your qualifications or those of your team and/or your organization** (if your proposal includes a qualifications section). Some proposal writers include only the qualifications of the organization in the summary.
- **Summarize the budget** (if your proposal includes a budget section). Summarize by stating the total cost of the proposed solution, product, service, or research. Some sales proposals purposefully leave the budget information out of the summary so the proposed product or service can be "sold" before giving the financial data. As Neil Cobb, executive director for AT&T, explains, if your product isn't the lowest priced on the market, tell readers about the product and the company before you give them the bottom line, so they will see its value in relation to its cost (Cobb 2008).

## TIPS FOR WRITING THE INTRODUCTION

- **Identify the problem or need that the proposal addresses.** Briefly describe that problem or need.
- **State the purpose of your proposal.** Although your readers will likely know the purpose, state it to ensure that you and your readers clearly understand the purpose of your document.
- **Describe what follows in the proposal.** Tell readers the organizational pattern that you follow in the proposal. For example, the writer in Figure 16.4 writes, "The following proposal describes our understanding of the required scope of work and our work plan."

- **Define the problem** in detail for an unsolicited proposal and with less detail for a solicited proposal.
- **Give the background of the problem or situation or explain how it developed** (primarily for unsolicited proposals). The background may help readers understand that a significant problem exists or that you understand their needs. For a research proposal, the background demonstrates that you understand prior research related to your proposed project.
- **Explain why the proposed solution, product, service, or research is necessary** (for unsolicited proposals).

For instance, if you are proposing a research project, explain why the research is important. As you prepare the problem definition, follow the Tips for Writing the Problem Definition.

Figure 16.5 presents the problem definition (called Scope of Work in this case) of a solicited proposal. The readers know what their needs are, so the primary purpose of this problem definition is to show that the writer understands the readers' needs. Thus, the writer restates the work the readers expect of his or her organization as well as what is not expected.

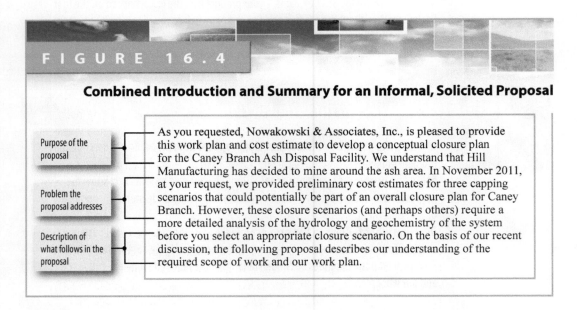

**FIGURE 16.4**

**Combined Introduction and Summary for an Informal, Solicited Proposal**

Purpose of the proposal

Problem the proposal addresses

Description of what follows in the proposal

As you requested, Nowakowski & Associates, Inc., is pleased to provide this work plan and cost estimate to develop a conceptual closure plan for the Caney Branch Ash Disposal Facility. We understand that Hill Manufacturing has decided to mine around the ash area. In November 2011, at your request, we provided preliminary cost estimates for three capping scenarios that could potentially be part of an overall closure plan for Caney Branch. However, these closure scenarios (and perhaps others) require a more detailed analysis of the hydrology and geochemistry of the system before you select an appropriate closure scenario. On the basis of our recent discussion, the following proposal describes our understanding of the required scope of work and our work plan.

FIGURE 16.5

## Problem Definition of a Solicited Proposal

**Scope of Work**

To define the problem, the writer restates the work the readers expect.

We understand that the scope of the work will include the following:
- developing a set of recommendations for capping and closing the ash area at the Caney Branch Ash Disposal Facility
- compiling a conceptual design document that describes and illustrates the recommended approach for capping and closing the ash area

The writer outlines the work the work plan does not include.

After developing the conceptual design document, we will, at the request of Hill Manufacturing, present the technical merits of the plan at a meeting with Hill and then with the state Water Commission. As you requested, the conceptual document will not include final design specifications or detailed cost estimates required to implement the recommended closure plan. However, we propose to develop a preliminary cost estimate as necessary to evaluate various closure alternatives.

## TIPS FOR WRITING THE PROBLEM DEFINITION

- **Define the problem or need.** If you are writing an unsolicited proposal, give the readers the details they require to understand the problem or need and explain why they should consider your proposed solution, product, service, or research. If you are writing a solicited proposal, include fewer details. Instead, give the readers only enough detail to know that you understand the problem. This information is important because proposals result in a deliverable, and you want a written record of your understanding of the problem or need. A *deliverable* is what you will "deliver" at the end of a project; for example, if you propose to design and build a website, the deliverable is the website.
- **Present the necessary background for the readers to understand the problem or need and the proposed solution.** Show the readers you have carefully studied the problem and/or their request—that you have done your homework. For example, if you conducted library research, summarize your research. If you examined company reports or interviewed people affected by the problem or need, use that information to give readers what they require to understand the context of your proposal.
- **Give the readers the information they require to understand why they should accept your proposal.** Explain why the proposed solution, product, service, or research is necessary to the readers, their organization, the community, or their field.

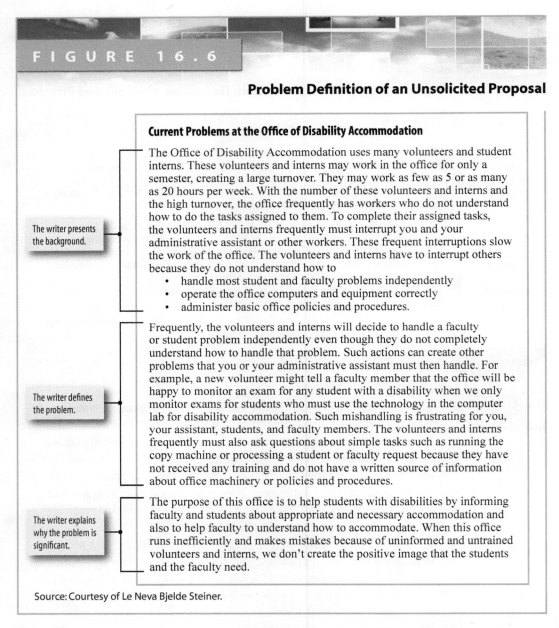

## FIGURE 16.6

### Problem Definition of an Unsolicited Proposal

**Current Problems at the Office of Disability Accommodation**

The writer presents the background.

The Office of Disability Accommodation uses many volunteers and student interns. These volunteers and interns may work in the office for only a semester, creating a large turnover. They may work as few as 5 or as many as 20 hours per week. With the number of these volunteers and interns and the high turnover, the office frequently has workers who do not understand how to do the tasks assigned to them. To complete their assigned tasks, the volunteers and interns frequently must interrupt you and your administrative assistant or other workers. These frequent interruptions slow the work of the office. The volunteers and interns have to interrupt others because they do not understand how to

- handle most student and faculty problems independently
- operate the office computers and equipment correctly
- administer basic office policies and procedures.

The writer defines the problem.

Frequently, the volunteers and interns will decide to handle a faculty or student problem independently even though they do not completely understand how to handle that problem. Such actions can create other problems that you or your administrative assistant must then handle. For example, a new volunteer might tell a faculty member that the office will be happy to monitor an exam for any student with a disability when we only monitor exams for students who must use the technology in the computer lab for disability accommodation. Such mishandling is frustrating for you, your assistant, students, and faculty members. The volunteers and interns frequently must also ask questions about simple tasks such as running the copy machine or processing a student or faculty request because they have not received any training and do not have a written source of information about office machinery or policies and procedures.

The writer explains why the problem is significant.

The purpose of this office is to help students with disabilities by informing faculty and students about appropriate and necessary accommodation and also to help faculty to understand how to accommodate. When this office runs inefficiently and makes mistakes because of uninformed and untrained volunteers and interns, we don't create the positive image that the students and the faculty need.

Source: Courtesy of Le Neva Bjelde Steiner.

Figure 16.6 shows the problem definition of an unsolicited proposal for a university Office of Disability Accommodation. Using examples and terms the readers will understand, the writer specifically explains the problems resulting from the turnover of volunteers and students. This problem definition (called Current Problems) points out why the problems are significant. The writer explains, for example, that these problems prevent the office from creating "the positive image that the students and the faculty need" and "slow the work of the office."

## Proposed Solution and Plan of Work

After you describe the problem or need, your readers will want to know how you plan to solve the problem or meet their needs—what you will deliver. They will especially want to see how you clearly link your proposed solution or plan of work to the problem or need. Readers will also expect you to present a detailed plan for carrying out the work. As you present this plan, consider the readers' questions. For example, they might ask: "How does your plan compare with other possible solutions?" "Why should we adopt your plan instead of another plan?" "Why is this plan better than the others?" (For more questions, see Figure 16.2.) You must persuade your readers that you have not only crafted a detailed plan, but also that your plan is the best solution to the problem.

In some work plans, you will need to explain not only what you and your organization will do, but also what you will not do. Your readers have a legal and ethical right to understand what you and your organization are proposing and what you are not proposing. If you

## FIGURE 16.7

### The Link between Hill Manufacturing's Problem and the Work Proposed by Nowakowski & Associates, Inc.

| Hill Manufacturing's Problem and Needs | How Nowakowski & Associates Plans to Solve the Problem and Meet the Needs |
|---|---|
| Set of recommendations for capping and closing the ash area at the Caney Branch Ash Disposal Facility | **Task 1**: Review data and develop preliminary closure options<br>**Task 2**: Collect and analyze additional data<br>**Task 3** (partial): Evaluate the closure alternatives |
| Conceptual design document that describes and illustrates the recommended approach for capping and closing the ash area | **Task 3** (partial): Develop a conceptual closure plan |
| Presentation of the technical merits of the plan at meetings with Hill Manufacturing and the state Water Commission | **Task 4**: Attend strategic planning meeting |

do not tell readers what you will and will not do, they may expect more than you intend. Prevent such miscommunication by spelling out exactly what you are proposing and are not proposing.

The proposed solution and plan of work in the proposal for Hill Manufacturing appear in the sections titled Work Plan and Schedule in Figure 16.8. (Proposal writers and companies use different titles to refer to the proposed solution and plan of work. Use the titles that the RFP or IFB requires or those that your organization prefers. If your organization doesn't have requirements, select the most appropriate titles for your readers.) In the proposal for Hill Manufacturing, the writer links the proposed solution and plan of work to the problem. Figure 16.7 shows how the writer (Nowakowski & Associates, Inc.) links the solution and plan of work directly to the readers' (Hill's) problems and needs. In the problem definition (called Scope of Work in Figure 16.8), the writer mentions three areas of work: "developing a set of recommendations for capping and closing the ash area," "compiling a conceptual design document," and "a meeting with Hill and then with the state Water Commission." In the Work Plan, the writer mentions these three areas in the list of tasks and explains how the tasks will fulfill the work requested by Hill. The proposal lists and describes the tasks necessary to carry out the work and then presents a schedule.

**TIPS** FOR WRITING THE PROPOSED SOLUTION AND WORK PLAN

- **Link the proposed solution (deliverable) to the problem by explaining how the solution will solve the problem and/or meet the readers' needs.** Tell your readers specifically how your proposed solution will solve the problem or address the needs that you described in the problem-definition section. Don't assume that readers will see the link; instead, directly state the link even in a solicited proposal.
- **Present a detailed, step-by-step plan for carrying out the work.** You want the readers to understand the scope of the work you are proposing. Justify your plan and anticipate readers' questions.
- **If necessary, explain specifically what you are and are not proposing to do.** You want readers to clearly understand not only what you and/or your organization will do as well as what you will not do.
- **Include a graphic to illustrate the schedule.** Many proposals include a graphic, such as a timeline or chart, illustrating the schedule (for example, see the Gantt chart in Figure 16.8).
- **Create a realistic schedule.** Be careful not to create an overly optimistic schedule in your eagerness to get your proposal accepted. Allow ample time to complete each phase of the work plan. Your readers and your organization want a realistic schedule, not one that is impossible to meet.

As you prepare the proposed solution and work plan, consider the questions in Figure 16.2 and follow the Tips for Writing the Proposed Solution and Work Plan.

## Qualifications

The *qualifications section*—sometimes called Project Team, Facilities, or Personnel—is important for readers who want to know whether you and/or your organization can carry out the work you propose. This section includes some or all of the following information:

- **Qualifications of the people (including yourself, if necessary) who will carry out the work.** Include a paragraph summarizing each person's qualifications for the project or attach résumés in an appendix. If you attach résumés, use the qualifications section to introduce the project personnel or summarize each person's qualifications; then refer readers to the appendix.
- **Qualifications of the organization.** For some proposals, you may need to "sell" your organization's qualifications. Demonstrate to readers that the organization has carried out similar work and has the facilities and capability to successfully and efficiently complete the work. In this section, give readers a brief background of your organization and projects it has completed successfully. Include as well information on specific facilities the organization will use to complete the work, especially if those facilities compare favorably with industry standards or with your competitors.

The sample proposal in Figure 16.8 includes a qualifications section. The writers summarize the qualifications of the personnel who will carry out the proposed work. The writers also include information about each person's responsibilities on the project and explain why each person is qualified to work on the project. The writers don't present resumés in an appendix because their organization has previously worked with Hill Manufacturing.

## Budget

The *budget*, sometimes called a Cost Estimate or Cost Proposal, is an itemized list of the estimated costs of the work. For some proposals, readers will expect a budget justification as well. The *budget justification* explains each budget item and its purpose. As you prepare your budget, follow the Tips for Preparing the Budget.

The budget for the Hill Manufacturing proposal (see Figure 16.8) is in a section titled Cost Estimate. There the writers present a total estimate for the project and separate estimates for each task.

**TIPS FOR PREPARING THE BUDGET**

- **Carefully estimate the cost of labor, equipment, and materials needed to carry out the work plan.** To ensure that you have included all costs, look at the budgets for similar projects or proposals or ask an experienced coworker to look at your budget.
- **Estimate accurately.** If you underestimate your costs in trying to get a proposal accepted, you may be bound by your estimate. If your estimate is too low, you or your organization could lose the goodwill of your client if you have to charge more money for the services. If you have contracted for a specific amount, you may not be able to ask the client for additional money; you or your organization may have to fund the additional expenses out of pocket.

## Conclusion

In most proposals, the *conclusion* briefly restates the problem or need and the proposed solution. The conclusion also restates

- what the proposal offers readers
- how the proposal will benefit readers
- why readers should accept the proposal
- why readers should accept you and/or your organization to carry out the proposed solution.

For shorter, less formal proposals in memo or letter format, the conclusion is likely to be a brief statement of whom readers should contact if they have questions.

 **TWO SAMPLE PROPOSALS**

Figures 16.8 and 16.9 illustrate the conventional sections for proposals. In Figure 16.8 an environmental services and engineering firm is responding to an RFP. The writer proposes to prepare a plan for capping and closing an ash area at a lignite mine owned by Hill Manufacturing. In Figure 16.9, as part of a service-learning project, a student proposes a procedures manual for the university's Office of Disability Accommodation. This office helps students with disabilities receive appropriate accommodation from the university and helps faculty members who have these students in their classes. The readers of her proposal are the director and assistant director of that office.

**Sample Solicited Proposal**

**Nowakowski & Associates**

Nowakowski & Associates, Inc.
243 26th Street, Suite 808
Montrose, CO 80303-2317
303/555-1823 Fax: 303/555-1836

> The writer uses the letter format.

March 24, 2012

Ms. Ginny Thompson
Hill Manufacturing
400 North Vintage Street
St. Louis, MO 75201

> The writer identifies the document as a proposal.

Re: Work Plan and Cost Estimate to Develop a Conceptual Closure Plan for the Caney Branch Ash Disposal Facility

Dear Ms. Thompson:

> The writer combines the summary and introduction. Here, the writer describes the problem and the organization of the proposal.

As you requested, Nowakowski & Associates, Inc. is pleased to provide this work plan and cost estimate to develop a conceptual closure plan for the Caney Branch Ash Disposal Facility. We understand that Hill Manufacturing has decided to mine around the ash area. In November 2011, at your request we provided preliminary cost estimates for three capping scenarios that could be part of an overall closure plan for Caney Branch. However, these closure scenarios and perhaps others require a more detailed analysis of the system's hydrology and geochemistry before you select an appropriate closure scenario. On the basis of our recent discussion, the following proposal describes our understanding of the required scope of work and our work plan.

**Scope of Work**

> Because the proposal is solicited, the writer uses "Scope of Work" to identify the problem definition and briefly states the scope of work. The writer also states the work that the project will not include.

We understand that our scope of work will include the following:

- developing a set of recommendations for capping and closing the ash area at the Caney Branch Ash Disposal Facility
- compiling a conceptual design document that describes and illustrates the recommended approach for capping and closing the ash area

After developing the conceptual design document, if desired by Hill Manufacturing, we will present the technical merits of the plan at a meeting with Hill and then with the state Water Commission. As you requested, the conceptual document will not include final design specifications or detailed cost estimates required to implement the recommended closure plan. However, we propose to develop preliminary cost estimates as necessary to evaluate various closure alternatives.

**Work Plan**

> The writer provides an overview of the work plan.

To develop the conceptual closure plan, we will balance the level of effort and associated costs for preparing the plan with the requirements to provide sufficient documentation and justification for addressing possible questions from the state Water Commission. We will work closely with Hill to ensure that the level of effort and work are consistent with Hill's objectives. We will carry out four tasks to complete the work that Hill requires.

# FIGURE 16.8

**Sample Solicited Proposal** *continued*

The writer describes in detail each task in the work plan.

G. Thompson, March 24, 2012, p. 2

## Task 1. Reviewing Data and Developing Preliminary Closure Options

We request that Hill Manufacturing provide any water level data, sump discharge volume data, and sump water quality data obtained at Caney Branch since the Phase II Investigation (2011). We will review these data, along with the historical data provided in the Phase II Report, to further develop closure options. In developing a preliminary list of closure options, we will review correspondence from the Water Commission and registration papers regarding Caney Branch. We will examine the Water Commission's precedents for closure of ash disposal facilities at other lignite mines in the state. We will also use these reviews to further evaluate possible data gaps in the various closure options.

## Task 2. Collecting and Analyzing Additional Data

During Task 2, we will evaluate the need for collecting additional data; we currently envision two specific needs. The latest water-level readings, taken in selected ash and overburden wells at Caney Branch, were measured in early May 2011. The last complete set of readings for all wells occurred in October 2011. Historically, water levels in the ash have generally exhibited an upward trend but may be approaching a quasistatic condition. The quasistatic water level in the ash under present stratigraphic conditions is important because it serves as a baseline when estimating the long-term water-level conditions in a post-mining scenario. Therefore, we propose to obtain another set of water-level measurements in wells within and near Caney Branch to evaluate the baseline condition.

We foresee the need for new data on the ground-water chemistry for ash and overburden wells. Because attenuation of ash leachate constituents will likely be a critical basis for limiting the scope of closure activities, we will collect samples from selected wells to confirm that ash leachate constituents are continuing to attenuate. We presently anticipate that collecting and analyzing the samples from six monitoring wells will be sufficient to document that attenuation.

We will collect and analyze the samples in the same manner as in the Phase II investigation. Field analyses would include Ph, Eh, specific conductance, and temperature. However, we will analyze the samples in the lab for a shorter list of constituents than those evaluated during the Phase II investigation. The proposed list of constituents includes calcium (dissolved), magnesium (dissolved), sodium (dissolved), potassium (dissolved), chloride, sulfate, alkalinity, boron (dissolved), and selenium (dissolved). We will be most interested in the key parameters of sulfate, boron, and selenium. To estimate cost, we have assumed that Core Laboratories, which analyzed the water samples for Phase II, will analyze the samples. However, if desired, the Hill Manufacturing lab could analyze the samples.

## Task 3. Evaluating Closure Alternatives and Developing a Conceptual Closure Plan

The current mine plan calls for mining within 400 feet of Caney Branch. This plan will have substantial effects on both the short- and long-term hydrogeologic conditions near the ash area. Therefore, we will consider these effects when evaluating the closure options:

- effects of mining on the rate of ash water leaching
- extent of ash area dewatering caused by adjacent mining and the possible effects on induration of the ash
- time required to resaturate the spoil and ash material after mining
- post-mining hydrologic conditions (effects of spoil characteristics, ponds, etc., on post-mining hydrology)

FIGURE 16.8

**Sample Solicited Proposal** *continued*

G. Thompson, March 24, 2012, p. 3

- historical and future attenuation of ash water constituents
- hydrologic effects of constructing a flow barrier between the ash area and Barrier Lake (a slurry wall is currently not a preferred option, but we will review it to address possible questions from the Water Commission or to provide an alternative)
- cost-feasibility of construction options
- applicability of the Water Commission's Draft Risk Reduction Rules to Caney Branch
- potential post-closure care requirements and costs

Although we don't anticipate substantial modeling efforts associated with developing the conceptual plan, the existing model developed during the Phase II investigation will help us address some of the hydrologic issues. In some cases, we can use previous model simulations to assess an issue; and in other cases, we anticipate performing additional simulations. We anticipate using the HELP (Hydrologic Evaluation of Landfill Performance) model to evaluate the hydrology of various capping scenarios. In other cases, we will draw on experience at the Barrier Lake Mine and perhaps simple hydraulic calculations of water imbalance to develop estimates. The actual level of effort and list of critical issues will depend on which closure options we evaluate.

We will develop a narrative to justify and describe the conceptual closure plan and simple conceptual design drawings to illustrate the closure concept. We will present the draft closure plan to Hill Manufacturing at a meeting (Task 4). The report to Hill will not include complete documentation of model results and analyses as part of the conceptual planning.

**Task 4. Attend Strategic Planning Meetings**
We will estimate the time and material required to prepare for and present the technical merits of the proposed conceptual closure plan in meetings with Hill Manufacturing and the Water Commission. Our cost estimate assumes two meetings, one with Hill Manufacturing and one with the Water Commission.

**Schedule**
We estimate eight weeks for drafting the conceptual closure plan. We assume that Hill Manufacturing can provide during the first week of the project any additional data they have collected since 2011 (see Task O). We anticipate performing the field work associated with Task 2 within the first two weeks of the project. We will proceed with Tasks 1 and 3 while the lab analyzes the additional water samples (two- to three-week turnaround). After we receive the sample results, we estimate that we can finalize the conceptual closure plan in approximately three weeks. Table I summarizes the tentative schedule.

> The writer describes the schedule for completing the work.

**Cost Estimate**
We propose to execute the work plan on a time-and-materials basis according to our 2013 Schedule of Charges. We will provide periodic reports to the Hill Manufacturing Project Manager detailing the project's progress and will work closely with Hill Manufacturing personnel to streamline the work and ensure the project deliverables are consistent with Hill Manufacturing expectations. We will not exceed the following total cost estimate without authorization from Hill Manufacturing. If the project requires less work, the invoiced amount will be less than the estimated budget. The itemized cost estimate appears in Table II (see page 5).

> The writer introduces the budget.

FIGURE 16.8

**Sample Solicited Proposal** *continued*

G. Thompson, March 24, 2012, p. 4

### Table I: Schedule of Tasks

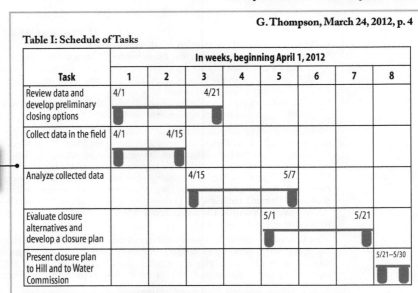

| Task | In weeks, beginning April 1, 2012 | | | | | | | |
|---|---|---|---|---|---|---|---|---|
| | 1 | 2 | 3 | 4 | 5 | 6 | 7 | 8 |
| Review data and develop preliminary closing options | 4/1 | | 4/21 | | | | | |
| Collect data in the field | 4/1 | 4/15 | | | | | | |
| Analyze collected data | | | 4/15 | | 5/7 | | | |
| Evaluate closure alternatives and develop a closure plan | | | | | 5/1 | | 5/21 | |
| Present closure plan to Hill and to Water Commission | | | | | | | | 5/21–5/30 |

The writer uses a Gantt Chart to show the schedule.

### Table II: Itemized Cost Estimates

| Task | Cost per unit in dollars | Total units | Total cost in dollars |
|---|---|---|---|
| **Task 1: Labor** | | | |
|   Principal | 100/hr | 4 | 400 |
|   Senior | 90/hr | 24 | 2,160 |
|   Staff | 55/hr | 4 | 220 |
|   Support Staff | 30/hr | 3 | 90 |
| **Task 1: Expenses** | | | |
|   Communications/Shipping | | | 75 |
|   Photocopies | | | 25 |
| **Task 1 Total** | | | 2970 |
| **Task 2: Labor** | | | |
|   Principal | 100/hr | 4 | 200 |
|   Senior | 90/hr | 24 | 1,440 |
|   Staff | 55/hr | 4 | 1,650 |
|   Support Staff | 30/hr | 3 | 60 |
| **Task 2: Expenses** | | | |
|   Vehicle | | | 200 |
|   Per Diem | 70/day | 2.5 | 175 |
|   Sampling Equipment | | | 100 |
|   Communication/Shipping | | | 200 |
|   Photocopies | | | 25 |
| **Task 2: Outside Services** | | | |
|   Lab Analysis | 108/sample | 6 | 648 |
|   10% Handling | | | 65 |

The writer presents a detailed budget for each task.

**Sample Solicited Proposal** *continued*

The writer presents a detailed budget for each task.

### Table II: Itemized Cost Estimates (continued)

| | | | |
|---|---|---|---|
| **Task 2 Total** | | | 4,813 |
| Task 3: Labor | | | |
| Principal | 100/hr | 32 | 3,200 |
| Senior | 90/hr | 140 | 12,600 |
| Project | 75/hr | 16 | 1,200 |
| Staff | 55/hr | 40 | 2,200 |
| Drafting | 40/hr | 24 | 960 |
| Support | 30/hr | 12 | 360 |
| Task 3: Expenses | | | |
| Communication/Shipping | | | 200 |
| Photocopies/Reproducing | | | 200 |
| **Task 3 Total** | | | 20,920 |
| Task 4: Labor | | | |
| Principal | 20/hr | 100/hr | 2,000 |
| Senior | 20/hr | 90/hr | 1,800 |
| Support Staff | 4/hr | 30/hr | 120 |
| Task 4: Expenses | | | |
| Travel | | | 200 |
| Communication/Shipping | | | 150 |
| Photocopies/Reproducing | | | 25 |
| **Task 4 Total** | | | 4,295 |
| **Estimated Project Total** | | | **32,998** |

The writer describes the qualifications of all the people who will complete the tasks.

### Qualifications

Bob Congrove, P.E., Senior Engineer, will serve as Project Manager and will provide much of the technical analysis and input for developing the conceptual closure plan. Mr. Congrove served as Project Manager for the Caney Branch Phase II Investigation and knows the conditions and Water Commission permitting processes and requirements.

Alejandro Martinez, P.E., Senior Civil Engineer, will provide conceptual design input on engineered components of the closure plan, such as capping specifications, and will assess the technical and financial feasibility of various closure options. Mr. Martinez has more than 22 years of applied engineering experience, including designing landfill caps, liner systems, and slurry walls, and developing landfill closure plans.

Brandon McCarroll, Principal Hydrogeologist, will provide input about geochemical processes affecting the mobility of ash leachate constituents. In addition, Donna Camp, Ben Armstrong, and Terry Huey (support staff) have recently worked on ash disposal projects and associated Water Commission permitting. As necessary, they will provide technical input and review. They will also participate in meetings with Hill Manufacturing and the state Water Commission.

The writer concludes by offering to answer questions.

If you have any questions about our recommended approach for developing the conceptual plan or about any other aspect of this proposal, please call me at (303) 555-1823.

Sincerely,

*Tom J. Nowakowski*

Tom J. Nowakowski
Senior Engineer

FIGURE 16.9

**Sample Unsolicited Proposal**

The writer uses a formal format.

## Proposal to Create a Training and Reference Manual for the Office of Disability Accommodation

The writer summarizes the problem, solution, schedule, and budget.

### Summary
The Office of Disability Accommodation does not have a Training and Reference Manual. We need a manual because our staff consists of only two full-time employees, many volunteers, and ten student interns. Our full-time employees are too busy to train new volunteers and to provide all the reference information for each situation that arises. We could use this manual to train volunteers and student interns. This manual will also consolidate the policies and procedures of our office, so that our staff can quickly refer to them.

I can complete the rough draft by May 24. The labor, materials, and supplies will cost approximately $1,048.74. However, I will donate my time to write and prepare the manual. This donation will reduce your cost for the manual to $48.74 for supplies and materials. If the rough draft is satisfactory, you will receive the final draft on June 1.

The writer uses informative headings.

### Current Problems at the Office of Disability Accommodation
The Office of Disability Accommodation uses many volunteers and student interns. These volunteers and interns may work in the office for only a semester, creating a large turnover. They may work as few as 5 or as many as 20 hours per week. With the number of these volunteers and interns and the high turnover, the office frequently has workers who do not understand how to do the various tasks assigned to them. To complete their assigned tasks, the volunteers and interns frequently must interrupt you and your administrative assistant or other workers. These interruptions slow the work of the office. The volunteers and interns have to interrupt others because they do not understand how to

The writer describes the nature of the problems.

- handle most student and faculty problems independently
- operate the office computers and equipment correctly
- administer basic office policies and procedures

Frequently, the volunteers and interns will handle a faculty or student problem independently even though they do not completely understand how to handle the problem. Such actions can create other problems that you or your administrative assistant must then handle. For example, a new volunteer might tell a faculty member that the office will be happy to monitor an exam for any student with a disability, when we only monitor exams for students who must use the technology in the computer lab for disability accommodation. Such mishandling is frustrating for you, your assistant, students, and faculty members. The volunteers and interns frequently must also ask questions about simple tasks such as running the copy machine or processing a student or faculty request because they have not received any training and do not have any written source of information about office machinery or policies and procedures.

The writer cites specific examples of the problems.

The purpose of this office is to help students with disabilities by informing faculty and students about appropriate and necessary accommodation and also to help faculty to understand how to make accommodations. When this office runs inefficiently and makes mistakes because of uninformed and untrained volunteers and interns, we don't create the positive image that the students and the faculty need.

FIGURE 16.9

**Sample Unsolicited Proposal** *continued*

The writer links
the solution to the
problems listed in
Current Problems.

**Proposed Solution: A Training and Reference Manual**
The proposed Training and Reference Manual will provide new volunteers and student interns with the training and information to
• handle most student and faculty problems independently
• operate the office computers and equipment correctly
• quickly learn the basic policies and procedures

I will write the Training and Reference Manual from my experience and will consult with your administrative assistant for technical information. The Training and Reference Manual will include the following sections.

**Answering Student Inquiries**
• Telephone Inquiries
• In-House Visits

**Working with New Students**
• Necessary Forms and Procedures
• Campus Offices of Assistance

**Working with Faculty Members**
• Pre-Semester Notification Packets
• Faculty Guide

The writer presents
a detailed outline
to show how the
proposed manual
will solve the
problem.

**Using Office Equipment and Computers**
• Equipment and Furniture
• Computers

**Understanding Procedures**
• Registering Students
  Early Registration
  Regular Registration
• Testing
  Regular Semester Exams
  Final Exam Procedures
• Filing
  Confidentiality
  Location of Different Files
• Issuing Elevator Keys
  Assigning Keys
  Returning Keys

**Working with Various Groups with Disabilities**
• Hearing Disabilities
• Visual Disabilities
• Motor/Mobility Disabilities
• Learning Disabilities
• Head-Injury Disabilities
• Hidden Disabilities
• Speech Disabilities

**FIGURE 16.9**

**Sample Unsolicited Proposal** *continued*

**Working with Volunteers**
- Applications
- On-Campus Service Groups

I can complete the Training and Reference Manual during the next seven weeks. During the week of May 17, the office volunteers and students will use the rough draft and give me their comments. I will then submit the draft to you on May 24. If the draft is satisfactory, you will receive the completed manual on June 1.

**My Qualifications for Writing the Proposed Manual**
I have worked in the Office of Disability Accommodation and in the computer lab for disability accommodation for three years as a student volunteer. I have seen and experienced first-hand the problems and frustrations of not understanding how to handle a student or faculty problem. I have worked in all phases of the office and am able to write the proposed manual. In addition, I am a senior majoring in rehabilitation therapy, so I understand the legal and ethical issues involved in working with students with disabilities.

**Budget**
The following table reflects the estimated cost of writing and printing the manual:

| Items | Time and Supplies | Cost (dollars) |
|---|---|---|
| Writing and Editing the Manual | 100 hours @ $10.00 per hour | $1,000.00 |
| Binding Costs | Vinyl Front and Back Spiral Binding | $5.18 |
| Colored Illustrations | 10 pages @ $2.50 per page | $25.00 |
| Tab Inserts | $0.89 for 5 pages x 4 packets | $3.56 |
| Copying Costs | 300 pages @ $0.05 a page | $15.00 |
| **Total Cost** | | **$1,048.74** |

I will donate my time in return for a receipt for my donation. Your cost for materials and supplies will be $48.74.

**Conclusion**
I am excited about the possibility of preparing this much-needed manual for our office. This manual will resolve our ongoing problem with training volunteers and student interns. I look forward to the possibility of working with you on this manual.

Source: Courtesy of Le Neva Bjelde Steiner.

*The writer includes a schedule.*

*The writer describes her experience.*

*The writer uses a table to present the budget.*

## With an *Eye* on Quality, Price Becomes Secondary in Awarding Bid[1]

### Background

A contract does not always go to the lowest bidder. When the city of Georgetown, Texas decided to accept bids for residential and commercial garbage collection, it left the guidelines open on its request for bids. Garbage disposal companies were encouraged to be creative in their bids to win the 4-year contract, which offered a renewal option for 10 years. The process was weighted toward quality, rather than price. The city council wanted to ensure it contracted a premium service for its nearly 11,000 combined residential and business accounts.

As city officials expected, they received a range of bids; but one, in particular, caught their attention. It was from Texas Disposal Systems (TDS) in Austin, Texas. Even though TDS didn't come in with the lowest price, it did offer an innovation to ensure quality. The disposal company offered to install video cameras on its garbage trucks to record its service.

TDS was awarded the contract, and the disposal company made an upfront investment of approximately $2,500 to install the cameras on each of its eight trucks. Some city officials were unconvinced that the added cost of awarding TDS the contract would pay off for either the city or the disposal company.

Soon after installation, however, the city and the disposal company began to realize rewards. Cameras on the front and back of the trucks captured customers' canister numbers, workers emptying containers, and the date and time of service. As a result, if a customer complained that his or her garbage was not picked up, TDS could go back and review videotapes to verify service to that customer's serial number on a particular day. In addition, TDS was able to review tapes to see which customers were illegally disposing of hazardous wastes and to improve worker procedures to ensure quality. In one instance, the tapes were even used to avoid a costly lawsuit when a customer claimed that a garbage truck had damaged her vehicle. The tapes showed no liability on TDS' part, and the customer dropped the claim. For its part, the city of Georgetown has received exemplary service as a result of TDS' cameras. Because the cameras catch every move, workers are more likely to pick up spills and errant papers, which improves quality and service in trash collection throughout the city.

[1] Compiled from wasteage.com/mag/waste_eye_collection_wins/.

## Assignment

1. Assume you are submitting a bid for a service that you know will be priced higher than your competitor's. You may be tempted to lower the price up front and then ask the customer to pay more later. Write a paragraph exploring the ethics of lowering the price simply to win a bid. Turn your paragraph in to your instructor.

2. Make a two-column list. On the left side, list some types of work where price is more important than quality. On the right side, list other types of work where quality is more important than price. Be prepared to present your list to your classmates.

DOWNLOAD A WORKSHEET FOR WRITING PERSUASIVE PROPOSALS ONLINE AT
WWW.GRTEP.COM

1. For your technical communications class, prepare a report or manual. Follow these steps to select a topic and write a proposal for that report or manual.
   a. Make a list of possible topics, and gather information about each one. You might select topics related to your major, to a need in your community, or to your current job. As you gather information, use some of the research techniques and tools you learned in Chapter 5.
   b. Brainstorm the feasibility of each topic. As you brainstorm, list the pros and cons of each topic and consider the amount of time you have to complete the project and the importance of the topic to you, your field, the readers, your community, or your workplace.
   c. After you've considered the pros and cons of each possible topic, select a topic and write a memo asking your instructor to approve your choice. In your memo, give your instructor enough information to understand and evaluate the topic.
   d. Include a list of possible sources of information in your memo to your instructor. Remember to follow either MLA, CSE, or APA style as you list your sources.
   e. After your instructor approves your topic, write a proposal addressed either to your instructor or to a person who would make a decision about your proposed topic. Include the conventional sections relevant to your proposal.

2. Evaluate your proposal using the questions in the online Worksheet for Writing Persuasive Proposals. After you have evaluated your proposal, revise it based on your answers to the questions.

3. Bring three copies of the proposal that you revised for Exercise 2 to class. Using the copies of your proposal, three of your classmates will read and evaluate your proposal based on questions in the online Worksheet for Writing Persuasive Proposals. Your instructor may ask you to post your proposal on the class website or bulletin board so classmates can use the comment function of a word-processing program to comment on your proposal.

4. Based on your classmates' answers to the questions in Exercise 3, revise your proposal as needed. Prepare a final draft proposal for your instructor.

# REAL WORLD EXPERIENCE

## Writing a Proposal to Solve a Problem in Your Community

You probably are aware of many problems and needs on your college or university campus or in the surrounding community. For instance, your campus may not have sufficient lighting for students walking across campus after dark; or in your community, some children may not receive toys at Christmas or Hanukkah; or some senior citizens may need their homes painted and work done in their yards.

### Assignment

Your team will write a proposal to solve a problem on your campus or in the surrounding community. To write this proposal, complete these steps:

1. Select a problem on campus or in the surrounding community. Make sure that you and all members of your team are familiar with the problem and that team members can gather the needed information about the problem to propose a persuasive solution in the allotted time.
2. Gather information about the problem and about the proposal readers. Develop possible solutions.
3. Discuss the advantages, disadvantages, and feasibility of each solution. Then determine the most effective solution for the readers.
4. Write the proposal and send it to campus or community leaders who could approve your proposal. Give a copy to your instructor.

# chapter *seventeen*

## Writing Reader-Focused Definitions and Descriptions

*Y*ou see and use definitions daily. For example, you might read a definition of a technical term used in one of your textbooks or you might read an extended definition of a complex term or concept such as bioengineering or nanotechnology. A *definition* tells the reader what something is; it can be as simple as a word or sentence or as complex as several paragraphs.

iStockphoto 2008.

You might describe how something looks or how something works. Descriptions create a picture using words and graphics. *Descriptions* in technical communications provide information on a product or a process for readers who need to know about it or how to use, produce, or purchase it. For example, if you work for a company that sells solar panels, you might write a description about how the solar panels work to generate electricity.

Definitions and descriptions often work together. For example, if you work for a pharmaceutical company, you might write a fact sheet to accompany a drug. The fact sheet would include a definition, but also a description of how the drug works and its side effects. Reader-focused definitions and descriptions use

- precise language
- a logical organization
- visual information when necessary

In this chapter, you will learn techniques for writing reader-focused definitions and descriptions. We will also focus on a common type of description: technical marketing materials.

##  PLANNING DEFINITIONS AND DESCRIPTIONS

To plan your definitions and descriptions,
- Find out about your readers.
- Anticipate and answer your readers' questions.
- Plan for precise, accurate language.
- Design the visual information.

### Find Out about Your Readers

Begin planning your document by learning about your readers' needs and expectations. Determine your readers' knowledge about what you are defining and what you are describing. Find out why your readers need the definition or description. For example, do they need to understand a technical term while they are reading a report? Or do they need to understand a technical concept so they can complete a task or use a product? Use the following questions to gather information about your readers. Once you have answered these questions, you can decide on the format and level of technical terminology appropriate for your readers.

- What do your readers know about what you are defining or describing?
- Why do they need the definition or description? To gather information? To understand technical terminology or concepts? To complete a task? To make a decision? To find out about your product?
- Are they internal or external to your organization?
- Will more than one group of readers read your definition or description?
- In what context will they read the description or definition? As consumers? As users? As decision makers?
- What level of technical terminology will they understand or expect?

## Anticipate and Answer Your Readers' Questions

To help readers understand your definitions and descriptions, gather the information necessary to answer their questions. This task may be as simple as determining if they understand specific terminology or as complex as employing primary and secondary research techniques (see Chapter 5). Although the specific questions vary with your purpose for writing, your readers will expect your definitions and descriptions to answer the questions in Figure 17.1.

## Plan for Precise, Accurate Language

Readers of technical documents expect precise
- measurements, weights, and dimensions
- locations and spatial relationships
- positions

Consider these examples:

| Imprecise | Precise |
|---|---|
| solar panels | monocrystalline silicon solar panels |
| near the power button | above the red power button |

When you use precise, accurate language, you eliminate language that focuses on individuals or opinions.

| Focuses on Opinions | Precise |
|---|---|
| The car gets **great** gas mileage. | The Toyota Prius gets 48 mpg on the highway and 45 in the city. |

**FIGURE 17.1**

### Questions Readers May Ask When Reading Definitions and Descriptions

- Why should I read this definition or description?
- What is the purpose of this definition or description?
- How do I know the information is honest, accurate, and complete?
- Are the information and the document credible?

## Design the Visual Information

As you plan your definitions and descriptions, decide what visual information, if any, your readers need. For example, if you are simply defining a technical term in a parenthetical definition, you probably do not need visual information. If you are describing for general readers what causes acid rain, a drawing will help them understand the process. For expert readers, you probably would not need a drawing.

The most commonly used graphics in definitions and descriptions are

- line drawings
- diagrams
- flowcharts
- photographs

If you decide to use graphics, plan for them early in the writing process. They take time to prepare; for example, if you plan to use line drawings or diagrams, you may need to hire someone to prepare them.

##  WRITING READER-FOCUSED DEFINITIONS

You can use three types of definitions: parenthetical, sentence, or extended. In this section, we discuss each type of definition.

## Parenthetical Definitions

*Parenthetical definitions* define a term by rephrasing it in words readers can understand. These definitions usually occur in parentheses immediately following the word(s) being defined. In these examples, the parenthetical definition appears in bold.

> Store the camera in an area where the ambient **(surrounding)** temperature reaches no higher than 86°F **(30°C)**.

> The Mini Cooper is equipped with a six-speed manual transmission or a continuously variable **(automatic)** transmission.

## Sentence Definitions

If your definition or your readers require more than a word or phrase, use a *sentence definition* with these elements of a formal definition: term to be defined, class of object or concept to which the term belongs and *differentia*. **Differentia** refers to what makes the term different from all other similar terms. Figure 17.2 shows examples of sentence definitions divided by the elements of a formal definition. Each of these examples uses words familiar to general readers.

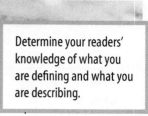

Determine your readers' knowledge of what you are defining and what you are describing.

Use sentence definitions when your readers require only a basic understanding of a term or concept. For example, the definition of radon in Figure 17.2 is appropriate for an informal report to a homeowner whose house you are inspecting. However, if you are writing a formal report for the U.S. Environmental Protection Agency on the effects of radon on public health, you would use an extended definition.

## Extended Definitions

For some readers and purposes, you may need an extended (expanded) definition. *Extended definitions* are explanations of a term, concept, or process. They are usually one or more paragraphs long, depending on your purpose and your readers. You have probably read extended definitions in textbooks or in user manuals. Extended definitions often begin with a sentence definition, as in this example:

> Bacteria are single-celled organisms that typically range in size from about 0.5 to 20 micrometers.

This definition tells you the classification of the organism and its size. However, it doesn't tell you how some bacteria cause illness or which bacteria are beneficial and which are harmful. Extend the definition to provide that information.

**Sentence Definitions**

| Term | Class | Differentia |
|------|-------|-------------|
| Ozone is | a gas | that occurs both in the Earth's upper atmosphere and at ground level. |
| Radon is | a natural radioactive gas | that you can't see, smell, or taste and that causes cancer. |
| Influenza is | an acute, highly contagious respiratory disease | that occurs sporadically or in epidemics, lasts up to a month, and rarely causes stomach upsets or diarrhea. |

## TIPS FOR WRITING READER-FOCUSED EXTENDED DEFINITIONS

- **Use language familiar to your readers.** If you define terms, concepts, or processes using unfamiliar language, your definition will not help your readers. Learn enough about your readers to write a definition appropriate to their level of knowledge and experience.

- **Use precise language.** For example, if you are defining ozone, don't write, "Gases combine with the air to create ozone." This language is imprecise. Write instead, "Ozone is created when NOx (nitrogen oxide) and VOC (volatile organic compounds) combine with heat and sunlight."

- **Use language accessible to readers of other cultures and languages.** Use Simplified Technical English to ensure that readers from other cultures and languages can understand your definitions. (See Chapter 8 for information on Simplified Technical English.) Avoid analogies that may not work for readers of other cultures and languages.

- **Use the standard patterns of organization to structure your extended definition.** Some of the more commonly used patterns include spatial order, partition, and comparison and contrast. (See Chapter 6 for information on these patterns.)

- **Use graphics when possible.** Graphics help readers to visualize a process or concept. (See Chapter 11 for information on creating graphics.)

- **Place the definition where the readers need it.** If your extended definition is part of a longer document, place the definition in the most convenient location so readers have the information they need to understand the rest of the document.

You can extend a definition using any of these techniques:
- examples
- partition
- principle of operation
- comparison and contrast
- negation
- history
- etymology
- stipulation
- graphics

## Extending with Examples

*Examples* are one of the most commonly used ways to extend definitions. Examples are especially helpful when you want to make an abstract term, concept, or unfamiliar process familiar to your readers. In the following extended definition of pesticide, the writer includes examples of common household pesticides. The examples help readers understand what pesticides are by associating a less familiar term (pesticide) with familiar examples (household products):

> A pesticide is any substance or mixture of substances intended to prevent, destroy, repel, or mitigate pests; a pest is any living organism that occurs where it is not wanted or may damage crops or injure humans or animals. Some common examples of pesticides found in many household products are
> - cockroach sprays and baits
> - insect repellents
> - rat and other rodent poisons
> - flea and tick sprays, powders, and pet collars
> - kitchen, laundry, and bath disinfectants and sanitizers
> - products that kill mold and mildew
> - some lawn and garden products, such as weed killers
> - some swimming pool chemicals[1]

## Extending with Partition

*Partition* is the division of an item into its individual parts, so readers can better understand the item as a whole (see Chapter 6). In the following example from the U.S. Department of Agriculture, the writer divides "grains" into two types: whole grains and refined grains. With this partitioning, readers can better understand the definition of all grains.

---

[1] Source: Adapted from "What is a Pesticide?" www.epa.gov/pesticides/about/index.htm#what_pesticide.

Grains are divided into two subgroups, **whole grains** and **refined grains**. Whole grains contain the entire grain kernel: bran, germ, and endosperm. Some examples of whole grains are

- whole-wheat flour
- bulgur (cracked wheat)
- oatmeal
- brown rice

Refined grains have been milled, a process that removes the bran and germ. Although this process gives grains a finer texture and improves their shelf life, it also removes dietary fiber, iron, and many B vitamins. Some examples of refined grain products are

- white flour
- white bread
- white rice[2]

## Extending through Principle of Operation

You extend a definition by explaining how something works, especially if you are defining a process or an object. To define gas turbine, the writer uses the principle of operation. The term is first defined as an internal combustion engine; however, some readers may not know how an engine works, so the writer explains how the engine—in this case, a gas turbine—works.

> A gas turbine engine is a type of internal combustion engine. The engine converts energy stored in the fuel to useful mechanical energy in the form of rotational power. The term "gas" refers to the ambient air that is taken into the engine and used as the working medium in the energy conversion process.
>
> This air is first drawn into the engine where it is compressed, mixed with fuel and ignited. The resulting hot gas expands at high velocity through a series of airfoil-shaped blades transferring energy created from combustion to turn an output shaft. The residual thermal energy in the hot exhaust gas can be harnessed for a variety of industrial processes.[3]

[2] Source: mypyramid.gov.
[3] Source: mysolar.cat.com/cda/layout?m=35442&x=7.

## Extending through Comparison and Contrast

You extend a definition by comparing or contrasting it to similar concepts, processes, or terms familiar to the reader. In Figure 17.3, the writer extends the definition of bonds to stocks and money market instruments. Notice how the writer has organized the definition by the type of investment tool and then used the same criteria (definition and risk) to define each tool.

**FIGURE 17.3**

### Using Comparison and Contrast to Extend a Definition

A *bond* is a debt security, issued by a government, municipality, corporation, other entity. The issuer promises to repay the buyer the amount of the bond (the principal) plus a specified rate of interest during the life of the bond. In the chart below, you can see how bonds compare with two other common investment tools: stocks and money-market instruments.

| Investment Tool | Definition | Level of Risk | Examples |
|---|---|---|---|
| Bond | A debt security, similar to an I.O.U., issued by a government, municipality, corporation, or other entity | Moderate | • U.S. government securities<br>• Municipal bonds<br>• Mortgage and asset-backed securities<br>• Foreign government bonds |
| Stock | Ownership shares in a company | High | • Shares in McDonalds<br>• Shares in Apple<br>• Shares in Dow Chemical |
| Money Market | Short-term, interest-bearing investments | Low | • Money market accounts<br>• Certificates of Deposit (CDs) |

TAKING IT INTO THE *workplace*

### Understanding the Technical Professional's Role in Writing Marketing Materials

Even when companies have marketing divisions responsible for preparing technical marketing materials, these divisions need experts to draft the technical information, such as specifications and process descriptions. In some smaller companies, the technical experts may be responsible not only for drafting the technical information, but also for writing and perhaps designing the marketing materials. You may work for such a company when you graduate.

### Assignment

1. Interview a technical professional who works for a company that manufacturers a product. You may conduct the interview by phone or by email. (For information on conducting interviews, see Chapter 5.) The purpose of your interview is to determine the professional's role in preparing the technical marketing materials.
2. Write a memo to your instructor summarizing what you learned from your interview. Attach the list of questions you used for the interview. (For information on writing memos, see Chapter 12.)
3. Write a follow-up thank-you letter or email to the professional whom you interviewed. (For information on writing follow-up letters, see Chapter 13.)

## Extending through Negation

You extend a definition by telling readers what the term, concept, or process *is not*. You must use negation with other techniques for extending a definition because once you have told a reader what a term, concept, or process is not, you should tell the reader what it is, as in the following example:

> In the U.S., football is not soccer. Football is played with a spherical ball whereas soccer is played with a round ball and has different rules.

## Extending through History

You extend a definition by giving historical or background information to help readers understand a term, concept, or process. In the example below, the writer extends the definition of mouse by giving its history:

> Invented by Douglas Engelbart of Stanford Research Center in 1963 and pioneered by Xerox in the 1970s, the mouse is one of the great breakthroughs in computer ergonomics because it frees the user from using the keyboard. The mouse is important for graphical user interfaces because you can simply point to options and objects and click a button on the mouse. The mouse is also useful for graphics programs that allow you to draw pictures by using the mouse like a pen, pencil, or paintbrush. Users can select from several types of mice such as:
> - **Mechanical.** On its underside, this mouse has a rubber ball that can roll in all directions. Mechanical sensors within the mouse detect the direction the ball is rolling and move the screen pointer accordingly.
> - **Optical.** This mouse operates similarly to the mechanical mouse, but uses LED optical sensors to detect the motion of the ball.
> - **Cordless or Infrared.** This mouse relays a signal to a wireless hub. The cordless mouse requires batteries.
> - **Trackball.** This mouse stays stationary as users use their thumb or index finger to move a ball that sits on top of the mouse.[4]

## Extending through Etymology

For some terms and concepts, you extend the definition through etymology. *Etymology* is defining a word by tracing its derivation. You may combine etymology with other techniques for extending a definition. In the following definition, etymology is used to define phishing.

> Phishing is the act of sending an e-mail to a user and falsely claiming to be a legitimate organization. The sender is attempting to scam the user to share private information. The e-mail redirects the user to a bogus Web site where he or she is asked to update personal information. The word phishing "comes from the analogy that Internet scammers are using e-mail lures to fish for passwords and financial data from the sea of Internet users. The term was coined in 1996 by hackers who were stealing AOL Internet accounts by scamming passwords from unsuspecting AOL users. Since hackers have a tendency to replace "f" with "ph" the term phishing was derived.[5]

[4] Source: adapted from Webopedia. http://www.webopedia.com/TERM/M/mouse.html
[5] Source: www.webopedia.com/DidYouKnow/Internet/2005/phishing.asp.

Use etymology to define an acronym, as in this example.

> LASIK stands for laser-assisted in *situ* keratomileusis and is a procedure that permanently changes the shape of the cornea.

### Extending through Stipulation

Use stipulation when you restrict (stipulate) the meaning of a term for a particular situation. In the following example, the writer stipulates the meaning of pesticide. The readers then know that any time the writers use pesticide, it refers to insecticides, herbicides, and fungicides.

> In this report, we use the term pesticide to refer to insecticides, herbicides, and fungicides.

### Extending through Graphics

Use graphics to extend a definition to help readers visualize a concept or a process. If you use graphics, incorporate callouts to help readers focus on what you want them to see. In the extended definition in Figure 17.4, the writer uses a diagram to show how ozone develops.

### A Sample Extended Definition

In the sample extended definition in Figure 17.5, the writer defines cochlear implant. The definition begins with a sentence definition, and then the writer uses the following techniques to extend the definition: graphics, partition, examples, comparison/contrast, and principle of operation.

## WRITING READER-FOCUSED DESCRIPTIONS

As a technical professional, you may need to describe any of the following:

- **Process.** A *process* is an action that brings about a result. Usually, the action takes place over time. You are familiar with many processes, such as digesting food or registering for classes. A process description differs from instructions; when you describe a process, you tell what happens, whereas in instructions, you tell the user how to perform the steps of the process.
- **Mechanism.** A *mechanism* is a machine—an object with parts that work together. For example, a helicopter, a car, and a coffeemaker are mechanisms. Each of these mechanisms has identifiable parts that work together.

FIGURE 17.4

**Using Graphics to Extend a Definition**

## What is Ozone?

### *Ozone: Good Up High - Bad Nearby*

Ozone (03) is a highly reactive gas composed of three oxygen atoms. Depending on where it is in the atmosphere, ozone affects life on Earth in either good or bad ways.

Stratospheric ozone is formed naturally through the interaction of solar ultraviolet (UV) radiation with molecular oxygen (02). The stratospheric "ozone layer" extends from approximately six to thirty miles above the Earth's surface and reduces the amount of harmful UV radiation reaching the Earth's surface.

Tropospheric, or ground-level, ozone forms primarily from reactions between two major classes of air pollutants: volatile organic compounds (VOCs) and nitrogen oxides (NOx). These reactions depend on the presence of heat and sunlight, meaning more ozone forms in the summer months.

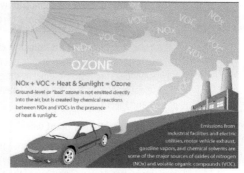

NOx is emitted by cars, power plants, industrial plants, and other sources. Significant sources of VOC emissions include gasoline pumps, chemical plants, oil-based paints, auto body shops, print shops, consumer products and some trees. Significant human made sources of VOC emissions include gasoline pumps, chemical plants, oil-based paints, auto body shops, print shops, and some consumer products.

Source: Downloaded from the World Wide Web, November 2008: www.epa.gov/airomsmo/airaware/day1-ozone.html.

- **Object.** An *object* is a single item. That item might be part of a helicopter, a car, or a coffeemaker. For example, if you describe the propeller of a helicopter, you are describing an object.

Descriptions of these items usually appear in documents used in the workplace: technical marketing brochures, instructions, manuals, proposals, websites, or even reports. For

FIGURE 17.5

## Extended Definition

### What is a cochlear implant?

The writer begins with a sentence definition.

A cochlear implant is a small, complex electronic device that can help to provide a sense of sound to a person who is profoundly deaf or severely hard-of-hearing. The implant consists of an external portion that sits behind the ear and a second portion that is surgically placed under the skin (see figure). An implant has the following parts:

The writer uses partition.

- A microphone, which picks up sound from the environment.
- A speech processor, which selects and arranges sounds picked up by the microphone.
- A transmitter and receiver/stimulator, which receive signals from the speech processor and convert them into electric impulses.
- An electrode array, which is a group of electrodes that collects the impulses from the stimulator and sends them to different regions of the auditory nerve.

The writer uses graphics to extend the definition.

An implant does not restore normal hearing. Instead, it can give a deaf person a useful representation of sounds in the environment and help him or her to understand speech.

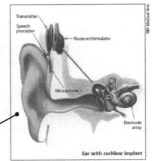

Credit: NIH Medical Arts
Ear with cochlear implant.

### How does a cochlear implant work?

The writer uses the principle of operation.

A cochlear implant is very different from a hearing aid. Hearing aids amplify sounds so they may be detected by damaged ears. Cochlear implants bypass damaged portions of the ear and directly stimulate the auditory nerve. Signals generated by the implant are sent by way of the auditory nerve to the brain, which recognizes the signals as sound. Hearing through a cochlear implant is different from normal hearing and takes time to learn or relearn. However, it allows many people to recognize warning signals, understand other sounds in the environment, and enjoy a conversation in person or by telephone.

Credit: Centers for Disease Control and Prevention (CDC)

### Who gets cochlear implants?

Children and adults who are deaf or severely hard-of-hearing can be fitted for cochlear implants. According to the U.S. Food and Drug Administration (FDA), as of December 2010, approximately 219,000 people worldwide have received implants. In the United States, roughly 42,600 adults and 28,400 children have received them.

Source: Downloaded from the World Wide Web, November 2008: www.nidcd.nih.gov/health/hearing/coch.asp. "Cochlear Implants." National Institute on Deafness and Other Communication Disorders.

**Extended Definition** *continued*

Adults who have lost all or most of their hearing later in life often can benefit from cochlear implants. They learn to associate the signal provided by an implant with sounds they remember. This often provides recipients with the ability to understand speech solely by listening through the implant, without requiring any visual cues such as those provided by lipreading or sign language.

Cochlear implants, coupled with intensive postimplantation therapy, can help young children to acquire speech, language, and social skills. Most children who receive implants are between two and six years old. Early implantation provides exposure to sounds that can be helpful during the critical period when children learn speech and language skills. In 2000, the FDA lowered the age of eligibility to 12 months for one type of cochlear implant.

### How does someone receive a cochlear implant?

The writer uses the principle of operation.

Use of a cochlear implant requires both a surgical procedure and significant therapy to learn or relearn the sense of hearing. Not everyone performs at the same level with this device. The decision to receive an implant should involve discussions with medical specialists, including an experienced cochlear-implant surgeon. The process can be expensive. For example, a person's health insurance may cover the expense, but not always. Some individuals may choose not to have a cochlear implant for a variety of personal reasons. Surgical implantations are almost always safe, although complications are a risk factor, just as with any kind of surgery. An additional consideration is learning to interpret the sounds created by an implant. This process takes time and practice. Speech-language pathologists and audiologists are frequently involved in this learning process. Prior to implantation, all of these factors need to be considered.

### What does the future hold for cochlear implants?

With advancements in technology and continued follow-up studies with people who already have received implants, researchers are evaluating how cochlear implants might be used for other types of hearing loss.

NIDCD is supporting research to improve upon the benefits provided by cochlear implants. It may be possible to use a shortened electrode array, inserted into a portion of the cochlea, for individuals whose hearing loss is limited to the higher frequencies. Other studies are exploring ways to make a cochlear implant convey the sounds of speech more clearly. Researchers also are looking at the potential benefits of pairing a cochlear implant in one ear with either another cochlear implant or a hearing aid in the other ear.

## TIPS FOR WRITING DESCRIPTIONS OF A PROCESS, MECHANISM, OR OBJECT

- **Introduce the description.** If the description will appear in a separate document, give it a title. If it will appear as part of another document, include an informative heading identifying what you are describing (see Figure 17.6).

- **Use the appropriate level of detail.** To determine how much detail is appropriate, you must know your readers and their expectations. For example, if you are describing for general readers the effects of nature on barrier islands, you would use less detail than if you were writing a report for the U.S. Geological Survey.

- **Use the standard patterns of organization.** For *process descriptions,* use the chronological pattern. For *mechanisms* and *objects,* use a spatial pattern or general-to-specific description. If you use the general-to-specific pattern, begin with a general definition of the object or mechanism and move to the specifics of how it functions or how it is used. For more complex objects or mechanisms, combine the organizational patterns. For example, if you are describing the human body, you could describe it spatially from the head to the toes. You could also describe it using a general-to-specific pattern, beginning with a definition of the human body and then describing the specific systems of the body: the nervous system, the digestive system, the musculoskeletal system, and the respiratory and circulatory systems.

- **Use language familiar to your readers.** Determine your readers' knowledge of your subject and use language they will understand.

- **Use present tense.** Unless you are describing a process, mechanism, or object that occurred in the historical past, use the present tense. For example, if you are describing how the Grand Canyon was created, you would use the present tense because it still exists. If you were describing how the Twin Towers, destroyed on 9/11, were built, you would use past tense because the towers no longer exist.

- **Use graphics.** To effectively describe most objects and mechanisms, use a graphic so readers get a picture of what you are describing. Graphics are especially important if you are describing a complex object or mechanism that is new or unfamiliar to most readers. The most commonly used graphics for descriptions are photographs, drawings, diagrams, and flowcharts. Figure 17.6 uses a drawing with numbers to orient the description and to help readers visualize the oven.

- **Place the description where readers will need it.** For example, if you are describing a product in a manual, place the description early in the manual before you tell the user how to use the product.

FIGURE 17.6

**Description Using a Graphic**

**How it works.**

The C3 oven uses patented technology to cook up to 10 times faster than the conventional methods.

1. Electricity heats a large volume of air outside the cooking chamber to approximately 500 degrees.
2. Heated air is circulated around the food at speeds up to 60 mph.
3. A vacuum at the bottom of the oven pulls the hot air down, forming a moving heat shroud around the surface of the food.
4. Air passes through a catalytic converter, is released, then returned to the top of the oven and into the cooking chamber again.
5. While the air is circulating a microwave system cooks food from the inside out, with precisely controlled bursts of energy.

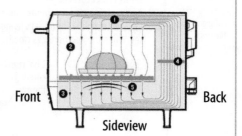

Source: Downloaded from the World Wide Web, November 2008: www.turbochef.com/commercial/our-products-how-it-works.htm. Used with permission.

example, if your company is writing a brochure on a new product, you would write a description of how the product works. If you are redesigning equipment in a manufacturing plant, you would describe how the redesigned equipment will work or how the parts of the equipment will work together.

Descriptions do not have a conventional structure like a proposal or a report. However, you can use the Tips for Writing Descriptions of a Process, Mechanism, or Object to ensure that you achieve your purpose and answer your readers' questions.

## Sample Descriptions

Figure 17.7 is an excerpt from a process description of cataract surgery. The description helps general readers who want to understand what to expect when having cataract surgery.

FIGURE 17.7

**Process Description**

The writer uses language familiar to and appropriate for the users.

## Cataract Surgery

### What is a cataract?

A cataract is a clouding of the eye's naturally clear lens. The lens focuses light rays on the retina—tile layer of light-sensing cells lining tile back of the eye—to produce a sharp image of what we see. When the lens becomes cloudy, light rays cannot pass through it easily, and vision is blurred.

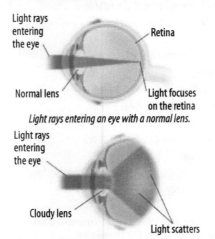

Light rays entering the eye

Retina

Normal lens

Light focuses on the retina

*Light rays entering an eye with a normal lens.*

Light rays entering the eye

Cloudy lens

Light scatters

*Light rays entering an, eye with a cataract. When a cataract forms, the lens of your eye is cloudy, light cannot pass through it easily, and your vision.*

### What causes cataracts?

Cataract development is a normal process of aging, but cataracts also develop from eye injuries, certain diseases or medications. Your genes may also play a role in cataract development.

### How can a cataract be treated?

A cataract may not need to be treated if your vision is only slightly blurry. Simply changing your eyeglass prescription may help to improve your vision for a while. There are no medications, eyedrops, exercises or glasses that will cause cataracts to disappear once they have formed. Surgery is the only way to remove a cataract. When you are no longer able to see well enough to do the things you like to do, cataract surgery should be considered.

In cataract surgery, the cloudy lens is removed from the eye through a surgical incision. In most cases, the natural lens is replaced with a permanent intraocular lens ( IOL) implant.

Source: Downloaded from the World Wide Web, November 2008: www.medem.com/MedLB/article_detaillb_for_printer.cfm?article_ID=ZZZY9VMAC8C&sub_cat=119. Courtesy of American Academy of Ophthalmology.

# FIGURE 17.7

**Process Description** *continued*

## What can I expect if I decide to have cataract surgery?

### Before Surgery

To determine if your cataract should be removed, your ophthalmologist (Eye M.D.) will perform a thorough eye examination. Before surgery, your eye will be measured to determine the proper power of the intraocular lens that will be placed in your eye. Ask your ophthalmologist if you should continue taking your usual medications before surgery.

You should make arrangernents to have someone drive you home after surgery.

### The Day of Surgery

Surgery is usually done on an outpatient basis, either in a hospital, an outpatient surgical center, or an ambulatory surgery center. You may be asked to skip breakfast, depending on the time of your surgery.

When you arrive for surgery, you will be given eye drops and perhaps a mild sedative to help you relax. A local anesthetic will numb your eye. The skin around your eye will be thoroughly cleansed, and sterile coverings will be placed amund your head. Your eye will be kept open by an eye lid speculum. You may see light and movement, but you will not be able to see the surgery while it is happening.

Under an operating mic ros cope, a small inci sion is made in the eye. In most cat ar act surgeri es, tiny surgical in struments are use d to break apart and remove the cl oudy lens from ti,e eye. The back membrane of the lens (ca lled the post eri or capsule) is left in place.

The writer organizes the process using a chronological pattern.

The writer uses simple graphics to help readers visualize the process.

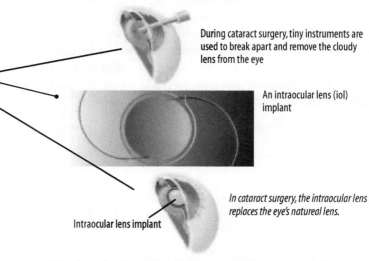

During cataract surgery, tiny instruments are used to break apart and remove the cloudy lens from the eye

An intraocular lens (iol) implant

Intraocular lens implant

*In cataract surgery, the intraocular lens replaces the eye's natureal lens.*

After surgery is completed, your doctor may place a shield over your eye. After a short stay in the outpatient recovery area, you will be ready to go home.

## Focus on Descriptions in Technical Marketing Materials

Technical marketing materials include product descriptions. As a technical professional, you may write descriptions to be included in these materials. You would describe the product accurately and persuasively encourage your readers to purchase the product. The readers may have any level of knowledge of your product and field—from general readers to expert. Technical descriptions help these readers visualize a product and determine how its features and specifications meet their needs.

Technical marketing documents come in many forms, such as:

- **Web pages.** Companies often put descriptions of products on their websites. These sites provide a flexible, inexpensive medium for presenting extensive descriptions. The Web page in Figure 17.8 is the home page for Cadillac. This page uses positive language, written in both general and precise language, and includes an attractive photo. Compare this page with Figure 17.9, another page from the same website. In Figure 17.9 the writers use precise language to back up some of the information on the home page (Figure 17.8).
- **Specification sheets, sometimes called fact sheets.** Specification, or fact, sheets focus on basic product information. They present the information more straightforwardly than do most Web pages and brochures. They may be printed double sided on 8½″ x 11″ paper. These pages can be more difficult to design because they are information rich, yet they must be attractive, inviting, and easy to access. You may also see specifications on consumer websites. Figure 17.9 from the Cadillac website includes a photo, the exterior dimensions, and precise information about the engine, transmission, and fuel system. The writer uses precise language and an appropriate amount of detail.
- **Brochures.** An effectively designed and written brochure can show readers the quality of your product. Brochures can be expensive to produce, and you must reprint them as the product changes. To save money, many organizations put PDFs of their brochures and fact sheets on their websites so readers can download them and the PDFs can be updated as the product changes.

FIGURE 17.8

**Technical Marketing Web Page**

## Using Persuasive, Accurate Language in Technical Marketing Materials

While your primary purpose in writing technical marketing material is to persuade, you also must give readers accurate, honest information about the product. You want to attract readers with positive, upbeat language to describe your product; however, for readers to trust that your claims are honest and accurate, you also must include precise information about its features and specifications. Readers may be suspicious of persuasive language that is unaccompanied by specific information about the product's features. For example, if you have a testimonial from a client who says the software is great and helped improve productivity, you must balance that testimonial with information on how the software improves productivity. In the following example from the Cadillac website, the writer says:

> As is the case with its design, the CTS Coupe Concept extends the acclaimed capabilities of the sedan in terms of performance technology. This includes the capability to support a broad engine range of gasoline and diesel engines. The CTS Coupe Concept supports the sedan's 3.6L V-6 engines, including the 304-horsepower (227 kW) Direct Injection power plant. The CTS Coupe Concept also is designed for a new 2.9L turbo diesel being developed for international markets. This new engine, tailored for use in the CTS, will deliver an estimated 250 horsepower (184 kW) and 406 lb.-ft. of torque (550 Nm). A six-speed manual transmission backs the engine, sending torque to an independently sprung rear axle. The CTS Coupe Concept's sport-tuned suspension gives it a slightly lower ride height than a production CTS – a look enhanced by the car's rakish shape and large, 20-inch front and 21-inch rear wheels. (adapted from Cadillac)

## ETHICS NOTE

### Earning Your Readers' Trust

When writing technical marking materials, you may be tempted to persuade readers by exaggerating what your product can do. While your purpose is to persuade readers of the merits of your product, your goal is also to inform.

You have an ethical obligation to make claims that you can substantiate. While you can appropriately use language to persuade your readers, you must be able to back up that language with data. When you use accurate information and are honest with your readers, you earn their trust and, hopefully, they will purchase your product. When you are honest and back up your claims, you are simply doing good business.

## FIGURE 17.9

**Excerpt from a Specification (Fact) Sheet**

The writer includes photos of different views to give the exterior dimensions of the car.

The writer uses precise language.

The writer details the car's specifications in a chart.

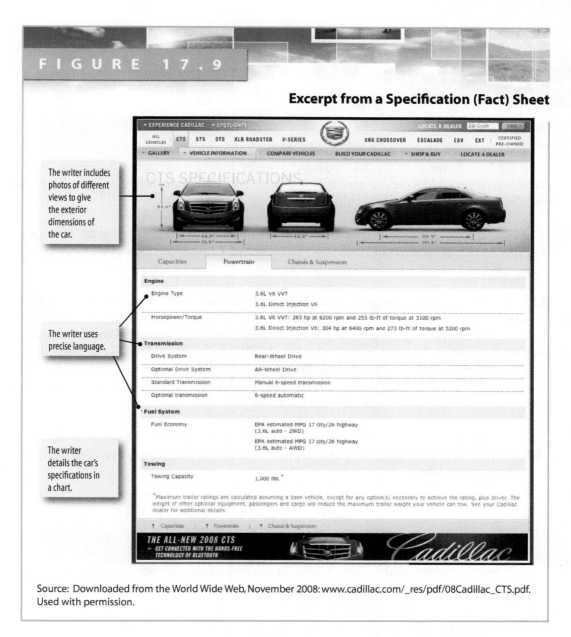

The writer begins with positive, upbeat promotional language in the first sentence, and then backs up that language with specific information in the sentences that follow.

## CASE STUDY ANALYSIS

### How Expanding the Definition of 'Obesity' Would Impact Children

#### Background

The old children's rhyme goes, "Sticks and stones may break my bones, but words will never hurt me." However, in 2006, a proposed change by a committee of the American Medical Association (AMA) and some federal government agencies could have hurt an untold number of children with one word, "obesity."

The AMA committee wanted to expand the definition of childhood obesity, effectively labeling nearly 25 percent of American toddlers and 40 percent of children between the ages of 6 and 11 with a medical condition known as "overweight and obese."

Critics of the proposed extended definition said the change would cause many children undue stress and could lead to teasing, to eating problems, and to avoiding physical activity. The critics were also concerned that labeling children with a medical condition would impact their future health care even though childhood obesity is not a good predictor of future weight or health problems as children grow into adults. The critics further cited that "overweight and obese" are arbitrary labels determined by a set cutoff point on the Body Mass Index, rather than a verifiable medical condition.

The AMA wanted to extend the definition of childhood obesity to align it with the adult definition of obesity. After receiving criticism for its proposed change, the AMA decided to reconsider the label.

#### Assignment

1. Assume you work for the AMA and are asked to write the extended definition of childhood obesity. Research the criteria for "obese."
2. Write a definition that informs readers of the revised obesity definition as it pertains to children. Avoid inflammatory language.
3. Email your definition to your instructor.

# EXERCISES

DOWNLOAD A COPY OF THE WORKSHEET FOR WRITING READER-FOCUSED DEFINITIONS AND DESCRIPTIONS

WWW.GRTEP.COM

1. Write a sentence definition for the following terms:
   a. zipper
   b. solar panel
   c. catalytic converter
   d. computer virus
   e. osteoporosis

2. Write an extended definition for a term in your field or for one of the terms below. Your definition should be 750–1,000 words. Cite any sources you use.
   a. virus
   b. cloning
   c. vaccine
   d. cancer
   e. telecommuting
   f. stem cells
   g. recycling

3. Write a memo addressed to your instructor to accompany the extended definition you wrote for Exercise 2. (See Chapter 12 for information on memos.) The memo should include the following:
   a. the techniques you used to extend your definition
   b. why you selected those techniques
   c. the standard pattern(s) of organization that you used

4. Visit the websites of three similar products. For example, you might visit the sites for three hybrid vehicles or three digital cameras. At the websites, look for product descriptions. Print a copy of the descriptions and answer the following questions:

a. Do the websites appropriately balance persuasive language with informative language? Explain your answer using examples.
b. Do the descriptions appear credible and trustworthy? Explain your answer using examples.
c. How appropriate is the language for the intended readers and for readers of other cultures and languages? Explain your answer using examples.

5. Write a 750–1,000-word process description of one of the following processes or a similar process that you understand and can describe. Along with your description, write a memo to your instructor describing the intended readers. In the process description, cite your sources.
   a. how electricity is generated
   b. how digestion works
   c. how cheese is made
   d. how tornadoes form
   e. how beaches erode
   f. how wind is used to generate electricity

6. Write a 500–750-word description for general readers of one of the following objects or mechanisms, or select one yourself. Cite any sources you use.
   a. garage door opener
   b. Geiger counter
   c. cloud computing
   d. blender
   e. helicopter

## Working with a Team to Create Technical Marketing Documents

Divide into teams of four. Your team works for a company that produces various types of mechanisms. Your team has been assigned the task of preparing technical marketing materials for one of the products.

### Assignment

1. Decide on a mechanism that you will market. The mechanism should be simple enough that all members of the team could understand or use it. You do not have to invent the mechanism; you may use an existing one.
2. Create a name and logo for your company.
3. Prepare a brochure and a fact sheet for the product.
4. Turn in your brochure and fact sheet to your instructor.

# Writing User-Focused Instructions and Manuals

W e use instructions daily at home and in the workplace. Whether we are cooking microwave popcorn or installing new software, we use instructions. Some instructions are short, simple, and informal—perhaps only a few steps. For example, Figure 18.1 presents brief instructions that tell users how to remove a battery. Other instructions may be hundreds of pages.

iStockphoto 2008.

The instructions that you write may be as simple as the list shown in Figure 18.1 or as complex as an entire manual. You might write instructions for tasks that you want your coworkers to complete or for tasks that consumers need to follow when using your company's products. Regardless of the number and complexity of the tasks, the same techniques apply. In this chapter, you will learn techniques to help you write effective, user-focused instructions.

**Simple Instructions**

## How to Remove the Battery

⚠️ CAUTION:  Before removing the battery, disconnect the computer from the electrical outlet.

**1.** Turn off the computer.
**2.** Slide and hold the battery latch.
**3.** Pull the battery out of the computer.

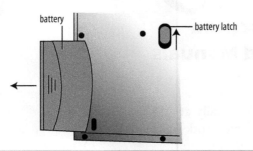

battery

battery latch

## FIND OUT HOW MUCH THE USERS KNOW ABOUT THE TASK

To write effective instructions, you need to know about your users. Who will use the instructions? How much do they know about the task? Will more than one group of users use the manual? Find out about users' backgrounds and training by answering these additional questions:

- Have users performed the task before? Have they performed similar tasks?
- Do all users have the same background or knowledge of the task?
- Will users have different purposes for using the instructions? Will their purposes for using the instructions change?
- How much detail do users need to complete the task? Do they want only minimal instructions?
- What are users' attitudes toward the task and toward the equipment used for the task (Brockmann 1990, 101)?

This information will help you decide how much detail users will need to perform the task correctly.

If you know how familiar users are with the task, you can include the appropriate level of detail. For example, if you know users have used a microscope, you won't have to tell them how to operate one; however, if you know they have never used one, you will need to include basic operating instructions. If you know users are familiar with a similar task, compare the familiar task to the new task to help them feel comfortable. You also help users feel comfortable with a task if you know their attitude toward the task and the equipment (ibid.). For instance, if you know the instructions will require the users to change a routine or habits, frequently reassure them and, whenever possible, link the new task to procedures they already know.

Depending on the users' needs, include detailed instructions and explanations or perhaps even the theory behind a procedure. For example, novice users may need detailed information to perform a task correctly, whereas expert users may need—and want—only minimal instructions. As you decide how much detail and explanatory information to provide, consider users' reasons for reading your instructions or manual. Users "with specific tasks in mind need little or no elaboration," but users "without specific goals benefit from explanations of how to apply procedures," not from elaborations that describe general concepts (Charney, Reder, and Wells 1988, 63). Users who have specific tasks to complete need little, if any, explanation of the procedure or the concept behind the procedure, and users without specific tasks will benefit from "how-to" statements, rather than "why" and "when" statements.

> Help users feel comfortable with a new task by building on knowledge they already have of similar instructions or equipment.

Consider the elaboration in a document on controlling thatch (Koop and Duble 1982).

| | |
|---|---|
| **General elaboration** | Mowers may scalp lawns that have excess thatch. |
| **How-to elaboration** | Use vertical mowers specifically designed to remove thatch. When using these mowers, make sure the blades penetrate the thatch to the soil surface. |

The general elaboration will not help users control thatch. However, the how-to elaboration gives users specific information about the type of mower to use and how to use it to remove thatch.

Find out if users will have varying backgrounds and knowledge of the task or if they will read the instructions for varying purposes. This information will help you determine how to organize the instructions to best meet the needs of all users. For instance, new users of a software application may first consult the manual to learn how to get started; therefore, they will want basic information. As these users learn more about the software, they may have questions about more advanced commands; they will then use the manual as a reference guide, not as a tutorial. Thus, the manual needs a tutorial section for new users and a reference section for users who have become familiar with the software.

## USE AN ACCESSIBLE DESIGN

As you plan your instructions and manual, decide how you will design the visual information. Select an appropriate typeface, layout, color, and page size for your purpose and your users. As you plan these elements, ask yourself how and where users will use the instructions. For example, will they use the instructions at a computer workstation? If so, you might use a spiral binding so the pages will lie flat, and a smaller-than-usual page size so the instructions will fit in a crowded workstation. Perhaps users will use the instructions outside the office. To select the design that best meets users' needs and environment, consider these questions:

- Will users use the instructions in an environment where the manual could get soiled or the pages crumpled?
- What typeface is appropriate for the instructions? Do users require a particular type size or page size to read the instructions?
- What layout will help users find and follow the instructions?

### Design Instructions Suitable for the Users' Environment

If users will use the instructions or manual outside the office, select a paper, typeface, type size, and page size that will make the instructions easy to use. For example, if users will use the instructions in a manufacturing or maintenance facility, use a laminated paper or card stock that users can easily clean.

If users must read the instructions from a distance, the type size and page size may need to be larger than usual. For example, the instructions for clearing the air passage of a choking victim in a restaurant might be on a poster in large type, so users can see the instructions while working with a victim. If users will use the instructions in a small area, the pages must be small enough to fit easily in the workspace. For example, quick reference information for some software programs is printed on the front and back of a card that users can place next to their computer.

## Liability and Safety Information—Could You or Your Company Be Liable?

Are companies liable for damages when instructions for their products are imprecise or inaccurate? In *Martin v. Hacker*, the New York Court of Appeals unanimously decided that companies indeed are liable. This decision is especially interesting to people who write instructions because the court carefully analyzed the language of the instructions in a lawsuit over a drug-induced suicide. Eugene Martin was taking hydrochlorothazide and resperpine for high blood pressure; although he "had no history of mental illness or depression, [he] shot and killed himself in a drug-induced despondency" (Caher 1995, 6). His widow alleged that the warning supplied with the drugs was insufficient. The court stated that the case centered on the drug manufacturer's obligation to fully reveal the potential hazards of its products. Therefore, the court specifically examined the safety warnings' accuracy, clarity, and consistency. The court scrutinized specific language that the writers used. The court dismissed the lawsuit, stating that the warnings "contained language which, on its face, adequately warned against the precise risk" (Martin v. Hacker 1993).

According to this case, courts will carefully analyze the specific language of technical documents and will hold companies liable for that language (Parson 1992). Companies and their writers, then, must be diligent in writing instructions—especially in terms of accuracy, clarity, and consistency because the "stakes are substantial" (Caher 1995, 10). When a writer's work is unclear and a user "inadvertently reformats a hard drive, that's unfortunate"; but if a writer's inaccurate or unclear language claims a life, that's another matter altogether" (Caher 1995, 10).

## Assignment

1. Locate a similar case where a consumer sued an organization for damages based on presumably faulty instructions and safety information.
2. Summarize the case and be prepared to discuss it with your classmates.

## Design Easy-to-Use Instructions

Instructions should be easy to use, so design the information to help users easily search for and locate specific instructions. When reading instructions, users have a problem to solve or a task to complete; they want to quickly locate the information needed to solve the problem or complete the task. For example, they may need to learn how to install a software program, how to maximize the storage space on a hard drive, or how to install a new filter in a refrigerator. Whatever the task or problem, users want to quickly locate the information they need.

A logical, consistent layout like the one in Figure 18.2 helps users find the information they need. The layout of this page from a user's guide is effective because of the headings, lists, color, and graphics. The headings suggest tasks that users will understand, and the flush-left format makes the headings easy to see. The numbered lists visually separate each step, so users can identify and perform each instruction. To design easy-to-use instructions, follow the Tips for Designing Easy-to-Use Instructions and review the guidelines for effective design in Chapter 10.

**TIPS** FOR DESIGNING EASY-TO-USE INSTRUCTIONS

- **Use ample white space.** Users prefer open, uncluttered pages so they can scan the page and locate the instructions.
- **Place the graphics near the related information.**
- **Use callouts to highlight information in the graphic.** As in Figure 18.2, use callouts to direct readers' attention to specific parts of the graphic.
- **Use a modified hanging or left-hanging format for headings.** The hanging format helps users locate instructions and scan for specific tasks (see Chapter 10).
- **When possible, use color to highlight important elements such as first-level headings and lists.** Use the same color consistently throughout the document so users know what particuar colors mean (Brockmann 1990). For example, if you use blue for one first-level heading, use blue for all first-level headings.
- **Use typefaces, type sizes, and other design elements consistently.** When you use these design elements consistently, you guide users through your instructions. For example, if you use a left-hanging format and a sans serif type consistently for first-level headings, users will recognize the level of information of those headings.

## Design the Safety Information

You have a legal and ethical responsibility to warn users about possible injury to themselves or others and possible damage to equipment and materials. In the introduction or in a separate section before or after the introduction, you must state the seriousness of the possible injury or damage, using the correct language and layout. The American National Standards Institute suggests specific terms for alerting users to hazards (see Figure 18.3). Figure 18.4 shows how to use these terms in safety alerts.

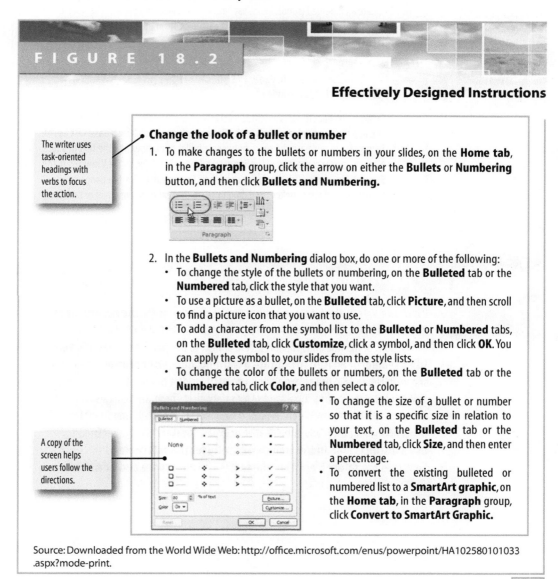

**FIGURE 18.2**

**Effectively Designed Instructions**

The writer uses task-oriented headings with verbs to focus the action.

A copy of the screen helps users follow the directions.

### Change the look of a bullet or number

1. To make changes to the bullets or numbers in your slides, on the **Home tab**, in the **Paragraph** group, click the arrow on either the **Bullets** or **Numbering** button, and then click **Bullets and Numbering.**

2. In the **Bullets and Numbering** dialog box, do one or more of the following:
   - To change the style of the bullets or numbering, on the **Bulleted** tab or the **Numbered** tab, click the style that you want.
   - To use a picture as a bullet, on the **Bulleted** tab, click **Picture**, and then scroll to find a picture icon that you want to use.
   - To add a character from the symbol list to the **Bulleted** or **Numbered** tabs, on the **Bulleted** tab, click **Customize**, click a symbol, and then click **OK**. You can apply the symbol to your slides from the style lists.
   - To change the color of the bullets or numbers, on the **Bulleted** tab or the **Numbered** tab, click **Color**, and then select a color.
   - To change the size of a bullet or number so that it is a specific size in relation to your text, on the **Bulleted** tab or the **Numbered** tab, click **Size**, and then enter a percentage.
   - To convert the existing bulleted or numbered list to a **SmartArt graphic**, on the **Home tab**, in the **Paragraph** group, click **Convert to SmartArt Graphic.**

Source: Downloaded from the World Wide Web: http://office.microsoft.com/enus/powerpoint/HA102580101033.aspx?mode-print.

**FIGURE  18.2**

**Effectively Designed Instructions** *continued*

The writer uses typeface, type size, and color consistently for the headings.

The writer uses redlines and callout numbers to highlight information.

• **Change list levels (indent), spacing between text and points, and more**

1. To create an indented (subordinate) list within a list, place the cursor at the start of the line that you want to indent, and then on the **Home tab**, in the **Paragraph** group, click **Increase List Level**.

   1. Decrease List Level (indent)
   2. Increase List Level (indent)

2. To move text back to a less indented level in the list, place the cursor at the start of the line, and then on the **Home tab**, in the **Paragraph** group, click **Decrease List Level**.
3. To increase or decrease the space between a bullet or number and the text in a line, place the cursor at the start of the line of text. To view the ruler, on the **View** tab, in the **Show/Hide** group, click the **Ruler** check box. On the ruler, click the hanging indent (as shown in diagram below) and drag to space the text from the bullet or number.

## TIPS FOR WRITING AND DESIGNING SAFETY INFORMATION

- **Place the safety alert before or next to the directions for the hazardous task, not after them.** If the hazard is severe, put the safety alert at the beginning of the instructions or manual and repeat it before or next to the task where the hazard occurs.
- **Use a symbol or an icon to indicate a warning, danger, or caution.** The warnings shown in Figure 18.4 use an exclamation point (!) inside a triangle to indicate a hazard. This symbol is the international symbol for safety alert. These warnings also use simple drawings to illustrate the potential hazard. Graphics are especially important for international users or for users who aren't native or expert speakers of technical English.
- **Use a distinct color and/or icon consistently for the safety alert.**
- **Separate the safety alert from the text with white space and/or a border.**

FIGURE 18.3

**Terms Used for Safety Alerts**

| Signal Word | Meaning | Example Graphic | Example Language |
|---|---|---|---|
| **Danger** | Alerts users to an immediate and serious hazardous situation, which will cause death or serious injury. | ⚠ DANGER | Danger: Moving parts can crush and cut. |
| **Warning** | Alerts users to a potentially hazardous situation, which may cause death or serious injury. | ⚠ WARNING | Warning: To reduce risk of electric shock, do not use this equipment near water. |
| **Caution** | Alerts users to the potential of a hazardous situation, which may cause minor or moderate injury. | ⚠ CAUTION | Caution: Do not use to exhaust hazardous materials and vapors. |
| **Note** | Gives users a tip or suggestion to help them complete a task or use equipment successfully. | *NOTICE* | Note: Turn off the mixer before scraping the bowl. |

Source: Downloaded from the World Wide Web: Danger/Warning/Caution/Notice Signs: www.compliancesigns.com/
index.shtml?kw=osha%20labels&gclid=CL6A4Y63upMCFQoRswodGAmUCA-1. Courtesy of www.compliancesigns
.com, supplier of high quality safety signs.

As you prepare the safety information, follow the Tips for Writing and Designing Safety Information. While preparing your instructions, consider these questions:

- Will the procedure or equipment endanger the users, their surroundings, or their equipment?
- Is the safety alert adequate for the circumstances and severity of the hazard (Brockmann 1990)?
- Is the safety alert located where users will see it *before* they perform the task that will endanger them?

## USE USER-FOCUSED LANGUAGE

To create user-focused language, use a ***talker*** style: Write as if you were speaking directly to your users (Brockmann 1990; Haramundanis 1992). The following examples contrast *talker style* with *writer style*:

**Safety Alerts**

Source: Downloaded from the World Wide Web: www.safetylabel.com/productsafetylabels/customization.php.

| Use Talker Style … | Not Writer Style. |
|---|---|
| Press <Enter> for help. | The user should press the <Enter> key for assistance. |
| Press the shutter-release button. | The user should press the shutter-release button. |
| Tighten the knobs on each side of the handle. | The knobs on each side of the handle should be tightened. |

Create *talker style* by using
- action verbs
- imperative sentences
- task-oriented headings
- simple, specific language
- language that users will understand

## Use Action Verbs

*Action verbs* tell users what to do. When writing step-by-step directions, use verbs such as *run, adjust, press, type,* and *loosen*—not verbs such as *is* or *have.* Notice the action verbs (in **bold**) in these directions:

> **Replace** the battery with a new one.
> **Enter** the phone number that you want to add to your contact list.
> **Press** the OK key.

Each action verb clearly indicates the action the user should perform. Each action verb is in the active voice (to review the difference between the active and passive voice, see Chapter 7).

## Use Imperative Sentences

Effective step-by-step directions consist of talker-style sentences with the understood *you* as the subject, as in Replace the battery—meaning [You] replace the battery. When the subject is understood to be *you,* the sentence is imperative. An *imperative sentence* is a command. Its main verb tells the user to carry out some action. Imperative sentences focus attention on what the user is to do, not on the user. Compare these two sentences:

Writer-style  You should locate a wall stud in the area where you want to install your flat-screen television.

Imperative  **Locate** a wall stud in the area where you want to install your flat-screen television.

The writer-style sentence focuses the user's attention on the subject *you.* In the imperative sentence, the user understands the subject is *you* and focuses on the main verb, *locate,* which expresses the action.

Let's look at two more examples:

Writer-style  Testing of emergency numbers should be performed during off-peak hours, such as in the early morning or late evening.

Imperative  **Test** emergency numbers during off-peak hours, such as in the early morning or late evening.

In the writer-style sentence, the verb is in the passive voice (be performed) and the action that the user is to perform is in the noun *testing*. The imperative sentence expresses the action in the verb *test*. By using imperative sentences, the writer eliminates passive-voice constructions and focuses the user's attention on the action.

EVALUATE INSTRUCTIONS IN THE INTERACTIVE STUDENT ANALYSIS ONLINE AT
WWW.GRTEP.COM

## Use Task-Oriented Headings

*Task-oriented headings* focus on the action by using verbs or the words *how to*. Consider these headings:

Not task-oriented  Slide Shows

Task-oriented  Running the Slide Show
How to Run the Slide Show

The non-task-oriented heading uses nouns instead of verbs to identify the tasks described in the section. The task-oriented headings use verbs to identify the tasks. Task-oriented headings
- suggest activities that users may already understand and can find immediately applicable (Brockmann 1990)
- help users locate the instructions for specific tasks

## Use Simple and Specific Language

Resist the temptation to use "fancy" or less familiar words. Instead, use words that users easily understand. If you are unsure whether users will understand a word, choose another word or provide a definition they will understand. See Chapter 8 for information on using simple language.

When writing instructions and manuals, use specific language. Otherwise, users might not gather the proper equipment and materials, or they might misunderstand the instructions and injure themselves or damage equipment. Consider these instructions for changing the oil in a car:

> Before changing the oil, run the engine until it reaches normal operating temperature. The engine has reached this temperature when the exhaust pipe is warm to the touch. You should run the engine to mix the dirt and sludge with the oil in the crankcase, so the dirt and sludge drain along with the oil.

Experienced automobile mechanics would know how long to let the engine run before the exhaust pipe became so hot that it would burn their hands. Novice users will not know how long to let the engine run. Thus, the writer should specifically state how long to let the engine run, so the novice won't get burned on a hot exhaust pipe. Specific language is crucial if users are to safely follow instructions.

## Use Language Users Understand

Use terminology that users will understand. To determine how *technical* your manual or instructions can be, consider these questions:

- What background and training do your users have? Will they understand technical terminology related to the task?
- Are the users native or expert speakers of technical English?

## ETHICS NOTE

### Protecting Your Users

You have a legal and ethical responsibility to protect users from possible injury to themselves or others and from possible damage to equipment or materials. Include whatever information is necessary to fully inform readers of dangers when following your instructions to use equipment. To ensure that you ethically provide users with safety information

- Make the safety information easy to see and read.
- Put the safety information where users need to see it. You cannot simply include the safety information in the introduction. You must place the safety alert above or next to the instructions.
- Use graphics for warnings and danger so users of all languages will see and understand.
- Include all information necessary to protect users.

## TIPS FOR USING USER-CENTERED LANGUAGE

- **Use action verbs.** When you use action verbs, you focus the sentence on the task.
- **Use imperative sentences.** Imperative sentences have an understood *you* subject; for example, "Turn off the speed control," rather than "You should turn off the speed control." Imperative sentences focus the users' attention on the action.
- **Use simple language.** Select words that users will understand.
- **Use specific language.** Without specific language, users could misunderstand the instructions and damage equipment or injure themselves or others.
- **Use language that users will understand.** Use technical terminology only if your users are familiar with it. If you must use technical terms that your users won't understand, define them.
- **Use technical terminology when your users expect it.** If your users are familiar with the technical terminology, they will expect you to use it.
- **If your users are nonnative English speakers, avoid connotative and ambiguous language and terms.** Such language and terms may have different meanings in other languages.
- **Follow the guidelines for Simplified Technical English.** See Chapter 8 for information on Simplified Technical English.

If you know that users have a background or training in a field related to the task, use technical terms that they will know and expect. If your users have little relevant background or training, avoid technical terms and, instead, use language they will understand. If your users are not native or expert speakers of technical English, avoid connotative and ambiguous language and terms that may have different meanings in other languages.

When writing for users of other cultures, be sensitive to the tone of your writing. For instance, imperative sentences make users in some cultures uncomfortable. For other users, you use labeled drawings and graphics, especially when the instructions are relatively simple and require few words (Brockmann 1990).

##  THE CONVENTIONAL SECTIONS OF INSTRUCTIONS AND MANUALS

The structure, length, and formality of instructions vary depending on the procedure and the users. To explain to your coworkers how to use a new copier, briefly introduce the procedure and then present the step-by-step instructions. You could send these instructions to the users in a memo or email or you could write the instructions on a card attached to the wall next to the copier. Your coworkers only want to know how to use the copier; they don't need to know how it works. However, suppose you are writing the instructions that go in the carton with the copier. These instructions have to be more formal than the ones for your coworkers, and the instructions must meet the needs of a diverse user group. These instructions would appear in a manual that has a table of contents and an index. Such a manual would also list the materials, equipment, and instructions for installing and using the machine. The manual would also have a troubleshooting section for solving common problems.

For informal instructions, include these sections:
- introduction
- step-by-step directions
- troubleshooting (not included with all instructions)
- reference aids (not included with all instructions)

For manuals, include these sections:
- front matter (cover, title page, table of contents)
- introduction
- step-by-step directions
- troubleshooting (not included with all instructions)
- reference aids (not included with all instructions)
- index

For information on front matter and indexes, see Chapter 15.

## Introduction

The *introduction* tells users about the purpose of the equipment or procedure and explains how to use the manual. Introductions often have titles other than Introduction such as Overview, Getting Started, or How to Use This Manual. In a manual, the introduction may have additional elements; it may explain how the manual is organized, who should use the manual, conventions used in the manual, and where to get additional information. Figure 18.5 lists questions that users may ask as they read the introduction (as well as other conventional sections of instructions and manuals). Figure 18.6 illustrates the introduction from a software manual. The introduction for instructions and manuals may include any or all of the information listed in the Tips for Writing the Introduction to Instructions and Manuals.

FIGURE 18.5

**Users' Questions about the Conventional Sections of Instructions and Manuals**

| Conventional Sections | User's Questions |
|---|---|
| Introduction | • What is the purpose of the instructions?<br>• What, if anything, should I know before beginning the task or using the equipment?<br>• What materials and equipment do I need?<br>• Is the equipment or the task safe? What do I need to do to protect the equipment or my surroundings from damage? What do I need to do to protect myself from injury?<br>• How is the manual organized? If I am familiar with the tasks or equipment, where do I begin using the instructions?<br>• What typographical conventions or terminology, if any, do I need to use the instructions? |
| Step-by-step directions | • What do I do first?<br>• What are the specific steps for performing the task?<br>• Can I perform the task in more than one way? |
| Troubleshooting | • How do I solve problem X? What do I do if X happens?<br>• Where can I get additional information if I cannot solve problem X? |

## Step-by-Step Directions

*Step-by-step directions* tell users exactly how to carry out a task. To determine how to organize the directions, consider these questions (Brockmann 1990):

• What action begins each task?
• What are the specific steps for performing the task? Can you group these steps into subtasks?
• What action ends each task?
• Can you perform the task in more than one way? If so, do users need to know both ways?

Once you have answered these questions, categorize the task into major steps and then divide the steps into appropriate substeps. For example, if you are explaining to a novice how to change the oil in a car, you might divide the task into four major steps: (1) drain the old oil, (2) remove the old oil filter, (3) install the new filter, and (4) refill the crankcase with oil. Then, subdivide each step into substeps. When you divide the steps into substeps, you help users understand the task and follow your directions. One long list of uncategorized

- **State the purpose of the instructions.**
- **State clearly who should use the instructions and what they should know about the task.** For example, the installation guide for a garbage disposal states the instructions are "for electricians with a Level 3 or higher certification according to Section 3 of the state electrical code." The writer, therefore, assumes that users know how to install similar equipment and that they understand the electrical code and related ordinances.
- **List all the materials and equipment that users need.** List all the materials and equipment in one place at the beginning of the procedure, so users can gather them before beginning the task.
- **Use drawings of unfamiliar materials and equipment to ensure that users know what tools they need and what they look like.** For example, if readers are unfamiliar with fasteners when installing a piece of equipment, you might include drawings of the fasteners (in their actual size), so users can keep track of and identify them. Some writers identify the materials and equipment in a separate section after the introduction but before the procedure.
- **Explain typographical conventions icons, color, and terminology used in the instructions.** If you use typographical conventions, icons, color, or terminology that your users may not understand or recognize, explain them in the introduction. If you use many terms that users may not understand, define them in a glossary and introduce the glossary in the introduction.
- **Explain the parts of the equipment (if equipment is involved).** For example, Figure 18.6 shows a drawing of a cell phone with callouts of the phone's features. These graphics help orient the user before reading the manual or using the phone.
- **Include other information necessary to help users follow the instructions.** For instance, if you've divided the manual into sections, tell users what information each section includes and perhaps when and how to use each section.
- **Explain all safety information and how you will note that information.** When users see the warning graphics and alerts, they will better understand the nature of the hazard.

steps is intimidating. The simple task of changing the oil could have as many as 30 steps. Most users would prefer four major steps with substeps to a list of 30 steps.

As you write the directions, follow the Tips for Writing Step-by-Step Directions. The instructions in the next several figures follow these tips.

FIGURE 18.6

## Introduction from a Software Manual

The introduction explains what the software does and what the user needs to know before using the software.

### Welcome to OptQuest®

Welcome to OptQuest® for Crystal Ball® 2000!

OptQuest enhances Crystal Ball by automatically searching for and finding optimal solutions to simulation models. Simulation models by themselves can only give you a range of possible outcomes for any situation. They don't tell you how to control the situation to achieve the best outcome.

OptQuest, through a new optimization technique, finds the right combination of variables that produces the best results possible. If you use simulation models to answer questions such as, "What are likely sales for next month?" now you can find the price points that maximize monthly sales. If you asked, "What will production rates be for this new oil field?" now you can additionally determine the number of wells to drill to maximize net present value. And if you wonder, "Which stock portfolio should I pick?" with OptQuest, you can choose the one that yields the greatest profit with the least risk.

Like Crystal Ball, OptQuest is easy to learn and easy to use. With its wizard-based design, you can start optimizing your own models in under an hour. All you need to know is how to create a Crystal Ball spreadsheet model. From there, this manual guides you step by step, explaining OptQuest terms, procedures, and results.

The introduction explains who should use the software.

### Who this program is for

OptQuest is for the decision-maker—from the businessperson analyzing the risk of new markets to the scientist evaluating experiments and hypotheses. With OptQuest, you can make decisions that maximize the use of your resources, time, and money.

OptQuest has been developed with a wide range of spreadsheet uses and users in mind. You don't need highly advanced statistical or computer knowledge to use OptQuest to its full potential. All you need is a basic working knowledge of your personal computer and the ability to create a Crystal Ball spreadsheet model.

*OptQuest User Manual* 7

- **Glossary**

  A compilation of terms specific to OptQuest as well as statistical terms used in this manual.

- **Index**

  An alphabetical list of subjects and corresponding page numbers.

### Additional resources

Decisioneering, Inc. offers three additional resources to increase the effectiveness with which you can use our products.

#### Technical support

If you have a technical support question or would like to comment on OptQuest, there are a number of ways to reach Technical Support. See the accompanying Crystal Ball README file for more information.

#### Consulting referral service

Decisioneering, Inc. provides referrals to individuals and companies alike. The primary focus of this service is to provide a clearinghouse for consultants in specific industries who can provide specialized services to the Crystal Ball and OptQuest user community.

If you wish to learn more about this referral service, call 800-289-2550 Monday through Friday, between 9:00 A.M. and 5:00 P.M. Mountain Standard Time.

The introduction directs users to additional resources.

*OptQuest User Manual* 9

FIGURE 18.6

**Introduction from a Software Manual** *continued*

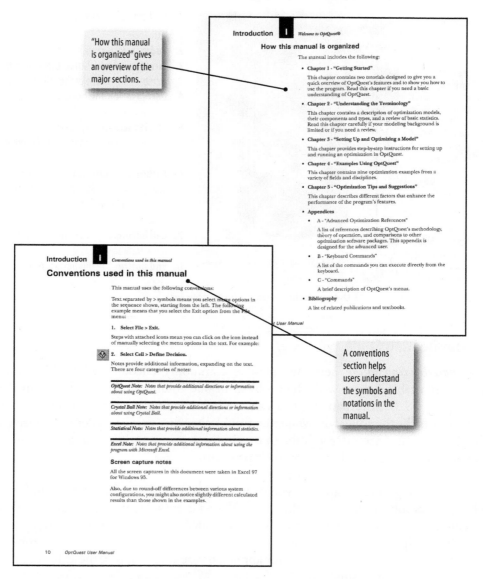

"How this manual is organized" gives an overview of the major sections.

A conventions section helps users understand the symbols and notations in the manual.

Source: Downloaded from the World Wide Web, November 2008: www.decisioneering.com. *OptQuest for Crystal Ball 2000 User Manual*, pages 7-10. Decisioneering, Denver, CO.

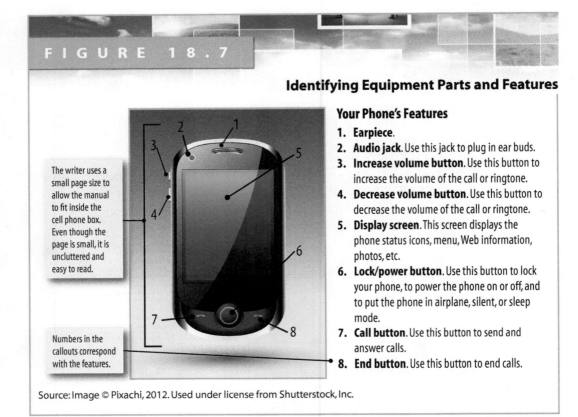

FIGURE 18.7

## Identifying Equipment Parts and Features

The writer uses a small page size to allow the manual to fit inside the cell phone box. Even though the page is small, it is uncluttered and easy to read.

Numbers in the callouts correspond with the features.

### Your Phone's Features

1. **Earpiece**.
2. **Audio jack**. Use this jack to plug in ear buds.
3. **Increase volume button**. Use this button to increase the volume of the call or ringtone.
4. **Decrease volume button**. Use this button to decrease the volume of the call or ringtone.
5. **Display screen**. This screen displays the phone status icons, menu, Web information, photos, etc.
6. **Lock/power button**. Use this button to lock your phone, to power the phone on or off, and to put the phone in airplane, silent, or sleep mode.
7. **Call button**. Use this button to send and answer calls.
8. **End button**. Use this button to end calls.

Source: Image © Pixachi, 2012. Used under license from Shutterstock, Inc.

## Troubleshooting Guide

A *troubleshooting guide* helps users solve commonly encountered problems. It often appears in a table format with the problem in one column and the solution in the other (see Figure 18.8). Alternatively, you can use left-hanging headings for the problem and bulleted lists for the solutions. Make the troubleshooting guide as a comprehensive as possible. A user can encounter a problem on almost any instruction or activity. Consult your company help desk for a list of common problems.

Troubleshooting guides can save you, your company, and your users time and money by helping users solve problems on their own. When users solve their problems on their own, the company reduces the amount of time and money it spends for online and phone support. By anticipating users' problems, troubleshooting guides let users solve common problems in less time than a trial-and-error approach would take and without having to call the company for technical support.

## Reference Aids

To help users find the information they need in your instructions and manuals, provide a variety of reference aids, depending on users' needs and the length and complexity of the instructions. Common reference aids include:

- **Table of contents.** Include a table of contents for all manuals (see Chapter 15 for information on preparing a table of contents.)
- **Index.** Include an index for all manuals. Indexes help users find specific information and instructions. (See Chapter 15 for information on preparing an index.)
- **Headings.** Headings help users locate information on the page and provide a road map to the instructions. (See Chapter 10 for information on designing headings.)
- **Quick-reference aids.** Quick-reference aids provide an overview of basic instructions or commands. These aids help users who are familiar with the task and who don't need extensive instructions. Quick-reference aids are usually a separate document from the manual; they may be in the form of a brochure, a sturdy card, a poster, or a flyer. You can also place a quick-reference aid on the back cover or inside the front or back cover. You might place the aid on walls or doors as with Figure 18.9. This quick-reference aid provides instructions and graphics for hand washing, with instructions in Spanish and English.

Your documentation is not complete until you test your instructions with the product before you release them to your primary users. A usable document contains accurate, complete information that is easy to use.

*Usability testing* is a process of conducting experiments with people who represent your users. The goal of usability testing is to determine how well users understand the document

### FIGURE 18.8

**Troubleshooting Guide**

| Troubleshooting Guidelines | |
|---|---|
| In the event that something is not working correctly on the oven, the display will show an error message that suggest that you call for service. Before calling for service, reference the following table for problems that you may be able to fix yourself. | |
| **Problem** | **Possible Solution (s)** |
| Displays and indicator lights are not working | Check that oven is receiving power. |
| Cook Navigator Screen is too dark or light | Adjust the brightness of the display. See Oven Setup, page 10. |
| Sounds are not working | Check that the volume is turned on. See Oven Setup, page 20. |
| Oven sounds are too loud or soft | Adjust the volume. See Oven Setup, page 20. |
| Menus are in the wrong language | Make sure tdesired language is selected. See Oven Setup, page 20. |
| Units and Measuremnets are displayed in metric and I want standard or vice versa | Change the Units and Measurements. See Oven Setup, page 20. |
| I forgot to save any changes to a recipe recently cooked | See Cooking a Recently Cooooked Dish, page 7, Select "Save as Favorites." |
| Clock is set at the wrong time | Use the Set Timer Knob to reset. See page 6. |
| Oven light bulb is burned out | Call Customer Service at 866.44serve to order a replacement bulb. Instructions and all necessary components included with each bulb. |
| Oven Timer does not count down | Make sure the Set Timer Knob is pressed back into its origional position. |
| I experienced interference with my wireless phone | 900MHz cordless phones are recommended to limit interference. Also try operating the wireless network on channel 1 if possible. |

Source: Downloaded from the World Wide Web, www.turbochef.com. *TurboChef 30" Double Wall Speedcook Oven Use and Care Guide,* page 37. Used with permission of TurboChef.

# FIGURE 18.9

**Quick Reference Aid**

Be a Germ-Buster...
# WASH YOUR HANDS!
*Elimine los gérmenes... LAVESE LAS MANOS*

**1. WET** REMOJE

**2. SOAP** ENJABONE

**3. WASH** LAVE

**4. RINSE** ENJUAGE

**5. DRY** SEQUE

**6. TURN OFF WATER WITH PAPER TOWEL** CIERRE LA LLAVE DE AGUA CON UNA TOALLA DE PAPEL

Health DOH Pub 130-012 8/2006

For persons with disabilities, this document is available on request in other formats. Please call 1-800-525-0127 (TDD relay 1-800-833-6388). Para personas discapacitadas, este documento está disponible a su pedido en otros formatos. Para hacer su pedido, llame a 1-800-525-0127 (TDD/TTY 1-800-833-6388).

The card includes numbers to show users the sequence for washing their hands.

The instructions appear in English and Spanish.

The simple graphics show users how to wash their hands properly without having to read the text.

Source: Compiled from information downloaded from the World Wide Web, July 16, 2009: https:// fortress.wa.gov/ doh/here/materials/PDFs/12_GermBust_B06L.pdf. DOH Pub 130-012, 8/2006. Courtesy of Washington State Department of Health.

and can carry out the functions they need to do the job. You can conduct usability testing on any technical document. Usability testing uncovers instructions that users cannot understand, where you have given too much or too little information, and where users need graphics. Usability testing tells you whether users can (1) locate the information they need to carry out the task and (2) use the information to carry out the task successfully.

To perform an effective usability test, you must put users in a realistic setting that simulates the actual situations in which they will use the document (Zimmerman, Muraski, and Slater 1999; Redish and Schell 1987). These users must be people who will actually use the document. Sometimes technical communicators conduct usability testing in the field (Zimmerman, Muraski, and Slater 1999). For example, researchers tested the effectiveness of pesticide warning labels with a group of farmers (ibid.).

Test instructions several times during the writing process:
- Test the prototype, or first draft, of a chapter or section. Prototype testing occurs early in the writing process before you draft the entire document. Prototype testing helps you see whether your layout, design, and style will work for your users.
- Test a complete, but preliminary, draft of the instructions.
- Test a revised, but not yet final, draft of the instructions.

Prototype testing provides feedback as you develop the document. If you wait to test until you are completely satisfied with the instructions, you probably will be near your final deadline and may not have time to revise the document after it is tested.

To conduct an effective usability test, you
- prepare for the test
- conduct the test
- interpret the test results to revise the document

## Prepare for the Test

To prepare and conduct an effective usability test, follow these steps:
1. **Determine the users' needs.** Many organizations conduct focus groups to determine what users need and want. Some groups are users who use similar products and documents. Other organizations conduct on-site interviews and observations of users. These focus groups, on-site interviews, and observations help testers find out what users already know about the task and in what situations they will refer to the instructions.
2. **Determine the purpose of the test.** What do you want to learn from the test? For example, you might want to test a prototype of the instructions. You can also test an advanced draft of your instructions.

3. **Design the test.** For most usability tests, you will work with a team. Each team member is responsible for carrying out one aspect of the test. The team as a whole or one member develops the test. Make sure that the test asks participants to focus on specific areas such as the following (Daugherty 1997):
   - *Content*. Are the instructions complete?
   - *Ease*. Can users easily complete tasks when following the instructions?
   - *Design*. Can users easily locate and read the information?
   - *Sentence structure and language.* Is the structure appropriate for instructions and straightforward? Is the language geared to the users?
   - *Graphics*. Would using more, fewer or different graphics help users follow the instructions?
4. **Select the test participants.** Test participants should mirror your intended users (Brockmann 1990).
5. **Reserve the testing facilities.** If you're simulating the situation in which users will perform the task, if possible, prepare two rooms: the participants' room with a camera to record the testing and the observers' room. The observers' room should have a one-way mirror so observers can see the participants, but participants can't see the observers. If you do not have access to a two-room setup, conduct the test up in one room with the observers in the back of the room out of sight of the participants. If you are testing software or online instructions, consider using eye-tracking equipment.
6. **Prepare a schedule of the testing day events.** Make sure that all participants and observers know when testing begins and what the goals are.

## Conduct the Test

To ensure that the test is reliable, conduct the test twice with different groups (Daugherty 1997) and follow these guidelines:
- **Explain the purpose of the test, either orally or in writing.**
- **Tell participants how they should note problems or make suggestions.** For example, you could give them a questionnaire to complete as they work through the test or give them a notepad to jot down ideas, questions, and criticisms.
- **Observe participants while they use the instructions.** Note exactly what problems they encounter.
- **Conduct an exit interview or debriefing with each participant.** Assign a team member to be in charge of the exit interviews to keep them consistent and organized. Prepare a brief questionnaire to give each participant at the end of the test. Either ask participants to complete the questionnaire in writing, or a team member can ask the questions, using the written questionnaire as a guide. Be flexible. If you or a team member has a question about the participants' actions or answers, ask—even if the question isn't on the questionnaire.

## Interpret the Results

After you have completed the usability test, tabulate and analyze the information from the questionnaires and notes. After your analysis, write a detailed report (usually an informal report) that includes the results and draws conclusions. (See Chapter 14 for information on informal reports.) For example, you may determine that you need to revise the format or the graphics and conduct more usability testing.

 SAMPLE INSTRUCTIONS

The instructions presented in Figure 18.10 are an excerpt from a user's manual for a cell phone. This figure illustrates effectively designed and written instructions. These instructions include task-oriented headings, user-focused language, effective page design, and clear graphics. Figure 18.11 shows a quick reference card for a coffee pot. The card uses graphics to identify the parts of the coffee pot and to illustrate how to make coffee. Figure 18.12 is a page from a manual for setting up a home and office network. These instructions include a graphic to show readers where to insert a network adapter.

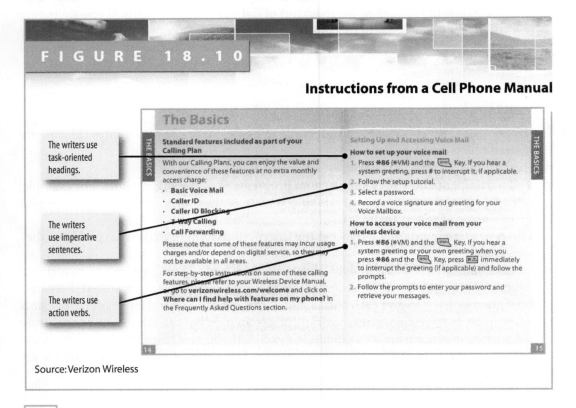

Source: Verizon Wireless

## Quick-Reference Card for a Coffee Pot

### Getting Started with your new Saeco Venus

Please check the contents of your box for the following items:

1 Saeco Venus
1 User Manual

Coffee Filter Basket
with Flip Top Lid

Filter Basket
Holder

Water Reservoir

Ceramic and
Stainless Steel
Thermal Carafe

Power Cord /
Storage

Control Pad

DO NOT turn machine on until water has been added to water tank.

Auto-on Button

Auto-on Light

Hour Program
Button

Digital Clock / Timer Window

On / Off Button

On / Off Light

Minute Program
Button

The ability to enjoy delicious coffee drinks has never been easier. Get ready to experience pure coffee nirvana.

Follow these three simple steps:
1. Add Water
2. Add Ground Coffee
3. Plug in Venus

**Step 1 - Add Water**
- Fill carafe with water and pour into reservoir (see figure 1)
- Place assembled carafe in brewing area, being sure to push all the way into the unit (see figure 2)

Figure 1

Figure 2

**Step 2 - Add Ground Coffee Beans**
- Open lid to coffee filter basket and fill with ground beans (see figure 3)
- Close flip top lid

Figure 3

**Step 3 - Plug in Venus**
- Plug power cord into outlet (see figure 4)

Figure 4

Now you are ready to enjoy delicious fresh brewed coffee from your new Saeco Venus.

**Simply**
- Press the On / Off Button
- Experience pure coffee nirvana

Source: © Koninklijke Philips Electronics N.V.

FIGURE 18.12

## Setting Up a Home and Office Network

Task-oriented heading

**Connecting Your Computer to a Network Adapter**
To connect your computer to a network, you will need a network cable.
If you did not receive a network cable with your computer, contact customer service at 1-866-543-1256.

Action verbs

**1.** Insert the network cable into the network adapter on your computer.
→ **TIP:** Insert the cable until it clicks into place.

**2.** Connect the other end of the cable to a network connection such as a network wall jack.
→ **TIP:** Do not use a network cable with a telephone jack. You could damage your computer.

Clear graphic

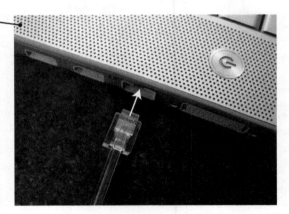

Setting Up a Home and Office Network • 25

### The Importance of the *Human Factor* in Product Design and Usability Testing

#### Background

When a medical device's design leads to patient death, more often than not, it can be attributed to human error. Often, the cause of human error can be traced to inadequate usability testing. The *human factor* has been recognized as a common problem in device failures. The U.S. Food and Drug Administration (FDA) published a report entitled "An Introduction to Human Factors in Medical Devices,"[1] in which it stated, "[D]evice design and related use errors are often implicated in adverse events." The purpose of the report was to "encourage manufacturers to improve the safety of medical devices and equipment by reducing the likelihood of user error." The FDA recommended usability testing as one avenue to address the problem.

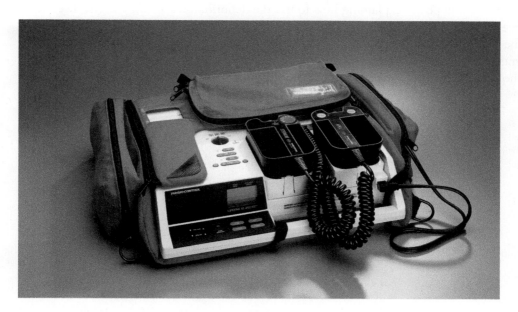

*The Lifepack 10 defibrilator featured improvements designed to make it easier to use. However, the company did not test the changes before the product was released, and unforeseen usability problems resulted in delayed treatment in real-world situations.*

Photo courtesy of Physio-Control.

---

[1] www.fda.gov/cdrh/humfac/doitpdf.

Usability testing is important even when a change will benefit a device's design. Consider the design of the Lifepak 10 defibrillator. An earlier version of the defibrillator featured paddles that had to be lifted and tilted to be removed from the base. The new model featured paddles that slid out toward the user, making them easier to disengage from the base. This change was promoted as an enhanced feature of the Lifepak 10, but it resulted in medical delays when staff had difficulty disengaging the paddles. The problem was compounded because the machine did not include visual clues, instructions, or warnings about how to remove the paddles. Usability testing would have identified the problem. Instead, delays resulted in user frustrations and patient death.[2]

## Assignment

1. Examine the photo of the Lifepak 10 defibrillator on the previous page. Create a graphic, instruction, or warning label for the device, explaining how to disengage the paddles. Turn in your design to your instructor with an explanation about where you would recommend attaching the label to the defibrillator.

2. Design a wall poster explaining how to use the defibrillator. For this exercise, use these five steps for the instructions: 1) turn on the defibrillator; 2) set the voltage; 3) remove the paddles; 4) administer the shock; 5) examine the patient for signs of revival. Use graphics and text to design your poster. Turn in your poster to your instructor with a short memo describing your design decisions.

[2] Compiled from www.health.qld.gov.au/patientsafety/documents/psmseptoct2006.pdf.

# EXERCISES

1. Locate some instructions that are hard to follow and print or copy them. (Your instructor may specify a length for these instructions.) Complete these tasks:
   a. Identify the intended users of the instructions. Analyze the organization, conventional sections, language, and design to determine if they are appropriate for the users. Based on your analysis, state why the instructions are hard to follow.
   b. Write a memo to your instructor describing the instruction's intended users and summarizing your analysis. Attach a copy of the instructions to your memo. (For information on memos, see Chapter 12.)
   c. Rewrite the instructions (or a portion of the instructions, as assigned by your instructor) so users can follow them easily. When you give the revised instructions to your instructor, attach a copy of the original.

2. Write instructions for one of the following tasks or for a task related to your major. When you have written the instructions, attach a memo to your instructor describing the intended users and the purpose of the instructions. Include graphics where appropriate, following the guidelines presented in this chapter. (For information on memos, see Chapter 12.)
   a. how to change the filters for the heating and air conditioning system in your house or apartment
   b. how to change a tire
   c. how to grill a steak

3. Write a troubleshooting guide for the instructions that you wrote in Exercise 2.

4. Analyze the language and design of the instructions in Figure 18.13. Write a memo to your instructor with your analysis.

5. Rewrite the instructions in Figure 18.13, eliminating the problems in language and design that you identified in Exercise 4.

6. Locate online instructions for a product or service related to your major. Evaluate the online instructions in an email to your instructor. Give the complete URL of the instructions to your instructor. In your email, answer these questions:
   a. Could you easily navigate through the instructions?
   b. Did the screen design help you locate information?
   c. How effectively did the writer design the instructions?
   d. How would you improve the instructions?

## FIGURE 18.13

## Sample Instructions for Exercises 4 & 5

### Operating Instructions: Humidity Sensor

Covered

Vented

Dry off dishes so they don't mislead the sensor.

**When using the Humidity Sensor...**

This microwave automatically adjusts cooking times based on the amount of humidity released during cooking. Various types and amounts of food release varying levels of humidity, guiding the sensor in detection of doneness.

Using the Humidity Sensor feature twice within a short period on the same food will likely result in severely overcooked or burnt food. If additional heating/cooking is desired after the first cooking period (using the Humidity Sensor), use the Time Cook feature.

The type of container used for heating food affects the Humidity Sensor. Tight sealing plastic containers do not allow steam to escape. Therefore, the Humidity Sensor is not able to detect cooking progress, resulting in over-cooked foods. The proper containers to use are those designed "microwave-safe." Cover them with their matching lids or use vented plastic wrap.

If wet or damp containers are used for heating food, the added steam will mislead the Humidity Sensor and food will likely be undercooked. This applies to the inside of the microwave as well–it must be dry in order for the Humidity Sensor to work accurately.

Operating instructions

*21*

# REAL WORLD EXPERIENCE

## Working with a Team to Write a Manual

You and your team will write a manual for a task for which written instructions are unavailable or are inadequate for users to complete the task. To write the manual, you and your team will complete these steps:

1. Select a task. Make sure that all members of your team are familiar with the task. If the task requires equipment, make sure your team has access to the equipment to prepare and test your instructions. Your instructor may want to approve your topic before you move to the next step.
2. Prepare a detailed outline of the manual. Submit this outline to your instructor for approval.
3. Decide on the reference aids you will include with the manual.
4. Prepare prototype pages showing the language, headings, and design that you plan to use in the manual.
5. Write the manual, dividing the writing tasks among your team members.
6. Test the instructions, following the guidelines for usability testing in this chapter.
   a. Find volunteer users. Ask these users to follow the step-by-step directions on the prototype pages. Watch these users as they follow the instructions, noting problems. After the users have completed the task, ask them whether the language, headings, and layout helped them follow the instructions and how you can improve the instructions.
   b. Revise the language, headings, and layout as necessary.
7. Revise the manual based on the test.
8. Turn in the final version of the manual to your instructor.

# chapter *nineteen*

## Creating User-Focused Websites

*iStockphoto 2008.*

**M**eredith is a technical writer for an engineering company. She will soon supervise a group that will redesign the company's external website. Meredith feels a little intimidated by the task. She visits websites to query consumers who use her company's products and services and to interact with friends and family through social media. However, she is not sure how to guide the group that will redesign the site. Meredith's manager assigned her to this group because she produces the print versions of the company's manuals, quick reference cards, and marketing documents.

Like Meredith, your manager may ask you to oversee the redesign of a website or to create one. In some companies, you may be responsible for the entire process of creating the site, from planning to maintaining it. Or you might work with a team to create a site. Or you might work with outside consultants, directing them to create the site using the feedback and guidance of your team. Whether you are solely responsible or you work with a team, you will create a more effective website when you know the characteristics that make a site user-focused and understand the process for creating that site.

##  CHARACTERISTICS OF A USER-FOCUSED WEBSITE

A user-focused website has these characteristics:

- **It is easy to scan.** Users "rarely read Web pages word by word; instead, they scan the page" (Nielsen 1997b, 1). Users want to scan a Web page, looking for keywords without scrolling through multiple text-filled screens. A scannable Web page has highlighted keywords, subheadings, and bulleted lists.
- **It uses concise language.** Users respond more positively to a website with fewer words. Because reading on a computer screen is about 25 percent slower than reading from paper, use about 50 percent fewer words when writing for the Web (Nielsen 1997a).
- **It is easy to navigate.** Users want to know how to navigate the site. They want to know where they are in the site and how to return to the home page. They want the navigation bar and hot buttons to appear in the same place on every page.
- **It is accessible.** Users may come from various cultures, may not be fluent in English, or may have disabilities. A successful website enables all users to access the information.
- **It is credible and trustworthy.** Because the Web is filled with unreliable information, make sure that readers see your site as credible. A credible and trustworthy site uses high-quality graphics, up-to-date links, worthwhile content, and effectively designed pages.

##  PLAN THE WEBSITE

As Figure 19.1 illustrates, the process of creating a website is recursive; you revisit steps of the process as the needs of your users change, as you receive input from usability testing and users, or as the product or process changes.

In this section, we focus on two steps of the planning process: (1) identifying the users and your purpose for the site and (2) determining the appropriate content.

### Identify the Users and the Purpose of the Site

To design a user-focused website, you need to first identify its purpose and its users. Begin by thinking about the purpose of the site. For example, do you want users to buy products

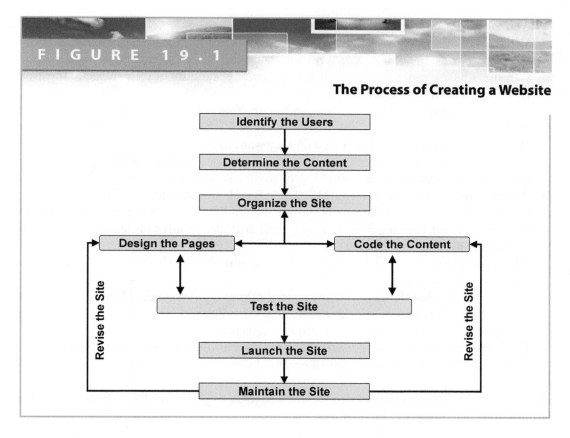

FIGURE 19.1

**The Process of Creating a Website**

Identify the Users

Determine the Content

Organize the Site

Design the Pages — Code the Content

Revise the Site

Revise the Site

Test the Site

Launch the Site

Maintain the Site

and services? Do you want users to learn how to use or install products? Do you want to provide answers to frequently asked questions or to provide information about your organization? The site may have more than one purpose; for example, you may want to provide information as well as answer frequently asked questions.

Successful websites also reflect an in-depth knowledge of the users. These websites build relationships with the users, and the users often participate in site design. To identify your users, conduct user research. For example, if the site is for people who use your products and services, send them a questionnaire to find out what information they would use on the site. Conduct a focus group with selected users. Through questionnaires and focus groups, you can learn more than the demographics of your users. You can also discover

- what your users want to learn or expect from a website
- how your users want information presented on the Web
- how your users search for information on the Web
- how your users might use the information you plan to present on your site

As you analyze your users, ask these questions:

- **What do the users know about the subject of the site?** Do the users have similar backgrounds? For example, if you are creating a site for NASA scientists, you can assume your users have similar backgrounds and some understanding of your subject. However, if you are creating a site for people interested in NASA, your users might be children, teachers, scientists, amateur scientists, and so on. Your users may or may not know much about your subject.
- **Why will users visit your site?** What do they want to do? Do they want to gather information, make a decision, or get an answer to a question? Do they want to perform a task, link to related sites, to make a purchase, or to download information?
- **Are the users internal or external?** Will only people in your organization use your site? Will people outside your organization use the site? If the users are external, what do they know about your organization? Are their attitudes positive or negative about your organization?
- **Will users view your site on a cell phone or other mobile device?** If so, create a version that users can view on those devices.
- **Are your users global?** Consider your users' culture and language. How will you meet the needs of global users? For example, will your organization and your users benefit from putting the site's content in multiple languages?
- **Do the users have disabilities that will affect their ability to access the information on your site?** Design your site so that all potential users can access the information.

When you launch your site, you can use the site itself to gather feedback from your users. Refine your site based on that feedback.

## Determine the Appropriate Content for the Site

After you have identified the users and purpose, identify the content that the site should include to meet the users' needs and expectations and to achieve your purpose. Jan Spyridakis recommends selecting "content that will be interesting and relevant" to the users (2000, 361). She explains that "readers comprehend better and retain more information when they are interested in the topic. …The more relevant users find content to be," the better they comprehend the information (Spyridakis 2000, 361–62). Before you begin to design the site, answer these questions: What are the parameters of the site? What is the purpose?

Think of building a website like building a house. Before you begin to draw the plans, you need to know what you want in the house. For example, how many people will live in it? Do you need two bedrooms or three? Do you want the house to have two stories? If you want two stories, will all members of the household be able to use the stairs? Do you want the master bedroom next to the other bedrooms? Will you need a garage? How many cars should the garage accommodate? What is your budget? You need to know your budget, users, and needs before you can design a house—or, in this case, a website.

A successful website reflects an in-depth knowledge of its users, building on that relationship and incorporating feedback received from them.

## TIPS FOR DETERMINING THE CONTENT OF THE WEBSITE

- **Select content that is interesting and relevant to the users.** Many Web authors fail to filter out irrelevant or uninteresting content because they can easily put the contents of existing paper documents into hypertext markup language (HTML) and place them on the site. These documents may be appropriate for paper, but they might not serve Web users well. Irrelevant or uninteresting content can include graphics or audio and video, as well as text. *Just because the information is available does not mean that it belongs on the site.*

- **Adapt existing content created for other media.** You may find that you already have some existing content suitable for your website. For example, you can convert content, such as text from online presentations, for Web pages. Some Web designers simply scan in paper documents and load them onto their sites. These documents may work effectively on paper, but not on the Web. Instead, decide what information from the paper document is appropriate for your purpose, your users, and the Web format. Then adapt that information for your site.

- **Decide if the content is best presented on paper or online.** Print is still a viable medium for some types of information and documents, and some content best meets readers' needs in print rather than online.

- **Ensure that all content helps the site achieve your purpose and meets users' needs.** The text, graphics, and links should relate directly to the purpose of the site. For example, a former IRS website began with the title The Digital Daily in a newspaper-style layout (see Figure 19.2). This layout and the title didn't help the site achieve its purpose because many users did not recognize the site as belonging to the IRS.

**Web Page without a User-Centered Title**

NEWS FOR YOU 2002

Source: Internal Revenue Service (December 19, 2001).

As you consider the information and the elements that you want to include and that your users need, answer these questions:

- **Will you use existing information from paper documents?** If so, you will have to adapt it for an online format. If the information is copyrighted, obtain permission to use the information (see Chapter 4 and the Ethics Note in this chapter).
- **Will you have to create new content?** Determine how much time you need to create the content, how much research you will have to do, and whether you will create the content alone or with a team.
- **Where will you get graphics for the site?** Do you have existing graphics you can use? If not, who will create them? If you plan to use existing graphics, are they copyrighted? Can you obtain permission to use them?

- **Will you include audio or video on your site?** If so, what is your budget for creating the audio and videos? Do you have the tools to create professional audio and videos?
- **What is the budget for creating the site?** Calculate the budget for each element: the graphics, audio, design, and so on.

You will think of other questions you need to consider as you think about the content. You can also use the Tips for Determining the Content of the Website.

##  ORGANIZE THE SITE

Once you determine the purpose and understand the needs of your users, organize the site. Use everything you know about your users to structure the site to meet their needs, accommodate their search methods, and appeal to their learning styles. In an effectively organized site, users can easily find the information they want.

Your users will visit the site for different purposes and will have different strategies to search for the same information. Therefore, organizing a site is complicated. Experiment with various layouts and designs to find the organization that best meets your needs and users' needs. For example, "role-play" each type of user, asking questions that a user would ask. For a product and services site, you might list products and services alphabetically, but find that users search in other ways, such as by keyword, product type, or product number. Ask focus groups of users how they would search for various types of information.

Once you have identified the types of content, consider how you will balance the amount of information with the ease of navigation. If a site is difficult to navigate your users may not be able to locate the information they need when they need it. Put information no more than three clicks away from the home page. That way, users are more likely to see the important information before they leave the site.

You can organize a website in several ways. One frequent organization appears in Figure 19.3. In this organizational chart (sometimes referred to as a *taxonomy*), users enter through the main page that serves as an entry point and links to other pages. From the homepage, users can directly access the pages About the Chamber of Commerce, Our Mission, Our Members, Our Community, and Links to Small Town, USA, Sites. However, from the homepage, user can't directly access the pages linked to Our Members. If these links appeared on the homepage, it would be overloaded with information.

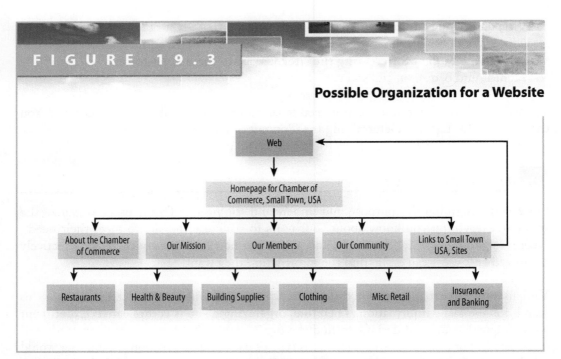

**FIGURE 19.3**

**Possible Organization for a Website**

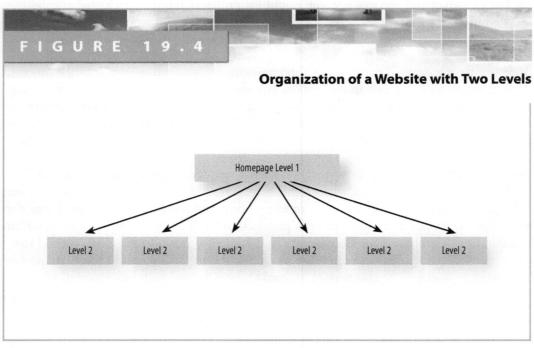

**FIGURE 19.4**

**Organization of a Website with Two Levels**

If your site is relatively simple, consider an organization with only two levels (see Figure 19.4). In this organization, all the second-level page links appear on the homepage. This two-level organization is easy to implement and easy for users to navigate. However, if your site is complex, this organization will clutter the homepage and overload users with information. For more complex sites, use a multiple-level organization such as the one shown in Figure 19.5. Here, only three links appear on the homepage, yet the site has more pages and levels. This site has four levels. If the Web author had put the links for all the pages on the homepage, the user would receive too much information.

When you have an idea of how you want to organize the site,
- Create an organization chart like those in Figures 19.3, 19.4, and 19.5.
- Use the chart as a guide. As you write, you may determine that you need more or fewer levels or that a page should appear at a higher or lower level.

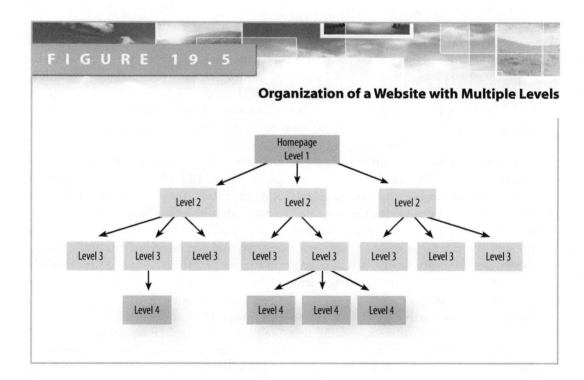

**FIGURE 19.5**

**Organization of a Website with Multiple Levels**

To design a user-focused Web page, you will use many of the principles that you learned for designing visual information and graphics in Chapters 10 and 11. This section focuses on how you can adapt those principles for the Web. To design an effective Web page, focus on these areas:

- Create an effective online layout.
- Write concise, scannable content.
- Make the site easy to navigate.
- Make the site accessible.
- Create a credible, trustworthy site.

## Create an Effective Online Layout

To create an effective online layout, use the principles of contrast, repetition, alignment, and proximity (see Chapter 10). These principles work just as effectively in online pages as in paper documents. The following guidelines will help you adapt these principles for Web pages:

- **Use ample white space.** Create contrast on the page by including ample white space (or empty space). If a Web page is filled with text and/or graphics, readers may not want to read the page or may not know what information is important. User-focused Web pages use white space to highlight and organize information. Don't be tempted to fill up the page just because you can. The sample Web pages throughout this chapter demonstrate effective use of white space.
- **Group related information together.** Use the principle of proximity to group related information (see Chapter 10). The Web page in Figure 19.6 effectively groups related information so users can scan the page and locate the information that meets their needs.
- **Use a consistent design for the pages.** The pages should look like they belong to the same website, so select an appropriate color scheme and use it consistently throughout the site. Use the same color for the same elements and the same background color for every page. For example, the two Web pages in Figure 19.7 from Kendall Hunt Publishing Company have a consistent page design: The navigation bar and the company logo are in the same place on both pages, and the pages use the same colors.
- **Include an informative title at the top of every page.** (Farkas and Farkas 2000; Spyridakis 2000). An informative, specific title "helps orient users" (Spyridakis 2000, 361). When users follow a link to a page, they want confirmation that they have arrived at the content they expected. Without a title to guide them, readers will be confused. For example, Spyridakis points to the former IRS website. The page title appeared to be

**FIGURE 19.6**

## Web Page with Related Information Grouped Together

Site Map    Frequently Asked Questions  Accessibility
Source: http://www.nature.nps.gov/

The Digital Daily. The page did not clearly indicate that the user had arrived at the IRS homepage (see Figure 19.2). The Web pages in Figure 19.7 have an informative title on each page: About and Contact Us.

- **Include the site name or logo on every page.** The title or logo should appear in the same place on every page to maintain site identity (Farkas and Farkas 2000). The Web pages in Figure 19.7 show the company's logo consistently in the top left corner.
- **Include an informative header and footer on every page.** Headers and footers add consistency and credibility to your site. The footer should include the copyright information and the title of the organization that is publishing the site. It may also include a link to the home page and the name of the Web master or page editor. Figure 19.8 is the footer from the NASA site. This footer includes the date the page was last updated, the page editor, the logo, and the links to a site map, other relevant information, and government sites.

- **Use graphics and color appropriate for the users and the topic.** For example, the photos in the Kendall Hunt Publishing Company site to the topic (see Figure 19.7).
- **Use graphics that download quickly.** Create an individual file for each graphic. Use a thumbnail sketch of the graphic with links to the image so users can click on it to link to the larger version of the graphic (Wilkinson 2000). You can find examples of thumbnail graphics on maps and weather sites.

## Write Concise, Scannable Content

Web users scan for information, so write content that lets them scan the page. You have options to consider as you create the content:

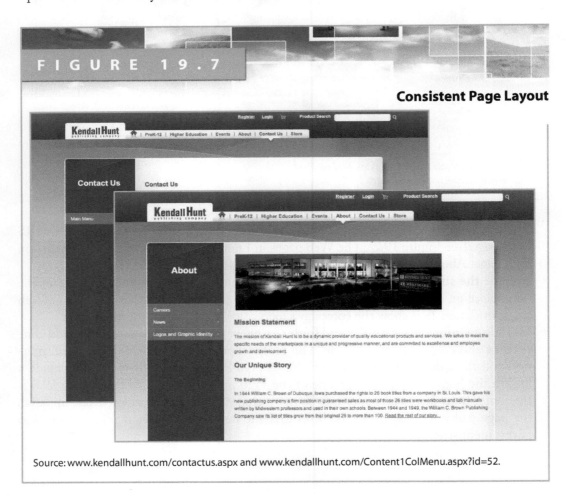

**FIGURE 19.7**

**Consistent Page Layout**

Source: www.kendallhunt.com/contactus.aspx and www.kendallhunt.com/Content1ColMenu.aspx?id=52.

**FIGURE 19.8**

**Footer on a Web Page**

- **Adapt existing content created for other media.** For example, you might adapt information from a paper document. However, content designed for other media, especially print, may not be appropriate for the Web. Analyze the content and decide whether you can use it. If you can use it, adapt it for the online format. For instance, a 15-page report may be appropriate for print; however, for the Web, you might summarize the report and provide a link to a PDF file containing the full report. If users want to read the report, they can download and print it. If you are creating a website, determine how it fits in with other kinds of organizational documents.
- **Write new content.** If you don't have content to adapt from other media or if the content from that media is inappropriate, write new content.
- **Select or create appropriate graphics.** As you select or create the graphics for the website, consider how the graphics will download. If the graphics take too long to download, users may abandon your site.

The guidelines you learned in Chapters 7 and 8 apply to Web documents as well as print. Follow these principles for writing reader-focused sentences and paragraphs and for using reader-focused language when writing the content for your Web pages. Be especially careful when selecting words for the headings, links, and pages. When users can easily read and understand the content, they can search more effectively and can better comprehend the information. The Tips for Writing User-Focused Content will help you to write better content for your website.

## Make the Site Easy to Navigate

With a book or magazine, you can see the entire document at once: You can flip from the beginning to the end. However, with a Web document, you can't see the "end" or even the "middle." You can't see the entire site at one time as you can with a book or a magazine.

*Creating User-Focused Websites* | 635

FIGURE 19.9

**Partial Site Map**

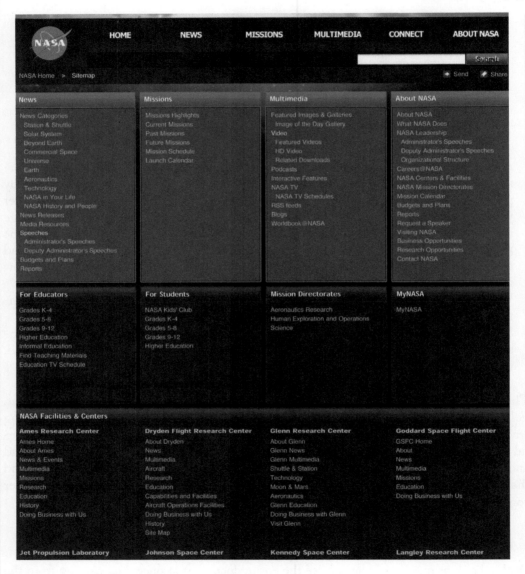

Source: www.nasa.gov/sitemap/sitemap_nasa.html.

## TIPS FOR WRITING USER-FOCUSED CONTENT

- **Write in small "chunks" and short pages** (Bradbury 2000; Spyridakis 2000). Small chunks help users scan pages. Break long paragraphs and pages into shorter ones. Put less information on each page (screen) and one idea in each paragraph (Bradbury 2000; Nielsen 1997b). In this way, users can "more easily find the information they need and read and retain it" (Spyridakis 2000, 363).
- **Use bulleted items and lists** (Bradbury 2000; Nielsen 1997b). Bulleted items and lists visually break up text, make pages easier to read, and guide users to information.
- **Include highlighted keywords.** These words help users scan for information.
- **Use subheadings.** Subheadings categorize information and help users scan the page. The Visitor Information page from the Denver Zoo website includes subheadings for admission and parking information (see Figure 19.11).
- **Use simple words and short sentences. Use words that users can easily read and understand** (see Chapter 8). Eliminate unnecessary detail and use only a few examples of a concept; don't provide "exhaustive coverage" (Spyridakis 2000, 363).
- **Use active-voice verbs whenever possible and appropriate.** Active voice helps users move more quickly through Web content (see Chapter 7).
- **Include an introduction or introductory sentence that identifies the purpose of the site and specifies the intended users** (ibid.). On the homepage, introduce the site's purpose. If you're writing for an organization, introduce the organization and state what it does or include a link to a page that gives information about the organization. This page might be called About Us.

Unlike a print document, a website lacks a linear organization with pages numbered consecutively from the first page to the last. However, a site does have an organization, and you should show your users how to navigate among the pages and how to return to the beginning, or homepage. Follow the Tips for Helping Users Navigate Your Website to make your site easy to navigate.

## Make the Site Accessible

Your site should be accessible for
- users with varied types of technology
- users of various cultures
- users with disabilities

Figure 19.13 is an example of a site that caters to a wide scope of users. To create an accessible site, follow the Tips for Creating an Accessible website.

## TIPS FOR HELPING USERS NAVIGATE YOUR WEBSITE

- **Include a site map.** A site map shows the *taxonomy,* or global structure of your site. It lists the site's pages, organized by category. Your site map will be more effective if you include a "You are here" or "Last page visited" marker (Farkas and Farkas 2000). Figure 19.9 from the NASA site illustrates a partial site map.
- **Include an index.** An index is an alphabetical listing of the pages and topics on your website. Often users select the beginning letter of their search item rather than having to scroll through the site to find what they want. Figure 19.10 illustrates an index. Notice how users can select a letter near the top of the page.
- **Provide a link to the homepage on every page.** Put the link in the same place on every page. Use your organization's logo as the Homepage link as on the Denver Zoo Web pages, Figure 19.11.
- **Include a navigation bar on every page.** Locate this bar in the same place on every page. For example, the navigation bar on the Denver Zoo site appears at the top of every page. On many sites, the navigation bar appears on the left side of the page and has a vertical, rather than horizontal, orientation.
- **Include a search function on every page.** Help users navigate the site by including a search box on every page. Locate the search function in the same place on every page.

## TIPS FOR CREATING AN ACCESSIBLE WEBSITE

- **Include a text-only version of all visual information.** Some users may use a text-only version of your site because their browsers are set to view text only. Other users may have limited ability to view the site because they are using a hand-held device or they are visually impaired. For example, if you rely solely on a graphic or on color to indicate a link, colorblind users may not find it.
- **Don't rely on color or graphics to convey information.** For example, if you use blue to indicate a link, also underline the link so colorblind users can see it.
- **Allow users to adjust the font size.** Website authors might use both a button and the words "text size" to show users they can adjust the text size.
- **Be sensitive to readers of other cultures.** Use Simplified Technical English. Avoid idioms. (See Chapter 8 for more information on writing for readers of other cultures and for readers who are not fluent in English.)

FIGURE 19.10

**Example of an A to Z Index**

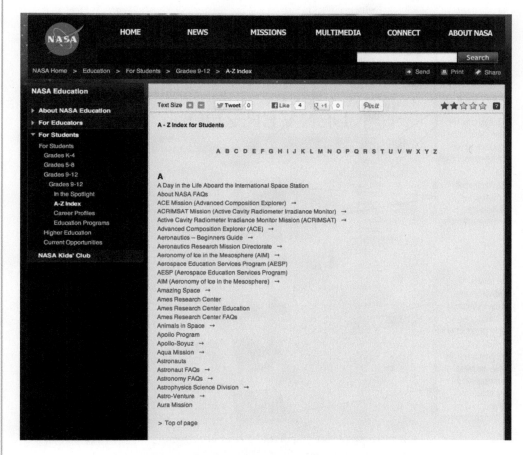

Source: www.nasa.gov/audience/for students/9-12/A-Z/index.html.

FIGURE 19.11

**Effective Page from the Denver Zoo Website**

The page is easy to navigate. It includes two navigation bars: the horizontal bar that appears on every page and the vertical bar that provides a table of contents for the information in the education section.

Even though the page is information-rich, users can easily scan the page.

The page includes a "quick links" feature to help users navigate frequently accessed areas of the website.

The information is chunked using subheadings.

The page is credible because of the high-quality photos.

The photos and the colors are relevant to the topic and appropriate for the users.

Source: Downloaded from the World Wide Web, November 2008: www.denverzoo.org/education/index.asp. Denver Zoo.

**Effective Page from a Company Website**

The page is easy to navigate because of the navigation bar and search box.

The logo is easy to see and appears in the header of every page.

The page uses text, not graphics, for the navigation bar, making the page accessible to those needing a text-only version.

The page uses the design principle of repetition by repeating the blue from the logo in the photo and the navigation bars.

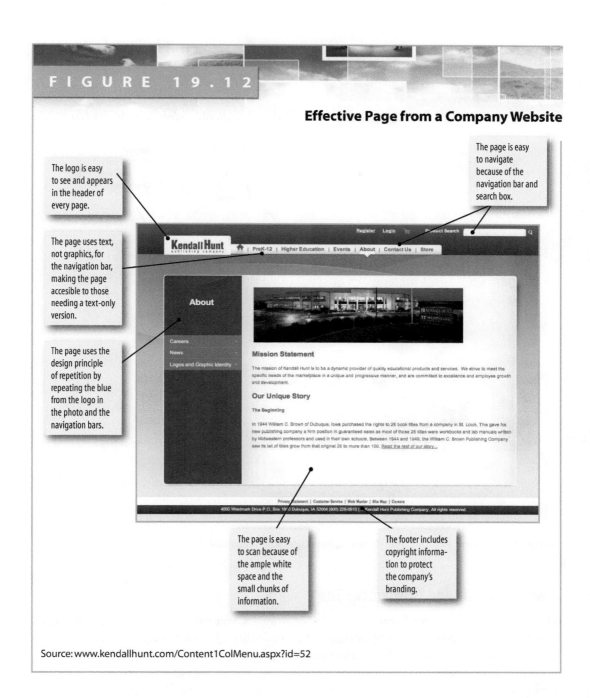

The page is easy to scan because of the ample white space and the small chunks of information.

The footer includes copyright information to protect the company's branding.

Source: www.kendallhunt.com/Content1ColMenu.aspx?id=52

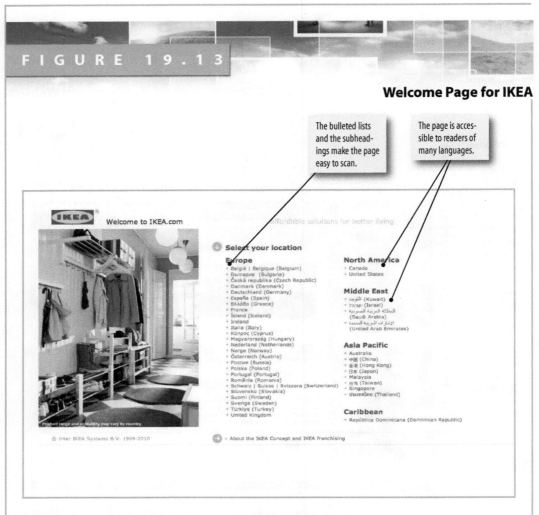

## FIGURE 19.13

**Welcome Page for IKEA**

The bulleted lists and the subheadings make the page easy to scan.

The page is accessible to readers of many languages.

Source: www.ikea.com/. IKEA. Used with the permission of Inter IKEA Systems BV.

## Create a Credible and Trustworthy Site

To encourage users to read your site and visit it again, you must establish credibility and gain their trust. According to Spyridakis, the credibility of a Web page is easily affected by the presence or absence of certain content. For some, the credibility of a company or institution may begin with its website. People may choose a graduate school or a future employer or purchase a specific brand of product in part because of how credible the company or agency appears to be in its website. (2000, 363)

### Copyright, Intellectual Property, and the Web

Have you ever found a graphic that you liked on a website and used it on your personal website? Have you copied code from a website and used it for your organization's site? Have you ever used a company's logo or trademark from a website? If so, you could be guilty of copyright, patent, or trademark infringement. U.S. and international laws protect every element of a website: the text, graphics, and the code (Le Vie 2000). Even if the authors of a site haven't filed a formal copyright application, the law protects their work. Along with copyrights, the law protects an organization's patents, trademarks, and trade secrets. You or your organization can "bruise its reputation by infringing on someone else's copyright" or intellectual property, and you could face legal penalties for it (Le Vie 2000, 21).

You must protect your website, your intellectual property, and your organization's products and services. For example, aspirin originally started as a trademarked product, but the manufacturer failed to protect its trademark, and aspirin became a name used by many manufacturers. To protect your website and your intellectual property—or that of your organization—follow these guidelines to maintain the uniqueness of your product or service:

- Place a copyright notice in the footer of every page, not just on the homepage.
- Link from the word "copyright" to another web page that defines what you own on the site (Le Vie 2000).

Protect yourself and your company from the legal penalties and bruised reputations that occur when you don't respect the copyrights and intellectual property of others:

- Obtain permission for any information, graphic, or code that you use from another site or printed document.
- Place the permission, copyright, and trademark information in a conspicuous place.
- ***Do not use any information, graphic, or code without the written permission of its authors.***

To make your site credible and trustworthy, follow the Tips for Creating a Credible and Trustworthy Website.

## TIPS FOR CREATING A CREDIBLE AND TRUSTWORTHY WEBSITE

- **Include your name and/or the name of the organization that maintains the site and contact information.** If you're writing for an organization, include the organization's name, its purpose, and contact information. If you are maintaining the site, include your credentials—some kind of affiliation or title that users can check (Spyridakis 2000).

- **Include the date the site was launched or the date of the last update.** Users want to know if the information is current. If you launch a site and don't update it frequently, the site will have little credibility. Users will be unable to trust that the information is accurate or up to date.

- **Check all links regularly to ensure they still work.** If you have linked to related sites, make sure those links still work and that the linked sites are relevant and current.

- **Periodically check to ensure the information on your site is accurate and free of typographical, spelling, and other mistakes.** These errors may cause users to assume the site is not credible. These errors can also "draw the user's attention away from the important information on the page and raise doubts about the author's credibility" (Spyridakis 2000, 373).

- **Use high-quality graphics.** High-quality graphics add credibility. Websites without high-quality graphics look amateurish and unprofessional, making the content and the site look untrustworthy.

- **Use a professional tone appropriate for your purpose and users.** Avoid hyped-up, unsubstantiated language, such as Scientific Breakthrough! or Best Weather Site on the Web.

- **Cite sources.** If you use information from other sources, tell users where you found the information.

- **Respond to reader feedback.** If you offer users the opportunity to contact the organization or provide feedback about the site, respond to user inquiries in a timely manner. You will anger, frustrate, and alienate users if you don't follow up on their inquiries. Offer users the option to send you email only if you can respond to them in a timely manner.

## Creating an ePortfolio

In Chapter 13 you learned about electronic career portfolios, often called **ePortfolios**. These portfolios are a Web-based collection of materials related to your job search and your career. As you begin your job search, employers may ask you for an ePortfolio or you may want to provide employers with additional information about you and your work.

## Assignment

1. Search the Web for examples of effective ePortfolios. The examples should have the characteristics of a user-focused website.
2. In an email to your instructor, send links to two effective ePortfolios.
3. Create your own ePortfolio. At a minimum, your portfolio should include
   a. an introductory (home) page
   b. a résumé with highlighted keywords
   c. several samples of your work
   You may include other relevant information. If you are unfamiliar with coding a website, locate tutorials on the Web or use Web-authoring software available at your college or university.
4. Test your ePortfolio.
5. Determine what users can access in your ePortfolio. Because you will have personal information on your ePortfolio, restrict access to those whom you trust: friends, family, professors, and potential employers.
6. Launch your ePortfolio. Send an email to your instructor with a link to your ePortfolio.

# CASE STUDY ANALYSIS

## Websites, Sustainability, and Environmental Stewardship

### Background

The U.S. Environmental Protection Agency describes sustainability with the term "environmental stewardship." The EPA describes how companies and nonprofit organizations can be stewards of the environment:

> From the way they manage their operations to the products and services they offer customers to the projects and activities they support in their communities, businesses and other institutions can play an important role in protecting the environment and preserving natural resources.[1]

Many U.S. companies use their websites to showcase their environmental stewardship and their commitment to sustaining the environment.

If you visit the websites of most U.S. global companies, you will find a section on environmental responsibility. The companies include sections such as Green (Google), Environment & Society (Shell Oil), Environmental Sustainability (Microsoft), and Sustainability (Kraft Foods). These environmentally focused pages are not limited to one industry. These pages provide an opportunity for consumers to see how an organization views environmental stewardship.

### Assignment

1. Locate the website for three global companies in different industries. These websites must include a section on sustainability and/or environmental stewardship.
2. Compare the three websites' approach to presenting the company's commitment to the environment (see Chapter 6). Your comparison should answer the following questions:
   a. What are the companies' commitment to the environment as presented on their websites?
   b. Who are the intended readers?
   c. Is the information credible? Explain your answer.
   d. What persuasive appeals do the websites use (see Chapter 9)?
   e. Which of the sites best presents the information for the intended readers?

[1] www.epa.gov/epahome/business.htm

# EXERCISES

1. Locate two websites on the same topic: one should be credible and trustworthy; one should be less credible and untrustworthy.
   a. Write a memo to your instructor comparing and contrasting the two sites. Include specific examples from the sites. (For help with the comparison/contrast pattern of organization, see Chapter 6).
   b. In your memo, include the URL for each Web page and attach a copy of the homepages.

2. Locate the website for a national or local nonprofit organization such as the Red Cross or the American Heart Association. Analyze the following aspects of the site:
   - consistency of the page design
   - color (see Chapter 11 to review the information on color)
   - ease of navigation
   - style of writing
   - appropriateness of content

   Write an informal report to your instructor analyzing problems with the site and recommending solutions. Print a copy of the organization's homepage to attach to your report. (Go to Chapter 6 to review the problem/solution pattern of organization and go to Chapters 14 and 15 for information on reports.)

3. Evaluate the website of your hometown and compare it to the sites of two cities of similar size. As part of your evaluation, consider whether the site has the characteristics of a user-focused website:
   - Is it easy to scan?
   - Does it use concise language?
   - Is it easy to navigate?
   - Is it accessible?
   - Is it credible and trustworthy?

Write an informative informal report to the mayor or city manager summarizing your evaluation and comparisons. Turn in a copy of your report to your instructor. (See Chapters 14 and 15 for information on reports.)

4. Expand your evaluation of your hometown's website. Determine
   • If the site has appropriately protected its copyright and other intellectual property, such as its logo (its branding).
   • If the site may have infringed on the copyrighted information or trademarks of others.

Based on your evaluation, write a memo to the webmaster explaining what you were looking for and whether the site adequately protects the city's intellectual property and branding and properly uses copyrighted information. Turn in a copy of your memo to your instructor.

# REAL WORLD EXPERIENCE

## Helping a Nonprofit Organization in Your Community

Nonprofit organizations are groups that provide a service without making a profit. Nonprofit organizations include groups such as Little League, Society for the Prevention of Cruelty to Animals (SPCA), Boys and Girls Clubs, and Big Brothers and Big Sisters. Some nonprofits don't have the budget or expertise to create a website. Even local and regional offices of some larger nonprofit organizations may not have the time, money, or staff to create and maintain a site. Sometimes these organizations have websites, but they are poorly designed and, therefore, are not credible and trustworthy. In your community, you can most likely locate nonprofit organizations that would benefit from a website or a redesigned website.

### Assignment

Working by yourself or with a team (according to your instructor), locate a nonprofit organization in your community. Go to the website for your city; this site may have links to contacts for local nonprofit organizations or for groups needing volunteers. You can also visit with volunteer groups in your community to find names of nonprofit groups. Some colleges and universities have volunteer groups that help local nonprofit organizations. When you have located a nonprofit organization:

1. Contact the organization and make an appointment to talk to a representative about designing a website.
2. Prepare interview questions before you arrive for the appointment (see Chapter 5 for information on interviewing). Develop questions about what types of information the organization would like to have on a website. Include questions for the representative on how the organization and its users would use the site.
3. Identify the users and the site's purpose.
4. Select and create content for the site. If you receive printed documents for the site, adapt them for the Web.
5. Create a site map.
6. Design the homepage and the additional pages.
7. Test your website and revise as necessary. Ask the staff at the organization to test the site.
8. Present your website to the organization and to your instructor. (The organization may launch the site on the Web; you will only create and test it.)

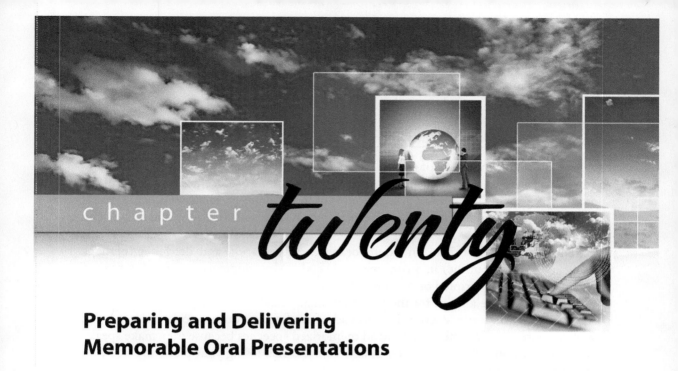

# Preparing and Delivering Memorable Oral Presentations

*A*re you uncomfortable speaking in front of strangers or even your peers? Do you enjoy talking in front of a group? Whether you dread or enjoy making presentations, you will make presentations as a professional. Oral presentations are an important part of technical communications; oral presentations allow professionals to interact with their audience and sell their ideas. You might make an oral presentation to any of these audiences:

- **Coworkers and decision makers in your organization.** For example, you might make a formal presentation to upper-level management on the results of a feasibility study. You might give an informal presentation on new software that the organization has adopted for tracking projects; or in a staff meeting, you might give a status report about a project.
- **Customers and clients.** You might make a presentation about a project or product to customers and clients.
- **Peers at a professional meeting.** You might present the findings of a research project. Your audience would be your *peers*—people who do the same type of work as you or who have a similar educational background.
- **General public.** You might make a presentation to a nonprofit, civic, or government group.

Whether you are speaking to coworkers, customers, clients, peers, or the public, the guidelines in this chapter will help you create and deliver memorable presentations.

##  UNDERSTAND THE TYPES OF ORAL PRESENTATIONS

Professionals might make any of the following types of oral presentations:
- **Impromptu**. You do not plan an impromptu presentation. You decide what you will say as you are speaking. You might give an impromptu presentation in a staff meeting when someone asks you about your research or wants a project update. You would talk briefly and answer questions.
- **Extemporaneous**. You plan an extemporaneous presentation and deliver it (perhaps using notes or an outline) in a conversational style. Most audiences prefer this type of presentation to the scripted or memorized types.
- **Scripted**. You write a script for the presentation and read it to the audience.
- **Memorized**. You write a script; but instead of reading it, you memorize it and speak without notes. Most professionals avoid memorized speeches because they make speakers appear stiff and formal (Pfeiffer 2002). You also risk losing your place or forgetting an important point.

Figure 20.1 presents advantages, disadvantages, and guidelines for each type of presentation. This chapter focuses on the two types of presentations that are most preferred and delivered in the workplace: extemporaneous and scripted.

## PLAN FOR THE AUDIENCE AND THE OCCASION

The process of preparing an oral presentation is similar to preparing most technical documents. You analyze your audience and the occasion (situation), gather and organize information, and prepare visual aids. To prepare the presentation, follow these guidelines:
- find out about the audience
- determine the purpose of the presentation
- plan for only the information that the audience can absorb
- anticipate the audience's needs and questions
- organize the presentation

### Find Out about the Audience

To deliver an effective presentation, you must first know who will be listening. To find out as much as possible about the audience, ask these questions:

**FIGURE 20.1**

**Advantages, Disadvantages, and Guidelines for
Four Types of Oral Presentations**

| Type of Presentation | Advantages | Disadvantages | Guidelines |
|---|---|---|---|
| **Impromtu** | • Delivered in a relaxed, conversational manner | • May be disorganized because the speaker can't prepare in advance<br>• May be rambling and unfocused | • Stop and think before speaking<br>• Ask the audience questions to determine what they want you to speak about |
| **Extemporaneous** | • Prepared ahead of time<br>• Delivered in a relaxed, conversational manner<br>• Allows speaker to adjust the presentation in response to the audience's reactions<br>• Takes less time to create than a scripted presentation | • Can run over the allotted time<br>• May cause the speaker to leave out information | • Rehearse the presentation<br>• Use visual aids to guide you as you give the presentation (these aids will also help the audience)<br>• Explain new information or terminology<br>• Define unfamiliar terminology<br>• Use simple, not fancy, language<br>• Prepare notes or an outline |
| **Scripted** | • Prepared ahead of time<br>• Allows the speaker to deliver complete, accurate information<br>• Helps the speaker stay within the time limit | • Often delivered in an unnatural, boring manner<br>• Doesn't allow the speaker to adjust to the audience's reactions<br>• Takes a long time to prepare | • Use when the audience expects precision<br>• Use visual aids and examples<br>• Explain new information or terminology<br>• Define unfamiliar terminology<br>• Use simple, not fancy, language |
| **Memorized** | • Prepared ahead of time<br>• Allows the speaker to deliver complete, accurate information<br>• Helps the speaker stay within the time limit | • Makes the speaker seem stiff and formal<br>• Without notes, the speaker may lose his or her place or forget part of the presentation<br>• Takes a long time to prepare | • When possible, select either the extemporaneous or scripted style instead of a memorized presentation |

- **What do you know about the demographics of your audience?** In this context, *demographics* are the characteristics of a group such as the size of the group, average age, gender, educational background, where they work, etc. The more you know about the demographics of your audience, the better you can deliver an audience-focused presentation.
- **What does the audience know about your topic?** With this information, you can determine what technical terminology you can use, what the audience will understand, and how much background, if any, your audience will need to understand your presentation.
- **What is your audience's attitude about your topic?** Do they have a positive, negative, or neutral attitude toward your topic? Will the audience have a mix of attitudes or opinions about the topic? For example, if you are delivering a presentation on cost-cutting initiatives for your department, will the audience favorably receive your message or will they feel threatened? The answers to these questions will help you know what types of information to include, what information to emphasize, and so on.
- **What is the audience's impression of you or your organization?** The audience may already have a positive, negative or neutral impression about you and the organization. Will your audience be hostile? Interested? Curious? Enthusiastic?
- **Why is the audience listening to the presentation?** The audience may attend the presentation because they have to; or they may attend because they want to gather information, to make a decision, or to learn something new.
- **What does the audience expect from your presentation?** Does the audience expect a formal presentation or an informal one? Does your audience expect certain types of visual aids? Be sure that your presentation is appropriate to the occasion and meets the expectations of your audience.

## Determine the Purpose of the Presentation

Once you have identified your audience and the occasion, define your purpose:

- **Why are you giving the presentation?**
- **What do you want to accomplish?** What are your goals for the presentation? Can you accomplish those goals in the time allotted? If not, adjust the goals so you can achieve them in the time allotted.
- **Is your goal to inform, to persuade, or both?** For example, if you are talking about how to use a new product

> To deliver an effective presentation, you must know your audience; determine your purpose; and plan, organize, and rehearse your material.

that the audience has just bought, your purpose is to inform. If you are discussing the benefits of this new product to an audience that might purchase it, your purpose is to persuade.

- **What do you want your audience to do with the information?** For example, do you want your audience to purchase a product, make a decision, or acquire information (Reiffenstein 2008)?

## Plan for Only the Information the Audience Can Absorb

Listening to information takes twice as long as reading the same information. If your audience can read 10 pages in 8 minutes, they can comprehend that same information through listening in about 16 minutes. The average adult has an attention span of about 18 minutes, so you should include only the amount of information that the audience can absorb in that time (ibid.). If your talk is longer than 20 minutes, break up the presentation with interactive exercises, lengthen the question-and-answer time, or perhaps supplement the presentation with handouts (ibid.).

Follow these guidelines to prepare a presentation, keeping in mind the length of adults' attention span. Remember that audiences want to hear only the information they need and no more.

- **Condense your presentation to its key points.** Don't try to give the audience every bit of information you have about a topic or all the details. Select the key points and present those. If necessary, you can refer the audience to your written research, to published articles, or to handouts you have prepared.
- **Stay within your allotted time and speak to the requirements of the occasion.** For example, if you are speaking at a professional conference, conference organizers will tell you how long they expect you to speak. If they give you 30 minutes, they expect you to make your presentation and answer questions during those 30 minutes. If you take more than your allotted time, other speakers may not have their full 30 minutes. When you speak longer than your allowed time, you are being inconsiderate and most audiences will begin to tune you out.
- **Plan the presentation to take slightly less than the allotted time.** Look for ways to tighten your presentation so you have time to answer the audience's questions. Most audiences prefer a presentation that is a few minutes short rather than a few minutes long.

## Anticipate the Audience's Needs and Questions

To prepare an audience-focused presentation, put yourself in their shoes and consider their needs, concerns, and perspectives. Focus on them, not yourself. Kathy Reiffenstein, author of "Five Things Not to Do in Front of an Audience," explains: "[W]e worry that we won't look knowledgeable, we won't be able to answer some questions, we'll appear nervous, or we'll forget what we wanted to say." While these worries are valid, the focus is wrong. Instead, we should concentrate on anticipating and meeting the needs of the audience. "Your presentation is not about you, it's *all* about your audience" (Reiffenstein 2008). To ensure that you focus your presentation on the audience, follow these guidelines:

- Define terminology the audience may not know. If audience members aren't experts in your field, avoid technical terminology when possible.
- Use specific, unambiguous examples to help audience members understand complicated or abstract concepts.
- Explain information that may be new to the audience.
- Clarify and support unfamiliar information, especially if the audience may disagree with or try to reject it.

As you anticipate the audience's questions, employ the *S.E.A.T.E.D.* approach to support your statements.

- **Statistics**: When possible, use statistics to support your statements. For example, if you are requesting the city council to authorize a traffic light at a dangerous intersection, you could tell them that 10% of the accidents at the intersection resulted in fatalities or that traffic has increased there by 30% in the past two years.
- **Example**: Examples help the audience relate to the topic of your presentation. For example, to support the need for the traffic light, you could describe accidents that have occurred at the intersection.
- **Analogy**: Use an analogy to compare your topic to something the readers will understand (i.e., one thing is like another thing). For example, you could compare the intersection to another one where the city council agreed to install a traffic light because of increased accidents.
- **Testimony of an Expert**: Experts or witnesses give *testimonials* when they authenticate information. A police officer might testify about the danger caused by the lack of a traffic light or a citizen who has been involved in an accident at the intersection might testify that the lack of a traffic light contributed to the accident.
- **Exhibit**: *Exhibits* are visual aids that demonstrate or support your statements. You could show a line graph indicating the upward trend of accidents at the intersection over the past two years.
- **Demonstration**: For example, you could show videos of accidents at the intersection. If time allows, you could take the city council members to the intersection to demonstrate why the intersection is dangerous without a traffic light.

## Organize the Presentation

Because most presentations have a specified length, prioritize the information according to the needs and expectations of the audience and your purpose. Imagine you are studying the effects of mercury emissions on health. At the end of the study, you will present your results to a group of public health experts. In a written document, you provide background information, methods, results, conclusions, and recommendations. However, the audience of public health experts will be interested primarily in your conclusions and recommendations. If you have only 20 minutes for your presentation, spend most of your time on your conclusions and recommendations. Briefly state the purpose of your research and how you conducted it. Only summarize the methods, if you mention them at all or refer the audience to a handout that describes your methods in detail.

Once you have prioritized the information you will present, prepare an outline of your presentation, as you would for a written document. Some speakers use a storyboard approach for their outline. A *storyboard* is a "sketch" of the document or presentation; it maps out each section or module of your document or presentation, along with the accompanying visual aids. For an oral presentation, the storyboard includes an outline on the left side of the page and the corresponding visual aids on the right. Add a description of the visual aids or attach small printouts or thumbnail sketches of the visual aids. Figure 20.2 illustrates

FIGURE 20.2

**Excerpt from a Storyboard for an Oral Presentation**

| Introduction<br>• Introduce myself<br>• Thank the audience for coming | Slide: **Title of presentation** |
|---|---|
| Outline the presentation | **Slide:** Photo of persons happy (to show that some people like to give presentations)<br>**Slide:** Photo of person crying (to show that some people don't like to give presentations)<br>**Slide:** List the sections of the presentation |
| Discuss the 3 purposes of presentations | **Slide:** List the purposes of presentations (inform, persuade, both) |

a storyboard for part of a presentation on delivering effective presentations. On the left side of the storyboard, the speaker outlines the presentation; on the right side the speaker lists the slides and handouts that will accompany the presentation. If you plan to use PowerPoint® slides, use its outline function. Figure 20.3 illustrates a portion of a PowerPoint outline for a presentation.

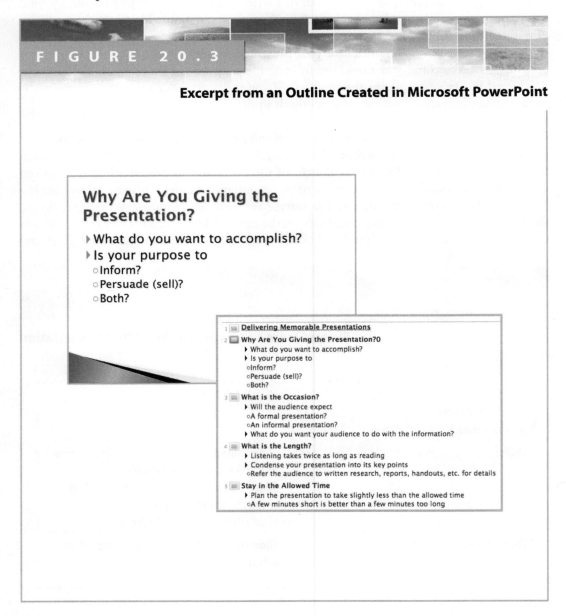

**FIGURE 20.3**

**Excerpt from an Outline Created in Microsoft PowerPoint**

When you have prepared your outline and/or storyboard, you are ready to prepare your notes for the presentation. You could

- prepare note cards
- prepare speaker notes, if you're using software such as PowerPoint. Figure 20.4 shows speaker notes.

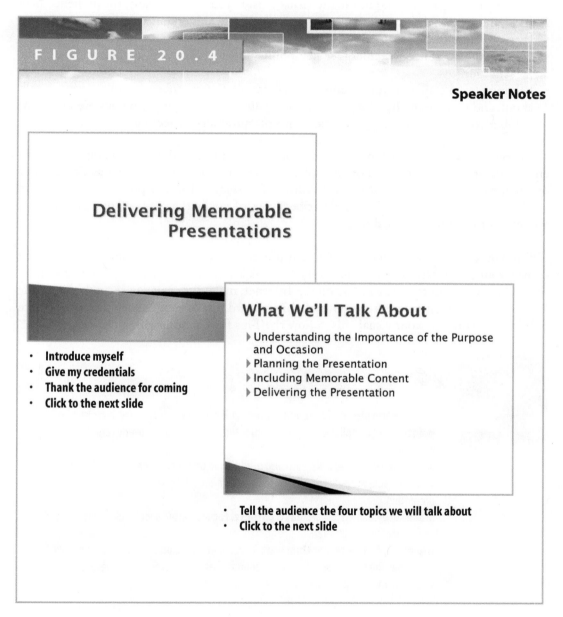

**FIGURE 20.4**

**Speaker Notes**

Audiences often have difficulty staying focused on an oral presentation even when the topic is interesting. Visual aids give the audience something to focus on while you're speaking. However, guard against using too many visual aids. If you use too many, the audience may focus on the visual aids instead of on your message. Visual aids enhance your presentation by

- keeping the audience focused on what you are saying
- helping the audience to remember key points and to follow the organization of your presentation
- helping you to stay with your planned organization, to remember what you want to talk about, and to use only the allotted time (especially with an extemporaneous presentation)
- helping you to concisely explain ideas, concepts, products, or technical information

Many types of visual aids are available to enhance your presentation and to help your audience understand your points. For example, use presentation software such as PowerPoint or Prezi to create professional-quality slides and displays. (Prezi is presentation software available at prezi.com). Figure 20.5 describes types of media that you can use and presents guidelines for using each medium.

Before you decide what visual aids you will use, find out about the room where you will deliver your presentation. Make sure the room has a screen on which to project the slides or video. If you plan to access media on the Internet, make sure you can securely access the Internet. If you plan to use a dry-erase (white) board, make sure the room has adequate lighting. As you plan your visual aids, follow the Tips for Creating Effective Visual Aids.

## TIPS FOR CREATING EFFECTIVE VISUAL AIDS

- **Use only the visual aids your audience will need to understand your key points.** Don't complicate your presentation with unnecessary or overly complex visual aids.
- **Select simple visual aids.** Each visual aid should present only one idea. The audience should be able to easily and quickly comprehend the information the visual aid is presenting.
- **Make sure each visual aid has a purpose.** Each visual aid should relate directly to a key point of your presentation.
- **Use brief phrases rather than sentences.** Sentences clutter a visual aid and make it illegible. The phrases should be clear enough that the audience can understand the visual aid after the presentation:

| **Not Effective** | Hydroelectric power has these disadvantages: |
| | It causes the loss of wildlife habitats. |
| | It takes significant amounts of land to construct the needed reservoir. |
| **Effective** | Disadvantages of hydroelectric power: |
| | Loss of wildlife habitats |
| | Loss of land |

- **Make sure everyone in the audience can read the visual aids, not only those in the front.** Remember that less is more, especially with slides created with presentation software. For example, instead of trying to fit all the information about a point on one slide by using a smaller type size or narrow margins, use two or more slides. Let's look at some examples: Figure 20.6 has too many words and the type is too small. Figure 20.7 has ample margins and uses an appropriate type size.
- **Use legible type.** Use legible typefaces and type size. If you are using presentation software, follow these guidelines:
  - Use 28–32 point type for text.
  - Use 36–44 point type for headings.
  - Use sans serif type, such as Tahoma or Arial, as they take less time to read.
  - Use upper- and lowercase letters, not all capital letters.
  - Avoid shadowed, underlined, or outlined type.
  - Use heavier, filled-in bullets, as they are easier to read (Reiffenstein 2006).
  - Use contrasting colors for the text and the background. For example, if you use a white or light background, use a dark type, preferably black or navy.
- **Use slide designs that are appropriate for the occasion and don't distract or hamper reading.** Some of the slide designs packaged in presentation software are distracting and make text difficult to read. Select backgrounds without images behind the words and with appropriate colors. The background in Figure 20.8 hampers reading, whereas the background in Figure 20.7 enhances reading.
- **Make sure that the visual aids are free of errors and contain correct, accurate information.** Your visual aids represent you and your organization. If they contain errors in grammar and style or if they contain incorrect information, you will lose credibility. Your audience may not trust you or the information that you are presenting because if the visual aids are sloppy or incorrect, then they might think your information, research, service, or product is also sloppy or incorrect.

## Types of Media for Visual Aids

| Type of Media | Advantages | Disadvantages | Guidelines for Using the Media Effectively |
|---|---|---|---|
| **Whiteboard** | • Flexible<br>• Excellent for informal presentations<br>• Excellent for incorporating audience ideas | • Appropriate only for small rooms and audiences<br>• Requires a room with good lighting | • Write legibly so everyone can read it<br>• Look at the audience, not at the board<br>• Don't forget to bring dry-erase markers |
| **Poster** | • Flexible<br>• No equipment required<br>• Inexpensive | • Appropriate only for small rooms and audiences<br>• Unprofessional appearance if not designed effectively<br>• Hard to transport | • Use at least 20"x30" sturdy poster board<br>• Use a simple, uncluttered design<br>• Make sure every person in the room can read it<br>• Use only in rooms with good light<br>• Use bright colors for greater contrast and readability |
| **Flip Chart** | • Flexible<br>• Excellent for incorperating audience ideas<br>• Inexpensive | • Appropriate only for small rooms and audiences<br>• Uprofessional appearance | • Use bright colors<br>• Keep the flip chart simple<br>• Don't put too much on one page<br>• Use only in rooms with good light<br>• Make sure every person in the room can read it<br>• Dont forget to bring markers |
| **Handouts** | • Excellent for presenting complex information<br>• Helps the audience to remember the information | • Distracts the audience from listening | • Give the audience the handouts at the end of the presentation<br>• Make sure the handouts are error free and have a professional appearance<br>• Number the pages |

**Types of Media for Visual Aids** *continued*

| Type of Media | Advantages | Disadvantages | Guidelines for Using the Media Effectively |
|---|---|---|---|
| **Opaque Projection** | • Excellent for displaying paper documents<br>• Requires little if any expense<br>• Flexible; lets you incorporate documents from the audience | • Poor image quality with may projectors<br>• Appropriate only for small rooms and audiences<br>• Room must be dark | • Leave the projector on until you are finished<br>• Make sure the audience is close enough to see the images<br>• Plan for a light source so you can see your notes |
| **Presentation Software (such as Prezi or PowerPoint)** | • Professional apprearance<br>• Versatile; multimedia capability<br>• Legible in small and large rooms<br>• Easy to transport | • Must be able to darken room<br>• Equipment may fail; have a backup | • Use a consistent design<br>• View the presentaion before speaking<br>• Rehearse using the equipment<br>• Bring more than one copy of the presentation file<br>• "Pack" the presentation to ensure that you can show it on most computers |
| **Film and Video** | • Excellent for presentations needing moving images and sound<br>• Versatile | • Expensive and time consuming to produce<br>• Requires high-quality equipment to produce professional quality<br>• Requires expertise to produce | • Introduce the film or video; tell audience what they will be viewing<br>• Practice setting up and operating the equipment<br>• Have a backup in case the equipment fails |

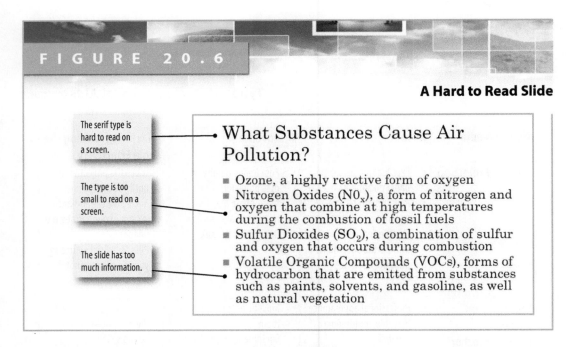

**FIGURE 20.6**

**A Hard to Read Slide**

The serif type is hard to read on a screen.

The type is too small to read on a screen.

The slide has too much information.

### What Substances Cause Air Pollution?

- Ozone, a highly reactive form of oxygen
- Nitrogen Oxides ($NO_x$), a form of nitrogen and oxygen that combine at high temperatures during the combustion of fossil fuels
- Sulfur Dioxides ($SO_2$), a combination of sulfur and oxygen that occurs during combustion
- Volatile Organic Compounds (VOCs), forms of hydrocarbon that are emitted from substances such as paints, solvents, and gasoline, as well as natural vegetation

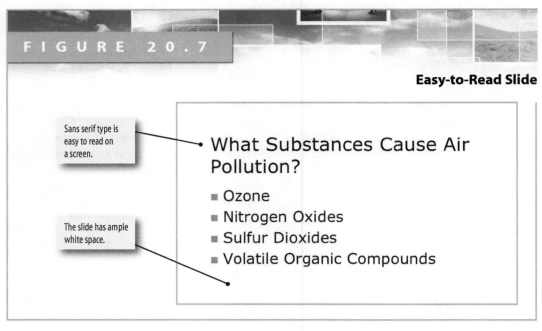

**FIGURE 20.7**

**Easy-to-Read Slide**

Sans serif type is easy to read on a screen.

The slide has ample white space.

### What Substances Cause Air Pollution?

- Ozone
- Nitrogen Oxides
- Sulfur Dioxides
- Volatile Organic Compounds

**FIGURE 20.8**

**Slide with a Distracting Background**

What Substances Cause Air Pollution?

- Ozone
- Nitrogen Oxides
- Sulfur Dioxides
- Volatile Organic Compounds

 USE EFFECTIVE STRATEGIES TO DELIVER MEMORABLE PRESENTATIONS

To deliver smooth presentations and to put yourself and your audience at ease, take ample time to get ready and use these effective strategies:
- rehearse your presentation
- plan for emergencies
- provide previews, transitions, and summaries to help the audience follow your presentation
- help your audience enjoy the presentation
- field questions effectively

## Rehearse the Presentation

Take plenty of time (more than you think you'll need) to rehearse and time your presentation. Check out the room and its equipment. Follow the Tips for Rehearsing and Preparing the Equipment.

**TIPS** FOR REHEARSING AND PREPARING THE EQUIPMENT

- **Make your rehearsal realistic.** If possible, rehearse your presentation with the actual equipment you will use and in the room where you will speak. As you rehearse, practice with the visual aids you will use.
- **Time your presentation.** Most presentations have an allotted time; so as you rehearse, time your presentation. If the presentation is too long, cut some of the text or some of the visual aids. Set aside some of your allotted time for questions from your audience.
- **Determine where you will use the visual aids in your presentation.** Mark your note cards or speaker notes for where to present each visual aid.
- **Check out the room and its equipment.** If you are speaking in an unfamiliar setting, check it out before you speak. Find the electrical outlets (if needed); look at the lighting; decide if you will need a microphone or a pointer.
- **Practice setting up the computer and projection equipment.** The setup can take more time than you think, so leave yourself plenty of time.
- **Review how to operate the presentation software.** Practice using the software efficiently to ensure that you don't distract the audience. Observe these tips if you plan to use PowerPoint:
  - **Press Ctrl-H after the slide show has started to keep the arrow or pointer from appearing on screen.** When you move the mouse, the arrow or pointer appears on screen, which is distracting to the audience. To cancel the arrow, press Ctrl-A. If the arrow appears while you are talking, don't press the escape button because it will stop the slide show.
  - **Pause the presentation by pressing W for a white screen or B for a black screen.** To resume the presentation, press W or B again.
- **Practice using the remote control that advances the slides.** Each remote control works differently, so get familiar with yours before the presentation.

## Prepare for Emergencies

Your presentation may not go as planned. Be prepared for emergencies and be flexible. You can lessen the likelihood of some emergencies by
- Bringing a backup of your slides and handouts.
- Having a backup plan in case the computer, projector, or DVD player doesn't work.
- Preparing notes. If you use note cards or speaker notes, number them. You may not need to refer to your notes often, but they will help if you lose your place while speaking.

## Provide Previews, Transitions, and Summaries to Help the Audience Follow Your Presentation

To help the audience follow your presentation, give them a road map with previews, transitions, and summaries.
- **Begin your presentation with a preview.** Tell (and possibly show) the audience what you will be talking about.
- **Introduce the key points you will discuss (in the order in which you will discuss them).** For example, you might say, "This morning, I will talk about X, Y, and Z." Use a slide that lists X, Y, and Z. Then discuss X, Y, and Z in the order in which you listed them on the slide.
- **Use clear transitions between topics.** *Transitions* tell the audience that you are changing the topic. Without transitions, the audience may misunderstand your words, get confused, or lose focus. To alert the audience to a change, use transitional phrases and sentences such as "My second point is" or "Next, I will discuss ..." Use visual aids, such as transition slides to signal a change in topics.
- **At the end summarize your presentation.** Tell the audience what you've told them by summarizing your key points. Use a visual aid to emphasize your summary.

## Help the Audience Enjoy Your Presentation

Use the Tips for Helping the Audience Enjoy Your Presentation to help the audience enjoy and focus on your presentation. If you are well prepared and have rehearsed your presentation thoroughly, these guidelines will be easy to follow because you will feel comfortable and confident.

**TIPS** FOR HELPING THE AUDIENCE ENJOY YOUR PRESENTATION

- **Talk slowly and distinctly.** Make sure the audience can understand your words.
- **Look the audience in the eye.** Audiences tend to be suspicious of speakers who don't maintain eye contact.
- **Speak with enthusiasm and confidence.** The audience doesn't want to listen to someone who seems uninterested or who lacks confidence.
- **Avoid verbal pauses (um, ah, uh, you know).** Rehearsing will help you eliminate them.
- **Don't read the slides.** When you read the slides, you are not maintaining eye contact or interacting with the audience.
- **Before you go on stage or to the podium, introduce yourself to some audience members.** Shake hands or make casual conversation.

## Field Questions Effectively

If you have prepared well and anticipated the audience's questions, you will be ready to field their questions. At the end of your presentation, ask the audience if they have any questions. If appropriate for the occasion, encourage the audience to ask questions during the presentation. For example, you can give the audience the opportunity to ask questions if you see they don't understand something.

As you field questions, follow these guidelines:
- Repeat the question to make sure you heard it correctly and that everyone in the audience knows the question you will be answering.
- Take a few seconds to think before you answer so you can respond in an organized, clear manner.
- If you don't know the answer to a question, say, "I don't know, but I'll find out" or "I don't know, but I will get you an answer." Your audience will sense if you are making up an answer. You will gain the respect of your audience if you are honest and ethical.
- If someone disagrees with you or criticizes your presentation, be respectful.

TAKING IT INTO THE *workplace*

## Taking Cues from the Audience

Your audience will give you cues if you are not meeting their expectations. Karl Walinskas, author of *Reading Your Audience* (2001), suggests you take in those cues and adjust your delivery. He identifies three cues the audience will give you:

- **"The eyes have it."** Your first clue to audience interest is the eyes of each person. (If the room and the audience are large, observe the people in the first few rows.) Walinskas suggests making sure "their eyes are *open!* ... Shut eyelids mean a bored crowd." (24) Is the audience looking around the room or at their laps rather than at you and your visual aids? If so, change your pace or volume.
- **"Actions speak louder than words."** The audience's body language will give you cues. For example, if people in the audience are leaning back in their chairs getting comfortable (perhaps for a nap), change the pace of your presentation or get the audience involved. You might ask them to look at something on the screen or in a handout.
- **"The engagement factor."** Walinskas explains that "the level to which your audience participates is a critical factor in determining how well they are receiving" your presentation (24). For example, even if you have asked them to hold questions until the end, someone in the audience may be so engaged that he or she can't wait. This signal tells you and the rest of the audience that your presentation is engaging.

| Audience Cue | What It Means | How to Adjust |
|---|---|---|
| Shut eyelids | Boredom, fatigue | Change pace, volume, and subject matter; use humor to get them laughing |
| Wandering eyes | Distraction | Use dramatic action; call attention to an important point and ask for audience focus; use humor |
| Mass exodus | Boredom; they've heard it before | Change tactics; use pointed humor; do something dramatic to reconnect; add controversy; move on to the next point; work on content for next time |
| Leaning back in seats | Apathy; waiting for something better | Use dramatic action; insert an exercise to involve them; use humor |
| Shaking heads | Disagreement | Confront a select head-shaker ("You disagree? Tell us why."); offer an alternative viewpoint that others embrace (even though you may not) |
| No questions | Disinterest, confusion, hesitation | Plant seed questions with several people in the audience ahead of time to get the ball rolling; call on people whom you read as being most engaged during the presentation |

Compiled from information downloaded from the World Wide Web: www.speakingconnection.com. Walinkskas, Karl, The Speaking Connection.

## Assignment

- Attend an oral presentation and evaluate how well the speaker delivers the presentation, based on audience cues.
- Write a memo to your instructor including the name of the speaker, the title, the date of the presentation, and your evaluation.

# CASE STUDY ANALYSIS

## An Award-Winning PowerPoint Hits Theaters

### Background

Few people would have bet that a PowerPoint presentation could win an Academy Award. Yet in 2007, that's exactly what happened. After bowing out of the political scene, former Vice President Al Gore wanted to spread the word about global warming. He created a PowerPoint presentation that became a book and an Academy Award–winning movie. Even though the medium changed from his oral presentation to a hit movie, the format of Gore's presentation remained virtually the same; the video was a film of Gore giving his oral presentation to a group.

Regardless of your beliefs about Al Gore or global warming (climate change), Gore's film, *An Inconvenient Truth*, is a classic study in oral presentations. Gore, who has been criticized for his dry vocal delivery style, uses many of the elements discussed in this chapter—including humor, varying intensity and pace, and visual aids—to create a memorable presentation.

### Assignment

Meet with a group of students (or as a class) and watch *An Inconvenient Truth*.
1. Take notes on the elements of Gore's presentation.
2. Write an evaluation of his presentation and turn it in to your instructor.
   a. In your evaluation, describe the audience to which Gore directs his presentation, the level of audience knowledge, the depth in which Gore covers the topic, the quality of the video used in the presentation, the typeface used in the slides, the delivery style and pace, etc.
   b. Discuss the effectiveness of Gore's oral presentation and style.

# EXERCISES

DOWNLOAD A COPY OF THE WORKSHEET FOR PREPARING AND DELIVERING MEMORABLE ORAL PRESENTATIONS AT

WWW.GRTEP.COM

1. Write instructions for creating a slide presentation using presentation software, available at your college or university. The audience for your instructions is your classmates. If you need help writing instructions, refer to Chapter 18.

2. Using presentation software, create a custom slide design that you can use as a master slide for an oral presentation. Make sure that your slide design follows the Tips for Creating Audience-Focused Visual Aids.

3. Create an oral presentation on one of the following topics to present to your classmates. Your presentation should include visual aids. Your instructor will tell you the time allotted for the presentation.
   a. Define a concept in your major.
   b. Explain a procedure you commonly follow at your workplace or will use as a professional in your field.
   c. Present the conclusions and/or results of a report that you prepared for your technical communications class.
   d. Present a visitors' guide to your hometown.
   e. Explain a procedure that students follow at your college or university.

4. Using the online Evaluation Sheet, evaluate the presentations of your classmates. Your instructor may ask you to complete this evaluation online and attach it to an email. The evaluation sheet is available on the the book's website.

DOWNLOAD A COPY OF THE SHEET FOR EVALUATING ORAL PRESENTATIONS ONLINE AT

WWW.GRTEP.COM

### Working with a Team to Prepare an Oral Presentation

You and your team have developed a product or service that community groups could use for fundraising. You want to get people to buy your product or service, so you have decided to prepare an oral presentation introducing your product or service to groups in your community. You and your team will work together to prepare and deliver the presentation. The purpose of your presentation is to
- introduce your product or service
- explain the advantages of your product or service
- persuade the group to use your product or service for its next fundraising project

### Assignment

Your team will complete the following activity:
1. Create a product or service you can use for your presentation. (You don't have to actually create a product; you can simply describe it.)
2. Decide what community group might use your product or service for fundraising.
3. Analyze the audience for your presentation. (This audience would be the group that you identified in Step 2.)
4. Plan your presentation.
5. Create appropriate visual aids.
6. Assign roles to each member of the team. Every member should have a speaking part in the presentation.
7. Rehearse the presentation.
8. Deliver the presentation to your instructor and classmates. They will use the evaluation sheet (available on the book's website) as they listen to your presentation.

DOWNLOAD A COPY OF THE SHEET FOR EVALUATING ORAL PRESENTATIONS ONLINE AT

WWW.GRTEP.COM

## Documenting Your Sources

Your organization or your instructor may have a preferred style for documenting sources. Find out what style they expect and use that style. Many instructors will expect you to use one of the following styles, which appear in this appendix:

- *Publication Manual of the American Psychological Association*, 6th ed. (Washington, DC: APA, 2009). This style is used in the social sciences and other fields.
- *MLA Handbook for Writers of Research Papers*, 6th ed. (New York: MLA, 2010). This style is used in the humanities.
- *Scientific Style and Format: The CSE Manual for Authors, Editors, and Publishers*, 7th ed. (Wheat Ridge: Council of Science Editors 2006). CSE style is one of many numerical documentation styles.

 **APA STYLE**

When you document information using APA style, consider two areas: citing the information in the text and preparing the references at the end of the document.

### Citing Information Using APA Style

When using APA style to cite information in a document, you typically will include the following information:

- author's last name
- year the source was published
- page number(s) if you are giving a specific fact, idea, or quotation

For example, a citation might read as follows:

> Thomas (2007) identified the reaction times while working in Alaska.

> Documents with an illogical structure make readers' tasks more difficult (Cobb 2011).

> Boswood (1999) states that "the professional applies a body of knowledge by exercising a range of skills in an ethical manner" (116).

The textual citations will vary depending on the type of information and context. If the models above don't fit your information, consult the *Publication Manual of the American Psychological Association*.

If you are citing a personal communication, use this format:

> N. Cobb (personal communication, June 29, 2008) suggested that …

## Preparing the Reference List Using APA Style

A reference list gives readers the information they need to find each source that you have cited in your document. Each entry in the reference list normally includes the following:
- author's name
- year of publication
- title of publication
- publishing information

In the reference list, include only those sources that you have actually used and cited in your document. Leave out sources that you used for background reading. When you prepare your reference list, follow these guidelines:
- **Put the sources in alphabetical order by the author's last name.** If you have more than one source from the same author, arrange the sources by date—beginning with the earliest source and moving to the most recent source. If the sources are from the same year, use lowercase letters to distinguish the articles (for example, Johnson 2008a, Johnson 2008b, and so on).
- **Use only initials for the author's first and/or middle name** (for example, Smith, E., not Smith, Ellen).
- **Capitalize only the first word of each title (and the first word of the subtitle, if necessary).** This guideline applies to all titles.

- **Italicize the names of journals, magazines, newspapers, and books.** Also italicize the volume and issue numbers.
- **End each reference with a period.**
- **Use a hanging indent of five to seven spaces to indicate the second (and subsequent) lines of a reference.** You can see this indent in the examples throughout this section.
- **Give the complete page numbers when citing a range of page numbers.** For example, write 345-352, not 345-52.

## Books

For books, include the following information in this order:
- last name(s) and initials of the author(s)
- publication year
- title (in italics)
- publication information (city and publisher)

### Books by One Author
Beaufort, A. (2000). *Writing in the real world: Making the transition from school to work.* New York: Teachers College Press.

### Book by Multiple Authors
Separate the authors' names with commas and use an ampersand (&) between the final two authors' names.

Miller, J. D., & Kimmel, L. G. (2001). *Biomedical communication: Purposes, audiences, and strategies.* San Diego, CA: Academic.

### Book in Edition Other Than First
When a book is in a later edition, include the edition of the book in parentheses.

Williams, J., & Colomb, G. G. (2010). *Style: Ten lessons in clarity and grace.* (10th ed.). Boston: Longman.

### Book Issued by an Organization
American Psychological Association (APA). (2009). *Publication manual of the American Psychological Association* (6th ed.). Washington, DC: APA.

## An Edited Book

When referencing an edited book, include the following information in this order:
- name(s) of the editor(s), following the same guidelines for multiple editors as for multiple authors
- publication year
- title of the book (in italics)
- publication information (city and publisher)

Kynell, T. C., & Moran, M. G. (Eds.). (1998). *Three keys to the past: The history of technical communication.* Stamford, CT: Ablex.

## Book, No Author or Editor

*Merriam-Webster's Medical Desk Dictionary.* (2002). Springfield, MA: Merriam-Webster, Inc.

## Journal, Magazine and Newspaper Articles

Include the following information in this order:
- author's last name and initials. If the article does not have an author, alphabetize the reference by the title of the article, ignoring all articles (*a*, *an*, and *the*).
- article's publication year. For magazines and newspapers, include as much detail as possible.
- title of the article
- title and volume number of the publication in italics
- issue number in parentheses immediately after volume number
- page number(s) of the article

## Journal Article, One Author

Smith, E. O. (2000). Points of reference in technical communication scholarship. *Technical Communication Quarterly*, *9*(4), 427–453.

## Journal Article, Multiple Authors

Separate the authors' names with a comma and an ampersand (&) and use the same format for each author's name: *last name first.*

Constantinides, H., St. Amant, K., & Kampf, C. (2001). Organizational and intercultural communication: An annotated bibliography. *Technical Communication Quarterly*, *10*(1), 31–58.

When a journal article has eight or more authors, list the first seven authors' names and finish the entry with *et al.*

Gilbert, D. G., McClernon, J. R., Rabinovich, N. E., Sugai, C., Plath, L. C., Asgaard, G., Zuo, Y. et al. (2004). Effects of quitting smoking on EEG activation ... and depressive traits. *Nicotine and Tobacco Research*, 6, 249–267.

## Magazine Article
Hindo, B. (2007, August 20 & 27). The empire strikes at silos. *BusinessWeek*, 63-65.

## Newspaper Article
For the pages of a newspaper article, use *p.* for a single-page article and *pp.* for a multipage article. If the article runs on continuous pages, separate the page numbers with an *en dash* (pp. 1-2). If the article runs on discontinuous pages, separate the page numbers with a comma (pp. 1, 3).

Young, J. R. (2000, November 9). Going to class in a 3-D lecture hall. *New York Times* (Late ed.). p. G8.

## Article or Chapter in an Edited Book
When referencing an article or a chapter in an edited book, include the following information in this order:
- last name and initials of the author
- publication year of the book
- title of the article or chapter
- the word *In* followed by the name of the editor (beginning with the editor's first initials) and the abbreviation *Ed.* in parentheses
- title of the book
- inclusive page numbers of the article or chapter
- book's publication information (city and publisher)

Ornatowski, C. M. (2000). Ethics in technical/professional communication: From telling the truth to making better decisions in a complex world. In M. A. Pemberton (Ed.). *The ethics of writing instruction: Issues in theory and practice* (pp. 139-166). Stamford, CT: Ablex.

## Journal, Magazine, or Newspaper Article with No Author Cited
Vista's Edge, Inc., wins technical writing award (2001, September 3). *San Diego Business Journal*, *36*(10), 24–28.

## Electronic Documents

## Document from a Website
When referencing a nonperiodical document from a website, include as much of the following information as possible:

- author of the document (if you cannot find the name of the author, begin with the title of the document)
- publication date or most recent update (or *n.d.* if the document doesn't have a publication date)
- title of the document (in italics)
- URL. If necessary, you may break a URL to a new line after a slash or before a period; do not insert a hyphen at the break. Omit the period following the URL.

Hansen, K. (n.d.). *Powerful new grad résumés and cover letters: 10 things they have in common.* Retrieved from http://www.collegerecruiter.com/pages/articles/article597.php

## Article in an Online Periodical
If you referenced an article online, provide the same information as you would for articles appearing in print. If the article appears in print,
- Do not include the URL.
- Include the words *Electronic version* in brackets after the title of the article.

Roy, D. (2008). Designing procedural graphics for surgical patient-education modules: An experimental study [Electronic version]. *Technical Communication Quarterly*, *17*(2), 173–201.

If the article is not available in print or if you are citing a different version from the printed version, include the
- Date you retrieved the article.
- URL. If the article is from a searchable website, include the URL for the site. If the article is not from a searchable site, include the URL for the article.

Hesseldahl, A. (2008, June 24). Technology: It's where the jobs are. *BusinessWeek*. Retrieved from http://businessweek.com

## Article Retrieved from a Database
Provide the same information as you would for articles appearing in print along with the following information:
- publication information
- name of the database
- item number if available

Morrice, J. (2008, March 1). Human influences on water quality in great lakes coastal wetlands. *Environmental Management*, *41*(3), 347–357. Retrieved from Agricola database (IND44015382).

**Email Message**

When referencing an email message in the text, cite the author of the message in the same way you would cite the source of a personal communication. Do not include the email in the reference list.

**Blog and Message Posted to Online Forums, Discussion Groups, or Electronic Mailing Lists**

If the posting is not archived (you cannot retrieve it), cite the posting as a personal communication and do not include it in the reference list. If you can retrieve the posting from an archive, provide the following information:
- author's name
- exact date of the posting
- title or subject line of the posting
- any identifiers such as a message number in brackets
- the words *Message posted to* followed by the URL. Omit the period following the URL.

DuBay, W. (2008, July 30). Journal readability. Message posted to http://lyris.ttu.edu/ read/?forum=attw-l

## Other References

**Article from a Volume of Proceedings**

When referencing an article from a volume of conference proceedings, include the following information in this order:
- author's last name and initials
- publication date of the proceedings
- title of the article
- title of the published proceedings
- publication information (city and publisher)

DeLoach, S. (2001). An overview of HTML-based help. *Proceedings of the 48th International Technical Communication Conference.* Fairfax, VA: Society for Technical Communication.

## Brochure, Corporate Author

When referencing a brochure written by a company or organization, include the following information in this order:
- corporation (company or organization)
- publication year
- title of the brochure (in italics) with the word *Brochure* in brackets following the title
- publication information (city and corporate publisher)

IBM. (2008). *IBM Annual Report 2008*. [Brochure]. White Plains, NY: IBM.

## Government Document
When referencing a document published by the Government Printing Office (GPO), include the following information in this order:
* author's last name and initials (if available)
* government agency that released the document
* publication year
* title of the document (in italics)
* publication information (city and publisher)

U.S. Department of Justice. (2000). *Bellows report: Final report of the attorney general's review team on the handling of the Los Alamos National Laboratory investigation.* Washington, DC: U.S. Government Printing Office.

## Technical Report
When referencing a technical report, include the following information in this order:
* author's last name and initials
* publication year
* title of the report (in italics)
* series name (if any) and number of the report
* publication information (city and publisher)

Scott, D. D. (2000). *Archeological overview and assessment for Wilson's Creek National Battlefield, Greene and Christian Counties, Missouri.* (Midwest Archeological Center technical report No. 66). Lincoln, NE: U.S. Department of the Interior, National Park Service, Midwest Archeological Center.

## Personal Interviews and Personal Correspondence

Treat personal interviews and correspondence like personal communications and do not include them in the reference list. Instead, cite them in the text as personal communications.

## Published Interviews

Include the following information in this order for published interviews:
* person(s) interviewing
* date

- title. If the interview doesn't have a title, include the word *Interview* with the subject's name in brackets
- publication information

Zachary, M., & Thralls, C. (2004). An interview with Edward R. Tufte. *Technical Communication Quarterly*, *13*(4), 447–462.

## MLA STYLE

When you document information using MLA style, you need to understand how to cite information in the text and how to prepare the Works Cited page.

### Citing Information in the Text Using MLA Style
When citing information in a document, you typically will include the following information:
- author's last name
- page number being referenced

For example, a citation might read as follows:

> Thomas identified the reaction times while working in Alaska during the 1950s (14–28).

> Documents with an illogical structure make readers' tasks more difficult (Cobb 18).

If you're citing an entire source, you would include only the author's last name. The textual citations will vary depending on the type of information and context. If the model above doesn't fit your information, consult the *MLA Handbook for Writers of Research Papers*.

## Preparing the List of Works Cited Using MLA Style

A list of works cited gives readers the information they need to find each source that you have cited in your document. Each entry in the list normally includes the following:
- author's name
- year of publication
- title of publication
- publishing information
- medium of the publication (print, eBook, Web)

In your works cited, include only those references that you have cited in your document. You should not include references that you used for background reading. When you prepare your list of works cited in MLA style

- **Put the references in alphabetical order by the author's last name.** If you are citing two or more references by the same author, arrange them by title. If you are citing references by an organization, alphabetize the work by the first important word in the name of the organization. For example, if the American Heart Association wrote the reference, alphabetize by the word *American*.
- **Use title-case capitalization.** Capitalize each important word in the titles and subtitles.
- **Italicize the names of journals, magazines, newspapers, and books.** Use the italics consistently.
- **Put the titles of articles and other short works in quotation marks.**
- **End each reference with a period.**
- **Use a hanging indent of one-half inch to indicate the second (and subsequent) lines of a reference.** You can see this indent in the examples throughout this section.
- **Give only the last two digits of the page number when citing a range of page numbers.** For example, write 345–52, not 345–352. Don't include *p.* or *pp.* to indicate page(s).
- **Follow this format for dates: day, month, year, without commas** (29 June 2002).

## Books

When referencing a book, include the following information in this order:
- author's name
- title of the book (in italics)
- publication information including the publisher's location and name and the date
- medium of the publication (print, eBook, Web)

**Book by One Author**

Beaufort, Anne. *Writing in the Real World: Making the Transition from School to Work.* New York: Teachers College Press, 2000. Print.

**Book by Multiple Authors**
- List the authors' names in the order they appear on the title page (which is not necessarily in alphabetical order).
- List the first author's name with the last name first followed by a comma, and then the next author's name beginning with the first name.
- Separate the last two authors with the word *and*. If a book has more than three authors, list the first author's name only followed by *et al*.

Miller, Jon D., and Linda G. Kimmel. *Biomedical Communication: Purposes, Audiences, and Strategies.* San Diego: Academic, 2001. Print.

### Book in Edition Other Than First
Williams, Joseph, and Gregory G. Colomb. *Style: Ten Lessons in Clarity and Grace.* 10th ed. Boston: Longman, 2010. Print.

### Book Issued by a Corporate Author
Include the following information in this order:
- name of the organization (omit a, an, the)
- title of the book (in italics)
- publication information including the publisher's location and name and the date. The organization and the publisher may be the same
- medium of the publication (print, eBook, Web)

American Psychological Association. *APA Style Guide to Electronic References.* Washington: American Psychological Association, 2007. Print.

### Book Compiled by an Editor or Issued Under an Editor's Name
Include the following information in this order:
- editor(s) names followed by the abbreviation *ed.* or *eds.*
- title of the book (in italics)
- publication information including publisher's location and name and the date
- medium of the publication (print, eBook, Web)

Kynell, Teresa C., and Michael G. Moran, eds. *Three Keys to the Past: The History of Technical Communication.* Stamford: Ablex, 1998. Print.

### Book, No Author or Editor
*Merriam-Webster's Medical Desk Dictionary.* Springfield, MA: Merriam-Webster, 2002. Print.

### Multiple Books by the Same Author
For the second and subsequent books by the same author, use three hyphens (or an em dash) instead of the author's name.

Horton, William. *E-Learning by Design.* San Francisco: John Wiley & Sons, 2006. Print.

—. *The Icon Book: Visual Symbols for Computer Systems and Documentation.* San Francisco: John Wiley & Sons, 1994. Print.

## Journal, Magazine, and Newspaper Articles

When referencing articles, include the following information in this order:
- full name(s) of the author(s) (last name first)
- title of the article (inside quotation marks)
- title of the journal, magazine, or newspaper (in italics)
- publication information, publication date, and page numbers
- medium of publication consulted (print, eBook, Web)
- date of access (day, month, and year) if the medium is Web

### Journal Article, One Author

Roy, Debopriyo. "Designing Procedural Graphics for Surgical Patient-Education Modules: An Experimental Study." *Technical Communication Quarterly* 17.2 (2008): 173–201. Print.

Roy, Debopriyo. "Designing Procedural Graphics for Surgical Patient-Education Modules: An Experimental Study." *Technical Communication Quarterly* 17.2 (2008): 173–201. Web. 19 Nov. 2012.

### Journal Article, Multiple Authors

- List the authors' names in the order they appear in the publication (which is not necessarily in alphabetical order).
- Put the first author's name with last name first followed by a comma, and the other authors' names beginning with the first name.
- Separate the last two authors with the word *and*.

Popham, Susan L. and Sage Lambert Graham. "A Structural Analysis of Coherence in Electronic Charts in Juvenile Mental Health." *Technical Communication Quarterly* 17.2 (2008): 149–72. Print.

When referencing a journal article with more than three authors, cite only the first author's name in full and add *et al*.

Smith, Elizabeth Overman, et al. "2000 ATTW Bibliography." *Technical Communication Quarterly* 10.3 (2001): 447–79. Print.

### Journal, Magazine, or Newspaper Article with No Author Cited

"Vista's Edge, Inc., Wins Technical Writing Award." *San Diego Business Journal* 3 Sep. 2001: 10. Print.

## Journal or Magazine Article Retrieved from a Database

When referencing an article retrieved from an electronic database, provide the same information as you would for nonprint articles along with the following information:

- name of the database
- medium (database)

Morrice, John A. "Human Influences on Water Quality in Great Lakes Coastal Wetlands." *Environmental Management*, 41.3 (2008): 347–57. *Agricola*. Database. 19 Nov. 2012.

## Magazine Article

- Do not list the magazine's volume and issue numbers.
- If the article is on more than one page, list the first page followed by a plus sign (+) with no intervening space.

Hindo, Brian. "The Empire Strikes at Silos." *BusinessWeek* 20 & 27 Aug. 2007: 63+. Print.

## Newspaper Article

- If the city of publication is not included in the name of a locally published newspaper, add the city in square brackets following the newspaper title.
- If the article is on more than one page, list the first page followed by a plus sign (+) with no intervening space.

Young, Jeffrey R. "Going to Class in a 3-D Lecture Hall." *New York Times* 9 Nov. 2000, late ed.: G8. Web. 15 June 2012.

## Article or Chapter in an Edited Book

When referencing an article or chapter in an edited book, include the following information in this order:

- author's full name
- title of the article or chapter (in quotation marks)
- title of the edited book (in italics)
- *ed.* for editor followed by the name(s) of the editor(s)
- publication information including the publisher's location and name, the date, and the page numbers of the article or chapter
- medium of the publication (print, eBook, Web)

Ornatowski, Cezar J. "Ethics in Technical/Professional Communication: From Telling the Truth to Making Better Decisions in a Complex World." *The Ethics of Writing Instruction: Issues in Theory and Practice.* Ed. Michael A. Pemberton. Stamford, CT: Ablex, 2000. 139–66. Print.

## Nonperiodical Web Publications

Nonperiodical publications do not appear regularly. Periodical publications appear regularly. Examples of periodical publications are newspapers, magazines, and scholarly journals.

### Publication Cited Only on the Web

When referencing a nonperiodical publication on the Web, include the following information in this order:

- full name of the author, compiler, director, editor, narrator, performer, or translator (if one is given)
- title of the publication (in italics if the publication is independent, in quotation marks if the work is part of a larger document)
- title of the website (in italics)
- name of the publishing organization
- publication date (if one is given)
- version or edition (if one is given)
- medium of publication (Web)
- date you accessed the publication (day, month, and year)

Hansen, Randall S. "Scannable Resume Fundamentals: How to Write Text Resumes." *Quintcareers.com*. Quintessential Careers. 30 July 2008. Web. 19 June 2012.

### Email Message

When referencing an email message, include the following information in this order:

- name of the writer
- title of the message taken from the subject line
- name of the recipient
- date of the message (day month year)
- medium of delivery (email)

Sims, Patrick. "Re: Graduate Program Questions." Message to Susan Audrain. 14 Nov. 2012. Email.

### Blog or Message Posted to Online Forums, Discussion Groups, or Electronic Mailing Lists

When referencing a blog or message posted to an online forum, discussion group or electronic mailing list, treat it like a nonperiodical Web publication. Include the following information in this order:

- author's full name
- title of the blog article or subject of the message followed by the description
- publisher or sponsor (blogs)

- forum name (messages)
- medium (messages)
- date the blog was published or the message was posted
- date retrieved
- URL in angled brackets (optional)

Goudreau, Jeanna. "Top 5 Interview Mistakes Millennials Make." *Forbeswoman*. Forbes. 26 Sept. 2012. Web. 19 Nov. 2012.

## Other References

### Article from a Volume of Proceedings
When referencing an article from a volume of conference proceedings, include the following information in this order:
- author's full name
- title of the article (in quotation marks)
- title of the proceedings (in italics)
- *ed.* for editor followed by the name(s) of the editor(s)
- publication information including the publisher's location and name, the date, and page numbers
- medium of the publication (print, eBook, Web)

DeLoach, Scott S. "An Overview of HTML-Based Help." *Proceedings of the 48th International Technical Communication Conference*. Ed. John Smith. Fairfax: Society for Technical Communication, 2001. Print.

### Brochure, Corporate Author
Treat a brochure or pamphlet the same way you would treat a book.

IBM. *IBM Annual Report 2008*. White Plains, NY: IBM, 2008. Print.

### Government Documents
When referencing a document published by a government agency, include the following information in this order:
- name of the government agency that released the document
- title of the document (in italics)
- publication information including the publisher's location and title and the date
- medium of the publication (print, eBook, Web)

U.S. Department of Justice. *Bellows Report: Final Report of the Attorney General's Review Team on the Handling of the Los Alamos National Laboratory Investigation*. Washington: GPO, 2000. Print.

## Interviews

Include the following information in this order for a published interview:
- person(s) interviewed
- title (in quotation marks). If the interview doesn't have a title, include the word *Interview* followed by a period
- publication information
- medium of the publication (print, eBook, Web). If the interview is published on the Web, include the date of access (day, month, and year)

Tufte, Edward R. "An Interview with Edward R. Tufte." *Technical Communication Quarterly* 13.4 (2004): 447–62. Print.

If you are citing a personal interview, include the following information in this order:
- person(s) interviewed
- type of interview (Personal interview, telephone interview, Web interview, etc.)
- date (day, month, and year)

Cobb, Neil. Personal interview. 29 June 2012.

 NUMBERED DOCUMENTATION STYLES

In a numbered documentation style, each reference is assigned a number the first time it is cited. The writer uses this number when referencing the article in the text. Numbered documentation styles are common in the physical sciences such as chemistry, physics, and geology and in the applied sciences such as computer science, engineering, and medicine. Each discipline has its preferred numbered style described in manuals such as
- American Mathematical Society, *A Manual for Authors of Mathematical Papers*
- American Chemical Society, *The ACS Style Guide for Authors and Editors*
- American Medical Association, *Manual of Style*

Many disciplines use the style guide published by the Council of Science Editors, *The CSE Manual for Authors, Editors, and Publishers*. This manual outlines the guidelines for a numbered-citation style. It also includes a name-year citation style that basically duplicates the APA documentation style.

### Citing Information in the Text Using CSE Numbered Style

In the CSE numbered citation style, cite the reference using a superscript number immediately following the reference.

This knowledge is based on extensive epidemiological studies of thousands of underground miners exposed to radon[1-3], carried out over more than fifty (50) years world-wide, including miners in the United States and Canada. One particular study by Wheeler[4] observed miners at relatively low exposure to radon.

When you refer to two or more sources in a single citation (as in the above example), separate the numbers by a hyphen if they are in sequence. If the references are not in sequence, separate them with a comma ([2,4,10]).

## Preparing the List of References in CSE Style

When preparing the list of references in CSE style,
- **List the references in the order in which they appear in the text.** Unlike APA and MLA styles, the references do not appear in alphabetical order.
- **List the author's name with the last name first and use initials for the first and middle names.** Do not use a comma between the last name and the initials.
- **For the titles of books and articles, capitalize only the first word of the title and all proper nouns.** Do not underline, italicize, or use quotation marks for titles of books or articles.
- **For the titles of journals, abbreviate the titles of journals that consist of more than one word.** Capitalize all words and abbreviations. Do not underline or italicize the titles.
- **For the publication information, include the publisher's location and name and the date published.**
- **Include the complete page ranges for articles and chapters:** 148-170 not 148-70. For chapters in edited volumes, use *p.* before the page numbers.

### Books

For all books, include the following information in this order:
- name of the author(s)
- title of the book (no italics)
- publication information including the publisher's location and name and the date
- number of pages

#### Books by One Author
1. Beaufort A. Writing in the real world: Making the transition from school to work. New York: Teachers College Pr; 2000. 239p.

#### Books by Multiple Authors
2. Patterson K, Grenny J, McMillan R, Switzler A. Crucial conversations: tools for talking when stakes are high. New York: McGraw-Hill; 2002. 240p.

### Books in Editions Other Than the First

Add the edition number along with *ed.* after the title.

3. Williams J. Style: ten lessons in clarity and grace. 9th ed. Boston: Longman; 2006. 304p.

### Book Issued by an Organization

4. American Psychological Association. APA style guide to electronic references. Washington, DC: American Psych Assoc; 2007. 24p.

### Book Compiled by an Editor or Issued Under an Editor's Name

5. Mirel B, Spilka R, editors. Reshaping technical communication. Mahwah, NJ: Lawrence Erlbaum; 2002. 216p.

### Book, No Author or Editor

Begin the reference with the title of the book

6. Merriam-Webster's Medical Desk Dictionary. Springfield, MA: Merriam-Webster; 2002. 928p.

## Journal, Magazine, and Newspaper Articles

When referencing articles, include the following information in this order:
- name of the author(s). For an article with up to 10 authors, list the names of all the authors. For an article with 11 or more authors, list the first 10 authors followed by a comma and *et al.*
- title of the article (no quotation marks)
- title of the journal (no italics)
- publication date, publication information, and page numbers

### Journal Article, One Author

7. Roy D. Designing procedural graphics for surgical patient-education modules: an experimental study. Technical Commun Q 2008; 17(2):173-201.

### Journal Article, Two or Three Authors

List the authors' names in the order they appear in the publication (which is not necessarily in alphabetical order).

8. Popham SL, Sage LG. A structural analysis of coherence in electronic charts in juvenile mental health. Technical Commun Q 2008; 17(2):149-172.

### Magazine Article

9. Hesseldahl A. Technology: it's where the jobs are. BusinessWeek. 2008 Jun 24:24.

### Newspaper Article

10. Young JR. Going to class in a 3-d lecture hall. New York Times (late ed.) 2000 Nov 9; Sect. G:8 (col. 2).

### Article or Chapter in an Edited Book

Include the following information in this order:

- name(s) of the author of the article or chapter
- title of the article or chapter
- *In* followed by a colon and the book editor(s) and the book title
- publication information including the publisher's location and name, the date, and the page numbers of the article or chapter

11. Ornatowski CJ. Ethics in technical/professional communication: from telling the truth to making better decisions in a complex world. In: Pemberton MA, editor. Ethics of writing instruction: issues in theory and practice. Stamford (CT): Ablex; 2000. p. 139-166.

## Web Publications

### Document Published on the Web

When referencing documents published on websites, include the following information in this order:

- name of the Author
- title of article (no quotation marks)
- medium (in brackets)
- publication information, including the place of the publication, the name of the publisher, and the date (include the date of update and the date you accessed the publication in brackets)
- the words *available from* followed by the URL of the publication

12. Hansen K. Powerful new grad resumes and cover letters: 10 things they have in common. [Internet] DeLand (FL): Quintessential Careers; 2008 [cited 2008 Jul 30; updated 2010 Jun 15]. Available from: http://www.collegerecruiter.com/pages/articles/article597.php

### Article in an Online Journal or Magazine

When referencing articles published in online journals or magazines, include the following information in this order:

- name of the author
- title of the article (no quotation marks)
- title of the journal or magazine (no itialics)
- medium (in brackets)

- publication information, including the year of publication, the volume and issue number, and the page numbers (if available)
- the words *available from* followed by the URL of the publication
- date you accessed the publication

13. Isaacs FJ, Blake WJ, Collins JJ. Signal processing in single cells. Science [Serial online]. 2005 Mar 25; 307(5717) [cited 2008 Aug 1]:1886-1888. Available from: http://www.sciencemag.org/cgi/content/full/307/5717/1886

## Article Retrieved from a Database

Treat articles retrieved from databases like articles published in online journals or magazines. Include the title of the database.

14. Morrice J. Human influences on water quality in great lakes coastal wetlands. Environmental Management 2008 March 1; 4(3):347–57. In: Agricola [database on the Internet]. New York: Springer-Verlag 2008 [cited 2008 Jul 30]: Available from: http://dx.doi.org/10.1007/s00267-007-9055-5; Article IND44015382.

## Email Message

"CSE recommends not including personal communications such as email in the reference list" (Hacker & Fister 2012) Instead, include a parenthetical note in the text as follows: (2008 email to author; unreferenced).

## Other References

## Article from a Volume of Proceedings

Treat an article from a volume of proceedings like a journal article.

15. DeLoach SS. An overview of HTML-based help. Proceedings of the 48th International Technical Communication Conference. Fairfax (VA): Society for Technical Communication, 2001. p. 26–30.

## Brochure, Corporate Author

Treat a brochure or pamphlet the same way you would treat a book.

16. American Funds. The income fund of America: annual report for the year ended July 31, 2007. White Plains (NY): American Funds; 2008. 36p.

## Government Documents

When referencing a government document, include the following information in this order:

- name of the government agency that released the document
- title of the document
- description of the report (if any)
- publication information including the publisher's location and title and date
- information that identifies the document, such as a document number
- the phrase *available from* followed by the name and location of the publishing organization

17. EPA's report on the environment 2008. Washington (DC): U.S. Environmental Protection Agency; 2008. 320p. Available from: EPA, Washington (DC): EPA/600/R-07/045F.

# appendix B

## Common Sentence Errors, Punctuation, and Mechanics

This appendix presents information about common sentence errors, punctuation, and mechanics. The topics in each section appear in alphabetical order, and an abbreviation (such as cs for comma splice) accompanies each topic. You can use these abbreviations as you edit your own documents or those of your team members. This appendix only briefly reviews grammar, usage, and mechanics; if you want complete information on these topics, consult a handbook for grammar or style.

 **COMMON SENTENCE ERRORS**

This section presents common sentence errors and suggests ways to eliminate these errors.

### Agreement Errors: Pronoun and Referent ( arg p )

A pronoun should refer clearly to a specific noun or pronoun—its referent (also called its *antecedent*)—and should agree in number and in gender with that referent.

Correct        **Gwen** paid cash for **her** new **car** although **it** cost more than **she** was hoping to pay.

Correct        The **students** received a trophy for **their** class project.

When you use a pronoun, make sure that its referent is clear.

| Vague | Douglas told Bill that he should move his car. |
| Clear | Douglas told Bill, "I should move my car." |
|  | Douglas told Bill, "You should move your car." |
|  | Douglas told Bill, "I should move your car." |

Pronoun-referent agreement becomes especially tricky with indefinite pronouns (such as each, everyone, anybody, someone, and none) and collective nouns. When an indefinite pronoun is the referent, the pronoun is singular, as in this example:

| Incorrect | **Each** student will receive **their** diploma through the mail. |
| Correct | **Each** student will receive **his or her** diploma through the mail. |

When a collective noun is the referent, determine whether the noun is singular or plural in its context. A collective noun may take a singular or a plural pronoun as its referent.

| Incorrect | The **university** will begin a new email service for **their** students. |
| Correct | The **university** will begin a new email service for **its** students. |

In this sentence, *university* refers to a single unit, not to individual members of the university community. In this context, it is singular, so the pronoun referring to it must also be singular.

A collective noun can also be plural, as in this example:

| Incorrect | The **faculty** can pick up **its** paychecks on Friday. |
| Correct | The **faculty** can pick up **their** paychecks on Friday. |

Here, *faculty* is a collective noun referring to the faculty in a context that emphasizes the individuals who comprise the group. The faculty wouldn't pick up their checks as a group.

## Agreement Errors: Subject and Verb    ( arg sv )

The subject and verb should agree in number. Often writers create subject-verb agreement errors when the verb follows a prepositional phrase:

| Incorrect | The **consequence** of the accidents **trouble** several board members. |
| Correct | The **consequence** of the accidents **troubles** several board members. |

The noun *accidents* in the prepositional phrase *of the accidents* does not affect the number of the verb; only the subject of the sentence affects the number of the verb.

## Comma Splice

A *comma splice* occurs when writers incorrectly use a comma to link two independent clauses, as in this example:

**Comma splice**     We baked 10,000 pretzels, we dipped them in dark chocolate.

To correct a comma splice:
- Change the comma to a period followed by a capital letter:
  Correct       We baked 10,000 pretzels. We dipped them in dark chocolate.

- Change the comma to a semicolon:
  Correct       We baked 10,000 pretzels; we dipped them in dark chocolate.

- Leave the comma and after it add an appropriate coordinating conjunction (and, or, nor, so, for, yet, but):
  Correct       We baked 10,000 pretzels, and we dipped them in dark chocolate.

- Add a subordinating conjunction to create a sentence consisting of one dependent and one independent clause. A *dependent clause* has a subject and a verb but can't stand alone; an *independent clause* has a subject and a verb and can stand alone. In the following example, the dependent clause begins with *after*:
  Correct       After we baked 10,000 pretzels, we dipped them in dark chocolate.

## Modification Errors: Dangling Modifiers  ( dgl )

See Chapter 8.

## Modification Errors: Misplaced Modifiers  ( mm )

See Chapter 8.

## Lack of Parallelism  ( // )

Use parallel structure when you put items in a series or in a list. All the items in a series or list must be *parallel*; that is, they must have the same grammatical structure. If the first item is a verb, the remaining items must be verbs. If the first item is a noun, the remaining items must be nouns.

**Not parallel** To complete the course, you will **write a research paper, take four exams, two collaborative projects,** and **participation**.

The first two items in the series are verb phrases, the third item is a noun phrase, and the fourth item is an unmodified noun. To make items in this series parallel, the third and fourth items must be verb phrases:

**Parallel** To complete the course, you will **write** a research paper, **take** four exams, **complete** two collaborative projects, and **participate** in class discussions.

## Run-On Sentences

A *run-on sentence* occurs when two or more independent clauses appear together without any punctuation (*independent clauses* have a subject and a verb and can stand alone). To correct a run-on sentence, use the same techniques you would use to correct a comma splice.

**Run-on** We baked 10,000 pretzels we dipped them in dark chocolate.

Correct We baked 10,000 pretzels. We dipped them in dark chocolate.

Correct We baked 10,000 pretzels; we dipped them in dark chocolate.

Correct We baked 10,000 pretzels, and we dipped them in dark chocolate.

Correct After we baked 10,000 pretzels, we dipped them in dark chocolate.

## Sentence Fragment

A *sentence fragment* is an incomplete sentence. Sentence fragments usually appear because the writer has left out the subject or the verb or failed to write an independent clause, which can stand alone.

### Fragments Resulting from Missing Subjects

**Fragment** Detached the coupon from the statement.

Correct Norma detached the coupon from the statement.

Correct Detach the coupon from the statement.

The fragment lacks a subject; no actor is doing the detaching. The first complete sentence has a subject—Norma. The second complete sentence has an understood *you* as its subject.

### Fragments Resulting from Missing Verbs

**Fragment**     Norma detaching the coupon from the statement.

Correct     Norma is detaching the coupon from the statement.

The fragment lacks a verb; the *-ing* form requires *is, was,* or *will be* to function as a verb in a complete sentence.

**Fragment**     The power surge caused by the thunderstorm.

Correct     The power surge caused by the thunderstorm damaged my computer.

In the fragment, *caused* functions as an adjective, not a verb.

### Fragments Resulting from Dependent Clauses

**Fragment**     You can use the cellular telephone. **If you charge the battery.**

Correct     You can use the cellular telephone if you charge the battery.

*If you charge the battery* (a dependent clause) cannot stand alone as a sentence because it begins with the subordinating word *if.* An ***independent clause*** has a subject and a verb, can stand alone, and does not begin with a subordinating word.

## Verb Tense Errors

Writers of technical material often misuse the present and the past perfect tenses and shift tense unnecessarily.

### Present Tense

Use the present tense to describe timeless principles and recurring events.

Incorrect     In 1997, the Mars *Pathfinder* scientists discovered that the climate of Mars was extremely cold.

Correct     In 1997, the Mars *Pathfinder* scientists discovered that the climate of Mars is extremely cold.

The scientists made their discovery in the past (in 1997) but the climate of Mars continues to be cold.

## Past Perfect Tense

Use the past perfect tense (indicated by had) to indicate which of two past events occurred first.

Correct        The presentation **had started** when we found the overhead projector.

The writer uses the past perfect tense to clarify that when the presentation started, they had not found the overhead projector.

## Unnecessary Shifts in Tense

Within a sentence, do not change tense unnecessarily.

Incorrect        He tested the new hardware, loaded the software, **adjusts** the computer settings, and waited for the network to respond.

Needless shifts in tense distract readers. In this example, the tense of the four verbs should be the same:

Correct        He **tested** the new hardware, **loaded** the software, **adjusted** the computer settings, and **waited** for the network to respond.

Correct        He **tests** the new hardware, **loads** the software, **adjusts** the computer settings, and **waits** for the network to respond.

## PUNCTUATION

This section presents information on how to use the apostrophe, colon, comma, dash, exclamation point, hyphen, parentheses, period, question mark, quotation marks, and semicolon.

## Apostrophe    ap

Use the apostrophe to indicate possession, to create some plural forms, and to form contractions.

### Apostrophes to Indicate Possession

Use apostrophes to indicate possession in the following situations:
• To create the possessive form of *most* singular nouns, including proper nouns, use an apostrophe and s, as in these examples:

gas's odor
Charles's calculator
student's book

If adding an apostrophe and *s* would create an *s* or *z* sound that is hard to pronounce, add only an apostrophe as in *Moses'*. (Try pronouncing *Moses's* and then *Charles's* to see the difference.) When a plural noun does not end in *s*, add an apostrophe and *s*. When a plural noun does end in *s*, add only an apostrophe:

men's               students'
children's          members'

- To indicate joint possession, add an apostrophe and *s* to the last noun. To indicate separate possession, add an apostrophe and *s* to each noun.

**Joint possession**      John and Stephanie's multimedia presentation

**Separate possession**  John's and Stephanie's multimedia presentations

- To create the possessive form of pronouns, add an apostrophe and *s* only to indefinite pronouns. Personal pronouns and the relative pronoun *who* have special forms that indicate possession.

**Possessives of Indefinite Pronouns**       **Possessives of Other Pronouns**
anyone's                                      mine (my)
everybody's                                   his, hers (her)
everyone's                                    yours (your)
nobody's                                      ours (our)
no one's                                      its
other's (also others')                        theirs (their)
                                              whose

Notice that the possessive form of *it* does not have an apostrophe. When you add an apostrophe and *s* to *it*, you create *it's*, the contraction for *it is*.

Incorrect      The city does not believe the pollution is **it's** problem.

Correct        The city does not believe the pollution is **its** problem.

## Apostrophes to Create Plural Forms

Use an apostrophe to create the plural form of letters and numbers:

a's and b's (or As and Bs)
8's and 5's (or 8s and 5s)

Some organizations prefer omitting the apostrophe in plural numbers. Check your organization's style guidelines to determine what your organization prefers.

## Apostrophes to Form Contractions

Use an apostrophe to indicate the omission of a letter or letters in a contraction.

| | |
|---|---|
| cannot = can't | who is = who's |
| you are = you're | let us = let's |
| it is = it's | they are = they're |
| does not = doesn't | she will = she'll |

## Brackets

Use brackets in the following situations:

To indicate that you've added words to a quotation:

**Correct**    The press release said, "They [Thompson and Congrove] voted against the amendment."

To identify parenthetical information within parentheses:

**Correct**    (For more information, see *The Publication Manual of the American Psychological Association* [Washington, DC: APA, 2009].)

## Colon

Use colons to introduce quotations and lists; to introduce words, phrases, and clauses; and to observe other stylistic conventions.

## Colons to Introduce Quotations

Use a colon to introduce a long or formal quotation:

**Correct**    In the Gettysburg Address, Lincoln began: "Four score and seven years ago our fathers brought forth on this continent, a new nation, conceived in Liberty, and dedicated to the proposition that all men are created equal."

## Colons to Introduce Lists

Use a colon to introduce a list when the introductory text would be incomplete without the list. A complete sentence must come before the colon:

| | |
|---|---|
| Incorrect | For the user testing, you will need: the beta version of the software, a flash drive, and a notepad. |
| Correct | For the user testing, you will need the following items: the beta version of the software, a flash drive, and a notepad. |

## Colons to Introduce Words, Phrases, and Clauses

Use a colon to introduce a word, phrase, or clause that illustrates or explains a statement:

| | |
|---|---|
| Correct | Our manager asked the following people to attend the meeting: production editor, art editor, and copy editor. |
| Correct | He suggested this solution: balancing the turbine to eliminate the vibration. |

The text before a colon must have a subject and verb and must be able to stand alone.

| | |
|---|---|
| Incorrect | We discovered problems in: the piping system and the turbine. |
| Correct | We discovered problems in the piping system and the turbine. |

In the incorrect example, *We discovered problems in* cannot stand alone; therefore, the colon is incorrect.

## Other Conventional Uses of Colons

- **Salutations**. Use a colon after the salutation (with a title such as Dr., Mr., or Ms.) in a letter: Dear Mr. Johnson:
- **Time**. Use a colon to separate hours and minutes: 8:30 A.M.
- **Subtitles**. Use a colon to separate the main title from a subtitle: *Creating Web Pages: A Handbook for Beginners*

# Comma

The following guidelines will help you to use commas correctly.

## *Commas to Separate the Clauses of a Compound Sentence*

A *compound sentence* has two or more independent clauses (*independent clauses* have a subject and verb and can stand alone). Use a comma to separate the clauses of a compound sentence when a coordinating conjunction (and, or, for, nor, but, so, yet) links those clauses.

Correct    We distributed 500 surveys to the shoppers, but we expect only 20 percent to return the surveys.

Often, the comma between the clauses of a compound sentence prevents readers from at first thinking that the subject of the second clause is an object of the verb of the first clause:

Incorrect    Bob will use the test results and the survey results will help him to prepare a prototype of the software.

Correct    Bob will use the test results, and the survey results will help him to prepare a prototype of the software.

Without the comma before *and*, readers at first may think that Bob will use both the test results *and* the survey results. The comma signals that an independent clause, not the object of the verb *use*, follows *and*.

## Commas to Separate Items in a Series

Use commas to separate items in a series composed of three or more items:

Correct    The assistant will deliver, collect, and tally the questionnaires.

The comma before the coordinating conjunction *and* is optional; however, many style manuals encourage writers to use the comma to distinguish items, prevent ambiguity, and prevent misreading.

## Commas to Set Off Introductory Words, Phrases, or Dependent Clauses

Generally, use a comma to set off an introductory word, phrase, or dependent clause from the main clause:

Correct    Therefore, NASA launched the shuttle two hours later.
           (introductory word)

| Correct | To localize documents, some companies hire translation agencies. (introductory phrase) |
|---|---|
| Correct | Because the team lost the debate, the school will not receive the prize money. (introductory dependent clause) |

A comma after an introductory clause can prevent misreading:

| Incorrect | After we completed bathing the cat jumped into the tub. |
|---|---|
| Correct | After we completed bathing, the cat jumped into the tub. |

Without the comma, readers at first might think the cat was being bathed. If the introductory text is short and readers can't misunderstand it, omit the comma.

## Commas to Set Off Nonrestrictive Modifiers

A *nonrestrictive modifier* is not essential to the meaning of a sentence. Writers can omit a nonrestrictive modifier and readers will still understand the sentence. When writers omit a restrictive modifier, they change the meaning of the sentence.

| **Restrictive** | Homeowners who **don't pay their property taxes** risk severe penalties. |
|---|---|
| **Nonrestrictive** | Homeowners, **whether novice or experienced**, can benefit from the seminar on home equity. |

The restrictive modifier makes clear that homeowners who don't pay their property taxes will risk severe penalties; homeowners who do pay their taxes will not risk penalties. The writer restricts, or limits, the homeowners to those who don't pay their property taxes. The restrictive modifier is essential, and commas should not be used. The nonrestrictive modifier is not essential, and commas should be used.

## Commas to Separate Coordinate Adjectives

Use a comma to separate *coordinate adjectives*—adjectives that modify the same noun equally.

| Correct | The company will test this fast, powerful computer next week. |
|---|---|
| Correct | The new design incorporates a bright, rectangular screen. |

When adjectives are coordinate, the sentence would still make sense if you replace the comma with the coordinating conjunction *and*. When adjectives are not coordinate, do not separate the adjectives with a comma. Adjectives are not coordinate when the noun and the adjective closest to the noun are closely associated in meaning, as in the following examples:

Incorrect    We will begin the test after the second, special session.

Correct    We will begin the test after the second special session.

In this example, the adjective *second* modifies the combination of the adjective *special* and the noun *session*.

## Other Conventional Uses of Commas

- **Dates**. Use commas to separate the parts of a date. (Some style guides omit the comma after the year: May 1, 1950 is his birthday.)

    Correct    After Friday, January 1, 2008, you may use your corporate card to charge your tickets and meals.

    Notice the comma after 2008. If you do not include the day (January 2008), omit the comma between the month and year. If you include the day before the month (1 January 2008), then don't use a comma.
- **Towns, states, and countries.** Use commas to separate the parts of an address. In the following example, notice the comma after Wisconsin. te. (Some style guides omit the comma after the state: Madison, Wisconsin was the first state capital we visited.)

    Correct    The senator from Madison, Wisconsin, asked the first question.

- **Titles of persons.** Use commas before and after a title that follows a person's name.

    Correct    Joseph Gerault, Ph.D., will address the board of directors on Tuesday.

- **Direct address.** Use a comma or commas to set off nouns used in direct address.

    Correct    My friends, I am happy to report the results of the second test.

    Correct    If you are willing to talk, Thomas, we will select a time convenient for you.

- **Quotations.** Use a comma to introduce most quotations.

    Correct    According to John Keyes, "Color grabs a reader's attention before the reader understands the surrounding informational context."

    Correct    They asked, "How long will the network be down?"

- **Interjections and transitional adverbs.** Use a comma or commas to separate interjections and transitional adverbs from the other words in a sentence:

Correct       Well, we did not budget any money for the new generator.

Correct       Therefore, we must wait until the next budget period to purchase the generator.

Correct       The old generator, however, is still fairly reliable.

## Dash   ( —/ )

Use an em dash (long dash) dash or two dashes to emphasize a parenthetical statement or to indicate a sharp change in thought or tone.

Correct       The United States is a locale, China is a locale, and India is a locale each has its own set of rules and cultural experiences.

Correct       The judge found the company guilty of deceptive advertising—as I remember.

## Exclamation Point   ( !/ )

Place an exclamation point at the end of an exclamatory sentence—a sentence that expresses strong emotion.

Correct       The new physics building, originally budgeted for $1.5 million, cost more than $5.5 million!

Because technical communication strives for objectivity, you will rarely use exclamation points in technical documents.

## Hyphen   ( -/ )

Use hyphens to form compound words, adjectives, fractions, and numbers and to divide words at the end of a line.

### Hyphens in Compound Words

A **compound word** consists of two or more words. Some, but not all, compound words are hyphenated. If you are unsure about whether to hyphenate a compound word, check your dictionary.

| Hyphenated | Not Hyphenated |
|---|---|
| up-to-date | workplace |
| editor-in-chief | proofread |
| self-image | bulletin board |

### Hyphens to Form Compound Adjectives

A *compound adjective* is two or more words that serve as a single adjective before a noun.

| | |
|---|---|
| **twenty-one-inch** monitor | **up-to-the-minute** news |
| **self-induced** attack | **reader-focused** sentences |
| **black-spotted** kitten | **general-to-specific** pattern |

### Hyphens in Fractions and Compound Numbers

Use hyphens to connect the numerator and denominator of fractions and to hyphenate compound numbers from twenty-one to ninety-nine when spelling out numbers. (Some style guides omit the hyphen when a fraction operates as a noun: Add one third of a cup of flour.)

one-third          seventy-seven

### Hyphens for End-of-Line Word Breaks

Use a hyphen to divide a word at the end of one line and continue it on the next line. Divide words only between syllables. Consult a dictionary to identify correct syllable breaks. Your word-processing software should automatically divide words between syllables.

Correct        Documents change across cultures just as body lang-
               uage, everyday expressions, and greetings change.

Whenever possible, avoid breaking a word at the end of a sentence. You can avoid end-of-line hyphens by using an unjustified right margin. You also can set your word-processing software not to hyphenate words at the ends of lines.

## Parentheses

Use parentheses—always in pairs—in the following situations:
- To enclose supplementary or incidental information:

| Correct | Please email me (jsmith@luminant.com) when you complete your section of the report. |
|---------|-----------------------------------------------------------------------------------|
| Correct | To readers in the United States, EPA (for Environmental Protection Agency) and IRS (for Internal Revenue Service) are common acronyms. |

- To enclose numbers and letters used to identify items listed within a sentence:

| Correct | To log on to the network, (1) type your login name, (2) press Tab, (3) type your password, and (4) press Enter. |
|---------|-----------------------------------------------------------------------------------|

Parentheses are unnecessary when you display a list vertically:

| Correct | To log on to the network, complete these steps: |
|---------|-------------------------------------------------|

1. Type your login name.
2. Press Tab.
3. Type your password.
4. Press Enter.

## Period

Use a period at the end of most sentences, after most abbreviations, and as a decimal point.

### Periods to Create an End Stop

Put a period at the end of any sentence that does not ask a direct question or express strong emotion (an exclamation):

| Correct | The Web has changed the way companies communicate with their employees. |
|---------|-------------------------------------------------------------------------|

### Periods After Abbreviations

- Use a period after most abbreviations:

  Ph.D.        etc.
  J.D.         U.S.

- Omit periods from abbreviations for the names of organizations such as corporations and government and international agencies:

  GM (for General Motors)
  NCAA (for National Collegiate Athletic Association)
  FBI (for Federal Bureau of Investigation)
  UN (for United Nations)

- Omit periods from acronyms—words (that you can pronounce) formed from the initial letters of the words in a name:

   NASA
   WHO
   DARE

## Periods as Decimal Points

- Use a period in decimal fractions and as a decimal point between dollars and cents:

   6.079        69.8%
   0.05         $789.40

# Question Marks

- Put a question mark at the end of a sentence that asks a direct question:

   Correct        How many volunteers participated in the survey?

- Don't use a question mark at the end of an indirect question:

   Incorrect      The director asked how many volunteers participated in the survey?

   Correct        The director asked how many volunteers participated in the survey.

- When a question mark appears within quotation marks, don't include any other end punctuation:

   Correct        The director asked, "How many volunteers participated in the survey?"

# Quotation Marks

Enclose short quotations and the titles of some published works in quotation marks. Many of us know when to use quotation marks but have trouble knowing how to use other marks of punctuation with them; therefore, this section also presents conventions for punctuation that accompanies quotation marks.

## Quotation Marks to Enclose Short Quotations

Enclose a quotation within quotation marks when it is short enough to fit within a sentence and takes up no more than three lines of text:

   Correct        According to Thompson, "Monarch butterflies have reddish-brown,
                  black-edged wings."

When a quotation is longer than three lines, follow these guidelines:
- Indent the quotation 10 spaces (or one-half inch) from the left margin.
- Omit the quotation marks. The indentation serves the same purpose as the quotation marks enclosing a short quotation.
- Introduce the quotation with a complete sentence followed by a colon.

Correct      Thompson (2000) writes the following about monarch butterflies:

> Monarch butterflies have reddish-brown, black-edged wings. The larvae of these butterflies feed on milkweed. These butterflies migrate hundreds of miles through North America. They have been sighted as far south as Mexico and as far north as Canada. (261)

## Quotation Marks Around the Titles of Some Works

Place quotation marks around titles of articles from journals, newspapers, and other periodicals:

Correct      Tumminello and Carlshamre's article "An International Internet Collaboration" …

## Conventional Punctuation with Quotation Marks

Follow the conventions presented below when using quotation marks with other punctuation.
- **Commas and periods.** Put commas and periods *inside* the quotation marks.

  Correct      Joanna Tumminello and Par Carlshamre wrote "An International Internet Collaboration."

  Correct      He cited "An International Internet Collaboration," an article by Joanna Tumminello and Par Carlshamre.

- **Semicolons and colons.** Put semicolons and colons *outside* the quotation marks.

  Correct      Joanna Tumminello and Par Carlshamre wrote "An International Internet Collaboration"; this article includes valuable information about collaborating to complete a research project.

- **Question marks, dashes, and exclamation points.** Put question marks, dashes, and exclamation points inside the quotation marks when they apply to the quoted material only and outside the quotation marks when they apply to the entire sentence.

| Correct | She asked, "Have you completed the audit?" (inside) |
| --- | --- |
| Correct | Did she ask, "Have you completed the audit"? (outside) |

## Semicolon    ( ;/ )

Use semicolons in the following situations.

### Semicolons to Link Independent Clauses

Place a semicolon between two independent clauses not linked by a coordinating conjunction (and, or, nor, so, for, but, yet):

| Incorrect | The newest version of the software has more options; but it requires more memory and a faster processor. |
| --- | --- |
| Correct | The newest version of the software has more options; however, it requires more memory and a faster processor. |

### Semicolons to Separate Items in a Series

Use a semicolon to separate the items in a series when any of the items already has internal punctuation:

| Correct | The production team consists of the following people: Patrick Sims, managing editor; Norma Rowland, production editor; Gwen Chavez, copy editor; and Thomas Thompson, art editor. |
| --- | --- |

 **MECHANICS**

This section includes information on how to use abbreviations, capitalization, italics, and numbers.

## Abbreviations    ( ab )

Generally, use abbreviations only when your readers are familiar with them. If you must use abbreviations, attach a list explaining what each one means. If you are uncertain about how to use an abbreviation, spell out the term. When using abbreviations, follow these guidelines:

- Use the singular form for most units of measure even when the word would be plural if spelled out:

psi      means either "pound per square inch" or "pounds per square inch"

oz      means either "ounce" or "ounces"

Use a period after the abbreviation for clarity if readers might confuse an abbreviation for another word. Otherwise, omit the period from technical abbreviations.
- Spell out short or common terms such as *ton* and *acre*.
- Abbreviate units of measurement only when a number precedes them:

| Incorrect | How many sq ft? |
|---|---|
| Correct | How many square feet? |
| Incorrect | 10 square feet |
| Correct | 10 sq ft |

## Capitalization

Follow standard capitalization conventions. The conventions listed here are the most important ones; for a more complete list, consult your style guides mentioned in Appendix A. If your style guide has no capitalization guidelines, consult your dictionary.
- Capitalize proper nouns, such as personal names, formal titles, place names, languages, religions, organizations, days of the week, and months:

    Kathryn Sullivan (personal name)
    American Association of Mechanical Engineers (organization)
    Chief Counsel (formal title)
    Europe (place name)
    Monday, Tuesday (days of the week)
    Chinese (language)
    Catholicism (religion)
    January, February (months)
- Don't capitalize seasons, compass directions (unless the reference is to a geographic region), and areas of study (unless the area already is a proper noun):

    winter, spring, summer, fall (seasons)
    We traveled north through Wyoming. (direction)
    The storm hit the Pacific Northwest. (geographic region)
    the study of language (area of study)
    the study of the French language (area of study)

- Capitalize the first word, the last word, and every important word in titles and headings:

  > Technical Communication in the Information Age (title)
  >
  > Research on Electronic Mail and Other Media (heading)
  >
  > If you are using the titles in a list of references, follow the guidelines for that style, such as APA, CSE, or MLA.

## Italics

Use italics in the following instances:
- For Latin scientific names:

  > *Lagerstroemia indica* (crepe myrtle)
  >
  > *Tryngites subruficollis* (buff-breasted sandpiper)

- For the titles of books, plays, pamphlets, periodicals, manuals, radio and television programs, movies, newspapers, lengthy musical works, trains, airplanes, ships, and spacecraft:

  > *War and Peace* (book)            *Madame Butterfly* (musical work)
  >
  > *Hamlet* (play)                   *Titanic* (ship)
  >
  > *American Idol* (television program)   *Apollo V* (spacecraft)
  >
  > *New York Times* (newspaper)

- For foreign words that are not widely considered to be part of the English language. If you are unsure, consult a dictionary. If it appears in the dictionary, do not italicize it.

  > The county levied an *ad valorem* tax.

- For words, letters, and numbers that you are referring to:

  > Use the coordinating conjunctions *and, so, nor, but, yet, for, or.*
  >
  > The students should work on writing lowercase *a* and *d* and the number *8.*

## Numbers

Guidelines for using numbers vary widely and in many instances differ from one field to another. Follow the standard practices of your field or organization, and use numbers consistently throughout each document. These guidelines will apply to most technical documents:
- When a number is the first word of a sentence, do not use numerals. Either spell out the number or, if you can't express it in two words, rewrite the sentence.

| | |
|---|---|
| Incorrect | 25 years ago, we began offering this degree. |
| Correct | Twenty-five years ago, we began offering this degree. |

| Incorrect | One thousand seventy-five of the 6,500 people we contacted returned the questionnaire. |
|---|---|
| Correct | Of the 6,500 people we contacted, 1,075 returned the questionnaire. |

- Use numerals for days and years in dates, exact sums of money, exact times, addresses, percentages, statistics, scores, and units of measurement:
  March 31, 1999 or 31 March 1999 (dates)
  $6,432.58 (money)
  6:34 P.M. (time)
  2600 St. Edwards Court (address)
  67 percent or 67% (percentage)
  a mean of 13 (statistic)
  a total score of 98.7 (score)
  37°P (unit of measurement)
- When mentioning rounded-off figures, use words:
  about five million dollars
  approximately nine o'clock
- When using two different numbers back to back, use numerals for one and spell out the other:
  nine 2-inch screws

references

All, Jim. Windowsteamblog, "Setting the Record Straight." Last modified 2006. Accessed November 20, 2012. http://windowsteamblog.com/windows/archive/b/windowsvista/archive/2006/12/12/title.aspx.

American National Standards Institute (ANSI). American National Standards for Product Safety Signs and Labels. Washington, DC: American National Standards Institute, 1989.

American Psychological Association (APA). *APA Style Guide to Electronic References*. 6th ed. Washington, DC: American Psychological Association, 2009.

Anderson, Paul. What Survey Research Tells Us About Writing at Work. *Writing in Nonacademic Settings*. Ed. Lee Odell and Dixie Goswami. New York: Guilford, 1985. 3–84.

The Associated Press (AP). Forest Service Uses Misleading Photo. April 12, 2004. Accessed November 25, 2012. www.msnbc.msn.com/id/4722630/.

Baker, William H. How to Produce and Communicate Structured Text. *Technical Communication*, 41 (1994): 456–66.

Barabas, Christine. *Technical Writing in a Corporate Culture: A Study of the Nature of Information*. Norwood, NJ: Ablex, 1990.

Barthon, Greg. Eat the Way Your Mama Taught You. November 28, 2007. http://www.mcneilml.com/html/referencelibrary_files/a_mama.htm.

Beal, Vangie 'Aurora'. *All About Phishing*. March 31, 2006. http://www.webopedia.com/DidYouKnow/Internet/2005/phishing.asp. Updated December 20, 2010.

Beason, Gary. Redefining Written Products with WWW Documentation: A Study of the Publication Process at a Computer Company. *Technical Communication* 43 (1996): 339-48.

Beauchamp, Tom L., and Norman E. Bowie. *Ethical Theory and Business*. 2nd ed. Englewood Cliffs, NJ: Prentice Hall, 1983.

Behn, Bill. Quoted in Zupek, Rachel. Career Builders. "15 Biggest Job Seeker Mistakes." Last modified December 12, 2007. Accessed November 20, 2012. http://www.careerbuilder.com/Article/CB-769-Job-Search-15-Biggest-Job-Seeker-Mistakes/.

Beil, Laura. Change of Heart: New Insights Gained as Cardiovascular Research Shifts More to Women. *Dallas Morning News* (February 6, 1995).

Bellis, Jack. "Information: What Should Go Online and What Should Go in Print?." *Intercom*, November 1996, 20–21.

Benson, Philippa J. Writing Visually: Design Considerations in Technical Publications. *Technical Communication*, 32, no. 4 (1985): 35–39.

Berger, Joseph. Consultant to First Lady Admits Error on Resume. *New York Times* (June 26, 1996).

Blain, Jennifer, and Taylor Lincoln. Make Yourself Essential. *Intercom* (April 1999): 9–11.

Boeing Corp. What Is Simplified English? Accessed November 25, 2012. http://www.boeing.com/phantom/sechecker/se.html

Bolles, Richard Nelson. *What Color Is Your Parachute?* Berkeley, CA: Ten Speed Press, 2009.

Bosley, Deborah S. International Graphics: A Search for Neutral Territory. *Intercom* (August–September 1996): 4–7.

Bradbury, S. Gayle. Writing for the Web. *Intercom* (November 2000): 24.

Braffman-Miller, Judith. When Medicine Went Wrong: How Americans Were Used Illegally as Guinea Pigs, *USA Today* (March 1, 1995).

Brockmann, R. John. *Writing Better Computer User Documentation: From Paper to Hypertext Version 2.0.* New York: Wiley, 1990.

Byerly, Gayla. Website Evaluation. Denton: University of Nort Texas Libraries, 2001. np.

Cadillac. CTS Coupe Concept Celebrates Cadillac's Design Renaissance. Accessed December 15, 2008. http://www.cadillac.com/cadillacjsp/experience/news_ctscoupe.jsp?evar10=CTS_MODEL_HOMEPAGE_MASTHEAD_CTS.

Caher, John M. Technical Documentation and Legal Liability. *The Journal of Technical Writing and Communication*, 25 (1995): 5–10.

Cash, J. I., Jr. A New Farmers' Market. *InformationWeek* (December 26, 1994): 60.

Charney, Davida, Lynee Reder, and Gail Wells. Studies of Elaboration in Instructional Texts. In *Effective Documentation: What We Have Learned from Research*, edited by Stephen Doheny-Farina, 47–72. Cambridge, MA: MIT Press, 1988.

Cobb, Neil. Email interview. December 8, 2008.

Coleman. *Gas Barbecue Use, Care and Installation Manual.* Neosho: Coleman, 1999.

College Board. *Writing: A Ticket to Work ... Or a Ticket Out: A Survey of Business Leaders.* Report of The National Commission on Writing for America's Families, Schools, and Colleges, 2004. http://www.collegeboard.com/prod_downloads/writingcom/writing-ticket-to-work.pdf. Accessed: November 28, 2012

Couture, Barbara, and Jone Rymer. Situation Exigence: Composing Processes on the Job by Writer's Role and Task Value. In *Writing in the Workplace: New Research Perspectives*, edited by Rachel Spilka, 4–20. Carbondale, IL: Southern Illinois University Press, 1993.

Crenshaw, W. Elmo, and Bruce Lawhorn. Tick-Borne Diseases of the Dog. (L-22667, Rpt. 10M-7-88). College Station, TX: Texas Agricultural Extension Service.

Daugherty, Shannon. The Usability Evaluation: A Discount Approach to Usability Testing. *Intercom* (December 1997): 16–20.

Davidson, Eli. Quoted in Zupeck, Rachel. 15 Biggest Job Seeker Mistakes December 12, 2007. http://www.careerbuilder.com/JobSeeker/Careerbytes/CBArticle. Accessed: April 22, 2008.

Dombrowski, Paul. *Ethics in Technical Communication*. Needham Heights, MA: Allyn & Bacon, 2000.

Dragga, Sam. Classifications of Correspondence: Complexity Versus Simplicity. *The Technical Writing Teacher*, 18, no. 1 (1991): 1–14.

Duin, Ann Hill. How People Read: Implications for Writers. *The Technical Writing Teacher*, 15 (1988a): 185–93.

———. Reading to Learn and Do. *Proceedings of the 35th International Technical Communication Conference*, Washington, DC: Society for Technical Communication, 1988b.

Ede, Lisa, and Andrea Lunsford. *Singular Texts/Plural Authors: Perspectives on Collaborative Writing*. Carbondale, IL: Southern Illinois University Press, 1990.

Eiseman, Leatrice. *Color: Messages and Meanings: A Pantone Color Resource*. Gloucester, MA: Hand Books Press, 2006.

Farkas, David K., and Jean B. Farkas. Guidelines for Designing Web Navigation. *Technical Communication*, 47, no. 3 (2000): 341–58.

Federal Emergency Management Administration (FEMA). Earthquake Safety Guide for Homeowners. Washington, DC: Federal Emergency Management Administration, 2005.

Felker, Daniel B., Frances Pickering, Veda Charrow, and V. Melissa Holland. *Guidelines for Document Designers*. Washington, DC: American Institutes for Research, 1981.

Flynn, Nancy. *The e-Policy Handbook: Rules and Best Practices to Safely Manage Your Company's E-Mail, Blogs, Social Networking, and Other Electronic Communication Tools*. New York: AMA Publications, 2001.

Forrester, S. Dru, and Bruce Lawhorn. Canine Epilepsy. College Station, TX: Texas Agricultural Extension Service, n.d.

Foy, Patricia S. The Reinvention of the Corporate Information Model. *IEEE Transactions on Professional Communication*, 39 (1996): 23–29.

Fugate, Alice E. Writing for Your Web Site: What Works, and What Doesn't. *Intercom* (May 2001): 39–40.

Golen, Steven, Celeste Powers, and M. Agnes Titkemeyer. How to Teach Ethics in a Basic Business Communication Class-Committee Report of the 1983 Teaching Methodology and Concepts Committee, Subcommittee 1. *Journal of Business Communication*, 22, no. 1 (1985): 75–83.

Gomes, Lee. Advanced Computer Screens Have Age-Old Rival. *San Jose Mercury News* (February 21, 1994).

GovLeaders.org. The 6 Golden Rules of Meeting Management. http://govleaders.org/meetings .htm. Accessed November 1, 2012.

Green, Marianne. Design Your Resume to Land an Internship. http://www.jobweb.com/ resumesample.aspx?id=250. Accessed: June 1, 2008.

———. Green, Marianne. Jobweb.com. "The Resume-Internship Connection." Accessed November 11, 2012. http://www.hofstra.edu/StudentAffairs/StudentServices/ career/career_internship_resume.html.

Greenly, Robert. How to Write a Resume. *Technical Communication* (1993): 42–48.

Hacker, Diana and Barbara Fister. Research and Documentation Online. 5th ed. http://bcs .bedfordstmartins.com/resdoc5e/RES5e_ch11_s1-0003.html. Accessed December 7, 2012.

Halpern, J. W. An Electronic Odyssey. In *Writing in Nonacademic Settings*, edited by Lee Odell and Dixie Goswami, 157–201. New York: Guilford, 1985.

Hansen, James B. Editing Your Own Writing. *Intercom* (February 1997): 14–16.

Hansen, Katharine. Quintessential Careers, "Powerful New Grad Resumes and Cover Letters." Last modified May 3, 2009. http://www.quintcareers.com/new_grad_resumes.html. Accessed November 20, 2012.

Hansen, Randall S. How to Write Text Resumes. August 31, 2001. http://www.quintcareers.com/scannable_resumes.html. Accessed November 25, 2012.

Hansen, Randall S., and Katharine Hansen. The Importance of Good Writing Skills. http://www.enhancemywriting.com/skills.html. Accessed November 27, 2012.

Haramundanis, Katherine. *The Art of Technical Documentation*. Maynard, MA: Digital Press, 1992.

Hayes, John R., and Linda S. Flower. On the Structure of the Writing Process. *Topics in Language Disorders*, 7 (1987): 19–30.

Helyar, Pamela S. Product Liability: Meeting Legal Standards for Adequate Instructions. *Journal of Technical Writing and Communication*, 22, no. 2 (1992): 125–47.

Holland, V. Melissa, Veda R. Charrow, and William W. Wright. How Can Technical Writers Write Effectively for Several Audiences at Once? In *Solving Problems in Technical Writing*, edited by Lynn Beene and Peter White, 27–54. New York: Oxford University Press, 1988.

Horton, William. The Almost Universal Language: Graphics for International Documents. *Technical Communication*, 40 (1993): 682–93.

———. *Illustrating Computer Documentation*. New York: Wiley, 1991a.

———. Overcoming Chromophobia: A Guide to the Confident and Appropriate Use of Color. *IEEE Transactions on Professional Communication*, 34 (1991b): 160–71.

Issacs, Kim. Monster.com, "Lying on Your Resume." Last modified November 11, 2012. Accessed November 20, 2012. http://career-advice.monster.com/resumes-cover-letters/resume-writing-tips/lying-on-your-resume/article.aspx.

Kellog, Ronald T. Attentional Overload and Writing Performance: Effects of Rough Draft and Outline Strategies. *Journal of Experimental Psychology: Learning, Memory, and Cognition* 14 (1988): 355–65.

Keyes, Elizabeth. Typography, Color, and Information Structure. *Technical Communication*, 40 (1993): 638–54.

Kintsch, Eileen. Macroprocesses and Microprocesses in the Development of Summarization Skill. *ERIC* Document ED305613. Washington, DC: Educational Research Information Center, 1989.

Klein, Fred. Beyond Technical Translation: Localization. *Intercom* (May 1997): 32–33.

Koehsler, Martina, Afschin Soleiman, Horst Aspock, Herbert Auer, and Julia Walochnik. *Onchocerca jakutensis Filariasis* in Humans, *Emerging Infectious Diseases Journal*, 13, no. 11 (November 2007). 1749-1752.

Koop, W. E., and R. L. Dubie. Thatch Control in Home Lawns. College Station, TX: Texas Agricultural Extension Service, 1982.

Kraft Foods. Our Way of Doing Business: The Kraft Foods Code of Conduct. March 2009. http://www.kraftfoodscompany.com/assets/pdf/codeofconduct.pdf. Accessed: August 15, 2012.

Krause, Jim. *Color Index*. (rev. ed.). Cincinnati: HOW Design Books, 2002.

———. *Idea Index*. Cincinnati: F & W Publications, 2000.

———. *Layout Index*. Cincinnati: North Light Books, 2001.

Krull, Robert, and Jeanne M. Hurford. Can Computers Increase Writing Productivity? *Technical Communication*, 34 (1987): 243–49.

Krull, Robert, and Philip Rubens. Effects of Color Highlighting on User Performance with Online Information, *Technical Communication*, 33 (1986): 268–69.

Lakoff, Robin Tolmach. Some of My Favorite Writers Are Literate: The Mingling of Oral and Literate Strategies in Written Communication. In *Spoken and Written Language*, edited by D. Tannen, 239–60. Norwood, NJ: Ablex, 1982.

Langewiesche, William. The Lessons of ValuJet 592. *The Atlantic Monthly*, 281, no. 3 (1998): 81–98.

Lawrence, Steve, and Lee Giles. Accessibility of Information on the Web. *Nature*, 400 (1999), 107–09.

Lay, Mary M. Nonrhetorical Elements of Layout and Design. In *Technical Writing: Theory and Practice*, edited by Bertie E. Fearing and W. Keats Sparrow, 72–89. New York: Modern Language Association, 1989.

Lee, Zonky, and Younghwa Lee. Emailing the Boss: Cultural Implications of Media Choice. *IEEE Transactions on Professional Communication*, 52, no. 1 (2009): 61–74.

Le Vie, Donald S., Jr. Internet Technology and Intellectual Property. *Intercom* (January 2000): 20–23.

Li-Ron, Yael. Office Assistant: Dog or Genius? *PC World*. 15.2 (1997): 116

Loar, J. M., and D. K. Cox. Biotic Characterization of Small Streams in the Vicinity of Oil Retention Ponds 1 and 2 Near the Y-12 Plant Bear Creek Valley Waste Disposal Area. Oak Ridge, TN: Oak Ridge National Laboratory, 1984.

Locker, Kitty O. *Business and Administrative Communication*. Homewood, IL: Irwin, 1989.

Lorch, Robert E., and Elizabeth Pugzles Lorch. Online Processing of Text Organization. *ERIC* Document ED245210. Washington, DC: Educational Research Information Center, 1984.

Louth, Richard, and Ann Martin Scott, eds. *Collaborative Technical Writing: Theory and Practice*. St. Paul, MN: Association of Teachers of Technical Writing, 1989.

Madden, Mary. *Older Adults and Social Media: Social Networking Use Among Those Ages 50 and Older Nearly Doubled over the Past Year*. Pew Internet & American Life. Washington, D.C.: Pew Research Center. August 27, 2010. Report URL: http://pewinternet.org/Reports/2010/Older-Adults-and-Social-Media.aspx.

Martin, Cynthia J. Individually and as Executrix of Eugene J. Martin, Deceased, v. Arthur Hacker, et al., and Chelsea Laboratories, Inc., et al. *83 NY2nd I*. November 23,1993.

Martinez, Benjamin, and Jacqueline Block. *Visual Forces*. Englewood Cliffs, NJ: Prentice Hall, 1988.

McCorvey, J. J. How to Create a Cell Phone Policy, *Inc.* (February 10, 2010). Accessed: November 28, 2012. http://www.inc.com/guides/how-to-create-a-cell-phone-policy.html

Metro Creative Communications. Employers Targeting Social Networking Sites. *Dallas Morning News* (May 3, 2009). Section 3J.

Mirshafiei, Mohsen. Culture as an Element in Teaching Technical Writing. *Technical Communication*, 41, no. 2 (1994): 276–82.

Nielsen, Jakob. Be Succinct! (Writing for the Web). *Jakob Nielsen's Alertbox*. March 15, 1997. http://www.useit.com/alertbox/9703b.html. Accessed: October 15, 2012.

——. How Users Read on the Web. *Jakob Nielsen's Alertbox*. October 1, 1997. http://www.useit.com/alertbox/9710a.html. Accessed: November 28, 2012.

Ong, W. J. Literacy and Orality in Our Times. In *The Writing Teacher's Sourcebook*, edited by G. Tate and Edward P. J. Corbett, 36–48. New York: Oxford University Press, 1981.

*OptQuest for Crystal Ball 2000 User Manual*. Denver, Colorado: Decisioneering, Inc., 2000.

Parker, Roger, and Patrick Berry. *Looking Good in Print*. 4th ed. Scottsdale, AZ: The Coriolis Group, 1998.

Parson, Gerald M. A Cautionary Legal Tale: *The Bose v. Consumers Union Case*. *The Journal of Technical Writing and Communication*, 22 (1992): 377–86.

Pavich, M. J., G. W. Leo, S. F. Obermeier, and J. R. Estabrook. *Investigations of the Characteristics, Origin, and Residence Time of the Upland Residual Mantle of the Piedmont of Fairfax County, Virginia*. (U.S. Geological Survey Professional Paper 1352). Reston, VA: U.S. Geological Survey, 1989.

Perl, Sondra. The Composing Processes of Unskilled College Writers. *Research in the Teaching of English*, 13 (1979): 317–36.

Pfeiffer, William S. *Pocket Guide to Public Speaking*. Upper Saddle River, NJ: Prentice Hall, 2002.

Plumb, Carolyn, and Jan H. Spyridakis. Conducting Survey Research in Technical Communication. *Technical Communication*, 39, no. 4 (1992): 625–37.

Quain, John R. Time for Face Time. *Fast Company* (October/November 1997): 232.

Raign, Kathryn, and Brenda Sims. Gender, Persuasion Techniques, and Collaboration. *Technical Communication Quarterly*, 2, no. 1 (1993): 89–104.

Raytheon. Ethics Quick Test. http://www.raytheon.com/Stewardship/ethics/ethics_answers/test/index.html. Accessesed: October 25, 2007.

Redish, Janice C. Adding Value as a Professional Technical Communicator. *Technical Communication*, 42, no. 1 (1995): 26–39.

Redish, Janice C., and David A. Schell. Writing and Testing Instructions for Usability. In *Technical Writing Theory and Practice*, edited by Bertie E. Fearing and W. Keats Sparrow, 61–71. New York: Modern Language Association, 1987.

Reiffenstein, Kathy. Five Things Not to Do in Front of an Audience. *Training Magazine*. May 22, 2008. http://www.trainingmag.com/article/five-things-not-do-front-audience. Accessed: November 27, 2012.

———. Harness the Power of PowerPoint Presentations. *WorldWIT Newsletter*. November 6, 2006. http://www.andnowpresenting.us/harness-the-power-of-powerpoint-presentations.html. Accessed: November 27, 2012.

Rottenberg, Annette T. *Elements of Argument*. 3rd ed. New York: St. Martin's Press, 1991.

Rubens, Philip M. Reinventing the Wheel? Ethics for Technical Communicators. *Journal of Technical Writing and Communication*, 11 (1981): 329–39.

Ruggero, Ed, and Dennis F. Haley, *The Leader's Compass*. 2nd ed. King of Prussia, PA: Academy Leadership Books, 2005.

Samuels, Marilyn Schauer. Scientific Logic: A Reader-Oriented Approach to Technical Writing. *Journal of Technical Writing and Communication*, 12, no. 4 (1982): 307–28.

Schrage, Michael. *No More Teams! Mastering the Dynamics of Creative Collaboration*. New York: Doubleday Business, 1995.

Scudder, Joseph N., and Patricia J. Guinan. Communication Competencies as Discriminators of Superiors' Ratings of Employee Performance. *Journal of Business Communication*, 26, no. 3 (1989): 217–29.

Selzer, Jack. Arranging Business Prose. In *Writing in the Business Professions*, edited by Myra Kogen. Urbana, IL: National Council of Teachers of English, 1989.

Shimberg, H. Lee. Technical Communicators and Moral Ethics. *Technical Communication*, 27 (1980): 10–12.

Shroyer, Roberta. Actual Readers versus Implied Readers: Role Conflicts in Office 97. *Technical Communication*, 47, no. 2 (2000): 238–40.

Simon, Jerold. How to Write a Resume. International Paper Company, 1981.

Sims, Brenda R. Electronic Mail in Two Corporate Workplaces. In *Electronic Literacies in the Workplace: Technologies of Writing*, edited by Patricia Sullivan and Jennie Dautermann, 41–64. Urbana, IL: National Council of Teachers of English, 1996.

——. Linking Ethics and Language in the Technical Communication Classroom. *Technical Communication Quarterly*, 2, no. 3 (1993): 285–99.

Sims, Brenda R., and Stephen Guice. Differences between Business Letters from Native and Non-Native Speakers of English. *The Journal of Business Communication*, 29, no. 1 (1992): 23–39.

Sims, William. Personal Interview. September 15, 2008.

Snow, Kathie. "To Ensure Inclusion, Freedom, and Respect for All, It's Time to Embrace People First Language." www.disabilityisnatural.com. January 2008. Accessed: December 2, 2012.

Solar Turbines. Gas Turbine Overview. http://mysolar.cat.com/cda/layout?m=35442&x=7. Accessed: November 28, 2012.

Sozo Firm Staff. When is the best time to conduct meetings and important business?. Last modified December 16, 2010. Accessed November 20, 2012. http://www.andrewjensen.net/when-is-best-time-to-conduct-important-business/.

Spivey, Nancy Nelson, and James R. King. Readers as Writers Composing from Sources. *Reading Research Quarterly*, 24, no. 1 (1989): 7–26.

Spyridakis, Jan H. Guidelines for Authoring Comprehensible Web Pages and Evaluating Their Success. *Technical Communication*, 47, no. 3 (2000): 359–82.

Stimpson, Brian. Operating Highly Complex and Hazardous Technological Systems without Mistakes: The Wrong Lessons from ValuJet 592. *Manitoba Professional Engineer* (October 1998). Accessed from http://web.archive.org/web/20070927004115/http://www.cns-snc.ca/branches/manitoba/valujet.html.

Strunk, William, and White, E. B. *The Elements of Style*. 4th ed. New York: Longman, 2000.

Sutton, Robert I. *The No Asshole Rule: Building a Civilized Workplace and Surviving One That Isn't.* New York: Warner Business Books, 2007.

Swallow, Erica. "How Recruiters Use Social Networks to Screen Candidates." *Mashable*, October 23, 2011. http://mashable.com/2011/10/23/how-recruiters-use-social-networks-to-screen-candidates-infographic/ Accessed: November 20, 2012.

Taylor, Barbara M., and Richard W. Beach. The Effects of Text Structure Instruction on Middle-Grade Students' Comprehension and Production of Expository Text. *Reading Research Quarterly*, 19, no. 2 (1984): 134–46.

Tebeaux, Elizabeth, and Driskill, Linda. Culture and the Shape of Rhetoric: Protocols of International Document Design. In *Exploring the Rhetoric of International Professional Communication: An Agenda for Teachers and Researchers*, edited by Carl R. Lovitt with Dixie Goswami, 211–52. New York: Baywood, 1999.

Tolman, Andrews L., Antonio P. Ballestero Jr., William W. Beck Jr., and Grover H. Emrich, Guidance Manual for Minimizing Pollution for Waste Disposal Sites. EPA-600/2-78-142. Washington, DC: Government Printing Office, 1978.

Tumminello, Joanna, and Par Carlshamre. An International Internet Collaboration. *Technical Communication*, 43, no. 4 (1996): 413–18.

University of Maryland Baltimore County. A Survey of the Frequency, Types, and Importance of Writing Tasks in Four Career Areas. August 29, 2001. http://userpages.umbc.edu/-rachdl/oral.html.

U.S. Copyright Office. *Fair Use*. Washington, D.C.: U.S. Copyright Office, June 2012. FL-102. http://www.copyright.gov/fls/fl102.html.

U.S. Office of Health, Safety, and Security. *DOE Openness: Human Radiation Experiment*. Washington, D.C.: Department of Energy. Updated: April 19, 2012. http://www.hss.energy.gov/healthsafety/ohre/ Accessed: November 27, 2012.

U.S. Patent and Trademark Office, "What is a trademark or service mark?" Last modified October 2012. Accessed November 20, 2012. http://www.uspto.gov/trademarks/index.jsp.

Walinskas, Karl. Reading Your Audience. *Intercom* (December 2001): 23–24.

White, Jan. *Visual Design for the Electronic Age*. New York: Watson-Guptill, 1988.

Wicclair, Mark R., and David K. Farkas. Ethical Reasoning in Technical Communication: A Practical Framework. *Technical Communication*, 31 (1984): 15–19.

Wilkinson, Theresa A. How to Increase Performance on a Web Site. *Intercom*, 47, no. 1 (2000): 38, 40.

Williams, Joseph M. *Style: Ten Lessons in Clarity and Grace*. 9th ed. New York: Longman, 2006.

Williams, Robin. *The Non-Designer's Design Book*. 3rd ed. Berkeley, CA: Peachpit Press, 2008.

Winsor, Dorothy A. The Construction of Knowledge in Organizations: Asking the Right Questions about the Challenger. *Journal of Business and Technical Communication*, 4, no. 2 (1990): 7–20.

Yeo, Sarah C. Designing Web Pages That Bring Them Back. *Intercom*, 43, no. 3 (1996): 12–14.

Zachary, Lois. Rekindling the Art of Persuasion. http://www.leadservs.com/artofpersuasion.html. Accessed: May 2008.

Zimmerman, Donald E., Michel Lynn Muraski, and Michael D. Slater. Taking Usability Testing to the Field. *Technical Communication*, 46, no. 4 (1999): 495–500.

Zickuhr, Kathryn, and Mary Madden. Older adults and Internet use. *Pew Internet and American Life Project*, Pew Research Center. June 6, 2012, n.p.

Zupek, Rachel. Career Builders, 15 Biggest Job Seeker Mistakes. Last modified December 12, 2007. Accessed November 20, 2012. http://www.careerbuilder.com/Article/CB-769-Job-Search-15-Biggest-Job-Seeker-Mistakes/.

# index

# I

Icons, 276
smart phone application, 278
*Idea Index*, 261
Idea sharing in collaborative writing, 55
Idioms
avoiding, for international readers, 225, 226
definition of, 225
IFB. *See* Information for bid
Implied warranties, 78
Important information, emphasis on, 192–193
Indentation, 489
Index, 497
Informal interviews
importance of, 108
tips for conducting, 109
Informal outline, 159
*vs.* formal outline, 161
Informal proposal, 542
Informal reports, 461, 467
directives (*See* Directives)
field and lab reports (*See* Field and lab reports)
*vs.* formal reports, 429
formats for, 433
email, 432
forms and templates, 432
letters, 432
memos, 432
meeting minutes (*See* Meeting minutes)
progress reports (*See* Progress reports)
readers' needs and expectations for, 430–432
trip reports (*See* Trip reports)
Information, 471, 487, 493, 506
complete and accurate, technical documents, 11–12, 107
kind of, 464

questions for evaluating, 127, 128
verifying, 107
Information for bid, 530
from *Commerce Business Daily*, 531
Information gathering
methods for, 107
in timely manner, 107
writing for others, 46
Information, organization of
definition of, 135
general-to-specific, 136, 138
illogical, 136, 137
importance of, 166
standard patterns for
cause-and-effect, 154, 157
chronological order, 144, 145
classification, 147, 148
comparison and contrast, 147, 151–154
general-to-specific, 144–147
most to least important, 158
order of importance, 154, 155
partition, 147, 149
problem-and-solution, 151, 154, 156
spatial order, 142–143
Information reports, 462–464
Information research
copyright laws and, 122–123
importance for professionals, 103
online, tips for, 124
planning for (*See* Research plan)
primary research methods for (*See* Primary research methods)
Information resource center
definition, 119
guidelines for using, 120
information collection by, 119
Information sharing
in collaborative writing, 57
using electronic tools, 61

qualifications, 547
readers, find out, 533–534
solution, product, service, and
research, 539–548
readers' questions and, 535
real-world experience, 560
assignment, 560
solve a problem, proposal
writing, 560
sample proposals, 548
Phoney research, case study analysis of,
129–130
Photograph, 321–324
comparing backgrounds in, 334
cropping, 324
of how something is done, 323
shows where something is located, 322
Pictographs, 324, 325
Pie charts, 324, 326
PIN. *See* Personal Identification Number
Plagiarism, 75
Planning, 562
Plastic spiral binding, 268
Point-by-point comparison, 152
Political constraints, in persuasive
arguments, 240
Poor writing skills, cost of, 200
Positive language, usage of, 220–222
Poster, 662
Post-interview follow-up letter, 418
Power plant, organizational chart for,
22, 23
PowerPoint presentation, 671
award-winning, 671
Preformatted template, 265
Preformatted templates and styles, 265
Preparations, used in story
descriptions, 497
PREPS. *See* Preparations, used in
story descriptions

Presentations
memorable, strategies for, 665–668
audience cue, 669–670
emergencies, prepare for, 667
field questions, 668
helping the audience enjoy your
presentation, tips, 667–668
provide previews, transitions, and
summaries, 667
rehearse, presentation, 666
oral (*See* Oral presentations)
Presidential election campaigns, 179
Primary readers, 32, 34, 492
Primary research, 108
Primary research methods, 106
inquiry letters and emails, 109
interviews, 108–109
observations and experiments, 116,
119
surveys and questionnaires, 110,
113–116
Problem-and-solution pattern, 151,
154, 156
information organized from, 156
tips for using, 151
Problem definition, 540–545
tips for writing, 542
of unsolicited proposal, 544
writing, 543
Process description, 572, 578–579
Proctor and Gamble, Worldwide Business
Conduct Manual of, 80–81, 83
Product, 532
Product design and human factor, 617
Professional image creation and
correspondence, 369–375
avoid overused phrases, 374, 375
follow grammar rules, 375
professional tone, use, 372–374
specific language, use, 374
understanding of reader, 369–372